Women, Medicine, Ethics and the Law

The International Library of Medicine, Ethics and Law
Series Editor: Michael D. Freeman

Titles in the Series

Women, Medicine, Ethics and the Law

Edited by

Susan Sherwin

Dalhousie University, Canada

and

Barbara Parish

Dalhousie University, Canada

Routledge
Taylor & Francis Group

LONDON AND NEW YORK

First published 2002 by Dartmouth Publishing Company and Ashgate Publishing

Reissued 2018 by Routledge
2 Park Square, Milton Park, Abingdon, Oxon OX14 4RN
711 Third Avenue, New York, NY 10017, USA

Routledge is an imprint of the Taylor & Francis Group, an informa business

Publisher's Note
The publisher has gone to great lengths to ensure the quality of this reprint but points out that some imperfections in the original copies may be apparent.

Disclaimer
The publisher has made every effort to trace copyright holders and welcomes correspondence from those they have been unable to contact.

A Library of Congress record exists under LC control number: 00053126

ISBN 13: 978-1-138-73048-9 (hbk)
ISBN 13: 978-1-138-73040-3 (pbk)
ISBN 13: 978-1-315-18941-3 (ebk)

Contents

Acknowledgements

The editor and publishers wish to thank the following for permission to use copyright material.

American Medical Association for the essay: Nancy S. Jecker (1993), 'Privacy Beliefs and the Violent Family: Extending the Ethical Argument for Physician Intervention', *JAMA*, **269**, pp. 776–80.

American Society of Law, Medicine & Ethics for the essay: Abby Lippman (1991), 'Prenatal Genetic Testing and Screening: Constructing Needs and Reinforcing Inequities', *American Journal of Law and Medicine*, **17**, pp. 15–50. Copyright © 1991 American Society of Law, Medicine & Ethics. Reprinted with the permission of the American Society of Law, Medicine & Ethics. All rights reserved.

Annual Reviews for the essays: George F. Brown and Ellen H. Moskowitz (1997), 'Moral and Policy Issues in Long-Acting Contraception', *Annual Review of Public Health*, **18**, pp. 379–400. Copyright © 1997 Annual Review Inc.; Sally Zierler and Nancy Krieger (1997), 'Reframing Women's Risk: Social Inequalities and HIV Infection', *Annual Review of Public Health*, **18**, pp. 401–36. Copyright © 1997 Annual Reviews Inc. Reprinted with permission, from the *Annual Review of Public Health*, vol. 18, www.Annual Reviews.org.

Alice Domurat Dreger (1998), '"Ambiguous Sex" – or Ambivalent Medicine? Ethical Issues in the Treatment of Intersexuality', *Hastings Center Report*, **28**, pp. 24–35. Copyright © 1998 Alice Domurat Dreger.

Duke University Press for the essay: Karen L. Baird (1999), 'The New NIH and FDA Medical Research Policies: Targeting Gender, Promoting Justice', *Journal of Health Politics, Policy and Law*, **24**, pp. 531–65. Copyright © 1999 Duke University Press. All rights reserved. Reprinted with permission.

Elsevier Science for the essay: Bonnie Kettel (1996), 'Women, Health and the Environment', *Social Science & Medicine*, **42**, pp. 1367–79. Copyright © 1996 Elsevier Science Ltd.

Indiana University Press for the essays: Kathryn Pauly Morgan (1991), 'Women and the Knife: Cosmetic Surgery and the Colonization of Women's Bodies', *Hypatia*, **6**, pp. 25–53; Susan Wendell (1989), 'Toward a Feminist Theory of Disability', *Hypatia*, **4**, pp. 104–24.

Kluwer Academic Publishers for the essay: Kirsti Malterud (1999), 'The (Gendered) Construction of Diagnosis Interpretation of Medical Signs in Women Patients', *Theoretical Medicine and Bioethics*, **20**, pp. 275–86. Copyright © 1999 Kluwer Academic Publishers. With kind permission from Kluwer Academic Publishers.

Oxford University Press for the essay: Catriona Mackenzie (1992), 'Abortion and Embodiment', *Australasian Journal of Philosophy*, **70**, pp. 136–55.

Population Council for the essay: Rebecca J. Cook (1993), 'International Human Rights and Women's Reproductive Health', *Studies in Family Planning*, **24**, pp. 73–86.

Princeton University Press for the essay: Elizabeth S. Anderson (1990), 'Is Women's Labor a Commodity?', *Philosophy & Public Affairs*, **19**, pp. 71–92. Copyright ©1990 Princeton University Press.

Saint Louis University School of Law for the essay: Christine E. Gudorf (1996), 'Gender and Culture in the Globalization of Bioethics', *Saint Louis University Public Law Review*, **15**, pp. 331–51. Copyright © 1996 Saint Louis University School of Law, St Louis, Missouri. Reprinted with permission of the Saint Louis University Public Law Review.

Swets & Zeitlinger Publishers for the essays: Lisa S. Parker (1995), 'Breast Cancer Genetic Screening and Critical Bioethics' Gaze', *The Journal of Medicine and Philosophy*, **20**, pp. 313–37; Kathleen Marie Dixon (1994), 'Oppressive Limits: Callahan's Foundation Myth', *The Journal of Medicine and Philosophy*, **19**, pp. 613–37.

Taylor & Francis Ltd for the essays: Marilys N. Guillemin (1999), 'Managing Menopause: A Critical Feminist Engagement', *Scandinavian Journal of Public Health*, **27**, pp. 273–78. Copyright © 1999 Scandinavian University Press; Robert H. Blank (1993), 'Maternal–Fetal Relationship: The Courts and Social Policy', *The Journal of Legal Medicine*, **14**, pp. 73–92. Copyright © 1993 Taylor & Francis. http:www.tandf.co.uk/journals.

University Publishing Group for the essay: Linda LeMoncheck (1996), 'Philosophy, Gender Politics, and In Vitro Fertilization: A Feminist Ethic of Reproductive Healthcare', *The Journal of Clinical Ethics*, **7**, pp. 160–76.

University of Toronto Press Inc. for the essay: Judith Mosoff (1995), 'Motherhood, Madness, and Law', *University of Toronto Law Journal*, **45**, pp. 107–42. Reprinted by permission of University of Toronto Press Inc.

Every effort has been made to trace all the copyright holders, but if any have been inadvertently overlooked the publishers will be pleased to make the necessary arrangement at the first opportunity.

Series Preface

Few academic disciplines have developed with such pace in recent years as bioethics. And because the subject crosses so many disciplines important writing is to be found in a range of books and journals, access to the whole of which is likely to elude all but the most committed of scholars. The International Library of Medicine, Ethics and Law is designed to assist the scholarly endeavour by providing in accessible volumes a compendium of basic materials drawn from the most significant periodical literature. Each volume contains essays of central theoretical importance in its subject area, and each throws light on important bioethical questions in the world today. The series as a whole – there will be fifteen volumes – makes available an extensive range of valuable material (the standard 'classics' and the not-so-standard) and should prove of inestimable value to those involved in the research, teaching and study of medicine, ethics and law. The fifteen volumes together – each with introductions and bibliographies – are a library in themselves – an indispensable resource in a world in which even the best-stocked library is unlikely to cover the range of materials contained within these volumes.

It remains for me to thank the editors who have pursued their task with commitment, insight and enthusiasm, to thank also the hard-working staff at Ashgate – theirs is a mammoth enterprise – and to thank my secretary, Anita Garfoot for the enormous assistance she has given me in bringing the series from idea to reality.

MICHAEL FREEMAN
Series Editor
Faculty of Laws
University College London

Introduction

Our Approach

In assembling this volume, we began by considering the distinct role that should be played by a collection of essays focused on women within a general series about medicine, ethics and the law. Although, clearly, we needed to seek out essays that address concerns specific to women, there are many different ways of interpreting this criterion. Simply raising the 'woman question' turns the focus towards gender and the meaning of gender difference. This is in marked contrast to works including the term 'man' or 'men' in their titles, since discussions of men's concerns typically omit any reflection on the relevance of gender. The term 'man' is commonly used to reflect gender-neutrality in the English language and, even when it is restricted to the male half of the species, the gendered implications of its usage are seldom addressed. It is as if women are defined by their difference from men but not vice versa, so that gender, and the difference it implies, only appear relevant from the perspective of women. Moreover, the generic male is usually taken to represent the norm for the entire species. His body and experience provide the standard measure against which everyone is to be compared. Women are seen as the alien 'other', approached as a source of complication if resources and interests permit. In other words, women are usually treated as being of secondary, not primary, importance.

In using gender as a fundamental organizing principle for this volume, we do not mean to imply that there is a straightforward basis for the apparent gender differences discussed. We recognize that it is no simple matter to decide on the precise nature of gender differences: they go well beyond 'mere' biological features. In fact, biology is an imperfect guide for assigning gender, let alone for interpreting its significance (see Dreger, Chapter 11). Nevertheless, most societies organize themselves on the basis of two mutually exclusive and exhaustive genders and, therefore, the assignment of gender influences most aspects of a person's social, personal and public life. Our own view is that gender is an important social category that is related to, but not defined by nor reducible to, biological characteristics.

Given the significance of gender to a person's life experience, we consider it remarkable that the worlds of medicine, law and ethics – like those of business, politics, religion and culture – have largely ignored the wide range of women's distinctive needs and experiences. The primary area in which any of these disciplines pay attention to women's concerns is that of reproduction (and, to a lesser degree, sexuality). In medicine, the speciality of obstetrics and gynaecology addresses women's reproductive and sexual organs and activities. Similarly, most of the literature in bioethics and health law that particularly focuses on women involves debates about the regulation of women's sexual and reproductive lives (for example, prostitution and abortion). Even in these matters, women often remain invisible within discussions that are directed towards abstract considerations about the rights of foetuses and the clients of prostitutes; often there is no acknowledgement of the impact of proposed policies on gender relations.

Where the institutions of medicine, ethics and the law intersect in their interest in women's reproductive and sexual lives, the impact on women can be profound. Most cultures have demonstrated a strong interest in controlling women's sexual and reproductive activities. In modern societies, medicine is a principal instrument for this activity, through its role in providing (or withholding) contraceptives, abortions, assisted conception, prenatal surveillance and advice regarding proper parenting techniques. Under the guise of concern about the well-being of (future) children, ethical arguments have been created which serve to demonize women (for example, crack cocaine users) who fail to conform to popular opinion about appropriate maternal behaviour (see Zierler and Krieger, Chapter 20), and the force of the law is sometimes invoked to enforce medical advice (Blank, Chapter 7). In such ways, these three social institutions often collaborate in support of a gendered social order.

Of course, women are more than vessels for the sexual and reproductive needs of others, and their encounters with medicine, ethics and the law involve many other aspects of their lives. Legal policies and dominant ethical beliefs have a significant impact on many aspects of women's health. For example, proposals that require the old to step aside in order to permit the use of limited health resources for the young have a differential impact on women since they constitute a significant majority of the elderly population (see Dixon, Chapter 16). Similarly, policies that require informed consent of clinical research subjects without reflecting on the selection criteria that determine who is invited to participate have supported research practices that often produce inadequate health information for the proper medical care of women (see Baird, Chapter 12).

Indeed, many of the health practices and policies of bioethics and health law tend to affect women and men in different ways. For instance, cultural attitudes about the unreliability of women's 'intuitive' knowledge may pervade the patient–physician relationship and distort the effect of standard approaches to informed consent and truth-telling (see Malterud, Chapter 13). In addition, principles that demand respect for the privacy of the family may be exceptionally dangerous for women caught in violent relationships (Jecker, Chapter 19). Yet, few discussions in the medical, bioethics or health law literature ask us to reflect on the possibility that women and men can be affected differently by the practices and policies discussed. Rather, most authors take the experience of men (and often that of white, middle-class, educated men) as representative of all patients (and providers) and ignore the social contexts of the participants.

In contrast, we propose that it is always meaningful to raise the question of gender within debates in medicine, ethics and the law. Whether exploring end-of-life decision-making, allocation of scarce resources, control of information, standards of consent, treatment of research subjects, implications of new genetic knowledge or the care of persons with mental illness, we need to consider how the proposed practices will affect both women and men.

Moreover, when focusing on the significance of gender differences in medicine, law and ethics, it is important not to lose sight of other important social differences. Individuals' social position and health status are affected not only by their gender, but also by their race, ethnicity, class, age, sexuality, religion, level of physical and mental ability and family relationships. In societies like our own, which attach different social power and opportunity to people according to their membership in groups defined by these categories, individuals' encounters with the health care system may be influenced by their position with respect to these socially significant categories. No one is simply a woman or a man; each of us is a woman or man whose identity has been shaped by the social meaning of our race, class, sexuality and so on.

Our approach to this collection is decidedly feminist. By that we mean that we consider the lives and experiences of women as primary. Hence, we focus on the question of how women's encounters with the health care system are structured by gender and other socially significant dimensions of their lives (rather than the question of how women differ from the male 'norm'). Our account is also feminist in that it is sensitive to issues of power and privilege between social groups. We perceive systematic patterns of oppression in society whereby multiple social institutions and practices jointly favour the interests of some social groups and disadvantage others and we believe, moreover, that such arrangements constitute a form of social injustice that demands correction. We are, then, particularly attuned to essays that seek to name and understand ways in which medical, legal and ethical assumptions and practices contribute to patterns of oppression involving gender and other social categories.

Inevitably, many of the essays included in this volume reflect our own feminist leanings. Not surprisingly, we are more likely to find such perspectives particularly compelling. It is not only our own biases at work here, however. It is also the fact that even putting women on the agenda of medicine, ethics or the law (with respect to issues outside of reproduction) is usually a feminist act. It is primarily feminists who tend to ask the 'woman question', exploring ways in which medical, legal, and ethical norms might affect women. That said, it is important to observe that the term 'feminist' is itself much contested and that there is much active debate among researchers and activists who adopt that label. The various authors included in this volume hold very different feminist (and occasionally non-feminist) perspectives.

The Selections

In organizing this collection, we began with a list of topics we considered to be relevant and then set about finding essays that would best represent the debates at issue. We sought provocative essays that make clear the relevance of their topic while presenting a strong argument for a particular position. Some essays are especially strong in the first category (explaining the importance of the subject), others in the latter (staking out an intriguing, but often contentious, position). A principal aim was to ensure a balanced set of topics reflecting the wide diversity of women's experiences and concerns in the realm of medicine, ethics and the law.

The Essays

We begin with a set of essays intended to situate our investigation within a global context. In Chapter 1, Christine Gudorf explores the significance of gender and culture in a global bioethics, noting the ways in which gender inequality is often preserved under appeals to protect local cultures. She discusses female circumcision and fertility reduction programmes to demonstrate the importance of broadening the focus of bioethics and health law beyond the perspectives and experiences of white, Western men (or women). These examples make visible some of the limits of a bioethics constructed from the apparently neutral position of abstract principles.

Bonnie Kettel (Chapter 2) is also sensitive to the relevance of women's geographical and political locations. She invites us to develop a gendered approach to environmental health policy and action. Differences in domestic responsibilities, employment, and socioeconomic status result in different environmental impacts on the health and well-being of women and men, even when they share the same households. Environmental health risks are especially serious for those women who have minimal economic resources whether they live in the developing or the industrialized world.

In Chapter 3 Rebecca Cook continues the international focus by reviewing the importance of promoting women's reproductive health. She stresses the importance of ensuring that women gain control over their reproductive lives and be given the tools to determine the number and timing of the children they produce. Her essay identifies the potential power of international human rights law to support this agenda, while documenting some of the barriers to implementing the needed laws in particular jurisdictions.

Access to voluntary, safe, and reliable contraceptives is a fundamental element of women's ability to control their reproductive lives. Yet, a legacy of morally problematic practices in the development and provision of various forms of contraception make it a sensitive practice in the minds of many. Abuses include coercion in the implementation of state-sponsored eugenics and population control policies, premature marketing of products before safety was established, and restrictions on access depending on a woman's marital status. In light of this sorry history, it is particularly urgent to attend to the many moral questions posed by new forms of long-acting contraception now being offered to women. In Chapter 4, George Brown and Ellen Moskowitz explore some of these issues and remind us of the importance of each woman's particular social location in her deliberations regarding participation in various contraceptive practices.

Contraceptives are not foolproof, however, nor are they always available or employed when necessary. Full reproductive control requires that women also have access to abortion which, nonetheless remains an extremely contentious practice in many parts of the world, particularly in the United States where it has assumed an enormous political significance. Accordingly, this topic remains the most widely discussed in the journals of medicine, bioethics, and health law, and the task of selecting one specific essay was particularly challenging. Even our preference for feminist perspectives was of limited assistance, since many feminists have written on the subject, and not always to the same end. While most feminist authors support a woman's right to choose, some do not, and there are many different arguments used to support the various positions. In the essay we have chosen, Catriona Mackenzie (Chapter 5) insists that abortion be understood as involving relationships between foetuses and the women in whose bodies they reside. Hence, she argues, we must attend to the phenomenological experiences of pregnant women when setting abortion policies.

Following on from this insight, we include two essays that deal with aspects of the complex experience of pregnancy. In Chapter 6, Abby Lippman explores the increasing pressure on pregnant women to undergo prenatal testing of their foetuses and identifies some of the dangerous assumptions behind this practice. She is especially concerned about the place of prenatal testing within a larger world-view that she dubs 'geneticization' – that is, the dominance of genetic explanations for health and illness over social understandings. She questions some of the particular implications this perspective holds for women.

Robert Blank (Chapter 7) addresses the fact that women's behaviour in pregnancy may affect the health of their children, taking as the focus of his concern those situations where women endanger the health of their foetuses through dangerous and often illegal acts (for example, illicit drug use). Some courts have responded to this problem by constructing the relationship between the pregnant woman and her foetus as adversarial and have taken upon themselves the responsibility of defending the interests of the foetus, using their judicial powers to coerce the woman's compliance and/or to punish her for her recklessness. Being decidedly non-feminist in his approach, Blank is sympathetic to the motivation behind these actions, but reluctantly concludes that there are severe practical limitations to the strategy of using judicial powers to force pregnant women to comply with medical advice. Better results can usually be achieved through a non-punitive, education-focused approach.

The subject of reproduction also extends to medicine's role in assisted conception. Hence, we include essays addressing two types of intervention aimed at facilitating reproduction: Linda LeMoncheck (Chapter 8) writes on in vitro fertilization (IVF) and Elizabeth Anderson (Chapter 9) discusses contractual pregnancies ('surrogacy'). These two technologies are significant because they represent the building blocks of most current reproductive technologies, including the use of donated eggs and embryos, pre-implantation diagnosis, and the deliberate division of fertilized eggs (a form of cloning). LeMoncheck reviews debates among feminists about the power and threat of IVF and proposes criteria for an approach to reproductive ethics that is consistent with feminist values, while Anderson explores the implications of importing the values and terms of the marketplace to women's reproductive labour and the production of children by commercial contract.

With Judith Mosoff's essay (Chapter 10), we make the transition from a focus on women's role in reproduction to other dimensions of women's medical encounters. Mosoff explores a particular hazard women face when diagnosed with mental illness. In such a circumstance, the normative demands of motherhood do not end with the completion of pregnancy but continue throughout the child's life, and the courts may intervene in women's lives at many stages for failure to conform to the norms of 'good mothering'.

The remainder of the book deals with a wide range of issues of particular significance to women. In Chapter 11, Alice Domurat Dreger examines some of the ethical issues surrounding the phenomenon of intersexuality, including the common medical response to perceived ambiguity in a newborn's sexual organs. She discusses the medical tendency to surgically assign a particular gender to each infant depending on the appearance of the child's genitalia. There are many ethical issues involved when invasive medical technologies are used to reinforce problematic cultural expectations about the nature of sex and gender.

Karen Baird (Chapter 12) provides an overview of the history of exclusion of women and minorities from many domains of medical research and also provides some of the key moral arguments for including both groups in clinical trials. By reviewing the ways in which two different US agencies (the National Institute of Health and the Food and Drug Administration) set about trying to correct the historical neglect of women in medical research, she is able to demonstrate the practical implications of alternative approaches.

In Chapter 13 Kirsti Malterud explores ways in which gender pervades encounters between individual patients and their physicians. Physicians tend to take the subjective complaints of men more seriously than those of women when there is no ready correlation between the symptoms described and some objective measure (such as x-rays). Working within a semiotic analysis of the communication patterns between patients and physicians, she argues that assigning greater validity to women's voices would result in improved health outcomes and experiences for women.

Like Gudorf, Lisa Parker (Chapter 14) turns her attention to the discipline of bioethics, investigating its responsibility in the development of a protocol for breast cancer genetic screening. In her view, bioethics should be playing an active role in identifying the complex political, cultural and conceptual complexities of this disease and the significance of a genetic test for certain forms of it. She recommends adoption of a form of 'critical bioethics' that interrogates its own normative and conceptual commitments.

In Chapter 15, Marilys Guillemin discusses some of the debates surrounding the medical management of the menopause, noting that women's resistance to the long-term use of hormone replacement therapy (HRT) has been constructed in medical terms as a problem of 'non-compliance'. This is viewed primarily as a public health problem because of the potential health costs of caring for a growing population of elderly women who fail to take advantage of the preventive health benefits of HRT. While objecting to many feminist critiques of HRT, she finds merit in feminism's commitment to focusing on the lives and needs of particular women.

Kathleen Marie Dixon (Chapter 16) moves the discussion further along the life cycle and examines the gendered implications of Daniel Callahan's influential recommendation that the proper response to scarcity of medical resources is to limit the medical care available to the elderly to comfort care, not to the extension of life. She warns of the potential implicit in this proposal to reconstruct the social order in ways that are particularly dangerous for women and she challenges four of its supporting assumptions ('myths').

In Chapter 17, Kathryn Morgan argues that bioethics must examine the widespread practice of elective cosmetic surgery, the primary users of which are women seeking to meet cultural norms of feminine beauty and youthful appearance. Adopting a Foucauldian perspective on the normalization of medical technology in women's lives, she asks what criterion of autonomy is appropriate for evaluating women's choices for these procedures when society so clearly prefers its women to be attractive.

Following on from this, Susan Wendell (Chapter 18) also asks us to reflect on cultural ideals of what is normal and acceptable and how such attitudes marginalize people with disabilities. She calls for a feminist theory of disability that would extend feminism's understanding of gender as a socially constructed category built on a biological reality and apply a similar analysis to the category of disability. Drawing a connection between the oppression of women and the oppression of people with disabilities, Wendell argues for the importance of accepting people with imperfect bodies or minds as full members of society.

Nancy Jecker's essay (Chapter 19) calls into question medicine's reluctant response to domestic violence, arguing that principles of beneficence and non-maleficence have proven inadequate in dislodging physicians' resistance to intruding on family matters. She proposes situating the problem under the principle of justice in order to make evident the moral necessity of intervening.

Sally Zierler and Nancy Krieger tie together many of the preceding themes in their focus on women and HIV (Chapter 20), arguing that social inequalities are at the heart of most risk factors for HIV infection among women. Reviewing the role not only of race and culture, but more accurately of racism and sexism, they explain how social and economic inequality contributes to particular women's vulnerability to infection. Gender inequalities associated with economic dependence on men and domestic violence undermine many women's ability to protect themselves against infection. Their analysis makes especially vivid the importance of economic security for women's health.

Our task in preparing this collection was complicated by the fact that the series is intended to bring together journal essays, and, sadly, most academic journals pay little attention to women's experiences beyond questions of reproduction. Fortunately, there is an abundant literature in the field of women, medicine, ethics and the law to be found in books. For readers interested in further explorations on the subject of women, medicine, ethics, and the law, we include below a list of some of many books that directly focus on this topic.

Acknowledgements

We were very fortunate to have benefited from the generous assistance of Patrycja Maksalon, Denise Ryder and Jocelyn Downie (along with the resources of the Dalhousie University Health Law Institute), in putting together the selections for this volume.

Further Reading

Adams, Diane (ed.) (1995), *Health Issues for Women of Color: A Cultural Diversity Perspective*, Thousand Oaks, CA: Sage Publications.

Apple, Rima D. (ed.) (1990), *Women, Health, and Medicine in America*, New York & London: Garland Publishing, Inc.

Bair, B. and Cayleff, S.E. (eds) (1993), *Wings of Gauze: Women of Color and the Experience of Health and Illness*, Detroit: Wayne State University Press.

Basen, Gwynne, Eichler, Margrit and Lippman, Abby (eds) (1993), *Misconceptions: The Social Construction of Choice and the New Reproductive and Genetic Technologies*, Prescott, ON: Voyageur Publishing.

Batt, Sharon (1994), *Patient No More: The Politics of Breast Cancer*, Charlottetown, PEI: Gynergy Books.

Boston Women's Health Collective (1976), *Our Bodies, Ourselves: A Book By and For Women*, New York: Simon and Schuster.

Boston Women's Health Collective (1992), *The New Our Bodies, Ourselves*, New York: Touchstone/ Simon and Schuster.

Brockman, Joan and Chunn, Dorothy E. (eds) (1993), *Investigating Gender Bias: Law, Courts and the Legal Profession*, Toronto: Thompson Educational Publishing, Inc.

Browne, Susan E., Connors, Debra and Stern, Nanci (eds) (1985), *With the Power of Each Breath: A Disabled Woman's Anthology*, San Francisco: Cleis Press.

Caplan, Paula (1995), *They Say You're Crazy: How the World's Most Powerful Psychiatrists Decide Who is Normal*, Reading, MA: Addison-Wesley.

Chesler, Phyllis (1972), *Women and Madness*, Garden City, NY: Doubleday.

Coney, Sandra (1988), *The Unfortunate Experiment: The Full Story Behind the Inquiry into Cervical Cancer Treatment*, Aukland, NZ: Penguin Books.

Corea, Gena (1985), *The Hidden Malpractice: How American Medicine Mistreats Women*, New York: Harper Colophon Books.

Currie, Dawn H. and Raoul, Valerie (eds) (1991), *The Anatomy of Gender: Women's Struggle for the Body*, Ottawa: Carleton University Press.

Dan, Alice J. (ed.) (1994), *Reframing Women's Health: Multidisciplinary Research and Practice*, London, England: Sage Publications.

Davis, Kathy (1995), *Reshaping the Female Body: The Dilemma of Cosmetic Surgery*, New York: Routledge.

Davis-Floyd, Robbie E. (1992), *Birth as an American Rite of Passage*, Berkeley, CA: University of California Press.

Davis-Floyd, Robbie E. and Sargent, Carolyn (eds) (1997), *Childbirth and Authoritative Knowledge: Cross-Cultural Perspectives*, Berkeley, CA: University of California Press.

Diprose, Rosalyn (1994), *The Bodies of Women: Ethics, Embodiment and Sexual Difference*, New York: Routledge.

Dobash, R.P. and Dobash, R.E. (1992), *Women, Violence and Social Change*, New York: Routledge.

Donchin, Anne and Purdy, Laura M. (eds) (1999), *Embodying Bioethics: Recent Feminist Advances*, New York: Rowman & Littlefield Publishers, Inc.

Donnison, Jean (1977), *Midwives and Medical Men: A History of Inter-Professional Rivalries and Women's Rights*, London: Heinemann.

Doyal, Lesley (1995), *What Makes Women Sick: Gender and the Political Economy of Health*, London: Macmillan Press Ltd.

Dreifus, Claudia (ed.) (1977), *Seizing Our Bodies: The Politics of Women's Health*, New York: Vintage Books.

Duden, Barbara (1993), *Disembodying Women: Perspectives on Pregnancy and the Unborn*, Cambridge, MA: Harvard University Press.

Dula, Annette and Goering, Sara (eds) (1994), *'It Just Ain't Fair': The Ethics of Health Care for African Americans*. Westport CT: Praeger.

Easlea, Brian (1981), *Science and Sexual Oppression: Patriarchy's Confrontation with Woman and Nature*, London: Weidenfeld and Nicolson.

Ehrenreich, Barbara (1973), *Complaints and Disorders: The Sexual Politics of Sickness*, New York: Old Westbury.

Ehrenreich, Barbara and English, Deirdre (1979), *For Her Own Good: 250 Years of the Experts' Advice to Women*, London: Pluto Press.

Faden, Ruth, Geller, Gail and Powers, Madison (eds) (1991), *AIDS, Women and the Next Generation: Towards a Morally Acceptable Public Policy for HIV Testing of Pregnant Women and Newborns*, New York: Oxford University Press.

Farquhar, Dion (1996), *The Other Machine: Discourse and Reproductive Technologies*, New York: Routledge.

Fausto-Sterling, Anne (1985), *Myths of Gender: Biological Theories About Women and Men*, New York: Basic Books Inc.

Fee, Elizabeth (ed.) (1993), *Women and Health: The Politics of Sex in Medicine*, Amityville, NY: Baywood.

Fee, Elizabeth and Krieger, Nancy (eds) (1994), *Women's Health, Politics, and Power: Essays on Sex/Gender, Medicine, and Public Health*, Amityville, NY: Baywood.

Fine, Michelle and Asch, Adrienne (eds) (1988), *Women with Disabilities: Essays in Psychology, Culture, and Politics*, Philadelphia: Temple University Press.

Fisher, Sue (1986) *In the Patient's Best Interests: Women and the Politics of Medical Decisions*, New Brunswick NJ: Rutgers University Press.

Ginsberg, Faye and Rapp, Rayna (eds) (1995), *Conceiving the New World Order: The Global Politics of Reproduction*, Berkeley, CA: University of California Press.

Gordon, Linda (1976), *Woman's Body, Woman's Right: A Social History of Birth Control in America*, New York: Penguin.

Grant, Nicole J. (1992), *The Selling of Contraception: The Dalkon Shield Case, Sexuality and Women's Anatomy*, Columbus, Ohio: Ohio State University Press.

Handwerker, W. Penn (ed.) (1990), *Births and Power, Social Change and the Politics of Reproduction*, Boulder, CO, San Francisco and London: Westview Press.

Hannaford, Susan (1985), *Living Outside Inside. A Disabled Woman's Experience. Towards a Social and Political Perspective*, Berkeley, CA: Canterbury Press.

Hanvey, L. and Kinnon, D. (1993), *The Health Care Sector's Response to Woman Abuse*, Health Canada, National Clearinghouse on Family Violence, June 1993.

Hartman, Betsy (1987), *Reproductive Rights and Wrongs: The Global Politics of Population Control and Contraceptive Choice*, New York: Harper and Row.

Hausman, Bernice (1995), *Changing Sex: Transsexualism, Technology, and Ideas of Gender*, Durham, NC: Duke University Press.

Hillyer, Barbara (1993), *Feminism and Disability*, Norman, OK and London: University of Oklahoma Press.

Hoangmai, Pham, Freeman, Phyllis and Kohn, Nancy (1992), *Understanding the Second Epidemic: The*

Status of Research on Women and AIDS in the United States, Washington, D.C.: Center for Women Policy Studies.

Holmes, Helen Bequaert and Purdy, Laura M. (eds) (1992), *Feminist Perspectives in Medical Ethics*, Bloomington and Indianapolis: Indiana University Press.

Jacobus, Mary, Fox Keller, Evelyn and Shuttleworth, Sally (eds) (1990), *Body/Politics: Women and the Discourses of Science*, New York: Routledge.

Jordanova, Ludmilla (1989), *Sexual Visions: Images of Gender in Science and Medicine Between the Eighteenth and Twentieth Centuries*, Brighton: Harvester Wheatsheaf.

Koblinsky, Marge, Timyan, Judith and Gay, Jill (eds) (1993), *The Health of Women: A Global Perspective*, Boulder, CO: Westview Press.

Komesaroff, Paul A. (ed.) (1995), *Troubled Bodies: Critical Perspectives on Postmodernism, Medical Ethics, and the Body*, Durham, NC: Duke University Press.

Laslett, Barbara, Kohlstedt, Sally Gregory, Longino, Helen and Hammonds, Evelynn (eds) (1996), *Gender and Scientific Authority*, Chicago: University of Chicago Press.

Leavitt, Judith Waltzer (ed.) (1984), *Women and Health in America*, Madison: University of Wisconsin Press.

Lewin, Ellen and Olesen, Virginia (eds) (1985), *Women, Health and Healing: Toward a New Perspective*, London: Tavistock Publications.

Lock, Margaret M. (1993), *Encounters with Aging: Mythologies of Menopause in Japan and North America*, Berkeley, CA: University of California Press.

Lock, Margaret M. and Kaufert, Patricia A. (1998), *Pragmatic Women and Body Politics*, New York: Cambridge University Press.

Lorber, Judith (1997), *Gender and the Social Construction of Illness*, Thousand Oaks, CA: Sage Publications.

McLaren, Angus and McLaren, Arlene Tigar (1986), *The Bedroom and the State: The Changing Practices and Politics of Contraception and Abortion in Canada*, Toronto: McClelland and Stewart.

Mahowald, Mary Briody (1993) *Women and Children in Health Care: An Unequal Majority*, New York: Oxford University Press.

Martin, Emily (1987) *The Woman in the Body: A Cultural Analysis of Reproduction*, Boston, MA: Beacon Press.

Mastroianni, Anna C., Faden, Ruth and Federman, Daniel (eds) (1994), *Women and Health Research: Ethical and Legal Issues of Including Women in Clinical Studies*, 2 vols, Washington D.C.: National Academy Press.

Messing, Karen (1991), *Occupational Health and Safety Concerns of Canadian Women: A Review*, Ottawa, ON: Labour Canada.

Messing, Karen (1998), *One-eyed Science: Occupational Health and Women Workers*, Philadelphia: Temple University Press.

More, E. Singer and Milligan, M.A. (eds) (1994), *The Empathetic Practitioner: Empathy, Gender, and Medicine*, New Brunswick, NJ: Rutgers.

Mort, Frank (1987), *Dangerous Sexualities: Medico-Moral Politics in England Since 1830*, London: Routledge and Kegan Paul.

Moss, Kary L. (ed.) (1996), *Man-Made Medicine: Women's Health, Public Policy, and Reform*, Durham, NC: Duke University Press.

Mukhopadhyay, Swapna (1998), *Poverty, Gender, and Reproductive Choice: An Analysis of Linkages*, New Delhi: Manohar.

Nechas, Eileen and Foley, Denise (1994), *Unequal Treatment: What You Don't Know About How Women are Mistreated by the Medical Community*, New York: Simon and Schuster.

Oakley, Ann (1984), *The Captured Womb: A History of the Medical Care of Pregnant Women*, Oxford: Basil Blackwell.

Oudshoorn, Nelly (1994), *Beyond the Natural Body: An Archeology of Sex Hormones*, New York: Routledge.

Overall, Christine (1987), *Ethics and Human Reproduction: A Feminist Analysis*, London: Unwin Hyman.

Overall, Christine (ed.) (1989), *The Future of Human Reproduction*, Toronto: The Women's Press.

Overall, Christine and Zion, William P. (eds) (1991), *Perspectives on AIDS: Ethical and Social Issues*, New York: Oxford University Press.

Perales, Cesar A. and Young, Lauren S. (eds) (1988), *Too Little, Too Late: Dealing with the Health Needs of Women in Poverty*, New York: Harrington Park Press.

Petchesky, Rosalind Pollack (1984), *Abortion and Woman's Choice: The State, Sexuality, and Reproductive Freedom*, Boston, MA: Northeastern University Press.

Petersen, Kerry Anne (1997), *Intersections: Women on Law, Medicine, and Technology*, Aldershot: Ashgate/Dartmouth.

Purdy, Laura (1996), *Reproducing Persons*, Ithaca, NY: Cornell University Press.

Ratcliff, Kathryn Strother, Feree, Myra Marx, Mellow, Gail O., Wright, Barbara Drygulski, Price, Glenda D., Yanoshik, Kim and Freston, Margie S. (1989), *Healing Technologies: Feminist Perspectives*, Ann Arbor, MI: University of Michigan Press.

Raymond, Janice (1993), *Women as Wombs: Reproductive Technologies and the Battle Over Women's Freedom*, San Francisco: Harper San Francisco.

Reed, James (1978), *The Birth Control Movement and American Society: From Private Vice to Public Virtue*, Princeton, NJ: Princeton University Press.

Rosser, Sue V. (1994), *Women's Health – Missing from U.S. Medicine*, Bloomington, IN: Indiana University Press

Rothenberg, Karen H. and Thomson, Elizabeth J. (eds) (1994), *Women & Prenatal Testing: Facing the Challenges of Genetic Technology*, Columbus: Ohio State University Press.

Rothman, Barbara Katz (1982), *In Labour: Women and Power in the Birthplace*, London: Junction Books.

Rothman, Barbara Katz (1986), *The Tentative Pregnancy: Prenatal Diagnosis and the Future of Motherhood*, New York: Viking Press.

Rowland, Robyn (1992), *Living Laboratories: Women and Reproductive Technologies*, Bloomington: Indiana University Press.

Russell, Denise (1995), *Women, Madness & Medicine,* Cambridge: Polity Press.

Ruzek, Sheryl Burt (1978), *The Women's Health Movement: Feminist Alternatives to Medical Control*, New York: Praeger Publishers.

Sargent, Carolyn and Brettell, Caroline (eds) (1996), *Gender and Health: An International Perspective*, Upper Saddle River, NJ: Prentice-Hall.

Saxton, Marsha and Howe, Florence (eds) (1987), *With Wings: An Anthology of Literature by and about Women with Disabilities*, New York: The Feminist Press at the City University of New York.

Scully, Diana (1980), *Men Who Control Women's Health: The Miseducation of Obstetrician–Gynecologists*, Boston, MA: Houghton Mifflin.

Sherwin, Susan (1992), *No Longer Patient: Feminist Ethics and Health Care*, Philadelphia, PA: Temple University Press.

Sherwin, Susan, Coordinator, The Feminist Health Care Research Network (1998), *The Politics of Women's Health: Exploring Agency and Autonomy*, Philadelphia: Temple University Press.

Shiva, V. and Moser, Ingunn (eds) (1995), *Biopolitics: A Feminist and Ecological Reader on Biotechnology*, London and Penang, Malaysia: Zed Books and the Third World Network.

Terry, Jennifer and Calvert, Melodie (eds) (1997), *Processed Lives: Gender and Technology in Everyday Life*, New York: Routledge.

Todd, Alexandra Dundas (1989), *Intimate Adversaries: Cultural Conflict Between Doctors and Women Patients*, Philadelphia: University of Pennsylvania Press.

Tong, Rosemarie (1997), *Feminist Approaches to Bioethics: Theoretical Reflections and Practical Applications*, Boulder, CO: Westview Press.

Wear, Delese (1997), *Privilege in the Medical Academy: A Feminist Examines Gender, Race, and Power*, New York: Teachers College Press.

Wendell, Susan (1996), *The Rejected Body: Feminist Philosophical Reflections on Disability*, New York: Routledge.

White, Evelyn C. (ed.) (1990), *The Black Women's Health Book: Speaking for Ourselves*, Seattle: Seal Press.

Whitford, Linda M. and Poland, Marilyn L. (eds) (1989), *New Approaches to Human Reproduction: Social and Ethical Dimensions*, Boulder, CO: Westview Press.

Wolf, Susan M. (ed.) (1996), *Feminism and Bioethics: Beyond Reproduction*, New York: Oxford University Press.

Women's Counselling Referral and Education Center (1985), *Helping Ourselves: A Handbook for Women Starting Groups*, Toronto: Women's Press.

Worcester, Nancy and Whatley, Marianne H. (eds) (1994), *Women's Health: Readings on Social, Economic, and Political Issues*, (2nd edn), Dubuque, Iowa: Kendall/Hunt Publishing Co.

[1]

GENDER AND CULTURE IN THE GLOBALIZATION OF BIOETHICS

CHRISTINE E. GUDORF*

In the last four decades, the field of western bioethics has broadened from its original focus on physician-patient issues (hence the name change from medical ethics) in three general areas: a tremendous expansion of issues involving both new technologies and research norms, as well as the challenges to both prevailing principles and practices from the women's movement.[1]

The latest challenge to the field of bioethics arises within the globalization of the field, and includes issues such as the shifting of technology from rich to poor nations, the health care brain-drain from poor to rich nations,[2] as well as the challenges to bioethic principles from both non-European cultures and the growing crisis of environmental degradation caused by overconsumption and overpopulation.

This paper will address two specific challenges to bioethics within the globalization process: 1) female circumcision, and 2) the role of health care personnel in fertility reduction. Both issues involve challenges to existing understandings of bioethics, affect largely female populations, and are highly charged religious issues in much of the world. Furthermore, there are dramatic implications in these issues for the future of American bioethics.

---

* Christine E. Gudorf is a Professor of Religious Studies, Florida International University, Miami. She has written extensively on ethics in international health, women's, and development issues. Her latest book is BODY, SEX, AND PLEASURE: RECONSTRUCTING CHRISTIAN SEXUAL ETHICS (Pilgrim 1994).

1. *See, e.g.,* Margaret A. Farley, *Feminist Theology and Bioethics, in* WOMEN'S CONSCIOUSNESS, WOMEN'S CONSCIENCE: A READER IN FEMINIST ETHICS 285 (Barbara H. Andolsen et al. eds., 1985); SUSAN SHERWIN, NO LONGER PATIENT: FEMINIST ETHICS AND HEALTH CARE (1992); JANET G. RAYMOND, WOMEN AS WOMBS: REPRODUCTIVE TECHNOLOGIES AND THE BATTLE OVER WOMEN'S FREEDOM (1993); Christine E. Gudorf, *A Feminist Critique of Biomedical Principlism, in* A MATTER OF PRINCIPLES?: FERMENT IN U.S. BIOETHICS 164 (Edwin R. DuBose et al. eds., 1994).

2. This is not always in the direction one might suspect. For example, there are recent years in which the entire graduating class of the medical school in Khartoum, Sudan has emigrated to Saudi Arabia. HANNY LIGHTFOOT-KLEIN, PRISONERS OF RITUAL: AN ODYSSEY INTO FEMALE GENITAL CIRCUMCISION IN AFRICA 49-50 (1989).

I. FEMALE CIRCUMCISION

Until fairly recently, relatively few persons outside affected nations had much knowledge of the various practices encompassed by the term female circumcision.[3] Individual Christian missionaries usually deplored the practice when they came into contact with it in the nineteenth century.[4] However, ignorance prevailed until international organizations, most notably UNICEF and the World Health Organization (WHO), began in the early 1980s to advocate the abolition of what was called "female genital mutilation," and women's groups around the world (in affected as well as unaffected nations) began publicizing the practices grouped under the term.[5]

The two bioethical principles relevant to female circumcision are beneficence, or a ban on maleficence (based on the pledge in the Hippocratic oath to do no harm) and informed consent. Female circumcision practices vary according to the age of the girl at the time of circumcision.[6] Most African cultures practicing female circumcision place it within puberty rituals,[7] though the Beja and the Beni Amir tribes of Sudan historically circumcised girls of seven to forty days old.[8] But the age of circumcision for girls in Africa seems to be dropping. Descriptions of groups of newly circumcised girls often report ages from four to nine years old, and in some groups the surgery is done on girls who are only twenty-four months old.[9] Very seldom are adults the subjects of female circumcision.[10] Normally, parents are the guardians of minor children, so informed consent for intervention in the health of a child

---

3. I use "female circumcision" both because it is the English translation for the most commonly used general term within the affected populations, and because it avoids the pejorative connotations in the term "female genital mutilation" used by western/northern organizations and individuals. Globally, over two million females are at risk of female circumcision yearly; currently, eighty-five to one-hundred-fourteen million females are circumcised. Nahid Toubia, *Female Genital Mutilation, in* WOMEN'S RIGHTS, HUMAN RIGHTS 224, 224 (Julie Peters & Andrea Wolper eds., 1995).

4. LIGHTFOOT-KLEIN, *supra* note 2, at 219-20.

5. Isabelle R. Gunning, *Arrogant Perception, World-Travelling and Multicultural Feminism: The Case of Female Genital Surgeries*, 23 COLUM. HUM. RTS. L. REV. 189, 242 (1991-1992).

6. LIGHTFOOT-KLEIN, *supra* note 2, at 52.

7. FRAN P. HOSKEN, THE HOSKEN REPORT: GENITAL AND SEXUAL MUTILATION OF FEMALES 28 (3d ed. 1982).

8. LIGHTFOOT-KLEIN, *supra* note 2, at 30.

9. *Id.* at 36, 51 (reporting that the age of circumcision is declining all over Africa in an attempt to avoid excessive pain, opposition and fear in the girls); *see also* ALICE WALKER & PRATIBHA PARMAR, WARRIOR MARKS: FEMALE GENITAL MUTILATION AND THE SEXUAL BLINDING OF WOMEN 43, 172-73 (1993) (reporting many female circumcisions on girls four to nine years old).

10. Barbara Crossette, *Female Genital Mutilation by Immigrants Is Becoming Cause for Concern in the U.S.*, N.Y. TIMES, Dec. 10, 1995, at 18.

must be obtained from the parent. In the case of female circumcision, mothers, usually with the tacit consent of fathers, arrange for the circumcision, often with the help and sometimes the prompting of both maternal and paternal grandmothers who, in many cultures undergoing modernization today, tend to have more loyalty to traditional cultural and religious practices.[11] Female circumcision, then, does not formally violate the principle of informed consent, since it is the guardian of the child (a guardian who herself likely underwent the same surgery as a girl) who arranges the surgery. It is more difficult to conclude that female circumcision does not violate the principle of beneficence.

This principle insists that any harm inflicted on patients be both temporary and outweighed by future health benefit. Different socio-religious cultures have different explanations of the benefits and necessity of female circumcision, depending upon both the type of procedure locally done and the cultural understandings of gender and sexuality.[12] Female circumcision is the term used to describe at least three different surgical procedures. The most simple is the removal of the clitoral hood, sometimes along with a piece of the labia minora (the inner lips of the vulva).[13] This form is appropriately called female circumcision, since the hood of the clitoris is the analogue of the foreskin of the male penis.[14] However, this mild form is clearly the least practiced form in the contemporary world.[15] The intermediate form is a clitoridectomy, or excision of the entire clitoris, hood, glans and shaft, sometimes along with some or all of the labia minora.[16] The most extreme form of female circumcision is genital infibulation, often called pharaonic circumcision in Africa, and includes a clitoridectomy as well as the excision of the labia minora and as much as possible of the labia majora.[17] As a part of this last form of circumcision, the edges of skin on either side of the labia are stitched together, leaving a straw or wood splinter to hold open a one-centimeter passage for urine and menstrual flow, after which the girl's legs are tied together for three or four weeks.[18]

The resulting health dangers from female circumcision depend upon both the type of circumcision done, and the degree of sanitation within the surgical situation. Female genital surgeries outside urban areas are performed either by

---

11. LIGHTFOOT-KLEIN, *supra* note 2, at 128.

12. Reasons given for the procedure include maintaining custom, controlling female sexuality, increasing fertility, and promoting cleanliness. HOSKEN, *supra* note 7, at 31-32.

13. LIGHTFOOT-KLEIN, *supra* note 2, at 32-33.

14. Toubia, *supra* note 3, at 226-27.

15. LIGHTFOOT-KLEIN, *supra* note 2, at 33.

16. *Id.*

17. *Id.; see also* HOSKEN, *supra* note 7, at 27.

18. LIGHTFOOT-KLEIN, *supra* note 2, at 33; *see also* WALKER & PARMAR, *supra* note 9, at 367; HOSKEN, *supra* note 7, at 27.

female midwives, most of whom learned their trade from mothers or grandmothers, or by male barbers or priests, none of whom have much knowledge of antisepsis.[19]   In the cities, some circumcisors have some medical training, but few circumcisions involve anesthesia or sterile conditions.[20] The most immediate health dangers are infection, hemorrhage, and tetanus.[21] Few reliable statistics exist on mortality or sickness following circumcision, despite the fact that experts estimate there are 84 to 200 million living women who have undergone one of these procedures, usually under appalling conditions.[22]   Deaths following circumcisions are attributed to everything from hostile spirits to bad humors in the blood. In those who survive both the procedure itself and the infections which commonly follow, there can be two different kinds of damage. One is the damage to the woman's health, and the other is the reduced ability to enjoy sex.

The first type of damage is more or less limited to the pharaonic circumcisions.[23] Women with pharaonic circumcisions experience extreme pain from vaginal intercourse since it involves the erect penis tearing through scar tissue.[24] Studies show that new husbands require as long as two to twelve weeks and alcoholic fortification to achieve full vaginal entry.[25] Doctors tell stories of frustrated men plagued with impotence as a result of weeks, months, and even years of trying to penetrate the scar tissue, and who finally secretly bring their wives to a doctor, who breaks scalpels and scissors cutting through.[26] Moreover, every new tear heals, leaving thickened scar tissue which is re-torn with succeeding intercourse.[27]

Further damage to a woman's health arises from medical complications with childbirth. Scar tissue is not nearly so elastic as normal skin, and thus will tear and bleed much more extensively, often delaying second stage labor.[28] But pharaonic circumcision is also a health risk apart from sex and

---

19. LIGHTFOOT-KLEIN, *supra* note 2, at 36.

20. *See* Lawrence P. Cutner, *Female Genital Mutilation*, 40 OBSTETRICAL & GYNECOLOGICAL SURVEY 437, 440 (1985) (noting that anesthesia is used in less than ten percent of the procedures).

21. LIGHTFOOT-KLEIN, *supra* note 2, at 57.

22. *See, e.g.*, LIGHTFOOT-KLEIN, *supra* note 2, at 31; WALKER & PARMAR, *supra* note 9, at 24; HOSKEN, *supra* note 7, at 34. WOMEN'S INTERNATIONAL NETWORK, FEMALE GENITAL MUTILATION (1994) (reporting a total of 132 million women in Africa alone).

23. Scholars usually trace the origins of genital infibulation to ancient Egypt, hence the title *pharaonic circumcision.* LIGHTFOOT-KLEIN, *supra* note 2, at 27-29.

24. Evelyn Shaw, *Female Circumcision*, 85 AM. J. NURSING 684, 685 (1985).

25. LIGHTFOOT-KLEIN, *supra* note 2, at 59.

26. *Id.* at 58-59, 145.

27. HOSKEN, *supra* note 7, at 3.

28. LIGHTFOOT-KLEIN, *supra* note 2, at 59 (reporting author's presence at over one hundred births by pharaonically circumcised women in Sudan in which none of them was able to dilate more than four centimeters); *see also* HOSKEN, *supra* note 7, at 29.

childbirth. Pharaonically circumcised women take fifteen to forty minutes to void their bladders, leaving residual urine and menstrual flow trapped behind the barrier of scar tissue to become a site of both vaginal and urinary tract infections.[29] There is also a strong link between pharaonic circumcision and high Acquired Immunodeficiency Syndrome (AIDS) transmission rates in parts of Africa.[30] This is due not only to the inevitable scar tissue tears in vaginal intercourse that allow HIV+ semen access to the female's blood system,[31] but also to the fact that many couples avoid the problems wrought by pharaonic circumcision on vaginal sex by shifting to anal sex,[32] which also poses high risks of HIV+ transmission. In addition, the more severe forms of pharaonic circumcision can remove so much skin, and even muscle, from the area around the crotch that free movement of lower extremities is permanently impeded; this is why investigators are frequently told that pharaonically circumcised women can be identified by their restrained walks.[33]

The second type of damage resulting from female circumcision is that both clitoridectomy and pharaonic circumcision procedures greatly reduce and often remove totally the woman's ability to enjoy sex.[34] This is usually an intended result for these forms of circumcision, because some cultures reason that if women do not experience pleasure in sex, they will have no reason to engage in fornication before marriage or in adultery after.[35] Others believe that uncircumcised women have voracious and promiscuous appetites for sex.[36] Circumcision, thus, protects a female's virtue, and in many cultures, protects the family's economic investment in her.[37] In cultures where polygamy is common, one of the many functions of the clitoridectomy is that it helps ensure that bonding occurs between co-wives, by discouraging sexual bonding between husband and wife.[38] Pharaonic circumcision is also acknowledged to benefit husbands in that it makes every act of sex "virginal," that is, tight.[39] For this reason, most women who have had pharaonic circumcisions are restitched after every birth to leave only the one centimeter aperture for urine and menses.[40]

---

29. *See, e.g.*, LIGHTFOOT-KLEIN, *supra* note 2, at 57, 161, 281.

30. *See* WOMEN'S INTERNATIONAL NETWORK, *supra* note 22.

31. Kenneth J. Bartschi, *Legislative Responses to HIV/AIDS in Africa*, 11 CONN. J. INT'L L. 169, 178 (1995).

32. LIGHTFOOT-KLEIN, *supra* note 2, at 58.

33. *Id.* at 57.

34. *Id.* at 40-41, 80-93, 97, 281, 284-86, 288.

35. *See, e.g.*, HOSKEN, *supra* note 7, at 31; LIGHTFOOT-KLEIN, *supra* note 2, at 39-40

36. LIGHTFOOT-KLEIN, *supra* note 2, at 39.

37. *Id.* at 38-41, 65-66, 70.

38. DENISE L. CARMODY, WOMEN AND WORLD RELIGIONS 29-30 (1989) (discussing the Sande of Sierre Leone).

39. LIGHTFOOT-KLEIN, *supra* note 2, at 35, 98-101.

40. *Id.* at 35, 98.

The examination of the damages caused by female circumcision illustrate that the rationales for circumcision involve only the enhancement of male prerogatives in sex. The practice of female circumcision is thus blatantly unjust in that all the benefits of the procedures accrue to men, while women suffer all the disabilities. But there are other religious-cultural purposes attributed to female circumcision. Particularly in sub-Saharan Africa, and varying a great deal from tribe to tribe, there is a general understanding that the clitoris is the analogue of the male penis, and in order for a female to be fertile, to display truly feminine characteristics, and to avoid rape, this male aspect must be removed.[41] Many tribes believe that if these particular parts of the female vulva are not removed, they will continue to grow until they emit noxious odors, facilitate vaginal worms, and disfigure a woman by dangling to her knees.[42] This explanation combines an intuitive apprehension of sexual biology and a specific cultural understanding of male/female complementarity, with a vivid historical association of the elongated labia of Hottentots, who pull their labia to elongate them as the emblem of their enslavement.[43] Male/female complementarity assumes that the two sexes are mirror reflections of each other, so that joined together they represent human wholeness, including reproductive capacity.[44] Anything which threatens to blur male/female differences obstructs wholeness.[45] Complementarity and the resulting culturally enforced distinctions between men and women have been the rule rather than the exception in human history, including much of recent history.[46]

The religious justification for female circumcision is chiefly associated with African Islam and indigenous African religions.[47] There also are some African tribes, which converted to Catholicism, that have long had Vatican permission for female circumcision, and some medical missionaries who have been performing clitoridectomies under anesthesia, in aseptic conditions.[48] In

---

41. *Id.* at 38-41.

42. *See, e.g., id.* at 38-39, 69; WALKER & PARMAR, *supra* note 9, at 139-40.

43. LIGHTFOOT-KLEIN, *supra* note 2, at 163-64.

44. *See* CHRISTINE E. GUDORF, CATHOLIC SOCIAL TEACHING ON LIBERATION THEMES 257-72 (1980) (discussing the sexual complementarity themes in papal teaching).

45. *Id.* at 269-72.

46. Americans, for example, may recall the difficulty that the majority of the United States population had thirty years ago with the concept of truly masculine men having long hair or wearing jewelry.

47. "Religion . . . should be acknowledged as a salient characteristic of the social and cultural scene of most countries . . . . 'Their perceptions of 'women's status' were still affected by numerous practices . . . Ranging in seriousness from relatively harmless folk beliefs . . . to the physically violent practice of female circumcision . . . .'" THEODORA FOSTER CARROLL, WOMEN, RELIGION, AND DEVELOPMENT IN THE THIRD WORLD 127 (1983) (citation omitted).

48. LIGHTFOOT-KLEIN, *supra* note 2, at 41-42.

Muslim Africa, both Arab and sub-Saharan, female circumcision is understood as Islamic practice and demanded of faithful Muslims.[49] However, the practice is historically unknown both in the cradle of Islam, Saudia Arabia, and among eighty percent of Muslims globally.[50] Many African Muslims claim that Mohammed commanded female circumcision, and point to the fact that female circumcision in many African nations is called *sunna*, the word used in Islam for sacred tradition.[51] But Islamic legal scholars contend that Islam modified the form of female circumcision it found practiced in Africa under the general Islamic ban on any cutting on the body unless the benefit exceeds the pain or injury suffered from it.[52]

Medical organizations in the developed world have tended to follow the lead of UNICEF in 1980 and WHO in 1984, by advocating the abolition of female circumcision as unnecessary mutilation which violates the bioethical principle to do no harm.[53] The mid-twentieth century saw the historic Jewish practice of infant male circumcision adopted virtually universally in the United States.[54] Only after decades of routine hospital circumcision of newborn males did the medical establishment recognize that male circumcision was not medically advisable.[55] However, most American newborn males are still routinely circumcised.[56] At the same time, increasing numbers of cosmetic surgeries on both men and women, especially to reverse the signs of aging, are undertaken in the West.[57] Virtually none of those surgeries are justified in terms of health benefits, and all carry some risk of infection, anesthesia complications, or other risks.[58] Yet, the principles of bioethics are virtually never used to brand these practices as mutilation.

Clitoridectomy and genital infibulation are impossible to justify, as both the risks and the usual consequences are so negative.[59] But the type of female circumcision which removes only the hood of the clitoris and perhaps a piece of the labia minora as a religious-cultural indication of sexual adulthood, fitness to marry, or ability to reproduce,[60] has a much better claim to legitimacy than

---

49. *See id.* at 42.

50. *Id.* at 41-42.

51. *Id.* at 30-31, 42.

52. *See Facts About Female Circumcision*, CAIRO FAMILY PLANNING ASS'N (50 Gumhouria St., Tel.: 914515), Mar. 1991, at 10.

53. *Id.* at 15-16.

54. *See* LIGHTFOOT-KLEIN, *supra* note 2, at 183.

55. *Id.* at 188.

56. *Id.* at 183.

57. Kathleen Kernicky, *A Stitch in Time*, SUN-SENTINEL (Ft. Lauderdale, FL), May 26, 1996, at 1E.

58. *Id.*

59. *See supra* text accompanying notes 9-16.

60. *Id.*

either cosmetic surgery or male circumcision of genitals, as long as it can be done in sanitary conditions and without excessive pain. This modified form of female circumcision should enjoy the same status as the ritual circumcision of Jewish males. The bioethical principal to do no harm should not prevent relatively minor surgeries, done in antiseptic circumstances, to enact some religiously or culturally sanctioned values.

Legally there is a dichotomy between developed nations which tend to ban all types of circumcisions, and African nations in which laws against pharaonic circumcision are not enforced. France, for example, has criminalized all forms of female circumcision, and has sentenced both circumcisors and the parents of a circumcised daughter to prison.[61] In comparison, in Sudan, where pharaonic circumcision has been illegal since 1974, eighty-three percent of women nevertheless have pharaonic circumcision.[62] Many local African Islamic authorities interpret opposition to circumcision, even infibulation, as anti-Islamic, and insist on female circumcision as a primary form of Muslim submission to Allah.[63] A compromise which allows circumcisions, excluding clitoridectomy or infibulation, to be performed with anesthesia, under antiseptic conditions, and by trained medical personnel capable of dealing with surgical emergencies, would be helpful but seems unlikely.

However, close regulation would be necessary to prevent the more severe forms of circumcision, since evidence suggests that medical settings tend to encourage *more extensive* cutting because the anesthesia prevents the children from struggling.[64] To facilitate such a compromise, the international medical establishment must agree that the weighing of benefits and harms includes benefits and harms both to health, and from the recognition or nonrecognition of the complete person in her socio-religious-cultural situation.

Integration of social and cultural variables into clinical bioethics will be strenuously opposed by many who insist that an effective and workable code of professional ethics must not rely on individual judgment, but must have some type of universal standards external to the individual in order to prevent xenophobic prejudice. For example, a nation which simultaneously condemns

---

61. Toubia, *supra* note 3, at 234.

62. LIGHTFOOT-KLEIN, *supra* note 2, at 31, 43. Likewise, in Egypt, the government banned female circumcision just months after the Ministry of Health authorized state hospitals to begin performing the procedure. *Egypt Again Forbids Girls' Circumcisions*, DALLAS MORNING NEWS, Dec. 30, 1995, at A11. Egypt previously allowed the procedure "in an attempt to curb botched operations by clumsy amateurs." *Id.* However, an official from the Ministry of Health stated that the ban was promulgated in response to "pressure from women's and human rights groups and fear of U.S. aid sanctions." *Id.*

63. *See* VERN L. BULLOUGH, THE SUBORDINATE SEX: A HISTORY OF ATTITUDES TOWARD WOMEN 143-44 (1974).

64. LIGHTFOOT-KLEIN, *supra* note 2, at 36.

surgery for cultural reasons in other countries, yet its citizens continue to practice the surgery will likely oppose any attempt at integration. Thus, concrete ethical directives are only possible in restricted settings, because the diversity of the world precludes universal concrete ethical directives. Furthermore, the health care profession cannot justly be made the sole moral arbiters of religious, cultural, and social practice. As in the case of cosmetic surgery in the United States, it is not advisable to ban all surgeries for non-medical reasons. Cosmetic surgeries for birth defects and disfiguring accidents are legitimate, and even some simple vanity surgeries, such as ear piercing, are easily accepted. The more basic moral problem with much of the current cosmetic surgery is the misogyny and intolerance of aging within the cultural standards of attractiveness which motivate the surgeries.

II. FERTILITY COERCION AS ENVIRONMENTALLY DICTATED

It should no longer be necessary to demonstrate that our biosphere is seriously endangered by a combination of overconsumption and overpopulation. The overpopulation is not the same as was feared in the fifties and sixties, when the issue was whether humans were having more children than could be fed. Food is not the central issue today, though it is increasingly clear that the majority of the nations in the developing world will not be able to grow or produce enough food by the end of this century to feed their populations.[65] Clean air; clean water; the survival of animal and plant species on land, seas, and in rivers; the adequacy of the cloud cover that filters ultraviolet rays; and global temperature stability are all at risk today as a result of the numbers of people on the earth and the superconsumption prevalent in developed nations.[66] Moreover, an increase in overall human population is inevitable for the next half century, simply because of lengthening lifespans and the huge proportion of children in the populations of developing nations who have yet to procreate.[67]

The 1994 United Nations' International Conference on Population and Development (ICPD) in Cairo declared that efforts to limit population growth could and would avoid national population targets and the resulting coercion

---

65. The United Nations' Food and Agriculture Organization (UNFAO) estimates that more than half of all developing nations may not be able to feed their populations in the year 2000 using current low levels of farming technology, and that most of these sixty-two nations will be able to feed less than half of their populations. Some, however, will be able to import more costly food, though only through using scarce foreign exchange which could otherwise be used to import materials for development. *The Environment and Population Growth: Decade for Action*, 20 POPULATION REP. 11, 13 (1992).

66. *Id.* at 12.

67. Wolfgang Lutz, *The Future of World Population*, 49 POPULATION BULL. 1, 34 (1994).

that a number of nations had used in the past to obtain those targets.[68] The ICPD constructed an agenda for achieving conditions under which couples around the world would voluntarily have fewer children. These conditions include: lowering infant and child mortality through increased access to potable water and child immunizations; increasing the health, education, and status of women; and, of course, making effective means of contraception available to the 470 million women who desire it but lack access.[69] There is no doubt that this agenda should be the foundation of global population concern. But, unfortunately, to the extent that this agenda aims at totally non-coercive solutions to overpopulation, it is doomed from the start to some degree of failure. We have simply waited too long in that we do not have enough lead-time left to make totally voluntary means work.[70]

The present population of the world is close to six billion people.[71] The most optimistic population projection published by the United Nations presumes that beginning in 1990, the global total fertility rate of 3.4 children per woman drops quickly to stabilize at 1.7 children per woman, significantly below the human replacement rate of 2.1 children per woman.[72] Based on this 1.7 fertility rate, world population size would rise significantly, then restabilize at six billion in 2100.[73] Presently, however, we are six years into this scenario, and there is no evidence supporting such a dramatic trend. In a second United Nations scenario, if the world fertility rate from 1990 onward was the replacement rate, 2.1 children per woman, the size of the youth population in the developing nations would dictate that the world population in 2100 would be eight billion.[74] In a third scenario, if the 1992 world

---

68. *The Programme of Action*, UNITED NATIONS INT'L CONFERENCE ON POPULATION & DEVELOPMENT (ICPD Secretariat, United Nations, 220 E. 42nd St., New York, NY 10017), 1994, at 12-13, 45; *see also The Cairo Consensus: The Right Agenda for the Right Time*, INTERNATIONAL WOMEN'S HEALTH COALITION (IWHC, Adrienne Germain & Rachel Kyte eds.), 1995, at 4-5.

69. *See The Programme of Action, supra* note 68, at 44-45.

70. There are technically possible scenarios which are not politically possible. For example, if the developed nations were to significantly cut their levels of production—energy, chemicals, and garbage—for the next decade, they might stave off further earth degradation until world fertility rates could further decline. The developing nations, who have two-thirds of the world's population and the highest fertility, only have a fortieth to a fiftieth of the per capita environmental impact of the developed nations. Paul Niebanck, *The Root of the Environmental Crisis, in* ON WORLD POPULATION . . . A COLLECTION OF WRITINGS 9 (Stan Becker & Cynthia Kerman eds., 1993).

71. Lutz, *supra* note 67, at 4.

72. *See, e.g.*, UNITED NATIONS, LONG RANGE WORLD POPULATION PROJECTIONS: TWO CENTURIES OF POPULATION GROWTH, 1950-2150 6-7 (1992); *The Environment and Population Growth: Decade for Action, supra* note 65, at 5.

73. UNITED NATIONS, LONG RANGE WORLD POPULATION PROJECTIONS: TWO CENTURIES OF POPULATION GROWTH, 1950-2150, *supra* note 72, at 14 (Table 4).

74. *Id.* at 13-14; Lutz, *supra* note 67, at 35.

fertility rate of 3.4 children per woman continues to decline then quickly stabilizes at 2.5 children per woman, we would have a population of nineteen billion in 2100, and world population would still be growing.[75] Thus, the lowest plausible, if still optimistic, projection is that of eight billion people by 2030, and ten billion people by 2100.[76] Many sources agree that even if fertility continues to decline around the world, we may well face a world population of twelve billion people, double the present number, by 2100.[77]

At the same time, ecologists' estimates of the carrying capacity of the earth over the next several centuries range from a conservative figure of one to two billion people with a consumption rate based on that of present-day developed nations, to a liberal figure of eight billion who consume at an adequate but much reduced level from that of developed nations today.[78] Given present trends regarding global warming, ozone holes, dropping global water tables, decreasing density in the oceanic fisheries, galloping deforestation, topsoil erosion, and decertification, not to mention increasing air and water pollution,[79] there is little reason to believe that these estimates for the carrying capacity will improve over the next few decades. In fact, many developing nations are just beginning to recognize, record, and report various types of ecological damage.[80] The likelihood is that our knowledge of local threats to the global ecosystem will continue to increase.

Our earth is overstrained today by a combination of poor use of farmland, poor extraction methods, excessive use of fossil fuels, overfishing, overuse of toxic chemicals and radioactive materials, and poor disposal of excessive

75. UNITED NATIONS, LONG RANGE WORLD POPULATION PROJECTIONS: TWO CENTURIES OF POPULATION GROWTH, 1950-2150, *supra* note 72, at 33.

76. Lutz, *supra* note 67, at 27.

77. *Id.* at 26-27.

78. *See, e.g., The Environment and Population Growth: Decade for Action, supra* note 65, at 23; H. R. Hulett, *Optimum World Population,* 20 BIOSCIENCE 160, 160 (1970); Arthur H. Westing, *A World in Balance,* 8 ENVTL. CONSERVATION 177 (1981); DONELLA H. MEADOWS ET AL., BEYOND THE LIMITS 194 (1992).

79. *See* Henry W. Kendall, *The Environmental Crisis Is Real, in* POPULATION: OPPOSING VIEWPOINTS 107 (David Bender & Bruno Leone eds., 1995).

80. See, for example, the account of the battle for the Brazilian rain forests and the indigenous rubber tappers led by Chico Mendes. WATERSHEDS: CLASSIC CASES IN ENVIRONMENTAL ETHICS 136 (Lisa H. Newton & Catherine K. Dillingham eds., 1994). The case details how the studies done on the effects of clearing the rainforest—effects on the land, the streams, the human inhabitants, the animal and plant species, and the surrounding climate patterns—all had to be organized and funded by foreign individuals and environmental groups, due to the cost and expertise required, as well as because the Brazilian government, for both economic and political reasons, was a major actor in the economic plans of clearing the rainforest. *Id.* The case mentions several other examples in developing nations. *Id.*

amounts of human generated waste.[81] The longer that overstrain continues, the smaller the population size the earth can support in the immediate future and still regain its capacity to sustain life. We are faced with the necessity not just of slowing population growth, but of actually reducing the size of the human population by somewhere in the neighborhood of three to six billion people, at least a quarter of the world's population, if we use the most optimistic estimates of the earth's carrying capacity. If we agree with the most conservative estimates of the earth's carrying capacity in the twenty-first century, then we must prepare to reduce our population by six to ten billion people, a reduction of between three-fourths and five-sixths of the total, within a century. There can be little doubt that reductions of twenty-five to eighty percent will require some form of coercion.

A. Population Control—A Developed World Problem, Too

Such coercion should not be and will not be an issue for the developing world alone. The developed nations are responsible for a major part of the world's problems in three different ways. First, the European nations secured extensive colonial and neo-colonial empires with which to absorb the population increases of their two-hundred-year demographic transition.[82] They sent many millions of their people to settle lands in the Americas, Australia and New Zealand, Africa, and Asia, and they used the resources of these colonial lands to supply their burgeoning home populations with food as well as industrial raw materials.[83] Moreover, in many parts of these European empires, the colonists were responsible for erasing or reducing the native population of these continents through policies including appropriation of land, enslavement, and even extermination.[84] All these events contributed to postponing demographic transition among the surviving native populations, not to mention denying them space in which to similarly expand.

Second, once Europe and the European-settled nations had completed their

---

81. Theodore Panayotou, *The Population, Environment, and Development Nexus*, in POPULATION AND DEVELOPMENT: OLD DEBATES, NEW CONCLUSIONS 169 (Robert Cassen ed., 1994).

82. R. R. PALMER & JOEL COLTON, A HISTORY OF THE MODERN WORLD 564 (3d ed. 1965).

83. *See id.*; JOSEPH REITHER, WORLD HISTORY: A BRIEF INTRODUCTION 311-16, 358 (1973).

84. The depopulation of Africa by millions of young people captured and exported as slaves is well known, as is the depopulation of Native Americans in North America through colonial and United States military campaigns, European diseases, and the reservation system. For a brief account of the depopulation within Latin America due to the Spanish conquest, see Hans Magnus Enzenberger, *Introduction* to BARTOLOME DE LAS CASAS, THE DEVASTATION OF THE INDIES: A BRIEF ACCOUNT 12-13 (Herma Briffault trans., 1974). The text present Las Casas' figures of four million dead from the conquest of Mexico, together with archeological estimates that almost five times fewer Indians died after the conquest of Mexico than was reported by other scholars. *Id.* at 13.

demographic transition, they completed the tightening of controls on immigration which had begun with the rise of modern states.[85] Today, the developing nations caught in demographic transition have been largely denied the most common historical method for societies dealing with overpopulation and ecological degradation: migration.

Third, the developed world not only set much of the world stage in which the present crisis occurs, but it continues through its superconsumption to present the single largest threat to the biosphere.[86] An American, for example, consumes an average of 900 kilograms of grain per year, compared to 180 kilograms of grain for the average Indian.[87] When we look at pollution, the imbalance increases. The average American adds 5.4 tons of carbon equivalent to the atmosphere per year, while the average Nigerian adds 0.8 ton, and the average Indian 0.4 ton.[88] Using these measures alone, each American child in her lifetime costs the earth as much as five to fifteen times more than do Indian children. When we consider individual use of water, waste production, and other measures of resource use, the environmental cost of an extra child in the developed world is somewhere between seventy and two hundred times that of a child in the developing world.[89] The argument of some in the developed world that "I can provide for my children; let those

---

85. For an alternative view of the entire issue of colonialization, population expansion and limits on immigration, see DANIEL QUINN, ISHMAEL (1990), which compares different ways that humans relate to the land and to other human groups. In general, the implementation of national boundaries and immigration controls victimized many formerly semi-nomadic peoples in Africa and North America, and the independence of colonial parts of the empires of European nations triggered stiffening of those nations' own immigration laws. This stiffening received an additional stimulus following the recent collapse of the communist regimes in Eastern Europe in 1989 and the creation of millions of would-be economic refugees. United States immigration policies became numerically restrictive in 1924 and have remained so through changes in 1953, 1965, and 1990. *The Population-Environment Connection: What Does It Mean for Environmental Policy*, ENVTL. PROTECTION AGENCY (Battelle Seattle Research Center, Seattle, WA), Dec. 1995, at 41-42.

86. Kendall, *supra* note 80, at 107-10.

87. JONATHAN TURK ET AL., ENVIRONMENTAL SCIENCE 350 (3d ed. 1983).

88. *Id.*; Allen L. Hammond et al., *Calculating National Accountability for Climate Change*, ENVIRONMENT, Jan./Feb. 1991, at 10, 14.

89. "Measured by commercial energy use, each American, on average, caused 70 time the environmental damage as a Ugandan or Laotian, 20 times an Indian, 10 times a Chinese, and roughly twice that of the U.K., France, Sweden or Australia." WATERSHEDS: CLASSIC CASES IN ENVIRONMENTAL ETHICS, *supra* note 80, at 197 (citation omitted). But the figures are telling even compared to *average* global per capita: the U.S. population of slightly over 250 million, and about 1/240th of the world's carbon dioxide, which is the major cause of the Greenhouse Effect. By comparison, in chlorofluorocarbon (CFC) production—the primary cause of ozone depletion—China and India, with fully one-third of the world's population, produced only two percent of global CFC emissions. *Id.* at 198-204.

who can't provide have fewer children" ignores the fact that we all draw our resources from the same common biosphere.

B. Steps in Coercion

Within the next twenty years many nations, both developed and developing, will see no other choice than to exert severe pressure on their populations to lower the total fertility rate. Production/consumption rates in the developed world, and reduced child mortality in the developing world, combine with the general rise in life expectancy, which increases the number of generations living at the same time, to overstrain the environment.[90] In developing nations where the average age of the citizenry is under twenty-five, and sometimes as young as fifteen,[91] and where the process of development expands the level of consumption as well as the expectation for continued expansion of consumption,[92] there simply is no alternative to restricting births. There is a great deal of diversity within developing nations. Some have long engaged in popular education campaigns regarding family planning,[93] and have instituted both positive and negative incentives.[94] An example of a positive incentive is the cash payment that India provides to individuals to be sterilized.[95] An example of a negative incentive is India's de facto practice of barring those with more than two children from civil service employment.[96] For nations such as India, which have managed to attain approximately half their demographic transition in the last twenty-five years by using incentives and popular education,[97] there are but two remaining options to further decrease the fertility rate: 1) increase the degree of both positive and negative

---

90. Panayotou, *supra* note 81, at 162-72.

91. Thomas W. Merrick, *Population Dynamics in Developing Countries, in* POPULATION AND DEVELOPMENT: OLD DEBATES, NEW CONCLUSIONS 92 (Robert Cassen ed., 1994).

92. Kaval Gulhati & Lisa M. Bates, *Developing Countries and the International Population Debate: Politics and Pragmatism, in* POPULATION AND DEVELOPMENT: OLD DEBATES, NEW CONCLUSIONS 47 (Robert Cassen ed., 1994).

93. *See* BETSY HARTMANN, REPRODUCTIVE RIGHTS AND WRONGS: THE GLOBAL POLITICS OF POPULATION CONTROL & CONTRACEPTIVE CHOICE 74-76 (1987) (describing the history of Indonesia's family planning program).

94. *Id.* at 65-73.

95. *Id.* at 66, 239.

96. This restriction is not universal throughout India, but is more or less *de facto* due to the general climate of support for strong incentives and even coercion which existed within the Indian government for most of the last quarter century—except for the period following Indira Ghandi's fall from power due to the sterilization campaign in the north in the late 1970s. See the sensitive language employed by SONALDE DESAI, GENDER INEQUALITIES AND DEMOGRAPHIC BEHAVIOR: INDIA 1-3 (1994).

97. With the exception noted below, see HARTMANN, *supra* note 93, at 281-83.

incentives, and 2) use outright physical coercion.[98] China is an example of a nation that has used physical coercion.[99] In fact, China is not the only nation to have already used physical coercion. In 1979, forced sterilizations of men as well as women in army campaigns in northern India were the major factor in the fall of Indira Ghandi's government.[100] Bangladesh, Indonesia, and a host of other nations have at various times also blurred the line between negative incentives and physical coercion.[101]

In the developed world, controls on energy use, waste production, and immigration are likely to precede coercion as tools to achieve fertility decrease. But, within the next twenty years, we are likely to see positive and negative incentives, such as tax deductions limited to first and second children and family health insurance limited to covering two children. Moreover, depending upon how successful efforts at energy and waste conservation are, some degree of physical coercion to limit fertility is likely to surface as well.

III.   COMMONALITY WITHIN RELIGION, FEMINISM AND BIOETHICS

Thus, there is a growing need for religious communities around the world to rethink traditional teachings which have often equated the right to marry with the right to procreate; which have condemned any form of non-consensual physical intervention within a human body as torture; and which have insisted upon the right of couples to decide the size of their families. Such an ethic is only appropriate for populations with unlimited resources, which has clearly never been the human situation. Religions in the West, such as Judaism, Christianity, and Islam, all have insisted on the goodness of reproduction, even the obligation to multiply the species, and have based this teaching on respect for both human life and for God's act of creation.[102] The new challenge is to preserve this foundational teaching, the respect for human life and for God's whole creation, through changing the shape of human activity and obligation.

Religions are not the only institutions which need to undertake such radical revision, however. Within American history, feminism and bioethics share a common origin in religion.[103] Feminism was born in this country within the context of nineteenth century liberal, revivalist Protestant social reform

---

98. Here I will reserve the word *coercion* for physical coercion, recognizing that there is some degree of coercion whenever a nation (in which millions live malnourished) pays enough cash to feed a family for weeks, in return for sterilization.

99. HARTMANN, *supra* note 93, at 150 (describing "reports of forced abortions and some of compulsory sterilization").

100. *Id.* at 237-38.

101. *Id.* at 77, 217.

102. E. CALVIN BEISNER, PROSPECTS FOR GROWTH: A BIBLICAL VIEW OF POPULATION, RESOURCES, AND THE FUTURE 50-51 (1990); HARTMANN, *supra* note 93, at 49-50.

103. H. TRISTRAM ENGELHARDT, JR., THE FOUNDATIONS OF BIOETHICS 5 (1986).

movements.[104] It developed within the abolitionist movement, which itself
was strongly religious.[105] However, some of the nineteenth century mothers
of feminism were not church-linked.[106] Similarly, the discipline of medical
ethics emerged in the twentieth century from religious and philosophical
reflection upon the religious teachings relevant to maintaining life in new
scientific situations.[107] At the core of mainstream, or modern liberal,
religious, feminist and bioethical thought is an understanding of the dignity and
rights of the individual human person as inviolable. All three assert the body
of the human person as radically personal, and, thus, not to be coerced.[108]
Religion imparts this belief about human beings in general; feminist principles
insist that this general theory applies to women, too, even in situations of
reproduction and mothering. Bioethics reminds us that patients do not, by
requiring medical care, forfeit this human dignity and right. The next section
explores some possible directions for bioethics, as it maintains that coercion is
necessary to preserve the biosphere.

A. Bioethics and Coercive Fertility Reduction

    Bioethics has drawn on liberal models of the human person that emphasize
individual autonomy, and therefore forbid virtually all forms of coercion.
Physical coercion such as forced vasectomy, tubal ligation, or treatment with
long-term injectable or implantable contraceptives violates the bioethical
requirement of informed consent. Constructions of Western bioethics have
focused on maintaining the integrity of the physician-patient relationship, and
hence the trust of patients.[109] Thus, though bioethics is divided as to those

---

    104. JOSEPHINE DONOVAN, FEMINIST THEORY: THE INTELLECTUAL TRADITIONS OF AMERICAN
FEMINISM 3, 21 (1992).
    105. *See* David A.J. Richards, *Public Reason and Abolitionist Dissent*, 69 CHI.-KENT L. REV.
787, 807-27 (1994).
    106. DONOVAN, *supra* note 104, at 12 (discussing Frances Wright, Sarah Grimke, and
Elizabeth Cady Stanton).
    107. *See* JOHN P. KENNY, O.P., PRINCIPLES OF MEDICAL ETHICS 1 (2d ed. 1962).
    108. *See* Ralph C. Conte, *Toward a Theological Construct for the New Biology: An Analysis
of Rahner, Fletcher, and Ramsey*, 11 J. CONTEMP. HEALTH L. & POL'Y 429, 441-42 (1995)
(discussing the analogy between the bioethical principle of autonomy and the theological value
of "freedom of the human spirit"); Sandra H. Johnson, *The Changing Nature of the Bioethics
Movement*, 53 MD. L. REV. 1051, 1053, 1060 (1994) (noting that bioethics is "essentially a
movement toward personal choice and autonomy" but that cultural and principlist paradigms have
been shifting the focus in bioethical thought away from autonomy); Susan Sherwin, *Feminist and
Medical Ethics: Two Different Approaches to Contextual Ethics*, in FEMINIST PERSPECTIVES IN
MEDICAL ETHICS 26-27 (Helen Bequaert Holmes & Laura M. Purdy eds., 1992) (discussing
freedom of coercion from reproductive technologies as a distinctive force in feminist ethics).
    109. TOM L. BEAUCHAMP & JAMES F. CHILDRESS, PRINCIPLES OF BIOMEDICAL ETHICS 202-03
(1979).

who insist and those who deny that there is an appropriate role for paternalism with patients, most agree that this paternalism should be in weak form. Moreover, most agree that, at most, recourse to paternalism should be in conjunction with the principle of beneficence understood in the sense of the good of the individual patient.[110] In this case, conversely, the compelling need or the good served is the common good, while the needs of the individual patient could be construed as sacrificed to the common good.

Despite this strong and enduring focus on the physician-patient relationship, bioethics has forcibly been reminded at various times that physician-patient relationships take place within a social context and not within a vacuum. Both physician and patient have obligations to other members of society and to society as a whole. States at various times in this century, for example, have demanded that doctors report child abuse, contagious diseases, and gunshot wounds to state authorities regardless of patient wishes.[111] Doctors have resented such regulations and have sometimes refused to comply, but the great majority have recognized that the public health of society required some such measure.[112] When bioethics has authorized doctors to perform *treatments* contrary to the wishes of patients, it has always been when the treatment was required by the interests of the patient, *and* after the patient has been judged incompetent and in need of a guardian who has authorized the treatment.[113]

Fertility control programs will be different not only because doctors will no longer provide the treatment patients desire, but also because they will, as doctors do presently, only ignore patients' desires for confidentiality about their conditions in cases of gunshot wounds and syphilis.[114] Instead, doctors will be called upon to provide treatment not only *undesired* by the patient (such as sterilization or long-term contraception), but also not required by the individual interest of the patient—treatment only desired by the larger society.

Perhaps the closest analogy in bioethics to fertility control is testing protocols for new drugs and treatments. While there is a decisive preference in testing for using research subjects who not only have given informed consent (autonomy principle), but are also able to participate in efforts to protect them from harm (beneficence principle), there is also a general insistence that the research be of at least potential benefit to the subject.[115] Thus, even toxicity studies—in which risks are relatively low—on drugs for sickle-cell anemia should be performed only on subjects of African descent who may carry the

---

110. *Id.* at 153-56.

111. *Id.* at 213.

112. *See id.* at 212-14; ENGELHARDT, *supra* note 103, at 299.

113. *See* BEAUCHAMP & CHILDRESS, *supra* note 109, at 84-85; ENGELHARDT, *supra* note 103, at 280-84.

114. ENGELHARDT, *supra* note 103, at 299.

115. *Id.* at 290-94.

348   *SAINT LOUIS UNIVERSITY PUBLIC LAW REVIEW*   [Vol. 15:2

sickle-cell trait, because only those individuals could benefit from the research study.

Even when it is assumed that subjects take risks which may outweigh potential benefits to them as individuals, it is also assumed that definite harm cannot be deliberately inflicted on an individual subject in order to further the general good of the program in which a subject participates.[116] Thus, not only do transplant programs lack donors offering organs to strangers, but the programs do not permit donations of one of a pair of organs by healthy persons, unless they have ties to a specific person in need of a donation.[117] Such a policy assumes that the loss of an organ is serious harm, even when the body ordinarily can function normally with only one of the original pair. Sterilization would seem a fitting analogy for this kind of harm, and thus would inevitably violate the principle of beneficence if the subject did not desire the treatment or require it for his or her health.

Obviously, the challenge to bioethical principles and the response of the health care profession both depend upon the measures each nation adopts; the sequencing of the various degrees of coercion in the adopted measures; and the equity, universality, and medical appropriateness within the application of the measures. Yet, once it has become clear that irresponsible reproduction by some segments of the population threatens both present lives and the ability of the environment to rebound and sustain future generations, health care professionals, too, have a social obligation to act to preserve human life.

This social responsibility does not authorize unilateral physician decisions to sterilize all patients with more than one child, but it does oblige physicians and other health professionals to take part in responsible social measures designed to preserve life on this planet. No individual or group of persons has the right to reproduce the earth to its severe detriment, despite the respect due to individual rights and responsibilities, including those governing one's body and reproduction.

Physicians and other health care personnel need to participate in creating public policy to address these issues. Physicians and other health care personnel have great contributions to make to both national policy debate and implementation measures regarding fertility reduction. The combination of their medical expertise, their professional solidarity, and their social status gives them a forceful voice in public debate. Moreover, their medical expertise and the relatively developed state of their professional ethics makes them a much safer resource for implementing complex and socially and ethically difficult

---

116. *Id.* at 294.

117. *See* Christian Williams, Note, *Combatting the Problems of Human Rights Abuses and Inadequate Organ Supply Through Presumed Donative Consent*, 26 CASE W. RES. J. INT'L L. 315, 334-35 (1994).

policies, such as those regarding coercion of human reproductive activity. The danger of entrusting such policy to a newly created class of medical technicians with no previous sense of professional identity, solidarity or ethics is substantial.

The health care profession needs to be a central part of the process of policy formation and implementation regarding fertility limitation. The health care profession has sometimes served its own interests, as have most professional groups. However, the fact that its ethics have been historically centered on patient rights[118] could help serve as a valuable corrective to the inevitable tendency of large, powerful bureaucracies to violate individual rights—especially the rights of the least powerful—in carrying out popular mandates.

The health care profession needs to carry with it into the coming national debates the following points, which are not exhaustive:

1. Any fertility reduction policy must be flexible enough to equitably deal with different circumstances. For example, a couple with a set of one-pound preemie triplets should not be referred to mandatory sterilization or long-term contraception, along with the parents whose healthy newborn child has two siblings ages seventeen and thirteen.

2. The policy should avoid both poor medical practice and reinforcing class and racial privileges. For example, while chemical contraceptives are contraindicated for women who are malnourished (one sign of which is chronic anemia), it would be unjust class/racial discrimination if poor or minority anemic women with three or four children were sterilized, while white middle-and upper-class couples get temporary injectable or implantable contraception.

3. One difficult issue is whether both members of a couple who have already exceeded their reproductive limit should be sterilized.[119] In deciding whether to force contraception on one or both members of a couple, medical factors such as contraindications for surgery or chemical contraceptives would be relevant, as would preferences of the couple. Estimates of the differential effects on the fertility rate would also be relevant.

4. Sexual equity should be a central concern. Women do not unilaterally produce offspring; therefore, fertility limitation, whether forced or voluntary, needs to be the equal responsibility of men and women.

5. Some assumptions in bioethics regarding autonomy need to be addressed. There is recent literature in theoretical bioethics which is largely, but not entirely feminist, attacking the term "autonomy" as reflecting a non-relational conception of the human person, and insisting that humans are relational and interdependent, not autonomous. Necessary, severe reductions in population

---

118. BEAUCHAMP & CHILDRESS, *supra* note 109, at 11, 41-53.

119. Of course, another alternative may be to remove the first excess child from its birth parents and place it for adoption, which should significantly lower the number of couples producing excess children.

(and in consumption) emerge from the need to preserve the biosphere yet demand respect for the agency and bodily integrity of both the patient and the health care professional.[120]

As this list of concerns illustrates, unethical health care practice is not a matter of certain actions being ethical and others not: many actions are ethically required under emergency circumstances and completely unethical under others. Ethical action does not always require consent; we are all familiar with some circumstances in which patients forfeit the right to give or deny effective consent.[121] Ethics is most often a matter of choosing the most appropriate, responsible option from among those available. Principles offer a kind of checklist to be consulted in each situation, but each principle seems to be more vital in the ethical reflection of some situations as opposed to others. Virtually all societies would agree that the life of the species, and obviously the life of the planet, take ethical priority over the rights of the individual to bodily integrity and self-determination. Moreover, the obligation to maintain patient trust and confidentiality are integral principles, but only for as long, and in the specific ways, that are necessary to preserve biospheric life.

To make this argument is not to condone any of the abuses that are likely to arise in the practice of such an ethic. As in any other emergency situation, there are always attempts of both individuals and groups to capitalize (both literally and figuratively) on the situation. The ability to predict these attempts should not paralyze social planning. The wedge argument, which predicts that any social permission granted less than ideal means will proliferate undesirable means and eventually make discrimination impossible, arises primarily from the pessimistic religious anthropology founded in Christian Protestant interpretations of original sin, and should be contested.[122] However, the predictability of abuse does not legitimate such abuse and should not lessen attempts to prevent it and disrupt it. The main focus of bioethics cannot center around keeping the hands of the health care profession clean by keeping them out of

---

120. *See* A MATTER OF PRINCIPLES?, *supra* note 1, at 99-208, 319-61. Moreover, to understand the patient as autonomous is to relieve the health care professional of any ethical responsibility whatsoever, and to make these professionals mere employees who do what they are told.

121. ENGELHARDT, *supra* note 103, at 275-76.

122. I refer here to the argument of William LaFleur, made at a Park Ridge Center conference—*Religion, Sexuality and Contemporary Crisis*, at Northwestern University on April 13, 1996. He stated that in Asia, and especially in the Buddhist religion, the "wedge argument" is unknown and incomprehensible; he provided the contrary religious example from Japan: in Japan, infanticide was the primary means of birth regulation until the mid-twentieth century, when abortion became the preferred method. Within the last two decades, contraception has replaced abortion as the primary method, and continues to gain ground with no legislative help. *Id.*

the work that needs to be done to preserve the life of the biosphere. Concepts like clean and dirty, ethical and unethical, must take their meanings from within the threatened, multi-shaded grey world we inhabit, and not from abstract, idealist thought.

[2]

Soc. Sci. Med. Vol. 42, No. 10, pp. 1367–1379, 1996
Copyright © 1996 Elsevier Science Ltd
Printed in Great Britain. All rights reserved
0277-9536/96 $15.00 + 0.00

 Pergamon

0277-9536(95)00285-5

WOMEN, HEALTH AND THE ENVIRONMENT*

BONNIE KETTEL

Faculty of Environmental Studies, York University, North York, Ontario, Canada M3J 1P3

Abstract—This paper develops a conceptual framework for gender-sensitive research and policy analysis that centres on women's interaction with the biophysical environment, and the implications of that interaction for their environmental health. The paper reviews the lack of data on women's non-reproductive health, and argues that there is a need for increased research and policy formulation dealing with women's environmental health in both the developing and the developed countries. One important dilemma for most researchers interested in women's environmental health is the lack of an appropriate conceptual model. The paper argues that attention to women's interaction with the biophysical environment within their own 'life spaces' reveals that women are exposed to the hazards of environmental illness in a manner that is clearly gender-differentiated. The paper reviews the impact of poverty, illiteracy and gender bias on women's life spaces, and argues that the failure to recognize and protect women's life spaces in economic policy and planning commonly leads to "disease environments" for women and their children. Evidence of the impact of such disease environments on women's environmental health is drawn from the urban setting and from women's experience of desertification in Africa and Asia. The paper reviews the policy issues that emerge from this analysis, and makes a series of suggestions for national and international policy and action in support of improvements in women's environmental health. Copyright © 1996 Elsevier Science Ltd

Key words—environmental studies, womens health, urban health

INTRODUCTION

The purpose of this paper is to identify some of the key issues relevant to the impact of the environment on women's health, and to formulate a conceptual framework that will facilitate gender-sensitive environmental health policy and action. Most existing discussions of women's health have considered only briefly aspects of women's health outside of their reproductive health [1]. At a health policy level, especially in the developing countries, women's primary significance has been as childbearers and childcarers.

Any adequate conceptualization of women's health involves women's total well being, a condition of life that is determined not only by women's reproductive

---

*This paper was originally prepared for the Fourth *Meeting of Commonwealth Ministers Responsible for Women's Affairs* in Cyprus in 1993. Substantial portions of the paper were also used as the basis for a discussion paper, "Beyond Nairobi and Rio: From Vision to Action for People and Nature", which was prepared for the Women's Environment and Development Organization in November, 1993. A summary of the paper is presented in the *Report of the Regional Workshop of Governmental and Non-governmental Organizations (East and Southeast Asia) on "Women, Economics and Sustainable Development"*, ENGENDER (Centre for Environment, Gender and Development), Singapore. The paper is published here with the permission of the Directorate of Women's and Youth Affairs of the Commonwealth Secretariat in London, and the Women's Environment and Development Organization in New York.

functions, but also by the effects of work load, nutrition, stress, war and migration, among other factors [2]. Among these additional factors are the environmental risks to women's health, particularly the risks arising from the "biophysical environment", a crucial domain that has been almost totally neglected in health research and policy analysis [3–4].

'Environmental health' is an arena for health policy that emerges from the inextricable link between human health and the environmental context within which people lead their daily lives [3]. The specific policy link between women's health, and the health of the local environment, is commonly established by women's environmental action as users and managers of a variety of resources in the 'biophysical environment', and by women's social and cultural involvements as health managers and care-givers.

In this paper, the 'biophysical environment' is understood as including both the natural and the constructed (or 'built') 'life space' within which women carry out their various gender-based involvements as domestic workers, producers and income-earners. Understanding the environment for human health as a biophysical 'life space' allows us to avoid arbitrary distinctions between natural and built environments, rural and urban areas, and developing and developed countries as contexts for women's environmental health concerns. Instead, the focus of policy attention is on the health implications of women's (and men's) direct and indirect *interaction* with the biophysical environment at the local level.

In all human communities, use and management of local life spaces is a gendered phenomenon, as women and men tend to occupy, use and manage aspects of the biophysical environment in a gender-differentiated manner. A detailed understanding of how women's (and men's) patterned interaction with the life space they occupy exposes them to health risks is central to articulating and promoting a gender-sensitive environmental health agenda. This paper uses a model developed by Roundy [5] to show how women's gender-based involvements with the biophysical environment can expose them to environmental illness in a gender-differentiated manner.

In both the developing and developed countries, women are also the primary day-to-day health managers. They manage health through their domestic work, through cleaning, sweeping, drawing water, washing clothes, dishes and children, and preparing food [6]. Women are central to maintaining the health and well being of their households through these activities. Women also manage health through their involvements as care-givers. Across the world, when people get sick, it is women who look after them.

As health managers, women are already providing a range of health care services, including tonics, herbal extracts, poultices, ointments and oils, and a variety of other medicines. MacCormack says: "To ignore their knowledge, curiosity and their social legitimacy to provide care is to squander a valuable human resource" [6] (p. 832). Many of the health care products and remedies that women provide are found in the biophysical environment within their life spaces. Women also have considerable knowledge about the appropriate use of the biophysical environment, including an awareness of how to use biophysical resources in a sustainable, healthy manner [7]. As environmental managers, they are, therefore, also important agents of disease control.

Women's knowledge about the sustainable use of the biophysical environment, and about health and care-giving, are still largely unrecognized assets for the promotion of their own health and the health of the natural and built environment. The failure to recognize women as environmental and health managers and decision-makers is a costly policy dilemma [8]. Where women's environmental interests and needs are not recognized—whether in the introduction of new technology, urban planning or overuse of the biophysical environment—the consequence is the creation of "disease environments" [9]. Where women's health interests and needs are not recognized—through gender-blind data collection, top-down health delivery or lack of concern for their participation—effective health promotion becomes impossible. A gender-sensitive approach to environmental and health policy formulation is a significantly lower cost alternative. In this paper, the participation of women is seen as central to policy formulation specifically in relation to their environmental health.

NEW PERSPECTIVES ON WOMEN'S ENVIRONMENTAL HEALTH

The *Safe Motherhood* conference, held in Nairobi in 1987, focussed the attention of health policy analysts on women's reproductive health. Maternal morbidity and mortality offers a useful domain for an illustration of the potential significance of the biophysical environment to women's health and well being. Five hundred thousand women, 99% of them in the developing countries, die every year from difficulties related to pregnancy and childbirth [10]. The preponderance of these deaths in the developing countries suggests that maternal health is not a simple consequence of reproductive risks *per se*, but an outcome of a host of maternal health hazards, among them social, economic and biophysical hazards, confronting women in these countries. These additional health risks have an important impact on maternal morbidity and mortality. They also affect women's health throughout the life cycle, and they do so, albeit in varying ways, and to varying degrees, in both the developing and the developed countries.

Koblinsky *et al.* offer a view of the possible impact of the biophysical environment on women's menstrual health, which in turn impacts on their success in pregnancy and childbirth, and their overall health and well being. Women's menstrual status affects issues as disparate as their recovery from breast cancer, their cardiovascular health and risk of osteoporosis. Yet, we have no idea how environmental impacts on women's menstrual health affect their long-term risk of cancer, heart disease or other illnesses, including mental illness. As Koblinsky *et al.* suggest, "...the reproductive system is responsive to a multitude of environmental signals, and systematic exploration of alternative (environmental) factors is clearly warranted" [10] (pp. 50, 55).

Menstrual health is an issue shared by women everywhere, in both the developing and the developed countries. Other aspects of women's environmental health may differ significantly between these two settings. In the developing countries, women experience a range of health problems that are clearly environmental in origin. Many of the leading causes of death in the developing countries, which are also known to cause significant morbidity, are either environmental in origin or exacerbated by environmental factors.

The leading causes of death in the developing countries are diarrhoeal diseases, acute respiratory conditions such as pneumonia and bronchitis, other infectious diseases, including tuberculosis, and vector-borne diseases such as schistosomiasis and malaria. Diseases such as diarrhoea, typhoid, schistosomiasis and malaria are caused by bacteria or other vectors (snails and mosquitos) in local water systems. Pneumonia and bronchitis are the common result of air-borne pollutants, including smoke. Tuberculosis is the result of air-borne bacteria, whose presence is generally increased by inadequate and unsanitary living conditions. Each of these diseases can best be controlled through careful management of the local biophysical environment. For the purposes of this paper, therefore, they are all considered to be 'environmental illnesses'.

Over 50% of all deaths from heart disease and cancer also occur in the developing countries [11] (p. 19). In the developed countries, these diseases are the leading causes of death, including deaths among women. Although it is not clear to what extent health problems such as heart disease and cancer, which are not commonly recognized as 'environmental illnesses', may be affected by environmental factors such as water and air pollution and toxic contamination, recent studies have drawn attention to the impact of the organochlorines, which are found in pesticides and refrigerants, on the incidence of breast and ovarian cancer [12].

The work of Koblinsky *et al.* [10] on female menstrual health also suggests the possible hidden impact of environmental factors on female morbidity and mortality rates due to cardiovascular disease and cancer. From this point of view, diseases such as schistosomiasis and malaria, which are vector borne, and diseases such as heart disease and cancer, which have important genetic components, may also be different expressions of 'environmental illness' experienced in different life spaces, especially the differing life spaces of the developed and the underdeveloped countries. In both settings, there may also be important epidemiological distinctions between life spaces in rural and urban areas, and even between neighbourhoods in the same rural area or city in exposure to a particular environmental disease.

This paper also suggests that the experience of environmental illness may differ significantly, not only between the developing and the developed countries, and rural and urban areas, but also between women and men within each of those settings. It argues, based on the initial evidence presented, that gender may sometimes be as important, or even more important, a factor in exposure to a particular environmental illness than is residence in a particular country or neighbourhood.

THE NEGLECT OF WOMEN'S HEALTH

The United States National Council on International Health (NCIH) held a path-setting conference on 'Women's Health' in 1991. The conference, which included representatives from 74 countries, provided a forum for the articulation of a new agenda for women's health policy [13]. This new agenda is centred in a holistic view of women's well being as a life-long phenomenon affected by a variety of mediating factors. Participants in the NCIH conference supported the view that, as a holistic phenomenon, women's well being cannot be addressed either piecemeal, or in isolation from the social, political, economic, cultural—and biophysical—

milieu in which women live [14–16]. Four guiding principles for new directions in international health policy for women were identified at the NCIH conference: the importance of gender-specific data, an end to gender discrimination in health policy and action, a life cycle approach to women's health, and support for women's empowerment as personal and family health decision-makers [13, 15] (pp. 12–16).

It is disconcerting to realize how little we actually know about women's health as compared to the health of men. Statistical health assessments in the developed countries, such as the United Kingdom, are "largely gender-blind, with an overwhelming focus on male mortality rates, and measures of morbidity" [17] (p. 86). In the developing countries, the emphasis on maternal morbidity and mortality has been accompanied by a lack of concern for data collection on other causes of illness and death among women. Koblinsky *et al.* argue that "women's health has been neglected in general, a neglect which fuels, and is fueled by, a lack of information" [10] (p. 43).

In the United States, health research funding and methodology have focused on the leading causes of male morbidity and mortality such as hypertension and lung cancer [1]. Although half a million American women die of heart disease every year, almost all of the significant studies on cardiovascular health have been done on men. Only 13.5% of American health research funding is devoted to health issues of particular importance to women [18] (pp. 164–165).

In part, this inadequacy is a consequence of the acute care bias that pervades health research and funding. The acute care bias is also a male bias, and not only in the disproportionate interest in men's health as compared to the health of women. The Asia and Pacific Development Centre (APDC) reports that 80% of national health budgets are commonly spent "to cure the illnesses of a minority through the training and equipping of doctors who are usually men" [19] (p. 14).

The lack of unambiguous data on female morbidity and mortality makes it difficult to identify and assess the factors, environmental or otherwise, that do affect women's health. Alanagh Raikes, writing about women's health in East Africa, suggests that one useful starting point for an improved understanding of factors relevant to women's health would be to analyse existing morbidity data by geographical region and gender specificity. However, as Raikes points out, morbidity data is often not good enough to allow for this breakdown. Not only are the data lacking in gender specificity, but their overall accuracy is often grossly inadequate as well [20] (p. 450).

Where they are available, it is interesting to see what commonly used statistical indicators of women's well being actually measure. *The World's Women: Trends and Statistics 1970–1990* [21], which was compiled from a variety of United Nations sources, provides measures of life expectancy, maternal mortality, infant mortality combined for males and females, mortality

1370   Bonnie Kettel

rates for girls, fertility, contraceptive use, availability of trained attendants at births and smoking rates. Such indicators tell us very little about women's non-reproductive well being [1, 4].

Identifying appropriate gender-specific indicators of women's well being is not an easy task. As Payne suggests, based on research in the United Kingdom:

at the centre...lies the fundamental problem of what is meant by health, how this varies...and how to reconcile the divide between positive concepts of health as more than an absence of illness, and the necessity of relying on the only regularly produced statistics which measure rates of death and sickness rather than health [17] (p. 94).

The NCIH guidelines suggest some important qualitative indicators of women's overall health status. Among these is the proportion of decision-making roles in health assessment, promotion and expenditure held by women. The amount of leisure time available to women, both in number of hours, and in comparison with men, is also a potentially important qualitative indicator of their health and well being, particularly with regard to mental illness.

Existing data show that the overall incidence of mental illness is highest amongst men [22], although this assessment certainly needs to be evaluated through better epidemiological studies on women's mental health. Paltiel suggests that women are more emotionally hardy than men; "...women are excellent copers. They are extraordinarily resourceful, creative members of their communities" [22] (p. 198). The challenge is not to stretch women's extraordinary coping skills past the limits of their mental and physical health. Instead, "we need more and better studies on the...effects of women's help-giving...as others rely on their strengths...to the detriment of their own well being, including burnout, a form of physical and emotional exhaustion" [22] (p. 210). We also need to assess the possible relevance of environmental factors to women's mental health, including factors as disparate as desertification and smog.

It is also important to identify unambiguously the leading causes of death among women. Data on the gender-specific incidence of environmental illness in the developing countries is almost totally lacking. In the developed countries, the absence of research on menstrual cycles, and their susceptibility to environmental impact, also makes it difficult to identify those environmental factors that are damaging to women's health and well-being. The apparent, but unaddressed significance of environmental factors to women's morbidity and mortality suggests three necessary improvements in the collection of female health indicators:

(a) Improved record keeping on all incidences of morbidity and mortality in the developing countries;

(b) Gender-disaggregated collection of data on diseases known to be environmental in origin, such as diarrhoea, relevant acute respiratory illnesses, and other relevant diseases such as tuberculosis, typhoid, schistosomiasis and malaria;

(c) A world-wide plan of action for research on women's menstrual cycles including cycle length, bleeding duration, hormonal patterns and metabolic impacts, together with epidemiological research on environmental determinants of variations in the menstrual cycle [10].

UNDERSTANDING ENVIRONMENTAL SYSTEMS AND THEIR IMPACT ON WOMEN'S WELL BEING

The prevailing inattention to the significance of the biophysical environment, which surrounds and affects women's health throughout the life cycle, is not only a gap in data, or relevant indicators. It is also a conceptual gap that affects our ability to understand a variety of environmental impacts on women's well being. The difficulty for many researchers and policy analysts interested in women's environmental health is knowing where to begin. The inclusiveness and generality of the term 'environment' often leads to ambiguity. The primary focus of attention in this paper is the 'biophysical environment' which includes both natural and built elements such as trees, water sources, mosquitos, houses and smokestacks. The biophysical environment may be distinguished from the social, economic and cultural or 'societal' environment and from the changing biophysical and societal circumstances that constitute the 'historical environment'. Women (and men) occupy all three environmental contexts simultaneously throughout their lives.

The biophysical life space forms the primary arena for environmental health policy analysis. Within their life spaces, women seek food, fuel, water, shelter, fodder, fertilizers, building materials, medicines, the ingredients of income generation and wages in support of their activities as individuals, wives and mothers. In the developing countries, women are the primary users and managers of the biophysical environment for human sustenance [7, 23]. In urban areas, and in the developed countries, women's roles as household provisioners and health managers also exposes them to particular environmental risks.

Societal and historical factors lead to variations and changes in their life spaces that are positive or negative for women's health, and the health of the environment. Societal factors, such as poverty, illiteracy and gender oppression, can significantly affect the quality of women's life spaces in both the developing and the developed countries (see below). Changes to women's life spaces, especially from the introduction of new technology, can transform local biophysical systems, thereby creating 'disease environments' that are hazardous to women's health.

'Disease environments' are aspects of, or places within, women's life spaces that support environmental illnesses [9]. These environmental illnesses may be new, furthered, or reintroduced by the disruption of equilibrium in the biophysical environment [3, 24]. In part, the widespread incidence and impact on women's health of such disease environments is the result of the current inattention to environmental and gender issues in economic development policy at the national and international levels [3, 25].

The creation of disease environments has often resulted from the introduction of irrigation systems, especially in the developing countries [4]. Both malaria, which is spread by mosquitos, and schistosomiasis, which is spread by snails, are water-dependant environmental diseases. Irrigation, especially inadequately designed and managed irrigation systems, provides new and better breeding grounds for the vectors that cause malaria and schistosomiasis. Hydroelectric development can have a similar effect. Irrigation and hydroelectric development establish simplified biosystems within which these disease vectors are able to flourish. Improved breeding areas further the spread of malarial mosquitos, while the spread of schistosomiasis requires the additional factor of inadequate sanitation, and improper disposal of human waste. The use of pesticides that often accompanies irrigation can establish vector resistance to insecticides, while the molluscicides used to attack snails are both hazardous and costly [24].

The changing patterns of labour utilization, migration and settlement that accompany technological development can also establish disease environments. In Swaziland, the changed patterns of migration and settlement that accompanied the introduction of citrus and sugar estates led to a resurgence of malaria across the lowland areas of the country [26] (p. 482). Crowded urban areas are almost, *ipso facto*, disease environments. Cities, which are central to modern transportation networks, and offer the possibility of rapid human transmission, create ideal disease environments for a variety of environmental illnesses [9], especially if pollutants and environmental toxins are allowed to accumulate in an uncontrolled manner.

The creation of disease environments can be prevented, or alleviated, by integrated planning that considers the biophysical and health consequences of proposed technological interventions. However, what few health policy analysts have recognized is that the 'disruption of equilibrium' in a local life space may also be a *gendered* phenomenon, with very different implications for women and men in the same biophysical environment [27]. The neglect and denial of women's environmental and health interests and needs with regard to their life spaces is a primary, but almost totally unaddressed, factor in the creation of disease environments for women and their children [15–16, 23].

SOCIOCULTURAL IMPACTS ON WOMEN'S ENVIRONMENTAL HEALTH

The well being of women world-wide is marked by significant 'epidemiological polarization', with some countries, and some communities, offering far greater hazards to women's well being than others. The wide regional disparities that exist in women's health status are reflected in female life expectancy data. As of 1988, 12 Sub-Saharan African countries had female life expectancies under the age of 50 [11]. Life expectancy rates for women of 50 years and under are also found in Bangladesh, Nepal and Pakistan, while women in India have a life expectancy of only 58 years [19] (pp. 292–295).

There are also significant differences in female life expectancy across social classes in the developed countries [11]. Thus, in the United Kingdom, the highest female mortality rates are found among unskilled (classified according to husband's occupation) married women, followed by women who are unskilled (classified by own occupation) and single [17] (p. 100). In both the developing and the developed countries, high female mortality is accompanied by significant levels of female morbidity. Spatial variations in disease patterns, such as national and neighbourhood variations, are often the consequence of interaction between the socio-economic and cultural context of life and the biophysical environment [9] (p. 1). Three broad parameters are clear: poverty; illiteracy; and gender oppression [8, 15].

The health risks of poverty are generally far greater for women than for men. Women are far more likely than men to be poor; women *worldwide*, in every income category, own less than men, work longer hours, and earn less income [28]. As a result, according to Jacobson, "poverty among females is more intractable than among males, and their health even more vulnerable to adverse changes in social and environmental conditions" [8] (pp. 4, 7).

In the developed countries, class can be as significant a factor in the determination of women's health and well being as is residence in a developing country. In the United Kingdom, "there is a powerful relationship between socio-economic status and poor health when measured by mortality and morbidity" [17] (p. 117). Female-headed households, which now include one-quarter to one-third of all households worldwide [29], are particularly vulnerable, even in the developed countries [17] (p. 121).

Several studies draw attention to inadequate housing as an outcome of poverty that creates health hazards for women. In India, Bhatt noted the detrimental impact of crude stoves, biomass fuels and poor ventilation on the respiratory health of women and children. She also comments that "infections and accidents, not the oft-touted problems of childbirth, are the leading killers of women during the reproductive age" [30] (pp. 14–16). For poor women in the United Kingdom, poor quality housing means poor heating, lack of space, damp living conditions, lack of hot water and inadequate furnishings [17] (p. 135). Both separately, and in combination, these difficult conditions impact on the health of women, and their children, in an ongoing manner.

Illiteracy is also an important factor in the creation of life spaces hazardous to women's health. The World Bank reports that education is 'strongly associated' with good health, while literacy plays an "extremely powerful role...in determining a population's level of mortality" [31] (p. 41). World-wide, women have a primary responsibility for the maintenance of the life space, especially the dwelling place, and the provision of family health care. Illiteracy, which is a common outcome of lack of education, denies women the opportunity for vital health learning, particularly the importance of sanitation and personal hygiene in personal and family health care.

There are now at least 597 million illiterate women in the world, compared to only 352 million men. Only 15% of African women are literate, and only one-third of women in Asia. According to Jacobson, "parents are apt to invest in educating girls only when they perceive long-term gains will outweigh immediate costs" [8] (pp. 11, 18). In urban Brazil, according to the World Bank, maternal education accounted for 34% and increased access to piped water for only 20% of mortality decline between 1970 and 1976 [31] (p. 52). Women's literacy is, therefore, a critical factor in environmental health promotion.

Gender oppression is also a significant factor in the creation of hazardous environmental conditions for women and girls. Gender discrimination in the allocation of food and health care has resulted in 'markedly higher' death rates for young girls than for young boys in the Middle East, North Africa and South Asia ([8], see also Refs [4, 15]). In India, "deaths of girls under the age of five exceed those of boys by nearly 330,000 annually", while women aged 15 and over die from tuberculosis, typhoid and gastroenteric infections "at consistently higher rates than for males" [8] (p. 9). One study from the Punjab indicated that mortality for girls under 15 years was almost 50% higher than for male mortality [32] (p. 21). Bhatt argues that "the expectation of life at various ages shows that ill-health stalks the Indian woman right through her life" [30] (p. 14). As a result, the ratio of women to men in India has declined, so that there are now only 929 women for every 1000 men [8] (p. 10).

Behal describes women in purdah in North Indian villages as "prisoners of the courtyard". She argues that, because of their limited mobility, "women's perceptions on issues such as health, hygiene and how to deal with them is very low" [33] (p. 28). Women in many countries experience a variety of difficulties in access to acute medical care, including their own unwillingness to visit male health professionals. Distance and poor roads, together with cultural restrictions on women's mobility, compound this effect, as does gender bias in health expenditures for wives and daughters [34].

Together, poverty, illiteracy and gender opppression have a deadly outcome on women's well being. Prakash describes the outcome for women in India:
...the image of woman as mother is not only consecrated but her sacrifices for the welfare of her family applauded. And what is the nature of her sacrifices...that she go hungry...that she work long hard hours...that she bear child after child...that she forego much-needed medical care...that she be abused, beaten, bruised and burnt alive...all for the sake of her family [35] (p. 33).

The deadly impact that Prakash describes affects women directly, through immediate assaults on their bodies and health, and indirectly, through the creation of biophysical environments that are hazardous for women's well being. In order to transform these hazardous life spaces, the social, economic and cultural factors that give rise to them, particularly poverty, illiteracy and gender oppression, must also be addressed. Thus, a gender-sensitive environmental health policy would necessarily include approaches to poverty alleviation, the promotion of literacy, and the eradication of gender bias both locally and nationally, as important factors in the creation of life conditions that are healthy for women.

UNDERSTANDING ENVIRONMENTAL HEALTH: A NEW MODEL

As this paper has suggested, women's 'spheres of activity', the amount of time that they spend in each, and also the intensity of their environmental involvements in these spheres, affect the nature and degree of their exposure to environmental health risks [1]. Roundy [5] has articulated a useful model which has so far received inadequate attention as a base-line for gender-sensitive environmental health research and policy formulation.

Roundy's model divides a particular human settlement into a series of activity spheres. For the community of Upper Bilajig in Ethiopia, Roundy delineates six activity spheres. These begin with an "individual cell", characterized particularly by behaviour such as personal hygiene, food and beverage consumption, and "ethnosurgery". (For this latter element, we might substitute use of traditional medicine as a form of behaviour with more general application.) This individual cell is the centre of a series of concentric circles, which include the household, compound, settlement, production area and a final "further ranging area of contact". Each of these activity spheres brings residents into contact with a varying place, and a varying disease environment, within the overall community and neighbourhood [5] (pp. 268–269).

While this model can be used for the delineation of activity spheres in any community, the particular spheres will vary from rural to urban environments, and from one region and country to another. It is the general, not the specific model, that is broadly relevant. The model also differentiates eight different behavioural subsystems that take place in these various activity spheres. These subsystems include family (household) interaction, extra-family (household) socializing, religious activities, primary production, trade, water use, animal contact and defecation. Each of these subsytems can be examined separately in relation to each activity sphere. Here again, behavioural subsystems will vary from one setting to another, and it is only the general model that is broadly applicable.

It is also possible to aggregate the behavioural subsystems, and to categorize the overall degree of interaction, in frequency and intensity, within each activity sphere as occasional, common or very great [5] (pp. 270–271). The clear advantage of the model is that it can be used for gender-sensitive research. Thus, Roundy shows how the degree of interaction with various activity spheres differs for adult males, adult females, working age children and non-working children. (Infants were categorized with adult females.)

The differences that emerge are striking. To all intents and purposes, these categories of people, who might otherwise be said to occupy the same community, actually live in different life spaces, and interact with different biophysical environments. In the process, they are also exposed to different diseases. In Upper Bilajig, it is men and working children who run the greatest risk of exposure to schistosomiasis, while women and younger children appear to have the highest rates of exposure to tuberculosis [5] (pp. 275–276).

This model has significant implications for research in support of gender-sensitive environmental health policy. It indicates the tremendous importance of understanding where and how women [and men] actually live in the biophysical environment, and the implications of their use of certain arenas of the biophysical environment for their own health. Presently, there is little relevant information on women's varying activity spheres and the health risks they are exposed to in the biophysical environment. This is a key area for research on women's health and well being that deserves significant policy attention.

WOMEN'S ENVIRONMENTAL HEALTH: URBAN ISSUES

In urban areas, the built aspects of the biophysical environment become comparatively more important as an aspect of the life spaces women occupy. This is not to say that the natural elements in the biophysical environment become irrelevant to women's health in urban areas. Instead, the major focus of concern is the impact of built elements on the natural aspect of the urban biophysical environment, and thus, on women's health.

Population is growing in many urban areas, particularly in the developing countries, at a phenomenal rate. By 2025, about 60% of the world's population is expected to live in urban areas [36]. Over 50% of urban dwellers in the developing countries live in slums and squatter settlements [36] (p. 122). There are two predominate forms of environmental health hazard that characterize life in urban areas. The first of these are the environmental problems faced by the urban poor, particularly slum dwellers and residents of squatter settlements. The second are the environmental difficulties shared by all urban dwellers, including those in high-income neighbourhoods.

All urban dwellers may be faced with air and water pollution, excess noise, traffic congestion and other urban hazards such as higher crime rates. Urban areas generally do not contain space for the natural absorption of garbage and sewage. Thus, sanitation and waste management is a much larger task in these areas, and even high income earners may be affected if these systems are inadequate. Industrial and toxic waste is a particular health hazard, especially when these pollutants are dumped into local rivers or onto open ground.

Squatters and slum residents must confront the environmental health hazards of overcrowding, inadequate sanitation and waste management, inadequate water supply and inadequate housing. The combined impact of these dilemmas can be a dehumanizing level of stress and discord. In some cities, such as Calcutta and Bombay, > 50% of the urban population lives in slum areas, with inadequate housing and a lack of basic services. Urban poverty often leads to inadequate housing. The Asia and Pacific Development Centre reports that over one billion people, or a quarter of the world's population are marginally housed or homeless [36] (pp. 121–122).

Environmental disease is prevalent in urban areas in the developing countries. Diarrhoea, dysentry, hepatitis and typhoid, all the result of environmental factors, are the major causes of death in such areas. Inadequate sanitation and contaminated drinking water are largely to blame. Rates of illnesses such as tuberculosis, diarrhoeas, leprosy and hookwarm are generally higher, sometimes very much higher, among slum dwellers [36] (p. 123).

However, the negative health impact of urban poverty is not limited to the developing countries. Payne argues that, in the United Kingdom, "unsafe public space...constitutes deprivation in the environment for women, as does inadequate public transport and poor public amenities". Racism adds a further dimension to the environmental impact of poverty "where women from some ethnic minority groups might have to go further to find shops selling food and other goods which they need, whilst racism makes the environment more dangerous" [17] (p. 136). Three-quarters of hazardous wastefill sites in the southeastern United States are located in low-income neighbourhoods, while at least one toxic waste dump can generally be found in communities occupied by African-Americans and Hispanic-Americans [37] (p. 21).

Women experience a disproportionate share of urban environmental difficulties as the result of their common gender-based roles as household provisioners and maintainers, especially of food, water, energy and shelter. Women's particular housing needs, such as adequate space, play areas for children, access to shopping and transportation, and security, are rarely taken into consideration in the design of urban structures and neighbourhoods, even in the developed countries.

Urban environmental hazards may also have a negative impact on women's maternal health. A report from Malaysia suggests that the rate of miscarriage among women in the state of Malacca increased 400% as the result of water shortages during a period of severe disruption of the local water system. These increased miscarriages appeared to be the result of water carrying by women who could not find, or afford, anyone to help them [36] (p. 127). Urban life, especially in crowded slums and squatter settlements, may also lead to increased stress, anxiety and mental illness. Payne's work on women's health in the United Kingdom suggests that this problem is not limited to the developing countries, but may also be found in low-income urban areas in the developed countries as well [17].

The environmental hazards of urban life may be compounded by the industrial hazards of women's work places. Women's health concerns arising from unsafe working conditions and long work hours have received surprisingly little attention [8] (p. 5). Packard also argues that greater attention needs to be paid to the health problems of female workers:

Women are frequently employed in the informal sector or in...work where wages are lowest, conditions are inferior and health and welfare benefits are nonexistent...Women also work a double day and are often expected to maintain the household as well as contribute to its income. This places a great deal of stress on women and may produce different health problems than those experienced by men [26] (p. 478).

Elements which are not hazardous in themselves can become so in the context of industrial work. Packard reports on the health problems of women workers in pineapple processing factories in Swaziland. Women in these factories stand in cold fruit juice for ten hours or more, without the protection of boots and gloves. As a result, they develop ulcers on their arms and legs [26] (p. 481). Women workers who live in slums or squatter settlements, or on the street, can face environmental threats to their well being throughout the day and night. Where these environmental difficulties are compounded by violence against women, from partners, employers, or government officials, the hazards to their well being can be literally life threatening.

In urban areas, women's health and the quality of the biophysical environment are intertwined issues. It is not possible to significantly improve women's health without improving their life spaces, and it is not possible to improve women's life spaces without recognizing women's interests and needs in the use and management of their own households and communities. Thus, women are central to environmental and health policy formulation in urban areas.

ENVIRONMENTAL DEGRADATION: SOURCES AND IMPACTS ON WOMEN'S HEALTH

'Environmental degradation' is the loss of biological productivity that results from erosion, the destruction of biodiversity, and factors such as salinization and sodication. Through its impact on the biophysical environment, environmental degradation has serious consequences for the health of women. Sontheimer comments that "over the last 20 years, the relationship between women and the living systems which support their life has changed drastically in response to heavy ecological stress in many areas of poor, developing countries" [38] (p. i).

'Desertification' is currently the most widespread form of global land degradation. Although vast areas may be affected by desertification, the phenomenon is always 'site-specific'. It always occurs within a local biophysical environment, and is always amenable to prevention through local and national strategies for desertification control and promotion of "land health" [39].

Desertification generally results from four common hazards: inappropriate irrigation; overcultivation; overherding; and deforestation. Population growth exacerbates the problem. However, it is a common misperception that desertification is most severe in the developing countries. As a proportion of existing dryland, moderate to severe desertification is most serious in North America. Asia contains the largest area of desertified dryland, followed by Africa. At least 50% of Australia's dryland is also moderately to severely desertified [39] (p. 19).

The developed countries, such as the United States and Australia, are better able to cope with the social and economic consequences of desertification, at least in the short term, through investment in reclamation, and the availability of non-agricultural employment. Among the existing consequences of desertification in the developing countries are crop failure, destruction of rangelands, reduction of woody biomass, reduction of surface and ground water, sand encroachment, flooding after sudden rains, overall failure of life support systems, famine and forced migration. In betweem 1984 and 1985, desertification produced 10 million environmental refugees in Africa [39] (pp. 3, 12). At least in Africa, the vast proportion of environmental refugees are men, who move to urban areas in search of employment, leaving the women and children behind in the desertified zones to fend for themselves [40].

As a result of their activities in producing food and gathering fuelwood and water, women in the developing countries are often held responsible for desertification [7]. This is also a misperception that denies the significance of profit-oriented strategies of production, such as agro-business, cash cropping, commercial meat production, timber and pulp extraction, and the impact of industry-oriented hydroelectric development, on the desertification process. As the United Nations Environment Programme points out in a recent report, "an over-riding socio-economic issue in desertification is the imbalance of power and access to strategic resources among different groups in a given society" [39] (pp. 3–4).

Gender bias, and the denial of women's needs and interests, is prominent amongst the social factors that lead to desertification [27, 40]. Profit-oriented strategies for dryland resource use typically rely on complex technologies such as irrigation, hybrid seeds, artificial insemination and industrial processing. Women in the developing countries have minimal access to these technologies, which are commonly expensive and require new skills, and little control over the land needed to use them. The technologies themselves may impact negatively on women's life spaces, and spread diseases such as malaria and schistosomiasis.

Very little of the money or other benefits gained from this profit quest flows back to women at the local community level, even though women may be a significant source of free or cheap labour for cash crop and plantation production. However, once the desertification process sets in, often as a result of the overuse of these technologies, women typically become the primary victims through the increasing difficulty they experience in the provision of food, water and fuelwood.

Desertification in Africa and South Asia has generally resulted in women having access to a smaller and smaller land base. As a result, women have often been forced to exploit land more intensively. This has furthered the spread of soil erosion and loss of vegetative cover. At the same time, the deforestation that has resulted from land clearing and timber cutting has also forced women to overuse remaining local sources, or to search further from home for fuelwood. As Monimart describes it, "fuel-gathering...becomes ever more time consuming and burdensome, to the point of becoming unbearable". Deforestation has also led to water shortages through loss of ground water, while the use of pesticides and fertilizers has further damaged women's water sources. In this way, shortages of water for domestic use in many areas of Africa and South Asia have reached a critical level. Ultimately, "the land and the women alike are exhausted. Neither gets any rest" [40] (p. 35).

The increasing female impoverishment that typically results from desertification also has profound consequences for women's health: "their health, that most precious asset, is severely undermined by privation of food, more frequent pregnancies, and the increasing burden of work" [40] (p. 38). The United

Nations Environment Programme now suggests that the solution to the problem of desertification lies largely in socio-political and socio-economic measures, rather than in technology [39] (pp. xiv–xv). Thus, desertification control must begin with "...solving problems such as poverty, food, housing, employment, health, education, population pressures and demographic imbalance". Furthermore, to achieve success, "broad-based public participation...including women...is essential" [39] (p. vii).

ENVIRONMENTAL IMPACTS ON WOMEN'S HEALTH: A CASE STUDY

Ferguson [41] provides a 'snapshot' of women's environmental health in a developing country in his study of Kibwezi Division of Machakos District in Kenya. Kibwezi is located in a marginal, semi-arid agricultural zone, with a low and unreliable rainfall. Population density is high and growing, with an average of only 0.23 ha of agricultural land per person. Shortages of food are both seasonal and chronic. Kibwezi is a division on the edge of the downward spiral of environmental decline.

The most commonly identified agricultural problem is a shortage of water, followed by shortages of equipment, seeds and labour. As in Kenya generally, women appear to contribute the major labour of food crop production, even in households headed by men. The health status of both adults and children is inadequate, with malaria, gastro-enteric and respiratory tract infections as the most common adult diseases.

About 30% of households have *de facto* female heads, and there is generally a high level of demographic dependency on women of child-bearing age. The crude birth rate is high. Women in the 40–44 age group have an average of 7.5 births, but life expectancy for men and women combined as of 1979 was only 47 years [41] (pp. 21, 26).

In these generally difficult circumstances, women also experience specific difficulties that emerge from their interaction with the biophysical environment. Water collection is particularly onerous: "on average, women are carrying 20–25 kg loads for 3.5 km, 1.5 times per day on rough terrain and in temperatures of up to 40°". Women carry water on their backs. When men do assist in water collection, they use bicycles, ox-carts or donkeys [41] (p. 25).

One-third of the women are suffering from parasitic infections, especially hookworm. Women generally are also shorter, and have less body fat than a comparison group from a more fertile area of Machakos District. They also have generally low haemoglobin levels, the apparent result of malaria and frequent pregnancy. Women with hookworm infestations have particularly severe anaemia [41] (p. 27). As a result of their difficulties:

...women of childbearing age form a cohort which is under heavy and almost constant stress...the majority of women...are undernourished and this condition is exacerbated by the widespread prevalence of intestinal parasitosis, normally considered to be less of a problem in Kibwezi than malaria, gastro-enteric infections and bilharzia...In many cases, chronic exposure to such stress leads to chronic disability and the burden on the more healthy women is concomitantly increased [41] (p. 28).

In between 1978 and 1983, over 100 community health workers were trained in Kibwezi through a community-based health project. However, the impact of these health workers on the health of women and children was limited. This limited outcome was due to the failure of the community to select women for these roles, and the failure of the project to encourage and support training of female health workers. Ferguson suggests an number of possible 'indirect' interventions: improved credit and extension services for women; encouraging men to take on water collection through the introduction of carrying methods that rely on bicycles, ox-carts or hand carts; and community-based grain stores. To this list he adds more direct strategies such as nutrition education, maternal and child health and family planning information, and evaluation and monitoring of health interventions [41] (p. 29).

It is typical that no direct recommendations for improvement of women's non-reproductive health, other than nutrition information are put forward. Specifically, nothing is said about interventions that might alleviate the prevalent environmental diseases in Kibwezi. A distressing vision appears from these recommendations of a group of tired, poor, environmentally sick women being instructed about the basic food groups. This vision is an all too frequent reality of women's health policy and planning, especially in the developing countries.

In order to move beyond this vision, we certainly need to begin with gender-sensitive environmental health research. Roundy's model [5] offers an excellent framework for the design and implementation of such research in both the developing and the developed countries. Such research would add a critically important epidemiological dimension, based on the notion of gendered life spaces, to the improvements in female health indicators discussed earlier in this paper. However, as Ferguson's research in Kibwezi also makes clear, we also need new policy approaches that will build on women's gender roles as environmental and health managers, and support women's participation in environmental and health decision-making at the local, national and international levels.

WOMEN'S ENVIRONMENTAL HEALTH: THE POLICY ISSUES

Several key points concerning the formulation of gender-sensitive environmental health policy emerge from the preliminary evidence reviewed in this paper. These key points are summarized briefly here as the basis for a delineation of the 'way forward'. First, appropriate health policy for women requires support for their overall well being, not only their reproductive health. Effective women's health policy also demands recognition of the full range of women's activities and responsibilities, including their involvements as domestic managers, producers, workers, care-givers and environmental managers. Better understanding is also required of the centrality of women to both environmental and health management, in the developing and the developed countries.

A gender-sensitive environmental health policy that will sustain women's health cannot be developed in an information vacuum. Far better data is needed on women's morbidity and mortality, and on women's gender-differentiated exposure to environmental illnesses. There is also a significant need for qualitative and participatory research to uncover women's existing environmental health problems as a basis for more detailed environmental health assessment, research and action. 'Silver bullet' approaches, which aim to improve women's overall health and well being through a particular strategic intervention, such as nutrition education or maternal health care, are unlikely to result in significant overall improvement in their health status, especially in their environmental health [14].

One fundamental reason why such approaches simply cannot work is that they fail to recognize that women and men do lead gender-differentiated lives, and that in many communities, in many countries, including communities in the developed countries, women and men really do not inhabit the same 'life spaces'. They may live in the same city or village, they may work on the same farm, they may sleep in the same room in the same household, but from the time they rise, until the time they go to bed, they may actually occupy and use very different life spaces, and they may be exposed to very different environmental illnesses as a result. For this reason, the differential attention paid to men's environmental needs and interests in a great deal of current national and international development policy and programming—in both the developing and the developed countries—may, in fact, be as significant an environmental health hazard for women, as is poverty, illiteracy and gender oppression [23, 27].

For this same reason, it is also not effective in terms of costs or outcomes to involve women only as implementors of health and environmental action plans arrived at by others, especially through top–down, male-oriented decision networks. Instead, the focus of policy attention has to be on women as key agents for the promotion of environmental and human health within their own life spaces. In the developing countries, local women's groups provide an important context for empowering women as environmental and health decision-makers. They offer women mutual solidarity and encouragement, and the benefit of shared knowledge and ideas [8]. In the developed

Women, health and the environment 1377

countries, women are beginning to discover that the walls of their homes, and the boundaries of their neighbourhoods, do not act as some 'magical detoxifying barrier' to the impact of pollutants and toxic contaminants on their life spaces [42]. In communities such as Love Canal in the United States, and Port Hope, Ontario, women have begun to participate in local action to prevent the spread of environmental pollution and inadequate disposal of nuclear waste [43].

However, such groups cannot operate in a policy vacuum [8]. They require support and affirmation at every level of environment and health action, from the community level up to national and international decision-makers. They also require access to the scientific and technological information, training and education that will serve their interests in environmental and human health. Ultimately what is necessary for environmental and human health policy that will protect and maintain healthy life spaces for women, in both the developing and the countries, is for women to participate in policy formulation, and related scientific and technological professions, in equitable numbers with men [4, 44].

THE WAY FORWARD

Women's participation as environmental and health professionals and decision-makers is a low-cost strategy for promotion of environmental and human well being. However, rehabilative and curative costs in both areas will continue to rise as long as policy in other areas, particularly economic policy, is prioritized over environmental and human well being [3, 8]. National and international decision-makers, both political and civil, have a key role to play in reorienting future development priorities towards a more cost effective, sustainable future through support for women's environmental and health knowledge and action.

Women who are poor, illiterate and oppressed, whether they live in the developing or the developed countries, cannot take on a meaningful, effective role as agents of environmental and human health. National and international decision-makers also have a central responsibility to support the alleviation of these hazards to women's well being through policy and action in support of better incomes, education and autonomy for women. This will require support for national and donor funding directly addressed to the alleviation of these barriers to women's well being and participation, including the barriers that currently deny women access to scientific and technological expertize and training, and political participation.

Research in both the developing [19, 36] and the developed countries [43] shows that women want to address their own environmental and health problems, and to do so in an integrated, effective, empowering manner. Top–down, male-oriented approaches to policy formulation will not include them effectively.

National and international decision-makers also have an urgent responsibility to ensure that women are included in decision-making frameworks at every level of policy forumlation. This will require support for the participation of women as key decision-makers at the national level, and at every level of government and community action. However, one woman cannot speak for all women. Women must have the opportunity and encouragement to participate in equal numbers, and with an equitable voice, in every level of environmental and health policy and decision-making.

In 1992, the World Health Assembly took what Yoon refers to as "a major step forward" by selecting "women, health and development" as the basis for its discussions [4] (p. 26). Many of the policy imperatives summarized here were supported by the Assembly in a set of recommendations which Yoon reviews. However, as Yoon points out, "although the expert group panel had emphasized linkages of gender and health to environment, particularly in areas of reproductive health, cancers, tropical diseases and occupational health...these were not specifically highlighted in the resolutions" [4] (p. 27). Member states were also encouraged only to "include at least one woman" in their delegations to the World Health Assembly. On the other hand, the Assembly recommendations did urge the Director-General of the World Health Organization to "maintain the target of 30% for the proportion of all professional and higher-graded posts...to be occupied by women" [45].

The forthcoming 1995 Fourth World Conference on Women will assess governmental progress on the *Forward Looking Strategies for the Advancement of Women* from the 1985 Nairobi conference [46]. The Forward Looking Strategies contain key sections in support of women as environmental and health decision-makers. In addition, Chapter 24 of *Agenda 21*, the global action plan adopted by the United Nations Conference on Environment and Development also contains key recommendations for the empowerment of women in these areas [47]. However, the *Forward Looking Strategies* and Chapter 24 of *Agenda 21* need to be ratified and *addressed*, through national policy formulation and implementation on the part of the member states of the United Nations. The *Women's Agenda 21*, from the World Congress of Women for a Healthy Planet, organized by the Women's Environment and Development Organization in Miami in 1991, also offers a valuable set of guidelines for the empowerment of women as participants in policy formulation for sustainable and equitable development [48].

All of these excellent policy guidelines, especially guidelines developed by women themselves in documents such as the *Women's Action Agenda 21*, are to no avail if they are not implemented. For this reason, key working groups and networks concerned with 'women, health and the environment', such as the

Women's Environment and Development Organiz-ation, are presently turning their attention to the formulation of specific, feasible recommendations for the improved participation of women in policy formulation [10] and relevant science and technology professions [4, 44].

A recent report from the *Expert Group Meeting: Women and Economic Decision-Making* calls this organizing for 'clout'. Of course, organizing for clout is not limited to women's participation in economic policy formulation, but has significant implications for women's involvement in environmental and health policy formulation as well. The report's view of what is essential in 'organizing for clout' is informative:

to be truly empowered...women need to break out of isolation and to organize into effective groups to influence local and national government...policies and resource flows, the media, and the social fabric as a whole. Women need to look beyond their immediate environments to create networks cutting across sectoral and professional boundaries and national border and so create new opportunities [49] (p. 17).

In the months leading up to the *Fourth World Conference on Women* in September 1995, 'women, health and the environment' is likely to be a key policy concern. The efforts to date of the working groups and networks organizing for a strategic change in women's participation in environmental health policy formu-lation suggest that what is really needed in the future is *partnership*—between policy-makers, researchers, government officials, non-governmental organiz-ations, and women's groups–both nationally and internationally, to recognize, protect and improve women's life spaces as a basis for a more equitable and sustainable approach to environmental and human health.

REFERENCES

1. Lewis N. and Kieffer E. C. The health of women: beyond maternal and child health. In *Health and Development* (Edited by Verhasselt V. and Phillips D.). International Geographic Union Commission on Health and Develop-ment. Routledge, London, 1994.
2. van der Kwaak A., van den Engel M., Richters A., Bartels K., Haaijer I., Mama A., Veenhoff A., Engelkes E., Keysors L. and Smith I. Women and health. *Vena J.* 3, 2, 1991.
3. Carr-Harris J. *New Dimensions of Eco-Health*. Eco-Health Series, South-South Solidarity, New Delhi, 1992.
4. Yoon S.-Y. Gender and health. Paper for the Gender Working Group, United Nations Commission on Science and Technology for Development. International Development Research Centre, Ottawa, 1994.
5. Roundy R. Human behavior and disease hazards in Ethiopia: spatial perspectives. In *Health and Disease in Tropical Africa* (Edited by Akhtar R.), pp. 261–278. Harwood, London, 1987.
6. MacCormack C. Planning and evaluating women's participation in primary health care. *Soc. Sci. Med.* 35, 831, 1992.
7. Dankelman I. and Davidson J. *Women and Environment in the Third World: Alliance for the Future*. Earthscan, London, 1988.

8. Jacobson J. Women's health: the price of poverty. In *The Health of Women: a Global Perspective* (Edited by Koblinsky M., Timyan J. and Gay J.), pp. 3–31. Westview, Boulder, 1993.
9. Akhtar R. Introduction. In *Health and Diseases in Tropical Africa* (Edited by Akhtar R.), pp. 1–12. Harwood, Chur, Switzerland, 1987.
10. Koblinsky M., Campbell O. and Harlow S. Mother and more: a broader perspective on women's health. In *The Health of Women: a Global Perspective* (Edited by Koblinsky M., Timyan J. and Gay J.), pp. 33–62. Westview, Boulder, 1993.
11. Jamison D. and Mosley W. H. Disease control priorities in developing countries: health policy responses to epidemiological change. *Am. J. Publ. Hlth* 81, 15, 1991.
12. Clorfene-Casten L. The environmental link to breast cancer. *Ms* May/June, 52, 1993.
13. Curlin P. and Tinker A. Introduction. In *The Health of Women: a Global Perspective* (Edited by Koblinsky M., Timyan J. and Gay J.), pp. 1–2. Westview, Boulder, 1993.
14. Brems S. and Griffiths M. Health women's way: learning to listen. In *The Health of Women: a Global Perspective* (Edited by Koblinsky M., Timyan J. and Gay J.), pp. 255–273. Westview, Boulder, 1993.
15. Tinker A., Daly P., Green C., Saxenian H., Lakshmi-narayanan R. and Gill K. *Women's Health and Nutrition: Making a Difference*. World Bank Discussion Paper No. 256, The World Bank, Washington, 1994.
16. Lewis N., Huyer S., Kettel B. and Marsden L. *Safe Womanhood: a Discussion Paper*. Gender, Science and Development Programme Working Paper Series No. 4. International Federation of Institutes for Advanced Study, Toronto, 1994.
17. Payne S. *Women, Health and Poverty: an Introduction*. Harvester Wheatsheaf, New York, 1991.
18. Freedman L. and Maine D. Women's mortality: a legacy of neglect. In *The Health of Women: a Global Perspective* (Edited by Koblinsky M., Timyan J. and Gay J.), pp. 147–170. Westview, Boulder, 1993.
19. APDC (Asian and Pacific Development Centre). *Asian and Pacific Women's Resource and Action Series: Health*. APDC, Kuala Lumpur, 1989.
20. Raikes A. Women's health in East Africa. *Soc. Sci. Med.* 28, 447, 1989.
21. UNIFEM (United Nations Development Fund for Women). *The World's Women: Trends and Statistics 1970–1990*. UNIFEM, New York, 1991.
22. Paltiel F. Women's mental health: a global perspective. In *The Health of Women: a Global Perspective* (Edited by Koblinsky M., Timyan J. and Gay J.), pp. 197–216. Westview, Boulder, 1993.
23. Kettel B. Gender and environments: lessons from WEDNET. In *EnGENDERing Wealth and Well Being* (Edited by Blumberg R., Rakowski C., Tinker I. and Monteon M.), pp. 365–398. Westview, Boulder, 1995 (in press).
24. Forget G. *Health and the Environment: a People-Centred Research Strategy*. International Development Research Centre, Ottawa, 1992.
25. Kettel B. New approaches to sustainable development *Can. Woman Stud.* 13, 11, 1993.
26. Packard R. Industrial production, health and disease in Subsaharan Africa. *Soc. Sci. Med.* 28, 475, 1989.
27. Kettel B. Gender distortions and development disasters: women and milk in African herding systems. *Natl. Women's Stud. Assoc. J.* 4, 23, 1992.
28. Ahooja-Patel K. *Linking Women with Sustainable Development*. The Commonwealth of Learning, Vancou-ver, 1992.
29. Chinery-Hessem., Agarwahl B., Ariffin J., Bare T., Ghai D., Henriques M. L., Jolly R., Mathews I., McAskie C. and Stewart F. *Engendering Adjustment for the 1990's:*

Report of a Commonwealth Expert Group on Women and Structural Adjustment. Commonwealth Secretariat, London, 1990.

30. Bhatt R. Why do daughters die. In *In Search of Our Bodies: a Feminist Look at Women, Health and Reproduction in India* (Edited by Bhate K., Menon L., Gupte M., Savara M., Daswani M., Prakash P., Kashyap R. and Patel V). Shakti, Bombay, 1987.

31. Wilson G. Diseases of poverty. In *Poverty and Development in the 1990's* (Edited by Allen T. and Thomas A.), pp. 34–54. Oxford University Press, Oxford, 1992.

32. Karkal M. Ill health, early death: women's destiny. In *In Search of Our Bodies: a Feminist Look at Women, Health and Reproduction in India* (Edited by Bhatt K., Menon L., Gupte M., Savara M., Daswani M., Prakash P., Kashyap R. and Patel V), pp. 20–25. Shakti, Bombay, 1987.

33. Behal M. Prisoners of the courtyard. In *In Search of Our Bodies: a Feminist Look at Women, Health and Reproduction in India* (Edited by Bhatt K., Menon L., Gupte M., Savara M., Daswani M., Prakash P., Kashyap R. and Patel V), pp. 28–30. Shakti, Bombay, 1987.

34. Timyan J., Brechin S., Measham D. and Ogunleye B. Access to care: more than a problem of distance. In *The Health of Women: a Global Perspective* (Edited by Koblinsky M., Timyan J. and Gay J.), pp. 217–234. Westview, Boulder, 1993.

35. Prakash P. Blind spot in health policy. In *In Search of Our Bodies: a Feminist Look at Women, Health and Reproduction in India* (Edited by Bhatt K., Menon L., Gupte M., Savara M., Daswani M., Prakash P., Kashyap R. and Patel V), pp. 31–35. Shakti, Bombay, 1987.

36. APDC (Asian and Pacific Development Centre). *Asian and Pacific Women's Resource and Action Series: Environment.* APDC, Kuala Lumpur, 1992.

37. Steady F. Women and children: managers, protectors and victims of the environment. In *Women and Children First: Environment, Poverty and Sustainable Development* (Edited by Steady F.), pp. 17–42. Schenkman Books, Rochester, Vermont, 1993.

38. Sontheimer S. (Ed.) *Women and the Environment: a Reader.* Earthscan, London, 1991.

39. UNEP (United Nations Environment Programme). *Status of Desertification and Implementation of the United Nations Plan of Action to Combat Desertification: Report of the Executive Director.* UNEP/GCSS.III/3, UNEP, Nairobi, 1991.

40. Monimart M. Women in the fight against desertification. In *Women and the Environment: a Reader* (Edited by Sontheimer S.), pp. 32–64. Earthscan, London, 1991.

41. Ferguson A. Women's health in a marginal area of Kenya. *Soc. Sci. Med.* **23**, 17, 1986.

42. Rosenberg H. The kitchen and the multinational corporation: an analysis of the links between the household and global corporations. In *Through the Kitchen Window* (Edited by Luxton M. and Rosenberg H.). Garamond, Toronto, 1990.

43. McIntosh S. On the homefront: in defence of the health of our families. *Can. Woman Stud.* **13**, 89, 1993.

44. Kettel B. *Key Pathways for Science and Technology for Sustainable and Equitable Development.* Expert Paper for the Gender Working Group, United Nations Commission on Science and Technology for Development. International Development Research Centre, Ottawa, 1994.

45. WHA (World Health Assembly). *Collaboration within the United Nations System: General Matters, Women, Health and Development (A45/VR/13).* World Health Organization, Geneva, 1992.

46. UN (United Nations). *The Forward Looking Strategies for the Advancement of Women.* United Nations, New York, 1985.

47. UN (United Nations). *Agenda* 21. United Nations, New York, 1992.

48. WEDO (Women's Environment and Development Organization). *Official Report: World Women's Congress for a Healthy Planet.* WEDO, New York, 1992.

49. UN (United Nations). *Expert Group Meeting: Women and Economic Decision-Making, Division for the Advancement of Women, (EDM/1994/1).* United Nations, New York, 1994.

[3]

International Human Rights and Women's Reproductive Health

Rebecca J. Cook

Neglect of women's reproductive health, perpetuated by law, is part of a larger, systematic discrimination against women. Laws obstruct women's access to reproductive health services. Laws protective of women's reproductive health are rarely or inadequately implemented. Moreover, few laws or policies facilitate women's reproductive health services. Epidemiological evidence and feminist legal methods provide insight into the law's neglect of women's reproductive health and expose long-held beliefs in the law's neutrality that harm women fundamentally. Empirical evidence can be used to evaluate how effectively laws are implemented and whether alternative legal approaches exist that would provide greater protection of individual rights. International human rights treaties, including those discussed in this article, are being applied increasingly to expose how laws that obstruct women's access to reproductive health services violate their basic rights. (STUDIES IN FAMILY PLANNING 1993; 24, 2: 73–86)

Protection of women's reproductive health has not been a priority for governments, as reflected by the laws they have created. Historically, the principal duty of women has been viewed as bearing children, particularly sons, and as serving as the foundation of families. The cost to women's health of discharging this duty went unrecognized. Poor health, influenced by early and excessive childbearing, and premature death during labor or from weakness or exhaustion due to pregnancy and close birth spacing, were explained as destiny and divine will. Maternal mortality and morbidity were, therefore, not considered amenable to control through health services, education, and law.

Women's reproductive health raises sensitive issues for many legal traditions because the subject is related to sexuality and morality. If women could enjoy sexual relations while preventing pregnancy and avoiding sexually transmitted diseases, then, many believed, sexual morality and family security would be in jeopardy. Such traditional morality is reflected in laws that attempt to control women's behavior by limiting or denying women's access to reproductive health services.

Many women die or are chronically disabled from complications of pregnancy. Maternal deaths are defined as deaths among women who are pregnant or who have been pregnant during the previous 42 days.[1] The World Health Organization has estimated that each year 500,000 women die from pregnancy-related causes and that unsafe abortion "causes some 25 to 50 percent of [maternal] deaths, simply because women do not have access to family planning services they want and need, or have no access to safe procedures or to humane treatment for the complications of abortion."[2] These statistics are only one indication of the neglect of women's reproductive health and well-being.

Epidemiological studies can be used to indicate which women have limited access to care and are therefore at higher risk than others of maternal mortality and morbidity. The universal risk factor is the fact of being female. Maternal sickness and death may be triggered by pregnancy, but frequently result from cultural, medical, and socioeconomic factors that devalue the status and health of women and girls. Maternal mortality

> often has some of its roots in a woman's life before the pregnancy. It may lie in infancy, or even before her birth, when deficiencies of calcium, vitamin D, or iron begin. Continued throughout childhood and adolescence, these faults may result in a contracted pelvis and eventually in death from obstructed labor or in chronic iron-deficiency anaemia and often death from haemorrhage. The train of negative factors goes on throughout the woman's life: the special risks of adolescent pregnancy; the maternal depletion

Rebecca J. Cook, J.D. is Associate Professor (Research) and Director, International Human Rights Programme, Faculty of Law, University of Toronto, Toronto, Canada M5S 2C5.

from pregnancies too closely spaced; the burdens of heavy physical labor in the reproductive period; the renewed high risk of childbearing after 35 and, worse, after 40; the compounding risks of grand multiparity; and, running through all this, the ghastly dangers of illegal abortion to which sheer desperation may drive her. All these are links in a chain from which only the grave or menopause offer hope of escape.[3]

There are, therefore, many causes that contribute to maternal death, and some combine with others to compound the risk of death.[4] For example, pregnant women whose blood is infected with human immunodeficiency virus (HIV) face aggravating factors that can lead to early death.[5]

Paternalistic control of women's sexual and reproductive behavior manifests itself in laws and policies. For example, access to voluntary sterilization services in some countries is contingent on the number of cesarian sections that a woman has undergone.[6] Laws and policies stereotype and punish women because of their role in reproduction, denying them equal opportunities with men. For example, laws that prescribe younger ages for women to marry than for men maintain the stereotype of women as restricted to childbearing and service roles, while denying them the years of education, preparation, and experience made available to men.[7]

Laws protective of women's health may be lacking; where they exist, they are rarely or inadequately enforced. In countries with no legal age of marriage, or where that age is low, or where the law is not enforced, adolescent pregnancy is common. Such pregnancies are associated with high obstetric risk and maternal mortality.[8]

In Nigeria, where there is no legal minimum age of marriage, 25 percent of all women are married by age 14, 50 percent by 16, and 75 percent by 18.[9] Kelsey Harrison and others have indicated the human cost of adolescent pregnancy in Zaria, Nigeria. Girls younger than age 15 constituted 30 percent of reported maternal deaths. A high proportion of teenage pregnancies ended in fetal loss, induced abortion, or infant death, as well as death or harmful consequences to the girl. Consequences included vesicovaginal fistulas (VVF), an injury to the bladder, urethra, and lower end of the bowel causing constant leakage of urine and, sometimes, vaginal excretion of feces. The adolescent VVF victims suffer infection and may be made infertile, becoming social outcasts as a result of divorce or of being forced into prostitution.[10]

Women's dignity and autonomy are abused during the delivery of reproductive health services, because the doctrine of informed consent is not enforced or is misapplied.[11] For example, the rate of cesarian sections is unnecessarily high in both developed and developing countries, in part because women are pressured to undergo the procedure without being given adequate information to make an informed choice between cesarian or vaginal delivery.[12]

In contrast to this traditional neglect, a humane view is emerging that women's reproductive health is defined as:

a condition in which the reproductive process is accomplished in a state of complete physical, mental and social well-being and is not merely the absence of disease or disorders of the reproductive process. Reproductive health, therefore, implies that people have the *ability* to reproduce, to regulate their fertility and to practice and enjoy sexual relationships. It further implies that reproduction is carried to a *successful outcome* through infant and child survival, growth, and healthy development. It finally implies that women can go *safely* through pregnancy and childbirth, that fertility regulation can be achieved without health hazards and that people are safe in having sex.[13]

Services to promote and maximize reproductive health include providing appropriate sex education and counseling, and the means to prevent unintended pregnancy, to treat unwanted pregnancy, and to prevent sexually transmitted diseases and other manifestations of sexual and reproductive dysfunctions, including infertility.[14] Epidemiological and related data show how reproductive health services can reduce maternal mortality and morbidity and contribute substantially to women's reproductive health.[15] Epidemiological data demonstrate life and health risks from pregnancies that come too early, too late, too often, or too close together in a woman's reproductive years.[16]

Laws that deny, obstruct, or limit availability of and access to reproductive health services are being challenged as violating basic human rights that are protected by international human rights conventions. The primary modern human rights treaty referred to in this article is the 1979 Convention on the Elimination of All Forms of Discrimination Against Women (the Women's Convention).[17] This treaty gives expression to the values implicit in the Universal Declaration of Human Rights,[18] and reinforces the Declaration's two initial implementing covenants, the International Covenant on Civil and Political Rights (the Political Covenant),[19] and the International Covenant on Economic, Social, and Cultural Rights (the Economic Covenant).[20] Similarly derived from the Universal Declaration are regional human rights conventions, including the European Convention for the Protection of Human Rights and Fundamental Freedoms (the European Convention),[21] the American Convention on Human Rights (the American Convention),[22] and the African Charter on Human and Peoples' Rights (the African Charter).[23] Other specialized conventions exist, such as the International Convention on the Elimination of All Forms of Racial Discrimination (the Race Convention),[24] which prevents discrimination against women of all racial groups, and the Convention on the Rights of the Child (the Children's Convention),[25] which protects the rights of girl children.

The Women's Convention obliges countries that have ratified it, known as states parties, in general "to pursue by all appropriate means and without delay a policy of eliminating discrimination against women,"[26] and in particular "to eliminate discrimination against women in the field of health care in order to ensure ... access to health care services, including those related to family planning."[27] States parties assume obligations to determine risks to women's reproductive health. The means chosen by states parties to address dangers to reproductive health are to be determined by national considerations, such as patterns of reproductive health-service delivery and the epidemiology of reproductive disability. The goal is the reduction of maternal mortality and morbidity and enhancement of the dignity of women and their reproductive self-determination.

If international human rights law is to be truly universal, it has to require states to take effective preventive and curative measures to protect women's reproductive health and to afford women the capacity for reproductive self-determination. International human rights treaties require international and national law to secure women's rights to: (1) freedom from all forms of discrimination; (2) liberty and security, marriage and the foundation of families, private and family life, and information and education; and (3) access to health care and the benefits of scientific progress.[28]

Treaty Interpretation

Empirical evidence and feminist legal methods can be used to reveal the law's neglect of women's reproductive health and expose legal bias that damages women. Empirical surveys and epidemiological studies, including those developed by the United Nations (UN) and its specialized agencies,[29] demonstrate how governmental neglect of reproductive health results in high levels of avoidable maternal and infant death and sickness, and in the exclusion of women from educational, economic, and social opportunities.

Empirical data show inequities in access to reproductive health services. Governments need to weigh evidence of how laws endanger the rights of women. Data are widely available showing that maternal and infant mortality and morbidity are associated with a dearth of family planning services.[30]

Rachel Pine has commented on evidence of the harmful consequences of laws requiring parental notification of their daughters' intended abortions, laws that are contrary to mentally competent minors' rights to confidential abortion services. Her observation is relevant both to national and international protection of human rights:

> At times it seems that the law's ignorance of its actual impact is one of the most severe threats to basic civil liberties. When justice is blind to the fruits of scientific and social research, and to the demonstrable effects of a statute in operation, rules of law are divorced from the empirical world. Courts are thus rendered impotent in the exercise of their duty to safeguard fundamental, constitutional guarantees, for rights may be violated in innumerable ways not apparent by speculation.[31]

Some national courts have taken account of data that demonstrate how applications of national laws do violence to international human rights values. In Canada, for instance, the Supreme Court struck down restrictive abortion provisions of the Criminal Code in 1988 for violating women's rights to security of the person protected by the Canadian Charter of Rights and Freedoms. The Court acted primarily on evidence from a government-sponsored report, which the government had failed to act upon, demonstrating that the law operated inequitably and delayed necessary health care.[32]

A modern development in the formulation of rights has been the emergence of feminist legal theories.[33] These theories, particularly those that are evolving from third world contexts,[34] recognize pluralism in feminist understanding of law and of legal institutions. Feminist theories provide a basis for the formulation and interpretation of laws designed to prevent and provide redress for violations of women's rights.

Feminist legal approaches start with the conviction of women's unjust subordination, and they evaluate law in terms of how it contributes to the dismantling of such injustice.[35] According to Bartlett, varying methods of evaluation "though not unique to feminists, attempt to reveal features of a legal issue which more traditional methods tend to overlook or suppress."[36] The challenge to feminists is to apply their methods of analysis to international human rights law[37] in order to remedy the legal neglect of women's reproductive health. Bartlett begins her analysis of feminist legal methods by explaining that:

> In law, asking the woman question means examining how the law fails to take into account the experiences and values that seem more typical of women than of men, for whatever reason, or how existing legal standards and concepts

might disadvantage women. The question assumes that some features of the law may be not only non-neutral in a general sense, but also "male" in a specific sense. The purpose of the woman question is to expose those features and how they operate, and to suggest how they might be corrected.[38]

Bartlett points out that this question challenges the assumption of the law's gender neutrality. She observes that:

> Without the woman question, differences associated with women are taken for granted and, unexamined, may serve as a justification for laws that disadvantage women. . . . In exposing the hidden effect of laws that do not explicitly discriminate on the basis of sex, the woman question helps to demonstrate how social structures embody norms that implicitly render women different and thereby subordinate.[39]

Feminist analysts try both to expose the negative effects of law on women's reproductive health and to make government more accountable for these effects. Bartlett notes that:

> For feminists . . . asking the woman question may make more facts relevant or "essential" to the resolution of a legal case than would more non-feminist legal analysis.[40]

Feminist thinking challenges the accuracy of prevailing presumptions about women's reality, and has "begun to expose the deeply flawed factual assumptions about women that have pervaded many disciplines, and has changed, in profound ways, the perception of women in . . . society."[41]

Epidemiological studies can help lawyers better understand and explain the impact that the neglect of reproductive health has had on women and their families. However, lawyers are not generally trained in the use of statistical data, and epidemiologists often lack understanding of legal process and reasoning, including the rules of evidence, the operation of burdens and standards of proof, and the adversarial use of analogies and hypotheses. The difficulties of interdisciplinary work can be overcome by understanding the limitations of each discipline. Some feminists have stressed

> both the indeterminacy of law and the extent to which law, despite its claim to neutrality and objectivity, masks particular hierarchies and distributions of power. These feminists have engaged in deconstructive projects that have revealed the hidden gender bias of a wide range of laws and legal assumptions. Basic to these projects has been the critical insight that not only law itself, but also

the criteria for legal validity and legitimacy, are social constructs rather than universal givens.[42]

Feminists have also offered the cautionary insight that empirical evidence

> tends to limit attention to matters of factual rather than normative accuracy, and thus fails to take account of the social construction of reality through which factual or rational propositions mask normative constructions.[43]

The International Protection of Women's Reproductive Rights

International protection of women's reproductive rights ranges from limited judicial or quasijudicial processes to the application of broader means of furthering accountability of states parties to human rights treaties. By their terms, such treaties establish committees to monitor compliance with their requirements. The Committee on the Elimination of Discrimination against Women (CEDAW), for example, is the treaty body established to monitor compliance with the Women's Convention. Other treaty-based bodies, such as the Human Rights Committee and the Economic Committee, are established to monitor compliance with the Political Covenant and the Economic Covenant, respectively.

All major human rights treaties provide for a system of reporting. Some of the treaties' bodies, such as the Human Rights Committee, also have the authority to receive petitions from individuals claiming that their governments violate the treaty. States parties are required to make regular reports to the responsible supervisory committees on the steps they have taken to implement their obligations and the difficulties they have experienced in doing so. Reports are examined by the relevant treaty bodies in the presence of representatives of the reporting states.

Treaty bodies have the power to make general comments or recommendations to indicate ways in which states parties should interpret and apply the respective treaties. These comments can be particularly useful for elaborating the specific content of broadly worded treaty guarantees. For example, the CEDAW General Recommendations indicate how states parties might formulate their practices under the convention and report periodically to CEDAW. They set goals by which to measure governments' observance of their international duties to put the rights of women into effect. Ratifying states are given latitude to choose the means to achieve those goals.

To date, the International Labour Organization (ILO) is the only specialized agency that has provided expert advice to CEDAW on the substance and working of the

General Recommendations relating to women and work.[44] The ILO, unlike most of the UN specialized agencies, integrates its development work with its human rights activities and provides assistance to most human rights committees on setting standards and making them operational. The World Health Organization (WHO), together with the United Nations Population Fund (UNFPA), might consider providing the same kind of assistance to CEDAW, the Human Rights Committee, and the Economic Committee to ensure that states parties address women's reproductive rights adequately through, for example, general recommendations for reporting states. International nongovernmental organizations (NGOs), such as the International Women's Rights Action Watch, are constantly working to maximize state compliance with the treaties.

National methods designed to protect women's reproductive rights will be more effective in the long run than international methods of protection, because the latter are too limited in number and scope to deal with the particular complexities of violations in different community contexts. National protection of human rights as defined by international treaties derives its legal force from the incorporation of those treaties into domestic law.

Application of international human rights at both levels is explored here in terms of discrete and legally distinguishable categories of rights. Women's reproductive health interests often cross the boundaries that separate one legally described right from another. Advocates tend to invoke several rights that are alleged to have been jointly violated. They identify specific articles of conventions that they claim have been violated; tribunals will distinguish one right from another in their judgments, but cases referring to reproductive health include all of the different rights implicated in particular grievances.

The following analysis proceeds from women's right to be free from all forms of discrimination through women's rights as enumerated in international treaties: rights to life, liberty, and security of the person, the right to marry and found a family, the right to private and family life, rights of access to information and education, the right to reproductive health and health care, and the right to the benefits of scientific progress. Explanations of how each of these rights has been or could be applied to reproductive health problems are given as examples. How these rights are applied differs depending on the patterns of reproductive health problems in individual countries and how these patterns are understood.

The Prohibition of All Forms of Discrimination

The Women's Convention characterizes women's inferior status and their oppression not just as a problem of inequality between men and women, but also as one of specific discrimination against women. The convention

goes beyond the goal of sexual nondiscrimination (as required by the UN Charter,[45] the Universal Declaration[46] and its two implementing covenants,[47] and the three regional human rights treaties[48]), to address the disadvantaged positions of women.

In contrast to previous human rights treaties, the Women's Convention frames its objective as the prohibition of all forms of discrimination against women, as distinct from the norm of sexual nondiscrimination. The convention develops the legal norm from a sex-neutral norm that requires equal treatment of men and women, usually measured by the scale of how men are treated, to recognize that the particular nature of discrimination against women and their distinctive characteristics is worthy of a legal response. The definition in article 1 of the Women's Convention reads:

> . . . the term "discrimination against women" shall mean any distinction, exclusion or restriction made on the basis of sex which has the effect or purpose of impairing or nullifying the recognition, enjoyment or exercise by women, irrespective of their marital status, on a basis of equality of men and women, of human rights and fundamental freedoms in the political, economic, social, cultural, civil or any other field.

When a law makes a distinction that has the effect or purpose of impairing women's rights, it violates this convention's definition of discrimination, and must accordingly be changed by the state party.

The inclusion in the title of the Women's Convention of the phrase "all forms" emphasizes the determination to adopt a treaty to eliminate "such discrimination in all its forms and manifestations" described in paragraph 15 of its preamble. The convention's preamble expresses concern in paragraph 8 "that in situations of poverty women have the least access to food, health, education, training and opportunities for employment and other needs." As a result, the convention entitles women to equal enjoyment with men not only of the so-called "first generation" of civil and political rights, such as the right to marry and found a family, but also of the "second generation" of economic, social, and cultural rights, such as the right to health care.

The Women's Convention, in prohibiting all forms of discrimination, including private discrimination, is intended to be comprehensive. It recognizes that women are not only subject to specific inequalities but that they are also subject to pervasive forms of discrimination that are woven into the political, cultural and religious fabric of societies. In addressing all the forms of discrimination that women suffer, the Women's Convention requires states to confront the social causes of women's inequality. Article 5(a) requires states parties to take all appropriate measures:

to modify the social and cultural patterns of conduct of men and women, with a view to achieving the elimination of prejudices and customary and all other practices which are based on the idea of the inferiority or the superiority of either of the sexes or on stereotyped roles for men and women.

Female circumcision, for instance, arises from the stereotypical perception that women are the principal guardians of a community's sexual morality, and also the primary initiators of unchastity. Article 5 (a) points to the need to examine such customary practices, and might be used to require states to educate those condoning and practicing female circumcision about its harmful effects[49] and to use legal sanctions where appropriate.[50]

Included in the goal of eliminating all forms of discrimination is the elimination of marital status discrimination. This objective is shown in the provision in the article 1 definition that offensive conduct is that which distinguishes on the basis of sex, and which has the effect or purpose of denying women "irrespective of their marital status" their human rights and fundamental freedoms in the "civil or any other field." For example, a practice of health clinics to require a wife, but not an unmarried adult woman, to obtain the authorization of a man, namely her husband, in order to receive health care constitutes marital status discrimination that violates the convention and would, accordingly, have to be changed.

UN documentation draws on extensive worldwide evidence to reach the conclusion that "the ability to regulate the timing and number of births is one central means of freeing women to exercise the full range of human rights to which they are entitled."[51] Women's right to control their fertility through invoking the prohibition of all forms of discrimination against women may be considered a fundamental key to women's entitlement to other human rights. Article 12 of the Women's Convention prohibits all forms of discrimination against women in the delivery of health care:

1   States Parties shall take all appropriate measures to eliminate discrimination against women in the field of health care in order to ensure, on a basis of equality of men and women, access to health care services, including those related to family planning.

2   Notwithstanding the provisions of paragraph 1 of this article, States Parties shall ensure to women appropriate services in connection with pregnancy, confinement and the post-natal period, granting free services where necessary, as well as adequate nutrition during pregnancy and lactation.

In considering whether a restrictive abortion law offends this article, the question must be asked:[52] Does the law have a significant impact in perpetuating either the oppression of women or culturally imposed sex-role constraints on individual freedom?

A restrictive abortion law exacerbates the inequality resulting from the biological fact that women carry the exclusive health burden of contraceptive failure. Contraceptive failure is defined as "counts of unintended pregnancies occurring during the practice of contraception and the number of months spent at risk." The estimated rates of contraceptive failure in the United States range from 6 percent of women who use the pill and experience failure during the first 12 months of use, to 14 to 16 percent for the condom, diaphragm, and rhythm method, and 26 percent for spermicides.[53] Moreover, a restrictive abortion law requires a woman with an unwanted pregnancy to carry that pregnancy to term with all the consequent moral, social, and legal responsibilities of gestation and parenthood.

Since such a law has this impact, is it justified as the best means of serving a compelling state purpose? The purpose of such a law is to serve the state's interest in the protection of prenatal life, which becomes more compelling as the pregnancy advances. A restrictive abortion law is only one means of protecting prenatal life, and the question has to be asked whether it is the *best* means. Other means include sex and reproductive health education and making contraceptive services widely available so that women will have only pregnancies that they desire, reducing the need for abortion services and the overall abortion rate.

In 1987 legal abortion rates "ranged from a high of at least 112 per 1,000 women of reproductive age in the Soviet Union to a low of 5 per 1,000 in the Netherlands."[54] The Netherlands has a liberal abortion law, but also public funding of sex education and accessible contraceptive information and services, resulting in low and declining abortion rates. The Dutch law enables postcoital treatment in the event of contraceptive failure. This law characterizes interceptive methods used before the pre-embryo has become implanted in the uterus as contraception and not as abortion. This description is consistent with the medical definition of pregnancy.[55] The Dutch approach presents the best means of serving a compelling state purpose in the protection of prenatal life that is consistent with the right to be free from all forms of discrimination.

The Rights to Life, Liberty, and Security

The Right to Life and Survival
The most obvious human right violated by avoidable death in pregnancy or childbirth is a woman's right to

life itself. Article 6.1 of the Political Covenant provides that "every human being has the inherent right to life. This right shall be protected by law. No one shall be arbitrarily deprived of his life."[56] The right to life is traditionally referred to in the context of the obligation of states parties to ensure that courts observe due process of law before capital punishment is imposed.[57] This understanding of the right to life is essentially male-oriented, since men consider state execution more immediate to them than death from pregnancy or labor. The feminist legal view suggests that this interpretation ignores women's reality. The Human Rights Committee has noted that "the right to life has been too often narrowly interpreted. The expression 'inherent right to life' cannot be properly understood in a restrictive manner, and the protection of this right requires that States adopt positive measures."[58]

The Committee considers it desirable that states parties to the Political Covenant take all possible measures to reduce infant mortality and to increase life expectancy. A compatible goal is reduction of maternal mortality, accomplished, for example, by the promotion of methods of birth spacing that would increase the likelihood of infant and maternal survival.

The argument that a woman's right to life entitles her to access to basic reproductive health services, and that legislation obstructing such access violates international human rights provisions, can be made on behalf of an individual woman. The argument must be expanded, however, where the threat to a pregnant woman's survival comes not from her medical condition, but from her membership in a group at high risk of maternal mortality or morbidity due to pregnancy. The collective right to life of women in groups at risk raises the question of whether states have a positive obligation to offer appropriate reproductive health services to such women, or at least provide education and counseling services that alert them to risks and to the means to minimize risks. The African Charter emphasizes collective rights in its preamble and might well be invoked to impose such obligations on African governments.

The Right to Liberty and Security
The strongest defense of individual integrity under the Political Covenant exists in article 9 (1), which provides that "everyone has the right to liberty and security of the person.... No one shall be deprived of his liberty except on such grounds and in accordance with such procedures as are established by law."[59] This right would seem to prohibit interference by the state in individual pursuit of means to limit, or to promote, fertility. A woman's right to liberty transcends her right to protect her life and health, and recognizes her right to reproduc-

tive choice as an element of her personal integrity and autonomy that is not dependent on health justifications.

Under international human rights law, states cannot compel women to conceive children against their will, nor force men to impregnate women. A violation of liberty and security occurs when the state denies women access to means of fertility control, leaving them to risk unintended pregnancy. For example, in El Salvador, where contraceptives are not widely available, women have about twice as many children as they want.[60] Further, a violation occurs when a state's laws allow husbands or partners to veto wives' or girlfriends' use of birth control. Courts in at least eight countries and a regional human rights tribunal have rejected applications by husbands or partners to prohibit abortions.[61] Parental veto laws may be condemned when they obstruct personal choices by mature or emancipated minors who are able to make their own sexual decisions, and to bear the consequences of their choices.[62]

The application of international human rights instruments to laws restricting women's choices has not been explored adequately. A special case for the protection of liberty and security concerns women who are imprisoned for terminating their own pregnancies. In Nepal women are often convicted for self-induced abortion, which is punishable by life imprisonment.[63] The offense, by definition, applies only to women, and may, therefore, constitute discrimination on the basis of sex. Article 2 (g) of the Women's Convention requires states parties "to repeal all national penal provisions which constitute discrimination against women." Women may be inappropriately charged for this offense, particularly if they had no access to contraceptive services, and be denied access to legal representation in court proceedings.

A barrier to the application of the right to liberty and security has been uncertainty about the interaction of free choice and wise or good decisions. Those with experience of life may well be able to make better choices than those without experience, but wisdom and experience are not legal conditions of freedom. Individuals may reach legal capacity for autonomous choice before they may appear trustworthy to exercise their freedom wisely. The tendency of the state to protect mature individuals against their poor choices, and to place them under the control of others whose judgment is deemed to be reliable, does violence to internationally legally protected rights to individual liberty.

Article 7 of the Political Covenant provides that "no one shall be subjected to torture or to cruel, inhuman or degrading treatment or punishment." The applicability of this provision to medical interventions, and to denial of desired medical care, is evidenced in the sentence of article 7 that provides: "in particular no one shall be subjected without his free consent to medical or scientific experimentation." Article 19 of the Children's Convention requires states "to protect the child from all forms of physical or mental violence, injury or abuse, neglect or negligent treatment, maltreatment or exploitation, including sexual abuse." These articles furnish grounds to oppose the cruelty, inhumanity, or degradation of compelling an adolescent to continue a pregnancy that endangers her life or health, and such treatment of children as female circumcision.

States ignoring the consequences for adolescents of the unavailability of contraceptives, the lack of services for unintended pregnancy, and the practice of female circumcision would be found in violation of the Political Covenant's article 7, as well as of article 19 of the Children's Convention.

The Right to Marry and Found a Family

In its origins, the recognition of the right to marry and found a family is a reaction to Nazi racial and reproductive policies that began with forced sterilization and culminated in genocide.[64] Article 23 of the Political Covenant and article 10 of the Economic Covenant both recognize the family as the "natural and fundamental group unit of society." The former states that "the right of men and women of marriageable age to marry and found a family shall be recognized."[65] The latter recognizes that "special protection should be accorded to mothers during a reasonable period before and after childbirth. During such period working mothers should be accorded paid leave or leave with adequate social security benefits."[66]

The Human Rights Committee's General Comments to article 23 of the Political Covenant explain that:

> the right to found a family implies, in principle, the possibility to procreate and live together. When States Parties adopt family planning policies, they should be compatible with the provisions of the Covenant and should, in particular, not be discriminatory or compulsory.[67]

The right to found a family is inadequately observed if it amounts to no more than the right to conceive, gestate, and deliver a child. An act of "foundation" goes beyond a passive submission to biology; it involves the right of a woman to plan, time, and space the births of children to protect their health and her own. Accordingly, article 16 (1) (e) of the Women's Convention requires states parties to ensure that women enjoy "rights to decide freely and responsibly on the number and spacing of their children and to have access to the information, education and means to enable them to exercise these rights."[68]

Maria Isabel Plata explained[69] that adopting the Women's Convention into Colombian law[70] made this article part of the 1991 Constitution of Colombia.[71] The Colombian Ministry of Public Health has interpreted the Women's Convention to establish a gender perspective in national health policies that considers "the social discrimination of women as an element which contributes to the ill-health of women."[72] A new ministerial resolution orders all health institutions to ensure women the right to decide on all issues that affect their health, their life, and their sexuality, and guarantees rights "to information and orientation to allow the exercise of free, gratifying, responsible sexuality which cannot be tied to maternity."[73] The new policy requires provision of a full range of reproductive health services, including infertility services, safe and effective contraception, integrated treatment for incomplete abortion, and treatment for menopausal women. The policy emphasizes the need for special attention to women at high risk, such as adolescents and victims of violence.

In some parts of the world, the right to found a family is threatened primarily by reproductive tract infections. In Africa, for example, such infections cause as much as 50 percent of infertility.[74] Government inaction that violates this right constitutes a basis for state political accountability, whether or not the law classifies the right as one that governments must protect through positive action. If the right is negative, in that a state must not obstruct its exercise, the state might still be liable, not because of the infertility itself, but because of the differential impact infertility has on the lives of women.[75]

The right to found a family incorporates the right to enhance the survival prospects of a conceived or existing child through birth spacing by contraception or abortion. This right is complementary to the right of a woman to survive pregnancy. The right to marry and to found a family can be limited by laws that are reasonably related to a family-based objective, such as laws requiring a minimum age for marriage. An objection to many age-of-marriage laws is that the age they set is too low for the welfare of women, and therefore of their families, and that they set lower ages for women than for men. Women are frequently induced to marry at the minimum legal age or a lower age through nonenforcement of the law or exceptions to the law, because they lack alternative opportunities.

Parental support obligations may terminate legally at the age of marriage, an age when most women have no means to support themselves through paid employment and no opportunities to pursue education or careers. They marry and bear children early because their societies recognize no function or worth for women except that defined by biology. Women need legal protection against being conditioned to serve prematurely in the founding of families. Human rights provisions that no one shall be obliged involuntarily to enter marriage fail to recognize that many women "volunteer" for marriage because they lack an alternative.

The Right to Private and Family Life

The right to private and family life is distinguishable from the right to found a family, although for some purposes the latter right may be considered to be part of the former. Article 17 of the Political Covenant provides that "no one shall be subjected to arbitrary or unlawful interference with his privacy, family, home or correspondence, nor to unlawful attacks on his honour and reputation."[76]

The European Convention specifies conditions under which private and family life may be compromised or sacrificed to interests of the state. Article 8 provides that:

1 Everyone has the right to respect for his private and family life, his home and his correspondence.

2 There shall be no interference by a public authority with the exercise of this right except such as is in accordance with the law and is necessary in a democratic society in the interests of national security, public safety or the economic well-being of the country, for the prevention of disorder or crime, for the protection of health or morals, or for the protection of the rights and freedoms of others.

This article was held not to have been violated in the case of *Bruggemann & Scheuten v. Federal Republic of Germany*.[77] Two West German women claimed that a 1976 restrictive abortion law interfered with respect for their private lives contrary to this article in that they were not permitted privately and alone to decide to terminate their unwanted pregnancies. The majority of the European Commission of Human Rights rejected the women's claims and found that the restrictive laws did not constitute an interference with private life.

Greater scope was given to a woman's right to private life in the case of *Paton v. United Kingdom*.[78] The European Commission upheld a British decision preventing a woman from being coerced to continue an unwanted pregnancy through her husband's veto of her abortion. The commission gave priority to respect for the wife's private life in her decision on childbearing over her husband's right to respect for his family life in the birth of his child, and found that the husband's right could not be interpreted to embrace even a right to be consulted on his wife's decision. The commission explained that a state's interest in an unborn life is not greater than that of the biological father's, so that preclusion of his right necessarily precludes the state's right to prevail.

Rights Regarding Information and Education

Rights to seek, receive, and impart information are protected by all the basic human rights conventions[79] and are essential to the realization of reproductive health. The Women's Convention explicitly requires that women have the right to information and counseling on health and family planning.[80]

Article 10 (1) of the European Convention protects "the right to freedom of expression [which] shall include freedom . . . to receive and impart information and ideas without interference by public authority and regardless of frontiers." The European Court of Human Rights in the recent case of *Open Door and Dublin Well Women v. Ireland*[81] found that the Irish government's ban on counseling women about where to find abortions abroad violates this article. In order to comply with this decision, the Irish government can no longer ban this counseling. This decision also applies to other countries that are members of the European Convention in the event that they try to restrict the counseling of women seeking services in other countries.

The right to education[82] serves the goal of individual and reproductive health. Women have greater access to contraceptives when they can read and understand the risks to their health and the health of their children caused by close birth spacing.[83] Education affecting sexual matters can raise issues, however, of rights to freedom of thought and religion.[84] Conflicts have arisen when public school systems have introduced health-oriented programs of instruction on sexual matters to which parents have objected on grounds of their religious convictions.

In the Danish Sex Education case,[85] some Danish parents objected to compulsory sex education in state schools. They complained that it violated the state's duty to respect "the right of parents to ensure such education and teaching in conformity with their own religious and philosophical convictions,"[86] and either jointly or alternatively it violated their right to religious nondiscrimination, rights to private and family life, and the right to freedom of thought, conscience, and religion as set out in the European Convention. The European Court held that compulsory sex-education classes in Danish schools violated none of these duties or rights because they were primarily intended to convey useful and corrective information which, though unavoidably concerned with considerations of a moral nature, did not exceed "the bounds of what a democratic state may regard as in the public interest."[87] The Court recognized, however, that

the State . . . must take care that information or knowledge included in the curriculum is conveyed in an objective, critical and pluralistic manner. The State is forbidden to pursue an aim of indoctrination that might be considered as not respecting parents' religious and philosophical convictions.[88]

The Right to Reproductive Health and Health Care

By article 12 (1) of the Economic Covenant, states parties "recognize the right of everyone to the enjoyment of the highest attainable standard of physical and mental health." Article 12 (2) provides that the steps to achieve the full realization of this right shall include those necessary for: a) The provision for the reduction of the stillbirth-rate and of infant mortality and for the healthy development of the child . . . d) The creation of conditions which would assure to all medical service and medical attention in the event of sickness.[89]

Article 12 addresses reproductive health services indirectly, in that multiple pregnancies and short birth intervals endanger infant survival and health. This article is reinforced by article 24 (f) of the Children's Convention, which requires that states parties "develop preventive health care, guidance for parents and family planning education and services." Epidemiological evidence demonstrates the significance of birth spacing to this goal.

The breadth of the concept of "health" is apparent in the preamble to the Constitution of the World Health Organization, which describes health as "a state of complete physical, mental and social well-being and not merely the absence of disease or infirmity."[90] In this sense, idealistic and ambitious though it may appear, the right to seek the highest attainable standard of health is inherent in every human being. Because mental and social well-being are components of health, unwanted pregnancy that endangers mental or social well-being is as much a threat to women's health as is pregnancy that endangers survival, longevity, or physical health.

States parties may be called upon to explain their failures to protect to such bodies as the Economic Committee.[91] The Economic Committee may want to seek assistance from WHO and UNFPA in the development of a general recommendation for reporting on the progress made in improving women's reproductive health, according to the WHO Indicators for Health for All by the Year 2000.[92] WHO indicators now include the reduction of maternal mortality by half by the year 2000.[93] Countries that are not moving progressively to meet this goal can clearly be found in breach of their human rights responsibilities to protect the lives and well-being of women. If, for instance, epidemiological or other evidence indicates that rates of maternal mortality or morbidity are rising without justified cause, the country may be asked to give promises of improved performance. Enforcement of promises will not be effected by such means as economic sanctions in most cases, but through, for example, international embarrassment generated by condemnation by nongovernmental organizations.

A general recommendation could explain that the right to reproductive health is part of the right to health care. This right includes the negative right of recourse to contraception and sterilization without legal obstruction, and also the positive right to be afforded access to related counseling and services. Similarly, women may claim a right to arrange an abortion, particularly when their personal history raises the medical risks of pregnancy above those faced by other women in their communities. Abortion is the practice of medicine, and women may claim access to physicians capable of undertaking the procedure safely. That is, the right to an abortion to preserve health may be claimed as a positive right where women are compelled to seek unqualified practitioners whose procedures are themselves a risk to women's health.

The Right to the Benefits of Scientific Progress

Article 15 (1) (b) of the Economic Covenant recognizes the right of everyone "to enjoy the benefits of scientific progress and its applications." Further, according to article 15 (3), states parties "undertake to respect the freedom indispensable for scientific research . . ."[94] Freedom of research requires states parties to tolerate and accommodate research on new techniques of fertility control and enhancement, and may require states to facilitate such research and development, particularly from women's perspectives.[95] The right to access to scientific advances is important, since so many of the modern techniques of fertility control and promotion, and of assisted reproduction, are the results of recent scientific research. Women's freedom from unwanted pregnancy by means of safe, effective, and convenient contraceptives has been achieved by scientific investigation.[96] These new means include male fertility regulating methods,[97] contraceptive implants,[98] nonsurgical abortion,[99] and contraceptive vaccines.[100]

The right to the benefits of scientific progress requires states parties to facilitate the use of birth-control methods proved to be safe and effective, and to favor interpretations of existing law that would facilitate their use. For example, some Islamic teachings allow abortion for up to 120 days of pregnancy, but abortion laws in some Islamic countries are not implemented accordingly.[101] Where abortion is already lawful, the right to the benefits of scientific progress and its applications requires governments to facilitate the availability of nonsurgical abortion, as was recently done in the United Kingdom by an amendment to the British Abortion Act of 1967.[102] Laws and practices obstructing drug approval and the importation of safe and effective drugs and other methods violate this right.[103]

States parties to the Economic Covenant are obliged to ensure that health professionals apply appropriate scientific knowledge according to the wishes and interests of their patients. When states delegate legal control of health professionals to self-regulating authorities that fail in this responsibility, the state may be held responsible in international law for treaty violation. A high rate of abortion performed by methods that are less than the safest available is one example of such failed responsiblity. Suction abortion is safer than dilatation and evacuation, but in many parts of the world physicians' retraining in the safer method is not required.[104] State responsibility might require the passage of such laws as one passed in Italy that requires "the use of modern techniques of pregnancy termination, which are physically and mentally less damaging to the woman and are less hazardous."[105]

To protect access to the benefits of scientific progress states might enact what are called "use it or lose it" patent provisions governing therapeutic, diagnostic, and preventive health-care products.[106] When such product patents have been granted to sponsors that subsequently fail or decline to market them, governmental authorities in several countries, including France,[107] have the legal power to transfer the patents to a new holder that will undertake or approve the marketing of the products. In conferring a patent on a drug manufacturer, a government is giving the manufacturer a monopoly to market a therapeutic product. In return for giving this monopoly, the government expects a health benefit for its population. The potential for involuntary transfer acknowledges that a drug patent serves not only the commercial interests of the holder, but also the interest of the government in the health of potential users. When the French patent holder indicated an intention to withhold RU 486 from the market, the then Minister of Health, Claude Evin, threatened to use this transfer power, describing the drug as "the moral property of women." [108]

Conclusion

The widespread disadvantage that women suffer through neglect of their reproductive rights, under laws and practices perpetuated by states, denies them more than their enjoyment of health. Women's reproductive functions have been used to control women themselves. States have advanced their chosen social, economic, and population agendas by implementing laws and employing practices that control women's reproduction. To gain autonomy, women must attain reproductive self-determination, their path to many of life's opportunities.

Respect for the human right of reproductive self-determination includes the prohibition of all forms of discrimination against women, and the changing of laws and of practices that are the instruments of such discrimination. Governments must be made accountable not only for their acts of discrimination and their failure to eliminate the discriminatory laws and practices that they have inherited, but also for the effects of their conduct on the status of women within their countries.

International governmental agencies and NGOs can monitor states' conduct. The Committee on the Elimination of Discrimination Against Women can be a catalyst for the advancement of women's reproductive rights by developing general recommendations on standards against which country performance can be measured. Such recommendations might include reducing maternal mortality, establishing minimum legal ages of marriage, and promoting healthy birth spacing. CEDAW can also hold states parties to strict account by scrutinizing national reports with help from international agencies and NGOs.

Family planning and women's associations are beginning to provide legal services to women in order to help them protect their reproductive rights.[109] Rights are worth little to women where there are no corresponding duties on the part of governments, organizations, and individuals to respect those rights. Violations of rights will go unrecognized and unremedied where there is no understanding of those rights or no legal services to advocate remedies.

Great potential exists to enforce state responsibility for the observance of women's reproductive rights by employing the resources of international law. These include mechanisms of account under the Women's Convention, the Political and Economic Covenants, and the regional human rights treaties. Of the human rights of particular concern to women, that which frequently exists as the precondition to the enjoyment of others is the right to reproductive self-determination. This right expresses the fundamental principle of respect for "the inherent dignity and ... the equal and inalienable rights of members of the human family," which the Universal Declaration of Human Rights observes to be the foundation of freedom, justice, and peace.[110]

References and Notes

1   World Health Organization. 1985. *Prevention of Maternal Mortality: A Report of a WHO Interregional Meeting.* Geneva: WHO. P. 5.

2   Safe Motherhood Conference Conclusions. 1987. *Lancet* i: 670.

3   Mahler, Halfdan. 1987. "The safe motherhood initiative: A call to action!" *Lancet* i: 668–670.

4   Fathalla, Mahmoud. 1987. "The long road to maternal death." *People* (IPPF) 14: 8.

5   Melica, F. (ed.). 1992. *AIDS and Human Reproduction.* Basel: Karger.

6   Brazilian Medical Code of Ethics, chapter VI. Article 52 (1965), cited in T. Merrick, "Fertility and family planning in Brazil." 1983. *International Family Planning Perspectives* 9: 110.

7   Cook, Rebecca and Jeanne Haws. 1986. "The United Nations Convention on the rights of women: Opportunities for family planning providers." *International Family Planning Perspectives* 12 : 49–53.

8   Population Information Program. 1985. "Youth in the 1980s: Social and Health Concerns." *Population Reports,* Series M, No. 9.

9   See Digest, *International Family Planning Perspectives.* 1985. 11:98, summarizing National Population Bureau, *The Nigeria Fertility Survey* 1981/82, Principal Report, 1984.

10 Harrison, Kelsey et al. 1985. "The influence of maternal age and parity on child-bearing with special reference to primigravidae aged 15 and under." *British Journal of Obstetrics and Gynaecology*, Supplement 5: 23–31.

11 Dickens, B. 1985. "Reproduction law and medical consent." *University of Toronto Law Journal* 35: 255–286.

12 Notzon, C. et al. 1987. "Comparisons of national cesarian-section rates." *New England Journal of Medicine* 316, 7: 386; Barros, F. et al. 1991. "Epidemic of caesarean sections in Brazil." *The Lancet* 338: 167–169.

13 Fathalla, Mahmoud. 1991. "Reproductive health: A global overview." *Annals of the New York Academy of Sciences* 626: 1–10.

14 Sai, Fred and J. Nassim. 1989. "The need for a reproductive health approach." *International Journal of Gynecology and Obstetrics*, Supplement 3: 103–114.

15 Maine, Deborah. 1991. *Safe Motherhood Programs: Options and Issues.* New York: Columbia University Center for Population and Family Health.

16 Royston, Erica and S. Armstrong (eds.). 1989. *Preventing Maternal Deaths.* Geneva: WHO.

17 18 December 1979, 34 United Nations (UN) GAOR Supplement (No.21) (A/34/46) at 193, UN Doc. A/Res/34/180.

18 GA Res. 217 A (III), UN Doc. A/810 (1948).

19 GA Res. 2200 (XXI), 21 UN GAOR Supplement (No. 16) at 52, UN Doc. A/6316 (1966).

20 *Id.* at 49.

21 213 U.N.T.S. 221 (1959).

22 OASTS at 1 (1969).

23 OAU Doc. CAB/Leg/67/3/ Rev. 5 (1981).

24 660 U.N.T.S. 195 (1965).

25 G.A. Res. 44/25, 44 UN GAOR, Supplement No. 49, UN Doc. A/44/736 (1989).

26 Article 2 of the Women's Convention.

27 Article 12 (1) of the Women's Convention.

28 Cook, Rebecca. 1992. "International protection of women's reproductive rights." *New York University Journal of International Law and Politics* 24: 645–727.

29 AbouZahr, C. and E. Royston. 1991. *Maternal Mortality: A Global Factbook.* Geneva: WHO; Law, M., Deborah Maine, and M. Feuerstein. 1991. *Safe Motherhood: Priorities and Next Steps.* New York: United Nations Development Program.

30 Winikoff, Beverly and Maureen Sullivan. 1987. "Assessing the role of family planning in reducing maternal mortality." *Studies in Family Planning* 18, 3: 128–142.

31 Pine, Rachel. 1988. "Speculation and reality: The role of facts in judicial protection of fundamental rights." *University of Pennsylvania Law Review* 136: 655–727.

32 *R. v. Morgentaler* (1988), 44 D.L.R. (4th) 385 (S.C. Can).

33 MacKinnon, Catherine. 1989. *Toward a Feminist Theory of the State.* Cambridge, MA: Harvard University Press; West, R. 1988. "Jurisprudence and gender." *University of Chicago Law Review* 55: 1–72.

34 See, generally, An-Na'im, A. 1987. "The rights of women and international law in the Muslim context." *Whittier Law Review* 9: 491–516; Plata, M. and M. Yanusova. 1988. *Los Derechos Humanos y La Convención Sobre la Eliminación de Todas las Formas de Discriminación Contra la Mujer 1979* (Human Rights and the 1979 Convention on the Elimination of All Forms of Discrimination Against Women). Bogotá, Colombia: Printex Impresores; Rahman, A. 1990. "Religious rights versus women's rights in India: A test case for international human rights law." *Columbia Journal of Transnational Law* 28: 473–98.

35 Lacey, N. 1987. "Legislation against sex discrimination: Questions from a feminist perspective." *Journal of Law and Society* 14: 411–420.

36 Bartlett, Katherine. 1990. "Feminist legal methods." *Harvard Law Review* 103: 829–888.

37 Bunch, C. 1990. "Women's rights as human rights: Toward a revision of human rights." *Human Rights Quarterly* 12: 486–498; Byrnes, A. 1992. "Women, feminism and international human rights law—methodological myopia, fundamental flaws or meaningful marginalization?" *Australian Year Book of International Law* 12: 205–240; Charlesworth, H., C. Chinkin, and S. Wright. 1990. "Feminist approaches to international law." *American Journal of International Law* 85: 613–645.

38 Bartlett, p. 837.

39 *Id.,* p. 843.

40 *Id.,* p. 856.

41 *Id.,* p. 871.

42 *Id.,* p. 878.

43 *Id.,* p. 871.

44 Byrnes, A. 1991. "CEDAW's tenth session." *Netherlands Quarterly of Human Rights* 3: 332–358.

45 Articles 13 (1), 55 (c) and 56.

46 Article 2.

47 Political Covenant: articles 2 (1), 3, 4, 14, 23, and 24; Economic Covenant: articles 2 (2) and 3.

48 European Convention: article 14; American Convention: article 1; African Charter: article 2.

49 Inter-African Committee on Traditional Practices Affecting the Health of Women and Children. 1987. *Report on the Regional Seminar on Traditional Practices Affecting the Health of Women and Children in Africa*; United Nations. 1991. *Report of the Working Group on Traditional Practices Affecting the Health of Women and Children,* E/CN.4/Sub.2 /1991/6.

50 Judgment of 10 July 1987, Case of Fofana Dala Traore, Cour d'Appel (convicted of circumcising her daughter contrary to French law). *Le Monde,* 13 July 1987; *Annual Review of Law and Population,* 1987, p. 205.

51 *Status of Women and Family Planning.* 1975. UN Doc. E/CN.6/575/ Rev.1.

52 Law, S. 1984. "Rethinking sex and the constitution." *University of Pennsylvania Law Review* 132: 955–1,040; *Andrews v. Law Society of British Columbia* (1989) 1 S.C.R. 143 (S.C. Can).

53 Jones, E. and J. Forrest. 1989. "Contraceptive failure in the United States: Revised estimates from the 1982 National Survey of Family Growth." *Family Planning Perspectives* 21: 103–109.

54 Henshaw, S. 1990. "Induced abortion: A world review." *Family Planning Perspectives* 22: 76–89.

55 Hughes, E.C. (ed.). Committee on Terminology of the American College of Obstetrics and Gynecology. 1972. *Obstetric-Gynecologic Terminology,* pp. 299 and 327; The Committee on Medical Aspects of Human Reproduction of the International Federation of Gynecology and Obstetrics unanimously agreed that "pregnancy is only

established with the implantation of the fertilized ovum." Fathalla, Mahmoud, Committee on Medical Aspects of Human Reproduction,' International Federation of Gynecology and Obstetrics, personal communication, 14 November 1985.

56 This article reflects article 3 of the Universal Declaration and is given further effect in, for instance, article 2 of the European Convention, article 4 of the American Convention, and article 4 of the African Charter.

57 Sieghart, P. 1983. *The International Law of Human Rights*. Oxford: Oxford University Press. Pp. 128–134.

58 CCPR/C/21/rev.1 at para. 5, 19 May 1989.

59 This article reflects article 3 of the Universal Declaration and is given further effect in, for instance, article 2 of the European Convention, article 4 of the American Convention, and article 4 of the African Charter. This right, protected in article 7 of the Canadian Charter of Rights and Freedoms, was held to be violated by the restrictive criminal abortion law by the Supreme Court of Canada in *R. v. Morgentaler* (1988), 44 D.L.R. (4th) 385 (S.C. Can).

60 Garcia, A. I. 1991. "Situación general de las mujeres en Centro America y Panama." In *Las Juezas en Centro America y Panama*. Ed. T. Rivera Bustamente. Center for the Administration of Justice, Florida International University, San José, Costa Rica, pp. 15–40, cited in C. Medina, "Towards a more effective guarantee of the enjoyment of human rights by women in the Inter-American system." In *Women's International Human Rights*. Ed. Rebecca Cook. Forthcoming. P. 344.

61 Cook, Rebecca and Deborah Maine. 1987. "Spousal veto over family planning services." *American Journal of Public Health* 77: 339–344.

62 Knoppers, B. et al. 1990. "Abortion law in francophone countries." *American Journal of Comparative Law* 38: 889–922; Paxman, J. and J. Zuckerman. 1987. *Laws and Policies Affecting Adolescent Health*. Geneva: WHO.

63 Women's Legal Service Project. 1989. *Female Inmates of Prisons in Nepal*. Kathmandu, Nepal: Women's Legal Service Project. P. 13.

64 Eriksson, M. K. 1990. *The Right to Marry and to Found a Family: A World-Wide Human Right*. Uppsala, Sweden: Justus Forlag.

65 This article reflects article 16 of the Universal Declaration and is given further effect in article 12 of the European Convention, article 17 of the American Convention, and article 18 of the African Charter.

66 Article 10 (2).

67 CCPR/C/21/Rev.1/Add.2, 19 Sept. 1990.

68 This right was first established in international law at the Women's Convention. The origins of the right date from a 1966 UN General Assembly Resolution on Population Growth and Economic Development [xxii] that recognized that "the size of the family should be the free choice of each individual family." This principle was proclaimed as a right in article 16 of the 1968 Teheran Proclamation on Human Rights, stating that ". . . parents have a basic human right to determine freely and responsibly the number and spacing of their children," and in article 4 of the Declaration on Social Progress and Development, stating that "parents have the exclusive right to determine freely and responsibly the number and spacing of their children." Article 22 of the same declaration obligates the state to provide families with "the knowledge and means necessary to enable them to exercise this right." (UNGA Res. 2545 [XXIV], 1969).

69 Plata, Maria. "New challenges for the Women's Convention: Re-

productive rights in Colombia." In *Women's International Human Rights*. Ed. Rebecca Cook. Forthcoming.

70 The Colombian Presidential Decree No. 1398 of 3 July 1990; Colombian Law 51 of 1981.

71 1991 Colombian Constitution, article 42.

72 Ministry of Public Health. 1992. *Salud para la mujer, mujer para la salud*. Bogotá: Ministry of Public Health.

73 Colombian Ministry of Public Health Resolution 1531 of 6 March 1992.

74 Wasserheit, J. 1989. "The significance and scope of reproductive tract infections among third world women." *International Journal of Gynecology and Obstetrics*, Supplement 3: 145–168; Germain, Adrienne et al. (eds.). 1992. *Reproductive Tract Infections: Global Impact and Priorities for Women's Reproductive Health*. New York: Plenum Press.

75 International Women's Health Coalition. 1991. *Reproductive Tract Infections in Women in the Third World*. New York: International Women's Health Coalition. Pp. 3–6.

76 This article reflects article 12 of the Universal Declaration and is given further effect in, for instance, article 11 of the American Convention and articles 4 and 5 of the African Charter.

77 3 Eur. H.R. 244 (1977).

78 Eur. H.R. Rep. 408 (1980).

79 Article 19 of the Universal Declaration, article 19 of the Political Covenant, article 10 of the European Convention, article 13 of the American Convention, and article 9 of the African Charter.

80 See articles 14 (b) and 16 (e).

81 64/1991/316/387-388, 29 October 1992.

82 Article 26 of the Universal Declaration, article 13 of the Economic Covenant, article 2 of protocol 1 of the European Convention, article 26 of the American Convention, article 17 of the African Charter, and article 10 (e) of the Women's Convention.

83 Casterline, John, Susheela Singh, John Cleland, and H. Ashurst. 1984. "The proximate determinants of fertility." In *World Fertility Survey Comparative Studies* No. 39. London: World Fertility Survey.

84 Article 18 of the Universal Declaration, article 18 of the Political Covenant, article 9 of the European Convention, articles 12 and 13 of the American Convention, and article 8 of the African Charter.

85 *Kjeldsen, Busk Madsen, and Pedersen v. Denmark*, 1 Eur. H. R. Rep. 711 (1976), referred to here as the Danish Sex Education case.

86 Article 2 of protocol No. 1 of the European Convention.

87 Paragraph 54 of the Danish Sex Education case.

88 *Id.*, paragraph 53.

89 This article reflects article 25 of the Universal Declaration and is given further effect in, for instance, article 13 of the European Social Charter, article 26 of the American Convention, and article 10 of its Additional Protocol in the Area of Economic, Social, and Cultural Rights (signed in San Salvador, El Salvador, "Protocol of San Salvador," *OEA Documentos Oficiales* OEA—Ser. A-44 [SEPF], 28 I.L.M. 156, 1989), article 16 of the African Charter, and article 24 of the Children's Convention.

90 The Preamble to the Constitution of the World Health Organization. In *Two Official Records of the World Health Organization*, 1948. Geneva: WHO. P. 100.

91 Leckie, S. 1991. "An overview and appraisal of the fifth session of the UN Committee on Economic, Social and Cultural Rights." *Hu-*

man Rights Quarterly 13: 545–572.

92 WHO. 1981. "Global Strategy for Health for All by the Year 2000." *Health for All* Series No. 4. Geneva: WHO.

93 Starrs, A. 1987. *Preventing the Tragedy of Maternal Deaths: A Report on the International Safe Motherhood Conference.* Nairobi, Kenya. Washington, DC: World Bank, p. 8.

94 This article reflects article 27 (2) of the Universal Declaration.

95 WHO and International Women's Health Coalition. 1991. *Creating Common Ground: Women's Perspectives on the Selection and Introduction of Fertility Regulation Technologies.* Geneva: WHO/HRP/ITT/91.

96 WHO. 1992. *Annual Technical Report 1991 of the Special Programme of Research, Development and Research Training in Human Reproduction.* Geneva: WHO/HRP/ATR/91/92.

97 *Id.,* pp. 59–76.

98 Dorig, B. and F. Greenslade (eds.). 1990. *Norplant Contraceptive Subdermal Implants.* Geneva: WHO.

99 Van Look, P. and M. Bygdeman. 1989. "Antigestational steroids: A new dimension in human fertility regulation." In *Oxford Review of Reproductive Biology,* vol. 11. Ed. S.R. Milligan. Oxford: Oxford University Press. Pp. 1–61.

100 Ada, G.L. and P.D. Griffin (eds.). 1991. *Vaccines for Fertility Regulation: The Assessment of Their Safety and Efficacy.* Cambridge, England:

Cambridge University Press.

101 Sachedina, Z. 1990. "Islam, procreation and the law." *Internationl Family Planning Perspectives* 16: 107–110.

102 The United Kingdom Human Fertilisation and Embryology Act of 1990, U.K. Stats. 1990, c. 37.

103 Pine, Rachel. 1992. "*Benten v. Kessler:* The RU 486 import case." *Law, Medicine and Health Care* 20: 238–242.

104 McLaurin, K. et al. 1991 "Health systems' role in abortion care: The need for a pro-active approach." *Issues in Abortion Care* 1: 1–34.

105 Sec. 15 of Law 194 of 22 May 1978 (Italy).

106 Boland, R. 1992. "RU 486 in France and England: Corporate ethics and compulsory licensing." *Law, Medicine and Health Care* 20: 226–234.

107 Code de Commerce, Brevets d'Invention, articles. 37–40, 2 January 1968.

108 Cook, Rebecca. 1989. "Antiprogestin drugs: Medical and legal issues." *Family Planning Perspectives* 21: 267–272.

109 Plata, Maria. 1988. "Family law and family planning in Colombia." *International Family Planning Perspectives* 14: 109–111.

110 Paragraph 1 of preamble.

[4]

Annu. Rev. Public Health 1997. 18:379–400

MORAL AND POLICY ISSUES IN LONG-ACTING CONTRACEPTION

George F. Brown

The Population Council, One Dag Hammarskjold Plaza, New York 10017; e-mail: gbrown@popcouncil.org

Ellen H. Moskowitz

The Hastings Center, Briarcliff Manor, New York 10510

KEY WORDS: long-acting contraception, moral issues, ethics, policy, contraceptive introduction

ABSTRACT

The advent of reversible long-acting contraceptives–IUDs, injectables and implants–has provided women throughout the world with valuable new fertility regulation options. These highly effective methods, together with male and female sterilization, have proven to be enormously popular and are now used by the majority of women and men who are currently contracepting worldwide.

Despite their remarkable popularity, long-acting contraceptives have engendered considerable controversy. Political, ethical, and safety questions have emerged, stemming from the ways in which these contraceptives have been developed and used over the course of this century. At the heart of the concern is the issue of reproductive rights and freedom.

This paper reviews the history of the development of long-acting contraceptives, including the prospect of new methods that will likely emerge from ongoing research and development. It also examines the history, in the United States and in developing countries, of the use and abuse of long-acting methods, including sterilization, in the context of eugenics and population control policies. It then describes a new paradigm of reproductive health and rights that has emerged from the International Conference on Population Development in Cairo, and which offers an enlightened approach to future policies and programs.

In light of the wide variety of ways in which long-acting contraceptives have been provided, the paper examines the rights and responsibilities of governments, family planning providers, and individuals. An ethical framework for the use of long-acting methods is discussed, and public policies for the future are proposed.

380   BROWN & MOSKOWITZ

DEVELOPMENT OF LONG-ACTING CONTRACEPTIVES: HISTORICAL PERSPECTIVES, FUTURE PROSPECTS

The development and introduction of modern intrauterine devices (IUDs) in 1960, shortly after the advent of oral contraceptives, marked the beginning of the modern era of long-acting reversible contraception (34). IUDs were seen to be a solution to the problem of inconsistent use associated with contraceptive methods requiring repeated action, and those methods that were coitus related.

The long-acting feature of the IUD was especially relevant for developing countries, where, in the 1960s, national family planning programs were rapidly expanding (11). This expansion was fueled by widespread anxiety about rapid population growth and its adverse societal consequences (27). There was a strong demographic rationale for family planning, and only a secondary emphasis on satisfying the fertility regulation needs of individuals.

This demographic imperative made it especially important for national leaders and international donors that high levels of continuous contraceptive practice be achieved. From their perspective, older methods such as the condom and diaphragm, as well as periodic abstinence and withdrawal, were less effective, difficult to use consistently, and required greater motivation.

Thus, the IUD rapidly became the method of choice in pioneering programs in Taiwan, Korea, and other countries; it had the advantages of high effectiveness over many years, no need for action by the user after insertion, and low cost (34). In developed countries, including the United States, the IUD was widely used as well, although oral contraceptives generally commanded greater popularity.

But the IUD clearly had drawbacks. It required carefully trained providers for insertion and removal, involved a pelvic examination, and often caused bleeding and pelvic discomfort. As a result, discontinuation rates were frequently high. Beginning in the late 1960s, there was a major, publicly financed initiative to develop new, more effective contraceptives, with priority given to long-acting methods. The World Health Organization launched a program of applied research in reproduction, as did the Population Council and a few other not-for-profit organizations based in United States. Several developing countries, notably Mexico, India, and China, also began research programs. The pharmaceutical industry, for the most part, concentrated on improving the highly profitable oral contraceptive method and steered away from the costly and risky development of long-acting methods. A notable exception was the development of injectable contraceptives (Depo-Provera and Noristerat) by two major pharmaceutical companies.

The public sector effort was financed largely by international development agencies, with the intent to develop new contraceptives appropriate for use in developing countries, although use in industrialized countries was also an important goal. The "ideal" contraceptive method would have the following characteristics:

long-acting
highly effective
safe
producing few or no side effects
fully reversible application, not coitus-related
little or no need for action on the part of the user, after initial acceptance
no need for continuing supplies
low cost (7).

While researchers agreed that there was little likelihood of fulfilling all of these criteria, multiple research leads were pursued between the 1970s and 1990s, with the intention of achieving as many of them as possible. One consequence of seeking to develop contraceptives with this profile was a research and development emphasis on provider-dependent technologies. A contraceptive meeting these criteria would most likely require the involvement of a health care provider to initiate contraception, and perhaps to stop it as well.

Initially, little attention was paid to the ethical aspects of provider-dependent methods. The reversibility of the IUD, and later of other long-acting methods, was seen as addressing the most pressing ethical issue surrounding contraception: the irreversibility of sterilization and the coercive ways in which sterilization procedures had been performed in some countries (49). Interestingly, despite its irreversibility, sterilization became increasingly widely used. Indeed, by 1980, sterilization had become the most widely used contraceptive method worldwide (45). The ethical problem of irreversibility was addressed in many countries by emphasizing voluntary informed consent. However, sterilization abuses continued, especially in China and, in the mid-seventies, during the governmental emergency in India (25).

The first implantable long-acting contraceptive, Norplant, was approved in Finland in 1983, after 15 years of research. By 1996, it was approved for use in 56 countries, including the United States in 1990. The first injectable method, Depo-Provera, was introduced in 1966, and it is now widely used in over 80 countries and territories. Controversy over animal toxicity delayed its approval in the United States until 1992 (66).

Currently, a wide range of contraceptive leads are under investigation by both public and commercial research groups. This review describes long-acting methods that show particular promise. Some of these methods are reasonably likely to be introduced within the next decade, although predictions in this field are notoriously difficult.

Intrauterine Devices

Over the past decade, a series of advanced copper-bearing IUDs have been developed. Currently, the two most widely utilized methods are the Copper-T

380 IUD (marketed in the United States as Paragard) and the Multiload IUD. Both are very long-acting, highly effective, and inexpensive. The Copper-T 380 has been recently approved for ten years of use.

Progestin-releasing IUDs are now being introduced in Europe. These IUDs release constant low doses of progestin and are extremely effective over a five-year period. They also prevent excess bleeding and have a therapeutic benefit for women with menstrual disorders. Although other IUDs are under study, there seems to be little likelihood of any substantial new developments in the near future (55).

Implant Systems

The successful development of Norplant implants has paved the way for a second generation of contraceptive implant systems. All implant methods require a trained health provider to insert flexible silastic rods beneath the skin in a minor surgical procedure. A similar intervention is required for removal. A two-rod implant was approved by the US Food and Drug Administration in 1996. This implant is as effective as Norplant for at least three years, and it has the advantage of greater ease of insertion and removal. It is unclear when this method will be introduced in the United States. Three single implant methods are under investigation, using different progestins. At least one of these new implant systems will likely be introduced (although not necessarily in the United States) by the end of this century or early in the next.

A two-implant system for men is under development. One implant releases an analogue of a hypothalamic hormone to suppress sperm production, while the other implant releases a synthetic androgen to maintain normal sexual function. While early research results are encouraging, it is too soon to predict when, or whether, this promising method will be available (60).

Injectables

The FDA approval in 1992 of Depo-Provera, a three-month progestin-containing injectable, was the last major regulatory hurdle for this method, which has been in wide use in many other countries since the late 1960s. Two other methods, Noristerat (a two-month progestin-containing injectable) and Cyclofem (a one-month combined progestin-estrogen injectable) are also widely available, although not in the United States. These contraceptives are relatively easy to use and are highly effective. As with other progestin-only methods, Depo-Provera and Noristerat cause menstrual irregularities. Since an injection cannot be reversed, the effects continue until the drug has worn off. New injectable methods for women are under investigation, but no new methods are likely to be available in the near future (22). An injection for men, using the hormone testosterone, has shown promise (69).

Immunocontraception

Contraceptives for women using methods to modify the immune system have been under investigation for two decades. Assuming that a safe and effective immunocontraceptive method can be developed, the anticipated advantages would be ease of administration, convenience, low cost, and the absence of any menstrual changes. Progress has been slow because of problems in developing the antigens needed to produce a strong immune response. Antibodies to human chorionic gonatrophin, a hormone essential for the implantation and development of the embryo, have been extensively studied. Given the complexity of this field, considerably more research is needed. Research is under way to develop a male immunocontraceptive method. Although efforts thus far have been encouraging, it is difficult to predict how soon a male method might be available (2).

Some women's health advocates have expressed particular disquiet about the possible coercive use of immunocontraceptives. They assert that this method's ease of administration, as well as its resemblance to existing vaccination programs for disease prevention, will lead corrupt health officials to temporarily sterilize individuals without adherence to principles of voluntarism or informed consent. To proponents of this position, these risks justify stopping all research in this area. Other advocacy groups have contested this position (46, 51, 68).

Research on Other Contraceptive Methods

Other important research leads are under investigation. Many of these are short-acting methods and would for the most part be user controlled, allowing the individual to initiate use and stop without recourse to a health provider. Some of these methods should become available in the next few years, and they would offer significant new alternatives to long-acting contraceptives.

Contraceptive vaginal rings containing estrogen and a progestin have been under investigation for over two decades. These rings do not require special fitting, and so are easier to use than the diaphragm. Different progestins are used in other ring formulations. This class of user-controlled contraceptives shows considerable promise (59).

The AIDS pandemic has focused attention on the need to develop a vaginal microbicide capable of preventing the transmission of HIV and other organisms that cause sexually transmitted diseases. Such a compound would be under the control of the woman herself and would be an alternative to the condom, which is currently the only technology available. Freeing women from reliance on their partner's willingness to use a condom would greatly enhance their reproductive autonomy and allow them to protect themselves effectively against STDs. Research efforts have been intensifying, but it is unlikely that a product will reach the market for several years (1).

384   BROWN & MOSKOWITZ

The antiprogestin compound mifepristone, developed in the early 1980s, has proved to be a highly effective medical abortifacient, providing an important alternative to surgical abortion. It has been introduced in France, Great Britain, China, and Sweden, and should become available in the United States and other countries soon. Research is under way to determine if mifepristone is useful for other indications, including emergency contraception (62).

One issue that has come to the fore in contraceptive development generally has been the importance of conducting ethically sound human subjects research during the development process. Special cultural sensitivity is necessary in order to ensure informed consent and the protection of the safety of the women and men who volunteer to participate in a study involving long-acting contraception. Assuring that a volunteer fully understands the research investigation can be difficult, especially where literacy is low and gender disparities are great (32).

Furthermore, each long-acting method, as it becomes available, will clearly require careful introduction. A key part of an introduction strategy must be a thorough examination of the ethical considerations inherent in the use of each method, and the potential for abuse that may exist in the specific setting of the potential user. There are undoubtedly circumstances where a given method should not be introduced in a particular country or service delivery system if appropriate ethical safeguards cannot be assured.

Finally, post-marketing surveillance, following the introduction of a new method, is important to assure scientists and users that there are no uncommon health problems that could not be uncovered in the research undertaken prior to regulatory approval, and to assure that particular countries or service delivery systems can make the method available in a competent manner. This kind of large-scale post-marketing surveillance has been conducted in eight countries over five years, following the introduction of Norplant.

CONTRACEPTIVE POLICY AND ETHICS: US HISTORICAL PERSPECTIVE

In the United States, long-acting contraceptives raise unique policy and ethical issues. Understanding these issues depends upon some knowledge of their history–a history characterized by two main themes.

The first theme, which emerged with the dawn of the US birth control movement during the late nineteenth century, relates to the double-edged quality of efforts to enhance the availability of contraceptives. Some activities were well-intentioned, ethical attempts to help women improve their own lives and those of their families by making available the power to control their own fertility. However, these coexisted with pernicious, coercive ventures to limit women's childbearing for eugenic purposes (40). Perhaps most confounding were instances where a single birth control endeavor seemed to contain both elements, raising the question of which portion was most predominant.

The second theme is one of suspicion about the safety of medical technologies used for contraception, forcefully articulated during the feminist movement of the 1970s. It was sparked by the heightened awareness of women's reproductive health and bodily autonomy engendered by that movement, as well as by the development and diffusion of more invasive hormone-based and implanted birth control techniques.

A Double-Edged Quality

About one hundred years ago, immigrant communities in the United States became the target of two very different family planning efforts, both focused on a strikingly similar goal. Proponents of "voluntary motherhood," hoping to improve the quality of life in poor urban locations, and eugenicists, worried about the "excessive breeding" of immigrant groups they viewed as socially undesirable, both sought to encourage the use of effective contraceptives among this same population (48).

At the time, contraception was largely unavailable to the struggling immigrants. Withdrawal and the rhythm method tended to be used by the poor, with predictably inferior results. When unwanted pregnancies ensued, dangerous, often self-induced abortions were relatively common, accompanied by high mortality levels. Against this backdrop of unequal access to the era's most effective contraceptives and all too frequent resort to unsafe abortion, federal and state laws were enacted making contraceptive devices and abortion illegal.

After the turn of the century, this repressive and dangerous climate was increasingly challenged by reformers, the most prominent of whom was Margaret Sanger. They promoted the importance of making information about human reproduction and birth control available to women, and worked for more ready access to contraception. While they advocated for improved access to birth control for all women, their efforts tended to focus on poorer women who lacked the financial resources to obtain contraceptives through private physicians, and whose more precarious circumstances made unwanted pregnancies particularly problematic (48).

Many historians view Sanger as motivated primarily by a desire to help and empower women trapped in the bonds linking unwanted pregnancy with poverty. However, others have viewed her activities as overtly eugenic (14, 23, 48). Whatever the truth of the matter, groups vigorously promoting birth control were unabashedly motivated by the goal of limiting the population growth of classes of persons they viewed as undesirable.

386   BROWN & MOSKOWITZ

The eugenicists feared that the availability of family planning methods among wealthier individuals would encourage persons they deemed productive and virtuous to control their fertility, while at the same time inadequate·contraceptive use and a presumed heightened fecundity would lead those they viewed as less worthy to bear children at a faster rate (23). The eugenic framework was society as a whole, and they classified parts of humanity as capable of substantially harming the general welfare based upon whether they were fit or unfit to have children. This assessment, in turn, rested on bad genetic science, leading eugenicists to identify a jumble of criteria for limiting other people's procreative capacities. These included ethnicity, poverty, intemperance, or criminal recidivism, having been a rapist or a prostitute, and having had epilepsy, venereal disease, advanced tuberculosis, mental illness or retardation (48).

The eugenicists' most egregious tool for promoting fertility regulation among target populations was involuntary sterilization. By the early 1900s, surgical procedures to sterilize men and women had been refined. Without the niceties of informed consent, physicians sterilized individuals found to fall within vague categories such as "mental defective" and "feeble-minded" (49). By the 1930s, 30 states had laws permitting compulsory sterilization. In 1927, the Supreme Court had upheld their constitutionality in *Buck v. Bell*, with the renowned jurist Oliver Wendell Holmes finding, "It is better for all the world, if instead of waiting to execute degenerative offspring for crime, or to let them starve for their imbecility, society can prevent those who are manifestly unfit from continuing their kind" (48).

Between 1920 and 1960 more than 60,000 persons were involuntarily sterilized under the authority of these eugenics measures. Although by the 1960s public sentiment had strongly turned against the idea of promoting public welfare through eugenic sterilization, scattered instances where sterilizations were performed without informed consent still occurred into the 1970s. Finally, federal regulations were issued requiring informed consent, a 30-day waiting period, and a ban on sterilizations for persons under the age of 21 (49).

Although the controversies surrounding involuntary eugenic sterilization have subsided, the double-edged quality of contraception, particularly as it relates to less advantaged populations, remains. The relatively recent emergence of a new generation of long-acting contraceptives has raised familiar questions about motives and goals. For example, following the US Food and Drug Administration's approval of Norplant in 1990, heated debate ensued about whether a range of efforts to facilitate, encourage, and in some proposals, mandate its use were best understood as empowering and affirming, or invidious and wrong. Clearly, this persistent historical tension challenges health professionals and policy makers to plainly distinguish one kind of activity from the other. Wrongful policies must be avoided, but positive policies must not be mistakenly condemned.

Is It Safe?

An important issue of the feminist movement in the 1970s was women's health and bodily autonomy, particularly with respect to reproduction. This feature of feminism was nicely captured by *Our Bodies, Ourselves*, first published in 1973 by the Boston Women's Health Book Collective, which found issues of power, justice, and solidarity implicated in women's reproductive health (9).

Intertwined with this innovative orientation was the emergence of more physiologically invasive birth control technologies, and a growing skepticism about the extent to which pharmaceutical companies, researchers, and physicians could be expected to consistently respond to women's need for fertility regulation with safe interventions. This skepticism had a salutary aspect, reflecting an increased sophistication in the general public about the fallibility and probabalistic quality of modern medicine, as well as about the sometimes dangerous effect of financial self-interest in technology development and diffusion. It also had an adversarial bent that in some cases led to deep and unfortunate divides between women strongly focused on the safety of contraceptive methods and members of the medical, research, and business communities–divides that linger today.

Certain watershed experiences with the new contraceptives helped mold this skeptical orientation. An important event occurred in the United States in the late 1960s, when it became known among lay persons that there were certain serious cardiovascular risks associated with the high-dose estrogen oral contraceptive. This information came to public attention almost a decade after the pill had been approved as safe by the Food and Drug Administration, and after millions of women had already used it regularly. Also, an initial source of the news was not a medical professional, but a feminist writer (53). Heightened federal regulation of contraceptive research and introduction followed (10).

Another milestone was the dramatic case of an intrauterine device, the Dalkon Shield, which was developed a decade after the first modern IUD, the Lippes Loop. Introduced in the United States in 1971 by the AH Robins Company and treated by the FDA as a medical device, not a drug, the Dalkon Shield avoided stringent reviews of safety and efficacy. However, by 1974, the company had stopped marketing this IUD, following growing evidence of cases of septic abortions and death caused by its defective design (24).

Too slowly for some, over the next ten years, AH Robins and government regulators racheted up their level of concern about and response to the safety issues raised by the Dalkon Shield. In 1975, the Food and Drug Administration began

388   BROWN & MOSKOWITZ

hearings on the Dalkon Shield, and in 1976, a law was passed requiring medical devices to be subject to the same monitoring and approval procedures as drugs.

In 1980, the company first formally advised physicians to remove Dalkon Shields from any women who still were using them. Only in 1983 did the FDA advise all women wearing Dalkon Shields to have them removed. About that same time the company filed for bankruptcy. Two years later, in 1985, AH Robins first publicly recommended to women, and not just to physicians, that they have their Dalkon Shields removed. By then over 300,000 women worldwide had filed legal claims against the company. The litigation was settled in 1988, when plaintiffs forced the sale of AH Robins for $3.3 billion. $2.5 billion of these proceeds went into a trust fund for the claimants (24). This massive product liability litigation was the largest to have ever occurred in the United States, although in 1992 the silicone breast implant litigation would usurp that dubious title–a legal action that is still unfolding (38).

The adverse health effects caused by the faulty design of the Dalkon Shield were unrelated to the Lippes Loop IUD, which continued to be safely used in many countries. Nonetheless, the negative publicity surrounding the Dalkon Shield controversy deeply affected the Lippes Loop and all other IUDs, especially in the United States, where IUD use is still much lower than in other industrialized countries.

Today, questions regarding safety and skepticism about contraceptive technologies persist in portions of the lay public, as does the specter of enormous lawsuits stemming from real or perceived problems associated with a new method. Regulatory oversight, safety research during product development, and pre- and post-marketing evaluation have been enhanced, and the new long-acting contraceptives have all benefitted from this greater attention.

Nevertheless, controversy continues. For example, less than four years after Norplant's FDA approval, product liability litigation had been instigated against Wyeth-Ayerst, the US distributor of the method–despite 20 years of intense study and a strong scientific consensus about Norplant's safety. The women involved have complained of ill health caused by removal and insertion procedures, side effects of the progestin, and illness purportedly stemming from the silicone composition of the implant tubing. Wyeth-Ayerst has countered that Norplant is safe, and the company will fight any class action (8, 16). The FDA issued a statement in 1995 declaring that its assessment of the safety of Norplant remains unchanged (58). The impact of the legal action has, however, resulted in a virtual collapse of the market for this method.

Sound, scientific proof of safety is clearly central in contraceptive development and diffusion, but if history is a guide, public skepticism and anxiety about invasive and provider-dependent long-acting contraceptives should be expected. If a method is truly safe and effective for most potential users, assuring continued access will depend not just on factors such as adequate supplies and good training of health care providers, but also on a vigilant response to misunderstandings and misrepresentations.

INTERNATIONAL EXPERIENCE WITH LONG-ACTING CONTRACEPTIVES

Internationally, long-acting contraceptives have figured prominently in the family planning programs of developing countries. An examination of the international experience with long-acting methods underscores the importance of maintaining a focus on individual users, and not simply demographic goals.

Although the first national family planning program was established in India in 1952, effective action in that country and in other Asian countries began in the early 1960s, stimulated by the introduction of oral contraceptives and the Lippes Loop IUD, as well as female and male sterilization. Long-acting methods were seen by national program managers and by international donor agencies as critical to large-scale acceptance of family planning, given their perceived advantages of ease of use, no need for repeated actions or supplies, and high level of effectiveness. Although there was great variation in the mix of methods used in different countries, by the mid-1990s long-acting methods were the dominant contraceptive technology in most countries. Over 170 million sterilizations have been performed, becoming the most important method in many countries, especially India, China, and other Asian countries, as well as in many Latin American countries (45).

In particular, initial enthusiasm for the IUD was great. In some countries, however, insufficient attention was given to counseling, especially for side effects–a problem that was mirrored in the 1980s with the introduction of Norplant. Health providers sometimes became fixated on numbers of individuals accepting methods. The IUD, especially in its improved copper-bearing versions, has continued to be widely used in many countries, especially in China, where there are currently an estimated 82 million users.

As noted above, the drive for quantity over quality was fueled by the fertility reduction targets established by governments, which were in turn translated into family planning acceptor targets set for health providers, requiring them to achieve fixed numbers of acceptors per year. In some countries, various incentives were offered to help meet these targets. The nature of these target-and-incentive schemes usually resulted in a heavy programmatic emphasis on sterilization and other long-acting methods. In India and other countries, for example, large sterilization recruitment efforts became dominated by sterilization "camps" where hundreds of women could receive a sterilization, or other methods, on a given day. User-controlled methods were frequently neglected,

390   BROWN & MOSKOWITZ

even though most programs theoretically adhered to a "cafeteria approach," offering a wide range of methods to all potential users. Some user-controlled methods, like the diaphragm, were dropped entirely.

While most national family planning programs adhered to the principle of voluntary decision-making, the target-and-incentive system also tended to reduce individual autonomy in decision-making. This was often coupled with provider dominance in the interpersonal exchange with the client, who was frequently poorly educated. The demographic dominance became acute in India the mid-1970s, when a government-launched "emergency campaign," designed to reduce high fertility, resulted in forced sterilizations of men and women and other coercive actions in some regions. After two years the program collapsed amid widespread popular resistance and the defeat of the government (25).

In China, the one-child policy established in the early 1980s included a wide range of governmental actions designed to control the reproductive behavior of individuals and couples. Incentives, disincentives, and intense control of reproductive behavior at the community level were effective demographically, but at the profound loss of individual reproductive freedom. Central mandates were implemented very differently at the provincial level, resulting in greater or lesser degrees of coercion (17). The widespread use of long-acting contraceptives in this political context clearly aided governmental directives aimed at population control.

Although most other countries did not pursue such demographically driven policies as China or India, the use of long-acting methods has been frequently stressed, always with a clearly stated policy of voluntarism. Nonetheless, some loss of voluntarism has frequently emerged, stemming from the need to fulfill targets, or the belief that poorly educated women are not capable of using barrier methods or oral contraceptives properly. In some Latin American countries, IUDs have been inserted immediately postpartum, sometimes with little or no informed consent given by the woman (19). For a time, Indonesia employed a version of India's "camp approach," emphasizing the Norplant method (47, 63). In many countries with weak health services women have received inadequate counseling regarding side effects, resulting in distrust and negative views about modern contraception.

Reminiscent of the IUD introductions in the 1960s, the introduction of Norplant internationally, beginning in 1983, was also accompanied by enthusiastic publicity that this method would be a major breakthrough in long-acting contraception. The method's high levels of effectiveness for five years, reversibility, and ease of use for the client following insertion seemed to offset problems of frequent side effects (principally menstrual irregularity) and the medical intervention required for both insertion and removal.

However, unlike the 1960s, the introduction of Norplant could take advantage of advances in contraceptive introduction theory and practice, and a careful international program of introduction of the method was undertaken (6, 56). High cost relative to IUDs and the requirement of careful training of providers for insertion, removal, and counseling made Norplant introduction efforts more complex and relatively slow.

Fifteen years after its initial introduction, Norplant has been approved for use in 56 countries, but only a handful of developing countries have incorporated the method into their national family planning programs in a substantial way. Indonesia, with by far the widest use of this method, has inserted over two million implants, which represents 5% of all contraceptive users in that country (33, 63).

Misgivings about the inadequate informed consent and coercive use of Norplant have emerged in several countries, despite strong initiatives to ensure careful counseling and adherence to voluntary use. A particular problem has emerged surrounding removal of the implants. In several countries, providers have refused to remove implants at the request of users, because of the cost involved, and the provider's insistence on maintaining continued contraceptive use. Women were urged to tolerate side effects and keep the implants in place. Thus the method, labeled as fully reversible, was not in fact reversible for some women who were denied this service.

Increasing international preoccupation in the 1980s with individual rights, voluntarism, and the need to respect the perspective of contraceptive users culminated in efforts to improve the quality of care of family planning programs. A quality of care framework enunciated by Bruce emphasized provider competence, client-provider interaction, the transmission of information, opportunity for choice, follow-up care, and availability of related health services (12). Increasing the availability of methods that could be controlled by the individual user–condoms, oral contraceptives, spermicides, diaphragms, periodic abstinence, and withdrawal–was promoted as a way to reduce dependence on provider-controlled long-acting contraceptives.

Despite the complex medical, programmatic, and ethical issues associated with long-acting contraceptives, their impact has been enormous throughout the world, and many millions of women and men have benefitted from their use. Contraceptive prevalence rates in the developing world have increased rapidly in the past three decades, reaching 55% in 1994, from less than 10% in the 1960s. Over 322 million women and men in the developing world currently use long-acting methods (sterilization, injectables, or IUDs), comprising over 72% of all contraceptive users (61).

The advent of the AIDS pandemic in the 1980s accelerated the urgent need to prevent the transmission of the human immunodeficiency virus (HIV) and other sexually transmitted diseases. As a result, family planning programs have been forced to reconsider the appropriate use of contraceptive technologies. Long-acting contraceptives do not prevent the transmission of HIV or other STDs, whereas several user-controlled barrier methods do so, notably condoms. In

392   BROWN & MOSKOWITZ

some countries, national family planning managers have struggled with the conflicting needs of expanding condom use, while at the same time increasing the use of long-term contraceptives. The role of family planning services in preventing AIDS and STD transmission has been actively explored, but much more work is needed to reconcile these two public health needs.

A high watermark for international family planning in the 1990s was The International Conference on Population and Development (ICPD), held in Cairo in 1994. The event brought into global prominence the importance of reproductive rights of the individual. The Conference's recommendations, which were approved by 180 country delegations, emphasized a focus on individual autonomy in reproductive choice and rejected targets and incentives in family planning programs (28). While it is too soon to predict what the impact of the ICPD will be on individual country's policies and programs, important conceptual changes are contemplated or under way in several countries. The Indian government, for example, has dramatically redesigned its program, placing greater emphasis on the needs of the user, quality of care, and placing family planning in a broader reproductive health framework. Contraceptive targets have been dropped in all states, and family planning services are being realigned into a reproductive health framework, including the expansion of user-controlled and long-acting reversible contraceptives as alternatives to sterilization (39, 65).

The Cairo Conference marked the forceful emergence of women's health advocacy groups in international family planning; many women's groups were active participants in the shaping of the ICPD recommendations. More generally, at both national and international levels, women's health advocacy groups have spoken vigorously for greater attention to women's reproductive autonomy, informed choice, and a wider range of user-controlled contraceptive methods, among other issues. In some countries, women's groups have sought to expose coercive measures, and as part of this effort have promoted blockage of the use of some long-acting contraceptives, including Norplant and Depo-Provera (41). Other groups have spoken out on reshaping contraceptive development strategy in favor of methods that can prevent STD transmission (67). While some have argued against immunocontraceptive research, in part because of its possible coercive use, others have disagreed with this position (46).

RIGHTS AND RESPONSIBILITIES: THE ETHICS OF LACs

A truism of family planning policy is that diversity counts. Sexually active individuals have a range of needs and confront a variety of personal, social, and health circumstances. Good reproductive health care depends on offering a varying selection of contraceptives. Different people will gravitate toward different approaches, and one person's preferences will vary over time. Increased birth control options improve the likelihood of user satisfaction and effective contraceptive use.

The advent of safe and effective long-acting contraception should therefore be welcomed. Diversity is enhanced by offering an alternative to the active, daily regimes of oral contraceptives and barrier methods, and many women have indeed been pleased by the new birth control options. However, as noted above, the methods have also invoked hostility and suspicion. In some cases, this negative reaction has been addressed to method safety, in keeping with the historical skepticism aroused by contraceptive technologies since the early 1970s.

However, a unique and ethically challenging aspect of this negativism concerns not safety, but reproductive freedom. To a degree not true of prior contraceptive technologies–other than permanent sterilization, the long-acting methods have sometimes been viewed less as means for enhancing reproductive choice than as potential instruments of gender or racial discrimination, class prejudice, and eugenic social control.

This section explores the unique questions of freedom and coercion raised by the available reversible long-acting contraceptives. It notes that ethical analyses of these technologies must take good account of their intrinsic properties, which lend themselves to surveillance and monitoring by third parties. It also suggests a perspective for grappling with questions of rights and responsibilities invoked by the methods that takes full measure of the individual interests at stake, as well as of the social dimension of reproduction and contraceptive decision making (37).

Freedom and Coercion

The long-term contraceptives developed thus far do not permit women to immediately initiate and discontinue use by their own actions: All rely on health care providers for initiation, and users cannot discontinue their contraceptive effect without substantial delay or professional assistance. As such, the contraceptives offer good opportunities for third parties to monitor a woman's period of infertility. While sterilization offers the same opportunities, other reversible contraceptives do not.

In some countries with demographic goals, these features have led to blatantly abusive population policies or practices where, for example, health providers have inserted IUDs without obtaining a woman's prior voluntary and informed consent (32). In the United States, these characteristics have led some to view long-acting methods as providing a means of addressing complex and severe social problems other than population growth, and ethical controversies have ensued.

For example, in the hope of addressing child abuse, some US judges have devised probation arrangements that require the use of Norplant (42). Seeking

394   BROWN & MOSKOWITZ

to decrease reliance on welfare, a number of state legislators have introduced, but not yet passed, bills requiring women who receive public assistance to accept Norplant implants (3, 4, 35, 64).

Similar issues have arisen at the clinical level. Providers sometimes serve sexually active clients who are unable to successfully use oral contraceptives or barrier methods, yet appear currently unready to take on the responsibilities of parenthood. Rather than simply prescribing another cycle of pills and awaiting the next abortion or child welfare crisis, some providers may instead try to encourage the use of a long-term method. If such a client wants to discontinue Norplant or an IUD, providers may resist those requests or attempt to change the client's mind.

These kinds of policies and clinical practices have led to charges of coercion and the violation of individual reproductive freedom. The charges rest on the principle that individuals have a fundamental right to control whether they will have children, and the notion that neither the government nor any individual is entitled to shape or influence a woman's contraceptive choices. The charges also reflect deep disquiet about discrimination in the United States on the basis of class, race, and gender, and the history, discussed above, of expressing those biases through resort to permanent birth control in the form of compulsory sterilization. Such charges have a parallel in other countries.

Reproductive Rights and Responsibilities

Sensitivity to these concerns is clearly essential for ethical analysis of the proposals and practices involving long-acting contraceptives. However, a more complete perspective requires taking note that all encouragement to use long-acting contraceptives is not necessarily unethical and coercive. Such encourgement is better understood as ubiquitous and inevitable. It should neither be dismissed nor mindlessly attacked, but examined carefully case-by-case.

In other words, the guiding normative idea that is most helpful in analyzing issues of freedom and coercion raised by long-acting contraceptives is not only the conception of individual reproductive rights, but rather a conception of responsible decision-making in the context of relationships. There is a strong social as well as individual dimension of reproduction and thus of contraceptive decision making, involving, for example, sexual partners and children. This dimension creates responsibilities that guide contraceptive choices as much as do individual rights and interests. True reproductive freedom needs to be set within relationships of involvement, concern, and respect for others (37).

Along with this fuller account of reproductive freedom and coercion, it is also important to remember the obvious: Unwanted, mistimed pregnancies can cause direct and foreseeable harm. For example, important injury can be done to a woman's opportunities to shape her life in accord with her own needs and goals, including her education and employment opportunities. In addition, serious harm caused by unwanted and mistimed pregnancy can befall other persons dependent on the woman, particularly vulnerable children.

All of this underlines the importance of access. Sound public policies and clinical practices involving long-acting contraceptives must rest on the availability of a range of contraceptives, including both user-controlled and long-term methods. Reproductive freedom and responsibility depend on effective choices.

Another point these observations suggest is the possibility of encouragement to consider the use of a long-term contraceptive. If it can be reasonably foreseen that an unwanted, mistimed pregnancy will cause substantial harm, and if the woman has not seriously considered using a long-acting method, it can be appropriate and responsible to provide information to enable the woman to consider the method. Under the proper circumstances (including strict adherence to principles of informed consent and voluntarism) such counseling can demonstrate the best kind of care, commitment, and respect (36).

At bottom, whether a particular policy or practice involving a long-acting method is sound will depend on a close, particularized, case-by-case analysis. This analysis must be attentive to the individual interests at stake, while keeping in mind the social dimensions and consequences of contraceptive decision making. The final decision to use a particular contraceptive method must rest with the individual woman, based on full information about the range of options available to her.

LACs AND PUBLIC POLICY

Government officials, policy makers in nongovernmental agencies, and health care providers are now confronting certain difficult issues raised by long-acting contraceptives: questions of access, research needs, and the ethics of government proposals to influence classes of women to use these methods. This section offers policy recommendations regarding these matters.

Access

Long-acting contraceptives should be available for informed, voluntary use by sexually active women. This requires service delivery systems that make these methods available and affordable, along with a wide range of user controlled contraceptives, and that also address the methods' special characteristics, including the need for removal by health care providers.

In light of the higher initial costs associated with some of the long-term methods, it is particularly important to prevent cost from becoming a substantial barrier to use. In nations lacking comprehensive health care coverage, such as the United States, this policy will depend on developing adequate public and private health insurance coverage for reversible contraception (20).

Where women have public or private insurance coverage for Norplant or IUDs at the time of insertion, they too often risk being uninsured when they seek removal (31). In some developing countries cost of removal has been a barrier. Accordingly, financial guarantees of removal must be extended at the time of insertion for any long-acting method requiring provider removal.

Appropriate access to long-acting methods also depends on the existence of suitable service delivery systems. Safe and respectful use of these contraceptives requires a local infrastructure of health services that can provide appropriate counseling, as well as skillful provision, continuing access to care and supervision, and, as necessary, removals. Other necessary elements include the availability of contraceptives other than long-acting methods, and sufficient numbers of trained and competent health care personnel. Family planning programs lacking a suitable service delivery system should not offer long-acting methods.

Furthermore, appropriate access should not be denied by reason of age or disability. For example, in the United States, adolescents have similar rates of sexual activity as compared with teenagers in other industrialized nations, but they have less sex education and lower contraceptive use, and higher incidence of unintended pregnancy (30). One study has shown that the selection of Norplant by adolescent mothers as a method of contraception is associated with higher rates of continued use and lower rates of new pregnancy than the selection of oral contraceptives (44). Appropriate access requires adherence to principles of informed consent and confidentiality; an adolescent's use of a long-term method should not be conditioned on parental consent or notification if the adolescent herself is capable of providing informed consent. In cases of women with mental illness or disability, access should not be categorically denied, but should rest on appropriate surrogate decision making processes that, as far as possible, respect the individual autonomy of each woman (15).

State Influences

While family planning counseling, including discussions and even recommendations about using long-acting contraceptives, may be appropriate for an individual woman in a clinic setting, strong governmental incentives and disincentives to lead broad classes of women to use a long-acting contraceptive method are generally unsound, even if they attempt to maintain adherence to principles of informed consent. This is true in both developing countries, where the goal of such policies might be decreasing population growth rates, and in developed countries, such as the United States, where such policies have been proposed to achieve other goals, for example, decreasing the numbers of persons dependent on public assistance, and addressing the problem of child abuse.

The most powerful sector of most societies, the government, cannot inoffensively use a heavy-handed prop to bring about two sensitive consequences: a bodily invasion and a single action with respect to fertility. Governments should be wary and reluctant about intruding on reproductive matters in this direct and invasive fashion (29).

LONG-ACTING CONTRACEPTIVES AND THE FUTURE: PERSONAL AND PUBLIC CHOICES

Long-acting contraceptives are here to stay. Their widespread use in virtually every country of the world, including those with strong records of respect for individual reproductive rights, demonstrates that long-acting contraceptives are popular and socially desirable. New methods are being developed, each designed to offer improvements, especially with regard to side effects, acceptability, and safety, as well as ease of use, both by the individual and the provider.

Thus the question must focus on *how* existing and new long-acting contraceptives are to be used, under what conditions, and with what degree of informed choice and quality of care. Who should establish the requirements for socially and ethically acceptable use? What mechanisms can be put in place to insure that these methods are employed properly?

A prior question focusses on the need for access to user-controlled methods for men and women as viable alternatives to long-acting methods. If the only realistic option in a given setting is a long-acting method, then access and choice is inadequate, and real reproductive freedom cannot be realized. It is imperative that women and men have a range of methods easily available to them, along with effective counseling as to their use, and a health infrastructure competent to support their choices and meet their needs.

The existing array of long-acting contraceptives, sterilization, and other methods has clearly been sufficient to achieve impressive levels of contraceptive use worldwide, but in many countries the real choices available are narrow. Heavy emphasis on long-acting methods in many countries continues, fueled by the fear that if more women opt for user-controlled contraceptives, they will use them incorrectly, or discontinue use, and as a result fertility will increase. This distrust of individual users frequently exists at the local level, even if it is not formally enunciated as national policy. Too often, local authorities and providers, motivated by demographic concerns, flout principles of voluntarism and informed consent. In the United States, special care must be taken to avoid involving governmental agencies in coercive programs aimed at nondemographic goals, such as welfare reform or child protection.

The moral and policy issues raised by long-acting contraceptives must be addressed by government leaders, family planning policy makers, and health care providers. In accordance with the ICPD recommendations, reproductive rights, as well as responsibilities, must be accepted and integrated into reproductive

398   BROWN & MOSKOWITZ

health. Choice of contraceptive methods must also be expanded, and a major program undertaken to train health care providers in the necessary counseling and technical functions. Policies and strong incentives involving numerical targets for contraceptive use should be eschewed. Comprehensive improvement of the quality of services should be the cornerstone to assuring that long-acting methods can be offered in a safe, voluntary, and ethically responsible fashion.

How can change be encouraged and monitored? Officials and health care providers must work actively to conform contraceptive policies and practices to these standards. Furthermore, the United Nations, as the sponsor of the ICPD, has a key role in encouraging the nations who are signatory to the ICPD Recommendations to honor their commitments. This work has already begun. An additional beneficial action at the international level would be to increase efforts to link reproductive rights to the wider human rights efforts of the UN. Moreover, women's health groups have been important agents for positive change; their efforts should be encouraged.

In future family planning research and practice, it can be expected that doubts will be voiced about the propriety of various contraceptive technologies. For a complex of historical, technological, and political reasons, long-acting contraceptives have been a locus of concern. Vigilance is critical for assuring the sound development of these important family planning tools. Also, inadequate policies and programs that deliver these methods must be identified and changed. Realizing the promise and avoiding the dangers of long-acting contraceptives requires taking good account of a rich mixture of clinical, social, political, and ethical factors.

Visit the *Annual Reviews home page* at
http://www.annurev.org.

Literature Cited

1. Alexander NJ. 1996. Barriers to sexually transmitted diseases. In *Science and Medicine*. March/April 32–41. New York: Sci. Am.
2. Alexander NJ. 1994. Contraceptive vaccines. See Ref. 61a, pp. 203–14
3. American Medical Association, Board of Trustees. 1992. Requirements or incentives by government for the use of long-acting contraceptives. *JAMA* 267:1818–21
4. Arthur SL. 1992. The Norplant prescription: birth control, woman control, or crime control. *UCLA Law Rev.* 40:1–101
5. Deleted in proof
6. Beattie KJ, Brown GF. 1994. Expanding contraceptive choice: the Norplant expe-

rience. See Ref. 61a, pp. 263–79
7. Berelson B. 1964. Application of intrauterine contraception in family planning programs. In *Intrauterine Contraception*, ed. SJ Segal, AL Southam, KD Schafer, pp. 9–13. New York: Excerpta Medica Found.
8. BNA Health Law Reporter. 1994. Products liability case filed against U.S. makers of implanted contraceptive. Sept. 22, p. 1310
9. Boston Women's Health Book Collective. 1992. *The New Our Bodies, Ourselves*, pp. 13–16. New York: Simon & Schuster
10. Boston Women's Health Book Collective. 1992. See Ref. 9, pp. 279–80
11. Brown GF. 1987. Family planning pro-

LONG-ACTING CONTRACEPTION 399

grams. In *Technology in Society*, ed. G Zeidenstein, pp. 465–80. New York: Pergamon

12. Bruce J. 1990. Fundamental elements of the quality of care: a simple framework. *Stud. Fam. Plan.* 21(2):61–91

13. *Buck v. Bell.* 1927. 274 U.S. 200

14. Chesler E. 1992. *Woman of Valor: Margaret Sanger and the Birth Control Movement in America.* New York: Simon & Schuster

15. Coverdale JH, Bayer TL, McCullough LB, Chervenak FA. 1993. Respecting the autonomy of chronic mentally ill women in decisions about contraception. *Hosp. Commun. Psychiatry* 44:671–74

16. Cowley G, Miller S. 1995. Norplant backlash: is it dangerous, or are lawyers exploiting it? *Newsweek*, Nov. 27, p. 52

17. Croll E, Davin D, Kane P. 1985. *China's One-Child Family Policy.* New York: St. Martin's Press

18. Feringa B, Iden S, Rosenfield A. 1992. Norplant: potential for coercion. In *Norplant and Poor Women*, ed. SE Samuels, MD Smith, pp. 54–56. Menlo Park, CA: Henry J. Kaiser Found.

19. Figureroa-Perea JG. 1994. The introduction of new methods of contraception: ethical perspectives. *Reprod. Health Matters* 3:13–19

20. Forrest JD, Kaeser L. 1993. Questions of balance: issues emerging from the introduction of the hormonal implant. *Fam. Plan. Perspect.* 25:127–32

21. Frost JJ. 1994. The availability and accessibility of the contraceptive implant from family planning agencies in the United States, 1991–1992. *Fam. Plan. Perspect.* 26:4–10

22. Garza-Flores J, Cravioto MC, Perez-Palacios G. 1994. Contraceptive research development: injectables. See Ref. 61a, pp. 53–68

23. Gordon L. 1981. *Women's Right: Birth Control in America*, pp. 95–115. New York: Penguin

24. Grant NJ. 1992. *The Selling of Contraception: The Dalkon Shield Case, Sexuality, and Women's Autonomy*, pp. 37–69. Columbus: Ohio State Univ. Press

25. Gwatkin DR. 1979. Political will and family planning: the implications of India's family planning experience. *Popul. Dev. Rev.* 5(1):29–59

26. Hardy E. 1996. Long-acting contraception in Brazil and the Dominican Republic. *Fam. Plan. Perspect.* 26:206–16

27. Harkavy O. 1995. *Curbing Population Growth: An Insider's Perspective on the Population Movement.* New York: Plenum

28. International Conference on Population and Development. 1994. Program of action. March 1995. *Popul. Dev. Rev.* 21(1):187–213; 21(2):437–61

29. Isaacs SL. 1995. Incentives, population policy, and reproductive rights: ethical issues. *Stud. Fam. Plan.* 26:363–67

30. Jones E, Forrest JD. 1985. Teenage pregnancy in developed countries: determinants and policy implications. *Fam. Plan. Perspect.* 17:53–63

31. Kaeser L. 1994. Public funding and policies for provision of the contraceptive implant, fiscal year 1992. *Fam. Plan. Perspect.* 26:11–16

32. Macklin R. 1996. Cultural difference and long-acting contraception. In *Coerced Contraception? Moral and Policy Challenges of Long-Acting Birth Control*, ed. EH Moskowitz, BJ Jennings, pp. 173–91. Washington, DC: Georgetown Univ. Press

33. Macro International Inc. 1995. *Indonesia Demographic and Health Survey 1994.* Calverton, MD: Macro Int. Inc.

34. Mauldin WP, Segal SJ. 1994. IUD use throughout the world: past, present, and future. *Proc. Int. Conf. IUDs, 4th*, ed. WC Bardin, DR Mishell Jr, pp. 1–10. Boston: Butterworth-Heinemann

35. Mertus J, Heller S. 1992. Norplant meet the new eugenicists: the impermissibility of coerced contraception. *St. Louis Univ. Public Law Rev.* 11:359–83

36. Moskowitz EH, Jennings B. 1996. Directive counseling on long-acting contraception. *Am. J. Public Health* 86:787–90

37. Moskowitz EH, Jennings B, Callahan D. 1995. Long-acting contraception: ethical guidance for policymakers and health care providers. *Hastings Cent. Rep.* 25(1) (Suppl.):S1–8). Reprinted in Ref. 32, pp. 3–19

38. Nocera J. 1995. Fatal litigation. *Fortune* Oct. 16:60–82

39. Pachauri S. 1995. Defining a reproductive health package for India: a proposed framework. In *The Population Council Regional Work. Pap.*, 4:7–66. New Delhi: Popul. Counc.

40. Pearce TO. 1996. Ethical issues in the importation of long-acting contraceptives to Nigeria. In *Coerced Contraception? Moral and Policy Challenges of Long-Acting Birth Control*, ed. EH Moskowitz, BJ Jennings, pp. 192–205. Washington, DC: Georgetown Univ. Press

41. Pearson CA. 1995. National Women's Network and the U.S. FDA: two decades

400   BROWN & MOSKOWITZ

of activism. *Reprod. Health Matters* 6:132–41

42. *People v. Johnson*, No. 29390 (Cal. Super. Ct. Tulare County 1990)

43. Planned Parenthood Federation of America. 1991. *Sexuality and reproductive behavior among U.S. teens*. Fact Sheet. Feb.

44. Polaneczky M, Slap G, Forke C, Rappaport A, Sondheimre S. 1994. The use of Levenorgestrel implants (Norplant) for contraception in adolescent mothers. *N. Engl. J. Med.* 331:1201–6

45. Pollack AE. 1994. One hundred and seventy million sterilizations later: what we know and what we wish to know. See Ref. 61a, pp. 215–32

46. Population Council, New York. 1994. Letter, with Vaccine Statement attached, to the Women's Global Network for Reproductive Rights, The Netherlands, June 28

47. Population Council. 1993. *1992 Indonesia Norplant User-Dynamics Study*. Asia Near East Operations Research and Technical Assistance Project, pp. 5, 28. New York: The Popul. Counc.

48. Powderly KE. 1994. Contraceptive policy and ethics: lessons from American history. See Ref. 21, pp. 23–33

49. Reilly P. 1991. *The Surgical Solution*. Baltimore: Johns Hopkins Univ. Press.

50. *Relf v. Weinberger*. 1974. 386 Fed. Suppl. 1384. DC. District Ct.

51. Richter J. 1993. *Vaccination against Pregnancy: Miracle or Menace?* Buko Pharma-Kampagne/Health Action International-Europe, Bielefeld

52. Robertson JA. 1994. *Children of Choice: Freedom and the New Reproductive Technologies*, Chapter 4. Princeton: Princeton Univ. Press

53. Seaman B. 1969. updated 1979. *The Doctor's Case Against the Pill*. New York: Dell

54. Segal SJ, Southam AL, Schafer KD, eds. 1964. *Intrauterine Contraception: Proc. Int. Conf., 2nd*. New York: Excerpta Media Found.

55. Sivin I. 1994. IUDs: a look to the future. See Ref. 61a, pp. 37–52

56. Spicehandler J. 1989. Norplant introduction: a management perspective. In *Demographic and Programmatic Conse-*

quences of Contraceptive Innovations, ed. SJ Segal, AO Tsui, SM Rogers. New York: Plenum

57. *State v. Carlton*, No. CR90–1937 (Neb. County Ct. Lincoln County 1991).

58. *Talk Paper*. 1995. Issued by the U.S. Food and Drug Administration. Aug.

59. Thau R, Jackanicz T. 1994. Contraceptive rings: a user-controlled long-acting method for family planning. See Ref. 61a, pp. 107–20

60. Thau R, Robbins A. 1994. New implant systems for men and women. See Ref. 61a, pp. 91–106

61. United National Population Fund. 1994. *Tech. Rep. No. 18: Contraceptive Use and Commodity Costs in Developing Countries 1994–2005*. New York: UNFPA

61a. Van Look PFA, Perez-Palacios G, eds. 1994. *Contraceptive Research and Development 1984-1994: The Road from Mexico City to Cairo and Beyond*. New York: Oxford Univ. Press

62. von Hertzon J, Van Look PFA. 1996. Research on new methods of emergency contraception. *Fam. Plan. Perspect.*, March/April:52–57

63. Widyantoro N. 1994. The story of Norplant implants in Indonesia. *Reprod. Health Matters* 3:20–29

64. Women's Legal Defense Fund. 1992. *Legislation and Litigation Involving Norplant*, pp. 1–5. Washington, DC: Women's Legal Defense Fund

65. World Bank. 1995. *India's Family Welfae Program: Toward A Reproductive and Child Health Approach*. Washington, DC: World Bank, Popul. Hum. Resourc. Oper. Div., S. Asia Country Dep.

66. World Health Organization. 1990. *Injectable Contraceptives*. Geneva: WHO

67. World Health Organization. 1991. *Creating Common Ground*. Geneva: WHO, WHO/HRP/ITT/91.

68. World Health Organization. 1992. *Fertility Regulating Vaccines*. Geneva, Switzerland: WHO

69. World Health Organization. 1996. Special group on male contraceptive methods, contraceptive efficacy of testosterone-induced azoospermia and oligospermia in normal men. *Fertil. Steril.* 65:821–29

[5]

Australasian Journal of Philosophy
Vol. 70, No. 2: June 1992

ABORTION AND EMBODIMENT[1]

Catriona Mackenzie

1. Introduction

Feminist perspectives on abortion focus on a fact the moral implications of which are either overlooked or considered unimportant by most other disputants in the debate. This is the fact that a foetus is not a free-floating entity about whom questions of potentiality and personhood arise as though in a vacuum. Rather a foetus is a being whose existence and welfare are biologically and morally inseparable from the woman in whose body it develops. From a feminist perspective the central moral subjects of the abortion question are thus not only, or not primarily, foetuses but women.

Within an influential strand of the feminist philosophical literature it has been usual to understand the moral dilemmas arising from this unique relationship between a foetus and a woman in terms of a conflict of rights and to defend a woman's right to abortion via the notion of bodily autonomy. In its crudest form, the alleged conflict is between a) the 'right to life' of the foetus, a right based on the presumption that it is a being deserving of some moral consideration, and b) the right of the woman to bodily autonomy, that is, her right to decide what happens in and to her body. In attempting to resolve this conflict in women's favour feminist defenders of abortion have taken two main lines of argument.

The first, articulated best by Mary Anne Warren, argues that in abortion decisions the woman's right to bodily autonomy must always prevail over any rights which may be claimed on behalf of the foetus.[2] This is because the only beings with full moral standing are persons. Not only are foetuses not persons,

---

[1] I am grateful to the editorial panel and to anonymous referees for their comments on earlier versions of this article. Earlier versions were also read to the Philosophy Department at Monash University, the Philosophy Society at Princeton University, and a seminar on 'Legal and Conceptual Aspects of Abortion' at the University of New South Wales. I would like to thank participants in those discussions for their comments. I would also like to thank the following people for their helpful discussions and/or comments: John Bigelow, John Burgess, Genevieve Lloyd, Michaelis Michael, Robert Pargetter, Peter Singer, Michael Smith, C.L. Ten.

[2] My argument in this part of the article refers to Mary Anne Warren's paper 'On the Moral and Legal Status of Abortion' in R. Wasserstrom (ed.) *Today's Moral Problems* (London: Macmillan, 1975). In a very recent paper, to which I refer in more detail later, Warren's characterisation of the foetus is markedly different although her basic position on a woman's right to bodily autonomy remains unaltered. See 'The Moral Significance of Birth', *Hypatia* 4 (1989) pp. 46-65. This paper is a modified version of an earlier paper with the same title which appeared in *Bioethics News*, Publication of the Centre for Human Bioethics, Monash University, vol.7, no. 2, January 1988.

they are not even personlike enough to warrant our regarding them as if they were persons. Indeed, Warren claims that an eight-month foetus is no more personlike than the average fish. On this view then, the 'right to life' of the foetus, to the extent that it has such a right, cannot possibly outweigh the right of a person to one of the fundamental rights of persons — the right to bodily autonomy. In fact, Warren claims that having an abortion is morally equivalent to cutting one's hair.

The second line of argument is best represented by Judith Jarvis Thomson and, following her, Christine Overall.[3] Their claim involves a sophisticated reinterpretation of the claim that even if a foetus does have a right to life, the woman's right to bodily autonomy overrides that right. By trying to show that even if the foetus is a being with moral standing it has no automatic right to occupancy of a woman's womb, their argument seeks to undermine the basic premise of the conservative position on abortion — namely the premise that if foetuses are persons, that is, beings with full moral rights, then abortion is necessarily wrong.

My aim in this article is to defend a feminist perspective on abortion by showing that questions of women's autonomy lie at the heart of the abortion issue. I shall argue, however, that the conflict-of-rights framework and rights-based models of bodily autonomy are liable seriously to misrepresent both the nature of abortion decisions and the reasons why the availability of abortion is essential to women's autonomy. My dissatisfaction with this kind of approach centres on four related concerns. Firstly, a conflict-of-rights approach fails adequately to address the issue of responsibility in pregnancy and abortion. Hence it mischaracterises both the nature of the moral relationship between woman and foetus and the kind of autonomy that is exercised in pregnancy and abortion. Secondly, it tends to oversimplify our conception of the status of the foetus. Thirdly, it leads to a misconstrual of the notion of bodily autonomy because it is inattentive to the kind of reflective bodily perspective that arises from a phenomenological account of pregnant embodiment. Finally, defending abortion solely on the grounds of women's right to bodily autonomy logically requires that the right to abortion cannot entail a right to secure the death of the foetus but only a right to foetal evacuation.

I shall argue that a strong feminist case for abortion needs to construe a woman's right to obtain an abortion as the right of an autonomous moral agent to be able to make a decision about whether she wishes to take responsibility for the future well-being of a being dependent upon her. In choosing an abortion in other words, a woman is not merely choosing not to allow the foetus occupancy of her uterus. Nor is she merely choosing not to undertake responsibility for a particular future child. Rather, as Steven Ross has pointed out, she is choosing that there be *no being at all* in relation to whom she is in a situation of such responsibility.[4] To require that a woman has no right to secure the death of the

---

3   Judith Jarvis Thomson 'A Defense of Abortion', *Philosophy and Public Affairs*, 1 (1971) pp. 47-66; Christine Overall, *Ethics and Human Reproduction* (Boston: Allen & Unwin, 1987) chs. 3, 4.

4   Steven Ross, 'Abortion and the Death of the Foetus', *Philosophy and Public Affairs* 11 (1982) pp. 232-245.

foetus, at least in the early stages of pregnancy, thus violates her autonomy.

Now against this claim it could be argued that here the woman is not only making decisions about her own life but about that of another. What entitles her to make such a decision? The next three sections of the article attempt to answer this question. In the second section I make some suggestions as to how we should understand the notions of responsibility and autonomy in pregnancy, while the third section assesses the moral status of the foetus both from the point of view of its intrinsic moral properties and from the point of view of its relationship with the woman in whose body it develops. Building on the previous two sections, the final section draws on a phenomenological account of pregnancy in order to explain the connection between autonomy, bodily autonomy and pregnant embodiment. My criticisms of the rights-based accounts of bodily autonomy emerge from this discussion.

II. Responsibility and Autonomy

Appeals to responsibility in the context of the abortion debate usually trade on the asymmetry between the situation of men and women with regard to pregnancy. The asymmetry is that while it is always possible for men to evade or even remain blissfully unaware of the consequences of their actions where those actions result in pregnancy, the same is not true for women. Further it is women alone who are physically able to sustain the foetus. Thus women come to be held 'responsible' for what was after all a joint action. Given this context it is hardly surprising that feminist defences of abortion often attempt to shift discussions of the abortion issue away from the question of responsibility. Thorny as it may be however, one of my central claims is that the issue of responsibility is crucial for an understanding of women's moral autonomy with respect to pregnancy and abortion. In this section I attempt to outline an adequate feminist approach to the question of responsibility in pregnancy and abortion.

A number of different aspects of responsibility are often conflated in the abortion debate. To disentangle these I want firstly to distinguish *causal responsibility* from *moral responsibility*. By causal responsibility I mean simply responsibility for the direct causal consequences of one's actions in cases where those consequences can be said to be reasonably foreseeable and where a person's actions were freely chosen. In this sense a woman can be said to be responsible for the existence of the foetus in much the same way as she can be said to be responsible for getting drunk, in that it is her actions, in this case along with those of another, which have brought about this outcome.[5] Although

---

[5] I discuss the question of men's responsibility below. Given this account of causal responsibility, a woman is, of course, not causally responsible in the case of rape. In cases where a woman cannot and cannot reasonably be expected to foresee the consequences of her actions (e.g. if she is a minor or mentally disabled), or if her actions were performed under duress (the distinction between rape and consent is not as hard and fast as many would think), or if she cannot be said to be acting autonomously (e.g. in a case of drug addiction or alcoholism or some other dependency), I would argue that, although a woman may have some causal responsibility for the outcome of her actions, she cannot be considered to be morally responsible for this outcome.

conservatives do not usually make an explicit distinction between causal and moral responsibility, the conservative claim seems to be that in the case of pregnancy, because the outcome here is to have brought into existence a being with full moral standing, then a woman's *causal responsibility* necessarily entails a moral responsibility towards maintaining the existence of the foetus.[6]

Feminists and liberals have responded to this claim in a number of ways. The approach of Warren and Tooley, for example, is to attempt to shift the focus of the abortion debate away from questions of moral responsibility and towards a consideration of the actual present status of the foetus with respect to personhood. Their argument is that because foetuses are not persons and therefore do not have rights, abortion is morally permissible.[7] A second approach aims to show that one does not necessarily have automatic moral responsibility to maintain the existence of a being dependent upon oneself — even if that being does have full moral standing and hence a right to life. This is Thomson's approach in the examples of the violinist and Henry Fonda.[8] As Warren and Feinberg have shown, however, this strategy fails because the examples chosen are disanalogous to the case of the foetus in one relevant respect, namely with respect to causal responsibility.[9] The strategy thus begs the question. Yet another tactic is to claim that the attribution of causal responsibility is a lot less straightforward than it might appear and thus to argue that causal responsibility for the existence of a being does not necessarily mean that one is required to assume moral responsibility for maintaining its existence. For to what extent is a person still morally responsible for the consequences of an action if she has taken reasonable precautions against those consequences occurring? Thomson's example of the house-owner covering her windows in wire mesh to prevent the entry of 'people-seeds' seeks to undermine in this way any necessary connection between causal and moral responsibility.[10]

While these responses have been partially successful in exposing some of the assumptions at work behind the seeming self-evidence of the conservative argument, they nevertheless fail adequately to come to terms with the question of moral responsibility in pregnancy because they concede too much at the outset to the conservative notion of moral responsibility. This is particularly true of the

---

[6] Somewhat surprisingly, some feminists have argued for a similar view. See Hilde and James Lindemann Nelson, 'Cutting Motherhood in Two: Some Suspicions Concerning Surrogacy', *Hypatia* 4 (1989) pp. 85-94.

[7] Warren, 'On the Moral and Legal Status of Abortion', *op. cit.*; Michael Tooley, 'Abortion and Infanticide', *Philosophy and Public Affairs* 2 (1972) pp. 37-65.

[8] The violinist example seeks to show that a person has no moral obligation to sustain the life of a famous violinist who has been attached to her without her consent, and whose survival is dependent on being connected to her circulatory system for nine months. The Henry Fonda example involves the case of a person who is dying but would be revived by the touch of Henry Fonda's hand on her brow. The example seeks to show that a person does not necessarily have a right to whatever is required to ensure her survival. See Thomson, 'A Defense of Abortion', *op.cit.* I discuss the problem with such examples in the final section of this article.

[9] Warren, 'On the Moral and Legal Status of Abortion', *op.cit.*; Joel Feinberg, 'Abortion', in Tom Regan (ed.), *Matters of Life and Death* (Random House, 1980).

[10] In this example 'people-seeds' are seeds which blow in through house windows like dust, take root in carpets, and then grow into people who demand food and shelter!

last approach which forces Thomson, after a series of increasingly bizarre examples, to attempt to dissolve the question of responsibility by an appeal to decency.[11] What needs to be pointed out is that the conservative account of moral responsibility is premised on a set of assumptions which are fundamentally oppressive to women. For it is significant that in this whole debate about responsibility there seem to be only two possible ways for women to get pregnant. Either they are raped, in which case they have no causal responsibility for the existence of the foetus — although according to some conservatives they nevertheless have a moral responsibility towards it. Or else they are not raped, in which case they are held to be fully responsible, in both a causal and moral sense. In neither case however is men's moral responsibility ever seriously discussed, despite their obvious causal involvement in the pregnancy. The consequence of this blindness is that moral responsibility in pregnancy gets construed extremely narrowly, as just responsibility towards the foetus, and in a way that seems to commit women to maternity.

The challenge then seems to be to envision a notion of moral responsibility in pregnancy that acknowledges the moral complexities of the situation, and of the decision facing a woman who is weighing up the choices of abortion or maternity, but that does not imply that the only possible morally responsible course of action is to choose maternity. My starting point here is to accept, without argument at this stage, both that the foetus does have some moral significance and that this is in part why causal responsibility does entail some kind of moral responsibility. Having conceded that much to the conservatives I want to disentangle two aspects of moral responsibility which are confused in conservative arguments.

The first aspect, which I call *decision responsibility*, emerges as a strong theme in Carol Gilligan's interviews with women making the abortion decision.[12] Gilligan's women reveal that in their thinking about abortion, acceptance of causal responsibility means assuming a moral responsibility to make a decision or a series of decisions about your future relationship with the being whose existence you have directly brought about. The decision process is focused on questions such as whether you are in a position adequately to care for it, both now when it is in the foetal stage and, more importantly, when it is an independent being; how and whether it can be integrated into your life and the lives of others, for example other children, whose lives will also be significantly affected by your decision; whether you feel yourself able, or prepared, to provide

---

11   I have in mind here Thomson's discussion of the woman who at seven months requests an abortion in order to avoid having to postpone an overseas trip. Thomson realises that her argument does not allow her to claim that such a request would be immoral, so she resorts to the claim that it would be indecent. This issue aside, Thomson's example is somewhat offensive in its presentation of women's moral attitude towards abortion. Those women seeking abortions at this stage of pregnancy are usually those whose health is in some way gravely threatened by continuation of the pregnancy, or those who, due to drug addiction, mental disability or some other such reason, cannot be said ever to have made a moral decision with regard to their pregnancies.

12   Carol Gilligan, *In A Different Voice* (Cambridge, MA: Harvard University Press, 1982). It should be noted here that the kinds of moral reflection in which these women engage is in part made possible by the fact that these women do have reproductive choice.

the physical and emotional care and nurture needed in order for both foetus and child to flourish. What emerges from these discussions of responsibility is that the assumption of moral responsibility in pregnancy cannot be construed just in terms of responsibility towards the foetus but has a wider focus — on the self, on relations with significant others, on a person's other commitments and projects. When responsibility is construed in such a way it is clear that exercising moral responsibility in no way entails a commitment to maternity and that the choice of abortion is in many cases the morally responsible decision.

The second aspect of moral responsibility in pregnancy, which I call *parental responsibility*, is the one which a person assumes when a commitment has been made to maternity.[13] What this kind of assumption of responsibility involves is a responsibility not just to maintaining the existence of the foetus, nor even just a commitment to providing the care and nurture needed for it to flourish, but a commitment to bringing into existence a future child. Often, though not necessarily, it also involves a commitment to long-term care and nurture of that future child. My claim is that the decision to abort is a decision, for whatever reason, that one is not prepared to bring such a child into existence.

It should be pointed out here that with respect to all aspects of responsibility the situation of men and women — in pregnancy at least — is asymmetrical. The asymmetry is that while men and women are equally responsible for pregnancy in the causal sense, causal responsibility and decision responsibility are in effect completely separable for men, but inseparable for women. This is because a woman's bodily connection with the foetus makes causal responsibility and hence decision responsibility inescapable for her.[14] On the other hand men's bodily alienation from the consequences of their actions and from the physical, psychic and emotional experience of pregnancy means that they may be in a position where they are either unaware of their causal responsibility for the existence of the foetus or *choose* not to acknowledge their causal responsibility or assume decision responsibility.

A sensitivity to this difference illuminates two important points. Firstly, if causal and decision responsibility are inseparable for women, then pregnancy cannot be thought of simply as a merely 'natural' event which just *happens* to women and in relation to which they are passive. Although pregnancy certainly involves biological processes which are beyond the woman's control, these processes are always mediated by the cultural meanings of pregnancy, by the woman's personal and social context, and by the way she constitutes herself in response to these factors through the decisions she makes. In other words,

---

13 As I have indicated, decision responsibility is a process, not a single decision. Thus a woman may change her mind a number of times before finally assuming parental responsibility. She may also change her mind after having assumed it. For reasons which I explain below I think there is a significant *moral* difference between such a change of mind in the first trimester or early in the second trimester and a change of mind during the latter half of pregnancy — except of course where such a change is made for medical reasons or because of foetal deformity discoverable only by amniocentesis during the second trimester. It does not follow from this however that women should be *legally* prevented from obtaining abortions for other reasons later in pregnancy. I discuss the distinction between moral and legal responsibility below.

14 I discuss the nature of this bodily connection in detail in section IV below.

pregnancy is never simply a biological process, it is always an active process of shaping for oneself a bodily and a moral perspective.[15] For this reason, the moral issues associated with pregnancy and abortion cannot be viewed in abstraction from the first-person perspective of the woman concerned.[16]

Secondly, because of the particularity of the woman's situation in pregnancy, in cases of conflict over abortion ultimately it should be up to the woman to decide whether or not she will choose abortion.[17] To say this does not imply, however, that in situations where men are aware of and do acknowledge causal responsibility, they should have no say in an abortion decision. In such circumstances, because the decision made will obviously affect their autonomy, they should also be party to, and involved in, both decision responsibility and, where appropriate, parental responsibility. Indeed after birth they may assume most, or even all, parental responsibility. Nevertheless prior to birth the impact upon their autonomy of any decision is very different from its impact on the autonomy of the woman. This is why in cases of conflict the woman's decision should prevail.

Two objections are likely to be raised at this point. The first is that a woman may also choose to relinquish moral responsibility, for example to others through adoption. Further it is often argued that abortion is just a relinquishing of moral responsibility for the foetus. From the preceding discussion it should be clear that this objection conflates the two senses of moral responsibility distinguished above. Deciding against assuming parental responsibility does not mean that one has relinquished moral responsibility, not even for the foetus. For no matter what a woman decides — maternity, abortion, adoption — she is still responsible to herself, to others, to the child if there is one, for the decision she has made. Further, as I have already pointed out, the decision to abort is often the most morally responsible course of action.

The second objection is that I have placed a great deal of moral weight on a decision process which in some cases just never occurs. For some women's lives are so chaotic and so little under their control that they cannot be said to be making any autonomous decisions about their own welfare, let alone about the welfare of any foetus that may be developing inside their body. My response to this objection, as I have already indicated, is to say that I would not attribute moral responsibility to a woman in such a situation. However given the difficulty of actually deciding, in any given case, whether or not a woman does have any moral responsibility for a pregnancy, what the objection forces us to recognise is that a distinction needs to be made between our moral assessment of a situation and the matter of legal sanctions. Although I have argued that the decision to continue with a pregnancy entails some kind of parental responsibility, this is

---

15   I develop this point in more detail in section IV below.
16   I would like to thank one of the Journal's anonymous referees for helping me clarify this point.
17   I have in mind here recent cases in the UK and Australia where men have attempted to obtain court orders, on the grounds of paternal right, to prevent women from obtaining an abortion. My analysis of the asymmetry in the positions of men and women with respect to responsibility in pregnancy should make it clear why feminists have been so outraged by the men's presumption in these cases that they should be able to overrule the decisions of the women concerned.

quite different from claiming that a woman should be legally liable for the foetus' welfare. Arguments to this effect must be vigorously resisted for they wrongly presume that foetuses are the moral and legal equivalents of women. In fact, as Mary Anne Warren has argued, 'There is room for only one person with full and equal [legal] rights inside a single human skin'.[18]

While this analysis of responsibility still leaves unanswered questions about the intrinsic moral status of the foetus, it does tend to suggest that, at least in part, its moral status is dependent on the relational properties it has with others and that the abortion issue cannot adequately be broached if we focus on intrinsic properties alone.[19] This relational aspect of the foetus' moral standing is best captured through the notion of moral guardianship. I want to suggest that although a foetus cannot be a bearer of full moral rights because, as I shall argue in the next section, it lacks the requisite intrinsic properties (namely personhood), nevertheless in a context in which some one or more members of the moral community have decided to take parental responsibility for its future well-being, it has moral significance by virtue of its relations with her or them. We might say that in such a case it has *de facto* significance through her or them, until such a point when it can be considered a full moral being in its own right. This significance does not guarantee the foetus a 'right to life' which overrides all other possible competing claims, but rather provides some grounds for the foetus' claims to nurture and care, that is, guardianship, from the woman who bears it and protection from harm from others.

In this context it should be noted that once again the situation of men and women with regard to moral guardianship is inescapably asymmetrical in pregnancy. A man, no matter how well-intentioned, cannot act as the primary guardian of an *in utero* foetus. The reason for this asymmetry is not hard to discern, namely the physical inseparability of the foetus from the woman, but its moral implications are often overlooked. The main implications are firstly that, as I argued earlier, in cases of conflict it should be the woman who has the right to decide the fate of the foetus. Secondly, this asymmetry makes it clear that, as Warren has argued, the event of birth is morally significant.[20] Its significance lies in the fact that at birth the infant becomes a member of the human moral community in its own right because its relationship with its mother and other human beings changes significantly. Not only is its body now separate from that of its mother, but it no longer needs to stand in a relation of moral and physical dependence on her in particular. Any responsible human adult will now be able to provide it with the care, nurture and moral protection required for it to flourish.

Having assessed the relational moral status of the foetus I want now to justify my earlier claim that causal responsibility for the existence of the foetus entails decision responsibility because the foetus is a morally significant being. A useful starting point for this discussion is Warren's account of foetal status.

---

[18]   My insert. Warren, 'The Moral Significance of Birth', *op. cit.*, p. 63.
[19]   Warren also criticises what she calls 'the intrinsic-properties assumption' on the grounds that it cannot account for the moral significance of birth. *Ibid*, pp. 47-56.
[20]   Warren, *ibid*, p.56.

III. Foetal Status and Potentiality

If, following Warren, we distinguish between 'human beings' and 'persons' and argue that only persons can be members of the moral community, then it seems clear that the foetus is not a bearer of moral rights in the same sense that a person is and so does not have the same 'right to life' as a person.[21] Nevertheless, as Warren herself argues with respect to infants, it does not follow from the fact that, because anyone who is a person is entitled to strong moral protections, that it is wrong to extend moral protections to beings that are not persons.[22] The more personlike the being, the more it should be treated as a person. The question arises therefore of how far advanced since conception a human being needs to be before it begins to have a right to life by virtue of being like a person, that is, at what stage should we start treating a foetus as if it were a person? On this point Warren in her earlier paper claims that the foetus of seven or eight months is no more personlike, or even less personlike, than the average fish and thus should not be treated as a person. For although, like the fish, the late term foetus is sentient, sentience is not sufficient for personhood. *Contra* Thomson, she thus concludes that 'whether or not it would be indecent (whatever that means) for a woman in her seventh month to obtain an abortion just to avoid having to postpone a trip to Europe, it would not, in itself, be immoral, and therefore it ought to be permitted'.[23]

Warren's comparison between foetuses and fish occurs in the context of a discussion of the nature of personhood. The intention of the comparison is to show that, while the foetus is indeed a member of the human species, as far as personhood and hence claims to rights are concerned the foetus is morally on a par with a fish. With respect to driving home the distinction between human beings and persons I do not dispute the effectiveness of Warren's comparison. However I want to suggest that the metaphor is problematic for two reasons. Firstly, it invites us to ignore the fact that, contingent though it may be,

---

[21] Warren, 'On the Moral and Legal Status of Abortion', *op.cit.* Warren supports this distinction by outlining five criteria for personhood, specifying that a person need not satisfy all these criteria but that a being which satisfied none of them could not be considered a person. The five criteria are:
1. Consciousness (of objects and events external and/or internal to the being), and in particular the capacity to feel pain;
2. Reasoning (the *developed* capacity to solve new and relatively complex problems);
3. Self-motivated activity (activity which is relatively independent of either genetic or direct external control);
4. The capacity to communicate, by whatever means, messages of an indefinite variety of types, that is, not just with an indefinite number of possible contents, but on indefinitely many possible topics;
5. The presence of self-concepts, and self-awareness, either individual or racial, or both.

[22] Warren, ' The Moral Significance of Birth', *op.cit.* I follow Warren here in using the term 'person' because I think that in the context of abortion the distinction between 'human beings' and 'persons' is an important distinction to maintain. However I am not happy with the legalistic and individualist connotations of the term which tend to downplay the intersubjective processes of development by means of which infants become self-conscious subjects.

[23] Warren, 'On the Moral and Legal Status of Abortion, *op. cit.,* p. 133.

personhood is constituted by a complex of properties which supervene on a specific physical constitution.[24] Yet despite its contingency, or perhaps because of it, I believe that this fact is morally significant. Secondly, although the foetus/fish metaphor should not be read as providing a model of the relationship between a woman and a foetus, it has the serious, if unintended, effect of downplaying the moral significance and particularly of this relationship. In particular, it has the effect of de-emphasising both the woman's role as moral guardian and her parental responsibility for the present and future well-being of the foetus. The force of the feminist defence of abortion must lie in its highlighting of the moral particularity of the relationship between a woman and a foetus.

On the question of foetal status and potentiality my claim is that foetuses are morally significant beings by virtue of the fact that they are potential persons. This makes them morally different in kind from fish. However, I think it is plausible to suggest that the moral value of the foetus' potential personhood is not static, but changes during the course of a normal pregnancy. This is because potential for personhood is not the only thing that bestows moral status on the being with that potentiality. Rather, the moral value of a being's potential personhood is related to the physical or biological basis of the potentiality, in particular it is grounded in the degree of complexity and development of this physical basis. Thus the more physically complex and developed the being is, the more value we attribute to its potential for personhood. There are two ways in which this claim could be developed. One way would accept an on/off view of potentiality and argue that potential for personhood remains constant although its moral significance changes. On this view conceptus and late term foetus both have the same potentiality but the moral value of those beings is different because the physical basis of the potentiality is different. In the one case we have a clump of undifferentiated cells, in the other a highly complex organism. Thus in the one case we have a being very far from being able to actualise its potentialities because it lacks the very physical basis to do so, in the other we have a being fairly close to being able to actualise its potentialities to the extent that the physical basis of those potentialities is highly developed.[25] Another way would be to question the on/off view of potentiality and to argue that potential for personhood itself changes as the foetus develops physically.[26]

For my purposes here nothing hinges on the differences between these positions. But what is appealing about the general suggestion is that it enables us to agree with Warren's criteria of personhood while nevertheless resisting the counter intuitive implications of these criteria, *viz.*, that a being has no intrinsic

---

[24] In stressing the connection between the development of subjectivity and physical development I am not denying the significance of the social relationships in the context of which these developments must occur.

[25] This argument is a simplified version of an argument of John Bigelow and Robert Pargetter. See 'Morality, Potential Persons and Abortion', *American Philosophical Quarterly* 25 (1988) pp. 173-181.

[26] An argument for this view is presented by Michaelis Michael in 'The Moral Significance of Potential for Personhood' (unpublished paper, Monash University, 1986). His view is that the potential for personhood of a being can be expressed as a function, from situations the being is (normally) in, to the probabilities of its giving rise to a person from those situations. We have greater potential when we have one function dominating another.

moral significance unless it is a person and that there is no important moral difference between a conceptus and a late term foetus. For now it can be argued that the intrinsic moral status of the foetus changes in direct relation to its changing physical basis. Thus, at least in terms of its intrinsic properties, an early stage foetus does not have great value. With respect to a highly developed foetus, although it is not a being with full moral rights, its gradually increasing moral significance warrants our treating it, in most circumstances at least, as if it were such a being.

Combining this view with the guardianship view outlined earlier we get the idea that the moral position of the foetus changes over the course of pregnancy. At the early stages its moral standing is defined in relational terms, because it is a being with moral significance for the woman in whose body it develops and who acts as its moral guardian. As the foetus develops physically however its intrinsic moral significance increases. Its moral standing is less and less dependent on its relational properties with the woman in whose body it develops and more and more tied to its own intrinsic value. This does not mean, however, that the foetus is ever the moral equivalent of the woman. Hence in cases where the foetus' continued existence severely threatens the woman's physical or mental survival, her interests should always prevail up until the moment of birth. It does however suggest that late term abortion is morally different from early abortion and that they cannot be justified on the same grounds.

On the question of guardianship, I suggested above that the rationale behind Warren's defence of abortion (namely that the foetus is not a person), particularly in the context of the foetus/fish comparison, has the effect of downplaying the moral significance of the woman's parental responsibility for the present and future well-being of the foetus. This effect is reinforced by Warren's claim, which she justifies on the grounds of a woman's right to bodily autonomy, that a decision to abort is morally permissible up until the moment of birth. For now it looks as though the foetus is a potential threat to the woman's bodily autonomy up until the moment of birth, rather than a being in relation to whom the woman has a unique bodily and moral connection. In the next section I shall argue that this view is based on a flawed conception of bodily autonomy. Here I simply want to point out that in pregnancy the assumption of parental responsibility necessarily involves a certain commitment of one's body. In other words, the decision to continue a pregnancy (and presumably by seven months some prior decision has been made) is a decision to assume responsibility (even if only for nine months) for the well-being of the foetus and this entails providing bodily nurture for it, perhaps even at some bodily risk to yourself. Now obviously there are limits to this risk. I am not suggesting that women have responsibility to the foetus whatever the risk. As I have already indicated, I am also not suggesting that parties other than the woman, for example the medical establishment, or the state-legal apparatus, have a right to determine the limits of that risk. Like many other feminists, including Warren, I am alarmed by the recent movements advocating both so-called 'foetal rights' and the introduction of charges of 'foetal abuse' against women who do not do what is required to nurture the foetus in the uterus. Further the whole question of what is 'required' for adequate nurture is open to much interpretation against women's autonomy as persons. Nevertheless, I think that my accounts of potentiality, guardianship and responsibility explain why there is a genuine moral requirement upon a woman to protect and nurture a foetus once she has assumed parental responsibility for its future well-being, without that requirement involving any infringement of her autonomy. In this context it should be noted that Warren's downplaying of the question of responsibility also fails to stress men's obligations with respect to a pregnancy.

IV. Pregnant Embodiment and Bodily Autonomy

I have argued so far that, at least in the early stages of its development, the moral standing of a foetus is dependent upon its relationship with the woman who bears it and who acts as its moral guardian. In terms of its own intrinsic properties its moral standing is not particularly significant. This is a necessary condition for the permissibility of abortion, but it is not sufficient. For it fails to explain why the availability of abortion is necessary for the moral autonomy of women and hence why a restriction on its accessibility violates their autonomy. In this section I attempt to explain and justify this claim. From my discussion it will also become clear why, in order to secure women's autonomy, abortion must be understood as foetal death rather than foetal evacuation.

What has emerged so far is that in order to understand the kind of autonomy that is exercised by women in pregnancy and abortion we must be attentive to the moral particularity of pregnancy. As we have seen there are a number of different factors which make pregnancy morally unique. To begin with, pregnancy is not simply a biological event with respect to which women are passive. Rather it is an active process and a social process which places women in a situation of moral responsibility — which I earlier called decision responsibility. This responsibility is due in part to the foetus' potential moral significance, but it is also due to the fact that the decision to commit or not to commit oneself to the existence of such a future person has far-reaching implications for the woman's own life as well as, possibly, for the lives of others — for example, the 'father' of the possible future child, other children, relatives, friends and so on. But pregnancy is also morally unique because the physical connection between the woman and the foetus, and the physical processes which occur during pregnancy, give rise to a unique bodily perspective.

In what follows I shall draw on a phenomenological account of pregnant embodiment in order to give an account of the kind of reflective bodily perspective that emerges out of the experience of pregnancy. I shall also suggest that the experience of moral responsibility in pregnancy, which I have detailed above, is mediated by this reflective bodily perspective, which both structures and points to the moral particularity of the relationship between woman and foetus —especially to the fact that this relationship and the responsibilities it entails cannot be conceived of as extrinsic to the woman's subjectivity. I want to make it clear that this phenomenological description is not a description of the subjective feelings of individual women, but is rather a normative and reflective apprehension of the way in which conscious experience is structured by our (bodily) situations, perspectives and modes of perception. The phenomenological experience I describe is therefore not meant to be an empirical description of the way in which all women experience or feel about their pregnancies, since women's individual bodily perspectives, feelings and experiences depend upon a wide range of factors, including the cultural, social and historical context in which they live their lives.[27]

My suggestion is that although in some ways (for example, biologically) it makes sense to speak of the foetus as a separate being from the woman, in other ways (for example in terms of talking of a conflict of rights), it makes no sense at all — especially in the early stages of pregnancy.[28] Phenomenologically, the experience of pregnancy, particularly in the early stages, is unique in the sense that it defies a sharp opposition between self and other, between the inside and the outside of the body. From the perspective of the woman, there *is* no clear-cut boundary between herself and the foetus, between her body boundaries and the body boundaries of the foetus. The foetus, to the extent that it is experienced as part of the woman's body, is also experienced as part of her self, but as a part that is also other than herself. On the one hand it is another being, but it is another being growing inside her body, a being whose separateness is not fully realised as such by her. This is the case even with an unwanted pregnancy. The uniqueness and intimacy of this kind of relationship, one where the distinction between self and other is blurred, suggests that the welfare of the foetus, at least early on, is not easily separable from that of the woman. The foetus is not simply an entity extrinsic to her which happens to be developing inside her body and which she desires either to remove or to allow to develop. It is a being, both inseparable and yet separate from her, both part of and yet soon to be independent from her, whose existence calls into question her own present and future identity.

The changing phenomenology of pregnancy also concurs with the account I have given of foetal status. For it seems to me that one of the main reasons for the experience I have described is that in early pregnancy, although the woman's body is undergoing massive changes, the foetus itself is not very physically developed. The foetus' separateness is thus neither physically well established nor is it felt as such by the woman. What happens as pregnancy continues is that, as the foetus develops physically, a triple process occurs. Firstly, from the perspective of the woman, the foetus becomes more and more physically differentiated from her as her own body boundaries alter. Secondly, this gradual physical differentiation (which becomes very pronounced as soon as the foetus

---

[27] My account here builds on psychoanalytic insights into the mother-child relation, on some of the descriptions of pregnancy and maternity in the work of Julia Kristeva, on Iris Young's phenomenology of pregnant embodiment, and on my own *a posteriori* reconstructions. See Julia Kristeva, 'Motherhood According to Giovanni Bellini' in *Desire in Language* (Oxford: Blackwell, 1980) and 'Stabat Mater' in T. Moi (ed.), *The Kristeva Reader* (Oxford: Blackwell, 1986); Iris Marion Young, 'Pregnant Embodiment: Subjectivity and Alienation', *The Journal of Medicine and Philosophy* 9 (1984) pp. 45-62.

[28] The rights-based model has also been criticised on different but related grounds by other feminists. See Janet Farrell Smith, 'Rights-conflict, Pregnancy and Abortion' in Carol Gould (ed.), *Beyond Domination* (Totowa, NJ: Rowman & Allanheld, 1984) pp. 265-273.

starts moving around — perhaps explaining why 'quickening' used to be considered morally significant) is paralleled by and gives rise to a gradual psychic differentiation, in the experience of the woman, between herself and the foetus. In other words, as the foetus' body develops it seems to become less and less a part of the woman and of her body although, as psychoanalysis reminds us, the psychic experiences of unity and differentiation continue to resonate for both mother and child right through infancy and early childhood. Thirdly, physical and psychic differentiation are usually accompanied by an increasing emotional attachment of the woman to the foetus, an attachment which is based both in her physical connection with the foetus and in an anticipation of her future relationship with a separate being who is also intimately related to her.

From the reflective perspective of the woman the foetus thus has a double and ambivalent status. On the one hand, it is experienced as interior to her own subjectivity, and this sense of interiority is grounded in the bodily connection between the woman and the foetus. On the other hand, this experience of interiority and connection is interrupted by an awareness that, if the pregnancy continues, this being which is now a part of her will become a separate being for whose welfare she is morally responsible. But this awareness itself arises in part from the woman's bodily experiences — for example, from the changes to her body shape and from feelings of the strangeness of her body to her — which remind her of the other being which is growing within her. I think it is this double character of the foetus' bodily and moral relationship to the woman that explains both why questions of responsibility are central to the experience of pregnancy and why the right of determination over the fate of the foetus is essential for a woman's autonomy.[29]

I think this reflective perspective also explains why it is a mistake to construe bodily autonomy in pregnancy and abortion simply as a matter of preserving the integrity of one's body boundaries. It is this kind of understanding of bodily

---

[29] At this point I would like to respond to an objection which is often made against the view I have proposed here. It could be argued that the woman's experience of the foetus as part of herself and as interior to her subjectivity is simply mistaken. So why should any moral weight be given to this experience? How is it different, for example, from the experience of a slave-owner who regards his/her slaves as a part of him/herself and thinks that because of this he/she has a right to determine their fate? My response to this suggestion is that these cases are completely disanalogous, and for two reasons. Firstly, I have argued that a necessary condition for the permissibility of abortion is that the foetus, especially in the early stages of pregnancy, has little moral value in and of itself, although it may have a great deal of value for the woman in whose body it develops. This is not a merely arbitrary claim, like the claim of the slave-owner who may think that his/her slaves have little moral value in and of themselves. Rather it is justified by the fact that the foetus simply does not yet have the capacities which ground the moral worth of persons, and by the fact that the foetus' possible potential for personhood has little significance until those capacities are close to being actualised.

But, secondly, this objection ignores what I have been insisting on throughout this article, namely that the relationship of the woman to the foetus is morally unique. It is not a relationship of domination and subordination and inhuman ownership, as in the case of the slave-owner. Rather, it is a relationship in which one human being grows and develops inside the body of another, and in which the moral significance of the foetus is in part bound up with its significance for the woman. The moral particularity of this situation, in other words, is grounded in the nature of the bodily connection between woman and foetus. The woman's sense of the foetus as a part of herself is thus not arbitrary. It arises, as I have

autonomy which seems to inform the views of Thomson and Warren, at least in her early paper, who construe the right to bodily integrity along the lines of a property-right. The idea seems to be that a woman has a right to preserve the integrity of her body boundaries, and to control what happens in and to her body, in the same way as she has a right to dispose of her property as she sees fit, and that the denial to women of access to abortion might be said to be akin to a system of coverture. I think this idea is quite explicit in such feminist slogans as 'Keep *your* filthy laws off *my* body' and in some of Thomson's metaphors — for example, the metaphor of the body as a house. Now it seems to me that underlying this view of the body is the mistaken idea that I am the owner of my body and my body parts and that, as their owner, I can dispose of them, use them, or contract them out for use as I see fit. This view of the body often underlies defences of surrogacy but I think it is also evident in Thomson's assumptions about pregnancy. In her argument pregnancy emerges as a kind of contract between the woman and the foetus such that she contracts with it for it to use her body for the required period until it is able to survive without her. Thus in Thomson's violinist example the idea seems to be that the unwanted foetus is attempting to use a woman's body without her having contracted with it to do so and it is this which makes abortion permissible. A similar kind of presumption seems to be operating in Warren's view that the foetus represents a potential threat to the woman's bodily autonomy up to the moment of birth.

For the remainder of this article I shall argue that this conception of bodily autonomy, and the rights-based model which provides the framework for it, are seriously flawed. My first set of objections to this way of defending abortion is that it misrepresents both the nature of pregnancy and the woman-foetus relationship. As a result, it is unable to come to terms with the question of moral responsibility in pregnancy. The second and connected objection is that it justifies the demand for abortion in terms of a right to an evacuated uterus, rather than a right to autonomy with respect to one's own life. This misrepresents the nature of the abortion decision. These two objections are explained in the next two subsections.

A. Bodily Autonomy, Subjectivity and Responsibility

It seems that underlying the property-contract model of bodily autonomy is a very inert view of pregnancy in which pregnancy is represented as a purely biological process with respect to which women are passive. It is as though, having agreed to the terms of the contract, the woman then simply allows her

---

[29] *continued* . . .

tried to show, from her own reflective bodily perspective and from the kind of moral reflection to which pregnancy gives rise.

Certainly it is possible to think up all kinds of examples in which the relationship between the woman and the foetus might have been different — as in Thomson's examples. But my point is that these examples cannot give us an adequate understanding of the moral complexities of the issues raised by pregnancy and abortion precisely because they overlook the context out of which these complexities arise, namely the bodily and moral connection between the woman and the foetus.

body to be used by the foetus. But this view of pregnancy blinds us to the fact that the relationship between the woman and the foetus is a special relationship of a very particular nature. The foetus is not a stranger contracting with the woman for use of her body but another, not yet separate, being growing within her body, a being implicated in her own sense of self and whose very existence places her in a situation of moral responsibility.

However, if we take seriously both the issue of responsibility in pregnancy and the kind of reflective bodily perspective that I have argued emerges from the process of pregnancy, then pregnancy seems to defy the making of a sharp distinction between a passive, unconscious, biological process and an active, conscious, rational process. To a large extent the biological processes occurring in a woman's body *are* beyond her control. Nevertheless, as I have already argued, these processes are always mediated by the cultural meanings of pregnancy, by the woman's personal and social context, and by the way she constitutes herself in response to these factors through the decisions she makes. Thus coming to terms with pregnancy and its implications, taking responsibility of whatever kind for the future of the foetus, are the activities of an autonomous moral agent. Bodily autonomy in pregnancy and abortion thus cannot be construed simply as the right to bodily integrity. Rather it is a question of being able to shape for oneself an integrated bodily perspective, a perspective by means of which a woman can respond to the bodily processes which she experiences in a way with which she identifies, and which is consistent with the decision she makes concerning her future moral relationship with the foetus.

To think that the question of autonomy in abortion is just a question about preserving the integrity of one's body boundaries, and to see the foetus merely as an occupant of the woman's uterus, is thus to divorce women's bodies from their subjectivities. Ironically it comes close to regarding women's bodies simply as foetal containers — the very charge which many feminists have levelled against the 'foetal rights' movement. If, however, we see our subjectivities as constituted through the constitution of our bodily perspectives so that, following Merleau-Ponty, we see the body as our point of view upon the world, then my body is no more my property than I myself am my own property.[30] Rather my body is my mode of being-in-the-world. Consequently changes to my body or to my perceptions of my body-image must affect my relation to the world. The experience of pregnant embodiment, that is, the gradual differentiation and development from within her own body of another being which is now a part of herself, thus affects a woman's mode of being-in-the-world both physically and morally and, as a consequence, re-shapes her sense of self. She is now no longer just herself but herself and another, but this other is not yet separate from herself. It is because of this psychic and bodily connectedness between the woman and the foetus that in pregnancy questions about the fate of the foetus cannot be separated out from the issue of a woman's right to self-determination.

---

[30]   I am drawing here on Maurice Merleau-Ponty's discussion of the body in *The Phenomenology of Perception* (1945), translated by Colin Smith (London: Routledge, 1962).

B. Evacuation and Abortion

If, as I have argued, the early stage foetus is both morally insignificant (in terms of its own intrinsic properties), and its identity and very existence are as yet indistinguishable from that of the woman, it becomes nonsensical to speak of a conflict of rights between them because we cannot talk about the needs and rights of the foetus in abstraction from those of the woman.[31] The idea of such a conflict only makes any sense later in pregnancy where the foetus is physically well developed and differentiated from the woman and where this physical basis now grounds a definite and significant moral value. Combining my earlier discussion of the moral insignificance of the early stage foetus with my claim that the early stage foetus is phenomenologically and psychically experienced by the woman as both part and not part of herself, thus grounds the moral permissibility of securing its death. At present the foetus is in itself a morally insignificant part of herself but it is a part of herself which, if the pregnancy continues, will become a separate, independent and significant being, for whose future existence she will be required to take parental responsibility and to whom she will become increasingly emotionally attached. What the abortion decision involves is a decision that this part of herself should not *become* a being in relation to whom such questions of parental responsibility and emotional attachment arise. In other words abortion is not a matter of wanting to kill *this particular being*, which is, after all, as yet indistinguishable from oneself. It is rather a matter of not wanting there to *be* a future child, so intimately related to oneself, for which one either has to take responsibility or give up to another.

Because property-contract models of bodily autonomy are inattentive to the phenomenological experience of pregnancy and ignore questions of moral responsibility they misrepresent the nature of this decision. For, if the demand for abortion is just the demand to control one's own body and use its parts as one sees fit, then abortion cannot involve the right to choose whether or not to bring a child into existence but only the right to evacuate a foetus from one's body. While Thomson and Warren explicitly acknowledge this as an implication of their account of bodily autonomy, they do not defend the position to which they are committed. In her discussion of abortion in *Ethics and Human Reproduction* Christine Overall does, however, attempt to defend this position even though she is explicitly critical of a property-contract view of women's bodies. My argument is that such a position is inconsistent with a concern for women's autonomy.[32] In what follows I shall develop this argument via a critical analysis of Overall's discussion.

Overall argues that abortion consists of two conceptually and morally distinct events which, though inseparable in current gynaecological practice may yet,

---

31 This does not, of course, mean that we cannot talk of what is physically harmful or beneficial to the development of the foetus.

32 Anne Donchin has expressed similar worries about the implications of Overall's position. See her review essay 'The Growing Feminist Debate Over the New Reproductive Technologies', *Hypatia* 4 (1989) pp. 136-149.

with the advancing state of technology, become separable. These are: (1) the evacuation of the foetus from the uterus, and (2) the destruction of the foetus. Overall's argument is that while (1) is morally permissible, (2) is not. In other words, if the foetus could be kept alive in some kind of incubator or if some form of foetal transplant and adoption were possible —that is, the evacuation of the foetus from one's woman's uterus and its implantation in the uterus of another — then such procedures would be morally required.

Overall's argument, which is very similar to a double-effect argument, involves a reconstrual of the alleged rights conflict in abortion. Where the original formulation is a conflict between (a) the foetuses' right to life, and (b) a woman's right to bodily autonomy, she reconstrues this, in terms of an absence of rights, as a conflict between (c) the pregnant woman (or anyone else, e.g. a physician) who has no right to kill the embryo/foetus, and (d) the embryo/foetus which has no right to occupancy of its mother's (or anyone else's) uterus. Overall's claim is that the right to bodily autonomy reconstrued as (d) does not entail (2). (d) involves a simple taking-over of Thomson's formulation without further argumentation. Overall's main argument in defence of (c) is an appeal to the foetus' potential personhood, but 'appeal' is all it is because Overall does not discuss the criteria for personhood, nor explain how we should understand the claim that foetuses are potential persons. In addition she simply assumes that foetuses at all stages of development have the same moral significance.[33]

Overall is aware that her position gives rise to many difficult questions: ought we to save all aborted foetuses?; should we try to adopt them out were that possible?; what if foetal adoption caused more suffering for women or for foetuses? She attempts to avoid some of these and to resolve the conflict between conflicting rights (c) and (d) by arguing that they apply to different periods of pregnancy. Hence right (d) may be regarded as overriding in early pregnancy (with abortion then resulting in the foreseeable but unintended death of the foetus), whereas right (c) may be regarded as overriding in late pregnancy.

---

[33] Overall offers three supposedly analogous cases which are supposed to back up this appeal and to show why the right to bodily autonomy, reconstrued as (d), does not entail a woman's right to demand (2), that is, the destruction of the foetus. The problem with these cases however is that Overall fails to make any moral discriminations between different stages of foetal development. The cases are as follows:
(A) If an aborted foetus lives we have no right to kill it, although we are not morally obliged to keep it alive. Here Overall seems to be appealing to the acts and omissions doctrine which in this context I would reject on compassionate grounds. If the foetus is likely to die and will presumably suffer more if simply allowed to die (which is pretty certain if we are talking about an abortion prior to twenty weeks), it seems morally preferable that we kill it.
(B) We have no right to kill premature babies in a case, for example, where the mother might have wanted an abortion but was prevented from obtaining one. But if there is no moral difference between a twenty six week premature baby and a twenty six week *in utero* foetus, it should be just as morally wrong to kill the foetus as the baby. Overall's argument here appeals to the claim that all foetuses, at whatever stage of development, are morally indistinguishable. I have already argued against this claim and have agreed that the killing of a late term foetus is morally different from killing an early foetus, although I have also indicated that I would not rule it out *a priori*, for example, in cases where it is unlikely it would ever acquire the complex physical basis required for personhood. I would agree though with Overall that were it possible to abort a late term foetus alive, in most cases

While I agree with Overall that, in most cases, it is morally indefensible to demand the death of a late term foetus, the problem with her argument is that she offers no reasons as to why this should be the case, nor does she offer an explanation as to why, if, as she thinks, there is no significant difference in moral standing between a conceptus and a late term foetus, the foreseeable consequence of the foetus' death should be any more allowable early in pregnancy than later on. As I have shown, however, there are a number of reasons why there is a morally significant difference between a conceptus and a late term foetus and it is this difference which makes foetal death in early abortions morally permissible. I conclude then that Overall's defence of abortion as foetal evacuation fails.

More importantly however, Overall's failure to make any significant moral discriminations between different stages of foetal development renders her 'solution' to the conflict between (c) and (d) arbitrary and far too contingent upon what is technologically feasible. For were it to become possible to evacuate an early stage foetus from the uterus of one woman and implant it into the uterus of another or to rear it in an incubator, Overall would be committed to the moral desirability of this procedure. Not only that, she would be committed to arguing that such a procedure, rather than abortion, is morally required. For the reasons outlined in this article, it seems to me disturbing that this outcome should seem to follow from a feminist defence of abortion. Apart from oversimplifying the complex issue of foetal status, this position ignores the fact that much more is at stake in the demand for abortion than the misconceived demand to dispose of or use one's own body parts as one sees fit. What is at issue is women's moral autonomy, an autonomy which, because of the specificity of women's embodiment, must include autonomy with respect to the fate of any foetus developing within her body. Because of the connection between the foetus, which is both part and not part of herself, and the woman's moral and bodily subjecthood, to allow the fate of the foetus to be settled by what is or is not technologically feasible once again removes from women what the availability of abortion helps make possible — the right to autonomous moral agency with respect to one's own life.

---

[33] *continued . . .*

where the foetus was likely to survive and become a healthy infant the mother would not have the right to kill it. Having said that I would nevertheless take issue with Overall's claim that there is no moral difference between a twenty six week premature baby and a twenty six week *in utero* foetus. Her claim assumes that birth has no moral significance. This is an assumption which I have already contested.

(C) At the other end of the process, Overall claims that neither foetus nor embryo is the property of the parents. Thus, she argues, just as parents involved in *in vitro* fertilization programmes should not have the right to demand the destruction of embryos, neither do women have the right to secure the death of the foetus. While I would agree with Overall that neither conceptus nor foetus is the property of its parents, I disagree that it is only on such grounds that we might regard it as their right to determine its fate. I don't want here to tackle the issue of the 'disposal' of *in vitro* fertilization embryos and/or foetal tissue. Suffice it to say that Overall's argument once again trades on the unargued claim that foetuses at all stages of development have intrinsic moral worth as 'potential' persons.

V. Conclusion: Metaphors, Experience and Moral Thinking

I shall conclude this discussion with some brief reflections on the methodological implications of the analysis I have given. A survey of the philosophical literature on abortion, including some of the feminist philosophical literature, shows that philosophical thinking on this topic has been dominated by bizarre metaphors and fantastic examples (Warren's fish, Tooley's kittens, Thomson's violinists, people-seeds, houses and so on) and has given rise to abstruse metaphysical speculations about the nature of personal identity (Parfit). These examples and speculations have undoubtedly served to question certain common unreflective prejudices and to highlight the philosophical ramifications and complexities of some of the questions raised by abortion. Unfortunately they have also contributed to the representation of pregnancy as a mere *event* which simply takes over women's lives and with respect to which women are passive. In addition, they have focused philosophical and moral reflection away from the contexts in which deliberations about abortion are usually made and away from the concerns and experiences which motivate those involved in the processes of deliberation. The result is that philosophical analyses of abortion often seem beside the point, if not completely irrelevant, to the lives of the countless women who daily not only have to make moral decisions about abortion but, more importantly, who often face serious risks to their lives in contexts where abortion is not a safe and readily accessible procedure. While I do not pretend to have addressed the social, religious, political and legal obstacles which give rise to this abhorrent situation, I do hope to have explained why the morality of abortion is not simply or even primarily about questions concerning personhood and foetal status but more fundamentally is about women's self-determination.

Macquarie University

Received September 1990
Revised July 1991

[6]

Prenatal Genetic Testing and Screening: Constructing Needs and Reinforcing Inequities

Abby Lippman*

This Article considers the influence and implications of the application of genetic technologies to definitions of disease and to the treatment of illness. The concept of "geneticization" is introduced to emphasize the dominant discourse in today's stories of health and disease and the social construction of biological phenomenon is described. The reassurance, choice and control supposedly provided by prenatal genetic testing and screening are critically examined, and their role in constructing the need for such technology is addressed. Using the stories told about prenatal diagnosis as a focus, the consequences of a genetic perspective for and on women and their health care needs are explored.

I. INTRODUCTION

During the past two decades, numerous techniques have been developed that allow geneticists to assess the physical status of the fetus during a woman's pregnancy. The variety of prenatal diagnostic techniques[1] and detectable/diagnosable fetal conditions continues to expand. These screening and testing procedures are already the most widespread application of genetic technology to humans.

This paper, part of an ongoing project, explores the genetic stories[2] told about health and disease today, the storytellers and the

---

* Associate Professor, Dep't of Epidemiology & Biostatistics, McGill University. Prenatal diagnosis, the focus of much of this paper, is troublesome for all women, users and critics alike. In no way do I intend my remarks about it to reflect on women who have considered or undergone testing; criticism of the technologies is not to be read as criticisms of them. Women considering childbearing today face agonizing issues I was fortunate enough not to have to confront, and I can only admire their resilience and strength.

[1] *See infra* notes 20-26 and accompanying text for a discussion of these techniques.

[2] In this Article, the word "stories" is not used to suggest that what is said is not true (this may or may not be the case). Rather it is used in a literary, not a legal, sense to capture the idea that how scientists present their observations and study results is no different from how novelists present *their* interpretations of the external world. "Raw" material is shaped and interpreted to convey a message by both groups, with their constructions reflecting the pre-

16 AMERICAN JOURNAL OF LAW & MEDICINE VOL. XVII NOS. 1 & 2 1991

cirumstances in which these stories are told. In this Article, I first discuss how disease categories and biomedical practices are constructed within their cultural context, and provide some technical information regarding prenatal diagnosis. I then examine the stories constructed about genetic testing and screening; the particular assumptions upon which they are grounded;[3] and the necessarily problematic nature of applications of these genetic technologies with respect to perceptions of pregnancy and the health care needs of women considering childbearing. I demonstrate how the approach implicit in the use of genetic technology is as much a cultural and social activity as it is scientific. Specifically, I examine why prenatal diagnosis is made available, discussing some of the rationales usually presented for its use, and explore how a "need" for prenatal diagnosis is currently constructed. I then consider how existing health, health care beliefs and North American social stratifications situate prenatal technologies and how these activities may themselves influence health and health care inequities.

II. HEALTH AND DISEASE AND THE STORIES TOLD ABOUT THEM

In today's western world, biomedical and political systems largely define health and disease, as well as normality and abnormality.[4] They also determine the individuals to whom each term will be applied. Western biomedicine does not just describe a pre-existing biological reality, but is grounded in particular social and cultural assumptions.[5]

---

vailing social/cultural context. Further, to the degree that the same story is repeated and becomes accepted and used, it will itself begin to shape this context.

[3] I attempt, in this way, to enter "an old text from a new critical direction." A. RICH, *When We Dead Awaken*, in ON LIES, SECRETS AND SILENCE 35 (1979). I consider how stories about prenatal diagnosis both reflect and affect the social process of geneticization, how they emerge from existing cultural values at the same time as they interactively influence this very culture, altering our values, redefining our reality. *See infra* notes 101-40 and accompanying text. Using the biomedical and social science literature, and switching analogies, I want to create a "femmage," a "sister concept" to the collage, wherein a composite describing these stories is created from multiple sources. *See* S. PRICE, PRIMITIVE ART IN CIVILIZED PLACES 4 (1989) (quoting Meyer & Shapiro, *Waste Not, Want Not: An Inquiry into What Women Saved and Assembled*, 4 HERESIES 66-69 (1978)).

[4] It should be emphasized that the priority given to matters of health is historically dependent and determined on a local level. These issues may not warrant political, economic or scientific attention in all places or at all times. A malady that is diagnosed and treated as a prevalent disease in one country may be diagnosed and treated completely differently in another country. *See generally* L. PAYER, MEDICINE & CULTURE (1988).

[5] *See* THE PROBLEM OF MEDICAL KNOWLEDGE: EXAMINING THE SOCIAL CONSTRUCTION OF MEDICINE (P. Wright & A. Treacher eds. 1982) [hereinafter THE PROBLEM OF MEDICAL KNOWLEDGE]; M. LOCK & D. GORDON, *Relationship Between Society, Culture, and Biomedicine: Introduction to the Essays*, in BIOMEDICINE EXAMINED 11, 11-18 (M. Lock & D. Gordon eds. 1988); Taussig, *Reification and the Consciousness of the Patient*, 14 SOC. SCI. & MED. 3, 3 (through reification, "disease is recruited into serving the ideological needs of the social order"); Young, *The Anthropologies of Illness and Sickness*, 2 ANN. REV. ANTHROPOLOGY 257 (1982) [hereinafter *The*

No strictly objective and value-free view of the biological world exists. Any attempt to explain or order it will be shaped by the historical and cultural setting within which it occurs.[6]

Although there is a biological reality to disease, biological processes take on particular forms in different human groups and in different periods of time.[7] Disorders and disabilities are not merely physiological or physical conditions with fixed contours. Rather, they are social products with variable shapes and distributions. Defining and studying these categories and the people assigned to them is necessarily subjective, reflecting how those with power at any particular historical time construct them as problems.

In studying the distribution of health and disease, any one of the factors influencing their occurrence (social and physical environments, economic conditions, heredity, personal behaviors, health services, etc.) may be chosen for attention and investment of resources. This choice and its subsequent expression in public policies and private practices reflect the assumptions, vested interests and ideologies of the investigators and those funding them.[8] Because "disease is socially mutable" and medical responses are "maleable,"[9] there is abundant raw material from which to create metaphors and stories describing health and disease. The same observations may be taken as evidence to construct very different hypotheses or stories.[10]

Today's stories about health and disease both in professional journals[11] and mass circulation magazines[12] are increasingly told in the lan-

---

Anthropologies of Illness and Sickness]; Young, *When Rational Men Fall Sick: An Inquiry into Some Assumptions Made by Medical Anthropologists*, 5 CULTURE MED. & PSYCHOLOGY 317 (1981) [hereinafter *When Rational Men Fall Sick*]; *see also* Young, *Rational Men and the Explanatory Model Approach*, 6 CULTURE, MED. & PSYCHOLOGY 57 (1982) [hereinafter *Rational Man and the Explanatory Model Approach*] (containing Young's replies to comments directed toward *When Rational Men Fall Sick, supra*).

[6] *See generally* S. TESH, HIDDEN ARGUMENTS: POLITICAL IDEOLOGY AND DISEASE PREVENTION POLICY 3 (1988) ("there is an inextricable interrelationship between facts and values, both in the search for the causes of disease and in the process of developing the best preventive policy").

[7] *See* Laurell, *Social Analysis of Collective Health in Latin America*, 28 SOC. SCI. & MED. 1183 (1989); M. LOCK, *Mind, Matter and Middle Age: Ideologies for the Second Sex, to be published in ANALYSIS IN MEDICAL ANTHROPOLOGY* (S. Lindenbaum & M. Lock eds.).

[8] *See* Winner, *Is There Any Light Under Our Bushel? Three Modest Proposals for S.T.S.*, 10 BULL. SCI. TECH. & SOC'Y 12 (1990).

[9] Woolhandler & Himmelstein, *Ideology in Medical Science: Class in the Clinic*, 28 SOC. SCI. & MED. 1205, 1206 (1989).

[10] *See generally* H. LONGINO, SCIENCE AS SOCIAL KNOWLEDGE: VALUES AND OBJECTIVITY IN SCIENTIFIC INQUIRY (1990).

[11] *E.g.*, Chui, Wong & Scriver, *The Thalassemias and Health Care in Canada: A Place for Genetics in Medicine*, 144 CANADIAN MED. ASS'N J. 21 (1991); Koshland, *The Rational Approach to the Irrational*, 250 SCIENCE 189 (1990); Stead, Senner, Reddick & Lofgren, *Racial Differences in Susceptibility to Infection by Mycobacterium Tuberculosis*, 322 NEW ENG. J. MED. 422, 426 (1990); Watson, *The Human Genome Project: Past, Present, and Future*, 248 SCIENCE 44 (1990).

18   AMERICAN JOURNAL OF LAW & MEDICINE VOL. XVII NOS. 1 & 2 1991

guage of genetics. Using the metaphor of blueprints,[13] with genes and DNA fragments presented as a set of instructions, the dominant discourse describing the human condition is reductionist, emphasizing genetic determination. It promotes scientific control of the body, individualizes health problems and situates individuals increasingly according to their genes. Through this discourse, which is beginning seriously to threaten other narratives, clinical and research geneticists and their colleagues are conditioning how we view, name and propose to manage a whole host of disorders and disabilities. Though it is only one conceptual model, "genetics" is increasingly identified as *the* way to reveal and explain health and disease, normality and abnormality. Baird, for example, sees the "major determinants" of disease as internal genetic factors.[14]

This conditioning directs how intellectual and financial resources are applied to resolve health problems.[15] More critically, it profoundly influences our values and attitudes. To capture this process, I use the term "geneticization."[16] Although most neologisms confuse rather

---

[12] *E.g.*, Alexander, *The Gene Hunt*, TIME, Mar. 20, 1989, at 52; Beers, *The Gene Screen*, VOGUE, June 1990, at 236, 237; Montgomery, *The Ultimate Medicine*, DISCOVER, Mar. 1990, at 60; Schmeck, *Battling the Legacy of Illness*, N.Y. TIMES GOOD HEALTH MAGAZINE, Apr. 28, 1990, at 36.

[13] *See* Council for Responsible Genetics, *Position Paper on Genetic Discrimination*, 3 ISSUES REPRODUCTIVE & GENETIC ENGINEERING 287 (1990) (criticizing the "blueprint" notion); Newman, *Idealist Biology*, 31 PERSPECTIVES BIOLOGY & MED. 353, 361 (1988) (DNA is one component of a "complex dynamical system," not a "command center" that is impervious to environmental input); Rose, *Human Perfectability*, 2 LANCET 1380, 1380-81 (1984) (emphasizing the effects of environment on DNA). *See generally* G. LAKOFF & M. JOHNSON, METAPHORS WE LIVE BY (1980).

[14] Baird, *Genetics and Health Care: A Paradigm Shift*, 33 PERSPECTIVES BIOLOGY & MED. 203, 203-04 (1990).

[15] *See* Lippman, *Genetics and Public Health: Means, Goals and Justices, to be published in* AM. J. HUM. GENETICS (1991) [hereinafter *Genetics and Public Health*]; Lippman, Messing & Mayer, *Is Genome Mapping the Way to Improve Canadians' Health?*, 81 CANADIAN J. PUB. HEALTH 397, 398 (1990) (noting that "undirected" studies of, for instance, "environmental protection against genotoxicants or of nutritional supplementation during pregnancy," will suffer financially because funds are going to human genome mapping).

[16] A. Lippman, La "Geneticization" de la Vie (unpublished manuscript presented at Seminaire, Lalonde-les-Maures, France, May, 1990). A few years ago, in an article only recently rediscovered, Edlin described a process he called "geneticizing" to refer to the tendency to label as "genetic" diseases and disorders "of possible polygenic-multifactorial origin" for which there was, in fact, "scant or no genetic evidence." Edlin, *Inappropriate Use of Genetic Terminology in Medical Research: A Public Health Issue*, 31 PERSPECTIVES BIOLOGY & MED. 47, 48 (1987). He argued that geneticizing led to premature categorization of diseases as genetic, and caused research funds to be allocated to genetic research to the detriment of other research. *Id.* at 48. I have deliberately chosen not to resurrect his term, since the processes I want to describe go beyond those that he emphasized. In this regard, too, the concept of geneticization goes beyond Yoxen's discussion of the "construction" of genetic disease. Yoxen, *Constructing Genetic Diseases*, in THE PROBLEM OF MEDICAL KNOWLEDGE, *supra* note 5, at 144. Apparently, the term "geneticism" was used even earlier in an essay by Sir Peter Medawar also to describe the inappropriate genetic labeling of variations between peo-

than clarify, enlarging our lexicon to interpret human genetics is appropriate. A new canon deserves a new vocabulary.

Geneticization refers to an ongoing process by which differences between individuals are reduced to their DNA codes, with most disorders, behaviors and physiological variations defined, at least in part, as genetic in origin. It refers as well to the process by which interventions employing genetic technologies are adopted to manage problems of health. Through this process, human biology is incorrectly equated with human genetics,[17] implying that the latter acts alone to make us each the organism she or he is.

Duster captures much of this in describing how prevailing social concerns of our age are leading us to see things through a genetic "prism."[18] "Geneticization" goes further, however, and poses genetics as the source of illumination itself, not merely one of the ways in which it might be refracted.

Prenatal diagnosis, already designated as a "ritual" of pregnancy, at least for white, middle-class women in North America, is the most widespread application of genetic technology to humans today.[19] It provides a central activity around which to explore geneticization and the health stories told in its language.

III. PRENATAL DIAGNOSIS: A TECHNICAL AND A SOCIAL CONSTRUCTION

Of all applied genetic activities, prenatal diagnosis is probably most familiar to the general population and is also the most used. Prenatal diagnosis refers to all the technologies currently in use or under development to determine the physi(ologi)cal condition of a fetus

---

ple. Medawar, *The Genetic Improvements of Man*, 18 AUSTRALASIAN ANNALS MED. 317, 319 (1969).

[17] *See* R. HUBBARD, THE POLITICS OF WOMEN'S BIOLOGY 52 (1990) (noting that in a less individualized society than ours, people might find many aspects of biology "more interesting than heredity, genes and . . . DNA"); Murphy, *The Logic of Medicine*, 66 AM. J. MED. 907, 908 (1979) (warning against a "narrow concern with single genes" that "destroys our vision of the human organism").

[18] T. DUSTER, BACKDOOR TO EUGENICS 2 (1990). Duster defines the "prism of heritability" as a "way of perceiving traits and behaviors that attributes the major explanatory power to biological inheritance." *Id.* at 164. In this definition, he is very close to Edlin's "geneticizing." *See supra* note 16. However, only when Duster notes, but without detailed development of the theme, that labels will determine how we choose to respond to a problem, does he begin to incorporate all that I place under the rubric of geneticization. The concept of geneticization explicitly makes this an essential part of the process.

[19] Rapp, *The Power of "Positive" Diagnosis: Medical and Maternal Discourses on Amniocentesis*, in CHILDBIRTH IN AMERICA: ANTHROPOLOGICAL PERSPECTIVES 103, 105 (K. Michaelson ed. 1988) [hereinafter CHILDBIRTH IN AMERICA]. *See generally* R. BLATT, PRENATAL TESTS: WHAT THEY ARE, THEIR BENEFITS AND RISKS, AND HOW TO DECIDE WHETHER TO HAVE THEM OR NOT (1988).

20   AMERICAN JOURNAL OF LAW & MEDICINE VOL. XVII NOS. 1 & 2 1991

before birth. Until recently, prenatal diagnosis usually meant amniocentesis,[20] a second trimester procedure routinely available for women over a certain age (usually thirty-five years in North America),[21]
for Down syndrome detection. Amniocentesis is also used in selected
circumstances where the identification of specific fetal genetic disorders
is possible.[22] Now, in addition to amniocentesis, there are chorionic
villus sampling (CVS)[23] tests that screen maternal blood samples to detect a fetus with a neural tube defect or Down syndrome, and ultrasound screening.[24] Despite professional guidelines to the contrary,[25]

---

[20] In amniocentesis, a hollow needle is inserted through a woman's abdomen and into the
amniotic sac in order to remove a small sample of the fluid that surrounds the developing
fetus. The procedure is usually preceded by an ultrasound examination to document the age
of the fetus and its location so that an appropriate site for insertion of the amniocentesis
needle can be chosen. The fluid that is removed — amniotic fluid — contains cells from the
fetus that, if allowed to divide in the laboratory, can then be analyzed. In particular, one can
count the number of chromosomes in the cells, determine fetal sex and carry out biochemical
and specific genetic analyses on these cells. Amniocentesis is performed at about sixteen to
twenty weeks' gestation, the second trimester of pregnancy: before this time not enough fluid
or enough cells are available. Once a fluid sample has been obtained, there is a further three
to four week wait for the analyses to be completed and results to be available, since it takes
this long to grow a sufficient number of cells for study. Thus, if a fetus is found to be affected
with the condition for which testing was done and the woman chooses to abort the pregnancy,
the abortion is not induced until about the twentieth week, which is halfway through the pregnancy. *See* E. NIGHTINGALE & M. GOODMAN, BEFORE BIRTH: PRENATAL TESTING FOR GENETIC
DISEASE 32-35 (1990) [hereinafter BEFORE BIRTH]. Recent technical developments that allow
diagnoses to be made following amplification of the genetic material in a single cell can
shorten considerably the time needed to obtain results. *See infra* note 23 and accompanying
text.

[21] *See infra* note 67 and accompanying text for a discussion of the social, rather than biological, bases for categorizing women over 35 as "at risk."

[22] Over 150 "single gene" disorders can now be detected, and testing may be carried out
for women who have a documented family history of one of these or who are otherwise known
to be at increased risk. Testing is not carried out for these disorders without specific indications. *See generally* Antonarakis, *Diagnosis of Genetic Disorders at the DNA Level*, 320 NEW ENG. J.
MED. 153 (1989) (reviewing recent progress in identifying single gene disorders).

[23] In chorionic villus sampling (CVS), a small tube (catheter) is inserted through the vagina and cervix. It is then advanced, under ultrasound guidance, until it reaches the placenta,
from which a small amount of tissue (chorionic villi) is removed. Some obstetricians now
obtain a sample through a needle inserted into the abdomen instead. Any chromosomal or
biochemical disorder can, in theory, be diagnosed with tissues obtained by CVS, because the
cells of the fetus and placenta (which are formed from chorionic villi) are genetically the same.
See Vekemans & Perry, *Cytogenic Analysis of Chorionic Villi: A Technical Assessment*, 72 HUM. GE-
NETICS 307 (1986). This procedure was first used successfully in China as early as 1975 to
determine fetal sex. Tietung Hosp. Dep't of Obstetrics & Gynecology, *Fetal Sex Prediction by
Sex Chromatin of Chorionic Villi Cells During Early Pregnancy*, 1 CHINESE MED. J. 117 (1975). CVS
can be done as early as eight or nine weeks after a woman's last menstrual period and, while
the results of tests carried out on the placental tissue can be available within hours, a two or
three day waiting period is usually required. *See* BEFORE BIRTH, *supra* note 20, at 35-36. If a
woman chooses to abort the pregnancy following CVS, the abortion can be carried out in the
first trimester. Finally, CVS does not appear more likely to cause a spontaneous abortion than
amniocentesis. Canadian Collaborative CVS - Amniocentesis Clinical Trial Group, *Multicentre
Randomised Clinical Trial of Chorion Villus Sampling and Amniocentesis*, 1 LANCET 1, 4 (1989).

[24] During an ultrasound examination, high frequency sound waves are projected into the

ultrasound screening is performed routinely in North America on almost every pregnant woman appearing for prenatal care early enough in pregnancy. And although ultrasound is not usually labeled as "prenatal diagnosis," it not only belongs under this rubric but was, I suggest, the first form of prenatal diagnosis for which informed consent is not obtained.[26]

Expansion of prenatal diagnosis techniques, ever widening lists of identifiable conditions and susceptibilities, changes in the timing of testing and the populations in which testing is occurring, and expanding professional definitions of what should be diagnosed *in utero*, attest to this technology's role in the process of geneticization.[27] But these operational characteristics alone circumscribe only some aspects of prenatal diagnosis. Prenatal diagnosis as a social activity is becoming

---

uterus; the sound waves that are reflected back are resolved visually to allow one to "see" the fetus on a television-like display screen. A. OAKLEY, THE CAPTURED WOMB: A HISTORY OF THE MEDICAL CARE OF PREGNANT WOMEN 155-68 (1984).

[25] *See* BEFORE BIRTH, *supra* note 20, at 31-32. A consensus development conference in the United States recently recommended reserving the use of ultrasound for pregnancies that may require it for specific medical reasons. PUB. HEALTH SERV., U.S. DEP'T OF HEALTH & HUM. SERVS., CONSENSUS DEVELOPMENT CONFERENCE: DIAGNOSTIC ULTRASOUND IMAGING IN PREGNANCY 11 (National Inst. of Health Publication No. 667, 1984). This recommendation is clearly not being followed and, at present, in many major North American teaching hospitals, almost all pregnant women are referred for two "routine" ultrasound examinations — one before the twentieth week and one in the third trimester — for purposes of dating the pregnancy, even though the benefits of such a policy have not been established. Even more frequent scans are considered routine in France. As a specific tool for prenatal diagnosis, ultrasound can be used to identify certain malformations such as neural tube defects, cleft lip, or limb shortening in fetuses known to be at risk for one of these abnormalities. It can also be used to identify fetal sex. Most subtle malformations will not be identified when ultrasound is applied routinely on a non-diagnostic basis, however; the detailed examination that would be necessary requires more than the time that is usually allowed (or the machinery that is employed) when the primary goal is pregnancy dating. Nevertheless, some fetal problems can be diagnosed and their recognition may influence subsequent decisions about how pregnancy is managed.

[26] *See* Chervenak, McCullough & Chervenak, *Prenatal Informed Consent for Sonogram*, 161 AM. J. OBSTETRICS & GYNECOLOGY 857, 860 (1989); Lippman, *Access to Prenatal Screening: Who Decides?*, 1 CANADIAN J. WOMEN L. 434 (1986) [hereinafter *Who Decides?*]. Chervenak and colleagues have recently called attention to the issue of informed consent for ultrasound, but their conclusions are troublesome. They consider the pregnant woman "the patient's fiduciary," the "patient" to them being the fetus. Chervenak, McCullough & Chervenak, *supra*, at 858. This suggests that the consent process they propose will be coercive.

It is also worth noting that ultrasound is no longer the only genetic technology applied without prior consent. Screening for carriers of hemoglobin disorders, for example, is also done unbeknownst to the individuals being tested in certain jurisdictions. *See* Rowley, Loader, Sutera & Walden, *Do Pregant Women Benefit from Hemoglobinopathy Carrier Detection?*, 565 ANNALS N.Y. ACADEMY SCIENCES 152, 153 (1989) [hereinafter Rowley]. These authors noted that consent for sickle cell and other hemoglobinopathies was not obtained because: "Consent for screening was not routinely sought; providers agreed that obtaining timely informed consent required counseling approaching that to be provided to identified carriers and many providers declined to participate if they had to obtain it." Rowley, *supra*, at 153.

[27] *See generally Who Decides?*, *supra* note 26, at 434.

22   AMERICAN JOURNAL OF LAW & MEDICINE   VOL. XVII NOS. 1 & 2 1991

an element in our culture and this aspect, which has had minimal attention, will be examined in depth.

A.   PRENATAL DIAGNOSIS AND THE DISCOURSE OF REASSURANCE

Contemporary stories about prenatal diagnosis contain several themes, but these generally reflect either of two somewhat different models.[28] In the "public health" model, prenatal diagnosis is presented as a way to reduce the frequency of selected birth defects.[29] In the other, which I will call the "reproductive autonomy" model, prenatal diagnosis is presented as a means of giving women information to expand their reproductive choices.[30] Unfortunately, neither model fully captures the essence of prenatal diagnosis. In addition, neither acknowledges the internal tension, revealed in the coexistence of quite contradictory constructions of testing that may be equally valid: 1) as an assembly line approach to the products of conception, separating out those products we wish to develop from those we wish to discontinue;[31] 2) as a way to give women control over their pregnancies, respecting (increasing) their autonomy to choose the kinds of children they will bear;[32] or 3) as a means of reassuring women that enhances their experience of pregnancy.[33]

The dominant theme throughout the biomedical literature, as well as some feminist commentary, emphasizes the last two of these constructions.[34] A major variation on this theme suggests, further, that

---

[28] *Id.*

[29] *See, e.g.*, Kolker, *Advances in Prenatal Diagnosis: Social-psychological and Policy Issues*, 5 INT'L J. TECH. ASSESSMENT HEALTH CARE 601 (1989); *see also* Dalgaard & Norby, *Autosomal Dominant Polycystic Kidney Disease in the 1980s*, 36 CLINICAL GENETICS 320, 324 (1989) (placing importance on "selective reproduction prevention").

[30] *See* PRESIDENT'S COMM'N FOR THE STUDY OF ETHICAL PROBLEMS IN MEDICAL AND BIOMEDICAL AND BEHAVIORAL RESEARCH, SCREENING AND COUNSELING FOR GENETIC CONDITIONS: THE ETHICAL, SOCIAL, AND LEGAL IMPLICATIONS OF GENETIC SCREENING, COUNSELING, AND EDUCATION PROGRAMS 55 (1983) [hereinafter PRESIDENT'S COMM'N] ("In sum, the fundamental value of genetic screening and counseling is their ability to enhance the opportunities for the individual to obtain information about their personal health and childbearing risks and to make autonomous and noncoerced choices based on that information.").

[31] *See* B. ROTHMAN, RECREATING MOTHERHOOD: IDEOLOGY AND TECHNOLOGY IN A PATRIARCHAL SOCIETY 21 (1989) (describing the "commodification of life, towards treating people and parts of people . . . as commodities . . . . We work hard, some of us, at making the perfect product, what one of the doctors in the childbirth movement calls a 'blue ribbon baby.' "). *See also* Ewing, *Australian Perspectives on Embryo Experimentation: An Update*, 3 ISSUES REPRODUCTIVE & GENETIC ENGINEERING 119 (1990); Rothman, *The Decision to Have or Not to Have Amniocentesis for Prenatal Diagnosis*, in CHILDBIRTH IN AMERICA, *supra* note 19, at 92, 92-98.

[32] *See* Hill, *Your Morality or Mine? An Inquiry into the Ethics of Human Reproduction*, 154 AM. J. OBSTETRICS & GYNECOLOGY 1173, 1178-80 (1986).

[33] *See generally* ROYAL COLLEGE OF PHYSICIANS OF LONDON, PRENATAL DIAGNOSIS AND GENETIC SCREENING: COMMUNITY AND SERVICE IMPLICATIONS (1989).

[34] *See, e.g.*, WOMEN'S RIGHTS LITIGATION CLINIC, REPRODUCTIVE LAWS FOR THE 1990s: A BRIEFING HANDBOOK (1987); *Who Decides?*, *supra* note 26, at 438.

PRENATAL GENETIC TESTING AND SCREENING   23

through the use of prenatal diagnosis women can avoid the family distress and suffering associated with the unpredicted birth of babies with genetic disorders or congenital malformations, thus preventing disability while enhancing the experience of pregnancy.[35] Not unlike the approach used to justify caesarean sections,[36] prenatal diagnosis is constructed as a way of avoiding "disaster."

The language of control, choice and reassurance certainly makes prenatal diagnosis appear attractive. But while this discourse may be successful as a marketing strategy,[37] it relates a limited and highly selected story about prenatal diagnosis. Notwithstanding that even the most critical would probably agree prenatal diagnosis *can be* selectively reassuring[38] (for the vast majority of women who will learn that the fetus does not have Down syndrome or some other serious diagnosable disorder), this story alone is too simplistic. It does not take account of why reassurance is sought, how risk groups are generated and how eligibility for obtaining this kind of reassurance is determined. Whatever else, prenatal diagnosis *is* a means of separating fetuses we wish to develop from those we wish to discontinue. Prenatal diagnosis does approach children as consumer objects subject to quality control.

This is implicit in the general assumption that induced abortion will follow the diagnosis of fetal abnormality.[39] This assumption is reinforced by the rapid acceptance of CVS, which allows prenatal diagnosis to be carried out earlier and earlier in pregnancy when termination of a fetus found to be "affected" is taken for granted as less problematic.[40] The generally unquestioned assumption that pre-implantation diagno-

---

[35] McDonough, *Congenital Disability and Medical Research: The Development of Amniocentesis,* 16 WOMEN & HEALTH 137, 143-44 (1990). McDonough notes that three rationales for amniocentesis emerged from her survey: "The procedure offered those at risk the possibility of 'health' . . . . [it] provided parents with reassurance and avoided abortion . . . . [and it] prevent[ed] disease and disability." *Id.*

[36] *See, e.g.,* McClain, *Perceived Risk and Choice of Childbirth Service,* 17 SOC. SCI. & MED. 1857, 1862 (1983).

[37] There is no evidence that control, autonomy and reassurance are actually enhanced and not merely assumed to occur. In fact, there have been very few in-depth studies in this area, and the conclusions of these investigations seem to vary with the orientation of the investigator. Studies reported in the social science and feminist literature suggest that prenatal diagnosis removes control; studies reported in the biomedical literature are interpreted to show how reassurance is provided. For an overview of these studies, see Lippman, *Research Studies in Applied Human Genetics: A Quantitative Analysis and Critical Review of Recent (Biomedical) Literature, to be published in* AM. J. MED. GENETICS (1991). Much more ethnographic work in this area is required.

[38] *See infra* text accompanying notes 48-51 for a reconstruction of the notion of reassurance.

[39] *See supra* notes 31-32 and accompanying text.

[40] This issue is discussed in A. Lippman, Led Astray by Genetic Maps (speech given, Ottawa, Canada, 1991). Treatment, often said to be a goal of early identification of affected fetuses, becomes even less likely with CVS. Pharmaceutical companies will not be motivated

24   AMERICAN JOURNAL OF LAW & MEDICINE VOL. XVII NOS. 1 & 2 1991

sis is better than prenatal diagnosis also undermines a monotonic reas-surance rhetoric.[41] With pre-implantation (embryo) diagnosis, the selection objective is clear: only those embryos thought to be "nor-mal" will be transferred and allowed to continue to develop.[42] Thus, embryo destruction is equated with induced abortion.[43] In perhaps the most blatant example, Brambati and colleagues have proposed the combined use of *in vitro* fertilization, gamete intrafallopian transfer, chorionic villus sampling and fetal reduction to "avoid pregnancy ter-mination among high risk couples" [sic], and have stated that the "fetus was reduced" when describing a situation in which this scenario actu-ally occurred.[44]

Thus, while no single storyline is inherently true or false, the reas-surance discourse appears to mask essential features of genetic testing and screening that are troubling. Reassurance — for pregnant women or for geneticists[45] — notwithstanding, the story is more complex. Pre-natal diagnosis necessarily involves systematic and systemic selection of fetuses, most frequently on genetic grounds.[46] Though the word

to invest in developing treatments for conditions that "need not occur." Rarely will they base business decisions on their social worth rather than on their financial value.

    This situation contains elements of an unusual conflict. Increasingly, geneticists are promising to have treatments available for a wide range of disorders and, for some conditions, therapeutic developments have occurred which make them far more benign than previously. The promises, and the available examples, are likely to to be sufficiently persuasive that wo-men "at-risk" may either make use of prenatal diagnosis less frequently or see less reason to abort an affected fetus than today. Yet, at the same time, the very availability of prenatal diagnosis and abortion may be seen as justifications for *not* investing in the further develop-ment of these therapies that parents will have been led to expect. *Cf.* Varekamp, Suurmeijer, Bröcker-Vriends, Van Dijck, Smit, Rosendaal & Briët, *Carrier Testing and Prenatal Diagnosis for Hemophilia: Experiences and Attitudes of 549 Potential and Obligate Carriers,* 37 AM. J. MED. GENET-ICS 147, 153 (1990) [hereinafter Varekamp] (noting decrease in hemophilia screening as treat-ment capabilities increased).

    [41] *See* Bell, *Prenatal Diagnosis: Current Status and Future Trends,* in HUMAN GENETIC INFORMA-TION: SCIENCE, LAW & ETHICS 18-36 (Ciba Foundation Series 1990). *See also* Kolker, *supra* note 29, at 612 (prevention is "clearly cheaper than providing services for those with genetic disorders"); Modell, *Cystic Fibrosis Screening and Community Genetics,* 27 J. MED. GEN. 475, 476 (1990) ("undesirable [diseases] may be all but eradicated"); Dalgaard & Norby, *supra* note 29, at 323-24 ("access to selective reproductive prevention" is important).

    [42] S. WYMELENBERG, SCIENCE AND BABIES: PRIVATE DECISIONS, PUBLIC DILEMMAS 130 (1990).

    [43] In fact, some consider the combined procedures of *in vitro* fertilization and embryo diagnosis to be "ethically better" than prenatal diagnosis for detecting problems because it "avoids" abortion. *See* Michael & Buckle, *Screening for Genetic Disorders: Therapeutic Abortion and IVF,* 16 J. MED. ETHICS 43 (1990). *But see* J. TESTART, LE MONDE DIPLOMATIQUE 24 (1990) (suggesting that it is the very need to consider abortion ("de terribles responsabilités") that is perhaps the best safeguard against ordinary eugenics ("l'eugenisme ordinaire")).

    [44] Brambati, Formigli, Tului & Simoni, *Selective Reduction of Quadruplet Pregnancy at Risk of B-Thalassemia,* 336 LANCET 1325, 1326 (1990).

    [45] If nothing else, it is certainly preferable for their public image if geneticists are seen as reassuring women, rather than selecting their offspring.

    [46] Much of importance has been written about the link between prenatal diagnosis and

"eugenics" is scrupulously avoided in most biomedical reports about prenatal diagnosis, except when it is strongly disclaimed as a motive for intervention, this is disingenuous.[47] Prenatal diagnosis presupposes that certain fetal conditions are intrinsically not bearable. Increasing diagnostic capability means that such conditions, as well as a host of variations that can be detected *in utero*, are proliferating, necessarily broadening the range of what is not "bearable" and restricting concepts of what is "normal." It is, perhaps, not unreasonable to ask if the "imperfect" will become anything we can diagnose.[48]

While the notion of reassurance has been successfully employed to justify prenatal testing and screening as responses to the problems of childhood disability, we need to question both the sufficiency and the necessity of its linkage to prenatal diagnosis. At best, reassurance is an acquired, not an inherent, characteristic of prenatal diagnosis. Even if testing provides "reassurance," it is of a particular and limited kind. For example, although the fetus can be shown not to have Down syndrome, most disabilities only manifest themselves after birth. Further, it is not the (only) way to achieve a global objective of "reassuring" pregnant women. Indeed, it may even be counterproductive. This becomes clear if one reconstructs the notion of reassurance. Assuming it is an acceptable objective of prenatal care, are there ways to reassure pregnant women desiring "healthy" children that do not lead to genetic testing and control?

Data from the United States Women, Infants and Children program leave little doubt that "low technology" approaches providing essential nutritional, social and other supportive services to pregnant women will reduce the low birth weight and prematurity responsible for most infant mortality and morbidity today.[49] Providing an adequate diet to the unacceptably large number of pregnant women living below the poverty line would clearly "reassure" them that their babies were developing as well as the babies of wealthier women. Similarly, alloca-

eugenics; this dialogue, despite its importance, will not be repeated here. *See generally* T. DUSTER, *supra* note 18; R. HUBBARD, *supra* note 17; Degener, *Female Self-determination Between Feminist Claims and "Voluntary" Eugenics, Between "Rights" and Ethics,* 3 ISSUES REPRODUCTIVE & GENETIC ENGINEERING 87 (1990); Hubbard, *Eugenics: New Tools, Old Ideas,* 13 WOMEN & HEALTH 225 (1987).

[47] This point is not merely an argument of critics of prenatal diagnosis. Shaw, a geneticist-lawyer who strongly defends the principle of fetal protection, has written that "any counselor who explains reproductive alternatives and offers a prenatal test to a counselee is a practicing eugenicist and any couple who chooses to avoid having babies with chromosome abnormalities or deleterious mutant genes is also practicing eugenics." Shaw, *Letter to the Editor: Response to Hayden: Presymptomatic and Prenatal Testing,* 28 AM. J. MED. GENETICS 765, 765-66 (1987).

[48] Rothschild, *Engineering Birth: Toward the Perfectability of Man?,* in 2 SCIENCE, TECHNOLOGY AND SOCIAL PROGRESS 93 (S. Goldman ed. 1989).

[49] *See* Anon, *WIC Program Shows Major Benefits,* NATION'S HEALTH, Dec. 1990, at 3.

26   AMERICAN JOURNAL OF LAW & MEDICINE VOL. XVII NOS. 1 & 2 1991

tion of funds for home visitors, respite care and domestic alterations would "reassure" women that the resources required to help them manage their special needs were readily available without financial cost, should their child be born with a health problem. It would also be "reassuring" to know that effective medication and simplified treatment regimes were available or being developed for prevalent disorders. Reassurances such as these may be all that many pregnant women want. Not only would these alternative approaches provide "reassurance" with respect to (and *for*) fetal disability, they would diminish a woman's feeling of personal responsibility for a child's health, rather than "exacerbate" it as does prenatal diagnosis.[50]

Genes may contribute to the distribution of low birth weight and prematurity in North America, and likely some investigators will seek their location and the order of their DNA base sequences on the human gene map. The social and economic inequalities among women with which they are associated,[51] however, are already well "mapped"; the "location" of women who are at increased risk is well known; the "sequences" of events leading to excessively and unnecessarily high rates of these problems have been well described. From this perspective, *gene* mapping and sequencing may be irrelevant as a source of reassurance in view of the most pressing needs of pregnant women. Even if genes were shown to be related to these problems, it must be remembered that the individuals to whom reassurance will be provided, as well as the concerns chosen for alleviation, rest on social, political and economic decisions by those in power. Such choices require continued analysis and challenge.

B.   CONSTRUCTING THE "NEED" FOR PRENATAL DIAGNOSIS

While reassurance has been constructed to justify health professionals' offers of prenatal diagnosis, genetic testing and screening have also been presented in the same biomedical literature as responses to the "needs" of pregnant women. They are seen as something they "choose." What does it mean, however, to "need" prenatal diagnosis, to "choose" to be tested?[52] Once again, a closer look at what appear to

---

[50] *See* Farrant, *Who's for Amniocentesis? The Politics of Prenatal Screening*, in THE SEXUAL POLITICS OF REPRODUCTION 96, 120 (H. Homans ed. 1985) [hereinafter THE SEXUAL POLITICS OF REPRODUCTION].

[51] *See* Yankauer, *What Infant Mortality Tells Us*, 80 AM. J. PUB. HEALTH 653 (1990).

[52] While those in need are identified explicitly as (certain) pregnant women, it is worth noting that clinical geneticists, themselves, have a need for this technology, too. For instance, when a child is born with a malformation, geneticists likely feel most "helpful" when prenatal diagnosis, a technological palliative for the pains of etiologic ignorance, can be offered. Saying that the malformation is not likely to happen again, given the usually low empiric recurrence risks associated with most of these problems, is not nearly as comforting for genetic counselors as is offering *in utero* detection. Counselors "need" this technique for the satisfac-

be obvious terms may illuminate some otherwise hidden aspects of geneticization and the prenatal diagnosis stories told in its voice.

We must first identify the concept of need as itself a problem and acknowledge that needs do not have intrinsic reality. Rather, needs are socially constructed and culture bound, grounded in current history, dependent on context and, therefore, not universal.

With respect to prenatal diagnosis, "need" seems to have been conceptualized predominantly in terms of changes in capabilities for fetal diagnoses: women only come to "need" prenatal diagnosis after the test for some disorder has been developed. Moreover, the disorders to be sought are chosen exclusively by geneticists.[53] In addition, posing a "need" for testing to reduce the probability a woman will give birth to a child with some detectable characteristic rests on assumptions about the value of information, about which characteristics are or are not of value and about which risks should or should not be taken. These assumptions reflect almost exclusively a white, middle-class perspective.[54]

This conceptualization of need is propelled by several features of contemporary childbearing.[55] First, given North American culture, where major responsibility for family health care in general, for the fetus she carries and for the child she births, is still allocated to a woman,[56] it is generally assumed that she must do all that is

---

tory performance of their jobs no less than they believe a family "needs" prenatal diagnosis to prevent the birth of a second affected child.

[53] See Lippman, *Prenatal Diagnosis: Reproductive Choice? Reproductive Control?*, [hereinafter *Reproductive Choice?*] in THE FUTURE OF HUMAN REPRODUCTION 182, 187 (C. Overall ed. 1989) [hereinafter THE FUTURE OF HUMAN REPRODUCTION] (consideration of prenatal diagnosis as a professional resource).

[54] See Nsiah-Jefferson, *Reproductive Laws, Women of Color and Low Income Women* in REPRODUCTIVE LAWS FOR THE 1990s 17, 17-58 (S. Cohen & N. Taub eds. 1988) [hereinafter REPRODUCTIVE LAWS FOR THE 1990s] (discussing potential areas of cultural conflict in genetic counseling).

[55] There is an extensive literature on "medicalization" in general and on the medicalization of pregnancy and childbirth *per se* in which this discussion is rooted and from which it derives guidance. *See, e.g.,* A. OAKLEY, *supra* note 24, at 275. ("The medicalization of everyday life is a phenomenon described in many radical and liberal critiques of medicine."); *id.* at 276 ("For both birth and death normal signs have become neon lights flagging risks which demand and validate medical intervention."); Raymond, *Feminist Ethics, Ecology, and Vision,* in TEST-TUBE WOMEN 427, 427-37 (R. Arditti, R. Klein & S. Minden eds. 1984) [hereinafter TEST-TUBE WOMEN]; I. ZOLA, *Healthism and Disabling Medicalization,* in I. ILLICH, I. ZOLA, J. MCKNIGHT, J. CAPLAN & H. SHAIKEN, DISABLING PROFESSIONS 41 (1977); Zola, *In the Name of Health and Illness: On Some Socio-Political Consequences of Medical Influence,* 9 SOC. SCI. & MED. 83, 85-87 (1975) (noting that control by medical value not achieved through political means but by "medicalization"); Zola, *Medicine as an Institution of Social Control,* 20 SOCIOLOGY REV. 487 (1972); *see also* Lewin, *By Design: Reproductive Strategies and the Meaning of Motherhood,* in SEXUAL POLITICS OF REPRODUCTION, *supra* note 50, at 123, 123-38 (1985) (women "must adapt" to "motherhood" but can also approach it as "active strategists").

[56] See Oakley, *Smoking in Pregnancy: Smokescreen or Risk Factor? Towards a Materialist Analysis,* 11 SOCIOLOGY HEALTH & ILLNESS 311 (1989).

28   AMERICAN JOURNAL OF LAW & MEDICINE VOL. XVII NOS. 1 & 2 1991

recommended or available to foster her child's health. At its extreme, this represents the pregnant woman as obligated to produce a healthy child. Prenatal diagnosis, as it is usually presented, falls into this category of behaviors recommended to pregnant women who would exercise their responsibilities as caregivers.[57] Consequently, to the extent that she is expected generally to do everything possible for the fetus/child, a woman may come to "need" prenatal diagnosis, and take testing for granted. Moreover, since an expert usually offers testing, and careseekers are habituated to follow through with tests ordered by physicians,[58] it is hardly surprising that they will perceive a need to be tested.[59] With prenatal diagnosis presented as a "way to avoid birth defects," to refuse testing, or perceive no need for it, becomes more difficult than to proceed with it.[60] This technology perversely creates a burden of not doing enough, a burden incurred when the technology is *not* used.[61]

A second feature, related to the first, is that women generally, and

---

[57] *See* Farrant, *supra* note 50, at 96; Oakley, *supra* note 56, at 311.

[58] *See* R. HATCHER & H. THOMPSON, SATISFACTION WITH OBSTETRICAL CARE AMONG CANA-DIAN WOMEN (Health Servs. Res. Unit, Department of Community Health, Queen's Univ., Kingston, Ontario 1987) (results of a survey showing pregnant women's reluctance to question medical authority).

[59] *See* Lippman, *supra* note 53, at 182. Physicians may pressure women into being tested, even using false information to do so. Marteau, Kidd, Cook, Michie, Johnston, Slack & Shaw, *Perceived Risk not Actual Risk Predicts Uptake of Amniocentesis*, 96 BRIT. J. OBSTETRICS & GYNAECOLOGY 739 (1989).

[60] *See* Hubbard & Henifin, *Genetic Screening of Prospective Parents and of Workers: Some Scientific and Social Issues*, 15 INT'L J. HEALTH SERVS. 231 (1985); Rothman, *The Meaning of Choice in Reproductive Technology*, in TEST-TUBE WOMEN, *supra* note 55, at 23. I have previously discussed the "burden" of decisionmaking in the context of genetic counseling and a similar "burden" would seem to exist here. *See* Lippman-Hand & Fraser, *Genetic Counseling I: Parents' Perceptions of Uncertainty*, 4 AM. J. MED. GENETICS 51, 58-63 (1979) [hereinafter *Genetic Counseling I*]; Lippman-Hand & Fraser, *Genetic Counseling II: Making Reproductive Choices*, 4 AM. J. MED. GENETICS 73 (1978) [hereinafter *Genetic Counseling II*]. This theme is present in contemporary literature as demonstrated by Goldstein's reference to the "momentous decision" that childbearing now involves. R. GOLDSTEIN, THE MIND-BODY PROBLEM 200 (1983).

Hubbard and Henifin, in fact, identify a "new Catch-22" wherein participating in a genetic screening program may lead to a person's being identified as a "genetic deviant," but failure to participate (or to abort a fetus diagnosed with a disorder *in utero*) may lead to her being labeled as a "social deviant." Hubbard & Henifin, *supra*, at 231-48.

[61] The degree of this burden is demonstrated by the frequency with which women queried about their reasons for having prenatal diagnosis say that they "had no choice." Sjögren & Uddenberg, *Decision Making During the Prenatal Diagnostic Procedure*, 8 PRENATAL DIAGNOSIS 263 (1988). *See* Kirejczyk, *A Question of Meaning? Controversies About the NRT's in the Netherlands*, 3 ISSUES REPRODUCTIVE & GENETIC ENGINEERING 23 (1990) (individuals often accept a medical technique because of fear that they might later regret not having done so); *see also* A. FINGER, PAST DUE: A STORY OF DISABILITY, PREGNANCY AND BIRTH (1990); Beck-Gernsheim, *From the Pill to Test-Tube Babies: New Options, New Pressures in Reproductive Behavior*, in HEALING TECHNOL-OGY: FEMINIST PERSPECTIVES 23 (1988) [hereinafter HEALING TECHNOLOGY]; Rapp, *Moral Pioneers: Women, Men and Fetuses in a Frontier of Reproductive Technology*, 13 WOMEN & HEALTH 101 (1987).

PRENATAL GENETIC TESTING AND SCREENING   29

pregnant women specifically, are bombarded with behavioral directives[62] that are at least as likely to foster a sense of incompetence as to nourish a feeling of control.[63] It is therefore not surprising that a search for proof of competence is translated into a "need" for testing; external verification takes precedence over the pregnant woman's sense of herself. Evidence that the fetus is developing as expected may provide some women with a sense that all is under control (although this suggestion has not been studied empirically to the best of my understanding). Personal experience is set aside in favor of external and measured evidence.[64] Moreover, given that a pregnant woman is more and more frequently reduced to a "uterine environment,"[65] and looked upon as herself presenting dangers to the fetus (especially if she eats improperly, smokes, drinks alcoholic beverages, takes medications, etc.), being tested becomes an early warning system to identify whether this "environment" is adequate. Women who share these suspicions and doubt that they can have a healthy baby without professional aid are likely to subject themselves to tests that are offered.[66]

Third, prenatal diagnosis will necessarily be perceived as a "need" in a context, such as ours, that automatically labels pregnant women thirty-five years and over a "high risk" group.[67] Although this risk la-

---

[62] B. ROTHMAN, *supra* note 31, at 92-97. Women are expected to behave in accordance with norms set up by those in power. *See* Rodgers, *Pregnancy as Justifications for Loss of Judicial Autonomy*, in THE FUTURE OF HUMAN REPRODUCTION, *supra* note 53, at 174.

[63] *See, e.g.*, Fleischer, *Ready for Any Sacrifice? Women in IVF Programmes*, 3 ISSUES REPRODUCTIVE & GENETIC ENGINEERING 1 (1990) (referring to a "code of good conduct" pregnant women ought to follow); *see also* M. DE KONINCK & F. SAILLANT, ESSAI SUR LA SANTÉ DES FEMMES (Conseil du Statut de la femme 1981); A. QUÉNIART, LE CORPS PARADOXAL: REGARDS DE FEMMES SUR LA MATERNITÉ (1988); Simkin, *Childbearing in Social Context*, 15 WOMEN & HEALTH 5 (1989) (all discussing the ideology of risk and behavioral expectations in pregnancy).

[64] *See* B. ROTHMAN, *supra* note 31, at 92; Leuzinger & Rambert, *"I Can Feel It — My Baby Is Healthy:" Women's Experiences with Prenatal Diagnosis in Switzerland*, 1 ISSUES REPRODUCTIVE & GENETIC ENGINEERING 1153 (1988).

[65] *Cf.* Levran, Dor, Rudak, Nebel, Ben-Shlomo, Ben-Rafael & Mashiach, *Pregnancy Potential of Human Oocytes — The Effect of Cryopreservation*, 323 NEW ENG. J. MED. 1153, 1154 (1990) [hereinafter Levran]; Sauer, Paulson & Lobo, *A Preliminary Report on Oocyte Donation Extending Reproductive Potential to Women Over 40*, 323 NEW ENG. J. MED. 1157, 1159 (1990).

[66] *See generally* R. BLATT, *supra* note 19; A. Lippman, *supra* note 40.

[67] *See* Fuhrmann, *Impact, Logistics and Prospects of Traditional Prenatal Diagnosis*, 36 CLINICAL GENETICS 378, 380 (1988). This categorization is more a cultural than biological creation. *See* Bourret, *Le temps, l'espace en Génétique: Intervention Médicale et Géographique Sociale du gène*, 6 SCIENCES SOCIALES ET SANTÉ 171 (1988); A. Lippman, *The Geneticization of Health and Illness: Implications for Social Practice* (manuscript in preparation based on presentation at National Ass'n for Science, Tech. & Soc'y, Washington, D.C., Feb. 2, 1991). It reflects prevailing ideas about the kinds of children women should have and when the probability for them is or is not diminished. *See* Finkelstein, *Biomedicine and Technocratic Power*, HASTINGS CENTER REP. 1990, at 13, 14-16; *see also infra* note 86 for a discussion of the role of genetics in creating these ideas. Age has thus become more than an event, a birthday; it has been redefined as a marker, a risk, although nothing inherent in it makes it so. *See* Fuhrmann, *supra*, at 380 (35 is the crucial age in North America); J. Moatti, J. Lanoë, C. LeGalés, H. Gardent, C. Julian & S. Aymé,

30 AMERICAN JOURNAL OF LAW & MEDICINE VOL. XVII NOS. 1 & 2 1991

beling is, itself, socially rather than biologically determined,[68] women informed that they are "at-risk" may find it hard to refuse prenatal diagnosis or other measures that are advertised to be risk-reducing. Once again, however, this "need" does not exist apart from the current context that created it by categorizing homogeneously those thirty-five and older who are pregnant as "at-risk." Mere identification of one's self as a member of a "high risk" group may influence the interpretation of an absolute risk figure[69] and the acceptance of a test. In this light, the additional screening and testing possibilities generated by genome projects are likely to expand greatly the ranks of those deemed "needy."[70] As the number of factors or people labeled as risks or at-risk increases, so, too, will offers of intervention.[71]

Fourth, as prenatal diagnosis becomes more and more routine for women thirty-five years and older in North America, the risks it seems to avoid (the birth of a child with Down syndrome) appear to be more ominous,[72] although the frequency of Down syndrome has not

---

Economic Assessment of Prenatal Diagnosis in France (unpublished manuscript presented at Joint Meeting of European Health Economic Societies, Barcelona, Spain, Sept. 21-23, 1989) (age 38 in France); Sjögren & Uddenberg, *supra* note 61, at 263 (age 37 in Sweden). This age marker may even serve to stigmatize the "older" woman. *See* Hubbard & Henifin, *supra* note 60, at 238 (1985). Further discussion of the arbitrariness of age 35 as a criterion for access to prenatal diagnosis can be found in *Who Decides?*, *supra* note 26, at 434; Vekemans & Lippman, *Letter to the Editor: Eligibility Criteria for Amniocentesis*, 17 AM. J. MED. GENETICS 531 (1986).

[68] The many ways in which the concept of "risk" is itself a cultural creation, unfortunately, cannot be given the attention they deserve here. However, it is useful to recall that the data used to assign people to risk categories reflects the information we choose to collect, and the problems that interest the collector. Alexander & Keirse, *Formal Risk Scoring*, in 1 EFFECTIVE CARE IN PREGNANCY AND CHILDBIRTH 345, 346-47 (I. Chalmers & M. Keirse eds. 1989). It is also important to note that changes in the nature and number of things counted as risks are more prevalent than changes in the actual number of people "at-risk"; and that even using the term "risk" to describe an event or experience is politically and socially dependent. *Cf.* L. WINNER, THE WHALE AND THE REACTOR: A SEARCH FOR LIMITS IN AN AGE OF HIGH TECHNOLOGY 142 (1986) (discussing risks versus hazards).

[69] *See* Botkin, *Prenatal Screening: Professional Standards and the Limits of Parental Choice*, 75 OBSTETRICS & GYNECOLOGY 875 (1990); Shiloh & Sagi, *Effect of Framing on the Perception of Genetic Recurrence Risks*, 33 AM. J. MED. GENETICS 130 (1989).

[70] A. Lippman, *supra* note 40. Human genome projects comprise the organized and directed international and national programs to map and sequence all human genes. Some of these genes will be associated with recognizable disorders; others will be associated with biological variations of varying and mostly unknown consequence. *See generally* McKusick, *Mapping and Sequencing the Human Genome*, 320 NEW ENG. J. MED. 910 (1989); Watson, *supra* note 11 at 44. Differences between people will be identified, and while knowing the location and composition of human genes will add to our information about the latter, it will not reveal how the person with these genes will "turn out." *See supra* notes 13-14 and accompanying text for a critical discussion of the limits of the genetic model.

[71] *Cf.* Vallgarda, *Increased Obstetric Activity: A New Meaning to "Induced Labor?"*, 43 J. EPIDEMIOLOGY & COMMUNITY HEALTH 48, 51 (1989) (hypothesizing that, among other factors, the availability of new technologies such as electronic fetal monitoring leads to an increased number of interventions by practitioners).

[72] This may be an example of what Tversky and Kahnemann have called the "availability" heuristic. Tversky & Kahneman, *Availability: A Heuristic for Judging Frequency and Probability*, 5

changed. This, too, may have a framing effect, generating a "need" for prenatal testing among women in this age group. Interestingly, however, this perception may inadvertantly influence both the implementation and efficiency of proposed screening programs designed to supplement risk estimates based on maternal age with information from maternal blood samples.[73] Having been socialized during the past fifteen to twenty years to view age thirty-five and over as the entry card to prenatal diagnosis, and convinced that once past this birthday they are "at risk," how will women beyond this age respond when blood test results remove them statistically from those in "need" of prenatal diagnosis? Will there be lingering doubts, and their sequelae, or will it be as easy to remove a risk label as it has been to affix one? What about the younger women who will have become prematurely aged (that is, eligible "by age" for prenatal diagnosis though not yet thirty-five)? As the title of a recent book phrases it, are pregnancy screening and fetal diagnosis *Calming or Harming?*[74] We neither have the data necessary to answer this question, nor do we give priority to studies that would be informative.[75] Instead, we proceed as if calming were a foregone conclusion. Programmatic changes such as these, no less than those subsequent to developments in genomics, underline how risk groups and needs are generated and constructed.

Fifth, on the collective level, prenatal diagnosis is generally presented as a response to the public health "need" to reduce unacceptably high levels of perinatal mortality and morbidity associated with perceived increases in "genetic" disorders. This reduction is of a special kind, in that prenatal diagnosis does not *prevent* the disease, as is

---

COGNITIVE PSYCHOLOGY 207 (1973). That is, having become familiar through constant reference to it and to prenatal diagnosis, Down syndrome may be perceived by the general population as "worse" and as more frequent than it is statistically.

[73] Until recently, the frequency of births of children with Down syndrome to women of different ages was the sole basis for estimating individual risks. Within the past few years, investigators have identified certain substances in blood samples from pregnant women that show a statistical association with the chromosomal status of the fetus. This additional information is now beginning to be used in conjunction with maternal age to estimate risks for Down syndrome. In some cases these data will increase a woman's putative risk above that associated with her age alone; in others, it will decrease it. When the numerical value of this risk equals or surpasses that associated with maternal age 35 alone, ("35-equivalent"), prenatal diagnosis is generally offered. *See* Wald & Cuckle, *AFP and Age Screening for Down Syndrome*, 31 AM. J. MED. GENETICS 197 (1988).

[74] J. GREEN, CALMING OR HARMING? A CRITICAL REVIEW OF PSYCHOLOGICAL EFFECTS OF FETAL DIAGNOSIS ON PREGNANT WOMEN (Galton Inst. 2d Series 1990). In this context, the notion of "iatrogenic anxiety" would seem pertinent. This anxiety may develop when laboratory analyses reveal chromosomal variations never before reported whose significance is unknown. The prevalence of iatrogenic anxiety among women being tested may be substantial, but its extent is currently unknown.

[75] *See* Lippman, *supra* note 37.

32   AMERICAN JOURNAL OF LAW & MEDICINE VOL. XVII NOS. 1 & 2 1991

usually claimed.[76] Yet, even this "need," ostensibly based on "hard" data demonstrating the size of these problems, is constructed. For example, geneticists say "their" kinds of diseases are increasing as the prevalence of infectious diseases decreases, making genetic intervention seem appropriate. But others construe the same data as evidence of an increase in the "new morbidity" of pediatrics (developmental delays, learning difficulties, chronic disease, emotional and behavioral problems, etc.), the problems of concern in *their* specialty.[77] Clearly, what one counts, emphasizes and treats as "evidence,"[78] depends on what one seeks as well as on the background beliefs generating the search. The numbers are then tallied, justifying a "need" to do something.[79]

Moreover, unacceptably high rates of morbidity generate all sorts of "needs."[80] Reducing these solely to biomedical problems hides the range of potential responses that might be considered.

Viewing needs and demands as cultural creations within a social context leads to doubts that assumptions of "free choice" with respect to the actual use of prenatal diagnosis are appropriate. It also clarifies why it is not fruitful to think that there may be a conflict between women who want prenatal diagnosis and critics who do not want them to have it. Not only does this polarization misinterpret the critics' position, it fails to recognize, for example, that prenatal diagnosis cannot really be a choice when other alternatives are not available,[81] or that accepting testing as "needed" may be a way for a woman to justify going through what is a problematic experience for her. Society does not truly accept children with disabilities or provide assistance for their nurturance. Thus, a woman may see no realistic alternative to diagnosing and aborting a fetus likely to be affected.

---

[76] *See, e.g.*, Modell, *Cystic Fibrosis Screening and Community Genetics*, 27 J. MED. GENETICS 475 ("Cystic fibrosis . . . is fast becoming preventable . . . . [because] [t]he gene in which mutation can lead to CF . . . has recently been identified . . . [This creates] an imminent need to set up population screening for CF carriers.").

[77] *See, e.g.*, N. ZILL & C. SCHOENBORN, DEVELOPMENTAL, LEARNING, AND EMOTIONAL PROBLEMS: HEALTH OF OUR NATION'S CHILDREN 190 (National Center for Health Statistics, Nov., 1990).

[78] *See* H. LONGINO, SCIENCE AS SOCIAL KNOWLEDGE: VALUES AND OBJECTIVITY IN SCIENTIFIC INQUIRY 38, 38-48 (1990).

[79] *See* Armstrong, *The Invention of Infant Mortality*, 8 SOCIOLOGY HEALTH & ILLNESS 211 (1986) (the idea of infant mortality was created by new measuring tools in statistics); Armstrong, *Use of the Genealogical Method in the Exploration of Chronic Illness: A Research Note*, 30 SOC. SCI. & MED. 1225 (1990) (how increases in chronic disease are constructed).

[80] Children with malformations and medical disorders will always be born, and avoiding their birth via prenatal diagnosis does not address the issue of preventing these problems or of ameliorating their effects on the child or the family. The former will require interventions that reduce environmental mutagens and teratogens, for example; the latter elicits interventions which have already been discussed. *See supra* text accompanying notes 42-44.

[81] *See* R. HUBBARD, *supra* note 17, at 198.

Parallel to the creation of a woman's "need" for prenatal diagnosis is the development of health professionals' "need" for technological solutions to problems of malformation. Thus, geneticists increasingly choose to use and develop prenatal diagnosis to deal with problems of malformation excluding, if not precluding, consideration of other approaches. They "need" to employ these technologies, and in doing so they establish professional norms about how much is needed. Individual decisions about when a woman needs testing accumulate, and rapidly establish new standards for the profession.[82] The routine use of ultrasound to monitor all pregnancies is probably the most obvious example. Regardless of the driving forces for dependency on this technology, the result is the construction of a particular "need": the basic "need" to know the gestational age of the fetus; the additional "need" to demonstrate that the pregnancy is progressing "normally." And the "needs" grow.

"Needs" for prenatal diagnosis are being created simultaneously with refinements and extensions of testing techniques themselves.[83] In popular discourse — and with geneticists generally silent witnesses — genetic variations are being increasingly defined not just as problems, but, I suggest, as problems for which there is, or will be, a medical/technical solution. With but slight slippage these "problems" come to be seen as *requiring* a medical solution. This again hides the extent to which even "genetic" disease is a social/psychological experience as much as it is a biomedical one.[84] This process is likely to accelerate as gene mapping enlarges the numbers of individuals declared eligible for genetic testing and screening. Given the extent of human variation, the possibilities for constructing "needs" are enormous.

C.   PRENATAL DIAGNOSIS AND THE SOCIAL CONTROL OF ABORTION AND PREGNANCY

The third element in the prenatal discourse that I will consider here stems from the often told story that testing is an option that increases women's reproductive choices and control. This claim has had

---

[82] *See* Beck-Gernsheim, *supra* note 61, at 28-29 ("It is characteristic that new technologies, once available, produce new standards of what we ought to have."); Lippman, *supra* note 53, at 182 (discussing professional establishment of criteria for testing and physicians' desires to comply with perceived medical standards).

[83] These techniques are likely to be driven by financial considerations of the pharmaceutical companies developing them. *See, e.g.*, D. NELKIN & L. TANCREDI, DANGEROUS DIAGNOSTICS: THE SOCIAL POWER OF BIOLOGICAL INFORMATION 33-36 (1989); A. Lippman, *supra* note 40; *cf.* Note, *Patents for Critical Pharmaceuticals: The AZT Case*, 17 AM. J.L. & MED. 145 (1991) (analyzing the validity of pharmaceutical companies' claims that without a federally-granted monopoly, they would not have the incentive to research and develop orphan drugs).

[84] *See* Shiloh, Waisbren & Levy, *A Psychosocial Model of a Medical Problem: Maternal PKU*, 10 J. PRIMARY PREVENTION 51 (1989).

34   AMERICAN JOURNAL OF LAW & MEDICINE VOL. XVII NOS. 1 & 2 1991

much attention in the literature and I will examine it only with respect to how some features of prenatal diagnosis do increase control, but allocate it to someone other than a pregnant woman herself. This is most apparent in the context of abortion.[85]

Without doubt, prenatal diagnosis has (re)defined the grounds for abortion[86] — who is justified in having a pregnancy terminated and why — and is a clear expression of the social control[87] inherent in this most powerful example of geneticization. Geneticists and their obstetrician colleagues are deciding which fetuses are healthy, what healthy means and who should be born, thus gaining power over decisions to continue or terminate pregnancies that pregnant women themselves may not always be permitted to make.

To the extent that specialists' knowledge determines who uses prenatal diagnosis and for what reasons, geneticists determine conditions that will be marginalized, objects of treatment or grounds for abortion.[88] Prenatal diagnosis is thus revealed as a biopolitical as well as a biomedical activity.[89] For example, an abortion may only be "legal" in some countries if the fetus has some recognized disorder,[90] and the justifying disorder only becomes "recognizable" because geneticists first decide to screen for it. Fuhrmann suggests that in Europe, in fact, geneticists significantly influenced legislators establishing limits within which abortion would be at all permissible, by arguing that access to abortion be maintained through a gestational age that reflected when results from amniocentesis might be available.[91] One wonders where

---

[85] For thorough analyses of the question of women's control, see generally Rapp, *Chromosomes and Communication: The Discourse of Genetic Counseling*, 2 MED. ANTHROPOLOGY Q. 143 (1988).

[86] In fact, the availability of amniocentesis "influenced legislation so that the upper limit of gestational age for legally tolerated termination of pregnancy was adjusted to the requirements of second trimester prenatal diagnosis in several countries." Fuhrmann, *supra* note 67, and 378. Evidently, geneticists can accomplish what women's groups cannot: a revisioning of abortion.

[87] The term "social control" is used in accord with its original use to embrace "the widest range of influence and regulation imposed by society upon the individual." D. GORDON, *Clinical Science and Clinical Expertise: Changing Boundaries Between Art and Science in Medicine*, in BIOMEDICINE EXAMINED, *supra* note 5, at 257.

[88] *Reproductive Choice?*, *supra* note 53, at 187-192.

[89] Finkelstein, *supra* note 65, at 14-16.

[90] Fetal abnormality as grounds for abortion is of fairly recent vintage, having first become "legal" in the United States in 1967 in response to a rubella epidemic. The Canadian Medical Association gave its approval the same year. Beck, *Eugenic Abortion: An Ethical Critique*, 143 CANADIAN MED. ASS'N J. 181, 181-84 (1990). Today, members of the general population as well as physicians regularly and strongly agree that fetal abnormality is a justification for abortion. *See* Annas, *The Supreme Court, Privacy and Abortion*, 321 NEW ENG. J. MED. 1200 (1989); Breslau, *Abortion of Defective Fetuses: Attitudes of Mothers of Congenitally Impaired Children*, 49 J. MARRIAGE FAMILY 839 (1987); Varekamp, *supra* note 40, at 147.

[91] *See* Fuhrmann, *supra* note 67, at 383-84. A recent example of the use of genetics to set social policy in this area is the position taken by the American Society of Human Genetics with

limits might have been placed had first trimester chorionic villus sampling been available *before* amniocentesis? Would they have been more restrictive?

Other potential participants in what should be an intensely personal matter for "control" include insurance companies and governments.[92] If either funds genetic screening programs or covers the cost of treatment for conditions diagnosable *in utero*, they may claim a say in determining which tests are carried out and what action the results entail.[93] Recently circulated reports about a health maintenance organization planning to withdraw medical coverage for a woman who could have avoided the birth of a child with cystic fibrosis if she had "chosen" to abort the pregnancy after the prenatal diagnosis was made, gives substance to concerns about changes in the locus of control.[94] While this kind of abuse of power grabs headlines — and gets discounted as something regulations can prevent — there are more subtle forms of control that achieve the same ends and actually result from seemingly benevolent regulations and public policies. For example, newborn screening for Phenylketonuria (PKU) is carried out in the United States with universal approval. However, in only four states are health insurers required to cover the cost of the special foods children with PKU need.[95] What choices/control does a woman have in this context? What are her options if prenatal diagnosis for PKU is offered? It would not be unreasonable to believe that a pregnant woman who learns that the fetus has the genes for PKU and does not see this as a reason for abortion may feel compelled to terminate her pregnancy because she could not herself finance the special diet her child would require after

---

respect to possible restrictions on abortion under consideration in various parts of the United States. This professional group has proposed as model legislation

> that any pregnant female whose pregnancy has not reached the point of viability and who has been informed by a licensed or certified health care professional that her fetus (or fetuses) is/are likely to have a serious genetic or congenital disorder shall have the right, among other options, to choose to terminate her pregnancy. This right shall extend to situations where the female is at significantly increased risk for bearing a child with a serious disorder for which precise prenatal diagnosis is not available.

Letter from Phillip J. Riley to the author. The merits for/against this position aside, it certainly demonstrates how geneticists seek to influence the resolution of fundamentally political, legal (and ethical) problems.

[92] Nsiah-Jefferson, *supra* note 54, at 31-37, 39-41.

[93] Billings, *Genetic Discrimination: An Ongoing Survey*, GENEWATCH, May 1990, at 7-15.

[94] *See* Billings, Kohn, de Cuevas & Beckwith, *Genetic Discrimination As a Consequence of Genetic Screening, to be published in* AM. J. HUM. GENETICS (1991); *see also* Gostin, *Genetic Discrimination: The Use of Genetically Based Diagnostic and Prognostic Tests by Employers and Insurers*, 17 AM. J.L. & MED. 109 (1991).

[95] Brody, *A Search to Ban Retardation in a New Generation*, N.Y. Times, June 7, 1990, at B9, col. 1 (citing Carol Kaufman) (the four states are Massachusetts, Montana, Texas and Washington). PKU reflects an inability to metabolize phenylalanine properly. It can be controlled by dietary restrictions.

36   AMERICAN JOURNAL OF LAW & MEDICINE VOL. XVII NOS. 1 & 2 1991

birth. Such pressures (explicit and implicit) exerted on a woman to abort a pregnancy following the prenatal diagnosis of some problem that makes her unable to keep a pregnancy she wants reveals another way in which social control over abortion may be genetically based.

Policy decisions establish control, too, in the guise of guidelines for seemingly straightforward features of prenatal screening and testing programs. For example, it has been shown that parents' decisions about pregnancy termination for the same chromosome abnormality are influenced by whether or not fetal anomalies are visualized on ultrasound.[96] Even *who* does the counseling associated with prenatal diagnosis can influence what a woman does after learning of a fetal chromosome abnormality;[97] rates of induced abortion are higher when obstetricians relate the results of testing than when geneticists do.[98] Similarly, the interval between prenatal diagnosis counseling and testing is of consequence. This is demonstrated clearly in the reported association between the rates of amniocentesis utilization and the interval between counseling and testing: the shorter the interval, the greater the use.[99] Pressure from state policies establishing when (as well as how)[100] genetic counseling will be provided to screening program participants may be covert, but this does not prevent it from being controlling. In sum, prenatal testing and screening may provide control. But for whom? To what ends? For whose benefit?

IV.   THE CONTEXT OF GENETICIZATION

I now turn from the specific stories being told about prenatal diag-

---

[96] Drugen, Greb, Johnson & Krivchenia, *Determinants of Parental Decisions to Abort for Chromosomal Abnormalities*, 10 PRENATAL DIAGNOSIS 483 (1990).

[97] *See Genetic Counseling I, supra* note 60, at 51; *Genetic Counseling II, supra* note 60, at 73; Harper & Harris, *Editorial: Medical Genetics in China: A Western View*, 23 J. MED. GENETICS 385, 386-388 (1986) (noting role of "genetic counselor as arbiter for permission to have additional children in China" or to abort child); Rapp, *supra* note 85, at 143 (analyzing messages conveyed in genetic counseling discourse); *see also* Puck, *Some Considerations Bearing on the Doctrine of Self-Fulfilling Prophecy in Sex Chromosome Aneuploidy*, 9 AM. J. MED. GENETICS 129 (1981) (noting use of term "syndrome" in prenatal diagnosis).

[98] Holmes-Seidle, Ryynanen & Lindenbaum, *Parental Decisions Regarding Termination of Pregnancy Following Prenatal Detection of Sex Chromosome Abnormality*, 7 PRENATAL DIAGNOSIS 239, 241-243 (1987). *See also* Robinson, Bender & Linden, *Decisions Following the Intrauterine Diagnosis of Sex Chromosome Aneuploidy*, 34 AM. J. MED. GENETICS 552 (1989). This raises an interesting question for the future as screening is further routinized and moves increasingly from geneticists to obstetricians.

[99] Lorenz, Botti, Schmidt & Ladda, *Encouraging Patients to Undergo Prenatal Genetic Testing Before the Day of Amniocentesis*, 30 J. REPRODUCTIVE MED. 933 (1985).

[100] As possibilities for screening and testing expand, so, too, will the need to provide genetic counseling services to participants. The size of the resources required to do this appropriately may be enormous, if existing models for genetic counseling are to be followed. *See* Fraser, *Genetic Counseling*, 26 AM. J. HUM. GENETICS 636 (1974). The consequences may also be enormous — however the programs are designed.

nosis to the circumstances in which they are being told, attempting to show the interactions between content and context. The links are numerous and the required analysis substantial. I shall concentrate here on the existence of the connections rather than on their critique. My overall thesis is that characteristics (political, economic, social) of the North American society in which prenatal diagnostic technologies have been developed determine how these techniques will influence how we define individual health, health care and the health care system. The same technology will have different consequences in different societies, so that exploring the characteristics of the system in which it is introduced is important.[101] The critical characteristics derive from current stratifications of North American society and the inequities with which they are associated.[102] These influence (and are influenced by) the use of prenatal technology in ways that laws, regulations or even ethical codes for screening and testing alone do not — and probably cannot — address.

A. IS THE "PLAYING FIELD" LEVEL?

Access to, a perceived need for and the use of either health care providers or the health care system vary markedly between people. The outcomes of these encounters (or of their non-occurrence) also are quite variable. A person with certain signs, characteristics or features may be referred to different people/services/systems for help.[103] Variations in the perspective and nature of the "help," along with variations in people's approach to and use of these different services, mean that disease and illness are labeled and socialized differentially according to where one becomes situated.[104] The definition of and help offered for

---

[101] Kranzberg, *The Uses of History in Studies of Science, Technology and Society*, 10 BULL. SCI. TECH. & SOC. 6 (1990). These technologies are not neutral objects waiting for us to make good or evil use of them. Rather, the "politics embodied in material things" from the very start, Winner, *supra* note 8, at 12, give them "valence" and make it essential to understand the social context in which a new device or practice is offered. Bush, *Women and the Assessment of Technology: To Think, To Be; To Unthink, To Free*, in MACHINA EX DEA: FEMINIST PERSPECTIVES ON TECHNOLOGY 154, 154-56 (J. Rothschild ed. 1983) [hereinafter MACHINA EX DEA]. The context, itself, not only influences the technologies we choose to develop but also presupposes certain approaches to their use. In turn, the use of any given technology will change the context, will change us. Technology is like a "new organism insinuating itself and altering us irrevocably." Boone, *Bad Axioms in Genetic Engineering*, HASTINGS CENTER REP., Aug.-Sept. 1988, at 9.

[102] This issue is presented in fairly general terms here without the in-depth consideration that is being (and will be) developed elsewhere in the context of my larger project.

[103] Waxler, *The Social Labeling Perspective on Illness and Medical Practices*, in THE RELEVENCE OF SOCIAL SCIENCE TO MEDICINE 283 (L. Eisenberg & A. Kleinman eds. 1980); *The Anthropologies of Illness and Sickness*, *supra* note 5, at 257; *Rational Men and The Explanatory Model Approach*, *supra* note 5, at 57.

[104] A recent example is the differential in rates of substance abuse reporting during pregnancy to public health authorities in Florida, with poor women being reported more often

38   AMERICAN JOURNAL OF LAW & MEDICINE VOL. XVII NOS. 1 & 2 1991

the same "sickness" or characteristic will vary according to an individual's economic and social power. This variability distributes inequities
in health problems and their resolution.

Moreover, since health-related naming and helping activities occur
in a cultural/political context where restraints on options vary with a
person's place in the society, "life choices,"[105] presented as ways to
manage or avert health problems, will not be randomly distributed.[106]
This certainly includes a "choice" of asking for or accepting information obtainable through genetic screening tests. Again, societal differences, no less than individual psychological ones, underlie these
differential behaviors.

Life circumstances, broadly defined, establish an individual's place
in society. They act, therefore, as powerful restraints on health options
from identification of a problem to approaches, by self or others, to its
resolution, and they influence possible options, expectations and responses.[107] These dynamics establish the inequities, the contours/ter-
rain of the society (the so-called "playing field"), that will modulate the
impact of genetic screening and testing just as the latter may themselves landscape the "playing field" and its inequities. To illustrate
this, I shall consider in very broad terms how two stratifications — gender and class — shape and are shaped by genetic testing and screening.[108] Although these are inseparably linked, I shall arbitrarily isolate
each one to clarify the discussion.

B. GENDER

Prenatal testing and screening represent techniques applied to women. How, when, why and by whom they are applied will be condi-

---

than others. Chasnoff, Landress & Barrett, *The Prevalence of Illicit Drug or Alcohol Use During
Pregnancy and Discrepancies in Mandatory Reporting in Pinellas County, Florida,* 322 NEW ENG. J.
MED. 1202 (1990). *See also* L. WHITEFORD & M. POLAND, *Introduction,* in NEW APPROACHES TO
HUMAN REPRODUCTION 1 (L. Whiteford & M. Poland eds. 1989).

[105] *See* Townsend, *Individual or Social Responsibility for Premature Death? Current Controversies
in the British Debate About Health,* 20 INT'L J. HEALTH SERVS. 373, 382-84 (1990) (noting that life
style is not just a matter of choice, and presenting an analysis of the many forces that shape
what we too easily call choice); *cf.* Rosén, Hanning & Wall, *Changing Smoking Habits in Sweden:
Towards Better Health, But Not for All,* 19 INT'L J. EPIDEMIOLOGY 316 (1990) (providing example
of where education contributes to increased inequities in health).

[106] *Rational Men and the Explanatory Model Approach, supra* note 5, at 57.

[107] *See* Kickbusch, *Self-Care in Health Promotion,* 29 SOC. SCI. & MED. 125 (1989).

[108] Other stratifications of consequence here based on ability, race, etc. are considered
elsewhere. *See generally* A. Lippman, *supra* note 40; T. DUSTER, *supra* note 18 (emphasizing
racial and ethnic strata). In addition, inequities attached to genetic screening and testing
relating to employment discrimination, insurance refusals and racial prejudice, for example,
have been considered in detail elsewhere and these situations will not be reviewed specfically
here. *See, e.g.,* T. DUSTER, *supra* note 18; N. HOLTZMAN, PROCEED WITH CAUTION: PREDICTING
GENETIC RISKS IN THE RECOMBINANT DNA ERA (1989); Billings, *supra* note 93, at 7, 15; Council
for Responsible Genetics, *supra* note 13, at 287.

PRENATAL GENETIC TESTING AND SCREENING   39

tioned by prevailing attitudes about women, their bodies and their roles. Because the world in which genetic and other reproductive technologies are developing is gendered, it would be naive to think that these technologies can escape gendered use.[109] In this world, women are disadvantaged, generally powerless, and frequently socialized to follow authority and acquiesce in certain norms surrounding maternity and motherhood.[110] Furthermore, because a child's disability is viewed as a private problem for the family, the gendered attribution of responsibilities for family health to women obligates them to deal with it alone whether by avoiding, reducing or managing disability. Prenatal diagnosis in such a context can hardly be "neutral."

Perhaps the most dramatic consequence of gender stratification for prenatal diagnosis is the (potential) use of genetic screening and testing to identify and select fetuses on the basis of their sex alone. Being female is of less value than being male, and the fetuses that are least valued are those most likely to be aborted.[111] Though generally condemned by North American geneticists,[112] and commonly considered unlikely when "selection" entails a second trimester abortion, the availability of chorionic villus sampling resurrects the problem anew, as if the timing of abortion were the (only) problematic aspect.[113] Because this use of prenatal diagnosis as a tool *against* women has had much attention in the literature, with one commentator calling it "previctimization,"[114] it will not be considered further here other than to emphasize that "sex selection" is problematic no matter when it is carried out, whether or not it requires some technological assistance, and that preconceptional selection differs from postconceptional selection only with respect to process, not principles.[115] However done, it

---

[109] Some even suggest that they have been developed and used specifically to maintain gendered distinctions and increase patriarchal power. *See, e.g.*, Morgan, *Of Woman Born? How Old Fashioned! — New Reproductive Technologies and Women's Oppression*, in THE FUTURE OF HUMAN REPRODUCTION, *supra* note 53, at 60; Rowland, *Reproductive Technologies: The Final Solution to the Woman Question?*, in TEST-TUBE WOMEN, *supra* note 55, at 356.

[110] *See* L. WHITEFORD & M. POLAND, NEW APPROACHES TO HUMAN REPRODUCTION 1, 8-9 (1989); Raymond, *Reproductive Gifts and Gift Giving: The Altruistic Woman*, HASTINGS CENTER REP., Nov.-Dec., 1990 at 7; *see also supra* note 61.

[111] *See, e.g.*, M. WARREN, GENDERCIDE: THE IMPLICATIONS OF SEX SELECTION (1985); Hoskins & Holmes, *Technology and Prenatal Femicide*, in TEST-TUBE WOMEN, *supra* note 55, at 237; Rothschild, *supra* note 48, at 107.

[112] *E.g.*, Fletcher, *Is Sex Selection Ethical?*, in RESEARCH ETHICS 333 (K. Berg & K. Tranoy eds. 1983); Wertz & Fletcher, *Ethics and Medical Genetics in the United States: A National Survey*, 29 AM. J. MED. GENETICS 815, 821 (1988) (Table V).

[113] *Who Decides?*, *supra* note 26, at 434; *Reproductive Choice?*, *supra* note 53, at 182.

[114] Raymond, *Introduction*, in THE CUSTOM-MADE CHILD? WOMEN CENTERED PERSPECTIVES 177 (H. Holmes, B. Hoskins & M. Gross eds. 1981) (defining previctimization as "the spectre of women being destroyed and sacrificed before even being born").

[115] *See generally* G. COREA, R. KLEIN, J. HANMER, H. HOLMES, B. HOSKINS, M. KISHWAR, J. RAYMOND, R. ROWLAND & R. STEINBACHER, MAN-MADE WOMEN: HOW NEW REPRODUCTIVE

40   AMERICAN JOURNAL OF LAW & MEDICINE VOL. XVII NOS. 1 & 2 1991

can only reinforce gender-based inequities.

Another consequence, less immediately obvious, is how the current applications of prenatal diagnosis are subtly entangled with another long-standing problematic for women: aging.[116] Not only has the availability of prenatal diagnosis and professionally imposed limits on access to testing created the "social category"[117] of "the older woman at risk," considered above,[118] but, not unlike cosmetic surgery or estrogen replacement regimens, testing has been presented as another way for women to circumvent features of aging,[119] with prenatal diagnosis supposedly a tool *for* women. The increasing probability of chromosomal nondisjunction associated with increases in a woman's age[120] can be managed, just as can other bodily changes associated with "getting older." The biological "failure" causing Down syndrome can be controlled and "older" women need not be "less fit"[121] for childbearing, just as wrinkles of the skin or hot flashes can be controlled. "Old enough" to warrant control is getting younger all the time.[122] When age, whether chronological or "equivalent,"[123] is used as a principal criterion for prenatal diagnosis, it appears to be essential for defining a woman (and women in general). Age-based strata come to be seen strictly as fixed "facts" of life, camouflaging the extent of their social production.[124]

TECHNOLOGIES AFFECT WOMEN (1987); Hanmer, *Reproductive Technology: The Future for Women?*, in MACHINA EX DEA, *supra* note 101, at 183, 191 ("The questions of social scientists imply that sex predetermination is an accepted and acceptable idea. It is just a matter of finding out which method is preferred and when and how many children are desired."); Rowland, *Technology and Motherhood: Reproductive Choice Reconsidered*, 12 SIGNS 512 (1987).

[116] *Cf.* E. MARTIN, THE WOMAN IN THE BODY: A CULTURAL ANALYSIS OF REPRODUCTION (1987).

[117] D. NELKIN & L. TANCREDI, *supra* note 83, at 17 (testing creates social categories "in order to preserve existing social arrangements and to enhance the control of certain groups over others").

[118] *See supra* notes 67-71 and accompanying text.

[119] These circumventions pale in comparison to the variety of pharmaceutical and surgical methods that can be applied to remove all age limits on the possibility of pregnancy for a woman. *See, e.g.*, Levran, *supra* note 65, at 1153; Sauer, Paulson & Lobo, *supra* note 63, at 1157.

[120] Hook, Cross & Schreinemachers, *Chromosomal Abnormality Rates at Amniocentesis and in Live-Born Infants*, 249 J. A.M.A. 2034 (1983).

[121] Hubbard & Henifin, *supra* note 60, at 238.

[122] R. HUBBARD, *supra* note 17; Hubbard, *Personal Courage Is Not Enough: Some Hazards of Childbearing in the 1980s*, in TEST-TUBE WOMEN, *supra* note 55, at 331, 339.

When amniocentesis was first introduced, 40 years was the age cut-off. This has dropped to 35 in North America, and recommendations that it be lowered further have been made. PRESIDENT's COMM'N, *supra* note 30, at 81; Crandell, Lebherz & Tabsh, *Maternal Age and Amniocentesis: Should This Be Lowered to 30 Years?*, 6 PRENATAL DIAGNOSIS 237, 241 (1986).

[123] *See supra* note 73.

[124] *See* Rindfuss & Bumpass, *Age and the Sociology of Fertility: How Old Is Too Old?*, in SOCIAL DEMOGRAPHY 43 (K. Taueber, L. Bumpass & J. Severt eds. 1978) (providing an overview of social definitions of childbearing age).

Existing gender (and age) strata mean that procreation-linked test-ing and screening cannot but be *of* major consequence to women (irre-spective of any consequences it may have *for* them).[125] Thus, the *geneticization* of pregnancy is following a trajectory similar to — but per-haps even more alienating than — that described and analyzed elo-quently by others studying the medicalization of pregnancy.[126] Once again, those with great power — physicians — control powerful tech-nologies to monitor, regulate and even obliterate the female body when they situate a fetus in conflict with a pregnant woman in the provision of obstetric care.[127] With dramatic images obtained by ultrasound, a presentation of the pregnant woman as a fetal container,[128] a uterine environment,[129] perhaps even a "fetal abuser"[130] gains force. Once again, an underlying ideological premise that women's inadequacy can threaten the success of reproduction justifies some technological inter-vention, and this time the "inadequacy" is innate. Purposefully or not, prenatal testing and screening reinforce stereotyped gender definitions of women and traditional values regarding their behavior. It would be particularly unfortunate, therefore, if realistic and serious concerns about increasing threats to women's already fragile abortion rights were to silence no less realistic and serious concerns about the place of prenatal diagnosis in a gendered society.

C. ECONOMIC CLASS

Morbidity patterns associated with all aspects of procreation (fertil-ity, abortion, pregnancy or birthing, for example) have repeatedly been

---

[125] Its impact on their experience of pregnancy is enormous but will not be considered here. *See* Beeson, *Technological Rhythms in Pregnancy*, in CULTURAL PERSPECTIVES ON BIOLOGICAL KNOWLEDGE 145 (T. Duster & K. Garrett eds. 1984); A. Lippman, *supra* note 40; *see also* B. ROTHMAN, THE TENTATIVE PREGNANCY: PRENATAL DIAGNOSIS AND THE FUTURE OF MOTHER-HOOD (1986).

[126] *See generally* K. MICHAELSON, *Childbirth in America: A Brief History and Contemporary Issues*, in CHILDBIRTH IN AMERICA, *supra* note 19, at 1; A. OAKLEY, *supra* note 24; Fraser, *Selected Per-inatal Procedures: Scientific Bases for Use and Psycho-social Effects. A Literature Review*, 117 ACTA OBSTETRICA ET GYNECOLOGICA SCANDANAVIA 6, 6 (Supp. 1983); O'Reilly, *Small "p" Politics: The Midwifery Example*, in THE FUTURE OF HUMAN REPRODUCTION, *supra* note 53, at 159.

[127] Board of Trustees, American Med. Ass'n, *Legal Interventions During Pregnancy. Court-Ordered Medical Treatments and Legal Penalties for Potentially Harmful Behavior by Pregnant Women*, 264 J. A.M.A. 2663 (1990); Landwirth, *Fetal Abuse and Neglect: An Emerging Controversy*, 79 PEDI-ATRICS 508 (1987) (discussing tension between fetal interests and maternal rights to privacy and self-determination).

[128] Petchesky, *Fetal Images: The Power of Visual Culture in the Politics of Abortion*, in REPRODUC-TIVE TECHNOLOGIES: GENDER, MOTHERHOOD AND MEDICINE 57 (M. Stanworth, ed. 1987).

[129] Morgan, *supra* note 109, at 65. For recent use of this term in the context of scientific studies, see *supra* note 65 and accompanying text.

[130] *See* Robertson, *Procreative Liberty and the Control of Conception, Pregnancy, and Childbirth*, 69 VA. L. REV. 405, 438-43 (1983); Shaw, *The Potential Plaintiff: Preconceptional and Prenatal Torts*, in 2 GENETICS AND THE LAW 225 (A. Milunsky & G. Annas eds. 1980).

42   AMERICAN JOURNAL OF LAW & MEDICINE VOL. XVII NOS. 1 & 2 1991

shown to be influenced by a woman's economic circumstances.[131] As
previously noted, these circumstances are created and result from general class- and power-based inequities that determine how illness is
named and treated (by self or others).[132] A woman's social (political)
status will also lead inescapably to "classist" effects in the use of genetic
testing, screening and the resulting information. Most simply, varying
circumstances (and psychological differences) cause individuals to react
to offers of testing and screening unequally, and differentials in the use
of genetic services have repeatedly been observed.[133] For example,
from the time amniocentesis first became available, utilization rates of
prenatal diagnosis among women thirty-five and over have been associated with a woman's socioeconomic status: those with more education
or wealth undergo amniocentesis more often than women with less
schooling or income. This is true even in Canada where there is no
direct financial charge for testing.[134] Whatever the exact reason,[135] the
potential consequences of this distribution are similar. One is the possibility of a substantial socially-created alteration in the epidemiology of
chromosomal disorders: Down syndrome, which heretofore was generally unrelated to sociodemographic factors might no longer be so in the
future. To the extent that use of prenatal diagnosis is class-specific,
and abortion of fetuses with trisomy 21 the general pattern, so, too, will
be the prevalence of this condition among births. Similarly, with "routine" prenatal care automatically including an ultrasound examination
of a woman early in her pregnancy, children with neural tube defects
may be born increasingly out of proportion to women whose circumstances prevent early prenatal care — the poor and the powerless.[136]

---

[131] *E.g.*, Lazarus, *Poor Women, Poor Outcomes: Social Class and Reproductive Health*, in CHILD-
BIRTH IN AMERICA, *supra* note 19, at 39; Silins, Semenciw, Morrison, Lindsay, Sherman, Mao &
Wigle, *Risk Factors for Perinatal Mortality in Canada*, 133 CANADIAN MED. ASS'N J. 1214 (1985)
(listing social class as risk factor in stillbirths and infant deaths up to seven years of age);
Yankauer, *Editorial: What Infant Mortality Tells Us*, 80 AM. J. PUB. HEALTH 653 (1990).

[132] *See supra* text accompanying notes 104-07.

[133] Beeson, *supra* note 125, at 145; Roghmann, Doherty, Robinson, Nitzkin & Sell, *The
Selective Utilization of Prenatal Genetic Diagnosis: Experiences of a Regional Program in Upstate New
York During the 1970s*, 21 MED. CARE 1111, 1122 (1983) (concluding that in use of prenatal
genetic testing, "[t]he primary factor appears to be emotional acceptance by the patient . . . .
[but] [l]ack of knowledge, financial barriers, earlier prenatal care, and cooperation from the
primary care sector are important"); Sokal, Byrd, Chen, Goldberg & Oakley, *Prenatal Chromosomal Diagnosis: Racial and Geographic Variation for Older Women in Georgia*, 244 J. A.M.A. 1355
(1980) (study showing that 15% of Georgia women 40 years and older underwent prenatal
chromosomal diagnosis; use ranged from 60% among whites in two large urban counties to
0.5% among blacks outside Augusta and Atlanta health districts).

[134] Lippman-Hand & Piper, *Prenatal Diagnosis for the Detection of Down Syndrome: Why Are So
Few Eligible Women Tested?*, 1 PRENATAL DIAGNOSIS 249, 250 (1981).

[135] Professional underreferral seems to be a factor in underutilization of prenatal diagnosis. *Id.* at 255.

[136] I do not suggest that all women *should* have an ultrasound exam early in a "normal"
pregnancy but merely point out what one of the effects of such a policy might be.

Leaving aside important questions about the priority to assign to this or any other sophisticated prenatal genetic screening program in a society that does not guarantee access to adequate prenatal care for all women, establishing such programs on today's "playing field" may be more likely to reinforce than to reduce existing inequalities in the distribution of health problems.[137] The failure to reduce inequalities in health among social groups during the past forty years, despite the proliferation of other biomedical developments during this interval,[138] strengthens this concern.

The conditions of this playing field also, and unfortunately, mean that posing "access" as an *isolated* problem of prenatal diagnosis may produce failure to grapple fully with the issue of who is (or can get) tested. If access is defined merely as having sufficiently affordable and geographically available services, class-based inequities will likely persist. Comparable availability does not automatically lead to equity, especially when individuals start off unequally. If nothing else, inequities in the distribution of information will keep the poor excluded in a class-stratified society.[139] "Access" may not even be a meaningful feature when the allocation of resources and services is controlled by those who develop and employ them, rather than by those on whom they are used.

With respect to genetic screening, particularly those programs likely to follow gene mapping, the "bumps" in the playing field deriving from class strata based on occupation may be of special pertinence, especially for women. The unequal distribution of workplace hazards by type of activity and the continued existence of female employment ghettos, combined with persisting racial discrimination, mean that some women will be seen as "more" eligible for certain genetic screening tests than others. To the extent that one finds what one is looking for, the identification of only certain groups of workers as "susceptible" to some putative workplace hazard might be used as a supposedly sci-

---

[137] Bowman, *Legal and Ethical Issues in Newborn Screening*, 83 PEDIATRICS 894, 895 (Supp. 1989) ("If we ask poor mothers to participate in newborn screening programs and do not fight for universal prenatal care, equitable health care delivery, education, and adequate housing and food, then we are coconspirators in health deception."); Lippman, Messing & Mayer, *supra* note 15, at 398; Lippman, *supra* note 15; Lippman, *supra* note 67.

[138] Acheson, *Public Health — Edwin Chadwick and the World We Live In*, 336 LANCET 1482, 1483 (1990) (United Kingdom study suggesting that inequalities in health are present everywhere).

[139] *Cf.* Stewart, *Access to Health Care for Economically Disadvantaged Canadians: A Model*, 81 CANADIAN J. PUB. HEALTH 450, 452-53 (1990) (advocating education as one of four strategies to increase health care access for the poor). Omitted from discussion here, since it is being treated in detail elsewhere, is the marketing of susceptibility screening as a form of preventive medicine and its failure to acknowledge the historical, political and economic determinants of health (by its focus on individuals) or the constraints on behavioral choice created by class (and other) stratifications. Lippman, *supra* note 67.

44 AMERICAN JOURNAL OF LAW & MEDICINE VOL. XVII NOS. 1 & 2 1991

entific justification for workplace discrimination.[140] Occupational segregation, no less than racial or residential segregation, is entangled with differential perceptions of the acceptability and "appropriate" applicability of genetic testing. Will testing level — or build up further — "bumps"?

V. CONCLUSION

There are an unlimited number of ways to tell stories about health and disease, and an extensive vocabulary exists for telling them. Yet today, an increasing number of these stories are being told in the same way and with the same language: genetics, genes and genetic technologies. These genetic presentations of health, disease and ways to deal with them are grounded in the political and social context of the storytellers. My concern has been to decipher some of the stories about prenatal genetic screening and testing, and to reveal alternative constructions and interpretations to those already written.

Prenatal testing and screening, as has been repeated throughout this text, are most often presented as ways to decrease disease, to spare families the pain of having a disabled child and to enhance women's choice. The best-selling stories about them speak of reassurance, choice and control. As has also been suggested, this discourse presents a child born with some disorder requiring medical or surgical care as (exhibiting) a "failure."[141] This failed pregnancy theme is reinforced in counseling provided to these families when counselors emphasize how most fetuses with an abnormality abort spontaneously during pregnancy, are "naturally selected," as it were, and how prenatal testing is merely an improvement on nature.

Just as there are several ways to construe reassurance, choice and control, the birth of a child with a structural malformation or other problem, "genetic" or otherwise, can be presented in other than biomedical terms. Is the story claiming that the pregnancy has malfunctioned (by not spontaneously aborting),[142] resulting in a baby with a malformation, any "truer" than the story suggesting that *society* has malfunctioned because it cannot accommodate the disabled in its midst?[143]

---

[140] *See* Andrews & Jaeger, *Confidentiality of Genetic Information in the Workplace*, 17 AM. J.L. & MED. 75 (1991).

[141] Dunstan, *Screening for Fetal and Genetic Abnormality: Social and Ethical Issues*, 25 J. MED. GENETICS 290 (1988).

[142] Dunstan thus sees genetic screening and "selective abortion" as a "rationalized adjunct to natural processes" in which "defective products" (babies) are "discard[ed] spontaneously." *Id.* at 292.

[143] For a full development of these ideas, see Asch, *Reproductive Technology and Disability*, in REPRODUCTIVE LAWS FOR THE 1990s, *supra* note 54, at 69; Asch & Fine, *Shared Dreams: A Left Perspective on Disability Rights and Reproductive Rights*, in WOMEN WITH DISABILITIES 297 (M. Fine & A. Asch eds. 1988).

Social conditions are as enabling or disabling as biological conditions. Why are biological variations that create differences between individuals seen as preventable or avoidable while social conditions that create similar distinctions are likely to be perceived as intractable givens?[144]

While "many people don't believe society has an obligation to adjust to the disabled individual,"[145] there is nothing inherent in malformation that makes this so. Consequently, arguing that social changes are "needed" to enable those with malformations to have rich lives is not an inherently less appropriate approach. Actually, it may be more appropriate, since malformation, a biomedical phenomenon, requires a social translation to become a "problem." Expanding prenatal diagnostic services may circumvent but will not solve the "problem" of birth defects; they focus on disability, not on society's discriminatory practices.[146] They can, at best, make only a limited contribution to help women have offspring free of disabilities, despite recent articles proposing prenatal diagnosis and abortion as ways to "improve" infant mortality and morbidity statistics.[147] Thus, as sociopolitical decisions about the place of genetic testing and screening in the health care system are made, it will be important to consider how problems are named and constructed so that we don't mistakenly assume the story told in the loudest voice is the only one — or that the "best seller" is best.

Unarguably, illness and disability *are* "hard" (difficult) issues,[148]

---

[144] There would seem to be similar assumptions beneath the transformation of problems with dirty workplaces into problems with women workers who may become pregnant. *See, e.g.*, Bertin, *Women's Health and Women's Rights: Reproductive Health Hazards in the Workplace*, in HEALING TECHNOLOGY, *supra* note 61, at 289, 297 (advocating legislation requiring safe workplaces and prohibiting sterility requirements); Woolhandler & Himmelstein, *supra* note 9, at 1205.

[145] Levin, *International Perspectives on Treatment Choice in Neonatal Intensive Care Units*, 30 SOC. SCI. & MED. 901, 903 (1990) (citation omitted).

[146] For a further discussion on this, see McDonough, *supra* note 35, at 149.

[147] Powell-Griner & Woolbright, *Trends in Infant Deaths from Congenital Anomalies: Results from England and Wales, Scotland, Sweden and the United States*, 19 INT'L J. EPIDEMIOLOGY 391, 397 (1990) (probable that level of infant mortality will be influenced by prenatal screening and selective abortion); Saari-Kemppainen, Karjalainen, Ylostalo & Heinonen, *Ultrasound Screening and Perinatal Mortality: Controlled Trial of Systematic One-Stage Screening in Pregnancy*, 336 LANCET 387, 391 (1990) (Researchers of ultrasound screening in Helsinki, Finland concluded that "[t]he decrease in perinatal mortality of about half in this trial can be explained mainly by the detection of major fetal anomalies by ultrasound screening and the subsequent termination of these pregnancies.").

[148] Lippman, *supra* note 15. *See* A. FINGER, *supra* note 61; P. Kaufert, The Production of Medical Knowledge: Genes, Embryos and Public Policy (paper presented at *Gender, Science and Medicine II* conference, Toronto, Ontario, Nov. 2, 1990). Moreover, illness and disability are *hard* (i.e., difficult) issues partly because society defines them as such, in its decisions about how (not) to allocate resources to deal with them. Unfortunately, since resources are always "scarce," the programs or projects that do (not) get supported will merely be those which policymakers choose (not) to fund. No specific choice is inherent in the limited budgets available, although the requirement that choices be made is. In choosing how to deal with health problems, budget limitations may sometimes be secondary to limitations in our visions about

46   AMERICAN JOURNAL OF LAW & MEDICINE VOL. XVII NOS. 1 & 2 1991

and no one wants to add to the unnecessary suffering of any individual. But being "hard" neither makes illness or disability totally negative experiences,[149] nor does it mean they must all be eliminated or otherwise managed exclusively within the medical system. Women's desire for children without disability warrants complete public and private support. The question is how to provide this support in a way that does no harm.

To date, support has been constructed to comprise genetic screening and testing. This construction is, in many ways, a result of the current system of health-care delivery in North America and the economic pressures on it. At a time when cost-containment is a dominant theme and a primary goal of policy makers, identifying those with, or susceptible to, some condition and preventing the occurrence of the anticipated condition seem to "make sense." It coincides, too, with the risk-benefit approach currently applied to most social and environmental problems.[150] It corresponds with middle-class attitudes toward planning, consumers' rights and quality. But while this approach seems to "make sense," it does not suffice as a justification for the use of these technologies. Though it is more than twenty years since the first fetal diagnosis of Down syndrome by amniocentesis, we do not yet know the full impact of prenatal testing and screening on women's total health, power and social standing.

When amniocentesis was introduced, abortion subsequent to a diagnosis of fetal abnormality was presented as a temporary necessity until treatment for the detected condition could be devised.[151] Advocates assumed that this would soon be forthcoming. With time, however, the gap between characterization and treatment of disease has widened.[152] New information from efforts at gene mapping will certainly increase the ability to detect, diagnose and screen, but not to treat. A human gene map will identify variations in DNA patterns. Genes that "cause" specific disease, as well as those associated with increased susceptibility to specific disorders, will be found. Simultaneously, prenatal screening and testing are evolving in a context where a "genetic approach" to public health is gaining great favor.[153] All the variations that will be mapped can become targets of prenatal testing. Which targets will be selected in the quest for improved public health? And who will deter-

---

what to do. And, in choosing how to approach (even) "hard" issues, genetic prevention is but one possibility.

[149] Asch, *Reproductive Technology and Disability, supra* note 143, at 70.

[150] *Cf.* L. WINNER, *supra* note 68.

[151] *See* Friedmann, *Opinion: The Human Genome Project — Some Implications of Extensive "Reverse Genetic" Medicine,* 46 AM. J. HUM. GENETICS 407, 412 (1990).

[152] *Id.* at 411.

[153] Lippman, Messing & Mayer, *supra* note 15, at 397.

mine that they have been reached? Given the extraordinary degree of genetic variability within groups of people, what does "genetic health" actually mean — and does it matter?

For society, genetic approaches to health problems are fundamentally expensive, individualized and private. Giving them priority diminishes incentives to challenge the existing system that creates illness no less than do genes. With prenatal screening and testing in particular, the genetic approach seems to provide a "quick fix" to what is posed as a biological problem, directing attention away from society's construction of a biological reality *as* a problem and leaving the "conditions that create social disadvantage or handicap . . . largely unchallenged."[154]

Justice in the domain of health care has several definitions, but only one is generally employed in contemporary choice-and-control stories of genetic screening and testing. In these stories, justice is defined by the extent to which testing and screening programs are available and accessible to all women.[155] Distributive justice is the goal: fair treatment requires access for all.

This definition seems insufficient. Access involves more than availability, even broadly defined. Not all individuals can respond similarly even to universally "available" services and, even if they can, unfairness and injustice may continue. Thus, perhaps we need to introduce other concepts of justice when thinking about prenatal testing and how these programs contribute to, or diminish, fairness in health and health care for women (and others). Do they ensure good for the greatest number (social justice)[156] given all the causes of perinatal morbidity and mortality? Do they recognize and seek to correct past discrimination (corrective justice) given current and historically-based inequities in health? Will they level the playing field for women, for the poor?

One approach to justice is not necessarily better than another. In fact, depending on the circumstances, each one might be seen as "better." We need to keep these multiple routes to fairness in mind as we determine those to whom we wish to be fair and that for which fairness will be sought. For instance, human relationality may be as worthy of guarantees and respect as human autonomy;[157] "individual good" is not always synonymous with "common good," though social responsi-

---

[154] McDonough, *supra* note 35, at 149.

[155] *See, e.g.*, Cunningham & Kizer, *Maternal Serum Alpha-Fetoprotein Screening: Activities of State Health Agencies: A Survey*, 47 AM. J. HUM. GENETICS 899 (1990) (arguing that state health agencies must accept that genetic services constitute a public health responsibility).

[156] Lippman, *supra* note 15. *Cf.* Shannon, *Public Health's Promise for the Future: 1989 Presidential Address*, 80 AM. J. PUB. HEALTH 909 (1990) (need for public health programs to promote social justice).

[157] Ryan, *The Argument for Unlimited Procreative Liberty: A Feminist Critique*, HASTINGS CENTER REP., July-Aug. 1990, at 6 (cautioning that human relationships must not be overlooked in the argument for an unlimited right to procreate).

48   AMERICAN JOURNAL OF LAW & MEDICINE VOL. XVII NOS. 1 & 2 1991

bility need not become paternalism. There are choices to be made and
the choices will reflect our values and ideology. How we choose our
culture (by the routes we take) is no less problematic than how we
choose our children, and consequences from both will be among our
legacies.[158]

Addressing these choices will itself be "hard," and will require we
recognize and grapple with disjunction[159] between goals and needs —
perhaps even "rights" — on the social and on the individual levels.
What seems to be appropriate or best for the individual may not be so
for the collectives to which we all belong.[160] We need urgently to address these contradictions now, using our energies to situate, understand and maybe even in some way resolve them, rather than keep them
at the periphery of our vision. We must confront the possible need to
choose between what is unfortunate and what is unfair in the distribution and reduction of risks to health and well-being. We must also acknowledge how our compassion for an individual's situation may harm
women's health in general if addressing private needs dislocates provisions required for the public or solidifies existing inequities in women's
position. This disjunction is not unique to genetic screening and testing,[161] but is certainly echoed with force in this area.

This disjunction will make dialogue about the place of prenatal diagnosis in women's health care especially difficult (and, on occasion,
tense). However, this only underscores the need to avoid premature
closure of discussion and to avoid reducing it to sterile debates be-

---

[158] See R. CHADWICK, Having Children, in ETHICS, REPRODUCTION AND GENETIC CONTROL 3
(R. Chadwick ed. 1987) (prenatal diagnosis is not only a private matter); see also Edwards, The
Importance of Genetic Disease and the Need for Prevention, 319 PHIL. TRANSACTIONS ROYAL SOC'Y
LONDON 211 (1988). Edwards identifies the "conveyance of our genetic material from one
generation to the next with the minimum of damage" as the "biggest public health problem
facing our species." Id. at 112. I adapt his comments as a further reminder of the essential
interconnections between genes and culture: mutations cause genetic damage and we do
make social and political choices that influence the rate of mutation.

[159] I thank Margrit Eichler for suggesting this term and apologize if my use distorts her
concept inappropriately.

[160] Cf. Danis & Churchill, Autonomy and the Commonweal, HASTINGS CENTER REP., Jan.-Feb.
1991, at 25 (suggesting we can no longer avoid the conflict between individual wishes and
societal needs and proposing, though with respect to other technologies, that we consider the
concept of "citizenship" in attempting to accommodate both levels); see also Fox, The Organization, Outlook and Evolution of American Bioethics: A Sociological Perspective, in SOCIAL SCIENCE PER-
SPECTIVES ON MEDICAL ETHICS 201 (G. Weisz ed. 1990) [hereinafter SOCIAL SCIENCE
PERSPECTIVES].

[161] Given that even viewing private and public as alternatives reflects our prior western
beliefs that these are necessarily distinct spheres, it is of interest that the notion of disjuncture
seems to echo the lingering historical debate between "healers" and "hygienists" about the
best way to deal with health problems. Generally, heroism in healing has had more appeal
than the supposedly less glamorous work of the hygienist. See Loomis & Wing, Is Molecular
Epidemiology a Germ Theory for the End of the Twentieth Century?, 19 INT'L J. EPIDEMIOLOGY 1
(1990).

tween "pros" and "cons." The issue is *not* between experts promoting technology and Luddites trying to retard science. It is not between women who "want" prenatal diagnosis and women who don't want "them" to have it. It is not a dispute between advocates of prenatal diagnosis who are seen as defending women's already fragile rights to abortion and critics who are said to be fueling "right to life" supporters seeking to impose limits on women (and their choices).[162] All of these themes are being played out, but to focus on them is to create false polarities and to trivialize the possible advantages and disadvantages of these technologies when trying to deal with women's health concerns. Moreover, it incorrectly decontextualizes these technologies, severing their essential relatedness to time and place and isolating them from the broader health and social policy agenda of which they are a part.

Consequently, it is imperative that we continue to listen to the stories being told about prenatal testing and screening with a critical ear, situate them in time and place, question their assumptions, demystify their language and metaphors and determine whether, and to what extent, they can empower women. These technologies warrant social analysis.[163] Not to examine repeatedly the tales and their tellers will be to abdicate responsibility to the generations that present and future genetic screening and testing programs will, or will not, allow to be born. A perspective that makes us responsible for the future effects of our current activities, the well-intentioned and the unintended, may stimulate the imaginative re-vision required so that we consider not just "where in the world" we are going with the new genetics,[164] but where we want to go and whether we in fact want genetics to lead us there.†

---

[162] Important to understanding this idea is the distinction between "fetalists" and "feminists." Raymond, *Fetalists and Feminists: They are Not the Same*, in MADE TO ORDER: THE MYTH OF REPRODUCTIVE AND GENETIC PROGRESS 58 (P. Spallone & D. Steinberg eds. 1987). "Feminist positions on the NRTs [new reproductive technologies] highlight the explicit subordination and manipulation of women and their bodies that are involved in these reproductive procedures . . . . [while f]etalists are concerned with what they express as the 'violence' done to the conceptus, embryo, or fetus in procedures such as IVF." *Id.* at 60-61.

[163] In fact, we must be careful not to assume that all the social implications are ethical ones and to acknowledge that even deciding *what* the moral/ethical questions are is not "value free." This is especially important because bioethical analyses tend to emphasize individual rights rather than the "mutual obligations and interdependence" that may be critical determinants. G. WEISZ, *Introduction*, in SOCIAL SCIENCE PERSPECTIVES, *supra* note 160, at 1, 3.

[164] Fletcher, *Where in the World Are We Going with the New Genetics?*, 5 J. CONTEMP. HEALTH L. POL'Y 33 (1989).

† This paper, and the larger project from which it derives, would have been impossible without the support (emotional and intellectual) of an especially generous and thoughtful number of friends and colleagues who have nurtured my work and ideas (and, not infrequently, me) during the past several years. Some of these individuals are personal friends; others I've either met only recently or know only through their writing because of our common interests in and concern about the impact on women or reproductive and genetic technologies. Among the latter, Peggy McDonough, Christine Overall, Rayna Rapp, Janice Raymond and Barbara Katz Rothman have been of particular influence. In many ways, this

50 AMERICAN JOURNAL OF LAW & MEDICINE VOL. XVII NOS. 1 & 2 1991

paper represents a synthesis of much of what they and I have said or written on various occasions in our interconnecting and overlapping commentaries. I have tried to disentangle who said/wrote what first so as to give credit where it is due, but I fear I have not always been successful. This means that the initiator of some argument or the coiner of some phrase may not be appropriately acknowledged in what follows. I request forgiveness for these citational lapses and count on those whose work I have unconsciously adopted and adapted without credit to point them out.

I extend special gratitude, too, to Louise Bouchard, Myriam Marrache and Marc Renaud, colleagues at the Université du Montréal who helped me think through some aspects of this project during its earliest stages in its — and their — mother tongue.

I have benefitted in many ways from my friends Gwynne Basen, Margrit Eichler, Patricia Kaufert, Karen Messing and Louise Vandelac. Their insightful ideas and comments have given depth and breadth to my own thinking about the issues discussed here, and their constant support has kept me going. Friendship with these very special women has enriched my life enormously.

The same is true of Ruth Hubbard, who graciously and thoughtfully shared her wisdom and provided encouragement. She was first to introduce many of the issues and concerns I address and her presence is apparent throughout this text. Her proposal that I use the opportunity of this paper to pull together several partial manuscripts I had been carrying around, on paper and in my head, was, moreover, just the stimulus needed to get me going at a time when this project was stalled and likely to remain so forever. But, while she is responsible for the process, any shortcomings in the product are mine alone.

There are others whom I would also like to thank: Marion Kaplan, the "best friend" everyone should have who, with Irwin, was an extravagent donor of bed and board during my sojourn in New York; the staff at the Hastings Center for their hospitality and the occasion to get carried away in their library during my month there as a visiting international scholar in 1989; Ryk Edelstein and Bill Swetland, who made emergency house calls when my limited word processing skills made manuscript drafts mysteriously disappear; Zeba Hashmi who put up with multiple document conversions trying to harmonize her WP 5.0 with my 4.2 as we created the text and its multiple annotations; the Social Sciences and Humanities Research Council of Canada for providing funds to support research assistants for project-related studies that allowed me to meet and work with Fern Brunger, a graduate student who held my hand during my first steps in the world of critical medical anthropology, and provided clear evidence of how the best learning is a two-way street; the National Health Research Development Program of Health and Welfare Canada for a Scholar Award that provides my personal support; and finally, but perhaps most of all and with much love, Christopher and Jessica for being in my life.

[7]

The Journal of Legal Medicine, 14:73-92
Copyright © 1993 Taylor & Francis
0194-7648/93 $10.00 + .00

MATERNAL-FETAL RELATIONSHIP

THE COURTS AND SOCIAL POLICY

Robert H. Blank, Ph.D.*

INTRODUCTION

We are in the midst of a revolution in biomedical technology especially in
human genetics and reproduction. Rapid advances in prenatal diagnosis
and therapy are joined with new reproductive-aiding technologies such as
in vitro fertilization and more precise genetic tests. Combined with the
burgeoning knowledge of fetal development and the causes of congenital
illness, these technologies are altering our perception of the fetus. As a
result, prevailing values are being challenged by the new biology, and the
courts are being confronted with novel, onerous cases that require a reevaluation of established legal principles.

One critical set of values undergoing reevaluation centers on the relationship between mother and fetus. The technological removal of the fetus
from the "secrecy of the womb" through ultrasound and other prenatal
procedures gives the fetus social recognition as an individual separate from
the mother.[1] The emergence of in utero surgery gives the fetus potential
patient status that at times might conflict with that of the pregnant woman
who carries it.[2] Moreover, conclusive evidence that certain maternal
actions during pregnancy, such as cocaine and alcohol abuse, can have
devastating effects on fetal health challenges conventional notions of ma-

---

* Senior Lecturer in Political Science, University of Canterbury. Address correspondence to Dr.
  Blank at Political Science Dept., University of Canterbury, P.O. Box 4800, Christchurch 1, New
  Zealand.
[1] In addition to ultrasound or sonography, other routinely used prenatal diagnostic procedures include
  amniocentesis, chorionic villus sampling, alpha-fetoprotein screening, and an expanding battery of
  DNA tests.
[2] The first reported surgery on a fetus in utero was performed in April of 1981, on a 31-week-
  gestation fetus suffering from a life-threatening urinary tract obstruction. *See* Golbus, Harrison,
  Filly, Callen, & Katz, *In Utero Treatment of Urinary Tract Obstruction*, 142 AM. J. OBSTETRICS &

ternal autonomy.[3] Together, these scientific trends are producing a context
in which women's procreative rights achieved only recently after decades
of struggle are threatened. In the words of legal scholar George Annas:
"Bodies of pregnant women are the battleground on which the campaign to
define the right of privacy is fought. The ultimate outcome will likely be
shaped at least as much by new medical technologies as by politics or
moral persuasion."[4] No applications of medicine promise more acrimoni-
ous and intense legal debate in the coming decades than the impact of these
technologies on the maternal-fetal relationship and on our notions of individual rights.

On the one hand, proponents of fetal rights contend that the health of
the unborn fetus must be protected even at the expense of maternal rights.[5]
They argue that the state's interest in protecting fetal health must take
precedence over the maternal right to privacy. In contrast, proponents of
maternal autonomy argue that no one but the pregnant woman can make
such intimate decisions.[6] Any attempt at state or third-party intervention,
therefore, represents unjustifiable constraints on women and is a return to
the days when enslavement of women was justified as biological destiny.

The more we understand about the relationship between the fetus and
the mother, the more validity must be ascribed to Aristotle's admonition to
pregnant women to "pay attention to your bodies . . . take regular exercise
and follow a nourishing diet."[7] It is clear that the well-being of the fetus is
inextricably bound to the actions of the mother. Although the courts largely
are cognizant of traditional maternal rights and have been hesitant to constrain those rights, recently they have shown a willingness to overrule
maternal autonomy and at times her physical integrity when the woman's

---

GYNECOLOGY 383 (1982). Other in utero surgeries have been performed to implant miniature shunt-
ing devices in the brains of fetuses diagnosed as having hydrocephalus, a dangerous buildup of fluid
in the brain, and heart valve operations. *See* Rosenfeld, *The Patient in the Womb*, 82 SCIENCE 18
(1982). The most dramatic type of fetal surgery involves the removal of the fetus from the uterus
with its return upon completion of the surgery. One recent application of this procedure was conducted to repair a diaphragmatic hernia on a 24-week-gestation fetus. *See* Harrison, Adzick, Longa-
ker, Goldberg, Rosen, Filly, Evans, & Golbus, *Successful Repair In Utero of a Fetal Diaphragmatic
Hernia After Removal of Herniated Visera from the Left Thorax*, 322 NEW ENG. J. MED. 1582
(1990).

[3] For effects of cocaine abuse on the fetus, see Chasnoff, *Drug Use in Pregnancy: Parameters of
Risk*, 35 PEDIATRIC CLINICS N. AM. 1403 (1988). For effects of alcohol abuse on the fetus, see
Wagner, *The Alcoholic Beverages Labeling Act of 1988*, 12 J. LEGAL MED. 167 (1991).

[4] Annas, *Predicting the Future of Privacy in Pregnancy: How Medical Technology Affects the Legal
Rights of Pregnant Women*, 13 NOVA L. REV. 329, 329 (1989).

[5] *See* Balisy, *Maternal Substance Abuse: The Need to Provide Legal Protection for the Fetus*, 60 SO.
CAL. L. REV. 1209 (1987).

[6] *See* Gallagher, *Prenatal Invasions and Interventions: What's Wrong with Fetal Rights*, 10 HARV.
WOMEN'S L.J. 9 (1987). *See also* Johnsen, *The Creation of "Fetal Rights": Conflicts with Women's
Constitutional Rights to Liberty, Privacy, and Equal Protection*, 95 YALE L.J. 599 (1986).

[7] ARISTOTLE, POLITICS, 7 XVI 14.

actions harm or represent probable danger to the life or health of the developing fetus.[8] As scientific evidence corroborates the deleterious effects of maternal behavior, the trend in the courts toward finding a cause of action against a pregnant woman for conduct injurious to her unborn child is bound to heighten.

In the last decade there has been a persistent intensification of policy issues surrounding attempts to define maternal responsibility.[9] Unfortunately, the current policy context and the government response to date have been inconsistent, haphazard, and often contradictory. Considerable interest has focused on the development of case law and the activity of the courts in redefining responsible maternal behavior and the standard of care owed the unborn.[10] It is clear that the courts are already heavily involved in revising conventional views of maternal autonomy and discretion in procreative matters. Trends in both tort and criminal law appear to be on a collision course with the traditional predominance given maternal autonomy.

An alternative approach to that which emphasizes maternal responsibility is to focus on the social responsibility to provide all pregnant women with access to proper nutrition, counseling, mental health and substance abuse services, and adequate general health care. Although there is a tendency for the public and the courts to emphasize maternal responsibility and castigate mothers of unborn who fail to act "responsibly," less attention has been directed at encouraging healthful behavior through public education. We have a health care system that stresses efforts to treat the medical problems at the expense of efforts to prevent them. The most pressing health problems of children continue to be related to deficiencies in access to essential basic maternal health services. Programs to provide adequate prenatal care to pregnant women usually return many dollars in benefits for each dollar spent, not to mention the reduction of less tangible social costs.[11] The costs of providing adequate maternal/child health care programs to educate pregnant women is meager compared to the neonatal intensive care costs of treating premature or disabled infants in fully pre-

---

[8] This can be seen in the willingness of many courts to constrain maternal autonomy in cases involving forced cesarian sections. For a summary of these cases and a discussion of the policy implications, see Kolder, Gallagher, & Parsons, *Court-Ordered Obstetrical Interventions*, 316 NEW ENG. J. MED. 1192 (1987).

[9] *See* Losco, *Fetal Abuse: An Exploration of Emerging Philosophic, Legal, and Policy Issues*, 42 W. POL. Q. 265 (1989).

[10] For a more detailed discussion, see R. BLANK, MOTHER AND FETUS: CHANGING NOTIONS OF MATERNAL RESPONSIBILITY (1992).

[11] THE INSTITUTE OF MEDICINE, PREVENTING LOW BIRTHWEIGHT (1985) (concluding that for each dollar spent on prenatal care, $3.38 is saved). *See also* Nagey, *The Content of Prenatal Care*, 74 OBSTETRICS & GYNECOLOGY 516 (1980) (finding a saving of $3.66 in hospital costs alone for each dollar spent for prenatal care).

ventable instances. Therefore, before society takes action to coerce responsible maternal behavior, substantial efforts must be made to provide proper
education, counseling, and health care to pregnant women, particularly
those in high-risk groups such as teenagers and the poor.

Even the most comprehensive and effective prenatal health program,
however, will not resolve problems with a minority of pregnant women
who are either unable or unwilling to alter their behavior that poses a risk
of harm to the unborn. Chronic alcohol abusers, drug addicts, and others
whose actions are undisputably harmful to the developing fetus, and who
are unresponsive to preventive efforts, might justly be precluded from
enjoying the rights of parenthood or legally required to take responsibility
for the consequences of their behavior, but only after society has better met
its responsibilities in averting such behaviors. Policy guidelines are needed
that encourage healthy maternal behavior, but also protect against unwarranted state intrusion into the procreative choice of women. This is a very
difficult, although critical, balance to achieve. The central question for
policy makers is when society has a duty to intervene in reproductive
decisions in order to protect the health or life of the unborn. If so, what are
the boundaries of governmental intrusion?

I. THE ROLE OF GOVERNMENT IN REDEFINING
PROCREATIVE RIGHTS

The progression of Supreme Court decisions on procreative privacy
culminating in *Roe v. Wade*[12] and reiterated in *City of Akron v. Akron
Center for Reproductive Health, Inc.* and *Thornburgh v. American College
of Obstetricians and Gynecologists,*[13] clearly enunciates the right of a
woman not to have a child if she so desires. Contraception and abortion in
theory at least, are guaranteed for all women, whatever their age and
marital status. Although abortion continues to be a volatile issue and recent
attention has focused on how tentative the legal context is in light of the
new alignment of the Supreme Court,[14] the complementary question of
whether all women, whatever their age, marital status, or other characteristics, have a corresponding right to have children is, perhaps, even more
problematic. If there is a right to have children, then are there any limits

---

[12] 410 U.S. 113 (1973).

[13] City of Akron v. Akron Center for Reproductive Health, Inc., 462 U.S. 416 (1983); Thornburgh v.
American College of Obstetricians and Gynecologists, 476 U.S. 747 (1986).

[14] Recent shifts in the Court's balance were initially reflected in Webster v. Reproductive Health
Servs., 492 U.S. 490 (1989), upholding a Missouri statute affirming that human life begins at
conception and prohibits the use of public funds, employees, and facilities for abortion-related
services not necessary to save the life of the mother. The replacement of Justice Thurgood Marshall
by Justice Clarence Thomas may have the effect of further undermining *Roe v. Wade.*

that can be imposed on the number or quality of progeny? Just as the right to abortion is not absolute,[15] it might be that the general right to have children ought to be circumvented under some circumstances. If so, who sets the limits and on what basis and how active a role ought the courts play in shaping these constraints?

Moreover, given the right to have children, do infertile couples or singles have a legitimate claim to new reproduction-aiding technologies such as in vitro fertilization and embryo lavage? Should Medicaid or some similar public program fund these procedures for those persons who cannot afford the high costs? Or does this right, if recognized, apply only to women who can afford the high costs of these technologies? What if a woman requires the services of a surrogate mother because she is unable to undergo pregnancy—does she have that right and, if so, who pays?[16] A public furor arose in response to a well-publicized case in which a woman on welfare had a child via artificial insemination by donor.[17] Although the notoriety of this case may not be commonplace, it is a cogent illustration of the dilemmas that arise in interpreting reproduction as a positive entitlement.

Another policy issue regarding the right to have children relates to persons who carry genetic diseases, particularly dominant genetic traits such as Huntington's Disease.[18] Social and legal pressures that will label parents as "irresponsible" who knowingly reproduce children with genetic disorders are likely to intensify. Do chronic alcohol abusers, drug abusers, or women with other high-risk conditions have a constitutional right to procreate without concern for the burden placed on their progeny and society? In the case of young teenagers who are emotionally and physically immature, is it fair to their potential children, others in society, or themselves to guarantee them an unfettered right to reproduce?

If one answers affirmatively that all women have a positive right to reproduce when they desire, then the social policy goals are reasonably straightforward—eliminate to the maximum extent possible any institutional, economic, and political infringements on the free exercise of that right. If one answers negatively, however, the policy context is significantly more troublesome because one must develop a strategy to set con-

---

[15] Even at the height of abortion rights immediately after *Roe v. Wade*, limits could be set by states after the end of the second trimester, or after viability, which is a changing concept due to medical technology.

[16] The other side of this question, which is at the center of the surrogate mother controversy, is whether a woman has a right to be a surrogate mother and be paid for her services. *See* M. FIELD, SURROGATE MOTHERHOOD (1988).

[17] *See Case Studies: AID and the Single Welfare Mother*, 13 HASTINGS CENTER REP. 22 (Feb. 1983).

[18] *See* Purdy, *Genetic Diseases: Can Having Children Be Immoral?*, in GENETICS NOW: ETHICAL ISSUES IN GENETIC RESEARCH 26 (J. Buckley ed. 1978).

straints without undercutting prevailing social values. Overall, then, in a democratic society, the policy issues in assuming complete reproductive freedom are less troublesome than those surrounding efforts to limit this freedom, because of difficulties in setting the boundaries of legitimate government involvement.

The potential governmental role in suppressing reproductive rights can take many routes depending on how these rights are defined by prevailing societal values. Because of the value that strongly supports the right of married couples to have children, there is a near consensus that few, if any, restraints ought to be placed on them. Social policies that focus on the education of high-risk parents to refrain from reproduction or provide other options for having children are likely to enjoy considerably greater support than coercive policies. Voluntary, not mandatory, genetic screening and prenatal diagnostic programs are most compatible with prevailing values concerning procreation in the United States. Although other inducements such as tax incentives might offer the means to supplement educational efforts, they result in inequities based on wealth. In contrast, the elimination or reduction of public support for the indigent, combined with the provision of a full range of family planning services, might encourage some people not to have children, but again at the cost of inequitable impact on various groups. More explicit policies to limit procreative choice historically have depended on sterilization programs.[19] These programs failed to reach even their most modest objectives and continue to personify state intrusion at its extreme for many people. Although new technologies in reversible sterilization and long-term subdermal implant contraceptives promise to ease rationalization of such policies, they will continue to be most controversial.[20]

The licensing of parents is abhorrent under the prevailing value system in the United States. Even if it could be demonstrated that requiring parents to undergo a series of genetic, medical, social, and personality exams would assure that children born have an adequate chance to compete in this complex world, any policy of this type understandably would be widely attacked and unenforceable within the pluralistic framework. Few elected officials are likely to advocate a policy that specifically delimits who can and who cannot have children.

Despite these caveats, the trends toward legal acknowledgement of fetal rights, torts for wrongful life, torts for prenatal damage, and criminal

---

[19] *See* P. REILLY, THE SURGICAL SOLUTION: A HISTORY OF INVOLUNTARY STERILIZATION (1991).

[20] I have argued elsewhere (R. BLANK, FERTILITY CONTROL: NEW TECHNIQUES, NEW POLICY ISSUES (1991)) that the routine availability of reversible techniques such as NORPLANT will undercut the major assumption of irreversibility that the courts have used to strike down involuntary applications of sterilization since Skinner v. Oklahoma, 316 U.S. 535 (1942).

liability of parents for abuse of their unborn children demonstrate a heightened acceptance by the courts and by the public to place limits on the reproductive choice of individuals.[21] Also, the expanding knowledge of fetal development, in combination with the emergence of intervention technologies, further shifts attention from the idea of reproduction as an unmitigated right to a responsibility to produce healthy children. Those persons who knowingly beget children born unhealthy are increasingly likely to be viewed as acting irresponsibly. They will have to endure mounting social pressure to conform to standards of "responsible" procreative action.[22]

To avoid exaggerating the conflict presented here, it is critical to note that the rights of the parents, affected offspring, and society in most instances will be congruent: all parties benefit by the birth of healthy children and most work toward that goal. Despite this fact, it is imperative to place the emergence of new medical knowledge and technologies within the context of the intense debate that surrounds the conflict over maternal-fetal rights. These technologies, in use now or available in the near future, promise to sharpen disagreement as to whether state intervention in reproductive decisions is ever justifiable, and if it is, under what conditions it is warranted. As they come into more routine usage, at a minimum they clearly support an argument for closer scrutiny of maternal responsibilities.

II. THE FETAL ENVIRONMENT: A SUMMARY OF MEDICAL EVIDENCE AND LEGAL TRENDS

A wide range of behavioral patterns and maternal characteristics have been found to be associated with deleterious effects on the fetus. In most cases, it appears that the critical period of development occurs between the third and twelfth weeks of human gestation.[23] However, each organ has its own critical period and for some, such as the brain where cell proliferation does not cease until at least six to eight months after birth, sensitivity to environmental teratogenic agents extends throughout the pregnancy. Although exposure to potential teratogens[24] later in gestation might not result

---

[21] Terms like "wrongful pregnancy," "wrongful life," and "wrongful birth" are constantly being added to the legal lexicon resulting in substantial questioning of previous legal and policy assumptions. It is not surprising that there is wide divergence in the reaction of the courts to these novel cases, both in recognizing a cause of action and determining the appropriate amount of damages, if any, to be awarded. See W. WINBORNE, HANDLING PREGNANCY AND BIRTHCASES 5 (1983) (the law in this area is far from being settled; it is just beginning to develop).

[22] In some ways, the combination of these more subtle, implicit pressures in the long run are more effective restraints on procreative freedoms in a democracy because explicit calls for the same result would be dismissed out of hand.

[23] H. NISHIMURA & T. TANIMURA, CLINICAL ASPECTS OF THE TERATOGENICITY OF DRUGS (1976).

[24] Teratogenesis is the development of abnormal structures in an embryo or fetus. Teratogens include any substances or agents that lead to such abnormal development.

in gross organ system abnormalities, it might still be associated with other serious dysfunctions.

Moreover, research on teratogens indicates that it is probable that most teratogenesis is caused by the combined effects of a number of more subtle agents acting in consort rather than a massive teratogenic action of a single agent. A "simple one-to-one correspondence does not exist for birth defects."[25] The problem is vastly more complex and, thus, the solution depends on unraveling the unique contribution of each of a multitude of intimately related factors. Accordingly, the challenge to the courts in judging proximate cause is formidable in many of these cases.

Despite the complex nature of the fetal environment and the variation of effects any single stimulus might have on a specific fetus, rapidly expanding medical evidence demonstrates that there are many ways in which maternal behavioral patterns and health status can impair the proper development of the fetus and, in some cases, cause irreparable harm. Although data remain inconclusive in many areas, there is evidence of the importance of providing as risk-free a fetal environment as possible. Maternal smoking, drinking, eating, and general lifestyle can and do have an effect on the fetus.[26] As more is known about the specific deleterious effects of certain maternal behavior, increased attention will be directed toward the responsibility of the mother to assure the fetus as normal as possible an environment throughout the gestation period. Unlike most other prenatal disorders, many of these threats to the fetus and newborn are completely avoidable. For law professor Patricia King this "increasing awareness that a mother's activities during pregnancy may affect the health of the offspring creates pressing policy issues that raise possible conflicts among fetuses, mothers and researchers."[27]

Within the context of the growing knowledge of these hazards, the question reemerges as to what right a child has to a safe fetal environment and as normal as possible a start in life? In turn, this demonstrates the potential conflict between the interests of the developing fetus and the mother. It is a tragedy that in an affluent country, such as the United States, children continue to be born with birth defects caused primarily by a lack of proper nutrition or the actions of the mother during pregnancy. However, in a democratic society, the primary responsibility belongs to the woman. She alone is the direct link to the fetus and she alone makes the

---

[25] Melnick, *Drugs as Etiological Agents in Mental Retardation,* in PREVENTION OF MENTAL RETARDATION AND OTHER DEVELOPMENTAL DISABILITIES 453 (M. McCormick ed. 1980).

[26] R. BLANK, *supra* note 10, at ch. 2.

[27] King, *The Juridical Status of the Fetus: A Proposal for the Protection of the Unborn,* in THE LAW AND POLITICS OF ABORTION 81 (C. Schneider & M. Vinovskis eds. 1980).

ultimate decision regarding whether to smoke, use alcohol or other drugs, maintain proper nutrition, and so forth.

Until recently, courts have been hesitant to recognize causes of action for prenatal injury in part because of the difficulty of demonstrating proximate cause and determining reasonable standards of care. Advances in medical technology and in knowledge of fetal development are rapidly altering this situation. In addition to increasing social recognition of and empathy for the fetus, innovative diagnostic and therapeutic technologies make prenatal injury cases increasingly similar to more conventional liability or injury torts.

As a result of these technological developments, there is a discernible trend in tort law toward recognition of a maternal responsibility for the well-being of the unborn child. Despite many inconsistencies across jurisdictions, there is an unmistakable pattern toward finding a cause of action against third parties for fetal death or prenatal injury even if it occurred at the previable stage.[28] The abrogation of intrafamily immunity and the willingness of some courts to hold parents liable for prenatal injury open the door for increased judicial involvement in defining parental responsibilities.[29] In a short time span, torts against parents for prenatal injury caused either by commission or omission have been recognized by some courts.[30]

---

[28] Increasing numbers of courts have either expressly renounced the viability rule or ignored it. The Georgia Supreme Court, in Hornbuckle v. Plantation Pipe Line Co., 93 S.E.2d 727 (Ga. 1956), held that viability was not the deciding factor in a prenatal personal injury action and that recovery for any injury suffered after the point of conception should be permitted. Similarly, in Wilson v. Kaiser Found. Hosp., 190 Cal. Rptr. 649 (Cal. App. 1983), the California Court of Appeal agreed with this reasoning and concluded that birth is the condition precedent that establishes the beginning of the child's rights. A tort action may be maintained if the child is born alive—whether the injury occurred before viability or after is immaterial once birth takes place. In a further extension of this logic, some courts have recognized a cause of action for personal injuries that occurred prior to conception. In Renslow v. Mennonite Hosp., 367 N.E.2d 1250 (Ill. 1977), a physician was held liable for injuries suffered by an infant girl as a result of a blood transfusion to the mother that occurred nine years before the child's birth. *See also* Turpin v. Sortini, 643 P.2d 954 (Cal. 1982); Harbeson v. Parke-Davis, 656 P.2d 483 (Wash. 1983).

[29] Over 40 states have abrogated the immunity doctrine. In the remainder, exceptions to the rule are freely granted such that it seems unlikely that prenatal injury torts against parents would be summarily dismissed. The courts generally agree that the child's personal rights are more worthy than property or contract rights, which are already protected. Hebel v. Hebel, 435 P.2d 8 (Alaska 1967). The courts see little family tranquility protected in denying a tort action solely on the basis of the immunity rule. Peterson v. Honolulu, 262 P.2d 1007 (Hawaii 1969). According to the Massachusetts Supreme Court in Sorenson v. Sorenson, 339 N.E.2d 907 (Mass. 1975), it is the injury, not the lawsuit, that disrupts harmonious family relations. The child's relationship to the tortfeasor should not result in denial of recovery for a wrong to his or her person. Briere v. Briere, 224 A.2d 588 (N.H. 1966).

[30] In Grodin v. Grodin, 301 N.W.2d 869 (Mich. App. 1980), the Michigan Court of Appeals recognized the possibility of maternal liability for prenatal conduct. The court upheld the right of a child allegedly injured prenatally to present testimony concerning his mother's negligence in failing to

III. DEFINING RESPONSIBILITY FOR FETAL HEALTH

The relationship between the pregnant woman and the developing fetus is a special one that is culturally as well as biologically unique. Although there are strong forces toward making this relationship adversarial, generally this situation serves neither party well. The fetus more than a born child needs the mother for its health and life. Any feasible strategy for dealing with the problems raised here must, therefore, emphasize the common, shared interests of the mother and fetus, not the conflicts. Unfortunately, the predominant influence of individual rights in American society, as reflected in legal thought, continues to focus inordinate attention on conflict between mother and fetus.

The problems in the mother-fetal relationship, then, cannot be separated from the broader social context. Vast socioeconomic inequities and the resulting lack of adequate primary care for a significant minority of the population continue to contribute to the health risks for women and for the fetuses they carry. Although large numbers of women who lack proper health care and education live in isolated rural areas, it is paradoxical that the most vulnerable women are congregated in urban areas, often within sight of the most impressive concentrations of medical technology in the world.

In addition to the macro-social context, one cannot explain an individual pregnant woman's behavior without knowledge of her personal experiences. The emphasis on punishing a pregnant woman diverts attention from the root causes of the woman's often self-destructive behavior that also happens to threaten the fetus. How many of these women were victims of sexual abuse, incest, and other denigration of their self esteem? In the long run, only by understanding why particular women act in ways dangerous to the health of their fetus and ameliorating these base causes can a policy to improve fetal health succeed.

Although no individual can escape ultimate responsibility for personal actions, the social and personal plight of an increasing number of young women makes rational choice problematic and elusive. The birth of ad-

---

take a pregnancy test when her symptoms suggested pregnancy and her failure to inform the physician who diagnosed the pregnancy that she was taking tetracycline, a drug that might be contraindicated for pregnant women. Noting that the Michigan Supreme Court had determined that a child could bring suit for prenatal injury and that the immunity doctrine had been discarded, the *Grodin* court ruled that the injured child's mother would "bear the same liability as a third person for injurious, negligent conduct that interferred with the child's 'legal right to being life with a sound mind and body.'" In Stallman v. Youngquist, 531 N.E.2d 355 (Ill. 1988), however, the Illinois Supreme Court held that no cause of action exists by or on behalf of a fetus, subsequently born alive, against its mother for unintentional infliction of prenatal injuries. In this case, in which action was brought by the infant against the mother for prenatal injuries sustained in an automobile accident, the supreme court reversed the appellate court's finding upholding a cause of action.

dicted, very premature, or otherwise ill babies to these women, however, only extenuates the problem and extends the dreadful cycle into another generation. Despite the expressed concern of policy makers for the health of the children and their right to be born with a sound mind and body, there has been a consistent lack of action. Unless society is willing to expend considerable resources to overcome the problems of poverty, illiteracy, housing, and lack of access to good prenatal care and meaningful employment for women of childbearing age, the future will continue to look bleak for many children.

IV. SOCIETAL RESPONSIBILITY: PREVENTIVE STRATEGIES FOR FETAL HEALTH

Society must place a much higher priority on prevention of health problems.[31] Nowhere is this strategy more essential than in the protection of fetal health. Health promotion activities, including education starting in the early grades, counseling—particularly of women in high-risk populations—and the provision of preemptive treatment programs, are critical societal responsibilities for reducing the occurrence of ill babies. Until society makes a concerted effort to carry out these responsibilities, efforts to protect fetal health by constraining women is premature and counterproductive. The current low priority put on prevention in the United States has, unfortunately, shifted attention toward attempts to deal with the resulting problems after the fact.

Coercive governmental action charging a woman who gives birth to a cocaine-addicted baby with a criminal offense or using the tort process to recover damages from a woman for injury to the fetus she is carrying is indicative of a failure of society to address the problem of high-risk behavior before the damage is done. Martha Field is correct when she concludes that if the real goal is not control of women but "protection of the child-to-be and creation of as healthy a newborn population as possible, then appropriate means are education and persuasion, free prenatal care, and good substance abuse rehabilitation programs, available free of charge to pregnant women."[32] Although this approach is more expensive in the short run and requires considerably more effort to implement than ex post facto coercive measures, in the long run it is more fair and cost effective, both monetarily and for the national psyche.

A growing realization of these facts was reflected in the report of many panels in the late 1980s. The Institute of Medicine,[33] the United

---

[31] See R. BLANK, RATIONING MEDICINE (1988).
[32] Field, *Controlling the Woman to Protect the Fetus*, 17 LAW, MED. & HEALTH CARE 114, 125 (1989).
[33] INSTITUTE OF MEDICINE, PRENATAL CARE (1988).

84   BLANK

States Public Health Service Expert Panel on the Content of Prenatal Care,[34] and the United States Congress Office of Technology Assessment[35] all called for universal access to prenatal care for pregnant women as the critical strategy to improve the health of infants. For instance, the Institute of Medicine concluded that the nation should adopt as a new social norm the principle that all pregnant women should be provided access to prenatal, labor and delivery, and post-partum services appropriate to their need.[36] It is admitted that this will require considerable resources to reorganize the entire maternity care system including the following: removal of all barriers (including personal and cultural) to such care; a vigorous education effort in schools, media, family planning clinics, social service networks, and places of employment; and, research on how to motivate women to seek this care.

The most comprehensive discussion of how to implement prenatal care to deal with these problems is found in the report of the Public Health Service Expert Panel on the Content of Prenatal Care.[37] This report demonstrates that the objectives of prenatal care, instead of pitting mother against fetus, are designed to serve the interests of the woman, the fetus/infant, and the family. Importantly, the panel places considerable emphasis on the need for preconception care to prepare for pregnancy, because it is often too late to ensure a healthy pregnancy once it has begun. In fact, the preconception visit "may be the single most important health care visit when viewed in the context of its effect on the pregnancy."[38] The birth of a healthy baby, then, depends in part on the woman's general health and well-being before conception as well as on the amount and quality of prenatal care. Health care before pregnancy can ameliorate disease, improve risk status, and help prepare the woman for childbearing.[39]

In addition to the risk assessment component, preconception care emphasizes health promotion. Promotion of healthy lifestyle choices, counseling about the availability of services, and education on the importance of ongoing prenatal care are critical to the success of this component. Finally, the preconception visit provides an opportunity to intervene in specific risks identified in the assessment phase. The panel correctly argues that it is "imperative that women who enter pregnancy at risk or develop medical or psychosocial risk during pregnancy receive an augmented program of

---

[34] PUBLIC HEALTH SERVICE, CARING FOR OUR FUTURE: THE CONTENT OF PRENATAL CARE (1989).

[35] OFFICE OF TECHNOLOGY ASSESSMENT, HEALTHY CHILDREN (1988).

[36] Zylke, *Maternal, Child Health Needs Noted by Two Major National Study Groups*, 261 J.A.M.A. 1687, 1687 (1989).

[37] PUBLIC HEALTH SERVICE, *supra* note 34.

[38] *Id.* at 26.

[39] Jack & Culpepper, *Preconception Care: Risk Reduction and Health Promotion in Preparation for Pregnancy*, 264 J.A.M.A. 1147 (1990).

care,"[40] and the report suggests what this might entail for specific risk factors such as substance abuse.

Unfortunately, the report does not satisfactorily answer how those women who are most at risk will be recruited into preconception care. Although the case for such care is persuasive and would appear to be the strategy of choice, even if significant additional funds were made available, it is unlikely that the most vulnerable women would be included. Evidence suggests that even when prenatal care is available, many pregnant women, particularly those at high risk, avoid it. Before preconception care can be assumed to be effective even with adequate funding, considerable research is necessary to understand more fully how to convince these women to seek prenatal care.

Society has a responsibility to ensure adequate prenatal care to all pregnant women. Even under the best of circumstances (expanded funding, universal availability, and effective outreach), however, there will be some situations in which a pregnant woman will clearly disregard all attempts to minimize her high-risk behavior and refuse to comply with counseling, referral, and treatment attempts. Reported cases of women who have given birth to two or more addicted babies, despite intensive efforts to encourage responsible behavior,[41] necessitate consideration of policies that encompass coercive intervention strategies. These extreme cases warrant more severe constraints on the woman's capacity to injure additional children.

V. THE RIGHTS CONTEXT: A FORMULA FOR CONFLICT

Although the primacy given individual rights in American political culture has worked to protect the interests of the most vulnerable groups in the past, it creates inexorable dilemmas when strictly applied to the maternal-fetal relationship. The problem is heightened by the fact that proponents both of women's rights and fetal rights often try to optimize their position by insisting that the rights they advocate must be absolute. Often the arguments are framed in either-or terms, emphasizing either the woman's right to privacy or the fetus's right to a sound mind and body. Moreover, the specter of the abortion debate underlies any discussion of this conflict.

Figure 1 demonstrates how the rights of the pregnant woman and the fetus can be distributed on two continua, each ranging from no rights to full or absolute rights. In quadrant I, the woman's rights to privacy are predominant and the fetus has no claim to rights. In contrast, quadrant IV

---

[40] PUBLIC HEALTH SERVICE, *supra* note 34, at 91.
[41] Logli, *Drugs in the Womb: The Newest Battlefield in the War on Drugs*, 9 CRIM. JUSTICE ETHICS 23 (1990).

recognizes a claim to fetal rights and the legitimacy of constraining maternal behavior by limiting the scope of her rights. In quadrant II, where both
the mother and fetus have full human rights, there is no problem so long as
the rights are congruent. However, when conflict arises between the interests of the mother and the fetus, this concept of rights does not allow for its
resolution. Quadrant III at the extreme represents a *Brave New World* scenario in which neither the woman nor the fetus has significant rights and
control of procreation is fully in the hands of the state.

Although much of the ethical debate in the literature is centered in
quadrant II, with advocates on either side arguing for full unfettered rights,
a diagonal line through quadrants I and IV largely defines the policy options that are meaningful within this context. In the upper left area, the

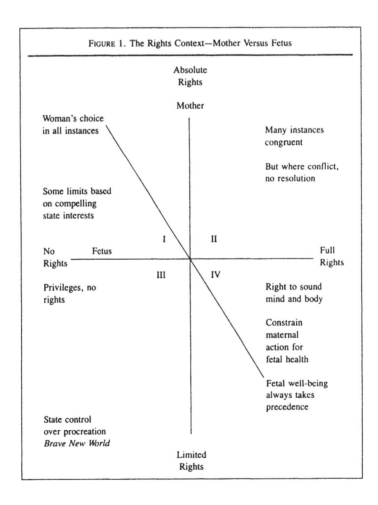

FIGURE 1. The Rights Context—Mother Versus Fetus

woman's freedom to choose on all the matters relating to procreation would be unquestioned. Conversely, in the lower right extreme, the fetal right to life and health would be the major criterion. Obviously, this position would negate abortions and force women not only to carry the fetus to term, but also to ensure fetal health, even in the face of potentially significant personal risk. The most feasible and fair policy options rest in the middle ranges of this diagonal.

Even this typology is deficient, however, because the term "fetal rights" is a distortion of the real issue and obscures what ought to be the primary concern—the health of the child when born. It is not the fetus that has rights; rather, it is the child once born that must be protected from avertable harm during gestation. The goal of any policies designed to make the fetal environment as safe as possible should be to maximize the birth of healthy children. The unfortunate, but conscious focus on fetal rights, instead of the rights of the newborn, intensifies opposition without contributing to resolution of the problem. Although the fetus may have interests to be protected that will materialize after birth, it is clear under *Roe v. Wade*[42] that fetuses do not even have a "right" to be born, at least throughout the first two trimesters.

Just as the concept of fetal rights is flawed, so the argument for a pregnant woman's absolute right to privacy is unwarranted in light of current knowledge of fetal development. Unless we are willing to give a woman license to practice infanticide, some constraints will always be imposed. Although in most cases the woman's right to procreative freedom ought to take precedence, in some instances state intervention is not only warranted but also obligatory to protect the interests of the future child by defining the woman's choices more narrowly. One major policy problem, then, is deciding how and where to set these limits. The second is who or what public agent has responsibility for doing so.

VI. THE POLICY PROBLEM: HOW TO BALANCE MATERNAL AND FETAL INTERESTS

Even if there were a consensus that a pregnant woman who chooses to carry her pregnancy to term has a moral responsibility to make reasonable efforts toward preserving fetal health, this would not necessarily translate into a legal duty to do so. By moving from a moral duty to a legal duty, we opt to permit state intervention to force the woman to make a particular moral choice. This may require, in some instances, the creation of a legal duty to accept medical procedures or treatments that benefit the

---

[42] 410 U.S. 113 (1973).

fetus even when it puts the woman at risk and requires invasion of her bodily integrity. But why should the pregnant woman be singled out for such a duty when other persons are not legally required to undergo medical risk for the benefit of someone other than themselves?[43]

Notwithstanding a hesitancy to move too readily to a legal duty for a pregnant woman, there are instances in which legal intervention is warranted. The problem still remains, however, as to what specific criteria should be used to determine when and how best to constrain maternal action to protect fetal interests. Actions of pregnant women that might affect normal fetal development include the following: abuse of illegal substances; use of alcohol; smoking or breathing secondary smoke; drinking coffee; not eating a balanced diet; use of over-the-counter and prescription drugs; working in a hazardous workplace; living in a high-risk environment; exercising too much or too little; travelling late in pregnancy; not obtaining adequate prenatal care; suffering physical harm through accident or illness; not following medical advice to avoid sexual intercourse, stay in bed for duration of pregnancy, agree to cesarean section, agree to stay on life-support system in interests of the fetus, or agree to surgery; being overweight or underweight; not entering a treatment or counseling program, if necessary; not using collaborative conception, if advised; not using prenatal diagnosis, if appropriate; and, not aborting a defective fetus diagnosed by prenatal diagnosis. Certainly, it would be ridiculous to develop a policy that restrains the pregnant woman's behavioral choices for all of the items listed. To do so would make the woman a slave of the fetus.

Moreover, such a policy would be impossible to implement and enforce and it would do little to protect the interests of the fetus. As noted earlier, it is unlikely that any mother consciously behaves in a manner designed to cause harm to her future baby. Although she might engage in behavior that entails a risk to the child she will bear, no rational woman purposely acts to do harm to a fetus she has chosen to carry to term. Although education, counseling, and provision of other services to reduce those actions of greatest risk are essential, to require a woman to comply with the above listed behaviors would be foolish and even counterproductive because it would divert attention from the few most critical deleterious actions.

It is unfortunate that, due to legislative inaction, the courts have been forced to take on the major policy-making role in this area. Although the courts are well-suited for adjudicating specific acts relevant to a particular case, judicial precedents often have broader social implications. The legal

---

[43] *See* Gallagher, *supra* note 6, at 57. *See also* Johnsen, *supra* note 6, at 625.

penalties that are available to influence the behavior of pregnant women fall into one of several categories. During pregnancy, the courts might order incarceration or detention of the woman to physically constrain her behavior out of concern for fetal health.[44] Legal penalties after birth include various civil tort actions or criminal sanctions.[45] All legal approaches have problems.

Part of the dilemma now facing pregnant women in tort liability cases stems from the acceptance of prenatal injury causes of action against third parties. The rapidly expanding number of tort claims for wrongful birth, wrongful death, and prenatal injury against third parties for commissions or omissions that result in the birth of affected children, have been motivated by a concern for the individual party to the case. However, these tort claims have produced a legal context in which it seems logically inconsistent to argue that the fetus has a cause of action against a third party, but not against the pregnant woman who might in fact be the proximate cause of the injury. By their nature, the courts are finding it difficult to draw lines that exclude the culpability of the mother and still protect the interests of the child, if born.

Criminal sanctions for maternal behavior also have inherent problems. Although a major argument for legal sanctions is deterrence, there is no evidence, for instance, that prosecution of pregnant drug abusers has

---

[44] One of the most publicized and controversial legal developments in the late 1980s was the increasing number of jurisdictions that tried to impose legal sanctions in an attempt to deter illegal drug use by pregnant women. Women have been prosecuted under statutes against child abuse and neglect, the delivery of a controlled substance to a minor, and involuntary manslaughter. It has been reported that the District Attorney of Butte County, California, announced his intention to prosecute all mothers of newborns with illegal drugs found in their urine; conviction would carry a mandatory minimum sentence of 90 days in jail. Chavkin & Kandall, *Between a "Rock" and a Hard Place: Prenatal Drug Use*, 85 PEDIATRICS 223 (1990). Likewise, other legal interventions such as civil detention have been sought to control the behavior of pregnant women deemed dangerous to the fetus. *See, e.g.*, United States v. Vaughn, 117 Daily Wash. L. Rep. 441 (D.C. Super. Ct. Mar. 7, 1989).

[45] Although the details of court cases involving drug abuse by pregnant women vary, several well-publicized cases clearly demonstrate the complex issues facing the courts. In 1989, Jennifer Johnson gave birth to a daughter. At the time, she advised hospital personnel that she was addicted to cocaine and tests confirmed traces of cocaine in her daughter's system. She was subsequently reported to the Florida Department of Health and Rehabilitation and charged with child abuse and delivery of a controlled substance during delivery of her daughter as well as during delivery of a son born in 1987. Although she was acquitted on the child abuse charge due to lack of evidence, she was found guilty on the controlled substance charge and sentenced to 15 years probation, 200 hours of community service, mandatory drug treatment, and participation in an intense prenatal program if she again became pregnant. Florida v. Johnson, No. E89-890-CFA (Seminole Cty., Cir. Ct. 1989). The judge reasoned that she had illegally introduced the cocaine into her body and then passed it on to the newborn children in the moments after delivery before the umbilical cord was cut. Children, like all persons, have the right to be born free from having cocaine introduced into their system by others. The Florida Supreme Court later reversed this decision. Johnson v. State, 602 So. 2d 1288 (Fla. 1992). For additional details of similar cases, see Janna Merrick's companion article, published as part of this Symposium at pages 57-71.

any deterrent effect. A report to the American Medical Association concludes that criminal penalties are unlikely to influence behavior because

> the use of illegal substances already incurs criminal penalties. Pregnant women who ingest illegal substances are obviously not deterred by existing sanctions; the reasons which prompt them to ignore existing penalties might very well also prompt disregard for any additional penalties. Also, in ordinary instances, concern for fetal health prompts the great majority of women to refrain from potentially harmful behavior. If that concern, generally a strong impetus for avoiding certain actions, is not sufficient to prevent harmful behavior, then it is questionable that criminal sanctions would provide the additional motivation needed to avoid behaviors that may cause fetal harm.[46]

To the contrary, there is some evidence that a major effect of such highly publicized cases is to discourage other pregnant women from obtaining proper prenatal care out of fear of criminal prosecution, thus potentially exacerbating the problem.[47] It seems reasonable that pregnant women who are substance abusers would avoid any medical treatment for fear that their physician's knowledge of their abuse might result in a jail sentence. Moreover, imposing criminal sanctions on pregnant women for potentially harmful behavior could provoke other women to seek abortions in order to avoid legal repercussions. Finally, evidence to date demonstrates that criminal prosecution of pregnant women has a clear bias against minority and low socioeconomic status women.[48] Although criminal sanctions might be successful in punishing a few women, the lack of deterrence and its likely inequitable application make it unattractive as a policy for assuring the birth of healthy children.

Although judicial intervention is warranted in exceptional cases, particularly when a pregnant woman refuses to undergo, with minimal risk to herself, lifesaving treatment for the fetus she is carrying, any such attempts should require a strict standard of review. Similarly, negligent conduct of a high degree—a conscious and reckless disregard for the welfare of the fetus by the pregnant woman—should be required before holding the woman liable for prenatal injury. Only with clear and convincing evidence, and a presupposition that the pregnant woman is to be given any benefit of doubt, should the case proceed. A closer reading of the trends in case law reviewed here demonstrates that the courts, in their understandable willingness to recognize the interests of those children born with injury, have created precedents that compromise the autonomy and physical integrity of pregnant women by creating increasingly stringent standards of care.

---

[46] AMERICAN MEDICAL ASSOCIATION, BOARD OF TRUSTEES REPORT: LEGAL INTERVENTIONS DURING PREGNANCY 14 (1990).

[47] Johnsen, *supra* note 6.

[48] Chavkin & Kandall, *supra* note 44.

The following statements are meaningful starting points for a vigorous dialogue on how to frame a workable and fair policy to deal with the maternal-fetal relationship that protects the rights of pregnant women in general, but also maximizes societal interest in the birth of healthy children.

1. The well-being of specific unborn children, as well as future generations, demands that pregnant women be educated as to the potential danger of their actions to the developing fetus.

2. The well-being of specific unborn children requires the widespread utilization of emerging technologies for prenatal diagnosis, monitoring, and therapy.

3. The provision of universal prenatal and preconception care for all pregnant women, along with adequate counseling and substance abuse treatment programs, is essential and would drastically reduce the problems leading to unhealthy maternal behavior.

4. In those instances in which preventive approaches fail and a pregnant woman refuses to modify her behavior, and thus minimize the risk of damage to her offspring, society, primarily through its courts and legislatures, has a duty to intervene to protect the interests of the defenseless fetus.

5. Intervention by the state in the maternal-fetal relationship should always be undertaken in the least intrusive, yet most effective, manner. Healthy children, not punishment of the mother, should be the primary objective of any intervention.

CONCLUSION

The balance between maternal autonomy and the interests of a child to be born with a sound mind and body is a delicate and elusive one, but all efforts must be made to arrive at this balance by fully taking into account these intertwined sets of rights and responsibilities.

The courts have played and will continue to play a central role in redefining the maternal-fetal relationship. In the absence of consistent, unambiguous statutory guidance, courts with little experience in these novel situations will be compelled to interpret the complex interaction of traditional values of rights and responsibilities, conventional legal principles, and a rapidly changing technological context. Although the extension of culpability for fetal harm from third parties to the pregnant woman, through her acts of commission or omission, might be legally consistent, it

92   BLANK

has dangerous policy ramifications. The courts face an unenviable balancing act within the adversarial context of mother and child in such cases.
Therefore, decisions must be tempered with the knowledge that actions on
behalf of infant plaintiffs against their mothers for prenatal injury have
severe implications for the way society reviews the rights and responsibilities of pregnant women. Furthermore, judicial rulings that might rightfully
compensate specific infant plaintiffs, cumulatively might divert needed attention from preventive strategies and do little toward the paramount policy
goal of healthy babies.

Philosophy, Gender Politics, and In Vitro Fertilization: A Feminist Ethics of Reproductive Healthcare

Linda LeMoncheck

In the feminist critique of reproductive technologies, it is not technology as an "artificial invasion of the human body" that is at issue--but whether we can create the political and cultural conditions in which such technologies can be employed by women to shape the experience of reproduction according to their own definitions.

–Michelle Stanworth

OVERVIEW

Feminists have long contended that men's control of women's reproduction has been crucial to men's oppression of women, individually and as a class. From a feminist perspective, men alienated from, envious of, and threatened by the reproductive power of women, use their hegemony in medicine and the law to define reproduction in terms of biological defect, illness, or disability needing medical treatment and legal regulation.[1] This male-identified construction of reproduction is then presented to women as the only means of ensuring a safe and satisfying reproductive life, the alternatives to which are described as dangerous, debilitating, or unpredictable. In this way, men can be assured of their social power and status by controlling the means and the resources by which future generations are created, and by restricting further women's reproductive role to that of domestic and sexual subordinate for whom economic independence and political power are deemed both unnatural and unfeminine. If a woman can be convinced that it is not possible or proper for her to exercise the freedom and power to determine if,

Linda LeMoncheck, *PhD, writes and lectures extensively on issues in feminist philosophy and women's sexuality in Seal Beach, Calif.*

when, with whom, and under what circumstances, she will have children, her reproductive autonomy can be undermined by a patriarchal medical and legal establishment that is interested in consolidating male power and authority.[2]

Thus, many feminists believe it is essential for all women to recognize that a woman's ability to conceive, gestate, and give birth is not solely, or even primarily, a natural or essential feature of women's biology. On the contrary, women's reproduction is a social construction, culturally contingent and politically circumscribed, whose patriarchal foundations in contemporary society can be undermined only when women begin to reconstruct and reevaluate the meaning and value of reproduction for women. Thus, the feminist challenge to male-identified constructions of women's reproduction is a twofold project: (1) to determine which alternative constructions of conception, pregnancy, and birth empower women and which do not, and (2) to recentralize such constructions in the choice and practice of women's reproductive healthcare.

The feminist debate over how best to achieve women's reproductive agency and self-definition is especially heated over the role of what have been called the "new" reproductive technologies: while the "old" technologies center around controlling fertility and managing labor and childbirth, the new reproductive technologies focus on treating infertility, reducing inherited disability or disease, and improving methods of selecting the sex of an infant.[3] Such technologies have their basis in extra-uterine conception: making fertilized eggs, called embryos or pre-embryos, available for transplantation into the womb of a woman otherwise unable to conceive, and also making embryos accessible to medical science for genetic evaluation and alteration, a part of what has come to be known as genetic engineering. The new technologies also include increased control of gestation in an effort to ensure that both traditional and high-tech pregnancies will yield an able-bodied, disease-free baby of the desired sex. Thus, the new reproductive and genetic technologies are symbiotically linked, offering the promise, not only of pregnancy and birth for infertile mothers, but of "perfect babies" with "designer genes," whose genetic characteristics (including sex) may be chosen or manipulated by parents themselves.[4] These technologies include in vitro fertilization (IVF) and embryo transfer, egg and embryo donation, egg and embryo freezing, genetic screening and gene therapy of embryos, prenatal diagnosis of genetic disability or disease of fetuses developing in utero, and technologies to select the sex of an infant.[5]

Many feminists who are critical of the new reproductive technologies regard them as little more than further advancements in the pervasive and institutionalized male control over women's reproduction.[6] Such feminists charge that the new technologies are particularly subversive because they disguise physically dangerous and emotionally debilitating experimentation on women's bodies as women's best and only hope for curing infertility and eliminating hereditary disease. They contend that practitioners of the new reproductive technologies often underestimate or ignore the real costs, benefits, risks, success rates of, and alternatives to new reproductive technologies in their rush to establish themselves in their fields and to ensure an ample supply of research subjects. Critics of the new technologies remind us that a feminist reading of the history of reproductive science over the last 150 years discloses a misogynistic and male-biased medical establishment that is willing to experiment on women with dangerous, untested drugs and devices without women's knowledge or consent, and that is willing to perform unnecessary operations on women, such as sterilizations, hysterectomies, and cesarean sections, to reduce "undesirable" populations and to fatten medical pocketbooks.[7] Underlying such reproductive intervention, according to feminist scientists like Renate Duelli Klein, is patriarchy's desire to *dictate* human reproduction, "to determine who produces what kind of

life, in which part of the world, at which time and how."[8]

Moreover, from this critical perspective, the mechanistic and sterile nature of the new reproductive technologies dehumanizes women by alienating them from their own bodies, and by commodifying women as wombs or as egg and embryo producers used to enhance the professional prestige and political power of medical practitioners who would breed selectively for social control. Such feminists predict that poor women and women of color will be denied infertility treatment or will be exploited as inexpensive surrogate mothers carrying the fertilized eggs of white and wealthy adoptive parents. These feminists argue that the development of technologies to select the sex of infants in a world that favors men and rewards women with social status and economic security for bearing sons, will inevitably result in abortions that are tantamount to prenatal femicide. Furthermore, by taking advantage of a pronatalist cultural ideology (an ideology that encourages women to reproduce and stigmatizes those who do not), practitioners of the new reproductive technologies can convince vulnerable women in a time of crisis in their reproductive lives to invest considerable amounts of time, money, and energy in technological baby making. Thus, some feminists charge that, even if a woman understands the risks of IVF and related technologies, she will still experience the kinds of medical, social, psychological, and often economic pressures that make a mockery of her "choice" to have children. Moreover, it is contended that, if women truly want to experience motherhood, there are plenty of unwanted children in the world to love and nurture. In short, according to many feminists critical of the new reproductive technologies, such technologies are harmful to women, because they promote the pathology and appropriation of what men have long regarded--with a kind of mystical fear and envy--as women's reproductive power.

On the other hand, feminists who support the use of the new reproductive technologies agree that there are risks, but that misinformation and abuse can be remedied with voluntary, woman-centered counseling, politically aware and socially responsible reproductive practitioners, and feminist oversight of reproductive research. Such counseling can help women understand their motives and needs for treatment of their infertility within a larger social context of compulsory motherhood; healthcare practitioners can apprise women of the successes and failures of reproductive science; and feminists can carefully monitor the technologies for dangerous commercial exploitation. From this perspective, to condemn the new technologies unequivocally shows a profound disregard for those women who wish to experience biological motherhood, but who may be infertile or at risk of passing genetic disease to their children. It is argued that such women can be fully apprised of the social implications, medical history, and physical risks of IVF but accept them in their search for the sense of accomplishment, loving commitment, and profound satisfaction that can accompany having a child "of one's own." Such condemnation also ignores the political impact of the use of new reproductive technologies by single women and lesbians whose mothering could help deconstruct the heterosexual, monogamous, nuclear family so often oppressive to women. Furthermore, even strongly vocal feminist critics of the new reproductive technologies warn that prohibition might be used against women to restrict other important reproductive freedoms with regard to contraception or abortion.[9] According to feminist supporters of the new technologies, if we are to "take back" our own bodies, we must be allowed to use the kinds of technology that will give each woman the experience of motherhood that she desires. To deprive women of this technology because of the existence of an oppressive pronatalism or a conspiratorial medical establishment is to preach a kind of technological and cultural determinism that defines women as no more than the reproductive subordinates of patriarchy.[10]

Such feminists are joined by infertile women and women who are carriers of genetically transmitted diseases who say that they cannot subscribe to a women's movement that sacrifices their real pain of childlessness for possible harms to unknown others. Such women claim that they should be free to use the new reproductive technologies without "maternalistic" feminists regulating their lives for them. In doing so, feminists who advocate prohibiting the new technologies appear to align

themselves with conservative moralists who want to keep motherhood as "natural" as possible and so restrict women's reproductive options. Clinicians, researchers, and commercial vendors add that they are only responding to the demands of patients or consumers, and that they do not appreciate being misrepresented as status-seeking profiteers who are ignorant of the real needs and sensitivities of women. Lawyers have taken up the cause of infertile women with arguments for a "right to procreate," which right would ensure that no government or individual interfere with women's pursuit of reproducing.[11] Even a feminist like Shulamith Firestone, who rejects biological motherhood outright as reproductive enslavement, regards woman-centered technologies as liberating as long as they free women from the social inequalities that accompany compulsory biological motherhood.[12]

Feminists continue to be deeply divided over the value of the new reproductive technologies in women's lives. At such an apparent philosophical impasse, as long as women are apprised of the content of the debates, it is tempting to leave individual women to decide for themselves if and how the new reproductive technologies will figure in their lives. This is particularly true in light of feminist agreement on all sides that women be given the freedom and power to determine our reproductive lives for ourselves. However, this attitude underestimates how profoundly women's decisions to use the new technologies are affected by medical clinicians, researchers, commercial vendors, family, or friends who may have little or no sense of the patriarchal politics of reproduction; nor does it properly account for how a woman's self-esteem is influenced by family and friends whom she perceives as expecting her to have children, and by clinicians in their assessment, use, and follow up of the new technologies for individual women.

In the remainder of this article, I argue for a feminist reproductive ethics that encourages IVF clinicians to treat their patients with an empathy and sensitivity to gender politics that can promote the reproductive interests of both their patients and of women as a class. I contend that in a collaborative co-partnership that particularizes the needs of each patient, clinicians can be instrumental in helping their patients make individually satisfying and socially responsible choices in their reproductive lives. Such an ethics encourages practitioners to understand the history and potential for abuse of the new reproductive technologies; to take seriously the stress, fear, guilt, grief, anxiety, and emotional rollercoaster of success and failure suffered by many IVF patients, each in her own way; and to share with patients' friends and loved ones how much patients' reproductive anxieties can be generated by the demands and expectations of others.[13]

To outline this reproductive ethics, however, requires negotiating some of the tensions in the

According to feminist supporters of the new technologies, if we are to "take back" our own bodies, we must be allowed to use the kinds of technology that will give each woman the experience of motherhood that she desires.

feminist debates over the new reproductive technologies detailed above. Such a negotiation is necessary so that practitioners are provided with an ethics that feminists from a wide variety of perspectives can endorse. Therefore, I will develop the feminist reproductive ethics described thus far from within a broader epistemological framework that circumscribes a woman's use of IVF in terms of a dialectic between the patriarchal politics of gender that constrain her reproductive options and the technological possibilities of reproduction that can liberate her gender. I will argue that such a dialectic mediates between those feminists who would prohibit the new reproductive technologies and those who would promote them; and I will use such a dialectic to generate the kind of particularizing, relational, and politically grounded ethics that feminists who would promote women's diverse expression of their reproductive agency could recommend to practitioners, patients, and their families.

In the following discussion, I offer a brief summary of IVF and embryo transfer procedures

and technologies so that I may later point to various stages of the IVF process to which a feminist reproductive ethics is particularly relevant. Such a summary is important for its own sake, however, since one of the complaints many feminists make with regard to the new reproductive technologies is that they are commonly described in ways that euphemize or sanitize the invasiveness, complexity, unpredictability, and risk of the relevant procedures. I then show how, given the concerns of feminists that were expressed in the beginning of this overview, neither an ethics of duty that is based on the autonomy and impartiality of moral agents, an ethics of utility that is grounded in promoting the social good, or an ethics of virtue that incorporates both our moral obligations to and our care about others will motivate IVF practitioners to particularize and politicize their treatment of women in ways that are essential to maximizing women's reproductive agency. I outline how conceiving of women's reproduction as a dialectic between oppressive gender politics and liberating reproductive technology can generate a feminist reproductive ethics that recommends specific ways that practitioners can promote women's reproductive empowerment. By way of conclusion, I offer some reasons for thinking that the current use by individuals and employers of health-maintenance organizations (HMOs) may inhibit medical practitioners from giving the additional time and support to their patients that would be required by a feminist reproductive ethics; and I suggest what practitioners and patients may do to begin restructuring the reproductive healthcare system to reward practitioners for treating their patients from a feminist perspective.

IVF AND THE TRANSFER OF EMBRYOS

The technologies that drive the latest developments in treating infertility are in vitro fertilization and the transfer of embryos. For a heterosexual couple to be fertile, the female must ovulate, there must be male sperm of sufficient number and motility to achieve fertilization, and there must be at least one female fallopian tube for picking up the egg and transporting it, fertilized, to the uterus for implantation and hormonal "priming."[14] Thus, infertility can be due to a variety of factors: women can become infertile as a result of tubal blockage, cervical cancer, inability to ovulate, or infection from prior surgery, sexually transmitted diseases, or IUDs (intrauterine devices); women can become infertile from being exposed to environmental toxins, from taking hormonal birth control, or from their mothers' use of DES during pregnancy (DES is the familiar name for diethylstilbestrol, a hormone prescribed widely in the 1940s and 1950s to prevent miscarriage); or from unknown factors. Men's sperm production can be too low; or their sperm can be of low motility, incapable of making sufficient headway up the uterine canal to reach the egg or to penetrate its membrane.[15] Every woman has all the eggs she will ever produce three months before she is born; however, the number and quality of these eggs diminish as she ages, with the most dramatic reduction in the quality and number of eggs beginning in her mid- to late-thirties.[16]

IVF and the transfer of embryos were technologies originally designed for women with functioning ovaries whose eggs could not reach the uterine canal for fertilization due to blocked or dysfunctional fallopian tubes. In IVF, eggs are retrieved from a woman's ovaries, fertilized by her partner's or a donor's sperm in a cultured medium in vitro (literally, "in the glass" of a petri dish), then placed in the woman's womb in a procedure known as embryo replacement or embryo transfer. Usually, three to four such embryos are transferred to increase the chances of any one of them remaining implanted in the womb. The process must often be repeated if embryos fail to implant or the embryos spontaneously abort.[17]

IVF and embryo transfer have expanded to include treatment of infertile women with mild endometriosis, women with cervical or immunological dysfunction, as well as fertile women whose husbands are infertile and who are participating in artificial insemination by donor (AID) programs. These technologies have also been expanded to include infertile or sterilized women whose ovaries do not yield the number or quality of eggs required for fertilization and implantation, since women may also donate eggs that have been fertilized using artificial insemination or IVF, for implantation in another woman's womb.[18] Parents who do not want to risk passing a genetic marker for disease to their children can use donor eggs or donor sperm for artificial insemination, or they can use IVF technology to diagnose the embryos before transfer to discern whether the negative trait is present in the embryo's DNA. In the United States, women who have had hysterectomies, severe endometriosis, or women in poor health for whom pregnancy is dangerous can legally contract with other women who act as surrogate gestators for eggs fertilized using IVF.[19] Single lesbians and gay men, lesbian couples and gay couples, and single heterosexual men and women also are increasingly taking advantage of IVF combined with AID and/or surrogacy, as fewer (but by no means all) IVF clinics are requiring their patients to be in stable, long-term, heterosexual relationships. IVF is now often used simply when the cause of a woman's infertility is unknown.[20]

IVF success rates vary from clinic to clinic: even the best clinics report an average "take-home baby" rate of approximately 20 percent, while new clinics or clinics with less-skilled staff may have success rates at or near zero. A single IVF procedure, including infertility testing for entry into an IVF program, can cost $6,000 or more; genetic testing adds another $2,000. Many couples spend five or six times this much to repeat the procedure after failures of egg retrieval, fertilization, or embryo transfer.[21] Such costs do not include costs for surgery caused by ectopic pregnancy or miscarriage, which occur at higher rates than in normal conception, nor do they usually include the costs of blood tests, urinalysis, fetal imaging, and amniocentesis during pregnancy, which are typical procedures during IVF follow up. The costs of premature births, multiple births, or cesarean sections, which also occur more frequently when IVF technology is used, are regarded as "extras."[22]

In order to have enough embryos for implantation, women who undergo IVF or women who donate eggs for IVF recipients are "superovulated" by hormone therapy that stimulates their ovaries to produce more than one ripe egg. The side-effects of such superovulation may include ovarian enlargement, burst ovaries, ovarian cysts, cancer, or permanent infertility; bloating, migraines, blurring, or dizziness are not uncommon. Researchers who report that they have found what they consider to be chromosomal anomalies in eggs after the use of hormones contend that more studies need to be carried out before an assessment of significant risk can be made.[23] "Egg harvesting" is typically achieved by laparoscopy, during which, under general anes-

> **IVF success rates vary from clinic to clinic: even the best clinics report an average "take-home baby" rate of approximately 20 percent, while new clinics or clinics with less-skilled staff may have success rates at or near zero.**

thesia, a laparoscope to locate the eggs and a catheter for suction are inserted thorough a small incision in a woman's abdomen. Carbon dioxide is used to bloat the abdomen, while forceps are used to manipulate the ovaries for harvesting the eggs. Transabdominal ultrasound directed oocyte recovery (TUDOR) is an ultrasound-guided technique for harvesting eggs in which a needle is inserted through a woman's bladder or vagina using local anesthetic. TUDOR is cheaper and less invasive than laparoscopy, but fewer eggs are retrieved using this method; many practitioners with access to embryo freezing prefer laparoscopy to retrieve a large number of eggs, which are then fertilized and frozen if repeated transfers, embryo donations, or embryo research is indicated.[24]

Fertilization occurs in a prepared culture in a dish, using sperm recently ejaculated from the male partner of the woman being treated, or from sperm frozen in a sperm bank. At this stage, for men whose sperm count is either low in number or motility, microinjection of a single sperm into an egg can be attempted to break through its membrane (the *zona pellucida*) for fertilization. The long-term effects on either the childhood or adulthood of those individuals reproduced in this manner are unknown.[25] Three to four embryos are typically transferred to each woman by catheter through the cervix to increase the chances of im-

plantation, although, as mentioned above, this also increases the chances of multiple births. If too many embryos remain implanted, a physician may recommend reducing the number of embryos in the womb by injecting an ultrasound-guided needle filled with a saline solution into the body of each developing fetus to terminate it. The fetus is then reabsorbed into the woman's body.[26] To increase the likelihood of implantation of a healthy embryo, practitioners can place the fertilized eggs in a sealed tube in the vagina for a two-day incubation period, at which time the tube is removed and the more mature embryo is implanted.[27] The hormone progesterone is usually administered after embryo transfer until a pregnancy is established to offset the high levels of estrogen that result from superovulation; high levels of estrogen appear to be implicated in the relatively high failure rate of implantation, where the IVF cycle fails most often.[28] Because of misgivings by moral and religious conservatives about "creating" embryos outside the body, scientists have developed an array of implantation techniques that do not require IVF, including gamete intrafallopian transfer (GIFT) in which eggs and sperm, separated by a bubble of air, are placed together in a woman's fallopian tube; transutero-tubal implantation (TUTI) in which sperm are injected directly into a uterus that has been hormonally stimulated to ovulate in conjunction with the injection; and tubal ovum transfer (TOT) in which superovulated eggs are placed in a woman's tubes while sperm are placed in the cervix which has been fitted with a cervical cap to prevent their escape.[29] With such a variety of new reproductive technologies at the clinician's disposal, many feminists are wary of their experimental nature and potential for abuse. It is to this subject that we can now turn.

THE INADEQUACY OF TRADITIONAL ETHICAL THEORY

As Susan Sherwin writes, "Few feminists object to reproductive technology per se; rather they express concern about who controls it and how it can be used to further exploit women. The problem with reproductive technology is that it concentrates power in reproductive matters in the hands of those who are not directly involved in the actual bearing and rearing of the child, i.e., in men who relate to their clients in a technical, professional, authoritarian manner."[30]

Traditional ethical theories might find more support among feminists if such models were to particularize and politicize women's reproductive lives. But do they? The Hippocratic oath is a professional promise that physicians make to hold the health and well-being of their patients as their highest medical priority. The moral requirements that are implied by taking such an oath form a part of what philosophers generally refer to as "duty ethics." Immanuel Kant set the standard for this ethics by advocating the autonomous and impartial endorsement of universalizable moral principles whose rightness derives from a willingness to act for the sake of moral duty alone. From this view, considerations of either personal or social good are irrelevant to a proper determination of right action. Moral agents are rational, mutually disinterested individuals who are morally obligated to respect themselves and others as free and equal persons under the moral law. Such respect requires, among other things, refraining from the violation, abuse, exploitation, or intimidation of others. In Kant's words, "Act in such a way that you always treat humanity, whether in your own person or in the person of any other, never simply as a means, but always at the same time as an end."[31]

This duty is particularly compelling concerning IVF and embryo transfer, since it forbids what feminist critics regard as the pervasive violence against, and exploitation of, women in potentially dangerous experimental IVF research. Such an ethics of duty also condemns the commodification and commercialization of women as wombs or embryo producers to enhance practitioners' professional prestige, their economic security, or even to promote the good of society as a whole. Women must not be misinformed as to the costs, benefits, success rates, or alternatives to IVF technology, nor should they be unduly pressured to undertake IVF procedures they might otherwise forego. So too, women must not be coerced or deceived into undergoing unnecessary surgery or ingesting hormones to provide researchers with a steady supply of eggs. A Kantian ethics of duty would also forbid discriminating against lesbians, single women, poor women, and women of color who may wish to take advantage of the new technologies in ways comparable to their white, affluent, heterosexual sisters, since all such women would theoretically be considered free and equal persons under the moral law.

Thus, there appears to be much about a Kantian ethics of duty to attract feminists interested in promoting women's reproductive agency. However, the disinterestedness and impartiality required of this ethics recommends that practitioners remain emotionally distant from their patients. Rationality authorizes those governed by this ethics to make moral decisions autonomously and decisively, in order that the requirements of moral duty be upheld. I contend that, as a result, practitioners who follow the recommendations of the IVF ethics of duty detailed above have no moral incentive to empathize with their patients or to politicize their practices in ways that promote women's reproductive empowerment. Indeed, the remarkable feature about this ethics is that it breeds the very kind of medical authoritarianism and moral elitism that feminists have complained are at the heart of abuses involving IVF.

Because the rational decisions of the autonomous IVF practitioner governed by a Kantian ethics of duty are deemed sufficient to determine right action, no incentive exists for the practitioner to question whether his or her universalizable moral judgments reflect the particular values or interests of the patient. Indeed, from this Kantian perspective, such considerations belie a partiality for and inclination toward others--which are not the proper domain of moral judgment. Therefore, such a practitioner will believe he or she can treat the patient with respect only by remaining sympathetically distant from what the IVF patient experiences *from her perspective*. Her anxieties about the risks or the ultimate success of IVF may be marginalized, because the practitioner has reasoned that the risks are minimal or that the success rates are high enough to justify the risks involved. Significantly, according to a Kantian ethics of duty, the patient's expression of these worries does not recommend that the clinician revisit the literature or get a second opinion, so long as, from the clinician's perspective, proceeding ahead does not constitute treating the patient "simply as a means." In fact, the practitioner may conclude that further psychological assessment of the patient, not further investigation into the benefits, risks, and possible alternatives for this patient, is indicated. Her complaints of side-effects from superovulation may be dismissed as symptoms of her initial anxiety over the procedure. If not ignored altogether, her feelings of humiliation, bewilderment, or discomfort from laparoscopy or embryo transfer may be interpreted clinically as an understandable but inconsequential hypersensitivity to new clinical procedures.[32] In short, as an autonomous and disinterested moral agent, the clinician is not required to create the kind of co-partnership with the patient that recommends a sensitivity and responsiveness to the reproductive needs and experiences of individual patients. Indeed, according to this ethics, moral judgments are universalizable in their scope and predictable in their content; therefore, duty-bound IVF clinicians may mistakenly apply the same moral guidelines to very different cases, because there is no moral motivation for the clinician to particularize the patient's condition or complaints.

Moreover, American IVF clinicians practice in a society where gender stereotypes exist that characterize women as dependent, emotionally labile subordinates of men, and not autonomous, rational agents in our own right. Therefore, a male IVF clinician or researcher governed by a Kantian ethics of duty may be convinced it is his moral duty not to include his patients' particular needs or interests in IVF decisions simply because his patients are not deserving of respect as equals under the moral law. Such speculations are borne out by the presumptive manner with which many clinicians assess the "medical suitability" of IVF patients, including whether such patients are "appropriately committed" to long-term heterosexual relationships or whether they are "psychologically stable" enough to handle the admitted stresses of the procedure. As mentioned above, clinicians may feel perfectly justified from a moral point of view in making their own assessments of the risks, benefits, costs, and chances of success of IVF and embryo transfer procedures, when nothing in a Kantian ethics of duty requires them to look further than their own rational assessments of what these are.

Even if clinicians believe that women and men are equally autonomous moral agents, an ethics of duty only requires clinicians to listen to patients respectfully, not sympathetically. Thus, there is no formal requirement that clinicians ask their patients for *their own assessment* of IVF procedures or protocol. What can appear to a clinician to be a "respectful" request for a laparoscopy patient's unused eggs may appear, *to the patient*, to be quite the contrary: an intrusive, even coercive suggestion whose positive response is regarded *by the patient* as an undesirable but necessary price for continuation in an IVF program with a long waiting list. The contention that the clinician did not intend to coerce the patient misses the point. My claim is not that an ethics of duty condones coercion, but that an ethics of duty does not encourage the clinician to see such a request *as this patient sees it*, in this case, as coercive. As a result, many clinicians virtually dictate the timing, frequency, and design of the procedures themselves, including follow-up examinations, in an environment where there are still few bona fide experts coupled with an increasing demand for IVF services.

Many feminists recommend that women inform themselves of the many alternatives to IVF motherhood, from homeopathic care to foster care, so that women are not caught in a cycle of debilitation and dashed hopes. For those women for whom IVF appears to be their best chance of bearing a healthy baby, feminists urge women to consider how clinicians often underestimate the risks involved in IVF treatment and prenatal diagnosis, how clinicians can mistake the long-term benefits, costs, and success rates of IVF and embryo transfer, and how commonly they presume to know which procedures, if any, will work for which sorts of patients and when.[33]

In addition, there is no moral obligation on the part of clinicians or researchers who follow an ethics of duty to make their moral judgments in light of the gender politics of women's oppression. Considerations of what might count as beneficial or equitable access to IVF *for this woman under these ideological constraints in this political climate* will never arise, when they are conceived as contributing to particularity and partiality, not universality and fairness. In this sense, an ethics of duty does not merely suffer from being practiced in a patriarchal society; an ethics of duty can itself be oppressive to women. Thus, despite a history of the medical abuse, exploitation, discrimination, and debilitating experimentation of women, a practitioner such as Samuel Gorovitz can say, "Collectively we [clinicians and researchers] have significant capacity to exercise judgment and control. . . . Our record has been rather good in regard to medical treatment and research."[34] While a Kantian ethics of duty would appear to condemn individual instances of abuse, exploitation, and intimidation, it only does so from the perspective of an apolitical and ahistorical rational agent whose moral judgments are, in principle, unaffected by the hierarchical and institutionalized social structures in which those judgments are embedded. As a result, an IVF practitioner who is governed by a Kantian ethics of duty may have no sense of, and no incentive to discover, the discriminatory and abusive history of women's reproductive lives, the ways in which a medical monopoly on reproductive healthcare limits a woman's choices of whether and how she may reproduce, or the oppressive pronatalist ideology that makes her feel guilty, depressed, and inadequate as a woman when she can bear no children. An ethics of duty will be unacceptable to feminists when obtaining consent from patients to perform IVF exists under conditions of medical authoritarianism and moral elitism that do not recognize the reproductive experience of women as expressed by women themselves, or under conditions that do not recognize the coercive and manipulative elements of women's reproductive lives that exist outside the practitioner's office.[35]

Utilitarian moral theory might appear to have more appeal to feminists interested in maximizing women's reproductive empowerment, because utilitarianism requires that moral agents make decisions based, not on a rational assessment of moral duty, but from considerations of which actions will promote the social good or produce the greatest happiness for all concerned. Thus, it might be thought that such an ethics would require IVF

practitioners to look beyond their own determination of clinical duty to what will promote the happiness of individual patients. From this point of view, to discover precisely what this happiness consists of would require an empathetic and politically sensitive assessment of each IVF patient's reproductive needs and experience. The medical authoritarianism and moral elitism of a Kantian ethics of duty would then disappear with the utilitarian requirement that clinicians give credibility to, and directly address, their patients' fears, anxieties, and expressions of real pain; clinicians would also be motivated to understand and to share with their IVF patients (and would-be patients) the social construction of reproduction that circumscribes women's choice to be mothers. In this way, clinicians may more accurately calculate individual patients' pleasures and pains at each point in the IVF process.

The problem with this interpretation of utilitarianism, however, is threefold: (1) it suggests that an IVF patient's happiness will never be sacrificed for what the clinician assesses is the "greater good"; (2) it implies that, even when an IVF patient's happiness is not sacrificed, the clinician is morally required to make his calculations based on *the patient's* assessment of her happiness, not his assessment; and (3) it assumes that the clinician's calculations of social utility must always be politically grounded. Indeed, there may be good reason to suspect the motives of the IVF clinician who is governed by utilitarianism, since a predominantly white, affluent, and male-identified medical establishment could morally justify limiting IVF procedures to those with gametes that are socially favored by race or sex, extending services only to those deemed psychologically and economically "fit" to parent, and using prenatal diagnosis to screen out "undesirables" in the name of strengthening the gene pool. Even less eugenically minded practitioners could rationalize regarding women as the natural and proper objects of experimental reproductive science, since they could argue that IVF and the transfer of embryos allow unprecedented study and control of reproduction, the pursuit of which would promote the long-term health and well-being of the children of both infertile and fertile parents. It is no wonder that so many IVF practitioners accuse feminists of a narrow-minded political correctness, when feminists would appear to deny reproductive science its progress toward such a profoundly important human goal.

A related objection concerns the many clinicians who would calculate that (1) their patients' and families' often desperate desire to have children "of their own," combined with (2) the advancement of reproductive research for the sake of future mothers and their children, and (3) the clinicians' own desire for professional prestige and financial reward, far outweigh any of the patients' emotional or physical distress before, during, or after the IVF process. It is noteworthy that there is no requirement in an ethics of utility that the clinician ask the patient for her understanding of the short- or long-term benefits of undergoing IVF, to compare the patient's utilitarian calculations with the clinician's own. A utilitarian might argue that both clinician and patient would be better served by following a rule that requires empathy in clinical relationships, even if individual acts do not always require it. However, neither act nor rule utilitarianism requires empathy unless it maximizes social utility; and it is unclear from either perspective just who determines whether or how empathy figures in "the social good." Thus, if the clinician feels that patients' unhappiness would only be exacerbated by their being informed of the relatively low success rates, real costs, controversial benefits, and associated medical risks of IVF, there is no apparent utilitarian incentive to disclose these facts. "What she doesn't know, won't hurt her" allows a utilitarian clinician to rationalize that, together with providing hope to desperate infertile women and prestige to the clinic, the clinician is doing what is best for all concerned. If the patient does discover what she considers to be misconduct on the part of the clinician, the clinician may still stand by the utility of his or her behavior, knowing that there are plenty of infertile women and profit-driven clinics eager for his or her services. Indeed, clinicians have been accused of using eggs and embryos from IVF patients without their consent to impregnate other patients for precisely the utilitarian reasons enumerated above.[36]

What these considerations suggest is that, without the moral requirement to empathize with the IVF patient in order to understand her reproduc-

tive needs from her own experience, the IVF practitioner who is governed by an ethics of utility may remain as stubbornly autocratic as his or her Kantian colleagues. When a patient opts to undertake the risks associated with IVF against the considered advice of her clinicians, many feminists would wish to give over the primacy of moral decision making to those IVF patients who judge the risks to be worth taking.[37] Moreover, without the moral requirement to politicize the IVF process, clinicians may fail to see how their calculations of the social good omit the oppressive elements of a pronatalist ideology, medical monopoly, and exploitative medical history of experimentation and selective breeding that would expand their understanding of the social good for women.

At this point, many clinicians may argue that they recognize the potential for medical insensitivity and moral autocracy in both the ethics of duty and an ethics of utility; and it is precisely to avoid such features that conscientious clinicians invoke an ethics of virtue that recommends justice, integrity, and charity to put the real "care" back in healthcare. The Hippocratic oath, it could be contended, has its roots in an ancient Greek moral tradition that ties human happiness quite closely with the possession of virtuous traits of character. A clinician's sense of moral obligation governed by an ethics of virtue is nuanced by a conscientiousness, forthrightness, and care about his or her patients' well-being, which are character traits good for clinicians to have--for their own sake, and for others. Such virtues as integrity and charity require a responsiveness to the needs of patients that militates against a clinician's self-deception or indifference and promotes the kind of partnership between clinician and patient that is to their mutual benefit. Moreover, the virtues are ideally instilled in clinicians so that their right actions are the result of habit, not the self-conscious assessment of social utility or clinical duty, neither of which require that clinicians listen to the reproductive experience of their patients as apprehended by the women themselves.[38]

My criticism of such a moral approach is that there is still nothing in an ethics of virtue to *politicize* the IVF process in ways that would help both the clinician and the patient to understand how subtle but real cultural and institutional influences shape the construction of a woman's infertility. If part of the role of the IVF clinician who is governed by an ethics of virtue is to provide his or her patient with the kind of counseling and treatment that will empower her to define her reproductive life in her own terms, then that counseling must include some sense of the pronatalist ideology under which they both work, the exploitative medical history of reproductive science, the medical monopoly on women's reproduction that marginalizes or ignores alternatives to technical baby-making, and the discriminatory ways in which IVF is currently practiced. Only then will each woman be able to make the kinds of personally beneficial and socially responsible reproductive choices that empower both herself and all women. With such considerations in mind, let me now propose a way of thinking and talking about women's reproductive lives that can generate a feminist ethics of reproduction for IVF clinicians that is responsive to a diverse population of women.

CLINICAL CARE AND SOCIAL RESPONSIBILITY UNDER A FEMINIST ETHICS OF REPRODUCTION

As Alison Jaggar writes, "Choosing between incompatible principles, weighing competing interests, and balancing the intensity of our socially constructed but nonetheless urgent emotional needs against the knowledge that fulfilling those needs may reinforce a social status quo we are deeply committed to changing provide feminists with a vivid sense that in the arena of family values, we are indeed living with contradictions."[39] The new reproductive technologies reveal the dilemma posed by the politics of women's personal choices alluded to by Alison Jaggar: If women use the new reproductive technologies, we will lose at least some control over women's reproduction by placing it in the hands of a technocratic medical, scientific, and pharmaceutical establishment with a clear history of abuse and exploitation of women; if women do not use the new technologies, we will fail to address the individual reproductive needs of many women whose lives undoubtedly will be enhanced by taking advantage of the new technologies. Using the new technologies tends to reinforce a strongly

pronatalist and discriminatory ideology that puts pressure on women to have children of the right kind and in the right way, which medical science claims only its technology can provide; not using the new technologies means women will remain identified with a reproductive "female nature" and committed to a patriarchal family structure that militates against women taking back our reproduction. For some women, motherhood will provide much of their experience of personal creativity, self-confidence, and emotional satisfaction; for others, motherhood will be given up altogether for economic, physical, or emotional well-being.[40] Thus, the new reproductive technologies challenge feminists to find common ground in our pursuit of women's reproductive agency and self-definition within caring communities, so that we may offer clinicians a feminist ethics of reproduction that allows women the opportunity to determine the nature and value of our own reproductive lives.

I contend that such common ground can be reached by understanding women's reproductive experience as a complex and variable dialectic that exposes the interplay between the oppressive politics of gender that constrain a woman's reproductive choices and the technological possibilities of reproduction that can liberate her gender. Such a dialectic characterizes women as both the subjects and the objects of our reproductive lives. As the subject of her reproductive experience a woman is able and willing to explore her reproductive identity to determine whether and how motherhood has meaning and value for her. She may define for herself the many possible ways there are for her to be a successful and satisfied mother, which may, in turn, encourage her tolerance for a wider range of reproductive expression by others. She takes responsibility for her reproductive life by practicing safer sex, by using contraceptive techniques when she does not wish to conceive, and by becoming informed of the variety of ways that economics, cultural ideology, and medical politics will figure in her own construction of her reproductive life. However, she is a reproductive subject who also recognizes her objectivity as a potentially exploitable and expendable means of furthering patriarchal reproductive science. As such, her own reproductive experience may be given little credence in a medical environment designed to authorize its

IVF clinicians and researchers as the final arbiters of her reproductive life. She also remains the object of strong pronatalist influences and discriminatory practices, which will constrain her decisions to reproduce.

The advantage of approaching women's reproduction from this dialectical perspective is that it allows feminists to claim that individual women can make positive reproductive choices for themselves and for women as a social class, while at the same time recognizing that those choices exist within a gendered social framework of powerful institutional hierarchies that constrain women's reproductive prospects and practices. Thus, any feminist ethics of reproduction that is generated from this perspective must recognize the real desires of individual women to be mothers and to use the new technologies to satisfy deeply felt needs. This ethics must also recognize that powerful ideological and gendered forces structure those needs, the satisfaction of which can result in the oppression of women as a class. As such, it is a dialectic that can generate the kind of particularizing, relational, and politically grounded ethics that more traditional ethical theories lack.[41]

A feminist ethics that is based on the dialectical relationship between gender and reproduction outlined above can offer specific guidelines to IVF clinicians and researchers. First, as Christine Overall points out, a feminist ethics of reproduction recommends that practitioners focus on women's relation to reproduction, as opposed to that of "society" or "the family," whose well-being women's reproduction has traditionally been designated to promote. In so doing, this ethics highlights how a woman's reproductive experience is interpreted and apprehended by the woman herself.[42] This focus in turn will require that clinicians spend more time with each patient, possibly in conjunction with a reproductive counselor, to discuss the patient's own needs and motivations for seeking IVF as she sees them. Therefore, preliminary IVF clinical discussions will include an evaluation of how much time, money, physical effort, and emotional commitment a patient may be willing to invest in the IVF process in order to have a child of her own, or how she will handle her relationships with a surrogate or an egg donor. The

clinician should ask: how will going through this procedure at this time in your life affect you and those you care about? Such evaluations should include a description of many of the physical and emotional set-backs she may experience, during preliminary testing through IVF follow up, from initial findings of pregnancy through birth, with the caveat that the problems she experiences cannot confidently be predicted, but should always be taken seriously. She would be encouraged to assess her own capacities to bear, give birth to, and rear a disabled child in a society that stigmatizes disability. If she does give birth to a disabled child, she would be directed to women-centered peer group counseling for information, resources, and support.[43]

The feminist ethics of reproduction outlined above also locates women's IVF experience within the larger social context of the reproductive exploitation and manipulation of women. Thus, guided by this ethics, clinicians will invite each prospective IVF patient to join them in evaluating the most current information concerning the risks, benefits, and success rates of IVF for this clinic with this group of practitioners. Such resources would include accessible and open forums for the exchange of IVF information and debate, detailing the history of dangerous reproductive experimentation on women, and the ideology of compulsory motherhood in which women's reproductive needs and experience are embedded. Such forums would also be designed to provide a variety of reproductive information regarding safe and reliable alternatives to IVF or hospital-based primary care, which may include homeopathic treatment, herbal prescriptions, acupuncture, self-insemination, home birthing, and the use of midwives; patients may also find advice regarding adoption, foster care, or other childcare options, as well as peer counselors who have chosen to remain childless. In this way, clinicians can encourage women to become informed, active, and critical subjects of our own reproductive care. Moreover, guided by this ethics, IVF clinicians would give equal time to poor women, women of color, women with disabilities, and single heterosexual women and lesbians who wish to be mothers, without subjecting them to the kinds of discriminatory "fitness" screenings that result from medical presumptions of moral elitism.

Under the feminist ethics of reproduction described thus far, regulation of IVF would be generated and inspired not just by the clinicians, researchers, lawyers, and government officials who are interested in maintaining a commercial and scientific stranglehold on women's reproduction; such regulation would also be informed by feminists, many of whom may be infertile women, IVF mothers, fertile mothers, post-menopausal women, and other women and men interested in removing the shame, worthlessness, and despair of involuntary childlessness and in defining a woman's value to herself, and to her community, in her own terms. Such individuals would sit on governmental regulatory commissions to help formulate guidelines for IVF research and development, for funding, for marketing, for gaining equal access to IVF information and resources, for monitoring, and for legal procedures for damages and violations of social policy. They would also participate in all of the aspects of the manufacture and distribution of the technologies associated with IVF. Clinicians, patients, and their families would thus be in a better position to assess the need for, and the benefits of, IVF and embryo transfer, and to allow individual women to make their own decisions as to whether or how such technologies figure in their lives. Such an ethics is true to feminist ideals in that it individualizes women's reproduction within a gendered social context that simultaneously acknowledges women's risks of reproductive exploitation and our capacity to liberate ourselves through the exercise of reproductive self-determination.[44]

A FEMINIST ETHICS OF REPRODUCTION FOR HMOs?

I would like to conclude with some reflections on whether IVF specialists and referring primary care physicians have sufficient incentive to adopt the feminist ethics of reproduction outlined above, given the current trend toward the use of HMOs (health maintenance organizations) by individuals and their employers. HMOs are designed to cut the costs of healthcare by promoting primary and preventive medical treatment that would minimize requirements for extensive, and expensive, medical service. Unlike traditional fee-for-service medical care, HMOs are designed to profit from their customers' use of fewer medical services, not more. HMOs employ physicians whose services to patients are typically capped as to how much each physician can spend per patient, based on HMO customers' monthly membership fees. If capitation is not used, HMO bonuses or "withholds" from physicians' fee-for-service payments or salaries are used as incentives for physicians to provide the kinds of medical treatment that keeps their patients healthy and "in-house." This strategy is aimed at minimizing unnecessary medical expenditures for specialized or extensive medical treatment, since less service required per patient is more money in the physician's (and HMO's) pocket.[45]

Feminists who are critical of the new reproductive technologies have often complained that if practitioners were truly interested in "curing" women's infertility, they would be performing preventive medicine in the form of providing a higher standard of basic health and prenatal care to all women, and of attacking the causes–iatrogenic, social, and environmental–of pelvic inflammation, endometriosis, inovulation, sterility, and cervical cancer.[46] If HMOs are designed to promote preventive healthcare and minimize referrals to specialists, then they seem ideally suited to a feminist ethics of reproduction that promotes women's long-term reproductive health and recommends exploring the many ways that women can experience motherhood and child care independent of the IVF specialist.

On the other hand, primary care physicians are already complaining that they are feeling squeezed by the demands of boards of directors of HMOs to fit more patients into already grueling clinical schedules and to withhold special treatment for the sake of higher profits for the organization. Specialists in virtually all medical fields are going out of business as their referral sources dry up.[47] In light of such considerations, neither primary care physicians nor specialists who belong to HMOs may have much incentive to adopt a feminist ethics of reproduction that recommends spending *more* time with their patients, not less, and spending *more* time learning about the broader social history, gender politics, and cultural ideology that circumscribe the reproductive treatments their patients' conditions may indicate. Indeed, primary care physicians who belong to HMOs may feel pressured to make their own in-house diagnoses of a woman's apparent inability to become pregnant, when they would otherwise have referred her to specialists more conversant with the causes and treatment of both male and female infertility.

Many physicians have begun to sponsor their own healthcare organizations, referred to as preferred provider organizations (PPOs), which they believe are more sensitive to the specialized needs of individual patients while they still promote preventive healthcare.[48] The prospective IVF patient who doubles as a feminist reproductive activist plays a crucial role here, since by demanding that primary care physicians and IVF practitioners particularize and politicize women's reproductive experience, women can help keep PPOs from recreating the gender hierarchies that are so oppressive to women. If PPOs do promote preventive care in the way more traditional fee-for-service physicians do not, then PPOs may be more conducive to the feminist IVF counseling, service, and follow up that are more typical of women's health clinics. Ironically, these clinics continue to suffer from a marginalization that is a direct result of their emphasis on the collaborative, holistic, and pro-active healthcare formerly deemphasized by much of mainstream medicine. However, because PPOs handle a wide variety of patients, they may be ideally situated to give feminist reproductive healthcare the stamp of legitimacy that would give clinicians more psychological and financial incentive to treat patients from a feminist perspective. Any fears that PPOs would lose money by turning off nonfeminist patients would be replaced with the confidence that their particularized and politicized healthcare could indeed save lives. If this is the case, then taking the Hippocratic oath requires providing reproductive healthcare from a feminist perspective.

Thus, a feminist ethics of reproduction recommends an individually responsive and socially responsible co-partnership between practitioner and patient that encourages *all* concerned to promote women's reproductive empowerment. As women's physician Christiane Northrup has pointed out, "There is no such thing as living in a fully empow-

ered partnership [between patient and practitioner] if you still fall into the damsel archetype and are waiting for your knight to rescue you."[49] Securing equal and informed access to a variety of reproductive alternatives is only the beginning of women's reproductive empowerment. Eliminating economic discrimination against women, improving our legislative power, and developing the self-respect and self-confidence to insist that our healthcare needs are met, whether or not we pursue motherhood, are its necessary accompaniments.

NOTES

The epigraph that opened this article is quoted from "Reproductive Technologies and the Deconstruction of Motherhood," in *Reproductive Technologies: Gender, Motherhood, and Medicine*, ed. Michelle Stanworth (Minneapolis: University of Minnesota Press, 1987), 35.

1. For feminist documentation of the medical pathology and appropriation of women's reproduction, see S. Arms, *Immaculate Deception* (Boston: Houghton Mifflin, 1975) and *Immaculate Deception II: A Fresh Look at Childbirth* (Berkeley, Calif.: Celestial Arts, 1994); D. Scully, *Men Who Control Women's Health: The Miseducation of Obstetrician-Gynecologists* (Boston: Houghton Mifflin, 1980); G. Corea, *The Mother Machine: Reproductive Technologies from Artificial Insemination to Artificial Wombs* (New York: Harper & Row, 1985), chap. 15 and 16; G. Corea, *The Hidden Malpractice: How American Medicine Mistreats Women*, 2nd ed. (New York: Harper & Row, 1985); G. Corea, "The New Reproductive Technologies," in *The Sexual Liberals and the Attack on Feminism*, ed. D. Leidholdt and J.G. Raymond (New York: Teachers College Press, 1990), 85-94; M. Daly, *Gyn/Ecology: The Metaethics of Radical Feminism* (Boston: Beacon Press, 1978); L. Coveney et al., *The Sexuality Papers: Male Sexuality and the Social Control of Women* (London: Hutchinson, 1984); B. Ehrenreich and D. English, *For Her Own Good: 150 Years of the Experts' Advice to Women* (New York: Anchor/Doubleday, 1978); A. Oakley, *Women Confined: Towards a Sociology of Childbirth* (New York: Schoecken, 1980); C. Dreifus, ed., *Seizing Our Bodies: The Politics of Women's Health* (New York: Vintage Books, 1978); B.K. Rothman, *In Labour: Women and Power in the Birthplace* (New York and London: W.W. Norton, 1982); J.G. Raymond, *Women as Wombs: Reproductive Technologies and the Battle over Women's Freedom* (New York: Harper Collins, 1993), 114-22; A. Direcks, "Has the Lesson Been Learned? The DES Story and IVF," in *Made To Order: The Myth of Reproductive and Genetic Progress*, ed. P. Spallone and D.L. Steinberg (Oxford, U.K.: Pergamon Press, 1987), 161-65; P. Bunkle, "Calling the

Shots? The International Politics of Depo-Provera," in *Test-Tube Women: What Future for Motherhood?* ed. R. Arditti, R.D. Klein, and S. Minden (London: Pandora Press, 1989), 165-87; R. Rowland, *Living Laboratories: Women and Reproductive Technologies* (Bloomington, Ind.: Indiana University Press, 1992).

2. The fight over contraception and abortion rights for women in the last two decades has been a fight over just this kind of reproductive self-determination for women.

3. See R.D. Klein, "What's 'New' about the 'New' Reproductive Technologies?" in *Man-Made Women: How the New Reproductive Technologies Affect Women* ed. G. Corea et al., (Bloomington, Ind.: Indiana University Press, 1987), 64-65; M. Stanworth, "Editor's Introduction," in *Reproductive Technologies*, 10-11.

4. See Corea, *The Mother Machine*, 133-34; P. Spallone, *Beyond Conception: The New Politics of Reproduction* (Granby, Mass.: Bergin & Garvey, 1989), 14-15; P. Spallone and D.L. Steinberg, "Introduction," in *Made to Order*, 15; F. Laborie, "Looking for Mothers, You Only Find Fetuses," in *Made to Order*, 51-54. For feminist concerns about the implications of genetic engineering in women's lives, see S. Minden, "Designer Genes: A View from the Factory," in *Test-Tube Women*, 92-98; S. Minden, "Patriarchal Designs: The Genetic Engineering of Human Embryos," in *Made to Order*, 102-9; L. Bullard, "Killing Us Softly: Toward a Feminist Analysis of Genetic Engineering," in *Made to Order*, 110-19.

5. Detailed descriptions of such technologies can be found in Rowland, *Living Laboratories*; Spallone, *Beyond Conception*; J.N. Lasker and S. Borg, *In Search of Parenthood: Coping with Infertility and High-Tech Conception* (Boston: Beacon Press, 1987); S. Fishel and E. M. Symonds, eds., *In Vitro Fertilization: Past, Present, Future* (Oxford, U.K.: IRL Press, 1986); P. Singer and D. Wells, *The Reproduction Revolution: New Ways of Making Babies* (New York: Oxford University Press, 1984); E.H. Baruch, A.F. D'Adamo, Jr., and J. Seager, eds., *Embryos, Ethics and Women's Rights: Exploring the New Reproductive Technologies* (New York: Harrington Park Press, 1988); B.B. Hoskins and H.B. Holmes, "Technology and Prenatal Femicide," in *Test-Tube Women*, 237-56; S. Minden, "Designer Genes"; B. Carey, "Chance of a Lifetime," *Health* (May/June 1994): 90-98.

6. For example, see Raymond, *Women as Wombs*; Rowland, *Living Laboratories*; Corea, *The Mother Machine*; Corea et al. ed., *Man-made Women*; Spallone and Steinberg, *Made to Order*; Spallone, *Beyond Conception*; Arditti, Klein, and Minden, eds., *Test-Tube Women*; R. Klein, ed. *Infertility: Women Speak Out about Their Experiences of Reproductive Medicine* (London: Pandora Press, 1989); C. Ewing and R. Klein, "Joint Resistance: Women Oppose the Technological Take-over of Life," *Reproductive and Genetic Engineering: Journal of International Feminist Analysis* 2, no. 3 (1989): 279-84; R. Hubbard, "The Case Against In Vitro

Fertilization and Implantation," in *The Custom-Made Child? Women-centered Perspectives*, ed. H.B. Holmes, B.B. Hoskins, and M. Gross (Clifton, N.J.: Humana Press, 1981), 259-62.

7. See G. Corea and S. Ince, "Report of a Survey of IVF Clinics in the USA," in *Made to Order*, 133-45; M. Soules, "The In Vitro Fertilization Rate: Let's Be Honest with One Another," *Fertility and Sterility* 43, no. 4 (1985): 511-13; B.K. Rothman, "The Meaning of Choice in Reproductive Technology," R. Hubbard, "Personal Courage Is Not Enough: Some Hazards of Childbearing in the 1980s," and R. Rowland, "Reproductive Technologies: The Final Solution to the Woman Question," in *Test-Tube Women*, 23-33, 331-69; T. Powledge, "Reproductive Technologies and the Bottom Line," in *Embryos, Ethics and Women's Rights*, 203-9; Rowland, *Living Laboratories*, 44-73; Raymond, *Women as Wombs*, 108-37; and note 1 above.

8. R. Klein, "Resistance: From the Exploitation of Infertility to an Exploration of In-Fertility," in Klein, *Infertility*, 256.

9. For example, see H.B. Holmes and B.B. Hoskins, "Prenatal and Preconception Sex Choice Technologies: A Path to Femicide?" and G. Corea, "The Reproductive Brothel," in *Man-made Women*, 15-29, 38-51; T.M. Powledge, "Unnatural Selection: On Choosing Children's Sex," in *The Custom-made Child?* 193-203; T. Powledge, "Reproductive Technologies and the Bottom Line."

10. This theme is echoed by writers who disagree about the exact form that a feminist reproductive technology should take. See Stanworth, ed., *Reproductive Technologies*; Holmes, Hoskins, and Gross, eds., *The Custom-made Child?*; C. Overall, "Access to In Vitro Fertilization: Costs, Care, and Consent," *Dialogue* 30 (1991): 383-97; M.A. Warren, "Is IVF Research a Threat to Women's Autonomy?" in *Embryo Experimentation: Ethical, Legal and Social Issues*, ed. P. Singer et al., (Cambridge, U.K.: Cambridge University Press, 1990), 125-40; Gordon, *Woman's Body, Woman's Right*, 457-69; N. Taub and S. Cohen, eds. *Reproductive Laws for the 1990s: A Briefing Handbook* (Newark, N.J.: Women's Rights Litigation Clinic, Rutgers Law School, 1988).

11. See J.A. Robertson, "Procreative Liberty, Embryos, and Collaborative Reproduction: A Legal Perspective," in *Embryos, Ethics and Women's Rights*, 179-94; J.A. Robertson, "Procreative Liberty and the Control of Conception, Pregnancy, and Childbirth," *Virginia Law Review* 69, no. 3 (1983): 405-14; L. Andrews, "Alternative Modes of Reproduction," in *Reproductive Laws for the 1990s*. For advice on how to take advantage of the new reproductive technologies, see L. Andrews, *New Conceptions: A Consumer's Guide to the Newest Infertility Treatments* (New York: Ballentine, 1985).

12. S. Firestone, *The Dialectic of Sex* (New York: Bantam Books, 1970), chapt. 1, 10, and "Conclusion."

13. For the purposes of this paper, IVF patients are female, unless otherwise noted.

14. See P.M. McShane, "In Vitro Fertilization, GIFT, and Related Technologies. Hope in a Test Tube," in *Embryos, Ethics and Women's Rights* 32. For a succinct overview of the physiology of reproduction, see A.F. D'Adamo, "Reproductive Technologies: The Two Sides of the Glass Jar," in *Embryos, Ethics and Women's Rights*, 10-14.

15. See Lasker and Borg, *In Search of Parenthood*, 2-4; Spallone, *Beyond Conception*, 71-75.

16. See *Health Matters, Long Beach* [Calif.] *Memorial Women's Hospital Newsletter*, (summer 1994).

17. See Rowland, *Living Laboratories*, 19; Lasker and Borg, *In Search of Parenthood*, 52; Spallone, *Beyond Conception*, 56-64; McShane, "In Vitro Fertilization," 34-38.

18. However, feminists have objected that such "donations" are often without the patient's consent, and that requests for eggs are often conceded to under clinicians' advice to "help other women who desperately want children." See Rowland, *Living Laboratories*, 91-94, 149-50; Raymond, *Women as Wombs*, 39-58; J. Marquis and M. Granberry, "Seven Couples Sue UC, Alleging Misuse of Eggs," *Los Angeles Times*, 8 August 1995.

19. See Singer and Wells, *The Reproduction Revolution*, 110-11, 128-30; Rowland, *Living Laboratories*, 156-58; McShane, "In Vitro Fertilization," 43-44.

20. See Spallone, *Beyond Conception*, 66; also see Lasker and Borg, *In Search of Parenthood*, 3-4, 52; McShane, "In Vitro Fertilization," 34, 39.

21. See Carey, "Chance of a Lifetime"; Raymond, *Women as Wombs*, xiv. Some clinics may have an IVF success rate of over 30 percent in women under 35 years of age, yet the same clinic may have less than a 10 percent success rate with women over 35. Thus, the age of patients admitted to any one IVF program over time can drastically affect a clinic's success in producing a sustainable IVF pregnancy.

22. For recent feminist discussions of the costs, risks, and success of IVF, see L.S. Williams, "No Relief Until the End: The Physical and Emotional Costs of In Vitro Fertilization," in *The Future of Human Reproduction*, ed. C. Overall (Toronto, Ont.: The Women's Press, 1989), 120-38; Rowland, *Living Laboratories*, 41-73; Spallone, *Beyond Conception*, 62-64; Raymond, *Women as Wombs*, 9-12; Corea and Ince, "Report of a Survey of IVF Clinics in the USA"; Soules, "The In Vitro Fertilization Rate."

23. See Rowland, *Living Laboratories*, 22-25, 49-63; Spallone, *Beyond Conception*, 57-60; Corea, *The Mother Machine*, 108-10; Klein and Rowland, "Women as Test-Sites for Fertility Drugs"; R. Klein, "The Making of This Book," and "Resistance," A. Belk-Schmehle, "Every Month a Little Miscarriage," and M. Humm, "Motherhood Has a History: Amenorrhea and Autobiography," in Klein, *Infertility*, 1-2, 28-34, 35-45, 234-48; Laborie, "Looking for Mothers." With this much documentation and more, it is depressing to find writers like Thomas Shannon asserting, "As yet [1987], no detrimental effects have been associated with this [su-

perovulating] use of hormones." See T. Shannon, "In Vitro Fertilization: Ethical Issues," in *Embryos, Ethics and Women's Rights*, 158.

24. See Lasker and Borg, *In Search of Parenthood*, 70; M. Wikland, L. Hamberger, and L. Enk, "Ultrasound for Oocyte Recovery" and J. Webster, "Laparoscopic Oocyte Recovery," in *In Vitro Fertilization*, 59-67, 69-76; Singer and Wells, *The Reproduction Revolution*, 84-98; Rowland, *Living Laboratories*, 25-30; Spallone, *Beyond Conception*, 60-61.

25. See Rowland, *Living Laboratories*, 39-40; D'Adamo, "Reproductive Technologies," 25-26.

26. See Rowland, *Living Laboratories*, 64, 68; Spallone, *Beyond Conception*, 62-63; Klein, "Resistance," 251; Raymond, *Women as Wombs*, 130-33.

27. See Rowland, *Living Laboratories*, 40-41; Klein, "Resistance," 251.

28. See D'Adamo, "Reproductive Technologies," 37, 42.

29. See Rowland, *Living Laboratories*, 30-32; Lasker and Borg, *In Search of Parenthood*, 55; Klein, "Resistance," 252-53; McShane, "In Vitro Fertilization," 43-44.

30. S. Sherwin, "Feminist Ethics and *In Vitro* Fertilization," in *Science, Morality and Feminist Theory*, ed. M. Hanen and K. Nielsen (Calgary, Alb.: University of Calgary Press, 1987), 281.

31. See I. Kant, *Groundwork of the Metaphysic of Morals*, trans. H.J. Paton (New York: Harper Torchbooks, 1964), 96.

32. See Williams, "No Relief Until the End"; J. Lorber, "In Vitro Fertilization and Gender Politics," in *Embryos, Ethics and Women's Rights*, 121-23; U. Winkler, "He Called Me Number 27," in Klein, *Infertility*, 90-100; Rowland, *Living Laboratories*, 73-80; Lasker and Borg, *In Search of Parenthood*, 57-64; Warren, "Is IVF a Threat to Women's Autonomy?"; Stuart, "Is It Worth It? I Just Don't Know," in Klein, *Infertility*, 82-89.

33. See Corea, "The New Reproductive Technologies"; C. Crowe, " 'Women Want It': In Vitro Fertilization and Women's Motivation for Participation" and A.R. Gomez dos Reis, "IVF in Brazil: The Story Told by the Newspapers," in *Made to Order*, 91-92, 120-32; A. Solomon, "Sometimes Pergonal Kills," in Klein, *Infertility*, 46-50; Klein and Rowland, "Women as Test Sites for Fertility Drugs"; R. Hubbard, "Prenatal Diagnosis Discussion," in *The Custom-Made Child?*, 106-7; Hubbard, "Personal Courage is Not Enough"; Carey, "Chance of a Lifetime"; M. Saxton, "Born and Unborn: The Implications of Reproductive Technologies for People with Disabilities," in *Test-Tube Women*, 298-312; Corea and Ince, "Report of a Survey of IVF Clinics in the USA"; Soules, "The In Vitro Fertilization Rate"; G. Corea, "What the King Cannot See," in *Embryos, Ethics and Women's Rights*, 77-93; Corea, *The Mother Machine*, chapt. 6, 8; Rowland, *Living Laboratories*, 49-73; A. Solomon, "Infertility as Crisis," in Klein, *Infertility*, 169-87.

34. S. Gorovitz, *Doctors' Dilemmas: Moral Conflict and Medical Care* (New York: Oxford University Press, 1982), 168, quoted in Sherwin, "Feminist Ethics and In Vitro Fertilization," 270. Similarly, Thomas Shannon, while calling for a national registry of research and practice on IVF, asserts, "Our American love affair with technology has been characterized by optimism, success, and a great deal of luck," in "In Vitro Fertilization," 158. From the perspective of feminists critical of the new reproductive technologies, the question is: whose optimism? whose success? whose luck?

35. For further discussion of how traditional ethics falls short of the requirements of a feminist ethics of reproduction, see Sherwin, "Feminist Ethics and In Vitro Fertilization," and S. Sherwin, "A Feminist Approach to Ethics," *Dalhousie Review* 64, no. 4 (1984-5): 704-13; M.A. Warren, "IVF and Women's Interests: An Analysis of Feminist Concerns," *Bioethics* 2, no. 1 (1988): 37-57. For specific feminist criticisms of a Kantian ethics of duty, often referred to as an "ethics of justice," as opposed to an "ethics of care," see M.J. Larrabee, ed. *An Ethic of Care: Feminist and Interdisciplinary Perspectives* (New York: Routledge, 1993); E.B. Cole and S. Coultrap-McQuin, eds., *Explorations in Feminist Ethics: Theory and Practice* (Bloomington, Ind.: Indiana University Press, 1992), section entitled, "The Care Debate"; C.R. Sunstein, ed., *Feminism and Political Theory* (Chicago, Ill.: University of Chicago Press, 1990), section entitled, "The Question of Different Voice: Care, Justice, and Rights."

36. See Marquis and Granberry, "Seven Couples Sue UC." In a follow-up story, it was reported that a clinic in Chile was so eager to lure one of the legally implicated IVF experts away from the United States that it dismissed as irrelevant the allegations against him, which include egg swapping without patients' consent and falsifying financial records. As one South American clinic official reportedly said, "We're not the FBI. We aren't an investigative body, we don't have anything to do with internal tax issues in the United States. All we know is we have an application from a man who is famous, who is an expert in fertility all over the world. We have to evaluate what the overall effect will be of having him join the clinic." The question remains: whose utilitarian evaluations will those be, the clinicians' or the patients'? See "Scandal Trails UCI Doctor Home," *Los Angeles Times*, 30 November 1995.

37. See Warren, "IVF and Women's Interests," 39. For further discussion of utilitarianism and its critics, see S. Scheffler, *The Rejection of Consequentialism* (Oxford, U.K.: Clarendon Press, 1982) and A. Sen and B. Williams, eds., *Utilitarianism: For and Against* (Cambridge, U.K.: Cambridge University Press, 1982).

38. For an excellent outline and critique of an ethics of virtue, see B.N. Moore and R.M. Stewart, *Moral Philosophy: A Comprehensive Introduction* (Mountain View, Calif.: Mayfield Publishing, 1994), 73-76; also see P. Foot, *Virtues and Vices* (Oxford, U.K.: Basil Blackwell, 1978); P.T. Geach,

The Virtues (Cambridge, U.K.: Cambridge University Press, 1977); A. MacIntyre, *After Virtue*, 2nd ed. (Notre Dame, Ind.: University of Notre Dame Press, 1984).

39. A. Jagger, "Introduction to Part V: Family Values," in *Living with Contradictions: Controversies in Feminist Social Ethics*, ed. A. Jagger (Boulder, Colo.: Westview Press, 1994), 386.

40. See K. Lindsey, "The Politics of Childlessness," in *Living with Contradictions*, 430-32; T. Mayrand, "Response," in *The Custom-Made Child?*, 249; M. Stanworth, "Reproductive Technologies and the Deconstruction of Motherhood," in *Reproductive Technologies*, 15-16.

41. This view is echoed by Sherwin in "Feminist Ethics and In Vitro Fertilization," 280; also see Overall, "Access to In Vitro Fertilization: Costs, Care, and Consent," 392-93.

42. C. Overall, *Ethics and Human Reproduction: A Feminist Analysis* (Boston: Allen & Unwin, 1987), 2.

43. See M. Saxton, "A Peer Counseling Training Program for Disabled Women," *Journal of Sociology and Social Welfare* 8, no. 2 (1981): 334-35; also see M. Saxton, "Prenatal Screening and Discriminatory Attitudes about Disability," in *Embryos, Ethics and Women's Rights*, 217-24; Saxton, "Born and Unborn"; A. Finger, "Claiming All of Our Bodies: Reproductive Rights and Disabilities," in *Test-Tube Women*, 281-97.

44. See V. Von Wagner and B. Lee, "Principles into Practice: An Activist Vision of Feminist Reproductive Health Care," in *The Future of Human Reproduction*, ed. C. Overall (Toronto, Ont.: Women's Press, 1989), 238-58; K. Kohlbert, "A Reproductive Rights Agenda for the 1990s," in Jaggar, *Living With Contradictions*, 292-97; Minden, "Designer Genes;" 97-98; Warren, "Is IVF Research a Threat to Women's Autonomy?" 137-38; Overall, "Access to In Vitro Fertilization," 393-95.

45. R.G. Shouldice, *Introduction to Managed Care: Health Maintenance Organizations, Preferred Provider Organizations, and Competitive Medical Plans* (Arlington, Va.: Information Resources Press, 1991), 11-16.

46. See Rowland, *Living Laboratories*, 14, 43; also see A. Pappert, "A Voice for Infertile Women," in Klein, *Infertility*, 201; U. Winkler and T. Schönenberg, "Options for Involuntarily Childless Women," in *Infertility*, 212, n.3, and 222-23; Solomon, "Infertility as Crisis," 186; Spallone, *Beyond Conception*, 27, 69, 183-84; P. Spallone, "Reproductive Technology and the State: The Warnock Report and Its Clones"; and H.P. Hynes, "A Paradigm for Regulation of the Biomedical Industry: Environmental Protection in the United States," in *Made to Order*, 78, 203.

47. See "The Health Care Revolution," *Los Angeles Times*, 27-31 August 1995 for how HMOs are changing the way physicians treat their patients and control standards of care.

48. Shouldice, *Introduction to Managed Care*, 65.

49. Quoted in K.H. Sullivan, "Mindful Medicine: An Interview with Pioneering Women's Physician Christiane Northrup," *Vegetarian Times*, July 1995, 10.

[9]

ELIZABETH S. ANDERSON   Is Women's Labor
a Commodity?

In the past few years the practice of commercial surrogate motherhood has gained notoriety as a method for acquiring children. A commercial surrogate mother is anyone who is paid money to bear a child for other people and terminate her parental rights, so that the others may raise the child as exclusively their own. The growth of commercial surrogacy has raised with new urgency a class of concerns regarding the proper scope of the market. Some critics have objected to commercial surrogacy on the ground that it improperly treats children and women's reproductive capacities as commodities.[1] The prospect of reducing children to consumer durables and women to baby factories surely inspires revulsion. But are there good reasons behind the revulsion? And is this an accurate description of what commercial surrogacy implies? This article offers a theory about what things are properly regarded as commodities which supports the claim that commercial surrogacy constitutes an unconscionable commodification of children and of women's reproductive capacities.

What Is a Commodity?

The modern market can be characterized in terms of the legal and social norms by which it governs the production, exchange, and enjoyment of

The author thanks David Anderson, Steven Darwall, Ezekiel Emanuel, Daniel Hausman, Don Herzog, Robert Nozick, Richard Pildes, John Rawls, Michael Sandel, Thomas Scanlon, and Howard Wial for helpful comments and criticisms.

1. See, for example, Gena Corea, *The Mother Machine* (New York: Harper and Row, 1985), pp. 216, 219; Angela Holder, "Surrogate Motherhood: Babies for Fun and Profit," *Case and Comment* 90 (1985): 3–11; and Margaret Jane Radin, "Market Inalienability," *Harvard Law Review* 100 (June 1987): 1849–1937.

commodities. To say that something is properly regarded as a commodity is to claim that the norms of the market are appropriate for regulating its production, exchange, and enjoyment. To the extent that moral principles or ethical ideals preclude the application of market norms to a good, we may say that the good is not a (proper) commodity.

Why should we object to the application of a market norm to the production or distribution of a good? One reason may be that to produce or distribute the good in accordance with the norm is to *fail to value it in an appropriate way*. Consider, for example, a standard Kantian argument against slavery, or the commodification of persons. Slaves are treated in accordance with the market norm that owners may use commodities to satisfy their own interests without regard for the interests of the commodities themselves. To treat a person without regard for her interests is to fail to respect her. But slaves are persons who may not be merely used in this fashion, since as rational beings they possess a dignity which commands respect. In Kantian theory, the problem with slavery is that it treats beings worthy of *respect* as if they were worthy merely of *use*. "Respect" and "use" in this context denote what we may call different *modes of valuation*. We value things and persons in other ways than by respecting and using them. For example, love, admiration, honor, and appreciation constitute distinct modes of valuation. To value a thing or person in a distinctive way involves treating it in accordance with a particular set of norms. For example, courtesy expresses a mode of valuation we may call "civil respect," which differs from Kantian respect in that it calls for obedience to the rules of etiquette rather than to the categorical imperative.

Any ideal of human life includes a conception of how different things and persons should be valued. Let us reserve the term "use" to refer to the mode of valuation proper to commodities, which follows the market norm of treating things solely in accordance with the owner's nonmoral preferences. Then the Kantian argument against commodifying persons can be generalized to apply to many other cases. It can be argued that many objects which are worthy of a higher mode of valuation than use are not properly regarded as mere commodities.[2] Some current argu-

2. The notion of valuing something more highly than another can be understood as follows. Some preferences are neither obligatory nor admirable. To value a thing as a mere use-object is to treat it solely in accordance with such nonethical preferences. To value a thing or person more highly than as a mere use-object is to recognize it as having some

73   *Is Women's Labor*
                                      a Commodity?

ments against the colorization of classic black-and-white films take this form. Such films have been colorized by their owners in an attempt to enhance their market value by attracting audiences unused to black-and-white cinematography. But some opponents of the practice object that such treatment of the film classics fails to appreciate their aesthetic and historical value. True appreciation of these films would preclude this kind of crass commercial exploitation, which debases their aesthetic qualities in the name of profits. Here the argument rests on the claim that the goods in question are worthy of appreciation, not merely of use.

The ideals which specify how one should value certain things are supported by a conception of human flourishing. Our lives are enriched and elevated by cultivating and exercising the capacity to appreciate art. To fail to do so reflects poorly on ourselves. To fail to value things appropriately is to embody in one's life an inferior conception of human flourishing.[3]

These considerations support a general account of the sorts of things which are appropriately regarded as commodities. Commodities are those things which are properly treated in accordance with the norms of the modern market. We can question the application of market norms to the production, distribution, and enjoyment of a good by appealing to ethical ideals which support arguments that the good should be valued in some other way than use. Arguments of the latter sort claim that to allow certain market norms to govern our treatment of a thing expresses a mode of valuation not worthy of it. If the thing is to be valued appropriately, its production, exchange, and enjoyment must be removed from market norms and embedded in a different set of social relationships.

---

special intrinsic worth, in virtue of which we form preferences about how to treat the thing which we regard as obligatory or admirable. The person who truly appreciates art does not conceive of art merely as a thing which she can use as she pleases, but as something which commands appreciation. It would be contemptible to willfully destroy the aesthetic qualities of a work of art simply to satisfy some of one's nonethical preferences, and it is a mark of a cultivated and hence admirable person that she has preferences for appreciating art. This account of higher and lower modes of valuation is indebted to Charles Taylor's account of higher and lower values. See Charles Taylor, "The Diversity of Goods," in *Utilitarianism and Beyond*, ed. Amartya Sen and Bernard Williams (Cambridge: Cambridge University Press, 1982), pp. 129–44.

3. This kind of argument shows why treating something as a commodity may be deplorable. Of course, more has to be said to justify prohibiting the commodification of a thing. I shall argue below that the considerations against the commodification of children and of women's labor are strong enough to justify prohibiting the practice of commercial surrogacy.

THE CASE OF COMMERCIAL SURROGACY

Let us now consider the practice of commercial surrogate motherhood in the light of this theory of commodities. Surrogate motherhood as a commercial enterprise is based upon contracts involving three parties: the intended father, the broker, and the surrogate mother. The intended father agrees to pay a lawyer to find a suitable surrogate mother and make the requisite medical and legal arrangements for the conception and birth of the child, and for the transfer of legal custody to himself.[4] The surrogate mother agrees to become impregnated with the intended father's sperm, to carry the resulting child to term, and to relinquish her parental rights to it, transferring custody to the father in return for a fee and medical expenses. Both she and her husband (if she has one) agree not to form a parent-child bond with her child and to do everything necessary to effect the transfer of the child to the intended father. At current market prices, the lawyer arranging the contract can expect to gross $15,000 from the contract, while the surrogate mother can expect a $10,000 fee.[5]

The practice of commercial surrogacy has been defended on four main grounds. First, given the shortage of children available for adoption and the difficulty of qualifying as adoptive parents, it may represent the only hope for some people to be able to raise a family. Commercial surrogacy should be accepted as an effective means for realizing this highly significant good. Second, two fundamental human rights support commercial surrogacy: the right to procreate and freedom of contract. Fully informed autonomous adults should have the right to make whatever arrangements they wish for the use of their bodies and the reproduction of children, so long as the children themselves are not harmed. Third, the labor of the surrogate mother is said to be a labor of love. Her altruistic acts should be permitted and encouraged.[6] Finally, it is argued that commer-

4. State laws against selling babies prevent the intended father's wife (if he has one) from being a party to the contract.

5. See Katie Marie Brophy, "A Surrogate Mother Contract to Bear a Child," *Journal of Family Law* 20 (1981–82): 263–91, and Noel Keane, "The Surrogate Parenting Contract," *Adelphia Law Journal* 2 (1983): 45–53, for examples and explanations of surrogate parenting contracts.

6. Mary Warnock, *A Question of Life* (Oxford: Blackwell, 1985), p. 45. This book reprints the Warnock Report on Human Fertilization and Embryology, which was commissioned by the British government for the purpose of recommending legislation concerning surrogacy and other issues. Although the Warnock Report mentions the promotion of altruism as one defense of surrogacy, it strongly condemns the practice overall.

75   *Is Women's Labor*
                                      a Commodity?

cial surrogacy is no different in its ethical implications from many already accepted practices which separate genetic, gestational, and social parenting, such as artificial insemination by donor, adoption, wet-nursing, and day care. Consistency demands that society accept this new practice as well.[7]

In opposition to these claims, I shall argue that commercial surrogacy does raise new ethical issues, since it represents an invasion of the market into a new sphere of conduct, that of specifically women's labor—that is, the labor of carrying children to term in pregnancy. When women's labor is treated as a commodity, the women who perform it are degraded. Furthermore, commercial surrogacy degrades children by reducing their status to that of commodities. Let us consider each of the goods of concern in surrogate motherhood—the child, and women's reproductive labor—to see how the commercialization of parenthood affects people's regard for them.

CHILDREN AS COMMODITIES

The most fundamental calling of parents to their children is to love them. Children are to be loved and cherished by their parents, not to be used or manipulated by them for merely personal advantage. Parental love can be understood as a passionate, unconditional commitment to nurture one's child, providing it with the care, affection, and guidance it needs to develop its capacities to maturity. This understanding of the way parents should value their children informs our interpretation of parental rights over their children. Parents' rights over their children are trusts, which they must always exercise for the sake of the child. This is not to deny that parents have their own aspirations in raising children. But the child's interests beyond subsistence are not definable independently of the flourishing of the family, which is the object of specifically parental aspirations. The proper exercise of parental rights includes those acts which promote their shared life as a family, which realize the shared interests of the parents and the child.

The norms of parental love carry implications for the ways other people should treat the relationship between parents and their children. If children are to be loved by their parents, then others should not attempt to

7. John Robertson, "Surrogate Mothers: Not So Novel after All," *Hastings Center Report*, October 1983, pp. 28–34; John Harris, *The Value of Life* (Boston: Routledge and Kegan Paul, 1985).

compromise the integrity of parental love or work to suppress the emotions supporting the bond between parents and their children. If the rights to children should be understood as trusts, then if those rights are lost or relinquished, the duty of those in charge of transferring custody to others is to consult the best interests of the child.

Commercial surrogacy substitutes market norms for some of the norms of parental love. Most importantly, it requires us to understand parental rights no longer as trusts but as things more like property rights—that is, rights of use and disposal over the things owned. For in this practice the natural mother deliberately conceives a child with the intention of giving it up for material advantage. Her renunciation of parental responsibilities is not done for the child's sake, nor for the sake of fulfilling an interest she shares with the child, but typically for her own sake (and possibly, if "altruism" is a motive, for the intended parents' sakes). She and the couple who pay her to give up her parental rights over her child thus treat her rights as a kind of property right. They thereby treat the child itself as a kind of commodity, which may be properly bought and sold.

Commercial surrogacy insinuates the norms of commerce into the parental relationship in other ways. Whereas parental love is not supposed to be conditioned upon the child having particular characteristics, consumer demand is properly responsive to the characteristics of commodities. So the surrogate industry provides opportunities to adoptive couples to specify the height, I.Q., race, and other attributes of the surrogate mother, in the expectation that these traits will be passed on to the child.[8] Since no industry assigns agents to look after the "interests" of its commodities, no one represents the child's interests in the surrogate industry. The surrogate agency promotes the adoptive parents' interests and not the child's interests where matters of custody are concerned. Finally, as the agent of the adoptive parents, the broker has the task of policing the surrogate (natural) mother's relationship to her child, using persuasion, money, and the threat of a lawsuit to weaken and destroy whatever parental love she may develop for her child.[9]

8. See "No Other Hope for Having a Child," *Time*, 19 January 1987, pp. 50–51. Radin argues that women's traits are also commodified in this practice. See "Market Inalienability," pp. 1932–35.

9. Here I discuss the surrogate industry as it actually exists today. I will consider possible modifications of commercial surrogacy in the final section below.

77   *Is Women's Labor*
                                      a Commodity?

All of these substitutions of market norms for parental norms represent ways of treating children as commodities which are degrading to them. Degradation occurs when something is treated in accordance with a lower mode of valuation than is proper to it. We value things not just "more" or "less," but in qualitatively higher and lower ways. To love or respect someone is to value her in a higher way than one would if one merely used her. Children are properly loved by their parents and respected by others. Since children are valued as mere use-objects by the mother and the surrogate agency when they are sold to others, and by the adoptive parents when they seek to conform the child's genetic makeup to their own wishes, commercial surrogacy degrades children insofar as it treats them as commodities.[10]

One might argue that since the child is most likely to enter a loving home, no harm comes to it from permitting the natural mother to treat it as property. So the purchase and sale of infants is unobjectionable, at least from the point of view of children's interests.[11] But the sale of an infant has an expressive significance which this argument fails to recognize. By engaging in the transfer of children by sale, all of the parties to the surrogate contract express a set of attitudes toward children which undermine the norms of parental love. They all agree in treating the ties between a natural mother and her children as properly loosened by a monetary incentive. Would it be any wonder if a child born of a surrogacy agreement feared resale by parents who have such an attitude? And a child who knew how anxious her parents were that she have the "right" genetic makeup might fear that her parent's love was contingent upon her expression of these characteristics.[12]

10. Robert Nozick has objected that my claims about parental love appear to be culture-bound. Do not parents in the Third World, who rely on children to provide for the family subsistence, regard their children as economic goods? In promoting the livelihood of their families, however, such children need not be treated in accordance with market norms—that is, as commodities. In particular, such children usually remain a part of their families, and hence can still be loved by their parents. But insofar as children are treated according to the norms of modern capitalist markets, this treatment is deplorable wherever it takes place.

11. See Elizabeth Landes and Richard Posner, "The Economics of the Baby Shortage," *Journal of Legal Studies* 7 (1978): 323–48, and Richard Posner, "The Regulation of the Market in Adoptions," *Boston University Law Review* 67 (1987): 59–72.

12. Of course, where children are concerned, it is irrelevant whether these fears are reasonable. One of the greatest fears of children is separation from their parents. Adopted children are already known to suffer from separation anxiety more acutely than children who remain with their natural mothers, for they feel that their original mothers did not love

The unsold children of surrogate mothers are also harmed by commercial surrogacy. The children of some surrogate mothers have reported their fears that they may be sold like their half-brother or half-sister, and express a sense of loss at being deprived of a sibling.[13] Furthermore, the widespread acceptance of commercial surrogacy would psychologically threaten all children. For it would change the way children are valued by people (parents and surrogate brokers)—from being loved by their parents and respected by others, to being sometimes used as objects of commercial profit-making.[14]

Proponents of commercial surrogacy have denied that the surrogate industry engages in the sale of children. For it is impossible to sell to someone what is already his own, and the child is already the father's own natural offspring. The payment to the surrogate mother is not for her child, but for her services in carrying it to term.[15] The claim that the parties to the surrogate contract treat children as commodities, however, is based on the way they treat the *mother's* rights over her child. It is irrelevant that the natural father also has some rights over the child; what he pays for is exclusive rights to it. He would not pay her for the "service" of carrying the child to term if she refused to relinquish her parental rights to it. That the mother regards only her labor and not her child as requiring compensation is also irrelevant. No one would argue that the baker does not treat his bread as property just because he sees the income from its sale as compensation for his labor and expenses and not for the bread itself, which he doesn't care to keep.[16]

---

them. In adoption, the fact that the child would be even worse off if the mother did not give it up justifies her severing of ties and can help to rationalize this event to the child. But in the case of commercial surrogacy, the severing of ties is done not for the child's sake, but for the parents' sakes. In the adoption case there are explanations for the mother's action which may quell the child's doubts about being loved which are unavailable in the case of surrogacy.

13. Kay Longcope, "Surrogacy: Two Professionals on Each Side of Issue Give Their Arguments for Prohibition and Regulation," *Boston Globe*, 23 March 1987, pp. 18–19; and Iver Peterson, "Baby M Case: Surrogate Mothers Vent Feelings," *New York Times*, 2 March 1987, pp. B1, B4.

14. Herbert Krimmel, "The Case against Surrogate Parenting," *Hastings Center Report*, October 1983, pp. 35–37.

15. Judge Sorkow made this argument in ruling on the famous case of Baby M. See *In Re Baby M*, 217 N.J. Super 313. Reprinted in *Family Law Reporter* 13 (1987): 2001–30. Chief Justice Wilentz of the New Jersey Supreme Court overruled Sorkow's judgment. See *In the Matter of Baby M*, 109 N.J. 396, 537 A.2d 1227 (1988).

16. Sallyann Payton has observed that the law does not permit the sale of parental rights, only their relinquishment or forced termination by the state, and these acts are subject to

Is Women's Labor
a Commodity?

Defenders of commercial surrogacy have also claimed that it does not differ substantially from other already accepted parental practices. In the institutions of adoption and artificial insemination by donor (AID), it is claimed, we already grant parents the right to dispose of their children.[17] But these practices differ in significant respects from commercial surrogacy. The purpose of adoption is to provide a means for placing children in families when their parents cannot or will not discharge their parental responsibilities. It is not a sphere for the existence of a supposed parental right to dispose of one's children for profit. Even AID does not sanction the sale of fully formed human beings. The semen donor sells only a product of his body, not his child, and does not initiate the act of conception.

Two developments might seem to undermine the claim that commercial surrogacy constitutes a degrading commerce in children. The first is technological: the prospect of transplanting a human embryo into the womb of a genetically unrelated woman. If commercial surrogacy used women only as gestational mothers and not as genetic mothers, and if it was thought that only genetic and not gestational parents could properly claim that a child was "theirs," then the child born of a surrogate mother would not be hers to sell in the first place. The second is a legal development: the establishment of the proposed "consent-intent" definition of parenthood.[18] This would declare the legal parents of a child to be whoever consented to a procedure which leads to its birth, with the intent of assuming parental responsibilities for it. This rule would define away the problem of commerce in children by depriving the surrogate mother of any legal claim to her child at all, even if it was hers both genetically and gestationally.[19]

---

court review for the sake of the child's best interests. But this legal technicality does not change the moral implications of the analogy with baby-selling. The mother is still paid to do what she can to relinquish her parental rights and to transfer custody of the child to the father. Whether or not the courts occasionally prevent this from happening, the actions of the parties express a commercial orientation to children which is degrading and harmful to them. The New Jersey Supreme Court ruled that surrogacy contracts are void precisely because they assign custody without regard to the child's best interests. See *In the Matter of Baby M*, p. 1246.

17. Robertson, "Surrogate Mothers: Not So Novel after All," p. 32; Harris, *The Value of Life*, pp. 144–45.

18. See Philip Parker, "Surrogate Motherhood: The Interaction of Litigation, Legislation and Psychiatry," *International Journal of Law and Psychiatry* 5 (1982): 341–54.

19. The consent-intent rule would not, however, change the fact that commercial surrogacy replaces parental norms with market norms. For the rule itself embodies the market

There are good reasons, however, not to undermine the place of genetic and gestational ties in these ways. Consider first the place of genetic ties. By upholding a system of involuntary (genetic) ties of obligation among people, even when the adults among them prefer to divide their rights and obligations in other ways, we help to secure children's interests in having an assured place in the world, which is more firm than the wills of their parents. Unlike the consent-intent rule, the principle of respecting genetic ties does not make the obligation to care for those whom one has created (intentionally or not) contingent upon an arbitrary desire to do so. It thus provides children with a set of preexisting social sanctions which give them a more secure place in the world. The genetic principle also places children in a far wider network of associations and obligations than the consent-intent rule sanctions. It supports the roles of grandparents and other relatives in the nurturing of children, and provides children with a possible focus of stability and an additional source of claims to care if their parents cannot sustain a well-functioning household.

In the next section I will defend the claims of gestational ties to children. To deny these claims, as commercial surrogacy does, is to deny the significance of reproductive labor to the mother who undergoes it and thereby to dehumanize and degrade the mother herself. Commercial surrogacy would be a corrupt practice even if it did not involve commerce in children.

WOMEN'S LABOR AS A COMMODITY

Commercial surrogacy attempts to transform what is specifically women's labor—the work of bringing forth children into the world—into a commodity. It does so by replacing the parental norms which usually govern the practice of gestating children with the economic norms which govern ordinary production processes. The application of commercial norms to women's labor reduces the surrogate mothers from persons worthy of respect and consideration to objects of mere use.

Respect and consideration are two distinct modes of valuation whose

---

norm which acknowledges only voluntary, contractual relations among people as having moral force. Whereas familial love invites children into a network of unwilled relationships broader than those they have with their parents, the willed contract creates an exclusive relationship between the parents and the child only.

81   *Is Women's Labor*
                                a Commodity?

norms are violated by the practices of the surrogate industry. To respect
a person is to treat her in accordance with principles she rationally accepts—principles consistent with the protection of her autonomy and her
rational interests. To treat a person with consideration is to respond with
sensitivity to her and to her emotional relations with others, refraining
from manipulating or denigrating these for one's own purposes. Given
the understanding of respect as a dispassionate, impersonal regard for
people's interests, a different ethical concept—consideration—is needed
to capture the engaged and sensitive regard we should have for people's
emotional relationships. The failure of consideration on the part of the
other parties to the surrogacy contract explains the judgment that the
contract is not simply disrespectful of the surrogate mother, but callous
as well.[20]

The application of economic norms to the sphere of women's labor violates women's claims to respect and consideration in three ways. First,
by requiring the surrogate mother to repress whatever parental love she
feels for the child, these norms convert women's labor into a form of
alienated labor. Second, by manipulating and denying legitimacy to the
surrogate mother's evolving perspective on her own pregnancy, the
norms of the market degrade her. Third, by taking advantage of the surrogate mother's noncommercial motivations without offering anything
but what the norms of commerce demand in return, these norms leave
her open to exploitation. The fact that these problems arise in the attempt to commercialize the labor of bearing children shows that wom-
en's labor is not properly regarded as a commodity.

The key to understanding these problems is the normal role of the
emotions in noncommercialized pregnancies. Pregnancy is not simply a
biological process but also a social practice. Many social expectations and
considerations surround women's gestational labor, marking it off as an
occasion for the parents to prepare themselves to welcome a new life into
their family. For example, obstetricians use ultrasound not simply for
diagnostic purposes but also to encourage maternal bonding with the fetus.[21] We can all recognize that it is good, although by no means inevitable, for loving bonds to be established between the mother and her
child during this period.

---

20. I thank Steven Darwall and David Anderson for clarifying my thoughts on this point.
21. I am indebted to Dr. Ezekiel Emanuel for this point.

In contrast with these practices, the surrogate industry follows the putting-out system of manufacturing. It provides some of the raw materials of production (the father's sperm) to the surrogate mother, who then engages in production of the child. Although her labor is subject to periodic supervision by her doctors and by the surrogate agency, the agency does not have physical control over the product of her labor as firms using the factory system do. Hence, as in all putting-out systems, the surrogate industry faces the problem of extracting the final product from the mother. This problem is exacerbated by the fact that the social norms surrounding pregnancy are designed to encourage parental love for the child. The surrogate industry addresses this problem by requiring the mother to engage in a form of emotional labor.[22] In the surrogate contract, she agrees not to form or to attempt to form a parent-child relationship with her offspring.[23] Her labor is alienated, because she must divert it from the end which the social practices of pregnancy rightly promote—an emotional bond with her child. The surrogate contract thus replaces a norm of parenthood, that during pregnancy one create a loving attachment to one's child, with a norm of commercial production, that the producer shall not form any special emotional ties to her product.

The demand to deliberately alienate oneself from one's love for one's own child is a demand which can reasonably and decently be made of no one. Unless we were to remake pregnancy into a form of drudgery which is only performed for a wage, there is every reason to expect that many women who do sign a surrogate contract will, despite this fact, form a loving attachment to the child they bear. For this is what the social practices surrounding pregnancy encourage. Treating women's labor as just another kind of commercial production process violates the precious emotional ties which the mother may rightly and properly establish with her "product," the child, and thereby violates her claims to consideration.[24]

22. One engages in emotional labor when one is paid to express or repress certain emotions. On the concept of emotional labor and its consequences for workers, see Arlie Hochschild, *The Managed Heart* (Berkeley and Los Angeles: University of California Press, 1983).

23. Noel Keane and Dennis Breo, *The Surrogate Mother* (New York: Everest House, 1981), p. 291; Brophy, "A Surrogate Mother Contract," p. 267. The surrogate's husband is also required to agree to this clause of the contract.

24. One might ask why this argument does not extend to all cases in which one might

83   *Is Women's Labor*
                                        a Commodity?

Commercial surrogacy is also a degrading practice. The surrogate mother, like all persons, has an independent evaluative perspective on her activities and relationships. The realization of her dignity demands that the other parties to the contract acknowledge rather than evade the claims which her independent perspective makes upon them. But the surrogate industry has an interest in suppressing, manipulating, and trivializing her perspective, for there is an ever-present danger that she will see her involvement in her pregnancy from the perspective of a parent rather than from the perspective of a contract laborer.

How does this suppression and trivialization take place? The commercial promoters of surrogacy commonly describe the surrogate mothers as inanimate objects: mere "hatcheries," "plumbing," or "rented property"—things without emotions which could make claims on others.[25] They also refuse to acknowledge any responsibility for the consequences of the mother's emotional labor. Should she suffer psychologically from being forced to give up her child, the father is not liable to pay for therapy after her pregnancy, although he is liable for all other medical expenses following her pregnancy.[26]

The treatment and interpretation of surrogate mothers' grief raises the deepest problems of degradation. Most surrogate mothers experience grief upon giving up their children—in 10 percent of cases, seriously enough to require therapy.[27] Their grief is not compensated by the $10,000 fee they receive. Grief is not an intelligible response to a successful deal, but rather reflects the subject's judgment that she has suffered a grave and personal loss. Since not all cases of grief resolve themselves into cases of regret, it may be that some surrogate mothers do not

---

form an emotional attachment to an object one has contracted to sell. If I sign a contract with you to sell my car to you, can I back out if I decide I am too emotionally attached to it? My argument is based upon the distinctive characteristics of parental love—a mode of valuation which should not be confused with less profound modes of valuation which generate sentimental attachments to things. The degree to which other modes of valuation generate claims to consideration which tell against market norms remains an open question.

25. Corea, *The Mother Machine*, p. 222.

26. Keane and Breo, *The Surrogate Mother*, p. 292.

27. Kay Longcope, "Standing Up for Mary Beth," *Boston Globe*, 5 March 1987, p. 83; Daniel Goleman, "Motivations of Surrogate Mothers," *New York Times*, 20 January 1987, p. C1; Robertson, "Surrogate Mothers: Not So Novel after All," pp. 30, 34 n. 8. Neither the surrogate mothers themselves nor psychiatrists have been able to predict which women will experience such grief.

regard their grief, in retrospect, as reflecting an authentic judgment on their part. But in the circumstances of emotional manipulation which pervade the surrogate industry, it is difficult to determine which interpretation of her grief more truly reflects the perspective of the surrogate mother. By insinuating a trivializing interpretation of her emotional responses to the prospect of losing her child, the surrogate agency may be able to manipulate her into accepting her fate without too much fuss, and may even succeed in substituting its interpretation of her emotions for her own. Since she has already signed a contract to perform emotional labor—to express or repress emotions which are dictated by the interests of the surrogate industry—this might not be a difficult task.[28] A considerate treatment of the mothers' grief, on the other hand, would take the evaluative basis of their grief seriously.

Some defenders of commercial surrogacy demand that the provision for terminating the surrogate mother's parental rights in her child be legally enforceable, so that peace of mind for the adoptive parents can be secured.[29] But the surrogate industry makes no corresponding provision for securing the peace of mind of the surrogate. She is expected to assume the risk of a transformation of her ethical and emotional perspective on herself and her child with the same impersonal detachment with which a futures trader assumes the risk of a fluctuation in the price of pork bellies. By applying the market norms of enforcing contracts to the surrogate mother's case, commercial surrogacy treats a moral transformation as if it were merely an economic change.[30]

The manipulation of the surrogate mother's emotions which is inherent in the surrogate parenting contract also leaves women open to grave forms of exploitation. A kind of exploitation occurs when one party to a transaction is oriented toward the exchange of "gift" values, while the other party operates in accordance with the norms of the market exchange of commodities. Gift values, which include love, gratitude, and appreciation of others, cannot be bought or obtained through piecemeal calculations of individual advantage. Their exchange requires a repudia-

---

28. See Hochschild, *The Managed Heart*, for an important empirical study of the dynamics of commercialized emotional labor.

29. Keane and Breo, *The Surrogate Mother*, pp. 236–37.

30. For one account of how a surrogate mother who came to regret her decision viewed her own moral transformation, see Elizabeth Kane: *Birth Mother: The Story of America's First Legal Surrogate Mother* (San Diego: Harcourt Brace Jovanovich, 1988). I argue below that the implications of commodifying women's labor are not significantly changed even if the contract is unenforceable.

85   *Is Women's Labor*
                             a Commodity?

tion of a self-interested attitude, a willingness to give gifts to others without demanding some specific equivalent good in return each time one gives. The surrogate mother often operates according to the norms of gift relationships. The surrogate agency, on the other hand, follows market norms. Its job is to get the best deal for its clients and itself, while leaving the surrogate mother to look after her own interests as best as she can. This situation puts the surrogate agencies in a position to manipulate the surrogate mothers' emotions to gain favorable terms for themselves. For example, agencies screen prospective surrogate mothers for submissiveness, and emphasize to them the importance of the motives of generosity and love. When applicants question some of the terms of the contract, the broker sometimes intimidates them by questioning their character and morality: if they were really generous and loving they would not be so solicitous about their own interests.[31]

Some evidence supports the claim that most surrogate mothers are motivated by emotional needs and vulnerabilities which lead them to view their labor as a form of gift and not a purely commercial exchange. Only 1 percent of applicants to surrogate agencies would become surrogate mothers for money alone; the others have emotional as well as financial reasons for applying. One psychiatrist believes that most, if not all, of the 35 percent of applicants who had had a previous abortion or given up a child for adoption wanted to become surrogate mothers in order to resolve their guilty feelings or deal with their unresolved loss by going through a process of losing a child again.[32] Women who feel that giving up another child is an effective way to punish themselves for past abortions, or a form of therapy for their emotional problems, are not likely to resist manipulation by surrogate brokers.

Many surrogate mothers see pregnancy as a way to feel "adequate," "appreciated," or "special." In other words, these women feel inadequate, unappreciated, or unadmired when they are not pregnant.[33] Lacking the power to achieve some worthwhile status in their own right, they must

31. Susan Ince, "Inside the Surrogate Industry," in *Test-Tube Women*, ed. Rita Arditti, Ranate Duelli Klein, and Shelley Minden (Boston: Pandora Press, 1984), p. 110.
32. Philip Parker, "Motivation of Surrogate Mothers: Initial Findings," *American Journal of Psychiatry* 140 (1983): 117–18.
33. The surrogate broker Noel Keane is remarkably open about reporting the desperate emotional insecurities which shape the lives of so many surrogate mothers, while displaying little sensitivity to the implications of his taking advantage of these motivations to make his business a financial success. See especially Keane and Breo, *The Surrogate Mother*, pp. 247ff.

subordinate themselves to others' definitions of their proper place (as baby factories) in order to get from them the appreciation they need to attain a sense of self-worth. But the sense of self-worth one can attain under such circumstances is precarious and ultimately self-defeating. For example, those who seek gratitude on the part of the adoptive parents and some opportunity to share the joys of seeing their children grow discover all too often that the adoptive parents want nothing to do with them.[34] For while the surrogate mother sees in the arrangement some basis for establishing the personal ties she needs to sustain her emotionally, the adoptive couple sees it as an impersonal commercial contract, one of whose main advantages to them is that all ties between them and the surrogate are ended once the terms of the contract are fulfilled.[35] To them, her presence is a threat to marital unity and a competing object for the child's affections.

These considerations should lead us to question the model of altruism which is held up to women by the surrogacy industry. It is a strange form of altruism which demands such radical self-effacement, alienation from those whom one benefits, and the subordination of one's body, health, and emotional life to the independently defined interests of others.[36] Why should this model of "altruism" be held up to *women*? True altruism does not involve such subordination, but rather the autonomous and self-confident exercise of skill, talent, and judgment. (Consider the dedicated doctor.) The kind of altruism we see admired in surrogate mothers involves a lack of self-confidence, a feeling that one can be truly worthy only through self-effacement. This model of altruism, far from affirming the freedom and dignity of women, seems all too conveniently designed to keep their sense of self-worth hostage to the interests of a more privileged class.[37]

34. See, for example, the story of the surrogate mother Nancy Barrass in Anne Fleming, "Our Fascination with Baby M," *New York Times Magazine*, 29 March 1987, p. 38.

35. For evidence of these disparate perspectives, see Peterson, "Baby M Case: Surrogate Mothers Vent Feelings," p. B4.

36. The surrogate mother is required to obey all doctor's orders made in the interests of the child's health. (See Brophy, "A Surrogate Mother Contract"; Keane, "The Surrogate Parenting Contract"; and Ince, "Inside the Surrogate Industry.") These orders could include forcing her to give up her job, travel plans, and recreational activities. The doctor could confine her to bed, and order her to submit to surgery and take drugs. One can hardly exercise an autonomous choice over one's health if one could be held in breach of contract and liable for $35,000 damages for making a decision contrary to the wishes of one's doctor.

37. See Corea, *The Mother Machine*, pp. 227–33, and Christine Overall, *Ethics and Hu-*

87   *Is Women's Labor
                                      a Commodity?*

The primary distortions which arise from treating women's labor as a commodity—the surrogate mother's alienation from loved ones, her degradation, and her exploitation—stem from a common source. This is the failure to acknowledge and treat appropriately the surrogate mother's emotional engagement with her labor. Her labor is alienated, because she must suppress her emotional ties with her own child, and may be manipulated into reinterpreting these ties in a trivializing way. She is degraded, because her independent ethical perspective is denied, or demoted to the status of a cash sum. She is exploited, because her emotional needs and vulnerabilities are not treated as characteristics which call for consideration, but as factors which may be manipulated to encourage her to make a grave self-sacrifice to the broker's and adoptive couple's advantage. These considerations provide strong grounds for sustaining the claims of women's labor to its "product," the child. The attempt to redefine parenthood so as to strip women of parental claims to the children they bear does violence to their emotional engagement with the project of bringing children into the world.

COMMERCIAL SURROGACY, FREEDOM, AND THE LAW

In the light of these ethical objections to commercial surrogacy, what position should the law take on the practice? At the very least, surrogate contracts should not be enforceable. Surrogate mothers should not be forced to relinquish their children if they have formed emotional bonds with them. Any other treatment of women's ties to the children they bear is degrading.

But I think these arguments support the stronger conclusion that commercial surrogate contracts should be illegal, and that surrogate agencies who arrange such contracts should be subject to criminal penalties.[38] Commercial surrogacy constitutes a degrading and harmful traffic in children, violates the dignity of women, and subjects both children and women to a serious risk of exploitation. But are these problems

---

man Reproduction (Boston: Allen and Unwin, 1987), pp. 122–28. Both emphasize the social conditions which undermine the claim that women choose to be surrogate mothers under conditions of autonomy.

38. Both of these conclusions follow the Warnock commission's recommendations. See Warnock, *A Question of Life*, pp. 43–44, 46–47. Since the surrogate mother is a victim of commercial surrogacy arrangements, she should not be prosecuted for entering into them. And my arguments are directed only against surrogacy as a commercial enterprise.

inherent in the practice of commercial surrogacy? Defenders of the practice have suggested three reforms intended to eliminate these problems: (1) give the surrogate mother the option of keeping her child after birth; (2) impose stringent regulations on private surrogate agencies; (3) replace private surrogate agencies with a state-run monopoly on surrogate arrangements. Let us consider each of these options in turn.

Some defenders of commercial surrogacy suggest that the problem of respecting the surrogate mother's potential attachment to her child can be solved by granting the surrogate mother the option to reserve her parental rights after birth.[39] But such an option would not significantly change the conditions of the surrogate mother's labor. Indeed, such a provision would pressure the agency to demean the mother's self-regard more than ever. Since it could not rely on the law to enforce the adoptive parents' wishes regardless of the surrogate's feelings, it would have to make sure that she assumed the perspective which it and its clients have of her: as "rented plumbing."

Could such dangers be avoided by careful regulation of the surrogate industry? Some have suggested that exploitation of women could be avoided by such measures as properly screening surrogates, setting low fixed fees (to avoid tempting women in financial duress), and requiring independent counsel for the surrogate mother.[40] But no one knows how to predict who will suffer grave psychological damage from surrogacy, and the main forms of duress encountered in the industry are emotional rather than financial. Furthermore, there is little hope that regulation would check the exploitation of surrogate mothers. The most significant encounters between the mothers and the surrogate agencies take place behind closed doors. It is impossible to regulate the multifarious ways in which brokers can subtly manipulate the emotions of the vulnerable to their own advantage. Advocates of commercial surrogacy claim that their failure rate is extremely low, since only five out of the first five hundred cases were legally contested by surrogate mothers. But we do not know how many surrogate mothers were browbeaten into relinquishing their children, feel violated by their treatment, or would feel violated had their perspectives not been manipulated by the other parties to the contract.

39. Barbara Cohen, "Surrogate Mothers: Whose Baby Is It?" *American Journal of Law and Medicine* 10 (1984): 282; Peter Singer and Deane Wells, *Making Babies* (New York: Scribner, 1985), pp. 106–7, 111.
40. Harris, *The Value of Life*, pp. 143–44, 156.

89   *Is Women's Labor*
                                  a Commodity?

The dangers of exploiting women through commercial surrogacy are too great to ignore, and too deep to effectively regulate.

Could a state-run monopoly on surrogate arrangements eliminate the risk of degrading and exploiting surrogate mothers?[41] A nonprofit state agency would arguably have no incentive to exploit surrogates, and it would screen the adoptive parents for the sake of the best interests of the child. Nevertheless, as long as the surrogate mother is paid money to bear a child and terminate her parental rights, the commercial norms leading to her degradation still apply. For these norms are constitutive of our understanding of what the surrogate contract is for. Once such an arrangement becomes socially legitimized, these norms will govern the understandings of participants in the practice and of society at large, or at least compete powerfully with the rival parental norms. And what judgment do these norms make of a mother who, out of love for her child, decides that she cannot relinquish it? They blame her for commercial irresponsibility and flighty emotions. Her transformation of moral and emotional perspective, which she experiences as real but painful growth, looks like a capricious and selfish exercise of will from the standpoint of the market, which does not distinguish the deep commitments of love from arbitrary matters of taste.[42]

The fundamental problem with commercial surrogacy is that commercial norms are inherently manipulative when they are applied to the sphere of parental love. Manipulation occurs whenever norms are deployed to psychologically coerce others into a position where they cannot defend their own interests or articulate their own perspective without being charged with irresponsibility or immorality for doing so. A surrogate contract is inherently manipulative, since the very form of the contract invokes commercial norms which, whether upheld by the law or by social custom only, imply that the mother should feel guilty and irresponsible for loving her own child.

But hasn't the surrogate mother decided in advance that she is not interested in viewing her relationship to her child in this way? Regardless of her initial state of mind, once she enters the contract, she is not

41. Singer and Wells support this recommendation in *Making Babies*, pp. 110–11. See also the dissenting opinion of the Warnock commission, *A Question of Life*, pp. 87–89.

42. See Fleming, "Our Fascination with Baby M," for a sensitive discussion of Americans' conflicting attitudes toward surrogate mothers who find they cannot give up their children.

free to develop an autonomous perspective on her relationship with her child. She is contractually bound to manipulate her emotions to agree with the interests of the adoptive parents. Few things reach deeper into the self than a parent's evolving relationship with her own child. To lay claim to the course of this relationship in virtue of a cash payment constitutes a severe violation of the mother's personhood and a denial of the mother's autonomy.

Two final objections stand in the way of criminalizing commercial surrogacy. Prohibiting the practice might be thought to infringe two rights: the right of procreation, and the right to freedom of contract. Judge Harvey Sorkow, in upholding the legality and enforceability of commercial surrogate parenting contracts, based much of his argument on an interpretation of the freedom to procreate. He argued that the protection of the right to procreate requires the protection of noncoital means of procreation, including commercial surrogacy. The interests upheld by the creation of the family are the same, regardless of the means used to bring the family into existence.[43]

Sorkow asserts a blanket right to procreate, without carefully examining the specific human interests protected by such a right. The interest protected by the right to procreate is that of being able to create and sustain a family life with some integrity. But the enforcement of surrogate contracts against the will of the mother destroys one family just as surely as it creates another. And the same interest which generates the right to procreate also generates an obligation to uphold the integrity of family life which constrains the exercise of this right.[44] To recognize the legality of commercial surrogate contracts would undermine the integrity of families by giving public sanction to a practice which expresses contempt for the moral and emotional ties which bind a mother to her children, legitimates the view that these ties are merely the product of arbitrary will, properly loosened by the offering of a monetary incentive, and fails to respect the claims of genetic and gestational ties to children which provide children with a more secure place in the world than commerce can supply.

43. *In Re Baby M*, p. 2022. See also Robertson, "Surrogate Mothers: Not So Novel after All," p. 32.

44. The Catholic Church makes this principle the fundamental basis for its own criticism of surrogate motherhood. See Congregation for the Doctrine of the Faith, "Instruction on Respect for Human Life In Its Origin and on the Dignity of Procreation: Replies to Certain Questions of the Day," reproduced in *New York Times*, 11 March 1987, pp. A14–A17.

91   *Is Women's Labor*
                                a Commodity?

The freedom of contract provides weaker grounds for supporting commercial surrogacy. This freedom is already constrained, notably in preventing the purchase and sale of human beings. Yet one might object that prohibiting surrogate contracts could undermine the status of women by implying that they do not have the competence to enter into and rationally discharge the obligations of commercial contracts. Insofar as the justification for prohibiting commercial surrogacy depends upon giving special regard to women's emotional ties to their children, it might be thought to suggest that women as a group are too emotional to subject themselves to the dispassionate discipline of the market. Then prohibiting surrogate contracts would be seen as an offensive, paternalistic interference with the autonomy of the surrogate mothers.

We have seen, however, that the content of the surrogate contract itself compromises the autonomy of surrogate mothers. It uses the norms of commerce in a manipulative way and commands the surrogate mothers to conform their emotions to the interests of the other parties to the contract. The surrogate industry fails to acknowledge the surrogate mothers as possessing an independent perspective worthy of consideration. And it takes advantage of motivations—such as self-effacing "altruism"—which women have formed under social conditions inconsistent with genuine autonomy. Hence the surrogate industry itself, far from expanding the realm of autonomy for women, actually undermines the external and internal conditions required for fully autonomous choice by women.

If commercial surrogate contracts were prohibited, this would be no cause for infertile couples to lose hope for raising a family. The option of adoption is still available, and every attempt should be made to open up opportunities for adoption to couples who do not meet standard requirements—for example, because of age. While there is a shortage of healthy white infants available for adoption, there is no shortage of children of other races, mixed-race children, and older and handicapped children who desperately need to be adopted. Leaders of the surrogate industry have proclaimed that commercial surrogacy may replace adoption as the method of choice for infertile couples who wish to raise families. But we should be wary of the racist and eugenic motivations which make some people rally to the surrogate industry at the expense of children who already exist and need homes.

The case of commercial surrogacy raises deep questions about the proper scope of the market in modern industrial societies. I have argued that there are principled grounds for rejecting the substitution of market norms for parental norms to govern the ways women bring children into the world. Such substitutions express ways of valuing mothers and children which reflect an inferior conception of human flourishing. When market norms are applied to the ways we allocate and understand parental rights and responsibilities, children are reduced from subjects of love to objects of use. When market norms are applied to the ways we treat and understand women's reproductive labor, women are reduced from subjects of respect and consideration to objects of use. If we are to retain the capacity to value children and women in ways consistent with a rich conception of human flourishing, we must resist the encroachment of the market upon the sphere of reproductive labor. Women's labor is *not* a commodity.

[10]

Judith Mosoff*

MOTHERHOOD,

MADNESS, AND LAW†

I *Introduction*

The ideas in this article originate from my practice as a lawyer representing clients at a large mental health facility. Shirley's situation stands out in my memory. A hospital social worker contacted me after a family court judge expressed concern at an initial apprehension hearing that no one appeared before him on behalf of the mother, that she was currently an involuntary patient in a psychiatric hospital, and that she had been given no notice of the proceeding. The superintendent of family and child services had apprehended the baby girl from the hospital because of the mother's prolonged, although non-violent and relatively uneventful, mental health history, as well as the numerous bizarre remarks that the woman had made in labour. When I first interviewed my client, this was her first psychiatric hospitalization. It was clear that she was heavily medicated and very sad. About seven weeks after her admission to hospital she was discharged. Over the next eight months Shirley was allowed supervised access visits to her baby, which were observed by those who would eventually be called to give evidence about her capacity as a mother. Her visits with the baby took place through the haze of medication which blurred her vision, made her mouth dry, and rendered her movements stiff. She was told to be spontaneous and demonstrative with the child. Talks with social workers, public health nurses, and psychiatrists strongly suggested to Shirley that her mental health prevented her from being a good mother. Eventually she agreed that she needed to remove herself from her child in the best interests of the child. The case ended with a consent order giving permanent custody to the superintendent so that the child could be adopted. Shirley told me that her own life was over. Less than two weeks after her decision she was again involuntarily committed to a psychiatric ward.

* Faculty of Law, University of British Columbia.
† An earlier version of this article was first presented at a meeting of the Canadian Law and Society Association, Ottawa, June 1993. The work is supported in part by a grant from the Social Sciences and Humanities Research Council of Canada. Among those friends and colleagues who gave helpful suggestions are Shoshannah Benmosche, Susan Boyd, Christine Boyle, Dorothy Chunn, Roberta Hamilton, Nitya Iyer, Fiona Kay, Marlee Kline, Bruce MacDougall, Don MacDougall, Jim Russell, and Claire Young. I am grateful for the invaluable research assistance of Carol Pakkala and Chantal Morton. Special thanks to Isabel Grant and Peter Carver.

As this story shows, mental health law and child protection law intersect in a manner that dramatically affects women with psychiatric disabilities,[1] particularly in situations where a mother is involuntarily committed to a mental health facility and her children are apprehended by the state. In combination, the apprehension proceedings and mental health history put both the woman's mental health and her relationship with her child in extreme jeopardy. Under the auspices of law and bureaucracies designed to protect certain vulnerable people, the state asserts its power in remarkably similar and interconnected ways in the mental health setting and in the child protection setting.

This article is concerned with the processes that lead to the state's removing children from mothers who are labelled mentally ill. While law is only one aspect of the process and is integrated with other state and civil processes, my focus here is on the relevant statutes and court decisions in these circumstances. My thesis is that the simultaneous operation of child protection law, mental health law, and the power of the psychiatric paradigm almost inevitably severs the relationship between mothers with mental health histories and their children.

The child welfare process is carried out through direct force of police or other entities and is legitimated through ideology.[2] I take ideology to mean the accepted, unquestioned ideas and values that guide the way people in a culture think and act. Ideology makes up the 'common sense' of a culture and pervades the conception of what are obvious 'natural' and true explanations. In the area of child welfare, ideas about who is an unfit mother are more powerful with the addition of the ideology of science. Specifically, modern science asserts

---

1 Throughout this article I use phrases such as 'women with a psychiatric disability,' 'women who have been psychiatrically labelled,' and 'women with mental health histories' interchangeably. I am referring to a large number of women who have been identified by the mental health system as having some form of mental illness, whether or not they have been hospitalized for the condition. I am specifically *not* referring to self-definitions of mental illness, although there is clearly overlap.

2 I use the term 'ideology' in the socialist feminist tradition as arising out of the material conditions and power relations of the social order. See S.A.M. Gavigan 'Paradise Lost, Paradise Revisited: The Implications of Familial Ideology for Feminist, Lesbian and Gay Engagement to Law' (1994) 31 *Osgoode Hall L J*; 'Law, Gender and Ideology' in A. Bayefsky (ed.) *Legal Theory Meets Legal Practice* (Edmonton: Academic Publishing 1988) 283–95. For a review of the variable ways that ideology has been defined, see T. Eagleton *Ideology: An Introduction* (London: Verso 1991); M. Barrett *The Politics of Truth: From Marx to Foucault* (Stanford: Stanford University Press 1991).

MOTHERHOOD, MADNESS, AND LAW 109

through psychology and psychiatry that the physical health, psychological well-being, and moral development of children is a direct result of child bearing and child rearing. These activities are viewed primarily as a mother's responsibility.[3]

In order to maintain its legitimacy, the liberal state must be seen as even-handed, neutral, and non-coercive. Although the state operates in complicated ways through various institutions at different sites of social life, the fundamental question is how the state can regulate and control people, discipline deviance, and at the same time maintain a benign or at least neutral face. One way of protecting vulnerable people from dangerous people is for the state to rely on the sciences of psychiatry and psychology as apparently objective expert discourses[4] to assess risk.[5] Because mothers with mental health histories are often portrayed as dangerous or potentially dangerous to their vulnerable children, the state looks to our society's collective understanding of psychology and psychiatry as capable of assessing, quantifying, and predicting risk.

Women most vulnerable to a process that undermines their fitness as mothers are those who are already marginalized.[6] In these circumstances women can expect the smallest and most intimate details of their lives to be considered legitimate subject matter of the public domain.[7] While this intrusion into the otherwise private is true of

3 For views of how medical experts contribute to the idea that mothers are responsible for their children's health, safety, and well-being, see B. Ehrenreich and D. English *For Her Own Good: 150 Years of the Experts' Advice to Women* (London: Pluto Press 1979); P.S. Penfold and G.A. Walker *Women and the Psychiatric Paradox* (Montreal: Eden Press 1983) 124–40.

4 See M. Foucault 'The Order of Discourse' I. MacLeod (trans.) in R. Young (ed.) *Untying the Text* (London: Routledge 1981) 69.

5 For a discussion of the increased use of risk assessment in the criminal context, see R.J. Menzies, D. Chunn, and C. Webster 'Risky Business: The Classification of Dangerous People in the Canadian Carceral Enterprise' in L.A. Visano and K.R.E. McCormick (eds) *Canadian Penology* (Toronto: Canadian Scholars Press 1992).

6 Others have written about how mothers with a 'difference' fare poorly in custody matters. See for example [on employment] S. Boyd 'Child Custody, Ideologies and Employment' (1989) 3 *Can. J. of Women & Law* 111; [on First Nations mothers] M. Kline 'Complicating the Ideology of Motherhood: Child Welfare Law and First Nation Women' (1993) 18 *Queen's LJ* 306; M. Kline 'Child Welfare Law, "Best Interests of the Child" Ideology and First Nations' 20 *Osgoode Hall LJ* 272; [on single motherhood] M. Fineman 'Images of Mothers in Poverty Discourses' (1990) 2 *Duke LJ* 274; [on lesbian mothers] K. Arnup '"Mothers Just Like Others": Lesbians, Divorce and Child Custody in Canada' (1989) 3 *Can. J. of Women & Law* 18.

7 I rely here on important feminist work on the role of the state regarding family, child care, and the public/private divide. See J. Ursel 'The State and the Main-

marginalized women in general, the special nuance for women with mental histories is the breadth of an official authorization to question whether her thoughts, perceptions, and feelings are 'normal.' Because of a medical/scientific assertion about a person that creates and names her difference, such women have little claim to any vestige of privacy. Once articulated, the label raises immediate concerns that her children are in jeopardy, not because of what she has done but what she might do in the future, based on who she is as defined by an expert.

Psychological and psychiatric theory influence a variety of social institutions and, in some cases, dominate them. The child protection system is an example, and, increasingly, psychiatry and psychology tend to govern most child protection proceedings. As a general rule, women involved in child protection proceedings are viewed as having serious inadequacies of a psychological or mental nature because of the implicit assumptions that they have failed as mothers. However, when there has been an independent psychiatric diagnosis of mental disturbance or inadequacy apart from the mothering question, there is even greater legitimation of the psychiatric paradigm and consequent reliance on the expertise of psychiatric professionals in the child protection proceedings. In such cases the judicial role is abdicated in favour of the psychological or psychiatric expert,[8] with the judge retaining only the power to monitor the most flagrant abuses of process.

For the sake of simplicity, I will use the terms psychiatrist/psychologist and psychiatry/psychology interchangeably to refer to the range of mental health personnel, particular theoretical models, and clinical practices which are associated with the analysis and treatment of the individual human psyche or individual behaviour.[9] For the purpose of this article, what unites the people who are associated with psychiatry, psychology, and related disciplines is that they are all seen in law to

tenance of Patriarchy: A Case Study of Family, Labour and Welfare Legislation in Canada' in J. Dickinson and B. Russell (eds) *Family, Economy and State: The Social Reproduction Process Under Capitalism* (Toronto: Garamond 1986) 150–91; J. Ursel *Private Lives, Public Policy: 100 Years of State Intervention in the Family* (Toronto: Women's Press 1992); N. Rose 'Beyond the Public/Private Division: Law, Power and the Family' (1987) 14 *J. of Law & Society* 61; F. Olsen 'The Family and the Market: A Study of Ideology and Market Reform' (1983) 96 *Harv. LR* 1487.

8 Compare the similar abdication of the judicial role in favour of the opinion of probation officers. M. Eaton *Justice for Women? Family Courts and Social Control* (Milton Keynes, UK: Open University Press 1986).

9 These would include psychoanalysis, psychology, psychiatry, certain forms of social work, and counselling.

MOTHERHOOD, MADNESS, AND LAW 111

have important expertise which assists in explaining how the human mind works, how a particular mind works, and how personality is formed.[10] In exercising the accompanying power these professionals all perform functions of surveillance and control as designated state agents in modern society.

My criticisms of how the child protection process works to disadvantage women with mental health histories is not meant to suggest that protecting children is not crucially important, nor do I mean that any mother, regardless of her actions, is entitled to remain a custodial parent with no intervention by the state or other entities. In my view, keeping children safe is the most justifiable reason for state intervention in our society. My quarrel here is with the twofold presumption that a mother is necessarily unfit because of a mental health diagnosis, and that psychiatrists and psychologists are the appropriate arbiters of questions about good mothering.[11] As psychological ideas become widely disseminated in our culture, 'pop' psychology is increasingly seen as the best explanation for much human behaviour. An accompanying set of values that favours those defined as mentally able results in discrimination and oppression of mothers who have been labelled mentally ill both before and during the legal proceeding. 'Sanism' does not stop at the courtroom door.[12]

The conclusions that arise from this study do not suggest an alternate model of child welfare nor advise that mothers with mental health histories be treated differently from other parents in child protection matters. More modestly, I recommend simply that judges act as they do

---

10 I recognize, however, that there are important distinctions among different mental health approaches. There is a particularly important difference between psychiatry and the others because of psychiatry's medical foundation and the important duties delegated to physicians or psychiatrists in mental health legislation. Besides the powerful position of doctors in mental health statutes, disability rights activists have criticized the influential medical model as an inappropriate way to understand disability issues because the most important aspects of disability are the socio-economic consequences and the attendant discrimination and oppression. See the medical, economic, and social/political models outlined in Jerome Bickenbach *Physical Disability and Social Policy* (Toronto: University of Toronto Press 1993) especially 61–179. See also Michael Oliver *The Politics of Disablement* (London: Macmillan 1990).

11 While this article is critical of the role of psychiatry in child protection matters, it takes no position on the value of therapy or counselling in any particular instance.

12 For some comments of the pervasiveness of 'sanism' in our culture, including jurisprudence and lawyering practices, see Michael L. Perlin 'On Sanism' (1992) 46 *So. Methodist ULR* 373.

on other matters and scrutinize the evidence of experts in child welfare cases with the same rigour as they would in other proceedings.

The study that forms the basis of this article is an analysis of each of the child protection statutes and mental health statutes in Canada and 61 judicial decisions made since 1980 on child protection matters where the mental health of the mother was an issue. The article is divided into four parts. In part II, I discuss the general similarities between child protection and mental health law and the particular effects of child protection law on women with mental health histories. In part III, I analyse judicial decision-making in child protection cases where the mental health of the mother is in issue. I argue that judges defer to mental health professionals on matters of substance and interfere with the actions of the professionals only when they have committed extremely serious breaches of required procedures. In particular, I argue that the occasional court 'victories' for women in these circumstances are often judicial pronouncements which authorize continuing vigilance of psychiatrists and psychologists by conditions attached to the order that returns the child to the woman. In the final part, I summarize my work and pose suggestions for future research.

II *Legislative provisions*

The notion of risk underpins both mental health and child protection legislation. Despite the numerous non-legal processes and actors that precede their application and enable the laws to be applied, these statutes operate as the ultimate tools to avert risk. Mental health statutes are premised on the idea that mentally disordered persons present a risk to society or to themselves. Child welfare statutes alert us to parents as present or future risks to their children's safety or well-being.

My general objectives in comparing child welfare and mental health legislation are threefold. First, I argue that since children and mentally disordered persons are seen to have limited legal capacity, similarities in the two systems are important indications of how the law reflects and contributes to the construction of disability. Second, I discuss how those mothers located in both systems may be particularly disadvantaged in trying to keep their children. Finally, I argue that mental health professionals are central in the operation of both statutes. Their role is expressed explicitly in mental health legislation and governs child protection proceedings by the ideology underlying the statutory framework. In each system the input of these professionals provides the substance for what protections are seen as needed and why.

MOTHERHOOD, MADNESS, AND LAW 113

1. GENERAL SIMILARITIES IN THE LEGISLATION

Establishing 'a separate body of law and specialized agencies to deal with abuse and neglect both justifies and ensures differential treatment of children.'[13] The existence of mental health law and mental health services ensures the same differential treatment for people with mental health diagnoses. Arguably, then, the common features in the legislation may reflect a more general orientation in law to disability and capacity. It follows that the philosophical and procedural connections between child protection and mental health legislation have a direct impact on mothers with mental health histories. If these women are perceived by law to be like children, they are not likely to be perceived by law as capable of taking care of children.

Although child welfare legislation is a matter within provincial jurisdiction, the schemes of the proceedings vary little from province to province. The stages in the procedures include: apprehension, an interim custody order, a determination by the court of whether the child is at risk, a disposition, and a means of reviewing court-ordered intervention. However, it is difficult to characterize clearly the nature of child protection proceedings.[14] The process has some elements common to a criminal adversarial model, some to a summary civil proceeding, and some to a quasi-administrative hearing. Although the state is clearly represented in court in such forms as a superintendent of a Child Welfare or a Children's Aid Society, the criminal law model has been rejected as inappropriate because the explicit purpose of the hearing is to protect a child, rather than to prosecute a parent. While the parent is recognized as an interested legal actor in the process, the subject is supposed to be the child; and the most important consequences of the court's decisions are the effects on the child and society generally, rather than on the parents. Rejecting a criminal law model means that there is no criminal standard of proof,[15] nor is there any

13 A. McGillvray 'Reconstructing Child Abuse: Western Definition and Non-Western Experience' in M.D.A. Freeman and P. Veerman (eds) *The Ideologies of Children's Rights* (Dordrecht: Martinus Nijhoff 1992).

14 See, for example, Lamperson J who declined to hear constitutional arguments not raised at trial and declined to overturn the trial judge's decisions, stating in *N.P. v. British Columbia (Superintendent of Family and Child Service)* [1992] BCJ No. 1828 (BCCA) that 'a child apprehension hearing is not a trial, but an inquiry to determine what is in the child's best interest.' The mother in this case was diagnosed as paranoid schizophrenic.

15 The American standard of proof in the termination of parental rights hearings is higher than the civil balance of probabilities, because a 'clear and convincing evidence' standard is a Fourteenth Amendment requirement. See *Santosky et al.* v.

equivalent to the presumption of innocence for the parent. The legal protections of the Canadian Charter of Rights and Freedoms may or may not be available to a parent in child protection proceedings.[16]

Probably the best formal description of a child protection matter is as a summary civil proceeding.[17] The summary nature of these proceedings means that there is no requirement for pre-trial disclosure, unless specifically required by the particular child welfare statute. Although reports are often exchanged by counsel, there is usually no requirement to do so. The other forms of disclosure normally available in civil proceedings, such as discovery of documents or discovery of witnesses and interrogatories, are usually absent in child protection proceedings. In combination, rejecting a criminal model and limiting pre-trial discovery means few of the usual procedural safeguards in law are available to the parent in a child protection proceeding.

The underlying legislative model of child protection statutes has been described as falling either into the 'rights' category where parents

Kramer, Commissioner, Ulster County Department of Social Services et al. (1982) 455 US 745, 102 S. Ct 1388, 71 L.Ed.2d 599, 50 USLW 4333. In *Re Chrysler* (1978), 5 RFL(2d) 50 (Ont. Prov. Ct, Fam. Div.) at 58, the court described the onus, while civil, as 'very demanding' where the contest of custody is between a mother and a Children's Aid Society.

16 The right to parent may be derived from the Supreme Court of Canada's decision in *Re Eve* (1986), 13 CPC (2d) 6, 31 DLR (4th) 1, 71 NR 1, 61 Nfld & PEIR 273, 185 APR 273 (sub nom. *E. v. Eve*) [1986] 2 SCR 388 (sub nom. *Eve v. E.*) 6 CHRR d/3733, reversing (1980), 27 Nfld & PEIR 97, 74 APR 97, 115 DLR (3d) 1283 (PEICA) additional reasons at (1981) 28 Nfld & PEIR 359, 79 APR 359, 115 DLR (3d) 383 at 320 (PEICA) in recognizing the importance of 'maintaining the physical integrity of the human being' in relation to the 'privilege of giving life.' See also *Antanopolous* v. *Gillespie* (28 January 1992) CA013573 (BCCA) allowing damages for the loss of ability to bear children. Probably the most important Charter argument for the benefit of parents in child protection proceedings that goes to substance involves the right of a child to remain with a family as a section 7 liberty interest. Other areas of Charter scrutiny are the standard of proof, legislation permitting apprehension without warrant generally, delays in proceedings, and notice proceedings. For commentary on the Charter and child protection, see: P. Zylberberg 'Minimum Constitutional Guarantees in Child Protection Cases' (1992) 10 *Can. J. of Fam. Law* 257; R.A. Thompson 'Why Hasn't the Charter Mattered in Child Protection?' (1989) 8 *Can. J. of Fam. Law* 133; and S. Toope 'Riding the Fences: Courts, Charter Rights and Family Law' (1991) 9 *Can. J. of Fam. Law* 55.

17 Exactly why certain legal proceedings are designated as summary rather than comprehensive procedures is somewhat mystifying to me. Two possibilities seem reasonable: that these are matters that have some urgency so that they should be adjudicated quickly, or that the interest is of lesser importance than others. Neither of these rationales seems to apply to child protection proceedings, since they are often protracted proceedings from start to finish and there is almost no interest more important than those involved here.

have a more substantial focus, or the 'social welfare' category where the child is supposedly more central.[18] There is a similar ongoing debate about mental health systems in which 'rights' models are distinguished from 'treatment models.'[19] The social welfare model envisions intervention by helping professionals in a troubled family and would avoid a legalistic court process. One extreme legislative niche of the social welfare model is the majority of child welfare statutes in Canada that now permit parents to terminate custody of their children on a permanent basis.[20]

However, the current trend in Canada is towards rights-based models,[21] and despite some differences in emphasis, there is a general similarity of the legislative schemes in both child protection statutes and mental health statutes across Canadian jurisdictions. Albeit through different mechanisms, both the social welfare and rights-based models of legislation reflect, in part, the ultimate reliance in these spheres on the wisdom of psychology and psychiatry. Underlying the social welfare model is the influence of psychology and psychiatry and the sociological knowledge which is reflected in the professional ideology of social work. The rights model contemplates resolution of the issues in court. It may describe the function of experts more directly in the legislation than in the social welfare model and/or will find psychiatrists and psychologists as expert witnesses in court.

Four important similarities can be drawn out of the legislative schemes: the responsibilities of the state, the implications of a 'crisis,' intrusions into privacy, and the notion of best interests.

18 See, for example, D.A. Rollie Thompson 'Taking Children and Facts Seriously: Evidence Law in Child Protection Proceedings – Part 1' (1988) 7 *Can. J. of Fam. Law* 11, 16.

19 For commentary on debates within the mental health law field, see: R.M. Gordon and S.N. Verdun-Jones 'The Trials of Mental Health Law: Recent Trends and Developments in Canadian Mental Health Jurisprudence' (1988) 11 *Dalhousie LJ* 833; and I. Grant 'Mental Health Law and the Courts' (1991) 29 *Osgoode Hall LJ* 747 [hereinafter Mental Health Law].

20 The mother who 'voluntarily' terminates her parental rights may be seen in a completely different and more positive light than a mother who resists the state. See Donald Poirier 'Social Worker Enforcement of Child Welfare Legislation: An Increasing Potential for Abuse of Power' (1986) 5 *Can. J. of Fam. Law* 215.

21 See, for example, the Ontario mental health statute and child welfare statute. The current Family and Child Services Act, RSO 1984, c. 55 is a rights-based model and replaced four pieces of legislation that were constructed around a social welfare model: Child Welfare Act, RSO 1980, c. 66; Children's Institutions Act, RSO 1980, c. 67; Children's Residential Services Act, RSO 1980, c. 71; Children's Mental Services Act, RSO 1980, c. 69.

a) Duty of the state

There is understood to be a positive duty on the state to intervene in the affairs of an apparently mentally disordered person or a child in certain circumstances. Both laws originate from the state's *parens patriae* power. Like adults who are labelled mentally ill, children are seen to need the protection of the state because they are both especially vulnerable to harm and limited in their capacity to avert the harm. Save for the legal legitimacy that arises from the notion of impaired capacity, such interventions in the lives of adults would be at least inappropriate, if not unlawful,[22] but people with mental disabilities are viewed as having 'immutable differences that set them apart from the rest of society and thus warrant different legal treatment.'[23] The legitimate target of state action becomes people who pose danger, because the state has a responsibility to protect people who are endangered.

What constitutes harm, however, is often nebulous. Child protection statutes specify the grounds upon which a child is considered in need of protection,[24] but may or may not outline the criteria to apply in making this determination. Even where the legislation includes criteria, these inevitably leave room for a large measure of interpretation by the apprehending authorities.[25] For example, while a parent's disability may be read into the meaning some of the vague criteria in deciding if a

---

22 If there were no issue of the capacity of the individual, the involuntary committal of an adult could otherwise constitute false imprisonment, and non-consensual treatment of an adult could otherwise constitute battery.

23 M. Minow *Making All the Difference: Inclusion, Exclusion and American Law* (Ithaca, New York: Cornell University Press 1990) 107.

24 Child Welfare Act, SA 1984, c. C-8.1, ss. 1(2), (3)(a)(c); Family and Child Service Act, SBC 1980, c. 11, s. 1; Child and Family Services Act, SM 1985-86, c. 8, CCSM C-80, s. 17; Family Services Act, SNB 1980, c. F-2.2, s. 31(1); Child Welfare Act, RSN 1990, c. C-12, ss 2(b), 12(4), 13(4)-(6), 34(7); Child Welfare Act, RSNWT 1974, c. C-3, ss 14, 14.1, 19(1); Children and Family Services Act, SNS 1990, c. 5, ss 22(2), 32, 40(1)(4)(5); Child and Family Services Act, RSO 1990, c. C.11, s. 37(2); Family and Child Services Act, RSPEI 1988, c. F-2, ss 1(2), 29(1); Child and Family Services Act, SS 1989-90, c. C-7.2, s. 11; Children's Act, RSYT 1986, c. 22, ss 116, 133.

25 Child Welfare Act, SA 1984, c. C-8.1, s. 2 outlines the matters to be considered in making any decision relating to a child in need of protective services; Children's Act, RSYT 1986, c. 22, s. 116(2) outlines considerations to be applied in determining whether a child is in need of protection, but only in situations where the use of physical discipline is at issue. Some child protection statutes list illustrations of a child in need of protection. These statutes do not, however, provide any considerations or standards in applying the list to a given situation. Such lists can be found in other child protection statutes: Family Services Act, SNB 1980, c. F-2.2, s. 31(1); Child and Family Services Act, RSO 1990, c. C.11, s. 37(2).

MOTHERHOOD, MADNESS, AND LAW 117

child is in need of protection, the legislation in British Columbia speaks more directly to the importance of disability. The statute specifies that a child may be found in need of protection on account of being 'deprived of necessary care through the death, absence or disability' of the parent.[26] Linking disability with death or absence of a parent is an astonishing codification of disability as a signal to the state of risk. The risk presented by situations where a parent is *disabled* is analogized to the risk where the parent is temporarily or permanently *non-existent.*[27]

Mental health legislation articulates the duty of the state in tests for involuntary committal. The law in Canadian jurisdictions maintains two general requirements for involuntary committals. First, there must be a finding of mental illness or mental disorder,[28] but the way to apply this test is unclear. For example, many of the statutes have circular definitions of mental disorder, defining it as any disease or disability of the mind, indicating obvious ambiguity between legal and medical conceptions.[29] The second statutory criterion for involuntary committal is usually two-pronged: protection of others or protection of self. Protection of self is especially problematic. The obligation to protect an adult from self-imposed harm or neglect raises important questions about what process ought to be in place to make such a determination.

Equally important is the question of what qualifications are necessary

---

26 See section 1 of the Act. As well, section 14(3)(a) of the BC Act directs that in making a permanent custody order, the court consider 'a parent's emotional condition, mental condition, mental deficiency or use of alcohol or drugs and whether these factors make the parent consistently or repeatedly unable to care adequately for the child.'

27 While new legislation has been introduced to replace the Family and Child Services Act and eliminates the direct reference to disability that carries with it a strong possibility of unconstitutional validity by violating section 15 of the Charter, the new Child, Family and Community Service Act creates a different method of alerting the court to disability. Section 59(1) states: 'On application, the court may order that a child or a parent of a child undergo a medical, psychiatric or other examination.' The Act does not specify by whom the application may be made, for what purpose, or at what stage of the proceeding.

28 For an overview, see H. Savage and C. McKague *Mental Health Law in Canada* (Vancouver: Butterworths 1987).

29 Mental Health Act, SNB 1985, c. 59, s. 1; Mental Health Act, RSN 1990, c. M-9, s. 2(g); Hospitals Act, RSNS 1989, c. 208, s. 2; Mental Health Act, RSO 1990, c. M.7, s. 1; Mental Health Act, RSPEI 1988, Cap. M-6, s. 1(j). Similarly, only Ontario (Mental Health Act, RSO 1990, c. M.7, s. 15) and the Northwest Territories (Mental Health Act, SNWT 1985 (2d), c. 6 as amended by 1989 c. 15, s. 9) have precise indicators for establishing the criterion for dangerousness.

for persons charged with the responsibility of committal. Under each mental health statute in Canada, doctors are made responsible for detaining a person in a mental health facility against the person's will. This process usually requires examining the person and completing the necessary documents, although the statutes often are silent about what constitutes an 'examination'[30] or the extent of detail necessary to complete documents properly.[31] Usually the doctor will be a psychiatrist, although the statute may not require this specialization.[32]

b) Response to crisis

Police powers of the state may be brought to bear when the situation is defined as a crisis. In adopting a quasi-criminal framework in both child protection and mental health law, an emergency permits the authorities, either police or social workers, to take an individual into custody without obtaining a warrant or without legal process of any kind. Inherent in the emergency provisions is wide discretion vested in

---

30 There is no definition for 'examination' in any of the mental health statutes. Some statutes even provide for a 'psychiatric assessment' and/or an 'examination' without differentiating or defining either term. See: The Mental Health Act, RSM c. M110, as amended, s. 10 (the emergency provision where an individual is brought in for an 'examination'), s. 16 (application for an involuntary psychiatric assessment); Mental Health Act, SNWT 1985 (2d), c. 6, as amended by 1989 c. 15, ss 9, 10, 11, 12, 13 allows for a psychiatric assessment, but in order to issue a certificate of involuntary admission, the medical practitioner must personally 'examine' the individual; Mental Health Act, RSO 1990, c. M.7, s. 15 provides for a physician to make application for a psychiatric assessment, while s. 17 requires an 'examination.'

31 The statutes generally require that the certificate of involuntary admission include the name and address of the individual in respect of whom the certificate is issued, as well as the issuing physician and facility; the date and time of the examination and issuing of certificate; and the facts upon which the physician formed his or her opinion that the individual is suffering from a mental disorder. Some, but not all, provisions require that the facts upon which the physician's opinion is based be those observed personally as differentiated from those communicated to the physician.

32 There is no requirement in any of the statutes that the initial examination for involuntary admissions be conducted by a psychiatrist. The Northwest Territories specifically allows for a *psychiatric* assessment to be conducted by a medical practitioner, which is defined separately from a psychiatrist in the statute (Mental Health Act, SNWT 1985 (2d), c. 6, as amended by 1989 c.15, ss 9, 10, 11, 12, 13). There are some statutes that require an examination by a psychiatrist at a later stage in the process. For example: in Nova Scotia, if an individual is admitted for observation, he or she shall be examined by a psychiatrist within three days (Hospitals Act, RSNS 1989, c. 208, s. 42); in Alberta, where a renewal certificate is issued, at least one of the two issuing physicians shall be a psychiatrist (Mental Health Act, SA 1988, c. M-13.1, s. 8).

the authorities to decide whether a child or apparently mentally disordered person should be taken into custody. Usually the emergency provisions in mental health legislation are provided as a last resort, at which point police become involved. Similarly, removing a child may be without incident and done with the complete cooperation of all concerned, but the full force of state police power is available to apprehend if deemed necessary.

The response to the crisis makes for an immediate imbalance in power between the legal actors:[33] that is, between the individual and the state in the mental health process, and between the state and the parent (usually a mother) in the child protection process. Given the unequal position created by an apprehension or committal, one might expect considerable legal process to precede an apprehension or committal in most instances. However, all legal process follows, rather than precedes, these events.

c) Intrusions to privacy
After an initial threshold has been crossed and the state has become involved, there is a wider definition of the legitimate spheres of an individual's life in which the state may rightfully involve itself.[34] Underlying these processes is an assumption that the triggering event, either a committal or an apprehension, opens an individual or a family to more state scrutiny than usual.[35] This is in contrast to the general belief

33 Compare with the description of the accused (referred to as a 'dependant' rather than a 'defendant') as a 'one-shot' or occasional actor in a system compared to the systematic organization of the rest of the actors in the criminal process. See R. Ericson and P. Baranek *The Ordering of Justice: A Study of Accused Persons as Dependants in the Criminal Process* (Toronto: University of Toronto Press 1982). See also M. Galanter 'Why the "Haves" Come Out Ahead: Speculations on the Limits of Legal Change' (1974) 9 *Law & Social Rev.* 95.

34 Although an apprehension or committal represents the official triggering event in these circumstances, a woman with a mental health history has almost certainly had prior contact with state agencies through income assistance programs, community health prenatal programs, or through the public school system. Because of this history, the state will have more information about this woman or her family prior to any emergency and will be particularly alert to any departures from some ill-defined standard of behaviour. Once the triggering event has occurred, there is already a body of evidence from the records of the state agencies that have been in touch with her.

35 The public/private sphere does not operate in the same way for all women regardless of their family situation. See S. Boyd '(Re) Placing the State: Family, Law and Oppression' (1994) *Can. J. of Law & Society* (forthcoming) where she describes the public/private sphere as a heuristic device.

120 UNIVERSITY OF TORONTO LAW JOURNAL

in our culture that there is a degree of autonomy of the family and a
right to privacy such that the state has no right to intervene or even to
pry.[36]

The power imbalance exists with respect to accessing information,
records, and resources. Regardless of any protests, the authorities often
remove personal items from an apparently mentally disordered person
if the items are considered dangerous. Such issues as medical information about a child who has been apprehended, consent to the child's
medical treatment, or inquiries and decisions about school progress all
become legitimate business of the state. The absence of pre-trial disclosure exacerbates the power imbalance between the parent and the
state, especially for the parent with a mental health history. In most
cases, the authorities have a vast array of documents that may be
entered at trial, anything from psychiatric hospital records to interview
notes of the parent with financial aid workers or comments on school
records.

Despite widely held beliefs about confidentiality as well as statutory
bars and common law holdings that such records are private, especially
doctor-patient communications, the courts tend to order production of
psychiatric records in child protection hearings. While not permitting a
fishing expedition, records may be admitted if they reasonably contain
information that may directly or indirectly enable the applicants either
to advance their own case or damage the case of their adversary.[37]
Hospital records may be admitted as business records[38] and, in some
cases, the records issue becomes a question of jurisdiction or abuse of
process.[39] The general reasoning for ordering production of records is
that the child's interests take precedence over the confidentiality
interest.[40] Because there is no formal mechanism to demand docu-

---

36 The right to a family's privacy is class-based. See: J. Donzelot *The Policing of Families*
    (New York: Pantheon 1979). I am not suggesting here that the private/public
    distinction is analytically useful to describe social life realistically, nor that the
    distinction applies in a universal way to women's lives. My point is only that the
    heightened scrutiny of matters seen to be private is excused and applauded in these
    circumstances.

37 *Dufault* v. *Stevens* (1978) 6 BCLR 199 (BCCA).

38 *T.(T.)* v. *Catholic Children's Aid Society of Metropolitan Toronto* (1984), 42 RFL (2d) 47.

39 See, for example, *Re: Clarke Institute of Psychiatry and Catholic Children's Aid Society of
    Metropolitan Toronto* (1981), 31 OR (2d) 486 (HC).

40 But see *R.* v. *O'Connor* (1994), 42 BCAC 105, which discusses the pre-trial disclosure
    order made by Associate Chief Justice Campbell on 4 June 1992, where the interest
    of the criminal accused is the reason for ordering the production of the psychiatric
    records of the complainant. Whether the woman with a mental health history is on

MOTHERHOOD, MADNESS, AND LAW 121

ments, discover witnesses, or pose interrogatories in advance of the hearing, this lack of pre-trial disclosure is one way in which the road is paved for an enormous reliance on psychiatric opinion at trial.

d) The 'best interests' standard
Because an individual is perceived as incapable or powerless to decide matters in his or her own interest, deciding in the 'best interests' of the individual pervades both the legal standards and procedures set out in both statutes. Long before any judicial consideration of 'best interests,' the agents of the state – social workers or mental health professionals – may insert their own definition of a person's best interests.[41] As a legal standard the best interests test assumes that it is necessary for an external authority to make the determination because an individual is unable to make a proper evaluation for himself or herself. Young children are presumed to be too inexperienced, not sufficiently developed cognitively, or otherwise powerless to make decisions in their best interests. A similar belief follows from the idea that psychiatric patients have diminished capacity. Like with children, someone else must make decisions for the benefit of that individual.[42]

At the disposition stage of child protection matters, the court must consider what is in the 'best interests of the child,' a much wider question and even more pliable concept than the standard of whether

the side of the state or not, it seems that confidentiality between her and her therapist is legally fragile. See also *Globe and Mail* Toronto, 15 July 1993, where a Vancouver psychiatrist, Dr Kay Parfitt, has refused to turn over her records about the mental health of a complainant in a sexual assault trial in the face of a Supreme Court order for production. She says: 'The seriousness of psychological damage does not seem to be appreciated by the courts or the public ... Talking with people who have been to court, this issue – that they feel they have been re-assaulted in court – has come up a number of times. People have come to me and said they would never have gone into therapy if they knew this would happen.'
41 Feminist scholarship has been highly critical of the value-laden interpretations of the 'best interests of the child' test as it affects women both in private custody disputes and in contests with the state. See supra note 6.
42 Recent debates about guardianship and substitute decision-making distinguish between various types of substitute decision-making: authorization obtained by a substitute of the person when the person was fully capable, standing in the shoes of the person, or acting in the best interests of the person. These reflect a hierarchy of the degree of agency of the person. Deciding in an adult's 'best interests' reflects the least recognition of autonomy and is a model of greatest dependence, yet some statutes specifically require a consideration of the 'best interests' of the person as the basis for substitute consent, albeit as a last resort. See, for example: Mental Health Act, RSO 1990, c. M.7, s. 2(6) and Mental Health Act, SA 1988, c. M-13.1, s. 28(3).

122 UNIVERSITY OF TORONTO LAW JOURNAL

a child is in need of protection. Many Canadian child protection statutes provide some principles or factors which must be considered in determining the best interests of the child.[43] Even when a statute does not state that the best interests of the child is the principle underlying a disposition, the courts have applied this test to child protection proceedings.[44]

43 See, for example, statutes outlining best interest considerations: Child and Family Services Act, SM 1985-86, c. 8, CCSM C-80, s. 2(1); Family Services Act, SNB 1980, c. F-2.2, s. 1; Child Welfare Act, RSN 1990, c. C-12, s. 4; Children and Family Services Act, SNS 1990, c. 5, s. 3(2); Child and Family Services Act, RSO 1990, c. C.11, s. 37(2); Family and Child Services Act, RSPEI 1988, c. F-2, ss 1, 2; Child and Family Services Act, SS 1989-90, c. C-7.2, s. 4; Children's Act, RSYT 1986, c. 22, ss 1, 30, 131. In two jurisdictions, the legislation alludes to the 'best interests' of the child, albeit not in those terms: the Child Welfare Act, SA 1984, c. C-8.1, s. 2 states that the interests of the child should be recognized and protected; and the Family and Child Service Act, SBC 1980, c. 11, s. 2 refers to the safety and well-being of a child as paramount considerations. The Child Welfare Act, RSNWT 1974, c. C-3 makes no reference to the 'best interests' of the child.

Some statutes require a child of a certain age to consent at the dispositional stage. The child's wishes then constitute some evidence to be weighed in the decision of what is in the child's best interest, a partial legal disability. See: Child Welfare Act, SA 1984, c. C-8.1, s. 2, which provides that the child's opinion should be considered; Family and Child Service Act, SBC 1980, c. 11, s. 11(2); Child and Family Services Act, SM 1985-86, c. 8, CCSM C-80, s. 2(2); Family Services Act, SNB 1980, c. F-2.2, s. 1 (where ascertainable, the child's views are to be considered); Child Welfare Act, RSN 1990, c. C-12, s. 18 (the right of a child to exercise free choice); Child and Family Services Act, RSO 1990, c. C.11, s. 4; Children's Act, RSYT 1986, c. 22, s. 168.

44 See: *Racine* v. *Woods* [1983] 2 SCR 173, where the Supreme Court of Canada emphasized that the best interests of the child is the paramount concern in child welfare and custody matters, particularly where psychological bonding has occurred. This case has been widely criticized because the 'best interests test' failed to consider the First Nations heritage of the child and concentrated on 'bonding.' The important principles, according to the critics, are whether the court will find collective or racial concerns as compelling as or more compelling than individual concerns. An underlying racist ideology has been thought to account for the failure to recognize the important ways in which First Nations culture affects custody decisions about children. *King* v. *Low* [1985] 1 SCR 87, 16 DLR (4th) 576, 3 WWR 1, 44 RFL (2d) 113, sub nom. *K.K.* v. *G.L. et al.*, 58 AR 275, 57 NR 17, sub nom. *King* v. *Mr. and Mrs. R.*, where the Supreme Court of Canada ruled that, even when a statute does not specify, the best interests test is the standard to be applied in questions of contested custody; *Dir. of Child Welfare* v. *L.(K.L.)* (1986), 5 RFL (3d) 53 (Alta QB) at 58, where the court held that the provincial court had erred by failing to find whether returning or failing to return a child to a parent within a reasonable time was in the child's best interests. The statute did not specify that the best interests test applied on this matter of timeliness, and the usual application is to more substantive considerations of best interests; and *Re: M.(S.J.)* (1990), 26 RFL

Mental health legislation incorporates the ideas of 'best interests' more indirectly. While doctors are charged with interpreting a legal question of what constitutes a mental disorder or mental illness in effecting a committal or extending a period of committal, their training and role tends to invoke a best interests interpretation of the definition.

In addition to specifying the threshold test for committal, mental health legislation outlines the requirements that the hospital authorities must fulfil in order to extend the period of committal once it has expired. Often there is less procedural protection and lower standards required for the authority to continue the hospitalization than there is for the initial committal. As well, after a person has been involuntarily committed, mental health statutes set out some process of external review of detention by a tribunal or by the courts. Some reviews have held that whether a person is benefiting from hospitalization is the test of whether the individual should continue to be detained in the hospital rather than whether the person could be involuntarily committed at the time of the review.[45] While a person may not meet the initial criteria for committal under the statute, the individual may not be released in the review process because the person is seen as 'better off' in hospital despite not being a danger to self or others. Usually, people who appear before tribunals have had their requests for release turned down by their doctors because, presumably, the doctors believed they were not ready for release, or were at risk in the community and therefore likely to be readmitted.[46] However, according to at least

(3d) 173 (BCSC) where the court notes that section 47 of the Law and Equity Act provides that in proceedings under the Family and Child Services Act, the court shall consider the best interests of the child.

45 See: *Hoskins* v. *Hislop* (1981) 26 BCLR 165 at 174, where the court held that under the Mental Health Act, RSBC, 1979, c. 256, it was authorized to order the continued detention of a patient 'whose mental state has improved due to treatment to the extent that he no longer requires care, supervision and control for his own protection or welfare or for the protection of others but who is still mentally ill and requires continued medical treatment in a provincial mental health facility if recovery is to be achieved or mental stability maintained.' But see *McCorkell* v. *Riverview Hospital (Director)*, [1993] BCJ No. 1518 (BCSC) stating that the standard for release by the tribunal is the same as the committal standard.

46 Except in circumstances where the person was extremely defiant or incompetent, the METFORS clinicians were reluctant either to 'excuse' or to institutionalize the people they assessed. They relied on outpatient treatment. See R. Menzies *Survival of the Sanest: Order and Disorder in a Pre-Trial Psychiatric Clinic* (Toronto: University of Toronto Press 1989).

one empirical study, the particular 'discharge route,' that is, via physician or via tribunal, is not a good predictor of readmission over the next year.[47] Arguably, then, once a person is caught by the net of the initial statutory criteria for involuntary admission, the process may allow a type of best interest test to be inserted implicitly in subsequent stages of the proceedings.

2. SPECIFIC EFFECTS FOR WOMEN WITH PSYCHIATRIC DISABILITIES

In general, mothers in child protection proceedings are treated poorly by the legal process and viewed as childlike themselves.[48] There are, however, specific aspects of the child protection process where mothers with psychiatric disabilities are especially devastated by the simultaneous application of child protection and mental health statutes. Two particular examples of these effects are pre-birth apprehensions where a mother is labelled with a mental disability, and the minimal notice provisions of post-apprehension hearings when a mother is in a psychiatric facility.

In pre-birth apprehension cases, the authorities decide that a pregnant woman is endangering the life or health of a fetus or that there is too high a risk that the woman will harm or neglect a newborn.[49] In anticipation of harm, the authorities apprehend a fetus *in utero* and may invoke mental health legislation specifically for the purposes of completing an apprehension. Cases such as these reflect a facile and unfair interpretation of mental capacity and assume that

---

47 The relative rate is 43 per cent vs. 45 per cent. See J. Parades et al. 'The Review Panel Process: Interpretation of the Findings and Recommendations' (1987) 32 *Can. J. of Psych.* 444.

48 Most court decisions refer to adult parties or witnesses with some degree of formality, the form of address being Mr, Mrs, Ms, but children are referred to by their first names. Routinely judges refer to women by their first names in child protection proceedings. See reference to Carrie, infra note 51, and to Marsha quote, cited in text referenced infra note 90. In my experience as an advocate, the same informal first-name form of address is used consistently to address patients at mental health tribunals.

49 The use of illegal drugs is often the reason given for pre-birth apprehensions or apprehensions shortly after birth. See *Superintendent of Family and Child Service* v. *M.(B) and O.(D.)* (1982) 28 RFL (2d) 278 (BCSC), where on appeal the court found that the child had been born abused and that the addiction made the child a 'high risk' baby. The court found further that a finding could be made on the basis of anticipated deprivation rather than actual deprivation. See L. Maher 'Punishment and Welfare: Crack Cocaine and the Regulation of Mothering' in C. Feinman (ed.) *The Criminalization of a Woman's Body* (Binghamton: Harrington Park Press 1992).

MOTHERHOOD, MADNESS, AND LAW 125

women with mental disabilities are inherently inadequate mothers.[50] If a person is deemed to be mentally disordered, both her own body and her children become legitimate objects of state protection because perceived incompetence in one area results in presumed incompetence in all.[51] In *Baby R.*[52] the medical authorities were concerned that the woman's refusal to consent to a Caesarian section posed grave dangers to the fetus, and they attempted to commit the mother under the Mental Health Act[53] so that the surgical delivery could occur without her consent.[54] The objective here was not to treat the woman for a medical or a psychiatric disorder, nor to protect her from herself or from others, but to deliver the fetus surgically because this was necessary in the medical view. In *Daigle*[55] the Supreme Court of Canada approved of the reasoning in *Baby R.* Because the court did not recognize separate legal personhood of the fetus, pre-birth apprehensions are unlawful.[56]

50 Sandra Goundry 'Women, Disability and the Law: Identifying Barriers to Equality in the Law of Non-Consensual Sterilization, Child Welfare and Sexual Assault,' The Canadian Disability Rights Council (15 April 1994) (unpublished).

51 Sometimes merely a threat of using mental health legislation is enough to obtain the mother's compliance. For a typical example, see *Children's Aid Society of Niagara Region* v. *W.(C.A.)* [1987] OJ No. 1838, where a mother with a mental health history, suspicious about hospitals, wanted a home birth. His Honour Judge Walmsley says: 'Carrie continued to display serious delusional thinking and to resist a hospital birth, because she thought a home birth would be healthier. Carrie's attitude so concerned the workers to the point that they demanded Carrie go to hospital on October 3rd, 1985, under threat of obtaining an order under Section 10 of the *Mental Health Act.* After much persuasion, Carrie agreed to go into hospital that day.' Her child was apprehended one day after his birth. There is nothing in the decision about why a home birth was particularly inadvisable.

52 *Re: Baby R.* (1988) 30 BCLR (2d) 237, 53 DLR (4th) 69, 15 RFL (3d) 225 (BCSC).

53 RSBC 1979, c. 256, as amended.

54 The psychiatry department refused to go along with this plan, presumably because the staff did not believe that the woman met the criteria for civil commitment. In my opinion the statute does not contemplate non-consensual *non-psychiatric* medical treatment, and such intervention would have been unlawful in any event. A similar situation arose in which medical authorities successfully used provisions of the Ontario Mental Health Act (then RSO 1980, c. 262, s. 10) to obtain an order requiring assessment by a physician of a pregnant woman who was thought to be negligent in attending to her needs when the birth was imminent. See *Re: Children's Aid Society of Belleville, Hastings County and T. et al.* (1987) 59 OR (2d) 204.

55 *Tremblay* v. *Daigle* [1989] 2 SCR 530 at 569–70.

56 For a view that appprehension of a fetus *in utero* may be lawful because a woman's lifestyle was negligent and posed a danger to the fetus, see *C.A.S., Belleville* v. *T.(L.)* (1987) 7 RFL (3d) 191 (Ont. Ct, Gen. Div.).

The minimal notice requirements for the post-apprehension court appearance in child welfare legislation is another way that the process has a specific negative impact on women who are hospitalized in a mental health facility. Within a specified and relatively short time the grounds of the apprehension must be presented and reviewed by a court. At this point the child is kept in care if there is continuing risk or, if not, the child is returned. Notice requirements for this first hearing are generally not stringent, and an initial hearing may take place without notice to the parents.[57] Often the first hearing is a rather pro forma affair. Counsel for the mother may not be present although the state is almost certainly represented by legal counsel in this first instance and throughout the proceedings. Whether any information about an impending hearing reaches a woman in a psychiatric facility may depend on the decision of her treatment team as to how such news would affect her. Even if she is informed of an important court matter, she may have limited access to counsel and to the courts because she is in a psychiatric ward, or she may not be well enough to attend the hearing or to represent herself. While there may be justifiable policy reasons for the lack of notice requirements for post-apprehension court appearances in some circumstances, such as cases where the location of the parents is unknown, a mother hospitalized in a psychiatric facility is at risk of being left out of the process from the beginning and of being separated from her child for lengthy periods. The separation has obvious negative effects on the parent-child relationship and significantly prejudices the mother's legal position.[58]

57 Child protection legislation generally provides for some form of notice prior to any initial hearing. In some jurisdictions, the legislation also provides either that the notice can be dispensed with (Family and Child Services Act, RSPEI 1988, c. F-2, s. 28) or that the validity of the proceedings shall not be affected if notice is not given in accordance with the Act (Child Welfare Act, SA 1984, c. C-8, s. 19). Quite clearly in some jurisdictions, initial hearings take place with notice to the parents only where practicable (Family and Child Service Act, SBC 1980, c. 11, s. 11(1.1)) or conceivably not at all (Child and Family Services Act, SS 1989–90, c. C-7.2, s. 20, where a family review panel hearing may be held without the presence of the parents, and where the panel is not bound by the rules of law).

58 In *Catholic Children's Aid Society of Metropolitan Toronto* v. *C.M.* (1994) 113 DLR (4th) 321, the Supreme Court of Canada acknowledged that the protracted nature of the proceeding, although unfortunate, had been a factor in the establishment of the bond between the child and her foster parents. Now there was a risk of emotional harm if the child was to be removed from her foster family. Therefore it was in the best interests of the child for the Children's Aid Society to have permanent custody of the child.

Usually there is a lengthy adjournment between the initial and the more comprehensive second-stage hearing. Therefore, despite the apparent interim nature of the orders at the initial hearing and the usual informality of the process, the court makes a custody and access ruling at this stage that potentially affects the remainder of the proceeding. The court's focus on bonding and stability in interpreting the best interests of the child leads to a preference for the status quo in the ultimate disposition.[59] Often the court will order supervised access at the initial hearing. The stress of such access visits cannot be exaggerated. Visits become sites where a mother must prove herself as competent, loving, and spontaneous, despite the effects of medication and obvious surveillance. Inevitably there will be conflict, or at best ambiguity, in the roles of various people who are involved with a woman with a psychiatric disability during this adjournment period. The supervisor is always a potentially adverse witness in the next stage of the proceedings. For the professionals involved, the objectives of caring and the objectives of social control present an inherent contradiction.

I became involved with Barbara's case after her child was permanently apprehended. She appealed the decision. Barbara's baby was apprehended at the hospital immediately after her birth. The public health nurse and a financial aid worker were worried that Barbara's mental disability would put the baby at risk. Before the second-stage hearing, where the judge would make a finding about whether the baby was at risk, the ministry arranged different sorts of supervised access visits for Barbara. Two such visits were to take place at Barbara and Vincent's apartment, where the ministry supplied 24-hour homemaker support. During the three-day visits Barbara noticed that the 'homemakers' were watching her closely and making notes. Barbara told me that the note-taking made her very nervous, that she couldn't concentrate well on taking care of the baby, and that she thought the notes might be important in court. She asked the homemakers if she could see the notes, but the homemakers said she couldn't. In response, Barbara and Vincent began making their own notes. Eventually, however, the homemakers found Barbara and Vincent's notes, and, over objections of Barbara and Vincent, the homemakers removed the notes from the apartment and never gave them back. On cross-examination at the hearing, the homemakers said that they could remember neither finding nor taking away any papers that belonged to Barbara and Vincent.

---

59 See *Racine* supra note 44; *Catholic Children's Aid Society of Metropolitan Toronto v. C.M.,* supra.

128 UNIVERSITY OF TORONTO LAW JOURNAL

III *Judicial decision-making*

1. GENERAL

Mothers with mental health histories may themselves be convinced that it is best to give up their child without a hearing, and the state may be able to remove a child from a mother with a mental health diagnosis without resorting to the court process. Yet some cases do reach the courts. My objective in this section is to explore the general tendencies in judicial decision-making in child welfare matters where the mother has a mental health history.[60] Specifically I will examine the tendency of judges to make their decisions by relying on the basic tenets of psychology as well as the particular opinions of the expert.

This analysis is based on child protection decisions since 1980 where the mental health of the mother was an issue. Since many decisions include extremely brief reasons, and the sample is not large enough to perform statistical analysis, this review suggests trends rather than conclusions.[61] Not surprisingly, very few of these cases reach the provincial courts of appeal,[62] and most cases are unreported.[63] Access to lawyers historically has been a matter of economic privilege, and poor people have not exercised their rights of appeal in legal matters. Despite the existence of legal aid, there are still few appellate decisions on any welfare matter. In this sample the low number of reported cases probably indicates that the people who decide which cases to report view these cases as fact-specific and not reflecting any important general legal principles.

---

60 I have not included cases where mental handicap is the issue unless the woman has a dual diagnosis, because cases involving mental handicap raise separate issues about such matters as predictability and dangerousness.

61 Sixty-one cases decided since 1980 were used as the sample. Cases originally reviewed (129 in total) were not subject to further analysis either when the decision was too brief to analyse the issues, or where the case was framed around a principle that was unrelated to the mother's mental health. An example of a case that was rejected because of brevity is *Child and Family Services of Central Winnipeg* v. *Poiron* [1989] MJ No. 651 (Man. CA), where the actual reasoning of the judgment was five lines long. An example of a case that was rejected because the issue of the case was completely separate from the mother's mental health was *Catholic Children's Aid Society of Metropolitan Toronto* v. *C.M.* (1991) 37 RFL 202 (Ont. Ct of Justice, Gen. Div.), where the issue was around the appointment of counsel for the child and the child's instructions to counsel.

62 Three cases or slightly less than 5 per cent of 61 cases.

63 Of the sample, 40 cases, or almost 66 per cent, were unreported.

In this section I focus on decisions where a custody order is made at the conclusion of the hearing.[64] I have defined the cases as 'unsuccessful' or 'successful' on the basis of the custody disposition at the end of the hearing. For the purpose of this analysis a case is defined as unsuccessful when the mother loses custody of her child at the conclusion of the hearing. Successful cases are decisions that result in the mother's retaining custody or regaining custody of her child at the conclusion of the hearing.

Where the mother has a psychiatric disability, child protection cases tend to be decided overwhelmingly against the mother.[65] Predictably these cases are characterized by the court's deference to the views of psychiatrists, psychologists, or social work authorities.[66] The deferential trend is consistent with Isabel Grant's work, which points to the general tendency of Canadian courts to adopt a paternalistic model in mental health cases rather than an explicit social control model that characterizes criminal cases.[67] However, the paternalistic attitude of the courts

64 Forty-seven cases ended with a custody order. The other major issue in these cases was the disclosure of psychiatric records. Disclosure of psychiatric records was the central issue in 14 cases, and the court ordered disclosure in 11 of these 14 cases.

65 In this sample, 29 of the 47 cases were unsuccessful, 10 of the cases were successful, and 8 could not be categorized. Of the 10 successful cases, the mother retained or regained custody without conditions in only one case.

66 There is a strain in American law that explicitly suggests judicial deferral to psychiatrists in mental health cases. In *Parham* v. *J.R.* (1979) 442 US 584, 99 S.Ct. 2493, 61 L.Ed.2d 101, the US Supreme Court restricted the right to procedural due process for children admitted to mental health hospitals and focused on these decisions as 'essentially medical.' The Court concluded that 'the supposed protections of an adversary proceeding to determine the appropriateness of medical decisions for the commitment and treatment of mental and emotional illness may well be more illusory than real' at (442 US 584) 609. See also *Youngberg* v. *Romero* (1982) 457 US 307 at 321, 102 S.Ct. 2452, 73 L.Ed.2d 28, where the court set an extremely high standard for judicial review of professional decision-making and held that it would be inappropriate 'for the courts to specify which of several professionally acceptable choices should have been made.' Even more extreme is the decision in *Washington* v. *Harper* (1990) 494 US 210, where the issue was the non-consensual administration of psychotropic drugs to mentally ill but competent prisoners. Here the court found that the decision to medicate was probably better made by the medical profession than the judiciary, and that due process requires no more than an administrative review by medical decision-makers to override a prisoner's decision not to accept drug therapy. But see also the cases in which a higher standard of due process protection is contemplated where a liberty interest is at stake: *Re Gault* (1967) 387 US 1, 18 L.Ed.2d 527; *Wyatt* v. *Stickney* (1971) 325 F. Supp. 781; and *Addington* v. *Texas* (1979) 441 US 418, 60 L.Ed.2d 323.

67 'Mental Health Law' supra note 19.

is inevitably connected to the advice of experts who act like legal agents of social control in their roles both before and during the court process. One explicit judicial statement that pronounces a paternalistic model in mental health cases states:

[T]he objects and purposes of criminal law and mental health legislation are so different that cases in one area will be of little guidance in the other. A protective statute and a penal statute operate in dramatically dissimilar contexts. Strict and narrow criteria for the detention of persons in a criminal law context reflect our society's notions of fundamental justice for an accused person and protection of the public is a foremost consideration. But in the field of mental health, the same criteria would defeat the purpose of the legislation which is to help seriously mentally ill people in need of protection.[68]

Underlying the paternalistic model is a view that all of the legal actors are seeking a solution in the best interests of the individual. Since there are no competing interests recognized by this model, the sensible approach would seem for judges to defer to those with the greatest expertise, the mental health professionals. The American courts have deferred to psychiatric opinion when an issue is interpreted as peculiar to the mental health context, such as a non-consensual treatment order, but may take a 'rights' approach on other issues brought by persons labelled mentally ill.[69] Canadian courts have taken a similar view.[70] Grant points out, for example, that psychiatric patients have generally lost their Charter challenges, but the few successful Charter challenges are cases where the court can analogize to some more familiar principle of law such as principles of administrative law or employment law.[71] That is, the court can view the case not as a 'mental health' case, where psychiatric and psychological knowledge may be more important, but as a question of 'statutory interpretation' or 'fairness,' where judicial knowledge is more immediately and obviously pertinent.

I argue that the courts adopt a paternalistic model in deciding child protection cases, as they do in deciding mental health cases. Just as

---

68 *McCorkell* supra note 45.
69 See 'Mental Health Law' supra note 19, 752–62.
70 *Fleming* v. *Reid* (1991) 82 DLR (4th) 298 is a notable exception in which the Ontario Court of Appeal held that it was unconstitutional for the review board to make treatment decisions on the basis of a person's best interests rather than the position expressed by the person while competent.
71 See *Dayday* v. *MacEwan* (1987) 62 OR (2d) 588; and *Fenton* v. *British Columbia (Forensic Psychiatric Services Commission)* (1992) 56 BCLR (2d) 170.

MOTHERHOOD, MADNESS, AND LAW 131

there are no competing interests recognized by a paternalistic model in deciding mental health cases, there is seen to be a common interest among the legal actors in a child protection proceeding, that is, the welfare of the child. For similar reasons judges tend to defer to the opinions of psychiatrists when the issues are defined as specific to the child protection context, such as mental health or child development questions. A rights approach may be more likely if the issue is defined outside the specific child welfare context and judges can analogize to some other area of law where psychiatric knowledge is not seen as superior.

2. UNSUCCESSFUL CASES

In deciding cases where the mother has a mental health history, judges are almost always presented with the evidence of mental health professionals about both the mother and the child. The particular opinions sought from the psychiatrist are usually how long the mother's problem is likely to last, how independent the mother can be as a parent, as well as the type and amount of support she would need.[72]

Inherent in such evidence are the postulates that inform psychiatric research and practice: a focus on the individual, the objectivity of (social) science, confidence in assessment, the predictive value of diagnosis, and the unreliability of lay observations of human behaviour. By accepting psychiatric evidence without serious scrutiny of the underlying assumptions and basic research leading to conclusions by psychiatrists and psychologists, the courts tend to remove children from mothers with mental health histories on the basis of psychiatric opinion that is not tested in the same ways as other expert evidence.[73]

---

72 See, for example, *Superintendent of Child Welfare* v. *P.(J.)* (1988) 15 RFL (3d) 216 (BCCA). See also *Winnipeg South Child and Family Services Agency* v. *W.(J.G.)* [1987] MJ No. 72 (Man. QB).

73 Courts have traditionally been reluctant to allow expert opinion on the 'ultimate issue.' The reason given is a concern that allowing such evidence would usurp the function of the trier of fact. Courts continue to be reluctant to admit this evidence, in that the closer the opinion gets to the ultimate issue, the more likely it will be rejected. The 'ultimate issue' phraseology is no longer used, but the reasoning is generally the same. The evidence will be rejected if the trier of fact does not need assistance in reaching a conclusion on the point in question (which will generally be the case with the 'ultimate issue'). *R.* v. *Graat* (1980) 55 CCC (2d) 429, 17 CR (3d) 55, 30 CR (2d) 247, 7 MVR 163, 116 DLR 143 (CA) aff'd [1982] 2 SCR 819, 2 CCC (3d) 365, 3 CR (3d) 289, 18 MVR 284, 144 DLR (3d) 267, 45 NR 451. The insanity defence is an exception to this pattern where courts almost always rely on psychiatrists on the ultimate issue.

Psychiatric opinions of what is in the best interests of the child are strikingly grounded in a medical model of mental disorder. A medical model assumes that disability originates from impairment, a defect in the individual which may be fixed by an appropriate professional.[74] Since judges seem to accept the general premise that psychiatrists know best what choices people with psychiatric diagnoses ought to make, the courts proceed as though the 'right' choice for people with mental illnesses is to do what the psychiatrist has recommended. As a consequence, mothers with psychiatric diagnoses do poorly in court when mental health professionals report that the women have refused to accept their advice. In *P.E.I. (Director of Child Welfare) v. H.(D.)*[75] the court was especially concerned that the mother had missed a number of counselling appointments and had terminated counselling although the counsellor thought that counselling should continue. Courts are far more persuaded by a psychiatric view that treatment is needed than by a mother's view that it is not. The medical model of mental illness is also clearly reflected in the decisions by the emphasis on drug therapy. Refusing to take medication is frequently mentioned in the reasons for the state to permanently remove a child,[76] as is a mother's 'resistance' to treatment.[77] In *W. (C.A.)*[78] although the court recognized a mother's right to refuse psychotropic medication, it decided that the refusal deemed her incapable of caring for a child. An identical concern about medication is very frequently the focus of hearings about releasing involuntary patients under mental health legislation.[79]

An especially ironic situation is demonstrated in the case of *L.(K.)*.[80] Here a mother diagnosed as a manic depressive was advised by her

---

74 See Bichenbach, supra note 10, c. 3.
75 [1989] PEIJ No. 60.
76 *C.A.S. of Niagara Region v. W.(C.A.)* supra note 51; *New Brunswick (Minister of Health and Community Services) v. N.J.C.* (1990) 239 APR 316 (QB); and *New Brunswick (Minister of Health and Community Services) v. C.(N.)* (1987) 9 RFL (3d) 332 (NBQB). Taking illegal drugs is also a reason for removing children. See Maher, supra note 49.
77 *New Brunswick (Minister of Health and Community Services) v. N.J.C.* supra. *Superintendent of Family and Child Services v. Alvarez* (2 February 1987) Vancouver CC860754 (BC Co. Ct).
78 Supra note 51.
79 See *Hoskins* supra note 45, where the intention to discontinue medication was a primary consideration in the decision not to release. This is certainly consistent with my experience in representing people at tribunals.
80 *L.(K.) v. C.A.S., Stormont, Dundas and Glengarry* (1988) 12 RFL (3d) 76 (Ont. Dist. Ct).

psychiatrist to discontinue lithium treatments during her pregnancy because the drug could harm the fetus. She stopped taking the drug while she was pregnant and consequently developed symptoms of shakiness and mood swings after the birth of the child. Because of these symptoms the psychiatrist recommended the child be placed in care until the mother's condition could be stabilized. Without any objection from the mother, the child was apprehended and found in need of protection. The mother consented to the child's remaining in care awaiting her own expected stabilization. Eventually the mother withdrew her consent, and a hearing was required to decide the question of whether the child was in need of protection and, if so, what was in the child's best interests. The court decided that there was no need to make a fresh finding that the child was in need of protection and that it was in the child's best interests to be permanently apprehended in order to be adopted. Here the mother had followed her psychiatrist's advice precisely concerning medication. She also cooperated fully with the legal process. Regardless of the fact that the mother cooperated with psychiatric officials, she lost her child. If she had not cooperated with her doctors and continued to take lithium during pregnancy or had objected to the child's being in care while she stabilized, one would expect exactly the same result.

Although the issue of child welfare is obviously intertwined with the fitness of the custodial parent, the courts tend to reorient these cases remarkably easily to make the central question the mother's mental health diagnosis. Exactly how a mother's diagnosis relates to a child's best interests is largely unexamined by the court. Regardless, the question in the hearing may become the mother's mental health rather than the child's best interests. Often applications for a mother's mental health records are made in child welfare cases without any argument as to how the records would answer the best interests question. In *C.L.M.*[81] the court ordered psychiatric disclosure of a mother's records because it was 'essential in the interests of justice.' The crown wardship application involved an application that the mother was unfit because of schizophrenia. The court found that psychiatric disclosure is essential when: '(1) The patient's psychiatric state is *the main issue being litigated* and (2) That issue cannot be determined through other evidence adduced' (emphasis added).

Besides generally accepting the medical model of mental illness, courts rely on the specific assumptions of the psychiatric paradigm.

---

81 In *Re: C.L.M.* (1982) 29 RFL (2d) 460 (Ont. Prov. Ct (Fam. Div.)).

134 UNIVERSITY OF TORONTO LAW JOURNAL

Judges accept the predictive value of psychiatric diagnosis in child protection proceedings despite the existing evidence that psychiatrists are poor assessors of risk.[82] Not only is the psychiatric diagnosis of the mother accepted relatively easily by the courts, children are assessed, labelled, and linked to the mother's label. In *W.(C.A.)*[83] the mother's diagnosis of personality disorder was linked to the assessment of learning disabilities in her children, thereby blaming the pathologically labelled mother for her children's label of pathology.

Even when the behaviour that led to psychiatric involvement in a woman's life has disappeared, the psychiatric diagnosis itself often serves as the pivotal point of the decision. Repeated apprehensions of a child or apprehensions of children born later occur because of a lingering psychiatric label.[84] In *N.B.* v. *C.(N.)*[85] a woman's paranoid delusions resulted in apprehension of two of her children shortly after their births. After her third child was born, this child too was permanently removed, although the mother demonstrated no psychiatric symptoms at this time and the diagnosis had changed from paranoid schizophrenia to schizoid personality disorder, considered a less severe condition. However, the psychiatric expert said that the mother's symptoms were 'lurking just below the surface' and this opinion led to the permanent removal of the child. In addition to accepting the 'truth' value of psychological prediction and assessment of an individual, judges are influenced by the psychological idea of the 'iceberg' nature of personality, that a person's motives and potential behaviour may be hidden behind a seemingly harmless exterior, especially in persons who are mentally ill.

According to the standard rules about opinion evidence, expert evidence is necessary only if the opinion tells the court something it would not otherwise know. In these circumstances it is only helpful to the court in making a decision if a diagnosis can lead to more accurate

---

82 See B.L. Diamond 'The Psychiatric Prediction of Dangerousness' (1974) 123 *U. of Penn. LR* 439; J.J. Cocozza and H.J. Steadman 'The Failure of Psychiatric Predictions of Dangerousness: Clear and Convincing Evidence' (1976) 29 *Rutgers LR* 1084; John Hinton (ed.) *Dangerousness: Problems of Assessment and Prediction* (London: Allen and Unwin 1983); C. Webster, M. Ben-Aron, and S. Hucker (eds) *Dangerousness, Probability and Prediction, Psychiatry and Public Policy* (New York: Cambridge University Press 1985).

83 Supra note 51.

84 See D.L. Rosenhan 'On Being Sane in Insane Places' (1973) 179 *Science* 250.

85 Supra note 76.

predictions about a mother's future behaviour. In *P.E.I.* v. *H.(D.)*[86] the medical diagnosis of 'borderline personality disorder,' for example, meant that the mother had 'difficulty dealing with the problems of day-to-day life,' and 'appears impulsive' and 'unable to establish priorities.' While not explored in the decision, this diagnosis is situated in a taxonomy or classification scheme shared by the psychiatric establishment.[87] Borderline personality disorder is not considered particularly amenable to therapy. As a result, the psychiatric prediction is that this woman is not likely to change. However, the judgment discloses no attempt to test the evidence or its context. For example, there is no indication of the basis of the assessment, no questioning about the research indicating that therapy is unlikely to work, and no empirical research to link the diagnosis to more general conclusions. In short, the more standard techniques of testing evidence in court or testing the basis of expert opinion seem to be passed over in these circumstances. Regardless, judges seem willing to accept psychiatric opinion as superior knowledge.

2. 'SUCCESSFUL' CASES

While mothers with mental health histories lose in the majority of cases, it is useful to look closely at the nature of the 'success' in the relatively few cases where the court decides in favour of the mother. Despite the apparent victories, these decisions reveal two important themes that point to the overarching influence of the psychiatric paradigm in the judicial process. First, judges are extremely reluctant to decide the question without arranging for an ongoing watchful eye of a psychiatrist or psychologist to attend the mother and/or child. Second, the decisions indicate a tendency to disagree with psychological or psychiatric evidence only in limited circumstances, these being only when the child protection authorities have demonstrated flagrant disregard for the required process.

86 Supra note 75.
87 S. Kaysen *Girl Interrupted* (New York: Turtle Bay Books 1993) gives an account of her own hospitalization and treatment for mental illness. She discovered, with the help of a lawyer to obtain her hospital records, that she was diagnosed as having a borderline personality. She needed to find a copy of the *Diagnostic and Statistical Manual of Mental Disorders* to 'see what they really thought of me.' She writes at 150–1: 'What does *borderline personality* mean anyhow? It appears to be a way station between neurosis and psychosis: a fractured but not disassembled psyche. Though to quote my post-Melvin psychiatrist: "It's what they call people whose lifestyles bother them." He can say that because he's a doctor. If I said it, nobody would believe me.'

136 UNIVERSITY OF TORONTO LAW JOURNAL

In *J.P.*[88] the mother had a vaguely described mental disability that suggested aspects of mental handicap and mental disorder. The British Columbia Court of Appeal quashed an order awarding permanent custody to the superintendent because the statute required the court to consider whether the condition was likely to be remedied.[89] The appellate court was not satisfied that the lower court had before it an appropriate assessment to make the determination according to the statutory requirement.

In *Children's Aid Society of Hamilton-Wentworth v. M.M.*,[90] a two-year-old child was apprehended on the basis of rather vague allegations of anticipated abuse. This case is somewhat exceptional in that the court examined the values underlying the psychological assessment. The mother was young, with a tendency to alcoholic binges. There were questions about her intellectual abilities and hints of mental health issues. Psychologists were called by both the Children's Aid Society and the mother, and each gave evidence of their assessments of both the mother and the child. Here the court describes a number of serious irregularities of process in this case. There was no indication that the mother was informed of her right to counsel at the beginning of the proceeding. The case took 24 months to come to trial, a delay that was primarily the fault of the CAS.[91] A further statutory breach occurred because CAS service providers did not ensure that the interests of the parents were represented at meetings where important decisions were made about their child. In considering the psychological evidence, the court decided that the main allegations about the mother reflected middle-class biases and were insufficient to make a wardship order.

As a matter of principle and social policy, family integrity should be maintained wherever it is reasonably possible. As I have already indicated, much of the criticism made with respect to M. seems to have been made from the perspective of middle-class values without sensitivity to the fact that Marsha, as do

---

88 Supra note 72.
89 Family and Child Services Act, SBC 1980, c. 11, s. 14(2)(b).
90 [1992] OJ No. 1704 (Unified Family Court).
91 Ibid. Judge Beckett was clear that the delay was attributable to the authorities: 'Delays in cases of this type are rarely in the best interests of the child or the family and almost always have an extremely serious deleterious effect on the child and the family. Certainly that is so in this case. It is not necessarily my function in this case to analyze the reasons why this case has taken so long to come to trial. The Unified Family Court and its system must bear part of the responsibility. However, the CAS had carriage of the case and the best interests of the child required the Society to move the case forward with dispatch. Certainly the CAS must bear the primary responsibility for the unconscionable period of time that has elapsed from apprehension to trial.'

thousands of others, lives in what for her has been perpetual poverty and deprivation. Added to this is her unfortunate cognitive disability. However, we have not reached the day in our society when being poor or homeless or unintelligent or unemployed can be viewed as a reason to send a child for adoption in a so-called normal, middle-class home. It may be argued that the child would be better off in a more affluent, socially acceptable home. That is not the test.[92]

The court ordered that the child be returned to the mother but with certain important conditions, almost all of which necessitated a continuing relationship between the mother, her child, and mental health professionals. These conditions included that the CAS supervise the case for twelve months; the CAS provide assistance in finding subsidized housing and necessary furniture; the child be enrolled in a day-care program, preferably a therapeutic day-care program where the mother could participate; the child be examined monthly by the family doctor and these reports be sent to the CAS and the mother; and the mother arrange counselling for her own problems and any deficiencies in parenting.[93]

In *Children's Aid Society of London (City) and Middlesex (County)* v. *H. (T.)*,[94] a Crown expert gained access to a mother's psychiatric records despite the fact that the mother had refused consent.[95] The Children's Aid Society secured the records for this purpose by obtaining consent from the grandmother who had interim custody of the child, and the CAS expert completed his report for trial with this information included. The mother successfully applied to exclude all of the evidence of this expert. The court was struck with 'the flagrant and wilful breach of T.H.'s rights' and viewed 'as of cardinal importance the protection of privacy of individuals such as T.H., who enter into a treatment facility for assistance to allow themselves to be questioned and assessed.' The court admonished counsel for the CAS further because 'the striking aspect of this fact situation is the number of other techniques available to the Society to have obtained the same information about T.H. in an entirely legitimate way.'

---

92 Ibid.

93 Other conditions were that no third party reside with her without the written consent of the CAS and that the child not be left alone with certain male family members.

94 (1992) 41 RFL (3d) 122 (Ont. Prov. Div.).

95 CAS obtained a release from the mother for her psychiatric records, but the mother did not consent for these records to be used in a psychological assessment.

A dramatic example is the case of *Re Pamela M.*[96] The court ordered costs against the Children's Aid Society, although such an order is acknowledged to be very unusual in custody matters 'at least where there has been good faith on the part of the contestants' and even more 'delicate' when one party is mandated by statute to protect children. Of greatest concern to the court was the CAS's apparent manipulation of the court process. Here the court found that the actions of the agency constituted exceptional circumstances, because not only was the original decision to apprehend 'a questionable exercise of state power but the conduct of the case thereafter is noteworthy as well.' The Court commented on the 'feeble attempt' by the social worker to make important contacts prior to the apprehension. At the initial hearing, a judge who was well acquainted with the family decided after three days of hearing that the original apprehension was not justified and the child should be returned home. In response, the CAS appealed the decision and moved to stay the order, filing 'a rather selective and biased representation of the facts ... [which] in the context of the whole of the evidence it is misleading as to the nature of the risks to Pamela.'[97]

The CAS never proceeded with the appeal of the order, and the trial was commenced. With one witness remaining, the trial judge anticipated the child's return home, made an access order for the mother to accelerate the proceedings and prepare for the child's return. The CAS did not comply with the access order and appealed it, but did not proceed with the appeal. At the conclusion of the trial the evidence was essentially the same as it was at the initial presentation hearing. In final argument, counsel for the CAS informed the court that it intended to proceed the way it had throughout the process, that is, to file an appeal of the decision and to keep the child in care pending the outcome. Despite court orders to the contrary, the CAS had retained custody of the child throughout the proceedings.

The first theme that characterizes the 'successes' in these cases is judges' tendencies to turn back the important matters in this area to the realm of psychiatry and psychology. In these circumstances, the courts definitely do not deem women fit, but simply divert them to a different system, which is likely to have even more complicated dynamics for these women than the judicial system. Whereas a woman's

96 *Re: Catholic Children's Aid Society and Pamela M.* (1982) 36 OR (2d) 462 (Ont. Prov. Ct (Fam. Div.)).
97 Ibid. 463.

experience with the courts is finite (although these experiences may certainly be repeated), her connection to the mental health system and related agencies is ongoing and perhaps permanent. The resulting 'victory' for women is a judicial endorsement of the need for psychiatry to monitor them as mothers and a prescriptive mandate for monitoring to continue.[98] Implicit in this trend is a message to a woman that she must conform to the ideology of motherhood as incorporated in psychiatry or psychology to retain her privilege as a mother,[99] or face further process to remove her as the guardian/custodian of her child.

For example, the pivotal issue in *J.P.*[100] is assessment, one of the basic premises of the psychiatric paradigm. Although the British Columbia Court of Appeal overturned the trial decision on a point of law, the court said that the trial judge did not have proper psychological evidence, or enough of it to make a permanent order: In its suggestion that the authorities could immediately reapprehend the child to begin the process anew, the court gives a clear message that an appropriately comprehensive assessment could well be sufficient. In *CAS of Hamilton-Wentworth* v. *M.M.*[101] there is considerable language acknowledging the value-laden ideals of motherhood, and the order returns the child to the mother. However, the court coincidentally returns the mother to the control and surveillance of psychologists and psychiatrists. In short, these cases conclude with orders where the authorities are directed to provide better and further assessment or where the mother must comply with conditions subjecting her to further psychiatric scrutiny so that the appropriate part of the taxonomy of pathology may be invoked, after which the court may comfortably make its decision.[102]

The second theme of the 'successful' cases is that courts tend to decide in favour of the mother not on the grounds of merit, but

---

98 The important point in these cases is that the court tends to impose an order to explicitly involve the mental health professionals. It is actually quite common that the return of children in child protection proceedings is accompanied by an order requiring continuing state involvement.

99 See M. Molloy 'Citizenship, Property and Bodies: Discourses on Gender and the Inter-War Labour Government in New Zealand' (1992) 1 *Gender and History* 301.

100 Supra note 72.

101 Supra note 90.

102 An incidental but potentially important consequence of an approach where the court requires more and better psychiatric/psychological evidence is the effect on the mental health system itself. Although I argue here that returning child protection questions to psychiatrists and psychologists makes the mother a further captive of the mental health system, it also puts the system on notice that it must be accountable, even if only on its own terms.

because the state authorities showed flagrant disregard for procedure. Where mothers have a mental health history the courts tend to seize on dramatic procedural or technical irregularities that have occurred in the child protection process, much as they have in the Charter challenges in child protection matters generally.[103] Although the courts give child protection authorities considerable latitude in their practice,[104] these cases represent situations where it appears to the judge that a critical line has been crossed, that the authorities have gone 'out of bounds' and that the judge must exercise judicial responsibility to avoid a public perception that

the state agency could act, ungoverned by law, to obtain evidence against a respondent in a child protection trial and that, although the legislature can

---

103 Two of the three successful Charter challenges in child protection law were decided primarily on procedural issues. First, imposing a 12-month, inflexible time limit for temporary custody was arbitrary and violated the rights of the child under section 7 of the Charter and was not saved under section 1. (See *R.A.J. (Re)* [1992] YJ No. 126. The provision was not stuck down, but the court merely exempted the application of the section to the child in question.) Second, authorizing warrantless searches without restriction for children in need of protection was too general and authorized searches too often. Section 15(1) of the Family and Child Services Act RSPEI 1974, c. F-2.0) was found to contravene section 8 of the Charter and was held to be of no force and effect (See *M.(H.)* v. *Director of Child Welfare for Prince Edward Island* (1989) 22 RFL (3d) 399 (PEISC (TD)).

In *Re: C.P.L.* (1988), 215 APR 287 (Nfld Unifed Fam. Ct), the only Charter decision that has been decided on substantive issues, the court held that the lack of notice of apprehension and granting consent to medical treatment without consultation with the parents deprived the baby of its right to liberty and security of the person. Here the court was appalled, not by a disregard for procedure, but by the procedures themselves: 'As can be seen from the evidence in this case total control is left in the hands of a medical practitioner. All he need do is call the Director or somebody who is a social worker and request that consent be given for treatment of a child. The consent may be given without further consultation. ... This effectively keeps the parents out of the picture. In this case it was not what was actually done but how it was done, which was the denial of the child's rights.'

104 See, for example, *Re: Clarke Institute of Psychiatry and Catholic Children's Aid Society of Metropolitan Toronto* supra note 39, where the mother, who was a patient in a psychiatric facility, and her child were apprehended shortly after birth. Her mental health records were subpoenaed under the child welfare legislation, although the process to release psychiatric records as outlined under the Mental Health Act was not exhausted. The authorities characterized their application as urgent in order to complete a quick investigation of child abuse under the Child Welfare Act because of the 'adoptability' of a ten-month-old baby. The court found that although it 'may have been preferable to complete the process contemplated by the *Mental Health Act*, application by the Society under the *Child Welfare Act* does not amount to an abuse of process.'

impose rules to protect people, those rules could be completely disregarded by an applicant Society in the prosecution of its case. I think a reasonable individual would be stunned by the prospect.[105]

Taken together, these two themes of the 'successful' cases represent a tacit division of responsibility between judges and psychologists/psychiatrists in child protection matters where a mother has a psychiatric label. Psychiatrists and psychologists are in charge of the substance of the matter, while the judge is to monitor the process, especially any serious abuses of the process.

Drawing on Grant's argument[106] that the courts are more likely to act independently when a mental health matter can be characterized as involving some other legal principle, the questions here are problematic for the courts because the most important issues all seem peculiar to the hybrid mental health/child protection proceeding and demand psychological answers rather than answers from law. The specific questions reduce to the stability of the mother and to the intellectual, social, and emotional development of the child. Occasionally, however, the issue in a child protection matter may be constructed outside this frame, most commonly as a question about procedure. If the authorities have ignored or sabotaged required procedures, the legal issues resemble questions of natural justice or contempt. In these cases the courts will be more comfortable in disagreeing with psychiatrists/psychologists because they are confronted with issues analogous to more familiar areas of law. However, this level of comfort rarely extends to releasing the mother or the child from additional involvement with the 'helping' professions. Indeed, the inferences about credibility that are normally applied to non-expert witnesses are not applied here. That is, the flagrant abuse of known process by these professionals is not used to question the diagnoses offered in their evidence.

IV *Conclusion*

To summarize, the legislative provisions of child protection law and mental health law resonate with each other, both in terms of process and in the underlying principles as perceptions about vulnerable people. The effects of these provisions are especially insidious for women with psychiatric disabilities, as demonstrated by the facts and

105 Supra note 89, 195.
106 The tendency of Canadian courts to adopt a paternalistic model and defer to 'experts': 'Mental Health Law' supra note 19.

underlying thinking behind pre-birth apprehension cases and the lax notice requirements for post-apprehension court appearances. Both statutes contemplate urgent situations which require state intervention, most often to protect the vulnerable person and also the public. The intervention legitimizes state scrutiny of otherwise private and personal spheres of life, although any court proceedings occur after the critical intervention.

I have argued that the structure of the law paves the way for the importance of the 'expert.' Women with mental histories tend to lose their children on the basis of psychiatric opinion. Because the legal model of a child protection proceeding is somewhat peculiar, and the disciplines of psychology and psychiatry seem so pertinent, judges tend to defer to the opinions of psychiatrists on the substantive matters and intervene where the authorities appear to have flagrant disregard for legal process. In effect, judges share their decision-making with psychiatrists by largely accepting psychiatric opinion on the substance and retaining the power to rule on breaches of procedure. Where the mother retains or regains custody the order almost always includes the condition of the ongoing watchful eye of a psychiatrist.

In trying to maintain or regain custody of their children, women with a psychiatric diagnosis are faced with an implicit presumption against their fitness. People with mental illnesses are often perceived as incomprehensible, unpredictable, and dangerous. Law operates here in tandem with psychology and other mechanisms of the state. Much like the paternalistic model that governs decisions in mental health cases and a certain modern ethos in criminal law, a 'judge thinks of himself as a therapist of the social body, a worker in the field of "public health" in the larger sense.'[107] What psychology and psychiatry offer to the court as scientific enterprises is the comfort of predictablity and knowledge. As a result, women with mental health histories continue to lose their children to the state through some combination of moral suasion, legal process, consent, and threat, all woven with the opinions of particular mental health personnel.

107 'The Anxiety of Judging' in Michel Foucault *Foucault Live: Interviews 1966–84)* (New York: Semiotexte Foreign Agents Series 1989) 168.

[11]

"Ambiguous Sex"— or Ambivalent Medicine?

Ethical Issues in the Treatment of Intersexuality

by Alice Domurat Dreger

Andrés Monreal, *Hiding*, 1985.

What makes us "female" or "male," "girls" or "boys," "women" or "men"—our chromosomes, our genitalia, how we (and others) are brought up to think about ourselves, or all of the above? One of the first responses to the birth of a child of ambiguous sex by clinicians, and parents, is to seek to "disambiguate" the situation: to assign the newborn's identity as either female or male, surgically modify the child's genitalia to conform believably to that sex identity, and provide other medical treatment (such as hormones) to reinforce the gender decided upon. The assumptions that underlie efforts to "normalize" intersexual individuals and the ethics of "treatment" for intersexuality merit closer examination than they generally receive. ➤

number of events have lately aroused substantial public interest in intersexuality (congenital "ambiguous sex") and "reconstructive" genital surgery. Perhaps the most sensational of these is the recent publication of unexpected long-term outcomes in the classic and well-known "John/Joan" case.[1] "John" was born a typical XY male with a twin brother, but a doctor accidentally ablated John's penis during a circumcision at age eight months. Upon consultation with a team of physicians and sexologists at the Johns Hopkins Hospital (circa 1963) it was decided that given the unfortunate loss of a normal penis John should be medically reconstructed and raised as a girl—"Joan." Surgeons therefore removed John/Joan's testes and subsequently subjected Joan to further surgical and hormonal treatments in an attempt to make her body look more like a girl's. The team of medical professionals involved also employed substantial psychological counseling to help Joan and the family feel comfortable with Joan's female gender. They believed that Joan and the family would need help adjusting to her new gender, but that full (or near-full) adjustment could be achieved.

For decades, the alleged success of this particular sex reassignment had been widely reported by Hopkins sexologist John Money and others as proof that physicians could essentially create any gender out of any child, so long as the cosmetic alteration was performed early. Money and others repeatedly asserted that "Johns" could be made into "Joans" and "Joans" into "Johns" so long as the genitals looked "right" and everyone agreed to agree on the child's assigned gender. The postulates of this approach are summarized succinctly by Milton Diamond and Keith Sigmundson: "(1) individuals are psychosexually neutral at birth and (2) healthy psychosexual development is dependent on the appearance of the genitals" (p. 298). While not a case of congenital intersexuality, the John/Joan case was nevertheless used by many clinicians who treat intersexuality as proof that in intersex cases the same postulates should hold. The keys seemed to be surgical creation of a believable sexual anatomy and assurances all around that the child was "really" the assigned gender.

But reports of the success of John/Joan were premature—indeed, they were wrong. Diamond and Sigmundson recently interviewed the person in question, now an adult, and report that Joan had in fact chosen to resume life as John at age fourteen. John,

now an adult, is married to a woman and, via adoption, is the father of her children. John and his mother report that in the Joan-years, John was never fully comfortable with a female gender identity. Indeed, Joan actively attempted to resist some of the treatment designed to ensure her female identity; for instance, when prescribed estrogens at age twelve, Joan secretly discarded the feminizing hormones. Depressed and unhappy at fourteen, Joan finally asked her father for the truth, and upon hearing it, "All of a sudden everything clicked. For the first time things made sense, and I understood who and what I was" (p. 300). At his request, John received a mastectomy at age fourteen, and for the next two years underwent several plastic surgery operations aimed at making his genitals look more masculine.[2]

Diamond and Sigmundson are chiefly interested in using this new data to conclude that "the evidence seems overwhelming that normal humans are not psychosocially neutral at birth but are, in keeping with their mammalian heritage, predisposed and biased to interact with environmental, familial, and social forces in either a male or female mode."[3] In other words, sexual nature is not infinitely pliable; biology matters.

In their report, Diamond and Sigmundson also take the opportunity of publication to comment on the problem of the lack of long-term follow-up of cases like these. But what is also troubling is the lack of ethical analysis around cases like this—particularly around cases of the medical treatment of intersexuality, a phenomenon many orders of magnitude more common than traumatic loss of the penis. While there have been some brief discussions of the ethics of deceiving intersex patients (that discussion is reviewed below), the medical treatment of people born intersexed has remained largely ignored by ethicists. Indeed, I can find little discussion in the literature of any of the ethical issues involved in "normalizing" children with allegedly "cosmetically offensive" anatomies. The underlying assumption grounding this silence appears to be that "normalizing" procedures are necessarily thoroughly beneficent and that they present no quandaries. This article seeks to challenge that assumption and to encourage interested parties to reconsider, from an ethical standpoint, the

Alice Domurat Dreger, "'Ambiguous Sex'—or Ambivalent Medicine? Ethical Issues in the Treatment of Intersexuality," *Hastings Center Report* 28, no. 3 (1998): 24-36.

dominant treatment protocols for children and adults with unusual genital anatomy.

Frequency of Intersexuality

Aside from the apparent presumption that "normalizing" surgeries are necessarily good, I suspect that ethicists have ignored the question of intersex treatment because like most people they assume the phenomenon of intersexuality to be exceedingly rare. It is not. But how common is it? The answer depends, of course, on how one defines it. Broadly speaking, intersexuality constitutes a range of anatomical conditions in which an individual's anatomy mixes key masculine anatomy with key feminine anatomy. One quickly runs into a problem, however, when trying to define "key" or "essential" feminine and masculine anatomy. In fact, any close study of sexual anatomy results in a loss of faith that there is a simple, "natural" sex distinction that will not break down in the face of certain anatomical, behavioral, or philosophical challenges.[4]

Sometimes the phrase "ambiguous genitalia" is substituted for "intersexuality," but this does not solve the problem of frequency, because we still are left struggling with the question of what should count as "ambiguous." (How small must a baby's penis be before it counts as "ambiguous"?) For our purposes, it is simplest to put the question of frequency pragmatically: How often do physicians find themselves unsure which gender to assign at birth? One 1993 gynecology text estimates that "in approximately 1 in 500 births, the sex is doubtful because of the external genitalia."[5] I am persuaded by more recent, well-documented literature that estimates the number to be roughly 1 in 1,500 live births.[6]

The frequency estimate goes up dramatically, however, if we include all children born with what some physicians consider cosmetically "unacceptable" genitalia. Many technically nonintersexed girls are born with "big" clitorises, and many technically nonintersexed boys are born with hypospadic penises in which the urethral opening is found somewhere other than the very tip of the penis.

Historical Background

I came to this topic as an historian and philosopher of science. My initial interest was actually in learning how British and French medical and scientific men of the late nineteenth century dealt with human hermaphroditism. The late nineteenth century was a time when the alleged naturalness of European social sex borders was under serious challenge by feminists and homosexuals and by anthropological reports of sex roles in other cultures. I wanted to know what biomedical professionals did, at such a politically charged time, with those who *inadvertently* challenged anatomical sex borders.

The answer is that biomedical men tried their best to shore up the borders between masculinity and femininity.[7] Specifically, the experts honed in on the ovarian and testicular tissues and decided that these were the key to any body's sexual identity. The "true sex" of most individuals thus by definition settled nicely into one of the two great and preferred camps, no matter how confusing the rest of their sexual anatomies. People with testicular tissue but with some otherwise "ambiguous" anatomy were now labeled "male pseudo-hermaphrodites"—that is, "true" males. People with ovarian tissue but with some otherwise ambiguous anatomy were labeled "female pseudo-hermaphrodites"—"true" females.

By equating sex identity simply with gonadal tissue, almost every body could be shown really to be a "true male" or a "true female" in spite of mounting numbers of doubtful cases. Additionally, given that biopsies of gonads were not done until the 1910s and that Victorian medical men insisted upon histological proof of ovarian and testicular tissue for claims of "true hermaphroditism," the only "true hermaphrodites" tended to be dead and autopsied hermaphrodites.

Nevertheless, new technologies—specifically laparotomies and biopsies—in the 1910s made this approach untenable. It now became possible (and, by the standing rules, necessary) to label some living people as "true" hermaphrodites via biopsies, and disturbed physicians noted that no one knew what to do with such people. There was no place, socially or legally, for true hermaphrodites. Moreover, physicians found case after case of extremely feminine-looking and feminine-acting women who were shown upon careful analysis to have testes and no ovaries. The latter were cases of what today is called androgen-insensitivity syndrome (AIS), also known as testicular feminization syndrome. We now know that individuals with AIS (roughly 1/60,000[8]) have an XY ("male") chromosomal complement and testes, but their androgen receptors cannot "read" the masculinizing hormones their testes produce. Consequently, *in utero* and throughout their lives, their anatomy develops along apparently "feminine" pathways. AIS is often not discovered until puberty, when these girls do not menstruate and a gynecological examination reveals AIS. Women with AIS look and feel very much like "typical" women, and in a practical, social, legal, and everyday sense they are women, even though congenitally they have testes and XY chromosomes.

In the 1910s, physicians working with intersexuality realized that assigning these women to the male sex (because of their testes) or admitting living "true hermaphrodites" (because of their ovotestes) would only wreak social havoc. Consequently, in practice the medical profession moved away from a strict notion of gonadal "true sex" toward a pragmatic concept of "gender" and physicians began to focus their attentions on gender "reconstruction." Elaborate surgical and hormonal treatments have now been developed to make the sexual anatomy more believable, that is, more "typical" of the gender assigned by the physician.

Dominant Treatment Protocols

Thus the late twentieth century medical approach to intersexuality is based essentially on an anatomically strict psychosocial theory of gender identity. Contemporary theory, established and disseminated largely via the work of John Money[9] and endorsed by the American Academy of Pediatrics,[10] holds that gender identity arises primarily from psychosocial rearing (nurture), and not directly from biology (nature); that all children must have their gender identity fixed very early in life for a consistent, "successful" gender identity to form; that from very early in life the child's anatomy must match the "standard" anatomy for her or his gender; and that for gender identity to form psychosocially boys primarily require "adequate" penises with no vagina, and girls primarily require a vagina with no easily noticeable phallus.[11]

Note that this theory presumes that these rules *must* be followed if intersexual children are to achieve successful psychosocial adjustment appropriate to their assigned gender—that is, if they are to act like girls, boys, men, and women are "supposed" to act. The theory also by implication presumes that there are definite acceptable and unacceptable roles for boys, girls, men, and women, and that this approach *will* achieve successful psychosocial adjustment, at least far more often than any other approach.

Many parents, especially those unfamiliar with sex development, are bothered by their children's intersexed genitals and receptive to offers of "normalizing" medical treatments. Many also actively seek guidance about gender assignment and parenting practices. In

> **In the United States today, typically upon the identification of an "ambiguous" or intersexed baby teams of specialists are immediately assembled, and these teams of doctors decide to which sex/gender a given child will be assigned.**

the United States today, therefore, typically upon the identification of an "ambiguous" or intersexed baby teams of specialists (geneticists, pediatric endocrinologists, pediatric urologists, and so on) are immediately assembled, and these teams of doctors decide to which sex/gender a given child will be assigned. A plethora of technologies are then used to create and maintain that sex in as believable a form as possible, including, typically, surgery on the genitals, and sometimes later also on other "anomalous" parts like breasts in an assigned male; hormone monitoring and treatments to get a "cocktail" that will help and not contradict the decided sex (and that will avoid metabolic dangers); and fostering the conviction among the child's family and community that the child is indeed the sex decided—"psychosocial" rearing of the child according to the norms of the chosen sex. Doctors typically take charge of the first two kinds of activities and hope that the child's family and community will successfully manage the all-critical third.

Clinicians treating intersexuality worry that any confusion about the sexual identity of the child on the part of relatives will be conveyed to the child and result in enormous psychological problems, including potential "dysphoric" states in adolescence and adulthood. In an effort to forestall or end any confusion about the child's sexual identity, clinicians try to see to it that an intersexual's sex/gender identity is permanently decided by specialist doctors within forty-eight hours of birth. With the same goals in mind, many clinicians insist that parents of intersexed newborns be told that their ambiguous child *does* really have a male or female sex, but that the sex of their child has just not yet "finished" developing, and that the doctors will quickly figure out the "correct" sex and then help "finish" the sexual development. As the sociologist Suzanne Kessler noted in her ground-breaking sociological analysis of the current treatment of intersexuality, "the message [conveyed to these parents] . . . is that the trouble lies

---

Not surprisingly, feminists and intersexuals have

invariably objected to presumptions that there is a

"right" way to be a male and a "right" way to be a

female, and that children who challenge these

categories should be reconstructed to fit into them.

---

in the doctor's ability to determine the gender, not in the baby's gender per se."[12] In intersex cases, Ellen Hyun-Ju Lee concludes, "physicians present a picture of the 'natural sex,' either male or female, despite their role in actually constructing sex."[13]

Because of widespread acceptance of the anatomically strict psychosocial theory of treatment, the practical rules now adopted by most specialists in intersexuality are these: genetic males (children with Y chromosomes) must have "adequate" penises if they are to be assigned the male gender. When a genetic male is judged to have an "adequate" phallus size, surgeons may operate, sometimes repeatedly, to try to make the penis look more "normal." If their penises are determined to be "inadequate" for successful adjustment as males, they are assigned the female gender and reconstructed to look female. (Hence John to Joan.) In cases of intersexed children assigned the female sex/gender, surgeons may "carve a large phallus down into a clitoris" (primarily attempting to make the phallus invisible when standing), "create a vagina using a piece of colon" or other body parts, "mold labia out of what was a penis," remove any testes, and so on.[14]

Meanwhile, genetic females (that is, babies lacking a Y chromosome) born with ambiguous genitalia are declared girls—no matter how masculine their genitalia look. This is done chiefly in the interest of preserving these children's potential feminine reproduc-

tive capabilities and in bringing their anatomical appearance and physiological capabilities into line with that reproductive role. Consequently, these children are reconstructed to look female using the same general techniques as those used on genetically male children assigned a female role. Surgeons reduce "enlarged" clitorises so that they will not look "masculine." Vaginas are built or lengthened if necessary, in order to make them big enough to accept average-sized penises. Joined labia are separated, and various other surgical and hormonal treatments are directed at producing a believable and, it is hoped, fertile girl.

What are the limits of acceptability in terms of phalluses? Clitorises—meaning simply phalluses in children labeled female—are frequently considered too big if they exceed one centimeter in length.[15] Pediatric surgeons specializing in treating intersexuality consider "enlarged" clitorises to be "cosmetically offensive" in girls and therefore they subject these clitorises to surgical reduction meant to leave the organs looking more "feminine" and "delicate."[16] Penises—meaning simply phalluses in children labeled male—are often considered too small if the stretched length is less than 2.5 centimeters (about an inch). Consequently, genetically male children born at term "with a stretched penile length less than 2.5 [centimeters] are usually given a female sex assignment."[17]

Roughly the same protocols are applied to cases of "true" hermaphroditism (in which babies are born with testicular and ovarian tissue). Whereas the anatomico-materialist metaphysics of sex in the late nineteenth century made true hermaphrodites an enormous problem for doctors and scientists of that time, clinicians today believe that "true hermaphrodites" (like "pseudo-hermaphrodites") can be fairly easily retrofitted with surgery and other treatment to either an acceptable male or acceptable female sex/gender.

One of the troubling aspects of these protocols are the asymmetric ways they treat femininity and masculinity. For example, physicians appear to do far more to preserve the reproductive potential of children born with ovaries than that of children born with testes. While genetically male intersexuals often have infertile testes, some men with micropenis may be able to father children if allowed to retain their testes.[18]

Similarly, surgeons seem to demand far more for a penis to count as "successful" than for a vagina to count as such. Indeed, the logic behind the tendency to assign the female gender in cases of intersexuality rests not only on the belief that boys need "adequate" penises, but also upon the opinion among surgeons that "a functional vagina can be constructed in virtually everyone [while] a functional penis is a much more difficult goal."[19] This is true because much is expected of penises, especially by pediatric urologists, and very little of vaginas. For a penis to count as acceptable—"functional"—it must be or have the potential to be big enough to be readily recognizable as a "real" penis. In addition, the "functional" penis is generally expected to have the capability to become erect and flaccid at appropriate times, and to act as the conduit through which urine and semen are expelled, also at appropriate times. The urethral opening is expected to appear at the very tip of the penis. Typically, surgeons also hope to see penises that are "believably" shaped and colored.

Meanwhile, very little is needed for a surgically constructed vagina to count among surgeons as "functional." For a constructed vagina to be considered acceptable by surgeons specializing in intersexuality, it basically just has to be a hole big enough to fit a typical-sized penis. It is not required to be self-lubricating or even to be at all sensitive, and certainly does not need to change shape the way vaginas often do when women are sexually stimulated. So, for example, in a panel discussion of surgeons who treat intersexuality, when one was asked, "How do you define successful intercourse? How many of these girls actually have an orgasm, for example?" a member of the panel responded, "Adequate intercourse was defined as successful vaginal penetration."[20] All that is required is a receptive hole.

Indeed, clinicians treating intersex children often talk about vaginas in these children as the absence of a thing, as a space, as a "hole," a place to put something. That is precisely why opinion holds that "a functional vagina can be constructed in virtually everyone"—because it is relatively easy to construct an insensitive hole surgically. (It is not always easy to keep them open and uninfected.) The decision to "make" a female is therefore considered relatively fool-proof, while "the assignment of male sex of rearing is inevitably difficult and should only be undertaken by an experienced team" who can determine if a penis will be adequate for "successful" malehood.[21]

The Problem of "Normality"

The strict conception of "normal" sexual anatomy and "normal" sex behavior that underlies prevailing treatment protocols is arguably sexist in its asymmetrical treatment of reproductive potential and definitions of anatomical "adequacy." Additionally, as Lee and other critics of intersex treatment have noted, "[d]ecisions of gender assignment and subsequent surgical reconstruction are inseparable from the heterosexual matrix, which does not allow for other sexual practices or sexualities. Even within heterosexuality, a rich array of sexual practices is reduced to vaginal penetration."[22] Not surprisingly, feminists and intersexuals have invariably objected to these presumptions that there is a "right" way to be a male and a "right" way to be a female, and that children who challenge these categories should be reconstructed to fit into (and thereby reinforce) them.

Indeed, beside the important (and too often disregarded) philosophical-political issue of gender roles, there is a more practical one: how does one decide where to put the boundaries on acceptable levels of anatomical variation? Not surprisingly, the definition of genital "normality" in practice appears to vary among physicians. For example, at least one physician has set the minimum length of an "acceptable" penis at 1.5 centimeters.[23]

Indeed, at least two physicians are convinced (and have evidence) that any penis is a big enough penis for male adjustment, if the other cards are played right. Almost a decade ago Justine Schober (neé Reilly), a pediatric urologist now based at the Hamot Medical Center in Erie, Pennsylvania, and Christopher Woodhouse, a physician based at the Institute of Urology and St. George's Hospital in London, "interviewed and examined 20 patients with the primary diagnosis of micropenis in infancy" who were labeled and raised as boys. Of the post-pubertal (adult) subjects, "All patients were heterosexual and they had erections and orgasms. Eleven patients had ejaculations, 9 were sexually active and reported vaginal penetration, 7 were married or cohabitating and 1 had fathered a child."[24]

Schober and Woodhouse concluded that "a small penis does not preclude normal male role" and should not dictate female gender reassignment. They found that when parents "were well counseled about diagnosis they reflected an attitude of concern but not anxiety about the problem, and they did not convey anxiety to their children. They were honest and explained problems to the child and encouraged normality in behavior. We believe that this is the attitude that allows these children to approach their peers with confidence" (p. 571).

Ultimately, Schober and Woodhouse agreed with the tenet of the psychosocial theory that assumes that "the strongest influence for all patients [is] the parental attitude." But rather than making these children into girls and trying to convince the parents and children about their "real" feminine identity, Schober and Woodhouse found that "the well informed and open parents . . . produced more confident and better adjusted boys." We should note that these boys were not considered "typical" in their sex lives: "The group was characterized by an experimental attitude to [sexual] positions and methods. . . . The group appears to form close and long-lasting relationships. They often attribute partner sexual satisfaction and the stability of their relationships [with women partners] to their need to make extra effort including nonpenetrating techniques" (p. 571).

"Ambiguous" genitalia do not constitute a disease. They simply constitute a failure to fit a particular (and, at present, a particularly demanding) definition of normality. It is true that whenever a baby is born with "ambiguous" genitalia, doctors need to consider the situation a *potential* medical emergency because intersexuality may signal a potentially serious metabolic problem, namely congenital adrenal hyperplasia (CAH), which primarily involves an electrolyte imbalance and can result in "masculinization" of genetically female fetuses. Treatment of CAH may save a child's life and fertility. At the birth of an intersex child, therefore, adrenogenital syndrome must be quickly diagnosed and treated, or ruled out. Nonetheless, as medical texts advise, "of all the conditions responsible for ambiguous genitalia, congenital adrenal hyperplasia is the only one that is life-threatening in the newborn period," and even in cases of CAH the "ambiguous" genitalia themselves are not deadly.[25]

As with CAH's clear medical issue, doctors now also know that the testes of AIS patients have a relatively high rate of becoming cancerous, and therefore AIS needs to be diagnosed as early as possible so that the testes can be carefully watched or removed. However, the genitalia of an androgen-insensitive person are not diseased. Again, while unusual genitalia may *signal* a present or potential threat to health, in themselves they just *look* different. As we have seen, because of the perception of a "social emergency" around an intersex birth, clinicians take license to treat nonstandard genitalia as a medical problem requiring prompt correction. But as Suzanne Kessler sums up the situation, intersexuality does not threaten the patient's life; it threatens the patient's culture.

Psychological Health and the Problem of Deception

Clearly, in our often unforgiving culture intersexuality can also threaten the patient's psyche; that recognition is behind the whole treatment approach. Nevertheless, there are two major problems here. First, clinicians treating intersex individuals may be far more concerned with strict definitions of genital normality than intersexuals, their parents, and their acquaintances (including lovers). This is evidenced time and again, for example, in the John/Joan case:

> John recalls thinking, from preschool through elementary school, that physicians were more concerned with the appearance of Joan's genitals than was Joan. Her genitals were inspected at each visit to The Johns Hopkins Hospital. She thought they were making a big issue out of nothing, and they gave her no reason to think otherwise. John recalls thinking: "Leave me be and then I'll be fine. . . . It's bizarre. My genitals are not bothering me; I don't know why it is bothering you guys so much."[26]

Second, and more basically, it is not self-evident that a psychosocial problem should be handled medically or surgically. We do not attempt to solve the problems many dark-skinned children will face in our nation by lightening their skins. Similarly, Cheryl Chase has posed this interesting question: when a baby is born with a severely disfigured but largely functional arm, ought we quickly remove the arm and replace it with a possibly functional prosthetic, so that the parents and child experience less psychological trauma?[27] While it is true that genitals are more psychically charged than arms, genitals are also more easily and more often kept private, whatever their state. Quoting the ideas of Suzanne Kessler, the pediatric urologist Schober argues in a forthcoming work that "Surgery makes parents and doctors more comfortable, but counseling makes people comfortable too, and [it] is not irreversible." She continues: "Simply understanding and performing good surgeries is not sufficient. We must also know when to appropriately perform or withhold surgery. Our ethical duty as surgeons is to do no harm and to serve the best interests of our patient.

Sometimes, this means admitting that a 'perfect' solution may not be attainable."[28]

Ironically, rather than alleviating feelings of freakishness, in practice the way intersexuality is typically handled may actually produce or contribute to many intersexuals' feelings of freakishness. Many intersexuals look at these two facts: (1) they are subject, out of "compassion," to "normalizing" surgeries on an emergency basis without their personal consent, and (2) they are often not told the whole truth about their anatomical conditions and anatomical histories. Understandably, they conclude that their doctors see them as profound freaks and that they must really be freaks. H. Martin Malin, a professor in clinical sexology and a therapist at the Child and Family Institute in Sacramento, California, has found this to be a persistent theme running through intersexuals' medical experience:

> As I listened to [intersexuals'] stories, certain leit motifs began to emerge from the bits of their histories. They or their parents had little, if any, counseling. They thought they were the only ones who felt as they did. Many had asked to meet other patients whose medical histories were similar to their own, but they were stonewalled. They recognized themselves in published case histories, but when they sought medical records, were told they could not be located. . . .
>
> The patients I was encountering were not those whose surgeries resulted from life-threatening or seriously debilitating medical conditions. Rather, they had such diagnoses as "micropenis" or "clitoral hypertrophy." These were patients who were told—when they were told anything—that they had vaginoplasties or clitorectomies because of the serious psychological consequences they would have suffered if surgery had not been done. But the surgeries *had* been performed—and they were reporting longstanding psychological distress. They were certain that they would rather have had the "abnormal" genitals they [had] had than the "mutilated" genitals they were given. They were hostile and often vengeful towards the professionals who had been responsible for their care and sometimes, by transference, towards me. They were furious that they had been lied to.[29]

Given the lack of long-term follow-up studies it is unclear whether a majority of intersexuals wind up feeling this way, but even if only a small number do we must ask whether the practice of deception and "stonewalling" is essentially unethical.

Why would a physician ever withhold medical and personal historical information from an intersexed patient? Because she or he believes that the truth is too horrible or too complicated for the patient to handle. In a 1988 commentary in the *Hastings Center Report*, Brendan Minogue and Robert Tarszewski argued, for example, that a physician could justifiably withhold information from a sixteen-year-old AIS patient and/or her parents if he believed that the patient and/or family was likely to be incapable of handling the fact that she has testes and an XY chromosomal complement.[30] Indeed, this reasoning appears typical among clinicians treating intersexuality; many continue to believe that talking truthfully with intersexuals and their families will undo all the "positive" effects of the technological efforts aimed at covering up doubts. Thus despite intersexuals' and ethicists' published, repeated objections to deception, in 1995 a medical student was given a cash prize in medical ethics by the Canadian Medical Association for an article specifically advocating deceiving AIS patients (including adults) about the biological facts of their conditions. The prize-winner argued that "physicians who withhold information from AIS patients are not actually lying; they are only deceiving" because they *selectively withhold* facts about patients' bodies.[31]

But what this reasoning fails to appreciate is that hiding the facts of the condition will not necessarily prevent a patient and family from thinking about it. Indeed, the failure on the part of the doctor and family to talk honestly about the condition is likely only to add to feelings of shame and confusion. One woman with AIS in Britain writes, "Mine was a dark secret kept from all outside the medical profession (family included), but this [should] not [be] an option because it both increases the feelings of freakishness and reinforces the isolation."[32] Similarly, Martha Coventry, a woman who had her "enlarged" clitoris removed by surgeons when she was six, insists that "to be lied to as a child about your own body, to have your life as a sexual being so ignored that you are not even given the decency of an answer to your questions, is to have your heart and soul relentlessly undermined."[33]

Lying to a patient about his or her biological condition can also lead to a patient unintentionally taking unnecessary risks. As a young woman, Sherri Groveman, who has AIS, was told by her doctor that she had "twisted ovaries" and that they had to be removed; in fact, her testes were removed. At the age of twenty, "alone and scared in the stacks of a [medical] library," she discovered the truth of her condition. Then "the pieces finally fit together. But what fell apart was my relationship with both my family and physicians. It was not learning about chromosomes or testes that caused enduring trauma, it was discovering that I had been told lies. I avoided all medical care for the next 18 years. I have severe osteoporosis as a result of a lack of medical attention. This is what lies produce."[34]

It is not at all clear if all or even most of the intersex surgeries done today involve what would legally and ethically constitute informed consent.

Similarly, as B. Diane Kemp—"a social worker with more than 35 years' experience and a woman who has borne androgen insensitivity syndrome for 63 years"— notes, "secrecy as a method of handling troubling information is primitive, degrading, and often ineffective. Even when a secret is kept, its existence carries an aura of unease that most people can sense . . . Secrets crippled my life."[35]

Clearly, the notion that deception or selective truth-telling will protect the child, the family, or even the adult intersexual is extraordinarily paternalistic and naive, and, while perhaps well-intentioned, it goes against the dominant trend in medical ethics as those ethics guidelines are applied to other, similar situations. In what other realms are patients regularly not told the medical names for their conditions, even when they ask? As for the idea that physicians should not tell patients what they probably "can't handle," would a physician be justified in using this reasoning to avoid telling a patient she has cancer or AIDS?

In their commentary in the *Hastings Center Report* Sherman Elias and George Annas pointed out that a physician who starts playing with the facts of a patient's condition may well find himself forced to lie or admit prior deception. "Practically," Elias and Annas wrote, "it is unrealistic to believe that [the AIS patient] will not ultimately learn the details of her having testicular syndrome. From the onset it will be difficult to maintain the charade."[36] They also note that without being told the name and details of her condition any consent the AIS patient gives will not truly be "informed." As an attorney Groveman too argues "that informed consent laws mandate that the patient know the truth before physicians remove her testes or reconstruct her vagina."[37]

Informed Consent and Risk Assumption

It is not at all clear if all or even most of the intersex surgeries done today involve what would legally and ethically constitute informed consent. It appears that few intersexuals or their parents are educated, before they give consent, about the anatomically strict psychosocial model employed. The model probably ought to be described to parents as essentially unproven insofar as the theory remains unconfirmed by broad-based, long-term follow-up studies, and is directly challenged by cases like the John/Joan case as well as by ever-mounting "anecdotal" reports from former patients who, disenfranchised and labeled "lost to follow-up" by clinicians, have turned to the popular press and to public protest in order to be heard. Of course, as long as intersex patients are not consistently told the truth of their conditions, there is some question about whether satisfaction can be assessed with integrity in long-term studies.

At a finer level, many of the latest particular cosmetic surgeries being used on intersexed babies and children today remain basically unproven as well, and need to be described as such in consent agreements. For example, a team of surgeons from the Children's Medical Center and George Washington University Medical School has reported that in their preferred form of clitoral "recession" (done to make "big" clitorises look "right"), "the cosmetic effect is excellent" but "late studies with assessment of sexual gratification, orgasm, and general psychological adjustment are unavailable . . . and remain in question."[38] In fact the procedure may result in problems like stenosis, increased risk of infections, loss of feeling, and psychological trauma. (These risks characterize all genital surgeries.)

This lack of long-term follow-up is the case not only for clitoral surgeries; David Thomas, a pediatric urologist who practices at St. James's University Hospital and Infirmary in Leeds, England, recently noted the same problem with regard to early vaginal reconstructions: "So many of these patients are lost to follow-up. If we do this surgery in infancy and childhood, we have an obligation to follow these children up, to assess what we're doing."[39] There is a serious ethical problem here: risky surgeries are being performed as standard care and are not being adequately followed-up.[40]

The growing community of open adult intersexuals understandably question whether anyone should have either her ability to enjoy sex or her physical health risked without personal consent just because she has a clitoris, penis, or vagina that falls outside the standard deviation. Even if we *did* have statistics that showed that particular procedures "worked" a majority of the time we would have to face the fact that part of the time they would not work, and we need to ask whether that risk ought to be assumed on behalf of another person.

Beyond "Monster Ethics"

In a 1987 article on the ethics of killing one conjoined twin to save the other, George Annas suggested (but did not advocate) that one way to justify such a procedure would be to take "the monster approach." This approach would hold that conjoined twins are so grotesque, so pathetic, any medical procedure aimed at normalizing them would be morally justified.[41] Unfortunately, the present treatment of intersexuality in the U.S. seems to be deeply informed by the monster approach; ethical guidelines that would be applied in nearly any other medical situation are, in cases of intersexuality, ignored. Patients are lied to; risky procedures are performed without follow-up; consent is not fully informed; autonomy and health are risked because of unproven (and even disproven) fears that atypical anatomy will lead to psychological disaster. Why? Perhaps because sexual anatomy is not treated like the rest of human anatomy, or perhaps because we simply assume that any procedure which "normalizes" an "abnormal" child is merciful. Whatever the reason, the medical treatment of intersexuality and other metabolically benign, cosmetically unusual anatomies needs deep and immediate attention.

We can readily use the tools of narrative ethics to gain insight into practices surrounding intersexuality. There are now available many autobiographies of adult intersexuals.[42] Like that of John/Joan, whether or not they are characteristic of long-term outcomes these autobiographies raise serious questions about the dominant treatment protocols.

Narrative ethics also suggests that we use our imaginations to think through the story of the intersexual, to ask ourselves, if we were born intersexed, what treatment we would wish to have received. Curious about what adult nonintersexuals would have chosen for themselves, Suzanne Kessler polled a group of college students regarding their feelings on the matter. The women were asked, "Suppose you had been born with a larger than normal clitoris and it would remain larger than normal as you grew to adulthood. Assuming that the physicians recommended surgically reducing your clitoris, under what circumstances would you have wanted your parents to give them permission to do it?" In response,

> About a fourth of the women indicated they would not have wanted a clitoral reduction under *any* circumstance. About half would have wanted their clitoris reduced *only* if the larger than normal clitoris caused health problems. Size, for them, was not a factor. The remaining forth of the sample *could* imagine wanting their clitoris reduced if it were larger than normal, but *only* if having the surgery would *not* have resulted in a reduction in pleasurable sensitivity.[43]

Meanwhile, in this study, "the men were asked to imagine being born with a smaller than normal penis and told that physicians recommended phallic reduction and a female gender assignment." In response,

> All but one man indicated they would not have wanted surgery under any circumstance. The remaining man indicated that if his penis were 1 cm. or less *and he were going to be sterile,* he would have wanted his parents to give the doctors permission to operate and make him a female. (p. 36)

Kessler is cautious to note that we need more information to assess this data fully, but it does begin to suggest that given the choice most people would reject genital cosmetic surgery for themselves.

As an historian, I also think we need to consider the historical and cultural bases for genital conformity practices, and realize that most people in the U.S. demonstrate little tolerance for practices in other cultures that might well be considered similar. I am, of course, talking about the recent passage of federal legislation prohibiting physicians from performing "circumcision" on the genitalia of girls under the age of eighteen, *whether or not the girls consent or personally request the procedure.* African female genital "cutting" typically involves, in part, excision of the clitoral tissue so that most or all clitoral sensation will be lost. While proponents of this traditional female genital "cutting" have insisted this practice is an important cultural tradition—analogous to male circumcision culturally—advocates of the U.S. law insist it is barbaric and violates human rights. Specifically, in the federal legislation passed in October 1996 Congress declared that: "Except as provided in subsection (b), whoever knowingly circumcises, excises, or infibulates the whole or any part of the labia majora or labia minora or clitoris of another person who has not attained the age of 18 years shall be fined under this title or imprisoned not more than 5 years, or both."[44]

Subsection "b" specifies that: "A surgical operation is not a violation of this section if the operation is (1) necessary to the health of the person on whom it is performed, and is performed by a person licensed in the place of its performance as a medical practitioner; or (2) performed on a person in labor or who has just given birth and is performed for medical purposes connected with that labor or birth."

Surgeons treating intersexuality presumably would argue that the procedures they perform on the genitals of girls (which clearly include excision of parts of the clitoris) are indeed "necessary to the health of the person on whom it is performed." While it is easy to condemn the African practice of female genital mutilation as a barbaric custom that violates human rights, we should recognize that in the United States medicine's prevailing response to intersexuality is largely about genital conformity and the "proper" roles of the sexes. Just as we find it necessary to protect the rights and well-being of African girls, we must now consider the hard questions of the rights and well-being of children born intersexed in the United States.

As this paper was in process, the attention paid by the popular media and by physicians to the problems with the dominant clinical protocols increased dramatically, and many more physicians and ethicists have recently come forward to question those protocols. Diamond and Sigmundson have helpfully proposed tentative new "guidelines for dealing with persons with ambiguous genitalia."[45]

As new guidelines are further developed, it will be critical to take seriously two tasks. First, as I have argued above, intersexuals must not be subjected to different ethical standards from other people simply because they are intersexed. Second, the experiences and advice of adult intersexuals must be solicited and taken into consideration. It is incorrect to claim, as I have heard several clinicians do, that the complaints of adult intersexuals are irrelevant because they were subjected to "old, unperfected" surgeries. Clinicians have too often retreated to the mistaken belief that improved treatment technologies (for example, better surgical techniques) will eliminate ethical dilemmas surrounding intersex treatment. There is far more at issue than scar tissue and loss of sensation from unperfected surgeries.

Acknowledgments

The author wishes to thank Aron Sousa, Cheryl Chase, Michael Fisher, Elizabeth Gretz, Daniel Federman, the members of the Enhancement Technologies and Human Identity Working Group, and Howard Brody, Libby Bogdan-Lovis, and other associates of the Center for Ethics and Humanities in the Life Sciences at Michigan State University for their comments on this work.

This article is adapted from *Hermaphrodites and the Medical Invention of Sex*, by Alice Domurat Dreger, to be published this month by Harvard University Press. Copyright © 1998 by Alice Domurat Dreger. All rights reserved.

References

1. Milton Diamond and H. Keith Sigmundson, "Sex Reassignment at Birth: Long-Term Review and Clinical Implications," *Archives of Pediatrics and Adolescent Medicine* 15 (1997): 298-304.

2. For a more in-depth biography, see John Colapinto, "The True Story of John/Joan," *Rolling Stone*, 11 December 1997, pp. 55ff.

3. Diamond and Sigmundson, "Sex Reassignment," p. 303.

4. I discuss this at length in Dreger, *Hermaphrodites and the Medical Invention of Sex* (Cambridge, Mass.: Harvard University Press, 1998); see especially prologue and chap. 1.

5. See Ethel Sloane, *Biology of Women*, 3d ed. (Albany: Delmar Publishers, 1993), p. 168. According to Denis Grady, a study of over 6,500 women athletes competing in seven different international sports competitions showed an incidence of intersexuality of one in 500 women, but unfortunately Grady does not provide a reference to the published data from that study (Denise Grady, "Sex Test," *Discover*, June 1992, pp. 78-82). That sampled population should not simply be taken as representative of the whole population, but this number is certainly higher than most people would expect.

6. Anne Fausto-Sterling, *Body Building: How Biologists Construct Sexuality* (New York: Basic Books, forthcoming 1999), chap. 2; Fausto-Sterling, "How Dimorphic Are We?" *American Journal of Human Genetics* (forthcoming); and personal communication. The highest modern-day estimate for frequency of sexually ambiguous births comes from John Money, who has posited that as many as 4 percent of live births today are of "intersexed" individuals (cited in Anne Fausto-Sterling, "The Five Sexes," *The Sciences* 33 [1993]: 20-25). Money's categories tend to be exceptionally broad and poorly defined, and not representative of what most medical professionals today would consider to be "intersexuality."

7. Dreger, *Hermaphrodites*, chaps. 1-5; for a summary of the scene in Britain in the late-nineteenth century, see Dreger, "Doubtful Sex: The Fate of the Hermaphrodite in Victorian Medicine," *Victorian Studies* 38 (1995): 335-69.

8. Stuart R. Kupfer, Charmain A. Quigley, and Frank S. French, "Male Pseudohermaphroditism," *Seminars in Perinatology* 16 (1992): 319-31, at 325.

9. For summaries and critiques of Money's work on intersexuality, see especially: Cheryl Chase, "Affronting Reason," in *Looking Queer: Image and Identity in Lesbian, Bisexual, Gay and Transgendered Communities*, ed. D. Atkins (Binghamton, N.Y.: Haworth, 1998); "Hermaphrodites with Attitude: Mapping the Emergence of Intersex Political Activism," *GLQ* 4, no. 2 (1998): 189-211; Anne Fausto-Sterling, "How to Build a Man," in *Science and Homosexualities*, ed. Vernon A. Rosario (New York: Rout-

ledge, 1997), pp. 219-25; and Ellen Hyun-Ju Lee, "Producing Sex: An Interdisciplinary Perspective on Sex Assignment Decisions for Intersexuals" (Senior Thesis, Brown University, 1994).

10. American Academy of Pediatrics (Section on Urology), "Timing of Elective Surgery on the Genitalia of Male Children with Particular Reference to the Risks, Benefits, and Psychological Effects of Surgery and Anesthesia," *Pediatrics* 97, no. 4 (1996): 590-94.

11. For example, see Patricia K. Donahoe, "The Diagnosis and Treatment of Infants with Intersex Abnormalities," *Pediatric Clinics of North America* 34 (1987): 1333-48.

12. Suzanne J. Kessler, "The Medical Construction of Gender: Case Management of Intersexed Infants," *Signs* 16 (1990): 3-26; compare the advice given by Cynthia H. Meyers-Seifer and Nancy J. Charest, "Diagnosis and Management of Patients with Ambiguous Genitalia," *Seminars in Perinatology* 16 (1992): 332-39.

13. Lee, "Producing Sex," p. 45.

14. Melissa Hendricks, "Is It a Boy or a Girl?" *John Hopkins Magazine* (November, 1993): 10-16, p. 10.

15. Barbara C. McGillivray, "The Newborn with Ambiguous Genitalia," *Seminars in Perinatology* 16 (1991): 365-68, p. 366.

16. Kurt Newman, Judson Randolph, and Kathryn Anderson, "The Surgical Management of Infants and Children with Ambiguous Genitalia," *Annals of Surgery* 215 (1992): 644-53, pp. 651 and 647.

17. Meyers-Seifer and Charest, "Diagnosis and Management," p. 337. See also Kupfer, Quigley, and French, "Male Pseudohermaphroditism," p. 328; Rajkumar Shah, Morton M. Woolley, and Gertrude Costin, "Testicular Feminization: The Androgen Insensitivity Syndrome," *Journal of Pediatric Surgery* 27 (1992): 757-60, p. 757.

18. Justine Schober, personal communication; for data on this, see Justine M. Reilly and C.R.J. Woodhouse, "Small Penis and the Male Sexual Role," *Journal of Urology* 142 (1989): 569-71.

19. Robin J.O. Catlin, *Appleton & Lange's Review for the US-MILE Step 2* (East Norwalk, Connecticut: Appleton & Lange, 1993), p. 49.

20. See the comments of John P. Gearhart in M. M. Bailez, John P. Gearhart, Claude Migeon, and John Rock, "Vaginal Reconstruction After Initial Construction of the External Genitalia in Girls with Salt-Wasting Adrenal Hyperplasia," *Journal of Urology* 148 (1992): 680-84, p. 684.

21. Kupfer, Quigley, and French, "Male Pseudohermaphroditism," p. 328.

22. Lee, "Producing Sex," p. 27.

23. See Donahoe, "The Diagnosis and Treatment of Infants with Intersex Abnormalities."

24. Reilly and Woodhouse, "Small Penis," p. 569.

25. Patricia K. Donahoe, David M. Powell, and Mary M. Lee, "Clinical Management of Intersex Abnormalities," *Current Problems in Surgery* 28 (1991): 515-79, p. 540.

26. Diamond and Sigmundson, "Sex Reassignment," pp. 300-301.

27. Cheryl Chase, personal communication.

28. Quoted in Justine M. Schober, "Long-Term Outcome of Feminizing Genitoplasty for Intersex," *Pediatric Surgery and Urology: Long Term Outcomes,* ed. Pierre D. E. Mouriquand (Philadelphia: William B. Saunders, forthcoming).

29. H. M. Malin, personal communication of 1 January 1997 to Justine M. Schober, quoted in Schober, "Long-Term Outcome."

30. Brendan P. Minogue and Robert Taraszewski, "The Whole Truth and Nothing But the Truth?" (Case Study), *Hastings Center Report* 18, no. 5 (1988): 34-35.

31. Anita Natarajan, "Medical Ethics and Truth Telling in the Case of Androgen Insensitivity Syndrome," *Canadian Medical Association Journal* 154 (1996): 568-70. (For responses to Natarajan's recomendations by AIS women and a partner of an AIS woman, see *Canadian Medical Association Journal* 154 [1996]: 1829-33.)

32. Anonymous, "Be Open and Honest with Sufferers," *British Medical Journal* 308 (1994): 1041-42.

33. Martha Coventry, "Finding the Words," *Chrysalis: The Journal of Transgressive Gender Identities* 2 (1997): 27-30.

34. Sherri A. Groveman, "Letter to the Editor," *Canadian Medical Association Journal* 154 (1996): 1829, 1832.

35. B. Diane Kemp, "Letter to the Editor," *Canadian Medical Association Journal* 154 (1996): 1829.

36. Sherman Elias and George J. Annas, "The Whole Truth and Nothing But the Truth?" (Case Study), *Hastings Center Report* 18, no. 5 (1988): 35-36, p. 35.

37. Groveman, "Letter to the Editor," p. 1829.

38. Newman, Randolph, and Anderson, "Surgical Management," p. 651.

39. "Is Early Vaginal Reconstruction Wrong for Some Intersex Girls?" *Urology Times* (February 1997): 10-12.

40. Intersexuals are understandably tired of hearing that "long-term follow-up data is needed" while the surgeries continued to occur. On this, see especially the guest commentary by David Sandberg, "A Call for Clinical Research," *Hermaphrodites with Attitude* (Fall/Winter 1995-1996): 8-9, and the many responses of intersexuals in the same issue.

41. George J. Annas, "Siamese Twins: Killing One to Save the Other" (At Law), *Hastings Center Report* 17, no. 2 (1987): 27-29.

42. See, for example, M. Morgan Holmes, "Medical Politics and Cultural Imperatives: Intersex Identities beyond Pathology and Erasure" (M.A. Thesis, York University, 1994); Chase, "Hermaphrodites with Attitude"; Geoffrey Cowley, "Gender Limbo," *Newsweek,* 19 May 1997, pp. 64-66; Natalie Angier, "New Debate Over Surgery on Genitals," *New York Times,* 13 May 1997; "Special Issue: Intersexuality," *Chrysalis: The Journal of Transgressive Gender Identities* 2 (1997). Intersexual autobiographies are also from peer support groups, including the Intersex Society of North America. For information about support groups see the special issue of *Chrysalis,* vol. 2, 1997.

43. Suzanne J. Kessler, "Meanings of Genital Variability," *Chrysalis: The Journal of Transgressive Gender Identities* 2 (1997): 33-37.

44. Omnibus Consolidated Appropriations Bill, H.R. 3610, P.L. 104-208.

45. Milton Diamond and Keith Sigmundson, "Management of Intersexuality: Guidelines for Dealing with Persons with Ambiguous Genitalia," *Archives of Pediatric and Adolescent Medicine* 151 (1997): 1046-50.

[12]

The New NIH and FDA Medical Research Policies: Targeting Gender, Promoting Justice

Karen L. Baird
Purchase College, State University of New York

Abstract   The National Institutes of Health (NIH) and Food and Drug Administration (FDA) have both recently revised their policies regarding the inclusion of women in clinical trials. Pressured by women's health activists and members of Congress, the NIH has vastly improved its policies; it now requires that women and minorities be included in clinical trials and that an analysis of gender and racial differences be performed. The FDA policy states that women and men should be included in clinical trials if both would receive the drug when marketed and that it expects a gender analysis to be performed. The FDA also lifted its 1977 ban on including women of childbearing potential in the early phases of drug studies. Analyzing these NIH and FDA policies according to a gender justice framework, I find that the NIH has moved significantly toward the institution of gender justice as it applies to medical research policies and that the FDA has taken only small steps toward this goal and lags behind the NIH.

For years, women have been excluded from or underrepresented in clinical research studies (IOM 1994; U.S. GAO 1990; Kinney 1981; LaRosa et al. 1995; Rothenberg 1996; but also see Kadar 1994).[1] But why have

This research was funded, in part, by the American Association of University Women (AAUW) Educational Foundation. The author held an American Fellowship. The author wishes to thank Mark Peterson and the anonymous reviewers for their helpful comments and suggestions.

  1. Clinical research or clinical study refers to "any investigation or analysis of a question, process, or phenomenon that has, or is presumed to have, some immediate or future clinical relevance" (IOM 1994, vol. 1: 95). In this article, the focus will be on clinical trials that can be defined as "experiment[s] designed to assess the safety and efficacy of one treatment relative to another in comparable groups of human beings treated according to a given protocol and observed for change in an outcome or measure or for occurrence of some event" (IOM 1994, vol. 1: 96). Furthermore, in a stricter sense, the term *clinical* refers to the subset of trials that are done in a clinical setting and based on outcome measures with obvious clinical implications (ibid.).

Journal of Health Politics, Policy and Law, Vol. 24, No. 3, June 1999. Copyright © 1999 by Duke University Press.

women been excluded or underrepresented?[2] Because of their reproductive capabilities, women or their potential fetuses have been viewed as needing protection from the possible harms of research. This concern for fetal protection is, in the words of one author, "the result of intellectual lassitude, defensive legalism, and a misplaced sense of obligation" (Moreno 1994: 29).

Though the problem of underrepresentation had been well documented for more than a decade, it was not until the early 1990s that federal policies governing women and medical research were revised. Pressured by women's health advocates and members of Congress, the NIH and the FDA revised their policies regarding the inclusion of women in research funded, supported, or approved by the respective institutions.

The purpose of this article is to examine the problem of women and medical research and the recently enacted policies. Because I, like others, argue that the past research practices were unjust, a framework of gender justice is employed here to analyze the recent policy efforts. I also assess the extent to which policy changes have eliminated bias and instituted justice for women with regard to research funded, supported, or approved by the NIH and FDA In other words, have the new policies rectified the past problems in medical and drug research and instituted gender justice?

To answer this question, a number of steps are taken here. First, background information regarding the recent historical context of medical and drug research in the U.S. is presented. Second, a framework of gender justice is introduced. Because we need some type of normative criteria by which to judge policies, and since what constitutes gender justice or gender equity is neither clear nor agreed upon, standards and questions that we can ask of public policies to assess their treatment of women are developed. Third, the FDA and NIH policies are judged according to the principles of gender justice in an effort to assess the manner and extent to which they have eliminated bias and instituted justice for women.

---

2. Some debate exists regarding the issue of the exclusion or underrepresentation of women in clinical trials. Specifically, the debate centers on the issue of what constitutes underrepresentation, and thus, in the converse, what constitutes adequate representation. See the IOM's report (vol. 1, 1994), pp. 47–70, for a full discussion of this issue.

History of Women and Medical Research:
The NIH and the FDA

Women and Medical Research

Women have been excluded from medical research since the late 1960s and early 1970s. As Tracey Johnson and Elizabeth Fee (1994) point out, this exclusion arose from a variety of political, social, and legal forces. Emphasis on the need to protect all subjects arose in the 1950s and 1960s in response to revelations of abuse of research participants by medical personnel. But particularly for women, cases of deformed infants resulting from drugs taken during pregnancy raised concerns about including women in drug trials. In the 1960s, many women took thalidomide, a drug used to prevent early miscarriages, and the drug caused over 1,000 birth defects. Inadequate research standards and failure of the manufacturer to acknowledge early evidence of side effects were blamed. Also, in the 1960s and early 1970s, problems with the drug diethylstilbestrol (DES) came to light. DES is a drug that women took in the 1940s and 1950s to prevent miscarriages; about twenty years later, many daughters of women who had taken the drug developed reproductive anomalies and had an increased risk of developing cancer of the vagina. From litigation brought by these daughters, the pharmaceutical companies incurred (and are still incurring) substantial costs. So in the 1960s, companies became more and more concerned about the liability issues surrounding the testing of drugs on women.

Furthermore, women's rights were sometimes abused and ignored. In a study of the side effects of oral contraceptives, dummy pills were given to women who sought treatment to prevent further pregnancies (Goldzieher et al. 1971a, 1971b). None of the women were told they were participating in the study, none gave their consent, and none were told they were given placebos; significantly, most of these women were poor Mexican Americans. There are also ethical questions about the initial testing of the oral contraceptive pill that was carried out on poor Puerto Rican women (Zimmerman et al. 1980).

People belonging to minority groups have historically been viewed as more expendable and used in dangerous and unhealthy research. One famous example is the Tuskegee syphilis experiment of four hundred African American males. From 1932 to 1972, the Public Health Service conducted a study of the effects of untreated syphilis on these men. Poor, illiterate, southern black men were watched for forty years to obtain data on the progression of syphilis and as many as one hundred

534   Journal of Health Politics, Policy and Law

men died (Jones 1981).[3] Most of the men were never told they had the disease, no drugs or treatments were given or tested in this experiment, and, in fact, most of the subjects did not even know that they were participating in the trial.

In 1974, the National Research Act was passed calling for the establishment of a National Commission to Protect Human Subjects to identify ethical principles and to develop guidelines for research. Political debates over abortion, artificial reproductive technologies, and fetal tissue research also raged at the time (Johnson and Fee 1994). With the legalization of abortion in *Roe v. Wade* in 1973, the antiabortion movement, with its emphasis on fetal rights, grew. Whether written policy or not, excluding women from most medical research became the established norm in the medical community.

In 1981, Elvin Kinney documented women's underrepresentation in drug trials and the problems associated with such exclusion. The article notes how the FDA's policy of excluding women of childbearing potential in early drug trial testing also led to their exclusion in later testing phases. The article received little attention and reflected the consensus of the time about the need for women, or their potential fetuses, to be protected from the potential harms of research.

NIH

In 1986, an NIH Advisory Committee on Women's Health Issues was established and announced a policy that *"urged* grant applicants to consider the inclusion of women in the study populations of all clinical research efforts" (U.S. GAO 1990: 3; emphasis mine). It also stated that if women were not to be included, a clear rationale for their exclusion needed to be given, and that researchers should evaluate gender differences in their studies. But despite these directives, little changed within the NIH or the research proposals it funded.

The real catalyst of the current surge in attention to women's health research was a 1990 General Accounting Office (GAO) report on the progress of the 1986–1987 NIH policy (Auerbach 1992). By this time, the women's health movement had gained force and was pressuring Congress for changes in many aspects of health care policy. A group of activists, who in 1990 formed the Society for the Advancement of

---

3. And as Karen Rothenberg (1996) notes, despite all the attention given to the Tuskegee experiment since the 1970s, little concern has been expressed about the women who were the sexual partners of the men exposed to syphilis.

Women's Health Research (SAWHR) and were led by Florence Haseltine of the NIH, began working with the Congressional Caucus for Women's Issues (CCWI). Haseltine, director of the Center for Population Research and a gynecologist herself, became involved because she wanted more gynecologists and gynecological research at NIH. Rep. Patricia Schroeder (D-CO) was interested in more contraceptive research; since abortion politics dominated most issues of women's health at the time, she wanted to shift the focus toward contraceptive research. Contraception should be an issue that could unite the various forces, Schroeder thought (Primmer 1998). At this time, Rep. Mary Rose Oakar (D-OH) and the National Breast Cancer Coalition (NBCC), led by Fran Visco, were working to increase funding for research on the prevention and cure of breast cancer. The AIDS activists had successfully fought for many changes in research funding and policies and they provided a model on which the women's health care activists could build.

When these women turned their attention toward the NIH and clinical research on women, they were quite disturbed by what they found. A major study of the effects of aspirin in reducing heart attacks used 20,000 males and no females; a study on heart disease risk factors was conducted on 13,000 men and not one female; and the National Institute on Aging's largest study excluded women for its first twenty years (Schroeder and Snowe 1994). And since NIH had a policy regarding the inclusion of women, this appeared to be an effective place to begin. The CCWI worked with Rep. Henry Waxman (D-CA), chair of the Energy and Commerce's Subcommittee on Health and the Environment, in requesting the GAO report. The report came to be the "smoking gun" for the government's neglect of women's health research (Schroeder and Snowe 1994: 95).

The CCWI and Henry Waxman scheduled a hearing for 18 June 1990 in which Mark Nadel of the GAO testified. The media were notified of the event and they gave it tremendous coverage. The 1990 GAO report noted that little progress had been made in carrying out the 1986–1987 policy: the new directive had neither been well communicated nor well understood within the NIH and the scientific community, it had been applied inconsistently, and NIH had been very slow to implement it. In fact, the application booklet used by most NIH grant applicants was not even updated to include the new information regarding gender until April 1991, over four years after the policy was first developed. Furthermore, the GAO report stated that the component of gender analysis—the evaluation of gender differences in a study—had not been implemented, and it was impossible to determine the impact of the policy as a whole because implementation began so late and no data had been kept on the gender composition of funded studies. Nadel testified that, as a result, significant gaps in knowledge exist regarding diseases that affect both men and women (U.S. GAO 1990). Following the hearing, articles entitled "In Research, Women Don't Matter" (Berney 1990), "Wanted: Single, White Male for Medical Research" (Dresser 1992), and "Report Says NIH Ignores Own Rules on Including Women in Research" (Jaschik 1990) were published all over the country.

Women's health activists argued that these NIH practices were discriminatory and unjust. Many contended that the NIH policies were biased against women and that women received substandard health care diagnosis and treatment; that they were systematically excluded from clinical drug trials; and that they were shortchanged and neglected. Patricia Schroeder and Olympia Snowe note, "We were outraged that women, who pay their fair share of tax dollars in this country, derived little benefit from these important federally funded research studies" (1994: 95). Others labeled this problem one of gender inequity and argued that women's autonomy and ability to give informed consent were not being respected because they were being told not to participate instead of being allowed to decide for themselves. Rep. Marilyn Lloyd (D-TN) concludes, "The result is unconscionable in a nation of such wealth and that professes equality for all of its people" (U.S. Congress 1990: 1).

So throughout the early 1990s, legislative packages were introduced in Congress that addressed women's health concerns regarding research, care, and prevention issues; these were coupled into a package called the Women's Health Equity Act. Initially, legislation regarding the NIH was vetoed by President Bush because of the inclusion of provisions regarding fetal tissue research. In 1990, the Office of Research on Women's Health (ORWH) was established within the NIH and was given the mandate to ensure that research supported by the NIH includes important issues that pertain to women's health, to ensure appropriate participation of women in clinical research that is supported by the NIH,[4] and to increase the participation of women in biomedical careers.

---

4. There are two important issues regarding women and medical research. One is the exclusion or underrepresentation of women in all medical studies of diseases common to women and men, and in studies of drugs or treatment for such diseases. The other issue is the study of diseases or conditions, such as breast cancer and osteoporosis, that only occur or more commonly occur in women. In 1987, only 13.5 percent of the NIH budget was devoted to the broadly defined category of women's health issues (Berney 1990), but this number is contested by some as constituting more than what men's issues receive (Kadar 1994).

In 1991, the NIH also established the Women's Health Initiative (WHI), a fourteen-year, $625 million effort to study approximately 150,000 women at forty-five clinical centers across the United States. The WHI is the largest research study ever funded by the NIH. Furthermore, after the election of President Clinton, the NIH Revitalization Act was signed into law in 1993. Among other things, it authorized additional funding for breast, ovarian, and other reproductive cancers and for osteoporosis research.

As part of this 1993 NIH Act and because of internal NIH policy changes, medical research policies regarding women and minorities were drastically revamped in the early 1990s. Now all applications, both for intramural and extramural research, are *required* to include women and minorities as research subjects.[5] "In conducting or supporting clinical research for purposes of this title . . . the director of NIH shall . . . ensure that—(A) women are included as subjects in each project of such research; and (B) members of minority groups are included as subjects in such research" (Pub. L. No 103–43, sec. 131, sec. 492[B][a], 107 Stat. 122, 123). The act also requires that a valid analysis be carried out to show whether the variables being studied affect the various subpopulations in different ways. Exemptions are allowed in cases where the research is inappropriate with respect to the health of the subjects, the purpose of the research, or other circumstances determined by the NIH. The 1993 act also requires that a "data system for the collection, storage, analysis, retrieval, and dissemination of information regarding research on women's health that is conducted or supported by the national research institutes" be established (IOM 1994, vol. 1: 68). In 1994, the NIH issued new guidelines for the inclusion of women in medical research in accordance with the 1993 act (U.S. DHHS 1994a).

The NIH also published an Outreach Notebook, which is not law but was published in an effort to help researchers understand and implement the new guidelines. It offers suggestions for deciding how to include women and minorities and recruitment strategies for obtaining such subjects. The ORWH held conferences with institutional review board (IRB) chairs in 1994 and again in 1996 to discuss and assess the progress of the implementation of the guidelines.[6] Also, as of February 1996, the ORWH

---

5. Extramural research is research performed outside of the NIH at other institutions, usually universities. Intramural research is research the NIH does in-house at its own facilities in Bethesda, Maryland.

6. An IRB is a local administrative body established to protect the rights and welfare of human research subjects participating in studies at the institution under the IRB's jurisdiction. All research involving human subjects must be approved by an IRB and it has the authority to

538   Journal of Health Politics, Policy and Law

had 5,000 clinical studies in its database and had issued preliminary results about the implementation and success regarding the inclusion of women and minorities in clinical research supported by the NIH.

Presently, the NIH will not fund "any grant, cooperative agreement, or contract or support any intramural project to be conducted or funded in fiscal year 1995 and thereafter which does not comply" with the new policy regarding the inclusion of women and minorities. Furthermore, researchers must report annually on the gender and ethnicity of the enrolled research participants (U.S. DHHS 1994a: 14509).

The FDA

Before reviewing the FDA policies regarding gender and research, I would like to point out the differences between the NIH and the FDA. The NIH funds medical research; as with any grant process, researchers submit detailed proposals that are reviewed and deemed fundable or not fundable, as judged by various criteria. The FDA does not fund research. It issues guidelines to aid organizations, typically pharmaceutical companies, involved in the evaluation of new drugs and medical devices for FDA approval. FDA guidelines specify information that they expect new applications to include.[7] In addition, the NIH conducts its own research —intramural research; the FDA does not. The FDA is only a regulatory agency with a mission of ensuring that drugs and medical devices are safe and effective. The agency sets parameters for the studies it reviews as part of the approval process for a new drug, but it does not usually ask that studies on certain drugs or devices be performed.

The FDA's 1977 guidelines stated that pregnant women and women who are at risk for becoming pregnant should be excluded from Phase 1 studies (U.S. DHEW 1977). They further recommended that women of

---

approve, require modifications, or disapprove research activities (IOM, vol. 1, 1994: 131). IRBs are composed of local scientists, ethicists, and nonscientists.

7. FDA approval for a new drug is a long, involved process. After preclinical testing (testing in laboratory and in animals), sponsors submit an investigational new drug (IND) application to the FDA. This application includes the plan for Phase 1 studies on humans. If approved by the FDA and a local IRB, clinical trials begin. Phase 1 involves twenty to eighty healthy individuals to determine safety and dosage of the drug. Phase 2 involves 100 to 300 subjects to evaluate effectiveness and to look for any side effects. Phase 3 uses 1,000 to 3,000 subjects to verify effectiveness and to monitor adverse reactions from long-term use. Each phase lasts one, two, and three years respectively. After this, a new drug application is filed with the FDA and the review/approval process begins. If the drug is approved, Phase 4 studies begin, which are post-marketing testing studies (Wierenga and Eaton 1993).

childbearing potential be excluded from large-scale clinical trials, which includes Phase 3 studies, until the FDA animal reproduction tests have been performed (IOM 1994, vol. 1: 137). Then, "if adequate information of efficacy and relative safety has been amassed during Phase 2, women of childbearing potential *may* be included in further studies" (U.S. DHEW 1977: 15, emphasis mine). *Childbearing potential* is broadly defined as a "premenopausal female capable of becoming pregnant" (15). Included in this category are women who are using contraception, celibate women, lesbians, and women whose male partners have been vasectomized.

After the women's health advocates had been successful with the NIH policy changes, they turned their eye toward the FDA. The awareness about research inequities raised by the NIH episode gave such visibility to the problem that there was little substantive argument against pressing for change when attention turned toward the FDA. David Kessler, commissioner of the FDA, brought in Ruth Merkatz, who was instrumental in obtaining many health victories for women at the FDA. Since the GAO report on the NIH policies proved to be so successful, the CCWI and Henry Waxman asked the GAO to investigate the FDA and the inclusion of women in drug and medical device research. The 1992 GAO report noted that women were underrepresented in drug trials and recommended that the FDA revise its policy to ensure the appropriate participation of women and to ensure that gender analyses be performed. Again, because of the established credibility of the issue, little opposition arose to the suggested changes.

In 1993, as a result of this report and public criticism, the FDA issued new guidelines (U.S. DHHS 1993). The guidelines state that subjects in a given clinical study should reflect the population that will receive the drug when it is marketed, and suggest that subjects include both genders in the same trial so that direct comparisons can be made. The FDA expects there to be an analysis of gender differences in terms of effectiveness and adverse effects of the drug. Though the 1977 guideline about excluding women of "childbearing potential" was lifted, the new guidelines do not require that women be included in the early phases of drug trials.

The new FDA guidelines specify precautions that are to be taken in clinical trials that include women of childbearing potential. Investigators should obtain the informed consent of the women, and the investigator should advise participants to take precautions to prevent the exposure of a fetus to potentially toxic drugs. Information should be provided about the risk of fetal toxicity and should recommend the use of contraception or abstinence. But the guidelines still recommend that large-scale exposure of women of childbearing potential should not take place until after the results of animal toxicity tests are analyzed.

The guidelines also contain exceptions and other provisions that weaken their ability to affect change in how drug research is actually performed. For example, the guidelines state that the FDA does not perceive a need "for requiring that women in general or women of childbearing potential be included in particular trials" (U.S. DHHS 1993: 39408; also see Rothenberg 1996, note 262). Also, the guidelines do not have the force of law; they are only recommended procedures to be followed and may or may not affect the approval of the drug. The FDA recognizes this drawback and states, "The change in FDA's policy will not, by itself, cause drug companies or IRBs to alter restrictions they might impose on the participation of women of childbearing potential" (39408; see also Rothenberg 1996: 1241). It further states that it is "confident that the interplay of ethical, social, medical, legal, and political forces will allow greater participation of women in the early stages of clinical trials" (39408–39409). The FDA is only "determined to remove the unnecessary federal impediment to inclusion of women" (39409). Moreover, no FDA policy mentions or addresses the need for more research on drugs and devices that could particularly benefit women, such as breast cancer drugs or more reproductive control devices.

In conclusion, by 1993 the NIH and FDA had revised their policies regarding the inclusion of women in clinical trials, though the NIH had enacted more radical alterations; most important, the NIH regulations have been written into law and no research will be funded that does not adhere to them. We have no similar guarantee about the FDA policy changes and do not know if the FDA will continue to approve drugs that have been tested in trials that exclude or underrepresent women. As one author noted, the NIH has moved from "encouragement to requirement" and the FDA has moved from "exclusion to encouragement" (Rothenberg 1996: 1230, 1236).

So, have these new policies eliminated bias and instituted justice for women? In order to answer such a question, we need some understanding of what principles of justice require when they include gender issues. In the next section, principles of gender justice that can be used to judge public policies and their treatment of women are presented.

Principles of Gender Justice

To date, there is no agreed-upon theory of justice for addressing gender inequities, inequalities, discrimination, and differences between the two sexes. Various theories abound, both within traditional political theory and feminist theory, but no consensus has been reached about justifiable standards or the proper methodology for addressing gender discrepancies. Thus, the literature is lacking a framework of what I will term *gender justice*.[8]

Historically, two approaches have been used to address issues of gender justice, equity, or equality. One approach tries to transcend the concept of gender and create systems, laws, and policies in which no gender distinctions are made, making the theoretical assumption that men and women are basically the same and that they should be treated as such. People are treated as citizens, employees, taxpayers, social security recipients, and even "nonpregnant persons" but never as men and women.[9] This approach assumes that people are equal in terms of gender (or at least that it is not an important characteristic), but different in terms of ability, education, intelligence, skills, vigor, and so forth, and that these differences have no relation to one's gender. Or on a slightly different note, some adherents to this approach believe that even if the differences are sometimes related to gender, the best way to remove this correlation is to treat people as if their gender does not matter; thus, in time, it truly will not matter. This approach has been called equal treatment, formal equality, symmetrical, assimilation, or the sameness model (Littleton 1987).

The other common approach to gender discrimination stresses the differences between women and men. In one version of this approach, the world is divided into the male world of politics, business, and competition—the public world—and the female world of home, family, and love—the private world. Each sex has its innate, natural, but different traits that allow them to fulfill their respective natural roles. The just social order is the "natural" order. Another version of this approach asserts that women are in fact different from men in that they are more nurturing, caring, and sensitive, but that these special functions and qualities have been devalued in society. Reform is needed so that women's special qualities do not result in their having less power in society. The

---

8. See also Baird 1998a, Bartlett and Kennedy 1991, Fraser 1994, and Rhode 1989.

9. In *Geduldig v. Aiello*, 417 U.S. 484 (1974), a case upholding the constitutionality of a California program that excluded pregnancy from insurance coverage but included disabilities affecting only men, the opinion noted that this case did not even involve "gender as such"; California had just made a distinction between "pregnant women and nonpregnant persons."

basis of both strands of thought is commonly derived from women's reproductive capabilities and assumptions about the family, though some argue that women's differences stem from gender role socialization and cultural expectations. This approach has variously been called the asymmetrical, sex-conscious relief, and difference model, and more negatively, has been described as essentialism, special treatment, protection, and reverse discrimination (Rhode 1989; Tong 1989; Wolgast 1980).

Both of these problematic approaches have been used in clinical research policies and health care practices. Women were considered different from men because of their ability to carry a fetus and thus were often excluded from research. The standard human research subject was not one who menstruated or had the ability to become pregnant, and, thus, women's differences from men disadvantaged them. But, oddly enough, at the same time, women were considered to be the same as men; it was thought that clinical research findings obtained from studying men could easily be applied to women. This practice also did not meet women's health care needs in that some diseases manifest themselves in (and treatments affect) women differently.

I reject these prior approaches and contend that neither is adequate to truly address issues of gender justice. A new approach is needed that focuses less on how women are the same as or different from men and more on how women, as a diverse group, are disadvantaged by certain policies or by the absence of specific policies to meet their needs. The principles of gender justice developed in the sections that follow recognize the complexity of issues surrounding the meeting of women's needs. The framework of gender justice gives explicit criteria by which to judge policies so we can specify where they succeed and where they fail.[10] The three principles of gender justice developed here are self-determination, equality of gendered consequences, and diversity.

Self-Determination

Typically, contemporary theories of justice focus on the distribution of benefits and burdens, or goods, in society. This is one important aspect of justice and is useful when discussing gender problems such as inequality of income, unequal distribution of high-status and high-paying jobs, or hours spent doing housework and taking care of children. Though

---

10. A much fuller development and explanation of the framework of gender justice is presented in Baird 1998a; only a brief outline is given here.

a distributive focus works well for material goods or clearly identifiable items, it works less well for nonmaterial items such as power, freedom, respect, opportunity, and participation in decision-making structures, and such issues are important for women (Young 1990). For example, domestic violence and rape are important topics in which distributive issues are not primary concerns; however, issues of autonomy, freedom, power, respect, and a right to live free of violence and coercion, to name a few, are important.

A focus on distribution also masks the institutional context in which distributions occur, gives primacy to "having" as opposed to "doing," and makes social groups invisible. Iris Marion Young's (1990) example is useful; she argues that when thinking about justice, one should start by thinking about injustice, and she then describes injustice as the existence of oppression and domination. Oppression is defined as the institutional constraint on self-development and domination as the institutional constraint on self-determination (37). We can formulate corresponding components of justice for these ideas of injustice. First, justice should be concerned with the degree to which a society's institutions and policies support the structural conditions necessary for developing and exercising one's capacities, that is, for supporting self-development (Young 1990). A related aspect of self-development is the ability to express one's self and to have others listen and legitimate one's experience, needs, values, view of the world, and so forth. Thus, justice should also be concerned with the degree to which societal institutions and policies support the expression and recognition of people's experiences.

Third, and corresponding to the concept of domination, justice should be concerned with the degree to which a society supports individuals in determining or at least participating in the determination of their actions (Young 1990: 37). I label this notion democratic freedom. These three criteria are discussed in further detail later in the article, but to review, the first principle of gender justice is self-determination and contains three subcomponents: self-development, recognition, and democratic freedom.

Self-Development. Developing one's abilities involves becoming the type of person one chooses and doing with one's life what one desires, and people should be given the right to do these things to some degree.[11] This

---

11. The concepts of development, human functioning, and capabilities, as well as the implications of these criteria of justice in a world setting, are discussed in Martha Nussbaum and Jonathan Glover's *Women, Culture, and Development* (1995).

is an important concept of gender justice because women have been hindered in this fashion by gender socialization, cultural constraints, reproductive concerns, educational limitations, business practices, and outright discrimination, to name a few. I agree with Martha Nussbaum, who quotes Aristotle: "A good political arrangement is one 'in accordance with which anyone whatsoever might do well and live a flourishing life'" (1995: 81). Therefore, we should judge public policies on their ability to further women's self-development, and policies may need to address past constraints on women's evolvement, if appropriate. We can ask: "Does the policy contribute to the ability of women to develop their capacities and abilities?"

Recognition. The next criterion of the principle of self-determination involves women being able to express themselves or have a voice, and others recognizing and respecting that voice. This suggests that people should pay attention to women and their needs and this is very important because many of women's concerns have historically fallen on deaf ears. For example, the public system of unemployment compensation in the U.S. mainly benefits men when they are out of work but there is no public system of child care so that women can work in the first place; we have a public system of workers' compensation for men when they are hurt and cannot work but no payment system whatsoever for traditional "women's work"—housework, child rearing, and care of other family members. Furthermore, rape has been used as a tool of terror in war for many years but only in 1996 was it recognized as a war crime, a crime against humanity, by the United Nations Court (Simons 1996). Previously, the crime of rape was not addressed and, of course, it is a crime that primarily affects women.

Public policies will never address women's concerns if policy makers do not first recognize women, their life experiences, and their needs, and then treat them as legitimate considerations—basically, respect women. As Young notes, "To treat people with respect is to be prepared to listen to what they have to say or to do what they request" (1990: 57).[12] So a criterion of recognition needs to be part of a framework of gender justice. Thus, we should ask of public policies: "Does the policy contribute to the ability of women to express their experiences and have them be recognized and legitimated?"

---

12. Young (1990) advances the idea of recognition and respect of group differences in *Justice and the Politics of Difference*.

Democratic Freedom. The ability of women to participate in determining their actions is another important aspect of self-determination and thus of gender justice. People should be able to decide where and how they would like to live their lives and what, where, how, and under what circumstances they will act and behave; control over one's life and choices about what and how to pursue one's goals and fulfill one's desires are very important. People should experience some set of liberties and participate in the defining of these freedoms; thus I call this criterion *democratic freedom.* We need a governmental commitment "to a society in which women as a group are not disadvantaged in controlling their own destiny" (Rhode 1989: 4). This is important for women because part of the injustice or inequality that they have historically experienced involves being controlled by others—husbands, fathers, male legislators, and so forth. A related aspect of this is that policies may need to address the specific past hindrances on women's ability to determine their own actions; policies may need to specifically address past problems and eradicate them.

Another important aspect of women determining their own actions is women's participation in the policy- and rule-making institutions of society. One reason women's needs have been overlooked in the policy-making process is that men have filled the rule-making institutions that define what policy needs to address. Historically, women have had little voice in such matters. But under a framework of gender justice, women's perspectives need to be taken into account, their experiences recognized, and their concerns legitimated so that their needs can be addressed by public policies. One very important step in this direction is to have women be present in the rule-making institutions of society. So, we should ask: "Does the policy further the ability of women to participate in determining their actions?"

Equality of Gendered Consequences

Another important principle of gender justice involves examining the actual consequences or effects of policies. We should not presume that policies produce sex-neutral outcomes just because they use sex-neutral terms; many policies have gendered consequences. When instituted in an unequal world, policies that treat everyone the same or equally all too often cause or reinforce existing inequalities and injustices. One example is employment practices and child care problems. Employers can and are even encouraged to hire women; all people, men and women, are (supposedly) treated the same in terms of hiring practices. But the world into which these sex-neutral hiring policies are instituted is gendered in terms of child-rearing practices, in that women are more often responsible for the care of small children. If a condition of employment is to be free from child care duties from nine to five, then many more women than men will not be able to fit the sex-neutral requirement. As Rhode states, "We need not simply mandates of equal treatment for women; we need strategies to secure women's treatment as equals" (1989: 319). This involves moving toward a framework that examines the results of—the actual applications of—policies and asks if women are disadvantaged in the outcomes.[13]

In practice, treating women as equals or keeping women from being disadvantaged can suggest different things. Sometimes an unequal distribution of a policy benefit to women would be justified if it was needed to secure women's treatment as equals. The idea is not so much to give women more because they are disadvantaged—a sort of compensation—even though this may be the case sometimes; the idea behind this application of the principle is to give women more so as to keep them from being disadvantaged. In the example described earlier about child care and employment, the women (and men) with young children would need to be provided with child care so they would not be disadvantaged in terms of employment. Then the consequences of the hiring practices would not be gendered. Some might argue that women are getting more in such situations, but since the goal is to have women be treated as equals and not be disadvantaged in policy outcomes, the different distribution could be justified in this light.

So we want to ask of public policies: "In the actual consequences of outcomes, do women achieve a lived-out equality or parity with men with respect to the policy's goals?"

Diversity

An issue that is closely related to all of these principles is diversity. For example, an examination of whether a policy helps or hinders the recognition of women's experiences should also pay close attention to the many differences among women. Minority women's experiences are more likely to be discounted than white women's experiences. Also, an analysis of the actual application and outcome of a policy forces us to recog-

---

13. Deborah L. Rhode (1989) advocates the use of a principle of gender disadvantage.

nize the diversity of people and the varieties of contexts to which the policy may be applied. Almost any policy will not have the same effect on all women or all men; class, race, ethnicity, sexual orientation, disability status, religion, and so forth are very important items to consider along with gender.

Furthermore, in recognizing the diversity of people and varieties of circumstances, we are forced to realize that one monolithic standard or guiding principle will not provide the solution to our gender justice problems. Claims of universalistic paradigms do not usually serve women's and society's diverse needs, and feminist theorists have been particularly successful in moving this point to the forefront. "Contemporary feminist theory offers no single view of our appropriate destination, but it does suggest certain preferred means of travel" (Rhode 1989: 317). Thus, the question to ask of a public policy becomes: "Does the policy recognize the diversity of women—age, class, race, ethnicity, sexual orientation, disability status, and so forth—and address their differing needs?"

To summarize, the framework of gender justice includes the principles of self-determination (composed of the criteria of self-development, recognition, and democratic freedom), equality of gendered consequences, and diversity. In the next section, the new NIH and FDA policies are analyzed according to the three principles. Once again, the questions remain: have the new policies rectified past problems and instituted gender justice? Do the new policies meet the criteria for a gender-just policy?

Are the NIH And FDA Medical Research Policies Gender Just?

Principle of Self-Determination

Self-Development. The question to ask about self-development is, "Does the policy contribute to the ability of women to develop their capacities and abilities?" So what might this mean for medical research policy? First, the purpose of medical research is to provide information to help all humans live healthier lives. The information obtained from small groups of subjects (trial participants) provides knowledge about diseases and treatments that can potentially help all of us. Also, clinical trials offer the potential benefit of new treatments or drugs to the actual participants in the research. Therefore, research helps people live healthier lives and healthier people are better able to develop their capacities and

abilities. Health is a first-order need like food and shelter, one that needs
to be addressed so that humans can satisfy higher-order needs.[14] And
women need information from studies done on women to know how diseases progress and manifest themselves within the female body. This, of
course, contributes to their ability to develop their capacities and abilities; the healthier one is, both mentally and physically, the better situated
one is to develop one's self.

We should also be concerned with the specific topics that are being
studied. Women want and need information about diseases and conditions
that affect women. Some of these diseases may also affect men—perhaps
in similar ways or perhaps in different ways—and some of the female
problems may not occur, or may only rarely occur, in men. Any research
that utilizes women as subjects needs to be part of a valid and scientific
project that will yield useful results for women. Precaution is needed so
that women are not used as guinea pigs for illegitimate experiments or for
legitimate experiments on subjects that are not useful for women. Furthermore, even if the project is a valid, scientific one concerning matters
that are beneficial for women and includes female subjects, the data must
also be collected and analyzed in a way that takes into account gender differences. In other words, gender must be a variable by which the data are
analyzed so we can know if differences exist between men and women
regarding the disease, treatment, drug, therapy, and so forth. In addition,
women need information from different races and ages of women to know
how race or age may affect the presence or progression of a disease or the
treatment of it with a drug. Just as medical knowledge needs to encompass
both sexes so as not to be biased, it also needs to encompass different ethnic and age groups so that we do not obtain information, for example, only
about middle-class, middle-aged white women.

Only if research is performed in this fashion will it provide useful
results for women that will contribute to their ability to develop themselves. So, much of the analysis of the new policies and gender justice
turns on whether or not these precautions are being taken and extra

14. Martha Nussbaum divides her conception of the human being into two levels of capabilities. The first level includes needs of the human body, and the second and higher-order level
includes items that if a person (or society) was to do without, we would not think that the person (or society) lived a good life. Incorporated into the second level are "being able to use the
senses; being able to imagine, to think, and to reason—and to do these things in a way informed
and cultivated by an adequate education. . . . Being able to form a conception of the good and
to engage in critical reflection about the planning of one's own life" (1995: 84). Justice is determined by a society's ability to further the quality of life as defined by these levels of needs.
Moreover, these items are very similar to what I am describing here about self-development.

efforts are being made. I first turn to the NIH policy to evaluate whether it meets the criteria of development and then I examine the FDA policy.

NIH

The 1994 NIH guidelines state that one of the major purposes of the new regulations for Phase 3 clinical trials is to "ensure that women and minorities and their subpopulations" are included "such that valid analyses of differences in intervention effect can be accomplished" (U.S. DHHS 1994a: 14508). They go on to state that "it is imperative to determine whether the intervention or therapy being studied affects women or men or members of minority groups and their subpopulations differently" (14508). These guidelines are "intended to ensure that all future NIH-supported biomedical and behavioral research involving human subjects will be carried out in a manner sufficient to elicit information about individuals of both genders and the diverse racial and ethnic groups and, in the case of clinical trials, to examine differential effects on such groups" (14508). The requirement of participation of different gender and race/ethnicity groups is with the goal of "detecting major qualitative differences (if they exist) among gender and racial/ethnic subgroups. . . . Other interpretations may not serve as well the health of women" (14512). So the policy is designed to ensure that women are included and that studies contain an analysis of gender differences.

The NIH guidelines also explain that the term *valid analysis* of gender and minority differences means an "unbiased assessment," an assessment that "will, on average, yield the correct estimate of the difference in outcomes between the two groups of subjects," and that it "does not need to have a high statistical power for detecting a stated effect" (14511). The principal requirements for a valid analysis are

- Allocation of the study participants of both genders and from different racial/ethnic groups to the intervention and control groups by an unbiased process such as randomization,
- Unbiased evaluation of the outcome(s) of study participants, and
- Use of unbiased statistical analyses and proper methods of the inference to estimate and compare the intervention effects among the gender and racial/ethnic groups (14511).

Many critiques have been made about the language used in the 1993 act, noting that it is unclear and that the congressional intent is left uncertain. In response, a working group of institute representatives, as well as

550   Journal of Health Politics, Policy and Law

clinical trialists, convened to address the interpretation of key phrases such as "valid analysis" and "significant difference" and their ideas were incorporated into the NIH guidelines. Debates ensued about the political meanings and intent of such terms and the scientific and ethical implications of them. Most applauded the appropriate representation of subjects of different genders but believed that the way the act is implemented will determine its actual effectiveness (Freedman et al. 1995; Woolson et al. 1995). Thus, the intent and wording of the policy itself support the principle of self-development by requiring that women be included and by requiring the analysis of gender differences, but the real success of the policy may only be measured over time as it is implemented.

The NIH guidelines also address the issue of when women and minorities can and cannot be excluded. Cost is not an acceptable reason. Women and minorities must be included "unless a clear and compelling rationale and justification establishes to the satisfaction of the relevant institute/center director that inclusion is *inappropriate* with respect to the health of the subjects or the purpose of the research" (U.S. DHHS 1994a: 14509; emphasis added); furthermore, if inclusion would duplicate data from other sources, certain groups may be excluded. These reasons appear to be catchall categories for various issues that may arise that would deem inclusion of women and minorities inappropriate and are not problematical unless the subjects are abused. But a trial may also include "only one gender where the disease, disorders, or conditions are gender specific. In all other cases, there should be approximately equal numbers of both sexes in studies of populations and subpopulations at risk, unless different proportions are appropriate because of the known prevalence, incidence, morbidity, mortality rates, or expected intervention effect" (14512). Thus only women or only men will be included in a study if the condition only affects one group, and more women will be included if the condition affects more women. This will ensure equality when appropriate, and inequality, to phrase it in one way, when appropriate to meet men's and women's various health needs. This will provide medical knowledge that will truly be beneficial for women, help them live healthier lives, and help them develop their capacities and abilities.[15] Yes, this is gender justice.

---

15. The tangible benefits of the policy may only be assessed after it is implemented, but initial analyses show that it has been quite effective (Hayunga, Costello, and Pinn 1997).

FDA

In the FDA's policy, the language used regarding the inclusion of women is much weaker. The FDA guidelines request that women, even those with childbearing capabilities, be included and state that men and women should be included in drug studies if both sexes would receive the drug when marketed. In fact, the population of a clinical study should reflect the population that will receive the drug when it is marketed. Furthermore, the FDA uses the weaker language of expecting that an analysis of gender differences be included as opposed to requiring it. Unfortunately, this is only a reiteration of a 1988 guideline,[16] and in 1992, despite the directive, the GAO found that in clinical trials (for new drugs), more than one-half of the studies did not analyze the results for gender-related effects. The GAO recommended that the FDA institute a stricter policy of *requiring* drug manufacturers to analyze trial data by gender (U.S. GAO 1992: 13).

The GAO also found that women were included in most drug trials but were underrepresented, meaning, women were not represented in the trial in the same proportion to the number of women in the general population that experience the disease or condition. The 1993 FDA guidelines do provide more explicit information regarding the FDA's expectations about the inclusion of both genders and the basis for the expectations so as to help drug researchers attain a better understanding. But it never states that new drug applications will be rejected if this information is lacking. Furthermore, the 1993 guidelines do not provide any information as to what constitutes an adequate representation of women in trials, despite the fact that the 1992 GAO report found that drug researchers were unclear about this and recommended that the FDA "tell drug manufacturers how to determine when enough women are included in drug trials" (U.S. GAO 1992: 13). In general, the new FDA research policy is an improvement over prior policy but is still fairly weak. The policy purports to have women included and thus have women obtain the health benefits that such inclusion provides, but it is difficult to make such a judgment since the policy offers no assurance that women will actually be included or that gender differences will be analyzed because the recommendation or expectation is not absolute. Overall, the FDA has made some progress toward a gender-just policy, but the improvements only slightly further the self-development of women.

---

16. The FDA issued *Guideline for the Format and Content of the Clinical and Statistical Sections of New Drug Applications* in 1988, in which it stated that it expects new drug applications to contain an analysis of gender differences.

Recognition. The question to ask about recognition is, "Does the policy contribute to the ability of women to express their experiences and have them be recognized and legitimated?" So how would medical research policies fulfill the criterion of recognition? One important facet is the awareness of past problems of women and medical research. As discussed previously, women and minorities have in the past been used in abusive research that, in part, led to their later exclusion. Because of this past exclusion and abuse, women—especially minority women—may be hesitant to participate, so researchers will need to make extra efforts to recruit and retain them.

Women may also not want to participate because medical research involves doctors—typically white, upper-class, male doctors—and many women have not had success in getting doctors to listen to their problems and treat them as legitimate. For example, a Commonwealth Fund survey found that one in four women reported they had been "talked down to" or treated like a child by a physician, as compared to 12 percent of men; 17 percent of women had been told a medical condition was "all in your head," as compared to 7 percent of men; and 41 percent of women had changed their physician because of dissatisfaction as compared to only 27 percent of men (Commonwealth Fund 1993). Women may fear coercion or belittlement and may not want to subject themselves willingly to a potentially oppressive situation. In addition, women may find participation difficult because of child care and family duties, as well as job commitments. Women's life experiences regarding these matters need to be recognized and addressed by the NIH and FDA policies if medical research is to be truly inclusive.

NIH

In noting important factors for the successful recruitment and retention of women, the NIH Outreach Notebook suggests that researchers recruit female, minority investigators and staff for the project (U.S. DHHS 1994b). It is thought that having more women researchers will help increase the attention given to women's issues and needs, as well as make female subjects feel more at ease and thus more likely to join and stay with the project.

The NIH guidelines state that with regard to recruitment strategies, "the purpose should be to establish a relationship between the investigator(s) and staff(s) and populations and communities of interest such that mutual benefit is derived for participants in the study" (U.S. DHHS

1994a: 14510). The outreach efforts should "represent a thoughtful and culturally sensitive plan of outreach and generally include involvement of other individuals and organization relevant to the populations and communities of interest, e.g., family, religious organizations, community leaders and informal gatekeepers, and public and private institutions and organizations. The objective is to establish appropriate lines of communication and cooperation to build mutual trust and cooperation such that both the study and the participants benefit from such collaboration" (14511–14512).

Furthermore, the Outreach Notebook specifically notes that many people of color remember the Tuskegee experiment and will be skeptical about participating; abuses of the past are well known in these communities and are often cited as reasons for not participating in clinical studies. The notebook suggests gaining the trust of opinion leaders so that they can become the primary link to many people of color.

The use of terms such as "mutual benefit," "culturally sensitive plan," and "cooperation to build mutual trust" show respect for the trial participants and recognition of possible gender or cultural problems for the investigator. The mention of the Tuskegee experiment shows an important recognition of people of color's experience and legitimates the skepticism that many may feel about participation. If these suggestions are followed, such efforts should ease some women's hesitation.

The NIH Outreach Notebook also notes that "in some instances, women may wish to share their decision to participate with family members or others in the community" (9) and states that other factors, such as child care, location of the research site, ease of access to it, transportation, and time off work, may affect the ability of women of differing ages and family statuses to participate. These factors should be weighed when designing recruitment and retention strategies (9).

Recognition of these issues is a very positive step for women and contributes to the recognition and legitimation of women's experiences. Of particular importance is the recognition of child care issues. Again, since costs cannot be considered as a reason for exclusion, the nonprovision of child care for study participants should not be an excuse either. And because women are more likely than men to have lower-status and lower-paying jobs that make taking time off more difficult, the Outreach Notebook states that researchers should consider such issues when designing recruitment plans.

Overall, women's needs that were previously unaddressed, and that partially formed the basis of their exclusion in research, are now recog-

554   Journal of Health Politics, Policy and Law

nized and legitimated. Investigators are now instructed to address these areas and are directed that such reasons cannot form the basis for women's exclusion. In terms of gender justice and the criterion of recognition, this is a great improvement over prior guidelines, prior medical research practices, and many other public policies; overall the NIH has made substantial progress.

FDA

Unfortunately, the FDA offers no such counterpart regarding the recognition of women's experiences. The FDA does not address issues of attracting minorities and women to research; it does not offer outreach programs to help pharmaceutical researchers include such people; and it has no examination or analysis of the relationship between the research project and the female subject. Again, the FDA only lifted its ban on including women of childbearing potential and says that it expects women to be included and a gender analysis to be performed. Therefore, the FDA barely heeds the criterion of recognition.

Democratic Freedom. Does the policy further the ability of women to participate in determining their actions? With regard to medical research, the issue of democratic freedom raises the matter of informed consent. Women must be fully informed of the risks and benefits of participation in any clinical trial and must be allowed to make their own decisions about participation. This is a point that women's health advocates clearly articulated in their arguments about the inequities of the earlier policies. Furthermore, it is important that all participants be provided with full information and that no coercion occur; this has particular implications for minority women.

Also, the representation of women in higher-level policy-making boards such as the NIH, FDA, and IRBs is important. The inclusion of women on IRBs is significant so that a female voice can be heard and be part of the evaluation of informed consent procedures;[17] research has shown that women policy makers can bring different considerations to the table when discussing issues and that they focus on certain

17. Of course, women should be adequately represented and at all levels—as principal investigators, at the NIH and FDA, and in Congress—but I have chosen to focus on IRBs because they actually evaluate the informed consent procedures of specific research projects. Moreover, a discussion of women as investigators, in high-ranking positions at the NIH, FDA, and in Congress is too extensive to be included here.

issues more often than men (Thomas 1994). Responsibilities given to IRBs include the review of risk-benefit ratios, confidentiality protections, informed consent processes and documents, and procedures for selection of subjects (IOM 1994, vol. 1: 40). Consequently, IRBs become important elements in the analysis of democratic freedom and informed consent procedures.

NIH

The NIH policy notes that as IRBs implement the new guidelines and include women and minorities, they must also continue to regulate for the protection of human subjects, including having informed consent procedures approved (IOM 1994, vol. 1: 130). The NIH Outreach Notebook explicitly states that it should be assumed that all Office for Protection from Research Risks' (OPRR) regulations concerning ethical considerations in clinical and community trials apply to all individuals regardless of gender, race, or ethnicity. "However, successful implementation of these regulations depends on the ability of the research team to understand implications of conducting research in particular populations, settings, and trials" (U.S. DHHS 1994b: 21). The NIH explains that different people may comprehend the purpose and benefits of participation in different ways; in fact, for some potential subjects, the purpose and benefits may be harder to understand. But issues of autonomy are "paramount in the decision to participate" and, as such, more time may be needed, multiple sessions may be required, and translators may need to be sought to further the potential participants' understanding so they can make informed choices. Significantly, the NIH is recognizing that the burden of informed consent rests with head investigators, as well as with the NIH, to do whatever is needed to ensure that women fully understand the benefits and risks of participation.

The Outreach Notebook states that "women of childbearing potential must understand the requirements of the study and decide whether it is appropriate for them to participate (e.g., do the benefits outweigh the risks?)" (9). So women must be fully informed and decide whether to participate—not the investigator, NIH, or the FDA; this is precisely what women's health activists argued for. Also the notebook points out that, even with IRB approval, researchers should make special efforts to ensure that women fully understand the demands of the study and what they will be asked to do. The NIH, with its focus on providing information and obtaining consent from women, is adhering to the criteria of democratic freedom and clearly addresses the past problems of excluding women from studies.

Regarding the possibility of coercion, the guidelines state that ethical concerns should be clearly noted so that there is minimal possibility of coercion or undue influence in the incentives or rewards offered for participation. IRBs should also address these concerns. The Outreach Notebook explicitly states that issues of coercion or undue influence are of particular importance for women, especially for minority women and women with lower economic resources. It goes on to note that incentives to participate should not be of the sort to seem coercive and that what is considered coercive may change from group to group or community to community. Once again, gender, cultural, and class differences are being acknowledged in a positive manner that helps women, especially minority women, determine their own actions and have greater control over their lives as applied to medical research issues.

With regard to the representation of women in policy-making positions, Bernadine Healy was appointed director of the NIH in 1991 and it is thought that her leadership brought many of the policy changes discussed here. Again, the ORWH was established with one of its goals being to increase the number of female researchers; furthermore, a woman, Vivian Pinn, was given leadership of the ORWH.

FDA

In its 1993 guidelines, the FDA is not as specific. But the FDA does revise the prior policy of excluding women of childbearing potential and states that one reason for the revision is that the initial determination of risk of fetal damage is "properly left to patients, physicians, local IRBs, and sponsors, with appropriate review and guidance by FDA, as are all other aspects of the safety of proposed investigations" (U.S. DHHS 1993: 39408). This is an important advancement in enabling women to determine their own actions regarding participation. The FDA guidelines discuss informed consent and state that all available information about the potential risk of fetal toxicity should be given to women. If no relevant information is available, the informed consent document should also reflect this. Furthermore, the guidelines state that a reliable form of contraception may be provided or abstinence recommended for the duration of drug exposure so that fetal exposure is limited. The FDA also developed an information document for IRBs that outlines the change in policy. It adds that women should be counseled about pregnancy testing and contraception, but the type of contraception is not specified because this decision is best left to a woman and her health care provider. Again, even though they are not as explicit, detailed, or advanced as the NIH's guidelines, the new FDA guidelines are certainly an advancement over the prior policy of excluding women of childbearing potential. Though a critique could be made regarding the continued focus on the fetus, this new FDA policy greatly increases the ability of women to determine their own participation in drug trials and thus adheres much more closely to the notion of democratic freedom.

In conclusion, regarding the principle of self-determination, the NIH has made great advancements toward this component of gender justice. Women's ability to develop themselves is enhanced by the new policy, a recognition of their concerns is articulated, many issues are addressed in the assistance documentation, and the ability of women to determine their own actions regarding participation in clinical trials is greatly increased. The FDA has made some tentative advancements: the policy changes *may* help women be healthier and thus develop themselves; they offer little recognition of women's experience but greatly increase a woman's ability to determine her actions regarding participation.

Principle of Equality of Gendered Consequences

In the actual outcomes, do women achieve a lived-out equality or parity with men with respect to the policy goals? This can mean many things with regard to medical research policies. First, their goal is to have women included in clinical trials, and the underlying goal is to have somewhat equal amounts of medical knowledge about men and women. As discussed previously, women's health activists forcefully pushed this point and argued that women were receiving substandard care and were being shortchanged in comparison to men; this was supported by the GAO reports on the NIH and FDA. But exactly what equal knowledge entails is very hard to specify. As stated before, some illnesses are more prevalent in women and some diseases are exclusive to women. So we also want an equitable number of studies done on diseases that are unique to women and on diseases that are unique to men. But how is this to be evaluated—by dollar amounts? By mortality or morbidity rates? By the number of people affected by certain diseases? These are difficult questions that are not answered in this article, but some evaluation of the NIH and FDA policy outcomes can be accomplished.

NIH

With regard to the inclusion of men and women, preliminary data are available. For Phase 3 trials awarded in 1994, considering only trials that include both men and women, 57 percent of the subjects were men and 42 percent were women; only about 7 percent of the applications were rejected for not including minorities and women (Hayunga 1996). The NIH has established a database so that such information can easily be obtained and analyzed. NIH does require that researchers make annual progress reports; the following year's funding depends on whether sufficient progress is being made. This has been standard NIH practice for many years, but now, additionally, researchers have to provide information on the gender and racial composition of the study group. Since this information is being computerized, the effectiveness of the new policy can be tracked.

I am hopeful about the outcome of this process for several reasons. First, the preliminary data show a fairly equitable distribution. And if the data gathered over time continue to indicate that progress is being made, then this principle is being followed. And the fact that the NIH is gathering this data places pressure on researchers to be sure that positive answers are given; the threat of losing funding for research projects is a formidable incentive for compliance. But even if the data show inequality, NIH personnel will know what the problems are and where the problems lie, such that a positive plan can be implemented to see that the required changes are made. As noted before, many state that the true success of the policy can only be determined by its implementation.

The other important issue is whether women's specific diseases are receiving adequate attention. The ORWH was established to address this need and has instituted the Women's Health Initiative (WHI) to study more than 150,000 women on a variety of important issues. This is one positive step. Moreover, Eugene Hayunga, Margaret D. Costello, and Vivian Pinn (1997) note that of single-gender studies funded by NIH in 1994, eleven involved women only and five involved men only Also, between 1990 and 1993, funding for breast cancer research increased almost fivefold (Weisman 1998: 88).[18] In conclusion, when the actual consequences of the policy are evaluated, an equality appears to be materializing with respect to the policy's goals.

---

18. This takes into account funds spent at the NIH as well as at the Department of Defense.

FDA

The FDA lifted its ban on the exclusion of women of childbearing potential. This is certainly a positive step and negates their total disregard for
the principle of equality of gendered consequences. But by not requiring
that women be included, the FDA may allow studies to exclude women
and hence they will be disadvantaged. The FDA's use of words such as
should and *expect* as opposed to *require* weakens the policy's potential
impact. And if the FDA does not require that researchers provide information on the gender and racial composition of the study groups, as
well as on the gender and racial composition of the group to which the
drug would be marketed, how will the FDA know if the guideline is
being followed?

With regard to the actual effect of the 1993 FDA guidelines, unfortunately neither the FDA nor any other agency has yet studied the effects
of the changes. No data have been gathered or studies implemented to
evaluate the consequences. This is a tremendous shortcoming of the
implementation (or lack of implementation) process of the guideline, particularly in light of the 1992 GAO findings noting the many problems
with the inclusion of women and analysis of gender-related differences.
Unfortunately, the FDA has made little progress toward the principle of
equality of gendered consequences.

Principle of Diversity

Does the policy recognize the diversity of women—in terms of age,
class, race, ethnicity, sexual orientation, disability status, and so forth—
and address their differing needs? One application of this principle of
gender justice with regard to medical research concerns the topics that
are studied. Women of various ages, races, and ability status have differing health care needs and all deserve to have their issues investigated.
Also important is the idea that women of various races and ages participate in studies, so investigators should develop appropriate and culturally
sensitive outreach programs and activities for such people. Thus, language issues are also important.

NIH

As discussed before, the 1994 NIH Act directly and explicitly addresses
many important issues regarding the diversity of women. Women and

members of minority groups and their subpopulations are to be included in research; investigators should develop appropriate and culturally sensitive outreach programs and activities for such people. The objective is to recruit the most diverse study population consistent with the goals of the research (U.S. DHHS 1994a: 14510). And, of course, a valid gender and racial analysis needs to be carried out so that differences in intervention can be detected. Beginning in fiscal year 1995, the NIH no longer awards any grant that does not comply with the new policy.

Regarding recruitment strategies, language issues are also addressed by the NIH in the Outreach Notebook, reminding researchers that they may not be familiar with a community's language, meaning of expressions, or colloquial phrasing. The literacy level of the individual in her first language and in English should be ascertained, and special efforts may be needed to develop and translate informational materials so that they are sensitive to the "linguistic and cultural differences among genders and subpopulations" because "outreach strategies that are productive in one population or setting may be counterproductive in another" (U.S. DHHS 1994b: 11, 12). This is, once again, recognizing the diversity of women's needs and addressing and thus legitimating them. Overall, the NIH policy does a very good job of explicitly recognizing and addressing the needs of a great diversity of women; in short, the policy institutes gender justice in this regard.

FDA

Once again, the FDA is not very explicit on diversity issues. The FDA states that "drugs should be studied prior to approval in subjects representing the full range of patients likely to receive the drug once it is marketed" (U.S. DHHS 1993: 39409). It does go on to state that researchers should do "analyses of effectiveness, adverse effects, dose-response, and, if available, blood concentration-response, to look for the influence of . . . demographic features, such as age, gender, and race" (39410). So, gender, race, and age are at least being mentioned in the policy and this is a positive step. But overall the FDA is fairly vague about the diverse women that need to be served. Just stating that studies should include the range of patients that will take the drug after approval is not particularly helpful. As noted already, the 1992 GAO report recommended that the FDA more clearly specify what constitutes an appropriate inclusion of women. The FDA did not do so.

Conclusion

The three principles used to analyze the NIH and FDA policies are self-determination, equality of gendered consequences, and diversity. Overall, the NIH has greatly improved its medical research policies and has made great strides toward instituting gender-just policies. The NIH guidelines contribute to the self-development of women, pay attention to women's experiences, and further the ability of women to enjoy democratic freedom. The initial information about the actual consequences of the policy show that it has been successful with regard to the inclusion of women and with regard to the funding of studies important for women. Furthermore, the diversity of women is recognized. The NIH still has considerable room for improvement, but overall, it has moved significantly toward gender justice.

The FDA has made slight improvements, though it lags quite far behind the NIH in comparison. The FDA has taken small steps toward improving justice for women in its policies for drug development, but it needs to do much more. The FDA has improved its policies, but not very substantially and certainly to a much lesser degree than the NIH.

It is interesting to note that the criticisms articulated by women's health activists about the inequities of the NIH policies were, for the most part, addressed by the changes. Their arguments centered on women increasing their capacities and abilities; women gaining more control over the decision of whether to participate or not; and women enjoying greater equality of consequences. The collective effort of women in the private sector together with women at the NIH and in Congress made it possible for the changes to occur. Many other factors contributed to the successful policy outcome: more women in higher-ranking positions in government, the prior success by AIDS activists, increased awareness of women's health issues, attention given to the issue by the media, and the change in administration with the election of President Clinton (Baird 1998b). Success occurred also because of the careful framing of the issue, namely exclusion of women, and the proposed solution, inclusion.

But why has the FDA lagged behind the NIH? Why the difference in policy? First, women's health activists purposely focused their initial attention on the NIH and only secondarily on the FDA. This was because the NIH is a government agency funding medical research with taxpayer dollars; the FDA is not. The FDA only regulates drugs and accepts or rejects applications for approval, and thus it has less control over its clientele Furthermore, the FDA issue was a much weaker one in that there were no glaring stories to tell about the exclusion of women in drug research such as there were regarding the NIH; as mentioned before, accounts about studies funded by the NIH that excluded women were highly publicized. Moreover, the GAO report on the FDA did not produce as much damning evidence as did the report on the NIH. The FDA and pharmaceutical groups performed their own studies providing counterevidence to the GAO report; their analyses showed that most drug trials included representative numbers of women. And the argument made about the FDA policy by the women's health activists centered upon women having more control over the decision of participation, or respecting a woman's autonomy and ability to give informed consent. In some manner, this was accomplished by the FDA policy change and thus the efforts of women's health activists could be construed as successful.

Also, in the early 1990s, the FDA was being scrutinized and criticized for the length of time it took to approve new drugs. Some argued that the FDA needed to decrease its regulations with regard to the drug approval process; and many such ideas were part of the FDA Modernization Act of 1997. So there was a countervailing pressure for deregulation at the FDA; and the lifting of the ban on including women of childbearing potential can be viewed as a deregulatory move. If the FDA required the inclusion of women, it would be instituting more constraints on the drug research and approval process that would have encountered great opposition.

The FDA has moved on two fronts since the publication of the guidelines. For one, they have sought to define more clearly how to present safety and effectiveness data by gender in new drug applications. They have also sponsored educational conferences for researchers and convened an internal gender analysis working group. And women's health activists, primarily the Society for the Advancement of Women's Health Research, have continued to work with the FDA and pharmaceutical companies to increase the participation of women. Thus, by education and persuasion, but without requiring their participation, the FDA may in the end accomplish objectives similar to those accomplished by the NIH. Perhaps in pharmaceutical research, as in medical research, we will eventually see gender justice.

References

Auerbach, J. D. 1992. The Emergence of the Women's Health Research Agenda: Some Preliminary Analysis. Paper presented at the annual meeting of the Association for Public Policy Analysis and Management, Denver, CO, 29–31 October.

Baird, K. 1998a. *Gender Justice and the Health Care System.* New York: Garland.

———. 1998b. The NIH and FDA New Medical Research Policies: A Case of Policy Streams or Advocacy Coalitions? Paper delivered at the 1998 annual meeting of the American Political Science Association, Boston, 3–6 September.

Bartlett, K. T., and R. Kennedy, eds. 1991. *Feminist Legal Theory.* Boulder, CO: Westview.

Berney, B. 1990. In Research, Women Don't Matter. *The Progressive,* October, 24–27.

Commonwealth Fund. 1993. *The Commonwealth Fund Survey of Women's Health.* New York: The Commonwealth Fund, 14 July.

Dresser, R. 1992. Wanted: Single, White Male for Medical Research. *Hastings Center Report,* January–February, 24–29.

Fraser, N. 1994. After the Family Wage: Gender Equity and the Welfare State. *Political Theory* 22(4):591–618.

Freedman, L., R. Simon, M. Foulkes, L. Friedman, N. Geller, D. Gordon, and R. Mowery. 1995. Response to Discussants' Letters. *Controlled Clinical Trials* 16:310–312.

Goldzieher, J. W., L. Moses, E. Averkin, C. Scheel, and B. Taber. 1971a. A Placebo-Controlled Double-Blind Crossover Investigation of the Side Effects Attributed to Oral Contraceptives. *Fertility and Sterility* 22(9):609–623.

———. 1971b. Nervousness and Depression Attributed to Oral Contraceptives: A Double-Blind, Placebo-Controlled Study. *American Journal of Obstetrics and Gynecology* 22:1013–1020.

Hayunga, E. 1996. Implementation of Inclusion Guidelines. From a workshop on the NIH inclusion guidelines, Office of Research on Women's Health (ORWH), 22 February. Bethesda, MD: Office of Research on Women's Health.

Hayunga, E., M. D. Costello, and V. Pinn. 1997. Demographics of Study Populations. *Applied Clinical Trials* 6(1):41–45.

Institute of Medicine (IOM), Division of Health Sciences Policy, Committee on the Ethical and Legal Issues Relating to the Inclusion of Women in Clinical Studies. 1994. *Women and Health Research, Volumes 1 and 2,* ed. A. Mastroianni, R. Faden, and D. Federman. Washington, DC: National Academy.

Jaschik, S. 1990. Report Says NIH Ignores Own Rules on Including Women in its Research. *Chronicle of Higher Education,* 27 June, A27.

Johnson, T., and E. Fee. 1994. Women's Participation in Clinical Research: From Protectionism to Access. In *Women and Health Research, Volume 2,* ed. Anna Mastroianni, Ruth Faden, and Daniel Federman. Washington, DC: National Academy.

Jones, J. 1981. *Bad Blood: The Tuskegee Syphilis Experiment.* New York: Free Press.

Kadar, A. 1994. The Sex Bias in Medicine. *Atlantic Monthly* 274(2):66–71.

Kinney, E. L. 1981. Underrepresentation of Women in New Drug Trials: Ramifications and Remedies. *Annals of Internal Medicine* 95(4):495–499.

LaRosa, J., B. Seto, C. Caban, and E. Hayunga. 1995. Including Women and Minorities in Clinical Research. *Applied Clinical Trials* 4:31–38.

Littleton, C. A. 1987. Reconstructing Sexual Equality. *California Law Review* 75(4):1279–1337.

Moreno, J. D. 1994. Ethical Issues Related to the Inclusion of Women of Childbearing Age in Clinical Trials. In *Women and Health Research, Volume 2*, ed. A. Mastroianni, R. Faden, and D. Federman. Washington, DC: National Academy Press.

Nussbaum, M. 1995. Human Capabilities, Female Human Beings. In *Women, Culture, and Development*, ed. M. Nussbaum and J. Glover. New York: Clarendon.

Nussbaum, M., and J. Glover, eds. 1995. *Women, Culture, and Development*. New York: Clarendon.

Primmer, L. 1998. Interview with author, Washington, DC, 26 March.

Rhode, D. L. 1989. *Justice and Gender*. Cambridge: Harvard University Press.

Rothenberg, K. 1996. Gender Matters: Implications for Clinical Research and Women in Health Care. *Houston Law Review* 32(5):1201–1272.

Schroeder, P., and O. Snowe. 1994. The Politics of Women's Health. In *The American Woman 1994–95*, ed. C. Costello and A. Stone. New York: Norton.

Simons, M. 1996. UN Court, for First Time, Defines Rape as War Crime. *New York Times*, 28 June, A1.

Thomas, S. 1994. *How Women Legislate*. New York: Oxford University Press.

Tong, R. 1989. *Feminist Thought*. Boulder, CO: Westview.

U.S. Congress. House. Subcommittee on Housing and Consumer Interests. Select Committee on Aging. 1990. *Women Health Care Consumers: Shortchanged on Medical Research and Treatment*. 101st Cong., 2d sess., 24 July.

U.S. Department of Health and Human Services (U.S. DHHS), Food and Drug Administration (FDA). 1988. *Guideline for the Format and Content of the Clinical and Statistical Sections of New Drug Applications*. Washington, DC: U.S. Department of Health and Human Services.

———. 1993. Guideline for the Study and Evaluation of Gender Differences in the Clinical Evaluation of Drugs. *Federal Register* 58(139):39406–39416.

U.S. Department of Health and Human Services (U.S. DHHS), National Institutes of Health (NIH). 1994a. NIH Guidelines on the Inclusion of Women and Minorities as Subjects in Clinical Research. *Federal Register* 59(59):14508–14513.

———. 1994b. *Outreach Notebook for the NIH Guidelines on Inclusion of Women and Minorities as Subjects in Clinical Research*. Bethesda, MD: National Institutes of Health.

U.S. Department of Health, Education, and Welfare (U.S. DHEW), Public Health Service, Food and Drug Administration (FDA). 1977. *General Considerations for the Clinical Evaluation of Drugs*. Washington, DC: U.S. Government Printing Office, HEW/FDA-77-3040.

U.S. General Accounting Office (U.S. GAO). 1990. National Institutes of Health: Problems in Implementing Policy on Women in Study Populations. Testimony of Mark Nadel before the Subcommittee on Health and the Environment, Committee on Energy and Commerce, House of Representatives. 101st Cong., 2d sess., 18 June.

————. 1992. *Women's Health: FDA Needs to Ensure More Study of Gender Differences in Prescription Drug Testing.* Washington, DC: U.S. Government Printing Office, GAO/HRD-93-17.

Weisman, C. S. 1998. *Women's Health Care: Activist Traditions and Institutional Change.* Baltimore, MD: Johns Hopkins University Press.

Wierenga, D. E., and C. Eaton. 1993. The Drug Development and Approval Process. In *In Development: New Medicines for Older Americans.* Washington, DC: Pharmaceutical Manufacturers Association.

Wolgast, E. H. 1980. *Equality and the Rights of Women.* Ithaca, NY: Cornell University Press.

Woolson, R., M. Jones, W. Clarke, and J. Torner. 1995. Discussion of "Inclusion of Women and Minorities in Clinical Trials and the NIH Revitalization Act of 1993–The Perspective of NIH Clinical Trialists." *Controlled Clinical Trials* 16:301–333.

Young, I. M. 1990. *Justice and the Politics of Difference.* Princeton, NJ: Princeton University Press.

Zimmerman, B., et al. 1980. People's Science. In *Science and Liberation*, ed. R. Aditta and S. Cavarak. Montreal: South End.

[13]

KIRSTI MALTERUD

THE (GENDERED) CONSTRUCTION OF DIAGNOSIS
INTERPRETATION OF MEDICAL SIGNS IN WOMEN PATIENTS

ABSTRACT. Medicine maintains a distinction between the medical symptom – the patient's "subjective" experience and expression, and the privileged medical sign – the "objective" findings observable by the doctor. Although the distinction is not consistently applied, it becomes clearly visible in the "undefined," medically unexplained disorders of women patients. Potential impacts of genderized interaction on the interpretation of medical signs are addressed by re-reading the diagnostic process as a matter of social construction, where diagnosis results from human interpretation within a sociopolitical context. The discussion is illustrated by a case story and empirical evidence of the gendering in the doctor-patient relationship. The theoretical analysis is supported by semiotic perspectives of bodily signs, feminist theory on experience, and Foucault's ideas about medical perception and gaze, and concludes that a medical diagnosis is seldom a biological fact, but the outcome of a process where biological, cultural and social elements are interwoven. Further deconstruction of the chain of signs from a feminist perspective, assigning validity to the voice of the woman patient, might broaden the understanding of women's health, illness and disease.

KEY WORDS: diagnosis, gaze, gender, medical reasoning, signs, symptoms

INTRODUCTION

Mainstream biomedicine maintains the ideal of a dichotomous distinction between the medical symptom and the medical sign.[1-4] While the former is a "subjective" matter, experienced and communicated by the patient (such as "pain in the neck"), the latter are assumed to be "objective" findings, observable by the doctor (for example "decreased mobility in the hip joint"). When the health care system operates in what Chinen calls the representational mode of medical understanding,[5] this dichotomy is emphasized, and symptoms are considered as secondary subjective reflections of an underlying objective reality. According to Foucault, medical signs are considered as objective facts, observable by the authority of the medical gaze.[1] The diagnosis – the name of the disease, which usually will explain the origin of the symptoms – is supposed to emerge as a fact which is discovered by the doctor when the puzzle of symptoms and signs has been sorted out and deciphered.[5,6]

Theoretical Medicine and Bioethics **20**: 275–286, 1999.
© 1999 *Kluwer Academic Publishers. Printed in the Netherlands.*

In this article I suggest that these "facts" emerge from interaction and interpretation of medical signs, and that this is a gendered process. I will demonstrate how medicine is inherently ambiguous on the symptom/sign dichotomy: on one hand, the epistemology of the representational mode is commonly referred to in medical theory and practice, implying that there are distinguished sources for clinical knowledge, with objective findings different from and ranking higher than subjective symptoms. On the other hand, subjective symptoms are nevertheless consistently valued as significant diagnostic information in everyday clinical judgement. I intend to explore this contradiction by focusing on situations when the patient's subjective symptoms are not accepted as valid medical signs – more specificly: the medically unexplained disorders of women patients.[7] From this point, I will reflect on gendered interaction in clinical medicine.

My approach is to replace the representational mode with a re-reading of the diagnostic process as a matter of social construction, where diagnosis results from human interpretation within a social and political context. From this position, it is possible to adress potential impacts of genderized interaction[8] on the construction of medical knowledge towards diagnosis by interpretation of medical symptoms and signs. Referring to semiotic perspectives on bodily signs,[9] I shall here deliberately use the word "sign" to denote anything which determines something about something to somebody, including the interpretant of the sign as a visible and situated actor. From this perspective, both patient and doctor are legitimate interpretants of medical signs. The discussion will be illustrated by a case story and supported by empirical evidence on the gendering of the doctor-patient relationship.

PAIN IN THE CHEST AND SHOULDERS –
THE CASE OF "JUDITH SMITH"

Judith Smith's story below is fiction, but draws on the author's similar experiences with authentic patients and doctors. The case story emphasizes experiences and consequences of pain, and how they are communicated, perceived and interpreted towards a diagnostic conclusion.[a]

Judith Smith (age 55) has pain in her chest and shoulders. She believes that this sign comes from her muscles, not from her heart. However, her mother died from a heart attack, and she is concerned. She has experienced that strain at work and at home increases her muscular tension, but she is not able to change her situation and relieve her symptoms.

One Wednesday morning Judith Smith is not able to go to work because of her pain. She needs a sick leave certificate, and she wants a medical explanation so that she can check her own understanding of the signs of pain and disability. The doctor listens to Judith

Smith's symptoms and story, which he recognizes from previous encounters with middle-aged women. The signs communicated by the patient are perceived by the doctor as not very serious. The doctor knows from experience that conditions like this tend to become chronic, and he has no effective cure. The doctor's interpretation is processed through a cultural grid of experience, emotions, attitudes, and preconception about this kind of patient and this kind of knowledges.

The doctor assumes that Judith Smith believes she has heart disease, that she does not attribute her symptoms to her life situation, and that she should be able to modify her daily life burdens. The clinical examination does not reveal any findings or sign considered significant by the doctor, and the medical signs represented by Judith Smith's experience, perception and story are not in this case considered relevant for the diagnosis of disease. The doctor's inference is that no signs of disease have been identified.

This conclusion is given to the patient (no diagnosis), and to the community (no sickness leave certificate). Judith Smith feels depressed and goes to work. Her symptoms and disability continue to increase.

GENDER IN DOCTOR-PATIENT INTERACTION

Judith Smith, a woman patient, has in this case consulted a male doctor.[b] Although many women patients prefer women doctors,[10–13] the gender distribution of doctors in the Western world is such that women patients most often meet a male doctor. This pattern is reinforced by the fact that women consult more often than men do. Referring to the typical participants of the consultation – the male doctor and the woman patient – the medical interaction is gendered from the initial moment, and even before that. The templates through which the doctor filters his perceptions of any sign, are embedded with his beliefs and sociocultural positioning.[14] The doctor's ability to perceive the signs of the patient is read through his sociocultural images of 55 year old women patients, as is the patient's image of herself. The overview below will illustrate the potential impact of gender in the doctor-patient relationship of the case story above.

Gendered assumptions about patients influence doctors' interpretation of medical symptoms and their management, as demonstrated in a study where 120 general practitioners assessed constructed case histories.[15] The cases were presented as identical, except for gender. Doctors who attributed the symptoms to women patients, gave significantly higher score for emotional explanations of the symptoms than doctors who thought the same symptoms belonged to men. Another study that compared examinations and tests for 181 patients with back ache, headache, dizziness, breast pain or fatigue, showed that men patients were significantly more comprehensively investigated than women patients with matching symptoms.[16] Among 2,231 patients in a postinfarction intervention trial, men were twice as likely to undergo an invasive cardiac procedure as women, despite stronger cardiac disability in these women patients.[17] In 82,782 patients hospitalized for coronary heart disease, consistent male-to-female odds ratios confirmed that women underwent fewer major diagnostic and therapeutic procedures than men with the same condition.[18] Women aged 46–60 years in the United States in long-term dialysis had less than half the chance of receiving a kidney transplant when compared with men of the same age and race.[19] Studies like these do not clarify whether such gender imbalances might be adequate, or whether they refer to social and gender bias. However, physician gender bias was identified in a recent longitudinal observation study of 1,546 patients of 349 physicians, where the odds of prescribed activity restrictions from the doctor were 3.6 times higher for women patients than for mens with equivalent characteristics.[20]

The doctor's gender also has an impact on the medical encounter. Women enrolled in a large health plan were more likely to undergo screening with Pap smears and mammograms when they saw women rather than men physicians.[21] A Dutch study including 47,254 consultations showed that women doctors spent more time on their patients and had a stronger tendency to provide continuity of care.[22] In a Canadian survey where 3,000 doctors were asked about prenatal diagnosis, women doctors reported more liberal attitudes than their men colleagues.[23] A case-control study from an urban outpatient practice in Boston demonstrated that women were more likely to be prescribed estrogen replacement therapy if they were cared for by women doctors than men doctors.[24] A survey among 1,000 primary care phycisians in Michigan showed that men doctors more often endorsed pharmacological treatment for depression in the elderly, while women doctors more frequently used conseling and exercise techniques.[25]

Communication between doctor and patient is affected by gender on both sides. Analysis of material from 336 audiotaped consultations revealed that women patients ask more questions to the doctor than men patients do, but although they proportionately have more responses from the doctor, the responses are less adequate.[26] In 21 videotaped consultations, men doctors were responsible for 67% of the interruptions during the medical conversation, while women doctors were responsible for 32%. A study of 100 videotaped consultations showed distinctive gendered patterns of doctor-patient communicative behaviour, especially in nonverbal communication.[27] Gender operates on diverse levels in medical interaction, and should also be adressed when it comes to the interpretative part of the diagnostic process.

WOMEN'S "UNDEFINED" MEDICALLY UNEXPLAINED DISORDERS

The case of Judith Smith portrays the "undefined", medically unexplained disorders – the commonly occurring conditions where the lack of observed findings is seen as significant, while the doctor's subsequent diagnostic interpretations discard the meaning of the patient's symptom experience. The logic of the representational mode of medicine implies that doctors can discriminate "real" disease from "unreal" disease by means of objective findings.[2] Symptoms without corresponding findings lack the structural correlation which signifies and legitimizes real disease, and will accordingly be refused the status of "real disease". The lack of signs in a strictly medical meaning justifies that these conditions are regarded as a vague or unspecific anomaly, classified as "other", "diverse" or "undefined", although the patients suffer from painful and disabling symptoms.[7] The medically unexplained disorders comprise a diversity of expressions, such as chronic pain syndromes, chronic fatigue, tension headache, irritable bowel, urinary tract inflammation, or whiplash trauma sequelae. The doctor does not understand the origin of the illness, and he does not know how to bring relief or cure.

Male patients may certainly experience the consequences of observable findings as privileged medical signs as compared to symptoms. However, there is a remarkable and consistent majority of women compared to men who suffer from the commonly occurring conditions mentioned above.[7] In these cases, where medical signs are interpreted according to the representational mode of medical understanding, subjective symptoms are overruled by objective findings, or rather the lack of such.

Women patients with chronic muscular pain report experiences of humiliation and distrust from the health care system when they present their symptoms.[28,29] The culturally impregnated judgement of the medical expert overrules and may even pervade the woman patient's bodily experience and interpretation.[30] Because an approved medical diagnosis is lacking, the patients risk being refused access to welfare benefits as sickness leave certificates or disability pension. They are concerned with the contested "reality" of pain, resist being blamed for this, and return the blame to the doctor who has not yet identified the cause of the pain.[31] Eccleston and co-workers comment that the place of power is an important issue in this web of blame, responsibility and identity.

Given the evidence on gender-biased interaction presented above, my hypothesis is that gender-biased interaction contributes to strategies of diagnostic reasoning where privilege is systematically given to the

280   KIRSTI MALTERUD

doctor's perception of medical signs, especially when the patient is a woman.

THE MEDICAL GAZE – PRIVILEGED SIGNS UNDER
CERTAIN CIRCUMSTANCES

Lilleaas's informants report the experiences of being labelled as whimpering, complaining or irrational if they tell their story and share the signs as perceived by them.[28] Due to the alleged scientific "objectivity" of medicine, doctors alone have the competency to make proper judgments about health and options.[32] Women's perceptions are communicated to the doctor, whose medical gaze[1] will interpret the signs and determine whether they are valid or not. Foucault comments that although the medical gaze is a collective mode of perception, shaped by issues related to politics and power as codes of knowledge, it is supposed to be open and receptive, not bound by the narrow grid of predefined structure.[c]

The "undefined" disorders emerge as an conceptual anomaly defined from within the representational mode of understanding. The indisputable existence of such disorders, portrayed by the large number of women with muscular pain syndromes, testifies that the medical culture of knowledge holds a hierachy of signs, where certain kinds of signs are more privileged than others. Symptoms are subordinate to findings, which are believed to be objective. Indirect evidence, as mediated by medical technology, seems to constitute to medical signs a stronger validity than direct evidence from the voice of the patient. However, this hegemony seems to deny that any indirect representation of disease is dependent on the contemporary scope, perspective and technological level. Illness which produces symptoms without leaving footprints available for the medical eye, may yet be visible tomorrow. The objectivity of indirect findings might certainly be contested.

Although gaze literally refers to visual perception, Foucault considered the medical gaze and its corresponding discourse to be a comprehensive mode of perception.[1] Auditiory perception may also be included in the gaze under certain circumstances. When auditive cues are mediated through medical instruments and analyzed by the doctor (listening to the heartbeats through the stethoscope), the problem of subjectivity seems to be no problem. However, when it comes to the voice of the patient with the medically unexplained disorder, this auditive cue can be discarded due to its alleged subjectivity. The medical gaze favours indirect and objectivized listening, preferably through technological devices.

THE (GENDERED) CONSTRUCTION OF DIAGNOSIS   281

Indirect visual signs, as x-ray pictures, are commonly considered as the absolute standard for objective diagnosis. The x-rays of women with "undefined" disorders are typically negative, with no pathological findings. I shall not deny the existence of x-ray pictures where any observer would agree upon the conclusion, and the progress of the case would confirm the correspondence between the interpreted signs and some significant clinical pattern. This might be the case when a broken leg is investigated and operated on. Ontologically, however, signs like these are just interpreted and indirect representations of selected elements of the body, perceived from specific positions and perspectives, and interpreted according to consensus values within radiology and clinical medicine. Empirical studies demonstrate considerable interobserver variation for clinical data assumed to be objective facts,[33] for example the problems of accuracy and variabiliy in mammographic interpretation.[34] This is not surprising, for even in experimental laboratory research, findings are the objects of human manipulation and interpretation.[35] Even within the most "objective" fields of medicine, human perception and interpretation can construct clinical knowledge presented as facts. The problem is not that this is happening, but that medical culture on certain frequently occurring occasions insists on the ideal of a diagnostic model in which signs and symptoms are separate phenomena.

While certain symptoms seem to require an objective correlate, others do not. Although patients with medically unexplained disorders experience that their symptoms are discarded, clinical decision-making is not consequent in sticking to the representational mode of understanding in any medical situation. The patient's symptom experience and story is actually very often attributed a strong impact and recognized as a medical fact in the construction of medical knowledge – not only in contexts classified as "undefined." In 77% of the cases at a British outpatient clinic, the diagnostic conclusion was mainly drawn from the story of the patient. Only in the remaining proportion, the clinical examination and technical tests contributed significantly to the diagnostic conclusion.[36] A gap between symptoms and findings is common even in supposedly "well-defined" conditions as pneumonia and dyspepsia.[37,38] Under such conditions, however, the discrepancy seems not to be held against the patients, as happens with the women who reported that they felt blamed for the disconcordance between symptoms and findings.[28]

282   KIRSTI MALTERUD

MEDICAL INTERPRETATION IN A SOCIAL AND CULTURAL CONTEXT

In the representational mode of medical understanding, a fact is a fact, unbiased by the observer as well as the context and the situation. What is not seen by the doctor, is not there.[1,5] The interpretative components of this activity and their contextual dependency are seldomly questioned. Perception and presentation of bodily symptoms are not just the simple exchange of facts, but a complicated hermeneutic process of reading and understanding the text of medical signs.[39] Von der Fehr used semiotic perspectives to elucidate the role of consciousness on the patient's perception and interpretation of bodily signs.[40] Rudebeck says that from a phenomenological perspective, a symptom is an act of perception, which contains both the meaning and its physical correlate, whereas the symptom presentation is a personal communication of a very private experience.[41] However, perception and expression of bodily experience are not solely "authentic" features, unbiased by the cultural context of the woman, but also constituted by historical context. Scott reminds us that what counts as experience is neither self-evident nor straightforward, – it is always contested and therefore political.[42] Even the bodily experience of a woman is influenced by the life she lives and the meanings of illness and womanhood in her culture.

The doctor is supposed to make sense of the patient's narrative. Rudebeck introduces the concept *"bodily empathy"* as a preconception for the clinical understanding of medical symptoms. We might suggest that the doctor's perception and response do not accommodate the bodily empathy needed to acknowledge the suffering of the women with medically unexplained disorders. The task of clinicians and clinical researchers is to extend and perfect the maps of illness, although each patient, and each instance of illness are yet uncharted territory.[43] Anomalies not fitting neatly into the puzzle of the doctor's mind, run the risk of being discarded, like the problems of Judith Smith. The doctor might forget that "the clinical entity" is only a preliminary typology[43] and blame the patient for not presenting a clearcut clinical pattern.

THE CONSTRUCTION OF MEDICAL "FACTS"

From a constructionist point of view, the validation of medical signs is not a mechanical procedure exposing undeniable facts, but a matter of perception, interpretation, narration, and negotiation.[33] The doctor's

THE (GENDERED) CONSTRUCTION OF DIAGNOSIS 283

inner images, constructed by previous medical science and history, are the template towards which the clinical signs are read by the medical gaze.

In fiction stories like the one presented in this article, the author has the freedom to exaggerate. In the story above, this was done to illustrate and emphasize the potential clinical impact of some of the gender issues which have been documented by empirical evidence. The reader should be warned not to interpret this story in an essentialist way, implying that all women patients are comparable to Judith Smith. Medical reality is not that simple, although stories from this reality sometimes may be read as simplified realities – even by the doctor.

Medical theory and practice have; for a long time, been constructed by men, with the clinical gaze of men, the cultural templates of men, and the perception and language of men. It is therefore not unexpected that the clinical signs presented by women patients are not always adequately embraced within the scope of contemporary medical epistemology. Theoretical and empirical evidence remind us that the interpretation of clinical signs depends on the position of the reader – even the gendered ones. From such a perspective, it is not surprising that medical signs in women have been denied medical validity.

A medical diagnosis is seldom a biological fact, but commonly the outcome of a process in which biological, cultural and social elements are interwoven through interaction and language. A semiotic perspective allows us to dispute the narrow conception of a medical sign as an observable, objective finding. The demonstration of the potentially gendered dynamics and effects of the interpretative and interactive elements of the diagnostic process calls for feminist perspectives on medical epistemology and clinical practice. Further deconstruction of the chain of signs from a feminist perspective, assigning validity to the voice of women patients, might broaden the understanding of women's health, illness and disease, and of the cultural construction of medical knowledge.

ACKNOWLEDGEMENTS

This article origins from a crossdisciplinary feminist collaboration about women's chronic muscular pain at the Center for Feminist Research, University of Oslo. I thank Ulla-Britt Lilleaas, sociologist, and Drude von der Fehr, literary theoretician, for their important contributions and critical comments.

284 KIRSTI MALTERUD

NOTES

[a] I admit that I might recognize myself in the role of the doctor, although I prefer to consider myself as more empathetic than the doctor portrayed here.

[b] I would not deny the possibility that what happened in this consultation, might have happened even with a woman doctor.

[c] This contradiction in logic attends to the relationship between ideals and practice mentioned initially.

REFERENCES

1. Foucault M. *The Birth of the Clinic. An Archaeology of Medical Perception.* New York: Vintage Books, 1994/73.
2. King LS. *Medical Thinking. A Historical Preface.* Princeton, New Jersey: Princeton University Press, 1982: 73–89.
3. Armstrong D. The patient's view. *Soc Sci Med* 1984; 18: 737–744.
4. Honkasalo, ML. Medical symptoms: A challenge for semiotic research. *Semiotica* 1991; 87: 251–268.
5. Chinen AB. Modes of understanding and mindfulness in clinical medicine. *Theoretical Medicine* 1988; 9: 45–71.
6. Albert DA, Munson R, Resnik MD. *Reasoning in Medicine. An Introduction to Clinical Inference.* Baltimore: The Johns Hopkins University Press, 1980.
7. Malterud K. Women's undefined disorders – A challenge for clinical communication. *Family Practice* 1994; 9: 299–303.
8. Code L. *What Can She Know? Feminist Theory and the Construction of Knowledge.* Ithaca & London: Cornell University Press, 1991.
9. Hoopes J, ed. *Peirce on Signs. Writings on Semiotic by Charles Sanders Peirce.* Chapel Hill/London: The University of North Carolina Press, 1991.
10. Graffy J. Patient choice in a practice with men and women general practitioners. *British Journal of General Practice* 1990; 40: 13–15.
11. Philliber SG, Jones J. Staffing a contraceptive service for adolescents: the importance of sex, race and age. *Public Health Report* 1992; 97: 165–169.
12. Brink Muinen A van der, Bakker DH de, Bensing JM. Consultations for women's health problems: factors influencing women's choice of sex of the general practitioner. *British Journal of General Practice* 1994; 44: 205–210.
13. Orzano AJ, Cody RP. Gender concordance between family practice residents and diagnoses in an ambulatory setting. *Family Medicine* 1995; 27: 440–443.
14. Pendleton D. Doctor – patient communication – a review. In: Pendleton D, Hasler J, eds. *Doctor – Patient Communication.* London: Academic Press Inc, 1983: 5–53.
15. Colameco S, Becker LA, Simpson M. Sex bias in the assessment of patient complaints. *Journal of Family Practice* 1983; 16: 1117–1121.
16. Armitage KJ, Schneiderman LJ, Bass RA. Response of physicians to medical complaints in men and women. *JAMA* 1979; 241: 2186–2187.
17. Peterson MC, Holbrook JH, von Hales D, Smith NL, Staker LV. Contributions of the history, physical examination, and laboratory investigation in making medical diagnosis. *West J Med* 1992; 156: 163–165.

THE (GENDERED) CONSTRUCTION OF DIAGNOSIS 285

18. Ayanian JZ, Epstein AM. Differences in the use of procedures between women and men hospitalized for coronary heart disease. *N Engl J Med* 1991; 325: 221–225.

19. Kjellstrand CM. Age, sex, and race inequality in renal transplantation. *Arch Intern Med* 1988; 148: 1305–1309.

20. Safran DG, Rogers WH, Tarlov AR, McHorney CA, Ware JE JR. Gender differences in medical treatment: The case of physician-prescribed activity restrictions. *Soc Sci Med* 1997; 45: 711–722.

21. Lurie N, Slater J, McGovern P, Ekstrum J, Quam L, Margolis K. Preventive care for women. Does the sex of the physician matter? *N Engl J Med* 1993; 329: 478–482.

22. Bensing JM, van den Brink Muinen A, deBakker DH. Gender differences in practice style: a Dutch study of general practitioners. *Med Care* 1993; 31: 219–229.

23. Bouchard L, Renaud M. Female and male physicians' attitudes toward prenatal diagnosis: a Pan-Canadian survey. *Soc Sci Med* 1997; 44: 381–392.

24. Seto TB, Taira DA, Davis RB, Safran C, Phillips RS. Effect of physician gender on the prescription of estrogen replacement therapy. *J Gen Intern Med* 1996; 11: 197–203.

25. Banazak DA. Late-life depression in primary care. How well are we doing? *J Gen Intern Med* 1996; 11: 163–167.

26. Wallen J, Waitzkin H, Stoeckle JD. Physician stereotypes about female health and illness: A study of patients sex and the informative process during medical interviews. *Women & Health* 1979; 4: 135–146.

27. Hall JA, Irish JT, Roter DL, Ehrlich CM, Miller LH. Gender in medical encounters: an analysis of physician and patient communication in a primary care setting. *Health Psychol* 1994; 13: 384–392.

28. Lilleaas UB. *Når forskjellen blir synlig – kvinner med kroniske muskelsmerter i et kjønnsrolleperspektiv.* [Making the difference visible – women with chronic muscular pain in a gender role perspective] Arbeidsnotat 8/95 – Senter for kvinneforskning. Oslo: Universitetet i Oslo, 1995 (in Norwegian).

29. Johansson EE, Hamberg K, Lindgren G, Westman G. "I've been crying my way" – qualitative analysis of allmenn group of female patients' consultation experiences. *Family Practice* 1996; 13: 498–503.

30. Lupton D. *Medicine as Culture. Illness, Disease and the Body in Western Societies.* London/Thousand Oaks/New Dehli: Sage Publications, 1994: 131–160.

31. Eccleston C, deWilliams C, Rogers WS. Patients' and professionals' understandings of the causes of chronic pain: Blame, responsitility and identity protection. *Soc Sci Med* 1997; 45: 699–709.

32. Sherwin S. *No Longer Patient. Feminist Ethics and Health Care.* Philadelphia: Temple University Press, 1992: 145–153.

33. Koran LM. The reliability of clinical methods, data and judgments. *N Engl J Med* 1975; 293: 642–701.

34. Elmore JG, Wells CK, Lee CH, Howard DH, Feinstein AF. Variability in radiologists' interpretation of mammograms. *N Engl J Med* 1994; 331: 1493–1499.

35. Latour B, Woolgar S. *Laboratory Life. The Construction of Scientific Facts.* Princeton/New Jersey: Princeton University Press, 1986.

36. Hampton JR, Harrison MJG, Mitchell JRA, Prichard JS, Seymour C. Relative contributions of history-taking, physical examination, and laboratory investigation to diagnosis and management of medical outpatients. *British Medical Journal* 1975; 2: 486–489.

286   KIRSTI MALTERUD

37. Melbye H. Diagnosis of pneumonia in adults in general practice. *Scandinavian Journal of Primary Health Care* 1992; 10: 226–233.
38. Johnsen R, Bernersen B, Straume B, Førde OH, Bostad L, Burhol PG. Prevalences of endoscopic and histological findings in subjects with and without dyspepsia. *British Medical Journal* 1991; 302: 749–752.
39. Daniel, SL. The patient as text: A model of clinical hermeneutics. *Theoretical Medicine* 1986; 7: 195–210.
40. Fehr D. Kropp og symptom i en tegnteoretisk kontekst. [Body and symptom in a semiotic theoretical context]. *Sosiologi i dag* 1996; (4): 65–77 (in Norwegian).
41. Rudebeck CE. General practice and the dialogue of clinical practice. On symptoms, symptom presentations and bodily empathy. *Scandinavian Journal of Primary Health Care* 1991; Suppl 1: 72–81.
42. Scott JW. "Experience". In: Butler J, Scott JW, eds. *Feminists Theorize the Political.* New York/London: Routledge, 1992: 22–40.
43. Hunter KM. *Doctors' Stories. The Narrative Structure of Medical Knowledge.* Princeton/New Jersey: Princeton University Press, 1991: 3–26.

Centre for Feminist Research
University of Oslo
P.O. Box 1040 Blindern
N-0315 Oslo
Norway

Address for correspondence:
University of Bergen
Ulriksdal 8C
N-5009 Bergen
Norway

[14]

LISA S. PARKER

BREAST CANCER GENETIC SCREENING
AND CRITICAL BIOETHICS' GAZE[1]

ABSTRACT. This paper illustrates a role that bioethics should play in developing and criticizing protocols for breast cancer genetic screening. It demonstrates how a critical bioethics, using approaches and reflecting concerns of contemporary philosophy of science and science studies, may critically interrogate the normative and conceptual schemes within which ethical considerations about such screening protocols are framed. By exploring various factors that influence the development of such protocols, including politics, cultural norms, and conceptions of disease, this paper and the critical bioethics' approach it endorses illuminate and critically assess some of the competing worldviews informing protocol development. One of the frequently neglected worldviews in traditional bioethics' treatment of protocols concerning breast care is constituted by women's own views of their breasts and breast cancer, both within the technologically-oriented social practice of American medicine and in light of the social construction of their breasted experience in American society. This paper attempts to redress and critically assess this neglect on the part of traditional bioethics. Finally, in contrast to traditional bioethics, critical bioethics critically interrogates its own normative and conceptual commitments. In this final capacity, a critical bioethics' approach makes a valuable contribution to the evolution of bioethics.

Key Words: bioethics, breast cancer genetic screening, conceptions of disease, conceptual frameworks

Through an exploration of the various factors that will influence the development of protocols for breast cancer genetic screening (e.g., BRCA1 screening), this paper will illustrate the role that bioethics should play in developing and criticizing such protocols. While some of these influences may be peculiar to the contexts of breast cancer, genetics, and screening interventions, others are of a more general nature. These influences include the politics of research funding, cultural conceptions of what is medically necessary (as opposed to elective), and cultural constructions of what is

Lisa S. Parker, Ph.D., Department of Human Genetics and Department of History and Philosophy of Science, University of Pittsburgh, 130 DeSoto Street, Pittsburgh, PA 15261 U.S.A.

The Journal of Medicine and Philosophy **20**: 313–337, 1995.

a matter of individual responsibility or choice (as opposed to what is socially influenced or beyond anyone's control). Therefore, making explicit how these factors will influence development of breast cancer genetic screening protocols will help to indicate how similar factors play roles in broader contexts. In addition, the process of revealing these influences will illustrate the contribution that a critical bioethics could make in these other contexts, such as health care reform. Cultural norms, like those concerning allocation of blame, the sick role, gender roles, and choice, influence, for example, the determination of which health care interventions are deemed medically necessary and, on this basis, which should be included in a package of basic health care benefits.

The development of breast cancer genetic screening protocols will also raise generalizable ethical concerns that have been the focus of much of traditional bioethics. Consideration of particular bioethical issues, such as how to preserve the confidentiality of BRCA1 carriers while providing them with appropriate social and psychological supports and medical interventions, cannot take place in isolation from consideration of the appropriateness and adequacy of the normative and conceptual schemes which frame the ethical concerns. Bioethics not only can consider possible solutions to specific ethical concerns, but also should offer critical analyses of the conceptual and normative frameworks within which these concerns arise. Analyses of this sort resemble contemporary work in philosophy of science, which has drawn attention to the need to examine carefully not only the content of science but also the conceptual frameworks within which scientific discoveries are made and used. They also resemble more recent work in the broader field of science studies with its more expansive view of its object of study and its interdisciplinary approach (Nelkin, 1989). Critical examination of factors influencing development of breast cancer genetic screening protocols affords an opportunity to witness the interplay among critical analysis of these frameworks, consideration of specific ethical concerns, and bioethics' own normative and conceptual commitments.

I. THE GAZE, OBJECTS, AND POWER OF CRITICAL BIOETHICS

Bioethics and bioethicists play a variety of roles within society and the social institutions of clinical medicine and medical science.

Bioethicists serve, for example, as teachers of clinical practitioners, as consultants and as patient advocates. They may play their most valuable and complex role, however, as critical commentators on the social practices that they witness (and in which they partici- pate). In this role, rather than merely seeking to identify and address ethical concerns arising within the social practices consti- tuting the clinical encounter, bioethicists can critically interrogate the values and conceptual schemes which ground the practices themselves.[2] Even in addressing the ethical conflicts that have tra- ditionally occupied both hospital-based bioethicists and classic bioethics texts – "May X breach Y's confidentiality?" "Who should make decisions about forgoing life-sustaining treatment?" – bio- ethics has long recognized that because the values and goals of patients and clinicians may differ vastly, the meanings of key con- cepts in their conceptual schemes pertaining to health and disease may also differ radically. The conceptual worlds inhabited by pa- tients and clinicians may indeed be as radically different as the social and economic worlds of laymen and the medical elite, or as the lived experiences of the sick and the well. In the light of this insight, bioethics can resemble contemporary philosophy of science, where investigation of science proceeds by focusing not only on the content of science but also by examining the concep- tual frameworks of science.

In its clinically-oriented roles of teaching and consultation, tra- ditional bioethics has, at least in part, cast itself as interpreter and reconciler of these different worldviews and seeks to make the values and worldviews of patients more intelligible to clinicians and vice versa. Of course, there is no value neutral patient-doctor, doctor-patient translation guide; there is no one-to-one correspon- dence between radically different worldviews. Consequently, tra- ditional bioethics frequently analyzes these competing conceptual schemes, seeking to make sense of each and to make each intelligi- ble to the other. In other words, depending upon the nature and degree of difference between the competing values or conceptual schemes involved, bioethics may call upon its interdisciplinary resources to address ethical concerns at the practical level (e.g., within the clinical setting). Variation in the degree to which such critical analysis proves necessary is evident since some bioethics consultations are solely a matter of facilitating communication be- tween various parties. In other cases, where the parties are "talking past each other" because of their radically different worldviews, the consultant working within a traditional bioethics' framework attempts to determine which set of values should prevail. Through tacit reference to its own normative and conceptual schemes, traditional bioethics endorses particular decisions and their underlying normative and conceptual frameworks. On the other hand, a critical bioethics would provide a normative critique of the competing conceptual and normative frameworks underlying such decisions. Moreover, recognizing that traditional bioethics has been engaged in a type of normative critique all along, albeit a rather univocal and unselfconscious one, inasmuch as it emphasizes the perspectives of a professional ethic and liberal pluralism, a critical bioethics would seek to make explicit bioethics' *own* normative and conceptual commitments.

In its traditional clinical role, perhaps even in its role as a participant in public policy debates, bioethics may quite appropriately seek common ground and compromise among parties with competing interests, claims and worldviews. In this role, bioethics as a social practice may achieve consensus on a particular issue, range of issues, or approach to problem solving. On the other hand, in its critical capacity, bioethics is unlikely to be so univocal. As they critically interrogate the values and conceptual schemes underlying various social practices (e.g., delivery of care by hospitals versus organizations, such as AIDS service organizations, or the structure of the clinical encounter versus peer intervention programs), individuals engaged in a critical bioethics' enterprise will likely come to endorse competing critiques and not permit anyone to dominate. Rather than rendering the field of bioethics inconsistent, this critical interrogation will enrich bioethics, which has hitherto preserved its relative univocality at the price of excluding various health-related practices (and their practitioners) as being outside of the domain of medicine and thus outside of its own domain. Recognition of the possibility, indeed the desirability, of competing critiques should, in turn, create a bioethics that is more explicit about and critical of its own normative and conceptual commitments.

As a mere critical observer of other social practices, bioethics may observe without being seen; i.e., criticize without itself being subject to observation and criticism, and without revealing the values and commitments underlying its own enterprise. However, insofar as bioethics makes claims to usefulness or to disciplinary validity, bioethics' norms and conceptual frameworks themselves should become subject to critical interrogation. Patients, understanding that bioethics purports to be a patient-centered ethic, may ask whether it truly attends to their experiences. Clinicians, viewing it as a professional ethic, may ask whether bioethics reflects the self-regulatory and exclusionary ethos of a profession. Cultural critics seeking an account of the social practice of medicine may ask whether bioethics is conscious of its own norms and its own role in various practical (or political) strategies.

The self-critical and strategic roles of bioethics deserve additional attention. Foucault suggests that much of modern disciplinary power lies in the ability of the observer to see without being revealed (Foucault, 1973). To re-interpret this insight slightly, it may be said that bioethics as an *inter*disciplinary enterprise is necessarily revealed and hence lacks disciplinary power. However, bioethics may gain interdisciplinary power by broadening its objects of study to include, for example, evidence about patient experiences and clinical practices, in a manner similar to science studies. For example, whereas traditional bioethics has sought to provide an account of *the* Jewish view of contraception without attending to Jews' actual contraceptive practices (Davis, 1994), a critical bioethics would include attention to lived experience as well as Talmudic authority. An additional source of power for a critical bioethics lies in its being an object of its own gaze. By providing a critique of its own normative and conceptual commitments, critical bioethics provides an analog of a disciplinary stance from which it may gain quasi-disciplinary power, albeit not the power of one who sees without being seen. In addition, a critical bioethics possesses strategic power by virtue of its discursive qualities and their potential as practical strategies or vehicles for effecting alliances both inside and outside of the social practice of medicine and among those with differing normative and conceptual commitments.

II. THE POLITICIZATION OF BREAST CANCER

Among the factors influencing the development of any breast cancer genetic screening protocol are the cultural, social, and political factors influencing the research, diagnosis, and treatment of breast cancer, combined with the norms surrounding genetic approaches to the detection and management of disease. Examination of these various influences is therefore essential to a critical analysis of the development of a protocol; such examination is part of the task of a critical bioethics that aims to crit-ically interrogate the normative and conceptual frameworks informing policy decisions.

Affecting the breasts of approximately 180,000 American women each year (Gail, 1992), and affecting still more women by striking their sisters and daughters with fear for their own health, with guilt about not being sick, and with a variety of other emotional, financial, and physical burdens, such as the provision of home health care, it is not surprising that breast cancer has taken center stage as a women's issue.

American women are told that they have an 11 percent lifetime risk of developing cancer, but that each woman needs to modify this "general population" risk to reflect a variety of factors (Gail, 1989; Gail, 1992; Marshall, 1993c). In contrast, women carrying the BRCA1 mutation have an approximately 85 percent lifetime risk of developing breast cancer, as well as an increased risk of ovarian cancer, with more than 50 percent of their breast cancers occurring before the age of 50 (Biesecker, 1993); 87 percent breast cancer risk by age 70 (Ford, 1994). Between 5 percent and 10 percent of breast cancers can be attributed to inherited or somatic gene mutations; the BRCA1 mutation is thought to be associated with 2–4 percent of breast cancer cases. Approximately one in 200 women – 600,000 American women – has inherited a susceptibility to breast cancer (King, 1993). Susceptibility is dominantly inherited from either mother or father; 50 percent of offspring will inherit the mutation (King, 1993; but see Gail, 1992).

A disease that one's grandmother might once have mentioned in a hushed tone as a "female problem," breast cancer has now become a highly politicized issue altering federal budgets, shaping the research agendas of the National Institute of Health (NIH), and reshaping coalitions within and between various communities. Breast cancer is at the center of not only political controversy, but also conflict between substantially different ways of understanding the goals and successes of various research agendas.

Since 1990 the NIH has taken steps to address charges that women have been discriminated against, because diseases in women are less likely to be studied than diseases in men, because women have been excluded from clinical trials, and because few women are senior research investigators (Dresser, 1992; Angell, 1993). Differing conceptions of being *affected* by disease and of being *disproportionately* affected will render different verdicts on this first discrimination charge and will suggest different actions to redress such alleged discrimination. Some diseases, like breast cancer, affect women almost exclusively, others affect them more often than men, and still others affect men and women almost equally. On the other hand, depending on how one conceives the notion of "being affected" by disease, it could be argued that almost all diseases disproportionately affect women who are typically the caregivers among the well. Women have indeed been excluded from studies of diseases that affect them and men equally. Whether diseases like breast cancer have in fact been ignored in favor of diseases affecting men (like prostate cancer) depends upon how attention to disease is to be measured. Although more research funds have been expended per life lost on breast cancer than prostate cancer (Angell, 1993), in terms of the number of people affected – e.g., living in fear of the disease or losing a partner, relative, or friend in midlife[3] – the amount spent on breast cancer could be claimed to be disproportionately low.

Breast cancer was also thrust onto center stage in the broader political arena of Congress. In an unusual case of the personal becoming political, coupled with a combination of traditional political maneuvering and anti-establishment political activism, Senator Tom Harkin managed to get 210 million dollars of the Department of Defense's budget earmarked for breast cancer. While Harkin may have been motivated by his experience with breast cancer in his family, other legislators were likely moved by the 600,000 letters delivered to members of Congress by the National Breast Cancer Coalition (NBCC) which was organized in January 1991. Emulating the tactics of ACT UP (AIDS Coalition to Unleash Power), the NBCC has become one of the most successful medical lobbying groups. Like ACT UP, the NBCC's activism is grounded in the principle that people living with or at risk for a disease should take an active role in drawing attention and resources to their experience. Like AIDS activism, the NBCC's activism is also grounded in medical expertise; prominent researcher, Kay Dickersin, and surgeon Susan Love are leading voices of the NBCC, which held technical meetings to inform Congress members about breast cancer (Love, 1993; Marshall, 1993a). Echoing the sentiments of AIDS activism, Love commented "what you can do...is get involved politically, because there's nothing else" (Morain, 1993, p. 15).

Finally, in recounting the course of breast cancer's service as a political strategic device, it should be noted that national agencies and national politics are not the only arenas in which it has been the catalyst for formation of alliances and for political activism. Within gay communities,[4] breast cancer has united and galvanized many lesbian women who found themselves alienated by these communities' attention to health concerns primarily associated with HIV/AIDS. Many lesbian women have thus found themselves aligned with nonlesbian women through their shared concern for the health of their breasts. In some cases, lesbian women have defined themselves as constituting a high risk group (Coward, 1992). The rhetorical, and thus political, power of (self-) constituting such a high risk group is instructive. Through such constitution, a largely invisible group of women, lesbians, gains visibility in relation to a disease which is attracting attention and financial resources. This visibility is purchased, however, at the price of being identified as (potential) victims. At the same time, on the model of AIDS activists, these (potential) victims deny their victim status even as they identify it; they assume the role of potential disease victims only as they refuse the sick role and become disease-oriented activists (Gessen, 1993).

One risk in this strategy is the phenomenon of "victim blaming." If victim blaming evolves with respect to breast cancer as it is evolving with respect to HIV/AIDS, this status of potential victim may disproportionately affect lesbian women whose increased risk for breast cancer is associated with factors deemed to be largely behavioral, or even *chosen* behaviors, such as forgoing childbearing or consuming alcohol or dietary fat.[5] Of concern in this regard are psychological and anatomical explanations, grounded in particular moral commitments and offered by some members of the far political right, for the "cancer-prone" lifestyle of feminists and the susceptibility to viral infection of gay men (Patton, 1993).[6]

Breast cancer genetic screening protocols will also be tremendously influenced by the increasing "geneticization" (Lippman, 1991) of disease. In part because of the enormous amounts of money being spent on the body of research collectively known as the Human Genome Project, and because of the public's perception of the recent successes in locating "genes" and developing treatments for genetic disease, breast cancer may become synonymous with genetically-linked breast cancer. This geneticization is dangerous in a number of ways. First, it will certainly influence the allocation of funds for research, diagnosis and treatment of breast cancer. In addition, geneticization is resulting in oversimplified social perceptions of breast cancer; instead of understanding and attempting to address breast cancer as a socially and environmentally mediated problem, people may come to see breast cancer as largely a matter of individual responsibility which may result in inappropriate victim blaming. Consequently, society may attribute irresponsibility to at-risk women who, for instance, refuse to undergo preventive mastectomy, or to parents who bear children despite knowledge of their increased risk. As a result, there may be pressure to craft public policies that penalize individuals for such behaviors (e.g., health care reform packages could fail to include adequate non-genetic screening for women at increased risk, or private insurance companies could refuse to insure infants who are carried to term despite parental knowledge of their increased risk).

Thus, scientific and medical facts about breast cancer, coupled with a variety of cultural norms, render it susceptible to being constituted as a device *within* various political strategies. These facts include that it is prevalent, that it can be genetically-linked, that it almost exclusively strikes women; that it strikes insidiously, and that it strikes women's breasts, which are both tissue with which women are often more closely identified (by themselves and others) than other body tissues, and objects so subject to cultural normative assessment as to almost constitute cultural artifacts. These facts and cultural norms also provide the raw materials for formulating political strategies to draw resources to breast cancer research, treatment and prevention.

III. THE BREAST CANCER EPIDEMIC: WHAT'S IN A NAME?

> *"If we told the men in this country that one in nine were going to lose a testicle, they'd think it was an epidemic and do something about it" – activist Eleanor Pred (Laurence, 1991).*

Although mortality rates from breast cancer have remained largely unchanged since the 1950s, the number of women diagnosed with breast cancer and age-specific incidence rates have risen in recent years (King, 1993). Not only are there more elderly women than ever before, but as the generation of women born after World War II reaches age 40, these women are becoming more at risk. Much of the rise in incidence rates may be attributable to early detection and lower mortality rates due to other causes (Feuer, 1993). Some report, however, that breast cancer risk has probably increased as the result of gradual changes in modern American women's lives (King, 1993). The average age of menarche is decreasing, perhaps because of improved nutrition and childbearing is being delayed.[7] Studies of environmental components, such as pollutants and increased dietary fat consumption, however, have generally proved inconclusive (Gail, 1992; Marshall, 1993b).

Some, especially NBCC members and affiliated researchers, have termed breast cancer a contemporary "epidemic" (Gorman, 1993; Kolata, 1994; Laurence, 1991; Morain, 1993; Zuckerman, 1992). They cite a 4 percent growth in incidence rates, as well as the seriousness of the disease: among women, breast cancer is the most frequent cancer and the second leading cause of death. Others, including some National Cancer Institute researchers, resist the epidemic label (Feuer, 1993; Marshall, 1993b). They argue that the increasing number of women diagnosed represent a one-time bulge in reported new cases, resulting from expanded use of mammography and detection of earlier and smaller tumors, as well as the shifting age demographics of women. These researchers also anticipate a declining mortality rate to result from the expanded mammographic screening of the 1980s. Even if members of these two camps could agree on the breast cancer "facts," they are likely to adopt different positions on the applicability of the epidemic label; moreover, because the "facts," for example, the explanation of the growth in incidence rates, are often themselves theoretical constructs, agreement on the facts is unlikely. The particular worldview of each camp is tied to its goals and values, to its understanding of key concepts (such as, risk of breast cancer), and to the "rhetorical mileage" inherent in the labels applied to breast cancer, e.g., whether it is termed a women's health issue or an epidemic.

Underlying application of the label of epidemic to breast cancer is recognition that one way in which to draw attention, and thus financial and intellectual resources, to a disease is to suggest that it is on the rise, spreading, or out of control. In the *us versus them* conceptualization of the healthy and the sick, the label of epidemic suggests that one's chance of becoming one of *them* is suddenly rapidly increasing. The rhetorical effect of the epidemic label is to create fear and to present the healthy with the choice of sticking their heads further into the sand of denial or of responding to the spread of disease by committing resources to its containment or eradication. In the early days when those living and dying with AIDS sought recognition of and resources for their battle with the disease, the label of epidemic suggested that AIDS was not (or soon would not be) an isolated problem affecting small numbers or isolated communities.

Nevertheless, a variety of liabilities attend the rhetorical power of the label of epidemic. Because of the demographics of early AIDS cases, for example, many of the healthy were allowed, even invited, by the epidemic label to deny that HIV/AIDS would spread to them. Much of the response to the epidemic of AIDS focused on the containment of the disease to members of relatively smaller communities already affected by it; eradication did not become a primary goal until HIV's spread from "high risk communities" to the "general population" became obvious. The us versus them strategy invited by the rhetoric of epidemic promoted denial and victim blaming: although hemophiliacs, children, and married women (of bisexual men) were viewed as innocent victims of HIV/AIDS, gay and bisexual men, injecting drug users, sex workers, and foreigners were seen as guilty victims and vectors of disease transmission. As information about HIV and its modes of transmission became more widespread, judgment of culpability for having the disease evolved: after a certain stage in the history of public health education about HIV/AIDS, one should have known better than to contract HIV, and one is, therefore, responsible for one's own illness.

With the advent of genetic screening for breast cancer, we may witness a similar eventual blaming of the victims of disease: at least those in "high risk communities," i.e., members of families with a history of breast cancer, should know better and take steps to prevent the onset of illness. Although members of such families have recognized that they are at increased risk, public attention has only recently become focused on families as high risk groups.[8] Time will tell whether the general cultural response is one of support for those at increased risk, or whether they will be blamed for developing their conditions. Unfortunately, as Love observes, some women already receive the message that they got their cancer because they did not do breast self-examinations (Morain, 1993). Failure to follow mammography screening protocols has been deemed somewhat understandable, partly because mammography is physically or psychologically uncomfortable for many; realizing the potential benefits of tumor detection involves facing both the possibility of having a potentially lethal disease entity in one's breast and the frightening nature of treatment alternatives (mastectomy, lumpectomy, radiation, and chemotherapy).[9] Moreover, for those without adequate insurance, mammography may be unaffordable.

While the burdens of prevention and treatment measures remain unchanged, development of a simple, relatively noninvasive, potentially inexpensive genetic test may undercut some women's excuses for not "learning the truth" about their breast cancer risk. Cases of inherited susceptibility to breast cancer may then be marked not only by self-blaming (for passing on a heritable trait) or blaming of one's parents, but also by social blaming. A woman who carries a mutation for breast cancer, but who chooses not to have prophylactic mastectomy or who fails to adhere to early detection protocols, may find herself with less sympathy from family, friends and society than she might have enjoyed prior to genetic screening. This is especially worrisome because carrying the genetic mutation is only a predictor of one's risk of developing breast cancer; in the case of BRCA1, one still has an approximately 13 percent chance of not developing breast cancer.[10] It is an open question whether society will grant the benefits of the sick role, and will assure quality health care, to female BRCA1 carriers who choose to keep their breasts, either because they gamble on being among the 13 percent escaping breast cancer or for some other reason, and who eventually develop the disease.

It is indeed likely that women's decisions concerning breast care and genetic screening will be subject to a great deal of scrutiny by clinicians, policy makers, feminists, bioethicists, and cultural critics. Such has traditionally been the case. One might say that women's decisions with respect to their breasts attract almost as much attention as the breasts themselves, but given the place of breasts in American culture, this would undoubtedly be an overstatement. The cultural construction of breasts, as well as the norms governing the treatment of women's choices about their breasts within a variety of social practices (e.g., clinical medicine or FDA regulation), help to constitute the competing normative and conceptual frameworks which will undoubtedly inform the terms of discussion of a breast cancer genetic screening protocol. Therefore, in addition to analyzing particular ethical concerns pertaining to such screening, bioethics will be called upon to critically interrogate these conceptual frameworks and social practices and to illuminate what is at stake for those who hold and participate in them.

IV. DIFFERENT WORLDVIEWS AND BORDER SKIRMISHES OVER WOMEN'S BREASTS

> *"Cosmetic surgery... is an ideological battlefield where women grapple... with opposing cultural constructions of femininity, beauty, and what should or should not be done about the female body"* – feminist *Kathy Davis (1991).*
>
> *"I would choose death over disfigurement. This is my reality"* – breast cancer patient and activist *Felicia Neal (FDA, 1992).*

The bodies of literature discussing breast surgery and recounting recent debates about the safety of silicone breast implants used for reconstruction and augmentation are replete with evidence of radically different views of women's breasts. Examination of the worldviews informing the breast implant debate will be instructive for the development of a breast cancer genetic screening protocol for two reasons. First, genetic screening for breast cancer and breast implantation obviously concern the same extremely personal, yet culturally constructed body tissue-women's breasts. Second, debate about access to breast implants and the development of criteria for access to screening both raise a traditional bioethical concern: the need to balance autonomous patient choice and considerations of patient welfare. Particularly important for a critical bioethics' analysis of this balance with respect to the development of breast cancer genetic screening protocols will be consideration of how women's decisions about breast surgery have been treated in relevantly similar contexts, as well as the reasons for this treatment.

Critical interrogation of the clinical practice of evaluating breast augmentation candidates, as well as the FDA's development of a protocol for studying the safety of silicone breast implants, reveals that women's breast surgery decisions are often not taken seriously. These decisions are subject to scrutiny, just as "a woman's chest, much more than a man's, is *in question* in this society, up for judgment, and whatever the verdict she has not escaped the condition of being problematic" (Young, 1990, p. 189). The scrutiny to which breast surgery decisions are subjected renders suspect both a woman's decisionmaking capacities and the personal experiences and values which inform her decisions. In short, her worldview is first rendered suspect and then, more often than not, is disregarded. Women who do not want to have their decisions about breast surgery disregarded learn to conform the expression of their choices to the terms which are deemed acceptable within the clinical and public health regulatory worldviews.[11] This scrutiny and disregard of women's decisions occur with frequency and in a characteristic style amounting to a *systematic* devaluation and disregard of the normative and conceptual frameworks within which women's breast care decisions are made. The worldviews of clinical, and especially acute care, medicine trump a view of breasts informed by the experience of actually having them. While traditional bioethics would likely conceive of this situation as a conflict between patient rights and professional ethics within the ethos of liberal pluralism that constitutes bioethics' own normative framework, a critical bioethics' perspective would critically interrogate these competing worldviews from a perspective informed by its own diverse normative commitments, not simply those assumed in liberal pluralism.

In the 1992 FDA policy governing access to clinical trials of silicone breast implants, candidates for breast reconstruction were guaranteed access to implants, while augmentation candidates' access was severely restricted. In justifying this differential treatment, FDA Commissioner David Kessler termed breast reconstruction a "public health need" and described it as "an integral part" of breast cancer treatment (Kessler, 1992).[12] Mastectomy constitutes a paradigmatic case of life-saving, acute care medicine, and reconstruction restores victims to their former, normal condition. In contrast, breast augmentation only restores recipients to a socially constructed norm. While the benefits of mastectomy are treated as objective, the benefits of breast implantation are largely subjective; i.e, the patient's values and goals serve to constitute the benefits of implantation. A breast cancer patient's desire for mastectomy and for breast reconstruction thereafter is deemed to be much more understandable than a woman's desire for breast augmentation. Little needs to be known about the breast cancer patient's individual values in order to understand her desire for implantation; her diagnosis justifies her desire to be made whole.

A breast augmentation candidate must model her desire for implantation on this acute care medical conceptualization of breasts; she must "justify her decision with accounts of extreme suffering. However, even these will require some special handling if she is not to appear psychologically unstable or overly dependent on the approval of men" (Davis, 1991, p. 24). A breast augmentation candidate must justify her decision by making her unhappiness with her "breasted experience" as acute as a mastectomy patient's, and she must do so without impugning her capacity to give informed consent (Parker, 1995). In order to walk this tightrope, she must make her suffering visible in a way that others (e.g., clinicians or members of the FDA advisory panel) may understand it. As she explains her decision to seek surgery, her prospective surgeon has the opportunity to determine whether the surgery is likely to afford the subjective benefits sought, to ensure a track record of good surgical results, and to avoid likely malpractice liability exposure. The norms governing this social practice of "assessing good candidates" allows clinicians to sustain "the belief in objective, factual, trans-situational grounds for aesthetic improvement – even as these are constructed from the particulars of the case at hand" (Dull, 1991, p. 61). In order for her decision to be intelligible to her surgeon (or other gate keepers, such as the FDA advisory panel), the breast surgery candidate must explain her breasted experience within the cultural construction of breasts, within the "male gaze" (Young, 1990), but not as inappropriately subordinated to that gaze. Candidates must explain that they desire augmentation for themselves, but they must make their desire understood to those who do not share their breasted worldview.

According to Young, before the normalizing, objectifying male gaze "what matters is the look of them, how they measure up... There is one perfect shape and proportion for breasts... The norm is contradictory..." (1990, p. 191). Young proposes a "conceptualization of a woman-centered experience of breasts" that is a "construction, an imagining," because no woman can experience her breasts utterly outside of the male gaze (1990, p. 192). Yet "from the position of the female subject, what matters most about her breasts is their feeling and sensitivity rather than how they look" (Young, 1990, p. 194). Indeed, because augmented breasts may lose some of their sensitivity, fail to move like organic breast tissue, and may suffer painful capsular contracture, informed augmentation candidates must be seeking implantation for reasons stemming from their breasted experience *within* the male gaze, i.e., within the cultural construction of breasts that is largely structured by the normative and conceptual framework of traditional, patriarchal, masculine culture.

Women who say that they seek breast augmentation "for themselves" to increase self-esteem or self-confidence or to improve self-image implicitly acknowledge that society not only treats physical appearance as a difference worth noting, but also link it to such social goods as regard, self-esteem, love, power, employment, and security. Some feminists have, therefore, concluded that women's decisions to have their breasts augmented are inauthentic or reflect false consciousness (e.g., Chapkis, 1986; Shapiro, 1992). Some have argued that women's decisions to have their breasts reconstructed following mastectomy similarly reflect false consciousness. They would prefer that women transform their bodily identities into those of one-breasted women and embrace a political strategy with the multiple goals of challenging the contradictory norm of breastedness within the male gaze and of allowing breast cancer patients to identify each other and to form a community of survivors (Lorde, 1980, p. 61; Young, 1990). Others recognize that women must make their choices within the prevailing cultural context and that it is, therefore, not unreasonable for them to consider cultural values in making their decisions (Davis, 1991). As Katha Pollitt notes, "self-esteem does not occur in a vacuum but in response to social pressures and rewards" (1992).

In this light, then, the importance that women place on the appearance of their breasts can be understood. Felicia Neal's choice of death over disfigurement becomes understandable (even to those who would disagree) only in light of a critical interrogation of the normative and conceptual frameworks within which Neal and other women make their choices about breast care. The importance that women generally place on their breasts' appearance may help to explain a variety of conflicting breast care behaviors. It may, for example, be employed to explain both adherence to and avoidance of breast self-examination and mammography protocols. It may help to explain ambivalent feelings, on the part of women at increased risk for breast cancer, about their breasts: their breasts may appear to them as time bombs that they desperately want to diffuse, but do not want to be rid of.

V. BREAST CANCER GENETIC SCREENING: BIOETHICS' OWN COMMITMENTS AND LESSONS FROM OTHER CONTEXTS

It remains to be seen precisely how differing worldviews will affect the development of protocols for breast cancer genetic screening. Already evident is the influence of the technology-driven, acute care conceptual scheme of American medicine. This conceptual scheme is reflected in the fact that the anticipated demand for breast cancer risk analysis (BCRA) is linked to the availability of a *medical* test, BRCA1 screening. Only 2–4 percent of current breast cancer cases are associated with the BRCA1 mutation. Given what is already known about other risk factors associated with breast cancer, as well as the anticipated link between early detection and reduced mortality and the established link between BCRA and adherence to detection guidelines, BCRA should already be much more widely offered by clinicians than it is currently (Kelly, 1987; Kelly, 1992; Mulvihill, 1989). Unfortunately, general clinical medicine does not share the view held by genetic counselors that the provision of information itself constitutes a medical intervention. Critical bioethics may play an important role in the development of protocols for breast cancer genetic screening, including BRCA1, by reflecting critically upon this technology-driven conceptual framework for according priority to medical interventions.

A variety of traditional bioethical concerns will be raised by the institution of breast cancer genetic screening programs. Many of these have been anticipated and already confronted at the intersection of research and clinical practice, where subjects, knowing that researchers were closing in on the BRCA1 mutation, sought researchers' medical advice about the risk for breast cancer and the advisability of prophylactic mastectomy (Biesecker, 1993; Breo, 1993). Their concerns included the preservation of privacy, confidentiality, insurability, employability, family relationships, and rights of self-determination of those seeking testing. As demand for population-based BRCA1 screening grows, those who would develop a BRCA1 screening protocol will confront the task of balancing patient choice and patient welfare. After identifying the "indications" for BRCA1 screening, i.e., after specifying the criteria for determining who should be offered or allowed access to it, a protocol will need to address two potential groups of women: (1) women who want BRCA1 screening, but for whom it is not deemed by the protocol to be medically indicated (perhaps because they have no family history of breast cancer), and (2) those for whom screening is deemed to be indicated, but who do not desire it. Here again critical bioethics may interrogate the normative and conceptual commitments of these women and of those who would act as gate-keepers of access to screening. This critical analysis will not purport to be value neutral, but will necessarily reflect diverse norms and conceptual commitments. Examining women's decisions to augment their breasts will reveal these diverse frameworks; depending upon the norms of the critic, a critical bioethics' analysis may endorse supporting women's decisions or challenging both the authenticity and the social construction of their choices. What is clear, however, is that bioethics will derive its greatest critical power from being explicit about its own normative and conceptual commitments.

Finally, using a methodology not unlike that evident in contemporary philosophy of science, bioethics may examine particular issues of concern within the purview of its critical interrogation, seeking both to examine differing (or possibly incommensurable) worldviews and to effect resolution of conflicting views where possible. In addition, in a manner paralleling recent interdisciplinary and self-critical approaches in science studies, bioethics may broaden its scope of study and self-consciously reflect the diverse normative and conceptual commitments which its analyses assume.

Drawing on critical analyses and successful resolutions in relevantly similar contexts, bioethics may consider how a BRCA1 screening protocol should treat the two groups of women identified above. Regarding the first group of women for whom screening is not "medically indicated," if the protocol fails to recognize the subjective benefits that women may realize from determining their BRCA1 carrier status (much as the FDA policy failed to recognize augmentation candidates' subjective benefits), genetic counselors are likely to find themselves in a situation similar to those who would have to commit insurance fraud to have their patients reimbursed for amniocentesis performed to relieve maternal anxiety (Kolker, 1994, p. 3).

In contrast, those in the second group who do not desire BRCA1 screening may eventually be pressured to undergo it. Although a nondirective ethos has dominated genetic counseling thus far, lessons to be learned from HIV screening suggest that some contexts may be more directive than others. Counseling following HIV screening in public health institutions – in contrast to that offered by AIDS service organizations – may be much more directive, particularly when a pregnant woman discovers that she is HIV-infected, or when an HIV-infected woman considers becoming pregnant. Although studies show she may have as low as a 13 percent chance of transmitting HIV to her fetus, termination of pregnancy has often been recommended (Andiman, 1990; European Collaborative Study, 1991; Field, 1993; Rogers, 1989; Altman, 1994). With the possibility that administration of AZT may improve fetal outcome, some have proposed, fortunately with little success thus far, unblinding anonymous testing or mandating screening and treatment with AZT of HIV-infected pregnant women or their infants. Critics cite the negative implications of such actions for rights of privacy and self-determination and question the degree of benefit to infants (Dao, 1994; Navarro, 1993).

Breast cancer genetic screening and prophylactic treatment could not currently be mandated on the basis of benefit to or protection of third parties. Indeed, in a departure from genetic counseling's nondirective ethos, commentators have argued against offering carrier screening or prenatal screening for breast cancer in the context of reproductive planning (Elias, 1994). The result of such a prohibition would be that only patients who know how to give the "right" reasons and hence "work the system," would have access to such prenatal diagnosis; a similar problem would likely occur with a prohibition on prenatal testing for sex selection (Parker, 1994).

Nevertheless, other social sentiments and objectives supporting calls for mandatory HIV screening and prophylactic treatment, particularly cost containment, might also be employed to justify pressuring or even compelling women, especially those at increased risk because of their membership in high risk communities (families), to undertake unwanted breast cancer screening. There would then be no *principled* reason not to compel women at increased risk because of various environmental or life-style factors to alter their behaviors, to undergo preventive treatment of mastectomy, or to for go either health care benefits for their disease should it develop or at least a sense of entitlement to sympathy and support. That this scenario is not so far fetched may be established by remembering that at one time women were given the unpleasant choice of either giving up their lucrative employment in the pigments department of an American Cyanamid plant or undergoing sterilization (*Oil, Chemical and Atomic Workers International Union v. American Cyanamid Co.*, 1984). Many who find this forced choice unacceptable would nevertheless suggest that women who choose to continue to work in higher risk environments may justifiably be asked to "contract out" of receiving health care benefits or seeking civil damages for health conditions associated with the increased risks their work environment presents. If similar sentiments prevailed with respect to breast cancer patients, this would constitute an unfortunate form of victim blaming.

VI. CONCLUSION

Like contemporary philosophy of science, critical bioethics interrogates differing normative and conceptual frameworks and brings to light what is at stake for those who employ them in various social practices. In effecting its analyses, critical bioethics also reveals its own (sometimes conflicting) normative and conceptual frameworks, such as its reflection of patient-centered experience and its role as a professional ethic. Using an interdisciplinary approach and attending to diverse health practices, not merely those occurring within traditional health care institutions, critical bioethics also parallels the methodological commitments of recent work in science studies.

Critical bioethics will play an important role in addressing particular ethical concerns arising in the context of developing breast cancer genetic screening protocols, including BRCA1 screening. Its most valuable role, however, may lie in illuminating and critically assessing the competing worldviews informing protocol development, especially women's own views of their breasts and breast cancer, both within the technologically-oriented social practice of

American medicine and in light of the social construction of their breasted experience in American society. Still more important for the evolution of the field of bioethics, however, may be critical bioethics' recognition that its own commitments constitute world-views that must be subject to its own analyses.

NOTES

[1] I am indebted to Donald Ainslie for our discussions of the critical capacities of bioethics and his criticism of the manuscript's penultimate draft, to Rachel Ankeny Majeske for her comments on earlier drafts, and to Elizabeth Gettig and Mona Stadler for information on breast cancer. I also thank SGP for her understanding and support.

[2] Jennings discusses the role of critical interrogation in his argument for a bioethics that is more communal and less individualistic. He writes also of bioethics giving medicine a vision of itself even as it develops a more communal vision (Jennings, 1990a; an eloquent shortened version is contained in Jennings, 1990b).

[3] Angell terms breast cancer a disease of middle age, while prostate cancer is one of old age. Even though breast cancer incidence rates rise steadily through age 79, the number of new cases decreases after age 69, because the higher rates are applied to successively smaller age-specific populations (Feuer, 1993).

[4] As Cindy Patton notes, 'community' has political valency, but is an inadequate analytic concept (1990, pp. 7–8). Gay communities are largely defined in virtue of being groups of nonheterosexuals; what constitutes members of these alleged communities as *communities* is not explicated. Other than their otherness, gay communities seem to have no essence; their membership is too diverse. For a brief discussion of this point, see Grover, 1988, esp. 24–25.

[5] Likely to be ignored in such victim blaming is that lesbian women, for whom heterosexual sex is generally not an option for reproduction, may fail to have a child because of a lack of resources for assisted reproduction. Similarly ignored may be the suspicion that increased alcohol consumption among lesbian, as compared to heterosexual, women may be a response to environmental (social) factors associated with their being marginalized in society, or may reflect attempted self-medication by women who do not have access to adequate mental health care benefits through their (or a male spouse's) employer.

[6] Such accounts are reminiscent of ante-bellum accounts of the physiological fitness for servitude of those of African descent.

[7] Compared to a century ago, these factors have doubled the period of exposure to hormonal stimulation of rapidly dividing breast ductal cells. This extended period would give abnormal cells more opportunity for clonal growth (King, 1993).

[8] If society generally, and mistakenly, begins to regard breast cancer as a preventable genetic disease, this social blaming of the approximately 90 percent of women whose breast cancers are sporadic may result.

[9] Testimony offered before the FDA by Esther Rome of the Boston Women's Health Book Collective, however, may dispute this point. She believes both that women know very little about specific breast cancer treatment options until the need to decide among them arises and that their decisions to seek mammograms are not influenced by the availability of options following diagnosis, including the option of breast reconstruction (FDA, 1992). Still, I would suggest that those who know anything about treatment options probably find them onerous; moreover, women should be informed of treatment options as part of the informed consent process for mammography.

[10] Indeed female BRCA1 carriers may die of another illness or accident before developing the disease. This somewhat macabre means of escaping the "death sentence" of HIV or AIDS or of carrying the Huntington disease gene is too often similarly ignored (Davison, 1994). Striking among those who do not ignore it are those with HIV or Huntington disease who describe their diagnoses as somehow liberating, as freeing them to "live for the present" or to take chances – emotional or financial risks or life-threatening chances – that they believe they would otherwise not take (Collard, 1994; Meissen, 1991). For them, having or being at greatly increased risk for a terminal disease does not mean having a disease that will take their lives, but having a diagnosis that justifies radically, qualitatively redefining their lives, perhaps to the extent of risking, or in some cases seeking, other means of dying. Medical and patient responses to terminal illness may differ radically depending upon the patients' or health care providers' (normative) conceptions of the "terminal-ness" of the disease.

[11] Similarly, women who make public their decisions to breast-feed, or who nurse in public, must conform their decision to the social norms that separate motherhood and sexuality; they must deny the erotic pleasure that may be taken in nursing. The political strategy grounding this "separation between motherhood and sexuality within a woman's own existence" seems to be "to ensure a woman's dependence on the man for pleasure" (Young, 1990, p. 198). Moreover, without this separation, "there can be no image of a love that is all give and no take" (Young, 1990, p. 198), the social ideal of self-less, feminine love.

[12] Kessler also set an unfortunate precedent in pointing to insurance industry practices (in this case, their usually reimbursing insureds for post-mastectomy breast reconstruction) in support of reconstruction's status as an integral part of cancer treatment. It would indeed be unfortunate if current insurance practices were used to inform public policy and clinical practice protocols or to define "medically necessary" interventions; many companies do not, for example, cover screening mammography despite the recommendation of screening by the American Cancer Society.

REFERENCES

Altman, L.: 1994, 'In major finding, drug limits HIV infection in newborns,' *The New York Times*, February 21.

Andiman, W., *et al.*: 1990, 'Rate of transmission of human immundeficiency virus type one infection from mother to child and short-term outcome of neonatal infection: results of a prospective cohort study,' *American Journal of Disabled Children* 144, 758–66.

Angell, M.: 1993, 'Caring for women's health – what is the problem?', *The New England Journal of Medicine* 329(4), 271–72.

Biesecker, B. B., *et al.*: 1993, 'Genetic counseling for families with inherited susceptibility to breast and ovarian cancer,' *Journal of the American Medical Association* 269(15), 1970–74.

Breo, D.: 1993, 'Altered fates – counseling families with inherited breast cancer,' *Journal of the American Medical Association* 269(15), 2017–22.

Chapkis W.: 1986, *Beauty Secrets*, South End Press, Boston.

Clancy, C. M., and Massion, C. T.: 1992, 'American women's health care: a patchwork quilt with gaps,' *Journal of the American Medical Association* 268 (14), 1918–20.

Collard, C.: 1994, *Savage Nights*, Quartet, London.

Coward, C.: 1992, 'Report: lesbian cancer risk is steep,' *The Advocate*, November 17, p. 22.

Dao, J.: 1994, 'Bill offered on requiring AIDS report,' *The New York Times*, March 8.

Davis, D. S.: 1994, 'It ain't necessarily so: clinicians, bioethics and religious studies', *The Journal of Clinical Ethics* 5(4), 315–319.

Davis, K.: 1991, 'Remaking the she-devil: a critical look at feminist approaches to beauty', *Hypatia* 6(2), 21–43.

Davison, C., *et al.*: 1994, 'The potential social impact of predictive genetic testing for susceptibility to common chronic diseases: a review and proposed research agenda,' *Sociology of Health & Illness* 16(3), 340–71.

Dresser, R.: 1992, 'Wanted: single, white male for medical research,' *Hastings Center Report*, January–February, pp. 24–29.

Dull, D., and West C.: 1991, 'Accounting for cosmetic surgery: the accomplishment of gender,' *Social Problems* 38(1), 54–70.

Elias, S., and Annas, G. J.: 1994, 'Generic consent for genetic screening,' *The New England Journal of Medicine* 330(22), 1611–1613.

European Collaborative Study: 1991, 'Children born to women with HIV-1 infection: natural history and risk of transmission', *Lancet* 337, 253–58.

Feuer, E. J., *et al.*: 1993, 'The lifetime risk of developing breast cancer,' *Journal of the National Cancer Institute* 85(11), 892–97.

Field, M. A.: 1993, 'Pregnancy and AIDS,' *Maryland Law Review* 52, 402–436.

Food and Drug Administration (FDA): 1992, General and Plastic Surgery Devices Panel Meeting, February 18–20, Bethesda, MD.

336   *Lisa S. Parker*

Ford, D., *et al.*: 1994, 'Risks of cancer in BRCA1-mutation carriers,' *The Lancet* 343, 692–95.

Foucault, M.: 1973, *The Birth of the Clinic: An Archaeology of Medical Perception*, Pantheon Books, New York.

Gail, M. H., *et al.*: 1989, 'Projecting individualized probabilities of developing breast cancer for white females who are being examined annually,' *Journal of the National Cancer Institute* 81(24), 1879–86.

Gail, M. H., and Benichou, J.: 1992, 'Assessing the risk of breast cancer in individuals,' *Cancer Prevention*, June, 1–15.

Gessen, M.: 1993, 'Lesbians and breast cancer,' *The Advocate*, February 9, pp. 44–48.

Gorman, C.: 1993, 'Breast-cancer politics,' *Time* 142(18), 74.

Grover, J. Z.: 1988, 'AIDS: keywords,' in Douglas Crimp (ed.), *AIDS: Cultural Analysis/Cultural Activism*, The MIT Press, Cambridge, MA, pp. 17–30.

Jennings, B.: 1990a, 'Bioethics and democracy,' *The Centennial Review* 34 (2), 207–25.

Jennings, B.: 1990b, 'Communal and individual values in biomedical ethics,' *Medical Ethics for the Physician* 5(2), 3–4.

Kelly, P. T.: 1987, 'Risk counseling for relatives of cancer patients: new information, new approaches,' *Journal of Psychosocial Oncology* 5(1), 65–79.

Kelly, P. T.: 1992, 'Breast cancer risk analysis: a genetic epidemiology service for families,' *Journal of Genetic Counseling* 1(2), 155–67.

Kessler, David A.: 1992, 'The basis of the FDA's decision on breast implants,' *The New England Journal of Medicine* 326, 1713–15.

King, M-C., *et al.*: 1993, 'Inherited breast and ovarian cancer: what are the risks? What are the Choices?,' *Journal of the American Medical Association* 269 (15), 1975–80.

Kolata, G.: 1994, 'Getting perspective: the latest news about breast cancer,' *Cosmopolitan* 216(2), 190–193.

Kolker, A. and Burke, B. M.: 1994, *Prenatal Testing: A Sociological Perspective*, Bergin and Garvey, Westport, CT.

Laurence, L.: 1991, 'The breast cancer epidemic: women aren't just scared, we're mad,' *McCall's* 119(2), 24–40.

Lippman, A.: 1991, 'Prenatal genetic testing and screening: constructing needs and reinforcing inequities,' *American Journal of Law and Medicine* 17(1–2), 15–50.

Lorde, A.: 1980, *The Cancer Journals*, The Crossing Press, Trumansburg, NY.

Love, S. M.: 1993, 'Breast cancer: what the department of defense should do with its $210 million,' *Journal of the American Medical Association* 269(18), 2417.

Marshall, E.: 1993a, 'The politics of breast cancer,' *Science* 259, 616–17.

Marshall, E.: 1993b, 'Search for a killer: focus shifts from fat to hormones,' *Science* 259, 618–21.

Marshall, E.: 1993c, 'Women's health initiative draws flak,' *Science* 262, 838.

Meissen, G. J., *et al.*: 1991, 'Understanding the decision to take the predictive test for Huntington diseases' *American Journal of Medical Genetics* 39, 404–410.

Breast Cancer Genetic Screening and Critical Bioethic   337

Morain, C.: 1993, 'Breast-cancer warrior,' *American Medical News* 36(22), 11–15.

Mulvihill, J. J.: 1989, 'Prospects for cancer control and prevention through genetics,' *Clinical Genetics* 36, 313–19.

Navarro, M.: 1993, 'Testing newborns for AIDS virus raises issue of mothers' privacy,' *New York Times* August 8.

Oil, Chemical and Atomic Workers International Union v. American Cyanamid Co., 741 *F.2d Series, 444 (1984)*

Parker, L. S.: 1994, 'Bioethics for human geneticists: models for reasoning and methods for teaching,' *American Journal of Human Genetics* 54, 137–147.

Parker, L. S.: 1995, 'Beauty and breast implantation: how candidate selection affects autonomy and informed consent,' *Hypatia* 10(1), 183–201.

Patton, C.: 1990, *Inventing Aids*, Routledge, Chapman and Hall, Inc., New York.

Patton, C.: 1993, 'Tremble, hetero swine!,' in Warner, M. (ed.), *Fear of a Queer Planet: Queer Politics and Social Theory*, University of Minnesota Press, Minneapolis, pp. 143–177.

Pollitt K.: 1992, 'Implants: truth and consequences,' *The Nation* 254(10), 325–329.

Rogers, M. *et al*: 1989, 'Use of the polymerase chain reaction for early detection of the proviral sequences of human immunodeficiency virus in infants born to seropositive mothers,' *The New England Journal of Medicine* 320, 1649–54.

Shapiro, L., Springen, K., and Gordon, J.: 1992, 'What is it with women and breasts?,' *Newsweek* 119(3), 57.

Young, I. M.: 1990, 'Breasted experience,' in *Throwing Like a Girl and Other Essays in Feminist Philosophy and Social Theory*, Indiana University Press, Bloomington, Indiana, pp. 141–159.

Zuckerman, M. B.: 1992, 'Battling breast cancer,' *U.S. News and World Report* 113 (20), 104.

[15]

Managing menopause: a critical feminist engagement

Marilys N. Guillemin

Alma Unit for Women and Ageing, Centre for the Study of Health and Society, University of Melbourne, Parkville, Australia

Scand J Public Health 1999; 27: 273–278

Feminist critiques of menopause have been beneficial in opening up important public health debates around menopause. One of the most contentious public health issues concerns the use of Hormone Replacement Therapy (HRT) for the prevention of osteoporosis, heart disease and, more recently, Alzheimer's disease, in postmenopausal women. For preventive purposes, it is recommended that women should take HRT for 10–15 years and preferably remain on the therapy for the remainder of their lives. This is despite reported increased cancer risks associated with HRT, side effects and considerable cost of the therapy. Various studies have shown that up to 50% of women stop taking HRT after 9–12 months. These figures are used in the medical literature as an indication of women's non-compliance. Extending earlier feminist critiques around menopause and HRT, this paper discusses a critical feminist engagement around issues of women's perceived non-compliance with HRT.

Key words: menopause, HRT, feminist critique, public health, non-compliance.

Marilys N. Guillemin, Alma Unit for Women and Ageing, Centre for the Study of Health and Society, University of Melbourne, Parkville 3052, Australia. Tel: +61 3 9344 0827, fax: +61 3 9344 0824, e-mail: m.guillemin@cshs.unimelb.edu.au

INTRODUCTION

The menopause arena is controversial, highly politicized and riddled with complexities. Some argue that menopause is a disease of deficient hormones requiring treatment, while others claim that it is a "natural" life event that should remain immune from the processes of medicalization. The most contentious issue centres on the use of Hormone Replacement Therapy (HRT). HRT is widely advocated for the treatment of the acute symptoms of menopause, including hot flushes, vaginal dryness, night sweats and mood swings. More recently, menopause and HRT have become public health concerns. HRT is widely considered to be a panacea for the prevention of the serious public health problems associated with menopause, namely, heart disease and osteoporosis, and, more recently, Alzheimer's disease (1–3). Although the use of HRT in the prevention of heart disease is still under debate (4), HRT is nonetheless seen to be a remedy not only for individual women, but also for the maladies of the public healthcare budget. This public health focus has become increasingly prevalent in Australia, which is the focus of this article. Although the article does not aim to make international comparisons of feminist arguments relating to HRT usage, the issues raised apply to most developed countries where the use of HRT is widespread.

The controversies around the use of HRT centre on its association with increased risks of breast and endometrial cancer. In addition, there are other concerns, such as the often serious side effects associated with using HRT, the costs related to HRT usage and the development of the so-called "menopause industry" (5). Advocates of long-term hormonal therapy recommend commencement of HRT for women from the age of 45–55 years. For maximum preventive benefit, it is recommended that therapy should continue for at least 10–15 years, and preferably be extended beyond the age of 65 years (6, 7). Concerns have been voiced about women's low rate of usage of HRT and the perceived lack of compliance in women prescribed long-term HRT (8–11). Amongst menopausal women commencing HRT, high proportions cease to take HRT after what some in the medical community perceive to be too short a period.

Feminists have been largely responsible for opening up the debates around menopause. Here, I trace the feminist concerns around menopause and HRT, and point to the contributions of feminists to the wider debate. However, I argue that gaps exist within these feminist critiques – gaps which I suggest fail to address adequately the public health concerns around menopause and its associated conditions. Critical feminist engagement is vital in addressing many public health issues. I show how extension of earlier feminist critiques of menopause can address the current public health issues of perceived non-compliance of women to HRT.

FEMINIST CONTRIBUTIONS TO CRITIQUES OF MENOPAUSE

Feminists[a] were significant in drawing attention to the lack of information on menopause during the early 1970s. Despite the increased use of HRT in the 1960s, many feminists wrote of the paucity of information about menopause during this period and noted that menopause had been a taboo subject for public discussion (18). What information was available during this period emphasized a notion of menopause as a psychological phenomenon (19). Biological explanations for menopause were under scrutiny during this time; whether menopause was a "real" phenomenon was actively questioned. It was largely feminists that drew attention to the complexities concerning menopause and, in particular, repudiated the notion of menopause as being "all in your head" while highlighting the reality of the problems women faced during the climacteric.

This paucity of information and discussion in the early 1970s soon changed as interest in menopausal issues increased. Influencing this burgeoning interest was the widespread promotion of HRT to prevent ageing, the reported link between HRT and endometrial cancer, together with the controversies surrounding the oral contraceptive pill and other hormonal preparations (20). Epidemiologists, medical practitioners, pharmaceutical companies, nurse practitioners and menopausal women all contributed to this growing interest. Feminists influenced the opening up of many of these issues to public debate as they argued against attempts to medicalize menopause (21–23). With the increased promotion of HRT and the prevailing understanding of menopause as hormone deficiency, feminists argued against the notion of menopause as a disease and promoted the concept of menopause as a social construction. In contrast to a biological understanding of menopause, feminists

argued that menopause drew its meaning from societal attitudes towards ageing, the role of women in the social structure and the prevalent view of women as reproductive beings. The social devaluing of older women was used to explain the depression and loss of confidence women experienced around the time of menopause. Menopause was constructed as a social problem, with menopausal women as the victims of demeaning cultural assumptions about older women. Anthropological studies of cultures in which ageing women are valued and have fewer perceived problems around menopause have been used to reinforce this social constructivist discourse around menopause (24–27).

Another important contribution from feminists has been in challenging what was perceived as the medicalization of women's lives by doctors and the health system (28–30). These critiques challenged the organization of menopause as a medical condition requiring the intervention of a patriarchal medical system. In addition, attention was drawn to the profiteering of the pharmaceutical industry and medical establishment from women's menopause, particularly in relation to the use of HRT. Sandra Coney in *The Menopause Industry* warns women against getting caught up in this market ideology, urging them to question the preoccupation of menopause as disease, which this ideology inculcates (5). Within this market ideology is the use of fear as an important selling point. Fear of ageing, together with a fear of succumbing to menopause-associated diseases, is played on to seduce women into the menopause market. Worcester & Whatley join in the chorus of their feminist sisters in their plea to wrestle control away from the profiteering market manufacturers towards self-help and real prevention for women (31).

LIMITATIONS OF FEMINIST CRITIQUES OF MENOPAUSE

Feminist analyses of menopause have been beneficial first in providing conceptual tools with which to critique the notion of menopause as a universal disease, and on a practical level, in improving health services for women. The feminist proposal of menopause as a social construction has provided a useful platform from which to expand options for the management of menopause and from which different kinds of understandings of menopause can emerge. However, feminist critics have been reluctant to extend the social construction argument to biology itself, thus limiting the scope and strength of their critiques. In this section I explore some of these limitations within the feminist critiques of menopause.

---

[a] I acknowledge that to group feminists in one category is an oversimplification. However, what I wish to highlight here are the common concerns of the various streams of feminism in their development of the notion of menopause as a social construction. Particularly important to the understanding of menopause as a social construct in the late 1960s and early 1970s was the establishment of the Women's Health Movement, which called for an end to sexism in the healthcare system and demanded that healthcare not only satisfy the physical needs of women, but also benefit their social needs (12, 13). Since the 1970s different notions of feminism have emerged (14–17).

I suggest that as menopause becomes a growing public health concern, there is an increased need for a different kind of feminist engagement with issues around the management of menopause, in particular the use of long-term HRT.

My first point is that previous feminist analyses of menopause have persisted in upholding various dichotomies, notably social versus biological and cultural versus natural divides. These analyses maintain these categories as pure. In these kinds of analyses, menopause as a social phenomenon is positioned in opposition to a biological understanding of menopause; menopause is either seen as a result of hormonal decline with resulting physical signs and symptoms, or it is perceived as an outcome of social influences (5, 32, 33). It is generally agreed in feminist debates on menopause that social forces, such as women's social devaluing, effects of the patriarchal medical system, and economic forces which maintain women's inferior social position, work together to produce the cultural understanding of menopause (30, 31). Relatively immune from debate, however, has been the social shaping of the biological knowledge of menopause. Most feminist critics argue that menopause has an underlying biological reality resulting in physical signs, but that the meanings of these physical signs are socially and culturally influenced (34). The biological raw material of menopause is taken for granted and accepted as given, while the social undergoes analysis for its role in the construction of particular understandings about menopause. Focus is placed on the meanings of menopause derived from social and cultural relations, while the biology of menopause is left unquestioned.

This separation of corporeality and culture has been the subject of an increasing number of more recent feminist analyses. Grosz argues against an automatic attribution of the biological body as natural (15). Furthermore, Grosz proposes a textured body that interacts with cultural, social and psychological factors. This viewpoint favours a notion of biology as interconnected with social relations, rather than one separated from the social.

My second criticism of the promotion of menopause as a social construction is the emphasis placed on menopause as ideology. Many feminist critiques assume a direct mapping of ideology onto practice, with little attention directed towards the analysis of practices. This analysis of menopause as ideology refuses to engage with the technologies and practices that confront women users as they seek to manage their menopause. Women experiencing serious problems during menopause must make decisions about whether to seek help, to take HRT, to have their bone density measured, or to remain on therapy and for

how long. Despite ongoing debates about the effectiveness of some of these interventions, women are urged to consider them for both their own individual health and the public good. For women faced with these decisions, feminist critiques that do not go beyond the level of ideology are of little help.

Third, I argue that approaching the social construction of menopause as a problem of ideology divorces the technical and material from the analysis. Situating menopause in relation to social conditions, class structures and economic relations is useful. However, this type of inquiry omits the technologies and material entities which are very much part of the world of menopause. The social and the material are inextricably intertwined when living with menopause. Women experiencing menopausal problems interact with a variety of different technologies including HRT, bone scans, ultrasound and mammograms. In analysing the practices of managing menopause we need to acknowledge that these are socio-material practices.

In the next section, I illustrate how we can take account of the limitations of earlier feminist critiques and incorporate them in different kinds of critical feminist engagement. The concerns around women's non-compliance with HRT offer an interesting and important starting point for this critical feminist analysis.

WOMEN'S "NON-COMPLIANCE" WITH HRT

Women's "lack of compliance" with regard to HRT has become a major public health concern (8–10, 35). Recent studies point to the variation in current HRT usage across different developed countries. Although the United States is reported to have one of the highest HRT usage rates (36), studies of European peri-menopausal women show wide variation in the current usage rate of HRT. Figures of current users of HRT range from 3% of women in Italy to 25% of women in Germany (37, 38). The current usage rate of HRT amongst peri-menopausal women in the general Australian community is 14–21% (39, 40). These usage rates are comparable to those reported in Scandinavian countries (41–43). In a sample of 4,525 Swedish women aged 46–62 years, 21% were reported to be currently using HRT (41). In a study of Norwegian women, it has been shown that in women in the age group 45–69 years, the usage rate of HRT increased from 16.3% in 1994 to 19.1% in 1996 (43).

Most studies indicate that many women cease to take HRT after a few months of commencing treatment. The Massachusetts Women's Health Survey of 2,500 women showed that 20% of women prescribed HRT stopped taking the drug after 9 months. Of greater interest is the fact that 20–30% of the women surveyed never had their prescriptions filled because they were either not convinced of the benefits of the therapy or were concerned about the risks associated with it (44). The Melbourne Women's Midlife Health Project involving 2,000 Australian women indicates that 50% of women stop taking HRT after 12 months (39). The reasons "non-compliant" women give for ceasing therapy vary. However, the main reasons include, first, side effects, such as bleeding, depression, weight gain and breast soreness, second, concern about long-term effects, in particular the likelihood of cancer, third, no further need for therapy, fourth, the high cost of therapy, and finally, dissuasion by the media (8, 9, 35, 39–41, 45).

These data have led to considerable concern among medical and public health practitioners who advocate the long-term use of HRT for women. Women who stop taking HRT are constructed as either ignorant or irresponsible. It has been suggested that it is women's lack of sufficient and accurate information about menopause that leads to their non-compliance with long-term HRT (10, 40, 43, 46). It is proposed that given adequate explanation, women will become convinced of the benefits of long-term HRT, leading to ensured compliance. Women who refuse to remain on long-term HRT are similarly constructed as irresponsible. This message is particularly obvious in relation to osteoporosis prevention in both the medical literature and promotional material from the pharmaceutical industry. These sources feature two predominating themes: first, they incite women's fear of developing osteoporosis, and second, women are made to feel responsible if they do sustain fractures and become dependent on the community to pay their healthcare costs. Examples include medical articles on menopause and osteoporosis that cite national health costs attributed to fractures in the elderly, particularly in older women (47, 48). The publication of such expenditure data and the estimated cost savings to the healthcare budget if women remained on long-term HRT indirectly urge women to be "responsible" both for their own sake and for the sake of the health budget.

WOMEN'S "NON-COMPLIANCE" TO HRT FROM A CRITICAL FEMINIST READING

A critical feminist reading of women's lack of compliance with HRT argues against the construction of women who cease to take HRT as either ignorant or irresponsible. Perceiving women as non-compliant does not address the legitimacy and seriousness of women's active decision-making to stop taking HRT, or in some cases, not to commence it at all. Women's

decision-making about whether to remain on long-term HRT operates within a complex milieu. In deciding whether first to commence and then to remain on HRT, women consider not only physiological aspects, but also the complex interrelation of their biology, emotional state, and related social and political concerns.

Women take into account the side effects of HRT – a serious consideration if you must remain on the therapy for the duration of your life, given that these side effects are undesirable and in some cases, debilitating. Women must individually consider their likelihood of actually developing osteoporosis or heart disease or Alzheimer's disease – some women are at much higher risk than others, depending on particular individual risk factors. Women's risk of developing cancer associated with taking HRT, in particular breast cancer, must be weighed up. The cost of the therapy and associated monitoring is a serious consideration, since for some women HRT is a proposition that may extend for 35 or more years. In addition, these women are concerned about having to take what they consider to be an unnatural therapy for the rest of their lives, as against maintaining a healthy and balanced lifestyle, which may in itself help alleviate the risks of osteoporosis and heart disease. Furthermore, there are uncertainties about the long-term effects of HRT that are still under investigation. Having weighed up these multiple factors, women then make informed decisions that are legitimated within their everyday contexts and by their individual circumstances. The early work of feminists alerted us to the long-term effects of hormonal therapies. Many of the women currently going through menopause are of the same generation of women who lived through the controversies surrounding the oral contraceptive pill, thalidomide, diethylstilboestrol (DES) and other hormonal drugs. Use of these drugs of the 1960s and 1970s resulted in dire consequences, with many women experiencing disastrous outcomes.

In calling for a critical feminist engagement with issues of HRT compliance, I am not arguing about whether the long-term use of HRT is right or wrong. My point is that promoting long-term compliance encourages women to be passively responsive to a dominant medical ideology, rather than encouraging considered decision-making. Ensuring women's compliance with HRT serves particular professional, social and economic interests. Many health practitioners are sincere in advocating the use of long-term HRT to improve the health and well-being of menopausal women. In addition, there is a genuine concern about reducing healthcare costs through the prevention of osteoporosis and heart disease. However, feminist critiques of menopause have pointed to the financial incentives that directly influence the promotion and long-term use of HRT. Keeping menopausal women on HRT for the remainder of their lives has obvious economic benefits to the pharmaceutical industry. There are also major financial benefits to be gained through the use of screening and monitoring technologies associated with the long-term use of HRT. Reading the practices of managing menopause as socio-material practices increases our awareness of the role of technologies. Technologies such as bone densitometry, used to measure women's bone density, and mammograms, used to screen for breast cancer, both associated with the use of HRT, are only two of the many examples of technologies used in menopausal and postmenopausal management. The use of these technologies requires appropriate medical referral and interpretation, necessitating additional visits to medical practitioners and further costs. These all add up to considerable expense – costs incurred by menopausal women and the community at large.

CONCLUSION

Feminist critiques of menopause have been beneficial first in opening up debate around menopause and HRT, and second, in guiding analysis of these debates. We need to extend these critiques to address the growing public health concerns that have arisen around the preventive use of HRT against conditions such as osteoporosis and heart disease. There has been widespread concern, expressed in medical journals, that despite the reported benefits of long-term HRT, many women do not remain on the therapy. These women are either portrayed as lacking information about the possible preventive benefits of HRT, or they are perceived as not taking responsibility for their long-term health or considering the costs the community will incur in caring for them.

A critical feminist engagement assists in addressing the issues of women's perceived non-compliance with HRT. This kind of engagement does not seek to take a judgmental stand in suggesting that a woman's decision to refuse long-term HRT is right or wrong. Menopause is not a uniform experience. It is therefore inappropriate and unreasonable to advocate uniform recommendations for all menopausal women. Long-term use of HRT for women at high risk of osteoporosis and heart disease may be beneficial. However, what this kind of critical feminist engagement does is acknowledge women's decision-making with regard to long-term HRT as responsible, legitimate and well-informed, and not as a problem of non-compliance. It reinforces the need for women to be fully informed about the relative merits and risks

of HRT, with due consideration to the consequences of long-term HRT. Furthermore, it challenges the use of long-term HRT as the only possible way of managing the potential problems of osteoporosis and heart disease in postmenopausal women. Feminist critical engagement forces us to consider assumptions about uniform menopausal management strategies and offers ways of thinking about other possibilities.

REFERENCES

1. Barrett-Connor E. Hormone replacement therapy Br Med J 1998; 317: 457–61.
2. Genazzani AR, Gambacciani M. Hormone replacement therapy: the perspectives for the 21st century Maturitas 1999; 32: 11–7.
3. Yaffe K, Sawaya G, Lieberburg I, Grady D. Estrogen therapy in postmenopausal women: effects on cognitive function and dementia JAMA 1998; 279: 688–95.
4. Hulley S, Grady D, Bush T, Urberg C, Herrington D, Riggs B, et al. Randomized trial of estrogen plus progestin for secondary prevention of coronary heart disease in postmenopausal women. Heart and Estrogen/progestin Replacement Study (HERS) Research Group JAMA 1998; 280: 605–13.
5. Coney S. The menopause industry. A guide to medicine's "discovery" of mid-life women. Auckland: Penguin, 1991.
6. Wren B. HRT benefits both women and society Australian Doctor, 1993; 10: 13.
7. Grady D, Cummings S, Petitti D, Rubin S, Audet AM. Guidelines for counselling postmenopausal women about preventive hormone therapy Ann Intern Med, 1992; 117: 1038–41.
8. Coope J, Marsh J. Can we improve compliance with long-term HRT? Maturitas, 1992; 15: 151–8.
9. Rebar RW, Thomas MA, Gass ML, Liu JH. Problems of hormone therapy: evaluations, follow up, complications. In: Korenman SG, editor. The menopause. Biology and clinical consequences of ovarian failure. Evolution and management. Norwell, MA: Serono Symposia, 1990: 145–56, 1992.
10. Silverman SL, Greenwald M, Huberman A. Decisions on menopausal therapy. In: Korenman SG, editor. The menopause. Biology and clinical consequences of ovarian failure. Evolution and management. Norwell, MA: Serono Symposia, 1992: 129–44.
11. Rozenberg S, Vandromme J, Kroll M, Twagirayezu P, Vyankandondera J. Compliance with hormonal replacement therapy Rev Med Brux, 1995; 16: 295–8.
12. Marieskind H. The women's health movement Int J Health Serv, 1975; 5: 217–27.
13. Broom DH. Damned if we do. Contradictions in women's health care. Sydney: Allen & Unwin, 1991.
14. Grosz E. Volatile bodies. Toward a corporeal feminism. Bloomington/Indianapolis: Indiana University Press, 1994.
15. Grosz E. Inscriptions and body maps: representations and the corporeal. In: Threadgold T, Cranny-Francis A, editors. Feminine/masculine and representation. Sydney: Allen & Unwin, 1990: 62–74.
16. Butler J. Gender trouble: feminism and the subversion of identity. New York: Routledge, 1990.

17. Gatens M. Towards a feminist philosophy of the body. In: Caine B, Grosz E, Lepervanche Md, editors. Crossing boundaries. Feminisms and the critique of knowledges. Sydney: Allen & Unwin, 1988: 59–70.
18. McKinlay SM., McKinlay JB. Selected studies of the menopause J Biosoc Sci, 1973; 5: 533–55.
19. Posner J. It's all in your head: feminist and medical models of menopause (strange bedfellows) Sex Roles, 1979; 5: 179–90.
20. Swartzman LC, Leiblum S. Changing perspectives on the menopause J Psychosom Obstet Gynaecol, 1987; 6: 11–24.
21. Lewis J. Feminism, the menopause and hormone replacement therapy Feminist Review, 1993; 43: 38–56.
22. Bell SE. Changing ideas: the medicalization of menopause Soc Sci Med, 1987; 24: 535–42.
23. Bell SE. Sociological perspectives on the menopause Ann N Y Acad Sci, 1990; 592: 173–8.
24. Flint M. The menopause: reward or punishment Psychosomatics, 1975; 16: 161–3.
25. Beyene Y. Cultural significance and physiological manifestations of menopause. A biocultural analysis Cult Med Psychiatry, 1986; 10: 47–71.
26. Flint M, Suprapti SR. Cultural and subcultural meanings of the menopause Ann N Y Acad Sci, 1990; 592: 134–48.
27. Toit BMD. Aging and menopause among Indian South African women. New York: State University of New York Press, 1990, 1990.
28. Klein R. Menopause malpractice: what's new about Hormone Replacement Therapy. In: Sorger R, editor. A critical look at Hormone Replacement Therapy. Melbourne: Healthsharing Productions,, 1990: 21–6.
29. MacPherson KI. Menopause as disease: the social construction of a metaphor Adv Nurs Sci, 1981; 3: 95–113.
30. McCrea FB. The politics of menopause: the "discovery" of a deficiency disease Social Problems, 1983; 31: 111–23.
31. Worcester N, Whatley MH. The selling of HRT: playing on the fear factor Feminist Review, 1992; 41: 1–26.
32. Dumble LJ. Hormone Replacement Therapy: the m(yth) of modern medicine. In: Sorger R, editor. A critical look at Hormone Replacement Therapy. Melbourne: Healthsharing Productions, 1992: 15–20.
33. Sheehy G. The silent passage. London: Fontana, 1992.
34. Theisen CS, Mansfield PK. Menopause: social construction or biological destiny? J Health Educ, 1993; 24: 209–13.
35. Wren BG, Brown L. Compliance with hormonal replacement therapy Maturitas, 1991; 13: 17–21.
36. Jolleys JV, Olesen F. A comparative study of prescribing of hormone replacement therapy in USA and Europe Maturitas, 1996; 23: 47–53.
37. Oddens BJ, Boulet MJ, Lehert P, Visser AP. Has the climacteric been medicalised? A study on the use of medication for climacteric complaints in four countries Maturitas, 1992; 15: 171–81.
38. Oddens BJ, Boulet MJ, Lehert P, Visser AP. A study on the use of medication for climacteric complaints in Western Europe. II Maturitas, 1994; 19: 1–12.
39. Shelley JM, Smith A, Dudley E, Dennerstein L. Use of hormone replacement therapy by Melbourne women Aust J Public Health, 1995; 19: 387–92.
40. MacLennan AH, MacLennan A, Wilson D. The prevalence of oestrogen replacement therapy in South Australia Maturitas, 1993; 16: 175–83.
41. Mattson LA, Stadberg E, Milsom I. Management of hormone replacement therapy: the Swedish experience Eur J Obstet Gynecol Reprod Biol, 1996; 64: S3–5.
42. Olesen C, Steffensen FH, Sorensen HT, Nielsen GL, Olsen J, Bergman U. Low use of long-term hormone replacement therapy in Denmark Br J Clin Pharmacol, 1999; 47: 323–8.
43. Sogaard AJ, Fonnebo V, Magnus JH, Tollan A. Hormone replacement therapy among Norwegian women. Self-reported use and sales of estrogen preparations Tidsskr Nor Laegeforen, 1998; 118: 590–5.
44. Ravnikar VA. Compliance with hormone therapy Am J Obstet Gynecol, 1987; 156: 1332–4.
45. Cano A. Compliance to hormone replacement therapy in menopausal women controlled in a third level academic centre Maturitas, 1995; 20: 91–9.
46. Rabin DS, Cipparrone N, Linn ES, Moen M. Why menopausal women do not want to take hormone replacement therapy Menopause, 1999; 6: 61–7.
47. Abbott TA, Lawrence BJ, Wallach S. Osteoporosis: the need for comprehensive treatment guidelines Clin Ther, 1996; 18: 127–49.
48. Johanesson M, Jonsson B. Economic evaluation of osteoporosis prevention Health Policy, 1993; 24: 103–24.

[16]

KATHLEEN MARIE DIXON

OPPRESSIVE LIMITS: CALLAHAN'S
FOUNDATION MYTH

ABSTRACT. Daniel Callahan has not simply proposed alterations of important features of the health economy. He has constructed a blue print for society drawing on concepts of what is natural and appropriate to human beings. He is, in effect, establishing a new social order. Like any social order, Callahan's system has its justificatory schemes or founding myths. This paper offers a feminist examination of the functions that these four myths – the concept of a whole of life; the stages of life; a tolerable death; and a reconstruction of the meaning of the aged in terms of sacrifice – fulfill in Callahan's new social order. Callahan's concept of a whole of life reflects the power he assigns to nature, and the futility and harm he associates with attempts to repudiate biological imperatives. It introduces the stages of human life, tolerable death, and aging. The paper critically examines these concepts.

Key Words: feminist medical ethics, aging, allocation of medical resources

In *Setting Limits*, Daniel Callahan embarks on a reconstruction of aging proceeding from a "societal perspective" (Callahan, 1987, pp. 28–29). Callahan rejects modernizing theories of aging that encourage the fulfillment of individual needs and pursuit of personal development. He argues instead that the "meaning of the aged"[1] must be recast in terms of self-sacrifice, particularly to younger generations. If this reconstruction were to emerge as a product of social consensus, Callahan argues, two intractable social problems could be resolved. First, the impending collapse of the health care economy could be forestalled by diminishing the demands on the system placed by the acute and chronic health care problems of the elderly. Callahan argues that a health care system which redistributes resources to meet the pressing needs of the young and the poor would better exemplify intergenerational justice. Second, personal and social crises resulting from the absence of a

Kathleen Marie Dixon, Ph.D., Philosophy and Women's Studies, Bowling Green State University, Bowling Green, Ohio 43403–0222, USA.

The Journal of Medicine and Philosophy 19: 613–637, 1994.
© 1994 *Kluwer Academic Publishers. Printed in the Netherlands.*

societally recognized meaning of aging and a significant social role for the aged could be avoided.

When this doctrine of aging is coupled with Callahan's concept of "a whole of life," the basic framework of a societally and biologically based rationing system emerges. Human life is understood in terms of a series of stages. Death is an absolute limit that need not be feared or avoided (Callahan, 1987, pp. 40–41). Aging is an inevitable saga of bodily decline and disengagement from the active management and administration of social power. From these premises, Callahan issues an injunction of sorts: to age graciously, ceding nature its due, and pursuing meaning and investment as moral conservators and guardians of the younger generation. Thus, his rationing system emphasizes care rather than cure in the last stages of life. It also prioritizes funding of research and treatment of those illnesses that would deprive the young of their potential to enjoy the opportunities that the various stages of human life afford.

In *What Kind of Life?* Callahan expands and refines this rationing system, building on the premise that the goal of the health care system is the attainment of the common good and the health and welfare of the society. The health care system is thus explicitly recognized as the life line of the state. It ensures levels of health sufficient to sustain important socio-political structures and institutions (Callahan, 1990, pp. 111–113). This theory results in the construction of a health pyramid. Callahan describes this pyramid, saying that the base consists of institutions emphasizing "the provision of caring in its most basic forms" including the needs for pain relief and companionship (Callahan, 1990, pp. 175–176). The next levels of the pyramid address public health concerns and provide preventive health programs. The narrowing of the pyramid reflects a shift from public health needs that if inadequately met would threaten social stability and welfare, to individual health problems and a move to more expensive, high-technology interventions aimed at prolonging individual life (Callahan, 1990, pp. 175–176). Callahan promotes a state sponsored program of universal access to care or support services, public health programs, preventive medicine, and primary care. With regard to more expensive or advanced, high-technology interventions, Callahan says:

Since at that point the benefits focus more on disparate and varied individual needs, the burden should be relatively more upon individuals to show that a claim for cure should be societally honored in the face of medical scarcity and other societal needs (Callahan, 1990, p. 179).

If the scope and daring of the project Callahan has undertaken in these two books is to be appreciated, we must recognize that he has not simply proposed alterations of important features of the health care economy. He has constructed a blue print for society drawing on concepts of what is natural and appropriate to human beings. He is, in effect, establishing a new social order. As with any social order, Callahan's system has its justificatory schemes or founding myths. This paper offers a feminist examination of these justificatory schemes, assessing their value and implications as founding myths. It reviews the functions that these four myths – the concept of a whole of life; the stages of life; a tolerable death; and a reconstruction of the meaning of the aged in terms of sacrifice – fulfill in Callahan's new social order. It should be noted that the metaphor of the founding myth does not function as a reductio. Instead it serves as a distancing lens that may allow us a more careful and reflective analysis of elements that not only play a key role in Callahan's system, but carry an important, if oppressive legacy in our own society.

The launching point of this paper's critical analysis is an assessment of Callahan's concept of a whole of life. The myth of a whole of life represents the ordering principle grounding Callahan's new society. Its central commitments reflect the power Callahan assigns to nature, and the futility and harm he associates with attempts to repudiate biological imperatives. As a framing principle, the concept of a whole of life introduces Callahan's notions of the stages of human life and a tolerable death. It also provides the foundation for his social reconstruction of aging.

If Callahan's notion of the stages of life is to be adequately understood, it must be recognized as a participant in a genre of myths. Myths of the stages of life represent an attempt to create order out of the chaos of life's possibilities. I provide an assessment of biological and cultural methods of modelling life. Special attention is paid to the myths' effects on women. Callahan's own offering is then situated within the broader framework provided by these types. I argue that although Callahan's own myth is presented as "unmarked" it is not gender neutral.

The mythic legacies of Callahan's concept of a tolerable death are subsequently described and explored. Constructions of tolerable death represent efforts to minimize the threat of death by situating it in accepted social or moral contexts. Myths of tolerable death are vehicles of social control, supporting specific social orders, offering meaning and transcendence only within the boundaries of particular practices and institutions. I briefly outline the social objectives of Callahan's version of the myth. The three components of Callahan's definition of a tolerable death are then reviewed. I discuss the integration of Callahan's myths of the stages of life and tolerable death, revealing elements of social role performance in Callahan's 'biographical' expression of a tolerable death.

The paper then turns to an examination of Callahan's reconstruction of aging. He argues that the appropriate social role of the aged is to serve as moral conservators of the past and advocates of the young. The central doctrine in this ideology is finding meaning through self-sacrifice rather than fulfillment of personal needs or exploration of personal identity. This reconstruction is remarkable for its resemblance to ideologies used to segregate the sexes and limit the social, political, and economic power of women. I will argue that Callahan uses the ethic of self-sacrifice unselfconsciously, failing to appreciate its legacy. I explore the socio-political motivations of his advocacy of this ethic, arguing that he attempts to limit intergenerational strife by creating a separate and unequal realm for the aged in which they allegedly have unique social and moral authority. This invites comparisons with the 18th century doctrines of sexual complementarity and Haraway's concept of the "natural mother" (Schiebinger, 1989, pp. 214–241; Haraway, 1990, p. 142).

The paper closes with a consideration of women's position in Callahan's new social order and the cumulative effect on women of the myths he adopts. Although Callahan constructs a society without explicit references to gender, his system offers limited views of the multifaceted experiences and insights of women. Rather than being gender neutral, Callahan's new social order is written from the vantage point of the universal masculine, assuming that this adequately reflects or captures women's voices. The univocal nature of Callahan's work and its lineage in socio-historical doctrines justifying the subordination of women disenfranchise women and represent important features of a repressive system. They may pale, however, when compared with the effects of adoption of his policies for allocation of medical resources. As a result of longer lifespans and lower incomes, women will suffer disproportionately in Callahan's medical rationing system and their sacrifice will be greater.

THE CONCEPT OF A WHOLE OF LIFE

The concept of a whole of life is the ordering principle that pervades Callahan's founding myth. Its presumptions and insights shape Callahan's social order, reflecting his conceptions of human nature and his quest for institutions and patterns of socialization that inculcate this view. Thus, the concept of a whole of life provides the telos for individual human beings and the ultimate reference point for societal structures.

The concept of a whole of life manifests the importance Callahan assigns to the search for a culturally authoritative definition of the good for human beings. Callahan argues in *Setting Limits* that there is a "perennial human need to find a way of envisioning the fullness of a life..." (Callahan, 1987, p. 66). Callahan asserts that cultural pluralism creates a void of meaning (Callahan, 1987, p. 60). Individuals are bereft of the sources of meaning that could help them endure suffering and illness or come to terms with death. Finally, in the absence of a culturally authoritative model of the meaningful life, social classes like the aged become absurd. Deprived of any social significance or unique status, the old ape their only models, the behaviors and practices of youth (Callahan, 1987, p. 60).

Although Callahan's concept of the whole of life is frequently expressed in cultural terms, it rests on a perception of the biological or natural realms. Callahan asserts that a concept of a whole of life requires us to recognize that: (1) life has relatively fixed stages; (2) death represents an "absolute limit"; (3) old age is necessarily an experience of decline, requiring a unique set of meanings, recognizing this biological fact; and (4) our society would be better off if it shared a common view of the whole of life (Callahan, 1987, pp. 40–41). The first three conditions express Callahan's understanding of human nature or our biological imperatives. Thus, they provide a fixed framework for social systems that they ignore at their peril. Indeed, Callahan argues that the health care crisis facing our own society is due in large part to a fruitless attempt to turn back the clock, wiping away the effects of aging and forestalling death.

Callahan also adopts the phrase "a natural life span" when he speaks about the wholeness of human life. While leaving open the possibility of "reading correct" moral and social theories of aging from nature, Callahan writes,

I want instead to use the term "natural" in a different way, that of pointing to a persistent pattern of judgment in our culture and others of what it means to live out a life, one that manifests a wholeness and relative completeness (Callahan, 1987, p. 64–65).

Thus, a natural life is measured in terms of cultural standards of human fulfillment (Callahan, 1987, p. 65). This is a misleading and unusual use. Talk of a natural life span or natural death suggests links with some precultural, physical or biological strata. This rhetoric draws on emotionally and psychologically charged terms that assign a privileged status to a biological order. It presents a critical social platform. Social institutions and practices become defective and foreign, "artificial", as they become distanced from this foundation. Callahan clearly expects the term 'natural death' to contrast favorably with a medically overmanaged or technologically inhibited death. To use the rhetoric of nature is also, oddly enough, to adopt a stance that limits or discourages diversity of approach. "Natural" is often characterized in terms of monolithic 'species' prototypes as when conservatives refer to "natural modes of sexual expression."

This combination of the biological and cultural in Callahan's concept of a whole of life expresses problematic trends. Callahan's goal is the construction of a culturally authoritative definition of a fulfilling human life. Use of a biological model reflects cultural assessments of science as an epistemically privileged activity and a prestigious occupation. Use of the biological or natural model also appeals to the naive realism of popular culture, apparently offering a firm and unbiased foundation for the formation of social policy. Finally, the biological model is suited to the development of a universal concept of a whole of life, surmounting the problems Callahan sees in pluralistic characterizations. Yet these very features of the myth create tensions within Callahan's new social order. Callahan perceives unchecked scientific expansionism as a threat to the developed society (Callahan, 1990, pp. 255–256). He argues for the inadequacy of the medical model, saying that it lacks any sense of appropriate ends. The society driven by the engine of medical science will endlessly pursue additional life years and relentlessly expand its onslaught on disease without radically and pervasively improving the quality of human life. Spending in other crucial social services would be neglected, effectively stunting social growth and hazarding social welfare. Thus, Callahan argues, the culture is enslaved by the powers of technology (Callahan, 1987, p. 173).

The cultural or societal model provides, from Callahan's perspective, an essential vantage point; supplying balance and direction, foreclosing medical expansionism. It provides the telos, the framework of individual meaning and social significance which determines the strategies and boundaries of scientific achievement (Callahan, 1987, p. 172). It also offers the opportunity for development of consensus with respect to the fulfilling human life, but seems more flexible than the biological model. It can respond to the levels of resources of particular societies. Callahan also hopes it can correct pervasive or dominant social ideologies. Finally, the cultural model provides clear and authoritative direction to individuals attempting to find meaning in their experiences of illness, aging, and death. It provides the framework for the construction of the social significance of specific classes or age groups, avoiding the harmful vacuum of meaning created by individualistic pluralism (Callahan, 1987, p. 60).

THE MYTH OF THE STAGES OF LIFE

Myths of stages of human life represent an attempt to create order out of the chaos of life's possibilities. They typically provide an overarching theme or organizing principle that unifies the complex, disparate phenomena of human life. Thus, they give life the simpler form of an unfolding narrative. Myths of the stages of life can also be used prescriptively. As such, they can demarcate periods characterized by shared attributes and compare individuals, charting their progress within or across these stages.

This genre of myths, the stages of human life, is quite diverse, including narratives organized around themes or principles of science and religion. Moreover, this myth has enjoyed a prominent representation in the arts. A literary or iconographic history of various myths of the stages of human life provides an interesting vantage point on human culture. I will, however, limit my consideration of myths of the stages of life to scientifically inspired or motivated modeling methods. This selection reflects the influences apparent in Callahan's own concept of the stages of life.

Within the framework of science, there are two prominent inter-related methods of modelling the human life: the life sciences and the social sciences. The former distinguish phases in the biological life cycle, demarcating periods characterized by specific physical or psychological achievements or tasks. The dominant characterization within this type casts the life story of the organism in reproductive terms. In this most basic version of the biological model we speak of fertilization, gestation, birth, infancy, pubescence, reproductive maturity, and reproductive senescence. It is important to remember, however, that this is not the only way of organizing the story. Life stages can be cognitively or psychologically based, allowing the narrative to emphasize the development of the brain or the psyche.

In the social sciences life stages express and demarcate social boundaries, thereby defining a course of human life. In this class, the concept of life stages most pertinent to Callahan's project is that of age-grades and age-sets.[2] Anthropologists use these concepts to describe the use of age as: a social principle of categorization by achieved or ascribed status; an ideology that may assist or hinder efforts to develop a sense of group identity or shared fate; and a salient category that can determine the locus and content of individuals' social activities (Keith, 1982, pp. 12–15, 33). These describe ways in which age operates as an organizing principle of the narrative.

An interesting feature of these narratives is reflected in the difference in the number of age-sets and age-groups for men and women that cultures recognize. Keith indicates that the most common number of grades for men is five, for women, two (Keith, 1982, pp. 17). One could readily speculate that if age-sets and age-grades describe cultural patterns of accession to, exploitation and ultimately renunciation or transmission of wealth or the means of commercial production, then given common cultural disenfranchisements of women, the number of female age-grades or age-sets would be limited. Alternatively, one could argue that the stereotypical productive modes allocated to women – childbearing, child-rearing, and commercial support or participation in a 'secondary economy' readily admit to binary classification. One is either pregnant or not, charged with the bulk of parenting obligations or not, and engaged in stop-gap or support employment or not.

Although Callahan assigns importance to a notion of the stages of life by asserting that it is an essential condition of a concept of a whole of life, he never systematically elucidates a doctrine of life stages. Callahan does, however, refer approvingly to Erikson's distinction of the characteristics of two stages of life, adult status and old age. Adult function is characterized in terms of generativity.

Its tasks include procreation, production, and creative activity. Old age is more ambiguously and less satisfactorily defined in terms of *"grand-*generative function" (Callahan, 1987, p. 41). Callahan himself recognizes at least three and possibly four stages of human life. He lists them and describes their tasks, indicating that the efforts of young children and young adults are expended in future role preparation and development of a pertinent sense of self. Mature adults are responsible for procreating and rearing the next generation and managing society. The indispensable social role of the elderly is as moral conservators of the past and advocates of the young (Callahan, 1987, p. 43). Callahan's reticence to fully explore all the stages of life can be explained as a matter of textual focus. Although he is deeply concerned with issues of integenerational equity, his approach suggests he believes that only one stage of life requires substantial reworking. The reconstruction of the meaning of aging that Callahan offers in *Setting Limits* represents his attempt to provide this.

Callahan's discussions of the stages of life presuppose the more detailed narratives provided by the biological and social sciences. Moreover, one could argue that they are intelligible only if they are situated within the frameworks these myths provide. Callahan frequently discusses the opportunities and obligations of adult life; reproduction and parenting appear prominently and are emphasized (Callahan, 1987, pp. 67–69). Familial relationships receive so much attention in *Setting Limits* that one is tempted to assume that Callahan considers reproduction an essential part of the adult stage. Callahan's view of aging as a saga of unavoidable bodily decline also empowers the biological model of the stages of life, this time stressing physical strength or capacity. Callahan's view of role preparation as one of the tasks of the immature stages is most readily assumed under the narrative of the social sciences. His views of the reproductive and administrative roles of adults must also be situated in cultural terms. Finally, Callahan's goal of a reconstruction of aging should be seen as an attempt to recast cultural age-grades.

Although Callahan makes no explicit references to sex or gender roles in his myth of the stages of life, he also makes no attempt to distance himself from those aspects of these narratives destructive to the interests of women. His references to those elements in the biological model whose historic emphasis offered the greatest impediment to full economic and political participation by women, without any overt recognition of this fact, could readily be seen as reinforcement of this myth. Callahan identifies adult tasks in terms of reproduction, parenting, and social administration, but ignores the all too common distribution of these tasks. Furthermore, his reconstruction of aging in terms of self-sacrifice could be characterized as an expansion of gender roles without adequate consideration of their pernicious effect.

If the harmful uses of these myths were trivial, then Callahan's oversight could easily be excused. Yet the damage these myths can wreak on women could hardly be more far-reaching. When the biological story is reduced to reproductive capacity or status, the full range of women's potential as human beings is disregarded. Women become reproductive vessels and their life stages are understood accordingly. From the vantage point of culture, the myth of the stages of life has been used to highlight the public and commercial labors of men, recognizing and rewarding their status in socio-political realms while obscuring or failing to recognize and reward the achievements of women.

In our society, the dominant or unmarked categories remain those of males and men. Thus, when we adopt biological or cultural myths of the stages of life, we automatically situate ourselves in this milieu. Entrance into the 'default' or alternate mode occurs through unambiguous reclassification or resistance. Unfortunately, in our culture when an author speaks of life stages, assigning adults the responsibilities of child bearing, parenting, and the administration of social power, it will typically be assumed, unless otherwise specified, that women largely bear the brunt of the first two, while men are the chief beneficiaries of the last. In our society, those who hope to avoid gender wars associated with myths of the stages of life will have to explicitly emphasize cognitive or psychological development within the biological model, arguing for parity of the sexes. Or they will have to explicitly address the inequities of cultural assignments of commercial and political authority and power. Silence fails to offer challenge to, and thereby only sustains, the harmful myths underlying status quo.

A TOLERABLE DEATH

Death remains one of the greatest human mysteries. As the essential unknown, it challenges sources of individual meaning. Its spectre of oblivionation, best represented in Shelley's Ozymandias, threatens to undermine the integrity of human projects, rendering our achievements, efforts, and trials absurd. Cultures attempt to minimize this threat through the mediation of ritual and integrating schemas offered by religion or philosophy. Myths of a tolerable death represent one such effort. They lessen death's sting by situating the awesome and fear provoking fact of human demise in accepted social or moral contexts. Callahan illustrates this point, positioning his own myth within the broader narrative of a concept of a whole of life. He quotes historian of religion, Frank E. Reynolds:

Deaths that are recognized as natural assume the realization of a cultural or religious model of human fulfillment. In each case there is a common understanding that if an individual lives his life properly and fully, his death is divested of its negative meaning and its destructive power (Callahan, 1987, p. 65).

A slight transposition of the elements of this explanation reveals another important feature of this genre, one that Callahan's concept shares. Myths of tolerable death support a specific social order, offering meaning or even transcendence of death only within the boundaries of particular practices or institutions. Thus, they are vehicles of social control. Callahan's myth of a tolerable death facilitates implementation of his rationing system. It allows him to cast the intentional death of a policy based withholding of life saving treatment in a new light. He can argue that such deaths are not evil and may even represent the fulfillment of these individuals' highest calling, i.e. self-sacrifice (Callahan, 1987, pp. 72–75). Thus, they can be encompassed by a just system and required by its administrators.

Callahan builds his notion of the tolerable death on the stages of human life. His underlying presumption, a common one in our culture, is that death in old age is neither a violation of the natural order nor an unjustified abridgement undermining the integrity of the elder's life story.

My definition of a "tolerable death" is this: the individual event of death at that stage in a life span when (a) one's life possibilities have on the whole been accomplished; (b) one's moral obligations to those for whom one has had responsibility have been discharged; and (c) one's death will not seem to others an offense to sense or sensibility or tempt others to despair and rage at the finitude of human existence. Note the most obvious feature of this definition: it is a biographical, not a biological, definition. A "natural life span" may then be defined as one in which life's possibilities have on the whole been achieved and after which death may be understood as a sad but nonetheless relatively acceptable event (Callahan, 1987, p. 66).

The first of these three components is the most interesting and controversial. Callahan, in elucidating this condition, draws further on his concept of the stages of life, asserting that life affords people a fairly fixed series of opportunities. We can work, love, bear and rear children, and pursue other intellectual, social, or aesthetic experiences (Callahan, 1987, pp. 66–67). Callahan indicates that by age 65, most of us will have had the opportunity to enjoy these activities. Nevertheless, he argues that what is essential to a tolerable death is not the range or depth of any pleasure or fulfillment associated with these activities, or their likely continuance, but the simple fact that we had these opportunities (Callahan, 1987, p. 67).

This might seem a slim reed from which to fashion a tolerable death. What, we might ask, happens to those who as a result of choice or circumstance, never availed themselves of these options? Callahan writes,

Many people, sadly, fail to have all the opportunities they might have: they may never have found love, may not have had the income to travel, may not have gained much knowledge through lack of education, and so on. More old age is not likely to make up for those deficiencies, however; the pattern of such lives, including their deprivations, is not likely to change significantly in old age, much less open up radically new opportunities hitherto missing (Callahan, 1987, p. 67).

Here Callahan acknowledges the fact of privation, some lives have a broader range of opportunities than others. Yet if the focus of a definition of tolerable death is the presence of opportunities, we ought to concern ourselves with the causes of their loss. Why have people lacked opportunities? Two explanations immediately come to mind. The absence of specific opportunities may have been the result of personal choices. This explanation expresses the primacy and might of the will and the power of unhampered personal choice to transform life.

The other explanation calls attention to limiting social conditions, arguing that privation is misunderstood if it is thought to result exclusively from the choices of those deprived. This explanation does not vitiate the will; it simply situates it within a broader socio-political context. The reality of privation is that it is also the product of choices made by those who are privileged. The achievement of many will be limited, their aspirations thwarted because they are approached through the limiting lenses of ethnic, gender, and class stereotypes. As a result of prejudice and social disenfranchisement, their window of opportunity is open only a crack.

The great tragedy of it all is that Callahan is correct, these barriers are unlikely to change. While personal effort may be sufficient to cast off the internal chains of limiting stereotypes, few will have enough strength to subdue the monster of prejudice themselves. For that, collective effort is required, effort aimed at widespread social change. Until our collective will levels the playing field, many will expend much effort, just to hold their present ground or make small advances. In such a context, Callahan's statement assumes a new and callous meaning. He seems to say, "I'm sorry you never had these opportunities, but additional life years won't really change your situation, because you're female, you're African-American, you're poor." Although Callahan can and should be criticized for failing to recognize and address limiting social conditions in his definition of tolerable death, he should not be pilloried unjustly. A major impetus for Callahan's system of health care rationing is his belief that reduced spending on health care will allow us to better attend to other, more pressing social ills.

Callahan calls his myth of tolerable death a biographical approach (Callahan, 1986, p. 66). Yet his elaboration of the components of a tolerable death is biographical only in the loose sense suggested by his concept of the stages of human life. "Biographical" here cannot be taken in any personal or subjective sense. This is the story of everyperson rather than any one person. For the central theme of Callahan's contention that "life's possibilities have on the whole been accomplished" is that the time frame has been sufficient to allow the individual the possibility of actualizing some culturally determined potentials (Callahan, 1987, pp. 66–67). It does not really matter whether the individual has actualized any or all of these in her own life. The systemic implications of this aspect of the myth are clear, the elderly cannot forestall or resist rationing by claiming that their particular range of actual experiences has been too small or that if allowed to die they would be cut off from important or essential opportunities.

A brief comment on the second component of Callahan's notion of a tolerable death seems warranted. Callahan indicates that in the tolerable death, "one's moral obligations to those for whom one has had responsibility have been discharged..." (Callahan, 1987, p. 66). He elaborates on this saying,

> When I speak of having discharged one's moral obligations, I have in mind primarily family obligations, particularly to one's children. Obligations to children are very special and inescapable. The death of parents at a time when children are still wholly dependent upon them is easily and rightly seen as particularly sad and wrong, and that is so even if others can step in and assume the parental role. It is a premature death not only biologically, but parentally and socially. Yet if the children are grown, and have achieved a self-supporting and self-directing status, it is then fair to say that the parents no longer have special obligations towards them. They have done their work in bringing their children to independence and maturity (Callahan, 1987, p. 69).

Callahan completes his picture of familial obligation arguing that in a marriage, death is premature when the deceased, because of lack of time, could not provide the foundation for the material security of the other partner (Callahan, 1987, p. 70).

These elaborations provide further evidence for the importance of the concept of life stages in determining a tolerable death. Recall that the central tasks of the adult stage are procreation, parenting, and social administration. Premature or intolerable deaths occur while individuals are still heavily engaged in these activities. Premature demise, then, precludes social role performance, impeding social function by burdening others who must assume the duties of the deceased. One possible explanation for Callahan's emphasis on the obligations of parenting could be the relative burdens associated with transfer of these duties. Perhaps Callahan presumes that the emotional and psychological components of the parental role can never be precisely duplicated, while replacements could more readily be found for those filling the role of spouse.

The final component of Callahan's myth of a tolerable death expresses the common interest of this genre in limiting the pain, loss, and shock associated with death. For such negative sequelae are not only personally disrupting for the dying and survivors, but strain existing social networks. A death that cannot be integrated into the strong and acknowledged patterns of meaning can threaten survivors' identities and lives. This final component of the definition is apparently produced by fulfilling the first two conditions. Yet, it works best given a local scale. Regardless of the context or age of a death, most such losses are not accorded the high social profile required to shake sense or sensibility or promote widespread

despair and rage. Only deaths that take on a social or iconic significance accomplish this.

CALLAHAN'S RECONSTRUCTION OF AGING

Callahan has strong motivation to reconstruct the meaning of the
aged. He believes such a change is required both to protect the
interests and status of elders and to preserve the social framework
from the stresses and degradation associated with increased intergenerational strife. Callahan argues that without a social consensus or "public philosphy" of the meaning of the aged, the old are
vulnerable. Individualism and pluralism create a vacuum of meaning, depriving the aged of firm foundations that would allow them
to understand and accept their ailments and death. The void of
meaning not only adversely affects individuals struggling to cope
with the difficult effects of aging, it compromises elders as a social
class. Old age itself become meaningless; devoid of any unique
status, it loses social value. Deprived of social significance, elders as
a class can make no justifiable claim to social protection. Callahan
argues that in the absence of a consensus view of the meaning of
aging and the social status of elders, any rationale for their protection results from sentimental benevolence (Callahan, 1987, p. 60).

Callahan's reconstruction of aging not only provides meaning
and secure social status to elders; it offers them the possibility of transcendence. This revision of aging eschews self-absorption, asserting
that altruism is the only available source of transcendence. Thus,
Callahan roots self sacrifice in biology, writing:

It may be only through passing life and culture along to the next generation – in
an active and responsible and yet gradually self–emptying way – that any kind
of transcendence can be found. Leon Kass has written suggestively that "...
biology has its own view of our nature and its inclinations. Biology also teaches
about transcendence, though it eschews talk about the soul. For self-preservation
is one thing, reproduction quite another; in bearing and caring for their young,
many animals risk and even sacrifice their own lives. Indeed, in all higher animals,
to reproduce *as such* implies both acceptance of the death of self and participation
in its transcendence. . . . human biology, too, teaches us how our life points beyond
itself – to our offspring, to our community, to our species. Man, like the other
animals, is built for reproduction. Man, more than the other animals, is also built
for sociality. And man, alone among the animals, is built for culture – not only
through capacities to transmit and receive skills and techniques, but also through
capacities for shared beliefs, opinions, rituals, traditions" (Callahan, 1987, p. 48).

In such a way Callahan can argue that the transcendence offered by his reconstruction of the meaning of the aged allows us to be fully human, actualizing our unique species potential.

Before the broader social objectives or systemic motivations for Callahan's reconstruction are considered in any detail, the elder-specific ends of Callahan's project should be assessed. Callahan argues that any effective characterization of aging will have to enjoy social dominance. If elders are to have meaning and direction in their lives or a secure social status, there will have to be near universal recognition of this new construction's legitimacy and power. Pluralism, Callahan argues, is a source of vulnerability for elders.

The presence, however, of dominant patterns of social meaning is not a sufficient condition for the protection of any group. Oppressive regimes require overarching schemas of value to legitimate subordination. A glimpse at any social history reveals the inadequacies of Callahan's claims. Societies have formulated ideologies rooted in concepts of nature, biology, and social significance to justify the subordination of women and ethnic minorities (Schiebinger, 1989, pp. 189–244).

Callahan's offer of transcendence is rich in irony. If biology speaks to the issue of transcendence it is only because it has placed phenomena within the broader interpretative, teological framework provided by culture. The brute facts of reproduction express no real acceptance of the death of self. After all, if Callahan and Kass were correct, few adults would rebel against or attempt to deny the reality of death. Yet death denial and avoidance are pervasive in our culture (Aries, 1981, pp. 559–601). It also seems fitting that the prize awarded for tireless self-sacrifice is transcendence. Few might expend any effort, however to achieve it, if its other face were revealed. After all, extinction of self is what remains after transcendence is stripped of euphemism.

Callahan believes that a reconstruction of aging is a matter of social survival. He argues that the unchecked demands of the elderly for personal gratification undermine the possibility of community (Callahan, 1987, p. 30). Maintenance of any social order requires the establishment of limits on the fulfillment of personal desires and needs, including those for medical treatment. Thus, the reconstruction of aging facilitates the development and application of a comprehensive system of medical rationing. If the state's expenditures for medical treatment for the elderly poor are contained, fewer costs will have to be passed to younger, commercially productive generations. This will minimize any sense of outrage experienced by younger workers at being forced to underwrite the costs of others' care. Social tensions between the generations will be reduced. Callahan suggests that the reconstruction of aging and implementation of a rationing system will also reduce social anxieties by allowing people to plan effectively for old age and clearly informing them of the precise nature and limits of their entitlements (Callahan, 1987, p. 60).

The final motivation for a reconstruction of the meaning of the aged is the most interesting and far-reaching. Although Callahan fails to clearly articulate this aim, it lies beneath his expressed motivation and systemic objectives. It may produce and drive all the founding myths. This motive is the reduction of intergenerational competition. If a unique status and social role for the aged can be prescribed, intergenerational competition for a full range of resources can be drastically reduced. In its designation of areas of privilege or special competency, prescriptive constructions of aging also create bounded social spaces or reservations. These reservations not only protect the aged from the effects of direct competition with younger generations by establishing and administering special entitlement programs. They also insulate the broader culture from the effects of social integration of elders, preventing them from continuing in their previous patterns of social production. Thus, the establishment of social preserves for the elderly ensures their transmission of social power and authority to a younger generation.

This strategy is remarkably similar to one used in Europe in the 18th century to resolve the *querelle des femmes*. The doctrine of sexual complementarity neatly settled some of the more troubling social implications of the revolutionary political doctrines of the Enlightenment (Schiebinger, 1989, pp. 213–216). This doctrine allowed a reconciliation between the postulate that all men are created equal and social policies that continued the subordination of women. Thus, it managed to sustain the separate preserve for women thought to be essential to the maintenance of middle-class values and structures. It also insulated the state, limiting the political influence and privilege of women by ridiculing the independence, intellectual power, and political ambition of the *salonnieres* (Schiebinger, 1989, pp. 217–218). Schiebinger describes this doctrine:

The theory of *sexual complementarity*, a theory which taught that man and woman are not physical and moral equals but complementary opposites, fit neatly into dominant strands of liberal democratic thought, making inequalities seem natural while satisfying the needs of European society for a continued sexual division of labor by assigning women a unique place in society. Henceforth, women were not to be viewed merely as *inferior to* men but as fundamentally *different from*, and thus *incomparable to*, men. The private, caring woman emerged as a foil to the public, rational man. As such, women were thought to have their own part to play in the new democracies – as mothers and nurturers (Schiebinger, 1989, pp. 216–217).

Two interesting features of the doctrine of sexual complementarity are shared by Callahan's reconstruction of the meaning of aging. The first could be cast as an attempt to remove the bitterness from the pill of segregation by adopting a rhetoric that recognized some moral virtue or unique social value associated with the limited activities of the subordinate group. Thus, motherhood was no longer considered an exclusively familial or personal phenomenon. It was transformed into a matter of essential interest to the state. Women, it was argued, were vested with a unique mission of the utmost importance; they produced and reared strong, healthy, and capable children (Schiebinger, 1989, p. 225). Thus, women were encouraged to attend to their duties with new diligence. A cult of domesticity arose, changing preexisting patterns of infant care (Schiebinger, 1989, p. 219).

Callahan offers elders a singular place of honor, arguing they alone are capable of supplying the historical perspective required to ground the visions of youth (Callahan, 1987, p. 43). He argues only elders have the insight, acquired by long experience, to consolidate existing social gains. Elders are, in Callahan's opinion, uniquely competent pilots, pointing out the perils and benefits associated with new and proposed policies (Callahan, 1987, pp. 43, 47). This tableau of the aged, like the doctrine of sexual complementarity, covers the reality of segregation and subordination. For in our culture, with its near instaneous and widespread access to information, elders become superfluous as social historians. Electronic and printed media can offer a living history, bringing legacies of the past alive. The allegedly unique and essential roles assigned to the aged vanish.

The second resemblance between the theory of sexual complementarity and Callahan's reconstruction of aging is the reliance of both systems on biology as an intellectual foundation and source of justification for their patterns of social segregation. Callahan finds support for his emphasis on altruism in the reproductive life cycle and interprets the transmission of culture as a species-specific, self-emptying activity. Sexual complementarians such as Rousseau, looked to anatomy to resolve the question of the social place of women. For Rousseau, the physical grounded the moral, and the constitution of women's bodies and minds determined their social roles (Schiebinger, 1989, pp. 220–222).

Callahan recognizes four social roles for the aged. He argues that elders function as social historians for younger generations, unifying and integrating the past and present (Callahan, 1987, p. 42). Younger persons can utilize elders as living museums, for elders bring the lessons of history alive and concretely demonstrate their meaning and significance. The aged also serve as "moral conservators of what has been" (Callahan, 1987, p. 43). Moral conservators seem to act as stewards of present social and natural resources, helping to preserve the inheritance of future generations. They also act as conservators by transmitting their understanding of culture, science, and moral values to younger generations. Callahan argues that the second role as conservator generates the third and most important social role for the elderly, that of advocates of a better future. Callahan writes:

We owe to those coming after us at least what we were given by those who came before us, the possibility of life and survival. We also owe to the future an amelioration of those conditions which, in our own life, lessened our possibilities of living a decent life and which, if they persist, will do the same for coming generations. If the aged, moreover, want to find meaning in their lives, and a significant place in society, then this is their most promising direction, drawing on that which only they can give (Callahan, 1987, p. 47).

The fourth social role of the aged is as life counsellors who teach the young to live fully in the present (Callahan, 1987, p. 42).

Callahan has little sympathy or patience with those who argue that old age should be a time of leisure and personal fulfillment. He writes:

If the old are to have meaning in their own lives and significance in the larger social world, they cannot claim a right to self-absorption or an exemption from civic duties (Callahan, 1987, p. 48).

A focus on pleasure or recreation in retirement can also become an exercise in death avoidance (Callahan, 1987, pp. 49–50). Callahan shares the sentiments of Cicero who argued that the old should structure their activities on their remaining capacities. As physical capacities decline, intellectual ones should be redoubled, and placed at the service of the young, friends, and country (Callahan, 1987, p. 50).

The net effect of Callahan's specifications is the construction of a relational meaning of the aged. The aged are defined and valued on the basis of the services they can offer to other groups, the goods they can secure for them. Thus, the aged are self-less in a fairly fundamental sense. As good conservators or stewards they are required to administer properties that are not their own, managing others' assets or resources. As conservators, their own interests become invisible within the boundaries of social role performance. Neither they nor others are permitted to notice them. Callahan's characterization of aging is one of self-diminution. The aged are on a voyage of self-denial and ultimately extinguishment as they socialize and educate the youth, emptying themselves of knowledge and power. Resources exhausted, skills and insights transmitted, the aged divest and withdraw, shrinking towards death.

Callahan's reconstruction of the meaning of the aged contains a number of the social roles that have long been incorporated into our concepts of gender. Although Callahan makes age rather than sex the salient characteristic for distribution of social roles, the roles of the aged bears a remarkable resemblance to the tasks of the good mother. The focus of both characterizations is the relational being whose chief virtue is her selflessness, her willingness and ability to sacrifice her own good for that of others. The good mother, like Callahan's elder, is a conservator of youth. She carefully monitors the family resources, typically distributing the benefits of another's commercially compensated production, just as the aged in Callahan's system concern themselves with the adequacy of a system they no longer control. The good mother's domestic skills and personal frugality ensure adequate supply and quality of goods required for her family's health and happiness. In a similar fashion, Callahan's elders accept rationing of medical treatment as a way of reducing economic demands on the health care system and reallocating capital to other pressing needs. The good mother is her children's first teacher, establishing important social and moral values early in the child's life, preparing the children to compete and succeed in their various roles in the broader culture. Finally, like Callahan's elders, the good mother is also a social historian, answering her children's questions about her own youth, describing the progress of her own life, using it as a model to impress various lessons or insights upon the children. Donna

Haraway aptly summarizes these characteristics of gender socialization in her description of the "natural mother." She is,

a being consumed and fulfilled by dedication to another; a being whose meaning
is the species, not the self; a being less than and more than human, but never par-
adigmatically man . . . (Haraway, 1990, p. 142).

What are the ramifications of Callahan's wider application of
stereotypical gender roles? Can his reconstruction be considered a
boon for women as it distributes their traditional labors across a
wider group? Or are we simply witnessing the expansion of the subordinate class? The fact that elders in Callahan's system are assigned
activities that have been historically devalued, without a clear
reconstruction of the social status or merit of these roles, should be
considered ominous. Like women, elders are given tasks rather
than jobs (Delphy, 1987, p. 96). They perform activities requiring
experience and skill that are similar or in some cases identical to
those required by certain occupations, but they receive no compensation for them. In our society, financial compensation is a rather
direct measurement of percieved social status or worth. Further,
the tasks they are given are massive, but they lack the administrative and social power to execute their policies or implement ideas.
Elders function as social housewives, offering advice that may never
be heard, lacking the socio-political status or financial resources to
enforce needed changes.

Two features of Callahan's system are indicative of the relega-
tion of elders to a subordinate social class. First, the ethic of stew-
ardship and sacrifice is imposed exclusively on the old. This cannot
be because the younger generations could not similarly benefit from
these virtues. Callahan might have a stronger case for his exclusive
focus if an attempt to acquire more and better things and to avoid
sharing them with others did not characterize much of American
adult life. Further, why should Callahan address his sermon on
the perils of self-absorption only to the aged? Do the younger generations not need these lessons? It self-absorption is a sin why not
castigate the middle aged? They are frequently consumed by the
competitive intrigues and anxieties of the work-place; they exhaust
themselves attempting to meet their own economic demands and
society's expectations. One is also left to wonder why an ethic of
sacrifice is pressed on those who have already divested themselves
of authority for social administration and who are, compared with

mature adults, economically disadvantaged.[3] It would seem that adoption of such an ethic could be encouraged with little risk of real change in existing social structures. Limitation of advocacy of an ethic of sacrifice to the aged also offers no challenge to the dominant pattern of resource distribution of the younger generations.

A second feature of Callahan's system reflects his tacit consignment of an ethic of advocacy to the subordinate classes. While Callahan argues that his goal is a social reconstruction of the meanings of aging and death, this reconstruction does not effectively permeate all socio-economic strata. Although adoption of an ethic of advocacy and personal sacrifice is encouraged for all elders, only indigent elders are forced to adhere to the policies associated with these reconstructions. Thus, Callahan's medical rationing system limits the access of the aged poor to those levels that provide support or basic medical care, while other elders may receive any level of care that their own or their families' resources will allow (Callahan, 1987, pp. 157, 199). Callahan explicitly rejects forcing changes in resource allocation on non-indigent populations, arguing that such action would represent a harmful incursion on familial protective power (Callahan, 1987, p. 157). He indicates that such a policy would be a "prescription for an authoritarian society" and that it could create crime and a dangerous black market in medical care (Callahan, 1987, pp. 157, 199). This glaring exception to the adoption of an ethic of advocacy and sacrifice for the aged reflects a de facto economic allocation of social value and status. For it is the aged poor whose adherence to an ethic of sacrifice is enforced, not those of better means, who could more readily afford it. From this vantage point the ethic of sacrifice seems to better reflect an attempt to preserve the resources of the privileged than to inculcate any noble moral ideals. Finally, this pattern of differential implementation would seem to preclude general adoption of the underlying views of aging. Social changes selectively targeted for the poor become socially stigmatized, limiting the willingness of other social groups to model the relevant values or practices. Thus, this would seem to be a particularly poor strategy to adopt if the goal were widespread social change.

WHAT KIND OF ORDER?

This paper has described and analyzed the myths that Daniel Callahan utilizes to establish his new social order. As the critical

stance adopted in this paper has been feminist, it seems appropriate to conclude with a brief assessment of the position of women
in this new society and the cumulative effect on women of the myths
Callahan adopts. Although Callahan constructs a society without
explicit references to gender, his system offers limited views of
the multifaceted experiences and insights of women. Rather than
being gender neutral or multivalent, Callahan's new social order
is written from the vantage point of the universal masculine,
assuming that this adequately reflects or captures women's voices.
Callahan describes aging in monolithic terms, failing to appreciate
that gender socialization and differential assignments of social
power and resources affect the way women and men approach
this event.

To simply cite one example, retirement has different connotations and implications in the context of women's labors. In a sense
women never completely retire. At retirement we are released
from one of our jobs, unfortunately it is the one that is compensated and may bring some broader socio-political identity or power.
Those elements of domestic activity that have been relegated to
women, that are rarely shared by men, remain (Hochschild, 1990).
Do these tasks suddenly become equally distributed in retirement?
In my experience, while retired men may take new interest in the
domestic economy, they attempt to carve out separate spheres
within the home, establishing their dominance within these realms.

Retired women also experience difficulties extricating themselves
from childrearing activities. Without adequate and affordable corporate or state sponsored child care, many grandmothers are placed
in an untenable position. They can ignore their adult children's
need for assistance in child care and watch their life worlds develop
slowly widening cracks under the stressors of multiple social
roles. Alternately, they can assume the strains and impediments of
rearing yet another generation themselves.

Callahan offers women no release from the burden and limitations of gender socialization, explicitly foreclosing prioritization of
personal needs or an exploration of personal identity. His sermons
on the virtues of sacrifice and the perils of self-absorption seem
unreflective and callous when applied to this group. He sustains
the subordination of a cohort of women subjected to particularly
brutal constraints of gender socialization, remaining blissfully
unaware of women's histories. Callahan argues that self-actualiza-
tion need not be prioritized amongst the aged because they already
have an adequately developed, stable sense of self (Callahan, 1987,

p. 42). Apparently, he does not realize that many of these women had been systematically denied the opportunity to discover themselves as unique individuals rather than as placeholders in a social role. The same rhetoric of self-sacrifice that Callahan would reinvigorate was used throughout their youth and maturity to limit their horizons. Apparently, Callahan would compel them to empty themselves further and permanently block any chance of self-realization.

The negative implications for women of Callahan's founding myths – their failure to reflect women's experiences and their lineage in socio-historical doctrines justifying the subordination of women – are important features of a repressive system. They may pale, however, when compared with the effects of adoption of his policies for allocation of medical resources. Callahan's distribution system prioritizes care rather than cure for the aged poor, providing them palliative support rather life-sustaining treatment. As a result of longer lifespans and lower incomes, women will suffer disproportionately in Callahan's medical rationing system. The potential effects of his proposal become shockingly widespread when one realizes that 24.4% of elder women had gross annual incomes of less than $5,000 in 1990. Another 37.0% of senior women made between $5,000 and $9,999 dollars in 1990 (U.S. Bureau of Census, 1992, p. 453). It would seem then that in the absence of dramatic and sustained contributions by extended families, a large percentage of elderly women will be at risk of death from a policy based failure to provide life sustaining medical treatment. Callahan's system forces these women to choose again between their own needs and the interests of their families. For they will only be able to sustain their lives at the cost of significant or perhaps even dramatic financial burden to their children. Many women may thus feel called upon to make the final sacrifice. In this context, Callahan's provision of palliative support may offer scant comfort to dying women who realize that life sustaining treatment is being withheld because they are poor. It certainly represents an ironic and tragic denouement for those whose social role has been defined in terms of care.

NOTES

[1] Callahan indicates that when he speaks of meaning in this sense:

I refer to the interior perception, backed up by some specifiable traditions, beliefs, concepts or ideas, that one's life is purposive and coherent in its way of relegating the inner self and the outer world – and that even in the face of aging and death, it is a life which makes sense to onself; that is, one can give a plausible, relatively satisfying account of oneself to oneself in aging and death (Callahan, 1987, p. 33).

² Jennie Keith offers a helpful description of the anthropological terms, age grade, age set, and age group. She writes:

The distinctions between age-grades, sets, and groups are parallel to the differences between the American concepts of senior year in high school (grade), the graduation class of a particular year (set), and the individuals who were senior together in a particular high school in a given year (group)... (Keith, 1982; 17–18).

³ Households headed by persons 75 years old or older had a 1990 pre-tax, average annual income between 47.74% and 43.71% of that of households headed by people 25–54 years old. Corresponding figures for persons 65–74 years old are 66.51% and 60.89%. Indeed, for households headed by those 75 and older, total expenditures exceeded pre-tax, average annual income in 1990 (U.S. Bureau of Census, 1992, p. 442).

REFERENCES

Aries, P.: 1981. *The Hour of Our Death*, Vintage Books, New York.
Callahan, D.: 1987, *Setting Limits: Medical Goals in an Aging Society*, Simon and Schuster, Inc., New York.
Callahan, D.: 1990, *What Kind of Life: The Limits of Medical Progress*, Simon and Schuster, Inc., New York.
Delphy, C.: 1987, 'Protofeminism and Antifeminism', in T. Moi (ed.), *French Feminist Thought: A Reader*, Basil Blackwell, New York, pp. 80–109.
Haraway, D.: 1990, 'Investment Strategies for the Evolving Portfolio of Primate Females', in M. Jacobus, *et al.* (eds.), *Body/Politics: Women and the Discourses of Science*, Routledge, New York, pp. 139–162.
Hochschild, A.: 1990, 'The Second Shift: Employed Women Are Putting in Another Day of Work at Home', *Utne Reader* 38, 66–73.
Keith, J.: 1982, *Old People as People: Social and Cultural Influences on Aging and Old Ages*, Little, Brown and Company, Boston.
Schiebinger, L.: 1990, *The Mind Has No Sex? Women in the Origins of Modern Science*, Harvard University Press, Cambridge, MA.
U.S. Bureau of the Census: 1992, *Statistical Abstract of the United States: 1992* (112th edition), Washington, D.C.

[17]

Women and the Knife:
Cosmetic Surgery and the Colonization of Women's Bodies

KATHRYN PAULY MORGAN

The paper identifies the phenomenal rise of increasingly invasive forms of elective cosmetic surgery targeted primarily at women and explores its significance in the context of contemporary biotechnology. A Foucauldian analysis of the significance of the normalization of technologized women's bodies is argued for. Three "Paradoxes of Choice" affecting women who "elect" cosmetic surgery are examined. Finally, two utopian feminist political responses are discussed: a Response of Refusal and a Response of Appropriation.

Introduction

Consider the following passages:

> If you want to wear a Maidenform Viking Queen bra like Madonna, be warned: A body like this doesn't just happen. . . . Madonna's kind of fitness training takes time. The rock star *whose muscled body was recently on tour* spends a minimum of three hours a day working out. ("Madonna Passionate About Fitness" 1990; italics added)

> A lot of the contestants [in the Miss America Pageant] do not owe their beauty to their Maker but to their Re-Maker. Miss Florida's nose came courtesy of her surgeon. So did Miss Alaska's. And Miss Oregon's breasts came from the manufacturers of silicone. (Goodman 1989)

> Jacobs [a plastic surgeon in Manhattan] constantly answers the call for cleavage. "Women need it for their holiday ball gowns." ("Cosmetic Surgery For the Holidays" 1985)

Hypatia vol. 6, no. 3 (Fall 1991) © by Kathryn Pauly Morgan

> We hadn't seen or heard from each other for 28 years. . . . Then
> he suggested it would be nice if we could meet. I was very
> nervous about it. How much had I changed? I wanted a facelift,
> tummy tuck and liposuction, all in one week. (A woman, age
> forty-nine, being interviewed for an article on "older couples"
> falling in love; "Falling in Love Again" 1990)

> "It's hard to say why one person will have cosmetic surgery done
> and another won't consider it, but generally I think people who
> go for surgery are more aggressive, they are the doers of the
> world. It's like makeup. You see some women who might be
> greatly improved by wearing make-up, but they're, I don't know,
> granola-heads or something, and they just refuse." (Dr. Ronald
> Levine, director of plastic surgery education at the University
> of Toronto and vice-chairman of the plastic surgery section of
> the Ontario Medical Association; "The Quest to Be a Perfect
> 10" 1990)

> Another comparable limitation [of the women's liberation
> movement] is a tendency to reject certain good things only in
> order to punish men. . . . There is no reason why a women's
> liberation activist should not try to look pretty and attractive.
> (Markovic 1976)

Now look at the needles and at the knives. Look at them carefully. Look at them for a long time. *Imagine them cutting into your skin.* Imagine that you have been given this surgery as a gift from your loved one who read a persuasive and engaging press release from Drs. John and Jim Williams that ends by saying "The next morning the limo will chauffeur your loved one back home again, with a gift of beauty that will last a lifetime" (Williams, 1990). Imagine the beauty that you have been promised. . . .

This paper is about women and about the knives that "sculpt" our bodies to make us beautiful forever. I want to explore this topic for five reasons. First, I am interested in the project of developing a feminist hermeneutics that tries to understand the words and choices of women situated in an interface position with various so-called experts in Western culture.

Second, I experience genuine epistemic and political bewilderment when I, as a feminist woman, think about contemporary practices and individual choices in the area of elective cosmetic surgery.[1] Is this a setting of liberation or oppression—or both?

Third, I have come to realize that this is a "silent" (if not silenced) topic both in mainstream bioethics and in recent ground-breaking discussions in feminist medical ethics.[2] Apart from some tangential references, there is virtually no discussion, feminist or otherwise, of the normative and political

Kathryn Pauly Morgan 27

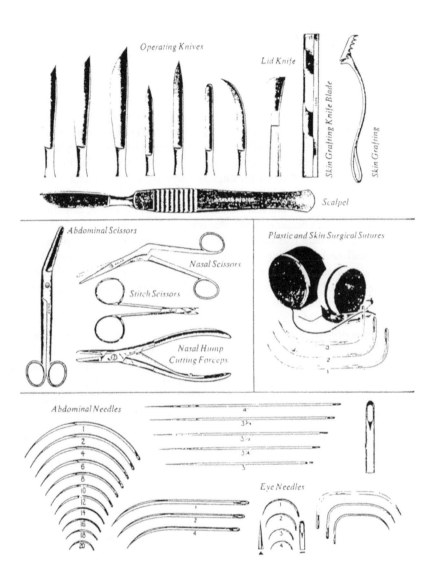

Originally published in Gina Luria and Virginia Tiger, *Every Woman*. Random House, 1974.

issues that might be raised in relation to women and elective cosmetic surgery. I believe we need a feminist framework and critique to understand why *breast augmentation*, until recently, was the most frequently performed kind of cosmetic surgery in North America ("New Bodies For Sale") and why, according to *Longevity* magazine, 1 in every 225 adult Americans had *elective* cosmetic surgery in 1989. We need a feminist analysis to understand why actual, live women are reduced and reduce themselves to "potential women" and choose to participate in anatomizing and fetishizing their bodies as they buy "contoured bodies," "restored youth," and "permanent beauty." In the face of a growing market and demand for surgical interventions in women's bodies that can and do result in infection, bleeding, embolisms, pulmonary edema, facial nerve injury, unfavorable scar formation, skin loss, blindness, crippling, and death, our silence becomes a culpable one.

Fourth, I situate this topic in the larger framework of the contemporary existential technologizing of women's bodies in Western culture. We are witnessing a *normalization* of elective cosmetic surgery. As the author of an article targeted to homemakers remarks, "For many women, it's no longer a question of *whether* to undergo cosmetic surgery—but what, when, by whom and how much" (McCabe 1990). Not only is elective cosmetic surgery moving out of the domain of the sleazy, the suspicious, the secretively deviant, or the pathologically narcissistic, *it is becoming the norm.* This shift is leading to a predictable inversion of the domains of the deviant and the pathological, so that women who contemplate *not using* cosmetic surgery will increasingly be stigmatized and seen as deviant. I believe it is crucial that we understand these normative inversions that are catalyzed by the technologizing of women's bodies.

Finally, I am intrigued by the deeper epistemological and metaphysical dynamics of the field of cosmetic surgery. For example, a recent hospital-sponsored *health* conference advertised a special session on "facial regeneration" by asking, "Are you looking in the mirror and, seeing the old you, wishing you could be seeing the you that you used to be?" and then promising that this previous, youthful "you" could be regenerated. As a philosopher, I am shocked at the extent to which patients and cosmetic surgeons participate in committing one of the deepest of original philosophical sins, the choice of the apparent over the real. Cosmetic surgery entails the ultimate envelopment of the lived temporal *reality* of the human subject by technologically created appearances that are then regarded as "the real." Youthful appearance triumphs over aged reality.

I. "Just the Facts in America, Ma'am"

As of 1990, the most frequently performed kind of cosmetic surgery is liposuction, which involves sucking fat cells out from underneath our skin with a vacuum device. This is viewed as the most suitable procedure for removing specific bulges around the hips, thighs, belly, buttocks, or chin. It is most appropriately done on thin people who want to get rid of certain bulges, and surgeons guarantee that even if there is weight gain, the bulges won't reappear since the fat cells have been permanently removed. At least twelve deaths are known to have resulted from complications such as hemorrhages and embolisms. "All we know is there was a complication and that complication was death," said the partner of Toni Sullivan, age forty-three ("hardworking mother of two teenage children" says the press; "Woman, 43, Dies After Cosmetic Surgery" 1989). Cost: $1,000-$7,500.

The second most frequently performed kind of cosmetic surgery is breast augmentation, which involves an implant, usually of silicone. Often the silicone implant hardens over time and must be removed surgically. Over one million women in the United States are known to have had breast augmentation surgery. Two recent studies have shown that breast implants block X-rays and cast a shadow on surrounding tissue, making mammograms difficult to interpret, and that there appears to be a much higher incidence of cancerous lumps in "augmented women" ("Implants Hide Tumors in Breasts, Study Says" 1988). Cost: $1,500-$3,000.

"Facelift" is a kind of umbrella term that covers several sorts of procedures. In a recent Toronto case, Dale Curtis "decided to get a facelift for her fortieth birthday. . . . Bederman used liposuction on the jowls and neck, removed the skin and fat from her upper and lower lids and tightened up the muscles in the neck and cheeks. . . . 'She was supposed to get a forehead lift but she chickened out,' Bederman says" ("Changing Faces" 1989). Clients are now being advised to begin their facelifts In their early forties and are also told that they will need subsequent facelifts every five to fifteen years. Cost: $2,500-$10,500.

"Nips" and "tucks" are cute, camouflaging labels used to refer to surgical reduction performed on any of the following areas of the body: hips, buttocks, thighs, belly, and breasts. They involve cutting out wedges of skin and fat and sewing up the two sides. These are major surgical procedures that cannot be performed in out-patient clinics because of the need for anaesthesia and the severity of possible post-operative complications. Hence, they require access to costly operating rooms and services in hospitals or clinics. Cost: $3,000-$7,000.

The number of "rhinoplasties" or nose jobs, has risen by 34 percent since 1981. Some clients are coming in for second and third nose jobs. Nose jobs involve either the inserting of a piece of bone taken from elsewhere in the body or the whittling down of the nose. Various styles of noses go in and out of fashion, and various cosmetic surgeons describe the noses they create in terms of their own surnames, such as "the Diamond nose" or "the Goldman nose" ("Cosmetic Surgery for the Holidays" 1985). Cost: $2,000-$3,000.

More recent types of cosmetic surgery, such as the use of skin-expanders and suction lipectomy, involve inserting tools, probes, and balloons *under* the skin either for purposes of expansion or reduction (Hirshson 1987).

Lest one think that women (who represent between 60 and 70 percent of all cosmetic surgery patients) choose only one of these procedures, heed the words of Dr. Michael Jon Bederman of the Centre for Cosmetic Surgery in Toronto:

> We see working girls, dental technicians, middle-class women who are unhappy with their looks or are aging prematurely. And we see executives—both male and female. . . . Where before someone would have a tummy tuck and not have anything else done for a year, frequently we will do liposuction and tummy tuck and then the next day a facelift, upper and lower lids, rhinoplasty *and other things.* The recovery time is the same whether a person has one procedure or *the works,* generally about two weeks. ("Changing Faces" 1989; italics added)

In principle, there is no area of the body that is not accessible to the interventions and metamorphoses performed by cosmetic surgeons intent on creating twentieth century versions of "femina perfecta."[3]

II: From Artifice to Artifact: The Creation of RoboWoman?

In his article "Toward a Philosophy of Technology," Hans Jonas (1979) distinguishes between premodern and modern technology. Part of what is especially characteristic of modern technology, he suggests, is that the relationship of means and ends is no longer unilinear but circular, so that "new technologies may suggest, create, even impose new ends, never before conceived, simply by offering their feasibility. . . . Technology thus adds to the very objectives of human desires, including objectives for technology itself" (Jonas 1979, 35). In 1979, Jonas only speculates about the final stage of technological creation: "Are we, perhaps, on the verge of a technology, based on biological knowledge and wielding an engineering art which, this time, has man [sic] himself for its object? This has become a theoretical possibility . . . and it has been rendered morally possible by the metaphysical neutralizing of .man" (Jonas 1979, 41). We now know that the answer to Jonas' question is yes. We have arrived at the stage of regarding ourselves as both technological subject and object, transformable and literally creatable through biological engineering. The era of biotechnology is clearly upon us and is invading even the most private and formerly sequestered domains of human life, including women's wombs. I interpret the spectacular rise of the technology of cosmetic surgery as a form of biotechnology that fits this dialectical picture of modern technology.

Kathryn Pauly Morgan   31

The domain of technolgy is often set up in oppositional relation to a domain that is designated "the natural." The role assigned to technology is often that of transcendence, transformation, control, exploitation, or destruction, and the technologized object or process is conceptualized as inferior or primitive, in need of perfecting transformation or exploitation through technology in the name of some "higher" purpose or end, or deserving of eradication because it is harmful or evil.

Although there continue to be substantive theoretical challenges to its dominant metaphors, Western scientific medicine views the human body essentially as a machine.[4] The machine model carries with it certain implica-tions, among which is the reduction of spirit, affect, and value to mechanistic processes in the human body. This perspective also facilitates viewing and treating the body in atomistic and mechanical fashion, so that, for example, the increasing mechanization of the body in terms of artificial hearts, kidneys, joints, limbs, and computerized implants is seen as an ordinary progression within the dominant model. Correlative with the rise of the modeling of the human brain as an information-processing machine, we are witnessing the development of genetic engineering; transsexual surgery; the technological transformation of all aspects of human conception, maternity, and birthing; and the artificial prolongation of human life.

What is designated "the natural" functions primarily as a frontier rather than as a barrier. While genetics, human sexuality, reproductive outcome, and death were previously regarded as open to variation primarily in evolutionary terms, they are now seen by biotechnologists as domains of creation and control. Cosmetic surgeons claim a role here too. For them, human bodies are the locus of challenge. As one plastic surgeon remarks:

> Patients sometimes misunderstand the nature of cosmetic sur-gery. It's not a shortcut for diet or exercise. *It's a way to override the genetic code.* ("Retouching Nature's Way," 1990; italics added)

The beauty culture is coming to be dominated by a variety of experts, and consumers of youth and beauty are likely to find themselves dependent not only on cosmetic surgeons but on anaesthetists, nurses, aestheticians, nail technicians, manicurists, dietitians, hairstylists, cosmetologists, masseuses, aroma therapists, trainers, pedicurists, electrolysists, pharmacologists, and dermatologists. All these experts provide services that can be bought; all these experts are perceived as administering and transforming the human body into an increasingly artificial and ever more perfect object. Think of the contestants in the Miss America pageant who undergo cosmetic surgery in preparation for participation. Reflect on the headline of the article in *Newsweek* (May 27, 1985) on cosmetic surgery: "New Bodies for Sale."

How do these general remarks concerning technology and the body apply to women—and to which women—and why? For virtually all women as women, success is defined in terms of interlocking patterns of compulsion: compulsory attractiveness, compulsory motherhood, and compulsory heterosexuality, patterns that determine the legitimate limits of attraction and motherhood.[5] Rather than aspiring to self-determined and woman-centered ideals of health or integrity, women's attractiveness is defined as attractive-to-men; women's eroticism is defined as either nonexistent, pathological, or peripheral when it is not directed to phallic goals; and motherhood is defined in terms of legally sanctioned and constrained reproductive service to particular men and to institutions such as the nation, the race, the owner, and the class—institutions that are, more often than not, male-dominated. Biotechnology is now making beauty, fertility, the appearance of heterosexuality through surgery, and the appearance of youthfulness accessible to virtually all women who can afford that technology—and growing numbers of women are making other sacrifices in their lives in order to buy access to the technical expertise.

In Western industrialized societies, women have also become increasingly socialized into an acceptance of technical knives. We know about knives that can heal: the knife that saves the life of a baby in distress, the knife that cuts out the cancerous growths in our breasts, the knife that straightens our spines, the knife that liberates our arthritic fingers so that we may once again gesture, once again touch, once again hold. But we also know about other knives: the knife that cuts off our toes so that our feet will fit into elegant shoes, the knife that cuts out ribs to fit our bodies into corsets, the knife that slices through our labia in episiotomies and other forms of genital mutilation, the knife that cuts into our abdomens to remove our ovaries to cure our "deviant tendencies" (Barker-Benfield 1976), the knife that removes our breasts in prophylactic or unnecessary radical mastectomies, the knife that cuts out our "useless bag" (the womb) if we're the wrong color and poor or if we've "outlived our fertility," the knife that makes the "bikini cut" across our pregnant bellies to facilitate the cesarean section that will allow the obstetrician to go on holiday. We know these knives well.

And now we are coming to know the knives and needles of the cosmetic surgeons—the knives that promise to sculpt our bodies, to restore our youth, to create beauty out of what was ugly and ordinary. What kind of knives are these? Magic knives. Magic knives in a patriarchal context. Magic knives in a Eurocentric context. Magic knives in a white supremacist context. What do they mean? I am afraid of these knives.

Kathryn Pauly Morgan 33

III. Listening to the Women

In order to give a feminist reading of any ethical situation we must listen to the women's own reasons for their actions (Sherwin, 1984-85 and 1989). It is only once we have listened to the voices of women who have elected to undergo cosmetic surgery that we can try to assess the extent to which the conditions for genuine choice have been met and look at the consequences of these choices for the position of women. Here are some of those voices:

Voice 1 (a woman looking forward to attending a prestigious charity ball): "There will be a lot of new faces at the Brazilian Ball" ("Changing Faces" 1989). [Class/status symbol]

Voice 2: "You can keep yourself trim. . . . But you have no control over the way you wrinkle, or the fat on your hips, or the skin of your lower abdomen. If you are *hereditarily predestined* to stretch out or wrinkle in your face, you will. If your parents had puffy eyelids and saggy jowls, you're going to have puffy eyelids and saggy jowls" ("Changing Faces" 1989). [Regaining a sense of control; liberation from parents; transcending hereditary predestination]

Voice 3: "Now we want a nose that makes a statement, with tip definition and a strong bridge line" ("Changing Faces," 1989). [Domination; strength]

Voice 4: "I decided to get a facelift for my fortieth birthday after ten years of living and working in the tropics had taken its toll" ("Changing Faces" 1989). [Gift to the self; erasure of a decade of hard work and exposure]

Voice 5: "I've gotten my breasts augmented. I can use it as a tax write-off" ("Changing Faces" 1989). [Professional advancement; economic benefits]

Voice 6: "I'm a teacher and kids let schoolteachers know how we look and they aren't nice about it. A teacher who looks like an old bat or has a big nose will get a nickname" ("Retouching Nature's Way: Is Cosmetic Surgery Worth It?" 1990). [Avoidance of cruelty; avoidance of ageist bias]

Voice 7: "I'll admit to a boob job." (Susan Akin, Miss America of 1986 quoted in Goodman 1986). [Prestige; status; competitive accomplishments in beauty contest]

Voice 8 (forty-five year old grandmother and proprietor of a business): "In my business, the customers expect you to look as good as they do" (Hirschson 1987). [Business asset; economic gain; possible denial of grandmother status]

Voice 9: "People in business see something like this as showing an overall aggressiveness and go-forwardness *The trend is to, you know, be all that you can be*" ("Cosmetic Surgery for the Holidays" 1985). [Success; personal fulfillment]

Voice 10 (paraphrase): "I do it to fight holiday depression" ("Cosmetic Surgery for the Holidays" 1985). [Emotional control; happiness]

Voice 11: "I came to see Dr. X for the holiday season. I have important business parties, and the man I'm trying to get to marry me is coming in from Paris" ("Cosmetic Surgery for the Holidays" 1985). [Economic gain; heterosexual affiliation"]

Women have traditionally regarded (and been taught to regard) their bodies, particularly if they are young, beautiful, and fertile, *as a locus of power* to be enhanced through artifice and, now, through artifact. In 1792, in A *Vindication of the Rights of Woman*, Mary Wollstonecraft remarked: "Taught from infancy that beauty is woman's scepter, the mind shapes itself to the body and roaming round its gilt cage, only seeks to adorn its prison." How ironic that the mother of the creator of *Frankenstein* should be the source of that quote. We need to ask ourselves whether today, involved as we are in the modern inversion of "our bodies shaping themselves to our minds," we are creating a new species of woman-monster with new artifactual bodies that function as prisons or whether cosmetic surgery for women does represent a potentially liberating field of choice.[6]

When Snow White's stepmother asks the mirror "Who is fairest of all?" she is not asking simply an empirical question. In wanting to continue to be "the fairest of all," she is striving, in a clearly competitive context, for a prize, for a position, for power. The affirmation of her beauty brings with it privileged heterosexual affiliation, privileged access to forms of power unavailable to the plain, the ugly, the aged, and the barren.

The Voices are seductive—they speak the language of gaining access to transcendence, achievement, liberation, and power. And they speak to a kind of reality. First, electing to undergo the surgery necessary to create youth and beauty artificially not only appears to but often actually does give a woman a sense of identity that, to some extent, she has chosen herself. Second, it offers her the potential to raise her status both socially and economically by increasing her opportunities for heterosexual affiliation (especially with white men). Third, by committing herself to the pursuit of beauty, a woman integrates her life with a consistent set of values and choices that bring her wide-spread approval and a resulting sense of increased self-esteem. Fourth, the pursuit of beauty often gives a woman access to a range of individuals who administer to her body in a caring way, an experience often sadly lacking in the day-to-day lives of many women. As a result, a woman's pursuit of beauty through transformation is often associated with lived experiences of self-creation, self-fulfillment, self-transcendence, and being cared for. The power of these experiences must not be underestimated.[7]

While I acknowledge that these choices can confer a kind of integrity on a woman's life, I also believe that they are likely to embroil her in a set of interrelated contradictions. I refer to these as "Paradoxes of Choice."

IV. Three Paradoxes of Choice

In exploring these paradoxes, I appropriate Foucault's analysis of the diffusion of power in order to understand forms of power that are potentially more personally invasive than are more obvious, publicly identifiable aspects of power. In the chapter "Docile Bodies" in *Discipline and Punish*, Foucault (1979, 136-37) highlights three features of what he calls disciplinary power:

> (1) The *scale* of the control. In disciplinary power the body is treated individually and in a coercive way because the body itself is the *active* and hence apparently free body that is being controlled through movements, gestures, attitudes, and degrees of rapidity.

> (2) The *object* of the control, which involves meticulous control over the efficiency of movements and forces,

> (3) the *modality* of the control, which involves constant, uninterrupted coercion.

Foucault argues that the outcome of disciplinary power is the docile body, a body "that may be subjected, used, transformed, and improved" (Foucault 1979, 136). Foucault is discussing this model of power in the context of prisons and armies, but we can adapt the central insights of this notion to see how women's bodies are entering "a machinery of power that explores it, breaks it down, and rearranges it" through a recognizably political metamorphosis of embodiment (Foucault 1979, 138).[8] What is important about this notion in relation to cosmetic surgery is the extent to which it makes it possible to speak about the diffusion of power throughout Western industrialized cultures that are increasingly committed to a technological beauty imperative. It also makes it possible to refer to a set of experts—cosmetic surgeons—whose explicit power mandate is to explore, break down, and rearrange women's bodies.

Paradox One: The Choice of Conformity—Understanding the Number 10

While the technology of cosmetic surgery could clearly be used to create and celebrate idiosyncrasy, eccentricity, and uniqueness, it is obvious that this is not how it is presently being used. Cosmetic surgeons report that legions of women appear in their offices demanding "Bo Derek" breasts ("Cosmetic Surgery for the Holidays" 1985). Jewish women demand reductions of their noses so as to be able to "pass" as one of their Aryan sisters who form the dominant ethnic group (Lakoff and Scherr, 1984). Adolescent Asian girls who bring in pictures of Elizabeth Taylor and of Japanese movie actresses (whose faces have already been reconstructed) demand the "Westernizing" of their own eyes and the creation of higher noses in hopes of better job and marital prospects ("New Bodies for Sale" 1985). Black women buy toxic bleaching agents in hopes of attaining lighter skin. What is being created in all of these instances is not simply beautiful bodies and faces but white, Western, Anglo-Saxon bodies in a racist, anti-Semitic context.

More often than not, what appear at first glance to be instances of choice turn out to be instances of conformity. The women who undergo cosmetic surgery in order to compete in various beauty pageants are clearly choosing to conform. So is the woman who wanted to undergo a facelift, tummy tuck, and liposuction all in one week, in order to win heterosexual approval *from a man she had not seen in twenty-eight years* and whose individual preferences she could not possibly know. In some ways, it does not matter who the particular judges are. Actual men—brothers, fathers, male lovers, male beauty "experts"—and hypothetical men live in the aesthetic imaginations of women. Whether they are male employers, prospective male spouses, male judges in the beauty pageants, or male-identified women, these modern day Parises are generic and live sometimes ghostly but powerful lives in the reflective awareness of women (Berger, 1972). A woman's makeup, dress, gestures, voice, degree of cleanliness, degree of muscularity, odors, degree of hirsuteness, vocabulary, hands, feet, skin, hair, and vulva can all be evaluated, regulated, and disciplined in the light of the hypothetical often-white male viewer and the male viewer present in the assessing gaze of other women (Haug, 1987). Men's appreciation and approval of achieved femininity becomes all the more invasive when it resides in the incisions, stitches, staples, and scar tissue of women's bodies as women choose to conform. And, as various theorists have pointed out, women's public conformity to the norms of beauty often signals a deeper conformity to the norms of compulsory heterosexuality along with an awareness of the violence that can result from violating those norms.[9] Hence the first paradox: that what looks like an optimal situation of reflection, deliberation, and self-creating choice often signals conformity at a deeper level.

Paradox Two: Liberation into Colonization

As argued above, a woman's desire to create a permanently beautiful and youthful appearance that is not vulnerable to the threats of externally applied cosmetic artifice or to the natural aging process of the body must be understood as a deeply significant existential project. It deliberately involves the exploitation and transformation of the most intimately experienced domain of immanence, the body, in the name of transcendence: transcendence of hereditary predestination, of lived time, of one's given "limitations." What I see as particularly alarming in this project is that what comes to have primary significance is not the real given existing woman but her body viewed as a "primitive entity" that is seen only as potential, as a kind of raw material to be exploited in terms of appearance, eroticism, nurturance, and fertility as defined by the colonizing culture.[10]

But for whom is this exploitation and transformation taking place? Who exercises the power here? Sometimes the power is explicit. It is exercised by brothers, fathers, male lovers, male engineering students who taunt and harass their female counterparts, and by male cosmetic surgeons who offer "free advice" in social gatherings to women whose "deformities" and "severe problems" can all be cured through their healing needles and knives.[11] And the colonizing power is transmitted through and by those women whose own bodies and disciplinary practices demonstrate the efficacy of "taking care of herself" in these culturally defined feminine ways.

Sometimes, however, the power may be so diffused as to dominate the consciousness of a given woman with no other subject needing to be present. As Bartky notes, such diffused power also signals the presence of the colonizer:

> Normative femininity is coming more and more to be centered on woman's body. . . . Images of normative femininity . . . have replaced the religious oriented tracts of the past. The woman who checks her makeup half a dozen times a day to see if her foundation has caked or her mascara has run, who worries that the wind or the rain may spoil her hairdo, who looks frequently to see if her stockings have bagged at the ankle, or who, feeling fat, monitors everything she eats, *has become, just as surely as the inmate of the Panopticon, a self-policing subject, a self committed to a relentless self-surveillance. This self-surveillance is a form of obedience to patriarchy.* (Bartky 1988, 81; italics added)

As Foucault and others have noted, practices of coercion and domination are often camouflaged by practical rhetoric and supporting theories that appear to be benevolent, therapeutic, and voluntaristic. Previously, for example, colonizing was often done in the name of bringing "civilization" through culture and morals to "primitive, barbaric people," but contemporary colonizers mask their exploitation of "raw materials and human labor" in the name of "development." Murphy (1984), Piercy (1980), and I (Morgan, 1989) have all claimed that similar rhetorical camouflage of colonization takes place in the areas of women's reproductive decision-making and women's right to bodily self-determination. In all of these instances of colonization the ideological manipulation of technology can be identified, and, I would argue, in all of these cases this technology has often been used to the particular disadvantage and destruction of some aspect of women's integrity.[12]

In electing to undergo cosmetic surgery, women appear to be protesting against the constraints of the "given" in their embodied lives and seeking liberation from those constraints. But I believe they are in danger of retreating and becoming more vulnerable, at that very level of embodiment, to those colonizing forms of power that may have motivated the protest in the first place. Moreover, in seeking independence, they can become even more dependent on male assessment and on the services of all those experts they initially bought to render them independent.

Here we see a second paradox bound up with choice: that the rhetoric is that of liberation and care, of "making the most of yourself," but the reality is often the transformation of oneself as a woman for the eye, the hand, and the approval of the Other—the lover, the taunting students, the customers, the employers, the social peers. And the Other is almost always affected by the dominant culture, which is male-supremacist, racist, ageist, heterosexist, anti-Semitic, ableist and class-biased.[13]

Paradox Three: Coerced Voluntariness and the Technological Imperative

Where is the coercion? At first glance, women who choose to undergo cosmetic surgery often seem to represent a paradigm case of the rational chooser. Drawn increasingly from wider and wider economic groups, these women clearly make a choice, often at significant economic cost to the rest of their life, to pay the large sums of money demanded by cosmetic surgeons (since American health insurance plans do not cover this elective cosmetic surgery).

Furthermore, they are often highly critical consumers of these services, demanding extensive consultation, information regarding the risks and benefits of various surgical procedures, and professional guarantees of expertise. Generally they are relatively young and in good health. Thus, in some important sense, they epitomize relatively invulnerable free agents making a decision under virtually optimal conditions.

Moreover, on the surface, women who undergo cosmetic surgery choose a set of procedures that are, by definition, "elective." This term is used, quite straightforwardly, to distinguish cosmetic surgery from surgical intervention for reconstructive or health-related reasons (e.g., following massive burns, cancer-related forms of mutilation, etc.). The term also appears to distinguish cosmetic surgery from apparently involuntary and more pathologically transforming forms of intervention in the bodies of young girls in the form of, for example, foot-binding or extensive genital mutilation.[14] But I believe that this does not exhaust the meaning of the term "elective" and that the term performs a seductive role in facilitating the ideological camouflage of the *absence of choice*. Similarly, I believe that the word "cosmetic" serves an ideological function in hiding the fact that the changes are *noncosmetic*: they involve lengthy periods of pain, are permanent, and result in irreversibly alienating metamorphoses such as the appearance of youth on an aging body.

In order to illuminate the paradox of choice involved here, I wish to draw an analogy from the literature on reproductive technology. In the case of reproductive self-determination, technology has been hailed as increasing the range of women's choices in an absolute kind of way. It cannot be denied that due to the advances in various reproductive technologies, especially IVF and embryo freezing, along with various advances in fetology and fetal surgery, there are now women with healthy children who previously would not have had children. Nevertheless, there are two important ideological, choice-diminishing dynamics at work that affect women's choices in the area of the new reproductive technologies. These dynamics are also at work in the area of cosmetic surgery.

The first of these is the *pressure to achieve perfection through technology*, signaled by the rise of new forms of eugenicist thinking. More profoundly than ever before, contemporary eugenicists stigmatize potential and existing disabled babies, children, and adults. More and more frequently, benevolently phrased eugenicist pressures are forcing women to choose to submit to a battery of prenatal diagnostic tests and extensive fetal monitoring in the name of producing "perfect" (white) babies." As more and more reproductive technologies and tests are invented (and "perfected" in and on the bodies of fertile women), partners, parents, family, obstetricians, and other experts on fertility pressure women to submit to this technology in the name of "maximized choice" and "responsible motherhood." As Achilles (1988), Beck-Gernsheim (1989), Rothman (1984), Morgan (1989) and others have argued, women are being subjected to increasingly intense forms of coercion, a fact that is signaled by the intensifying *lack of freedom* felt by women to refuse to use the technology if they are pregnant and the technology is available.

The second important ideological dynamic is *the double-pathologizing of women's bodies*. The history of Western science and Western medical practice is not altogether a positive one for women. As voluminous documentation has shown, cell biologists, endocrinologists, anatomists, sociobiologists, gynecologists, obstetricians, psychiatrists, surgeons, and other scientists have assumed, hypothesized, or "demonstrated" that women's bodies are generally inferior, deformed, imperfect, and/or infantile. Medical practitioners have often treated women accordingly. Until the rise of the new reproductive technologies, however, women's reproductive capacities and processes were regarded as definitional of normal womanhood and normal human reproduction. No longer is that the case. As Corea (1985) and others have so amply demonstrated, profoundly misogynist beliefs and attitudes are a central part of the ideological motivation for the technical development of devices for completely extrauterine fetal development. Women's wombs are coming to be seen as "dark prisons." Women are viewed as threatening irresponsible agents who live in a necessarily antagonistic relationship with the fetus. And women's bodies in general are coming to be viewed as high-risk milieus since fetal development cannot be continuously monitored and controlled in order to guarantee the best possible "fetal outcome" (particularly where middle- and upper-class white babies are concerned).

Increasingly, "fully responsible motherhood" is coming to be defined in technology-dependent terms and, in a larger cultural context of selective obligatory maternity, more and more women are "choosing to act" in accord with technological imperatives prior to conception, through conception, through maternity, and through birthing itself. Whether this is, then, a situation of increased choice is at the very least highly contestable. Moreover, in a larger ideological context of obligatory and "controlled" motherhood, I am reluctant simply to accept the reports of the technologists and fertility experts that their patients "want access" to the technology as a sufficient condition for demonstrating purely voluntary choice.[15]

A similar argument can be made regarding the significance of the pressure to be beautiful in relation to the allegedly voluntary nature of "electing" to undergo cosmetic surgery. It is clear that pressure to use this technology is on the increase. Cosmetic surgeons report on the wide range of clients who buy their services, pitch their advertising to a large audience through the use of the media, and encourage women to think, metaphorically, in terms of the seemingly trivial "nips" and "tucks" that will transform their lives. As cosmetic surgery becomes increasingly normal-ized through the concept of the female "make-over" that is translated into columns and articles in the print media or made into nationwide television shows directed at female viewers, as the "success stories" are invited on to talk shows along with their "makers," and as surgically transformed women win the Miss America pageants, women who refuse to submit to the knives and to the needles, to the anaesthetics and the bandages, will come to be seen as deviant in one way or another. Women who refuse to use these technologies are already becoming stigmatized as "unliberated," "not caring about their appearance" (a sign of disturbed gender identity and low self-esteem according to various health-care professionals), as "refusing to be all that they could be" or as "granola-heads."

And as more and more success comes to those who do "care about themselves" in this technological fashion, more coercive dimensions enter the scene. In the past, only those women who were perceived to be *naturally* beautiful (or rendered beautiful through relatively conservative superficial artifice) had access to forms of power and economic social mobility closed off to women regarded as plain or ugly or old. But now womanly beauty is becoming technologically achievable, a commodity for which each and every woman can, in principle, sacrifice if she is to survive and succeed in the world, particularly in industrialized Western countries. Now technology is making obligatory the appearance of youth and the reality of "beauty" for every woman who can afford it. Natural destiny is being supplanted by technologically grounded coercion, and the coercion is camouflaged by the language of choice, fulfillment, and liberation.

Similarly, we find the dynamic of the double-pathologizing of the normal and of the ordinary at work here. In the technical and popular literature on cosmetic surgery, what have previously been described as *normal* variations of female bodily shapes or described in the relatively innocuous language of "problem areas," are increasingly being described as "deformities," "ugly protrusions," "inadequate breasts," and "unsightly concentrations of fat cells"—a litany of descriptions designed to intensify feelings of disgust, shame, and relief at the possibility of recourse for these "deformities." Cosmetic surgery promises virtually all women the creation of beautiful, youthful-appearing bodies. As a consequence, more and more women will be labeled "ugly" and "old" in relation to this more select population of surgically created beautiful faces and bodies that have been contoured and augmented, lifted and tucked into a state of achieved feminine excellence. I suspect that the naturally "given," so to speak, will increasingly come to be seen as the technologically "primitive"; the "ordinary" will come to be perceived and evaluated as the "ugly." Here, then, is the *third paradox*: that the technological beauty imperative and the pathological inversion of the normal are coercing more and more women to "choose" cosmetic surgery.

V. Are There Any Politically Correct Feminist Responses to Cosmetic Surgery?

Attempting to answer this question is rather like venturing forth into political quicksand. Nevertheless, I will discuss two very different sorts of responses that strike me as having certain plausibility: the response of refusal and the response of appropriation.[16] I regard both of these as utopian in nature.

The Response of Refusal

In her witty and subversive parable, *The Life and Loves of a She-Devil*, Fay Weldon puts the following thoughts into the mind of the cosmetic surgeon whose services have been bought by the protagonist, "Miss Hunter," for her own plans for revenge:

> He was her Pygmalion, but she would not depend upon him, or admire him, or be grateful. He was accustomed to being loved by the women of his own construction. A soft sigh of adoration would follow him down the corridors as he paced them, visiting here, blessing there, promising a future, regretting a past: cush-

ioning his footfall, and his image of himself. But no soft breath-
ings came from Miss Hunter. [He adds, ominously,] . . . he would
bring her to it. (Weldon 1983, 215-216)

But Miss Hunter continues to refuse, and so will many feminist women. The
response of refusal can be recognizably feminist at both an individual and a
collective level. It results from understanding the nature of the risks
involved—those having to do with the surgical procedures and those related
to a potential loss of embodied personal integrity in a patriarchal context. And
it results from understanding the conceptual shifts involved in the political
technologizing of women's bodies and contextualizing them so that their
oppressive consequences are evident precisely as they open up more "choices"
to women. "Understanding" and "contextualizing" here mean seeing clearly
the ideological biases that frame the material and cultural world in which
cosmetic surgeons practice, a world that contains racist, anti-Semitic, eugenicist, and ageist dimensions of oppression, forms of oppression to which current
practices in cosmetic surgery often contribute.

The response of refusal also speaks to the collective power of women as
consumers to affect market conditions. If refusal is practiced on a large scale,
cosmetic surgeons who are busy producing new faces for the "holiday season"
and new bellies for the "winter trips to the Caribbean" will find few buyers of
their services. Cosmetic surgeons who consider themselves body designers and
regard women's skin as a kind of magical fabric to be draped, cut, layered, and
designer-labeled, may have to forgo the esthetician's ambitions that occasion
the remark that "the sculpting of human flesh can never be an exact art" (Silver
1989). They may, instead, (re)turn their expertise to the victims in the
intensive care burn unit and to the crippled limbs and joints of arthritic
women. This might well have the consequence of (re)converting those surgeons into healers.

Although it may be relatively easy for some individual women to refuse
cosmetic surgery even when they have access to the means, one deep, morally
significant facet of the response of refusal is to try to understand and to care
about individual women who do choose to undergo cosmetic surgery. It may
well be that one explanation for why a woman is willing to subject herself to
surgical procedures, anaesthetics, postoperative drugs, predicted and lengthy
pain, and possible "side-effects" that might include her own death is that her
access to other forms of power and empowerment are or appear to be so limited
that cosmetic surgery is the primary domain in which she can experience some
semblance of self-determination. Lakoff and Scherr comment on this:

No responsible doctor would advise a drug, or a procedure,
whose clearly demonstrated benefits do not considerably outweigh its risks, so that a health-threatening drug is not prescribed responsibly except to remedy a life-threatening

> condition. But equally noxious drugs and procedures are medi-
> cally sanctioned merely to "cure" moderate overweight or flat-
> chestedness—hardly life-threatening ailments. . . . The only
> way to understand the situation is to agree that those conditions
> *are*, in fact, perceived as life-threatening, so dangerous that
> seriously damaging interventions are justified, any risk worth
> taking, to alleviate them. (Lakoff and Scherr 1984, 165-66)

Choosing an artificial and technologically-designed creation of youthful beauty may not only be necessary to an individual woman's material, economic, and social survival. It may also be the way that she is able to choose, to elect a kind of subjective transcendence against a backdrop of constraint, limitation, and immanence (in Beauvoir's sense of this term).

As a feminist response, individual and collective refusal may not be easy. As Bartky, I, and others have tried to argue, it is crucial to understand the central role that socially sanctioned and socially constructed femininity plays in a male supremacist, heterosexist society. And it is essential not to underestimate the gender-constituting and identity-confirming role that femininity plays in bringing woman-as-subject into existence while simultaneously creating her as patriarchally defined object (Bartky 1988; Morgan 1986). In these circumstances, refusal may be akin to a kind of death, to a kind of renunciation of the only kind of life-conferring choices and competencies to which a woman may have access. And, under those circumstances, it may not be possible for her to register her resistance in the form of refusal. The best one can hope for is a heightened sense of the nature of the multiple double-binds and compromises that permeate the lives of virtually all women and are accentuated by the cosmetic surgery culture.

As a final comment, it is worth remarking that although the response of refusal has a kind of purity to recommend it, it is unlikely to have much impact in the current ideological and cultural climate. In just one year, the number of breast augmentations has risen 32 percent; eye tucks have increased 31 percent; nose jobs have increased 30 percent; face lifts have increased 39 percent; and liposuction and other forms of "body contouring" have become the most popular form of cosmetic surgery ("New Bodies for Sale" 1985). Cosmetic surgeons are deluged with demands, and research in the field is increasing at such a rapid pace that every area of the human body is seen as open to metamorphosis. Clearly the knives, the needles, the cannulas, and the drugs are exercising a greater and greater allure. Nevertheless, the political significance of the response of refusal should not be underestimated in the lives of individual women since achieved obligatory femininity is a burden borne by virtually all women. And this response is one way of eliminating many of the attendant harms while simultaneously identifying the ways that the technological beauty imperative increasingly pervades our lives.

The Response of Appropriation

In their insightful essay, "The Feminine Body and Feminist Politics," Brown and Adams remark that "since the body is seen as the site of *action*, its investigation appears to combine what are otherwise characterized as discrete sites, the theoretical and the political, in an original unity" (Brown and Adams 1979, 35). Rather than viewing the womanly/technologized body as a site of political refusal, the response of appropriation views it as the site for feminist action through transformation, appropriation, parody, and protest. This response grows out of that historical and often radical feminist tradition that regards deliberate mimicry, alternative valorization, hyperbolic appropriation, street theater, counterguerrilla tactics, destabilization, and redeployment as legitimate feminist politics. Here I am proposing a version of what Judith Butler regards as "Femininity Politics" and what she calls "Gender Performatives." The contemporary feminist guerrilla theater group Ladies Against Women demonstrates the power of this kind of response. In addition to expressing outrage and moral revulsion at the biased dimensions of contemporary cosmetic surgery, the response of appropriation targets them for moral and political purposes.

However, instead of mourning the temporal and carnal alienation resulting from the shame and guilt experienced prior to surgery and from the experience of loss of identity following surgery, the feminist theorist using the response of appropriation points out (like postmodernists) that these emotional experiences simply demonstrate the ubiquitous instability of consciousness itself, that this is simply a more vivid lived instance of the deeper instability that is characteristic of *all* human subjectivity. Along with feeling apprehension about the appropriation of organic processes and bodies by technology, what this feminist theorist might well say is that the technologies are simply revealing what is true for *all* embodied subjects living in cultures, namely, that *all* human bodies are, and always have been, dialectically created artifacts (Lowe 1982; Haraway 1978, 1989). What the technologies are revealing is that women's bodies, in particular, can be and are read as especially saturated cultural artifacts and signifiers by phenomenologically oriented anthropologists and forensic archaeologists (even if they have never heard about Derrida or postmodernism). Finally, present practices in cosmetic surgery also provide an extremely public and quantified reckoning of the cost of "beauty," thereby demonstrating how both the processes and the final product are part of a larger nexus of women's commodification. Since such lessons are not always taught so easily or in such transparent form, this feminist theorist may well celebrate the critical feminist ideological potential of cosmetic surgery.

Rather than agreeing that participation in cosmetic surgery and its ruling ideology will necessarily result in further colonization and victimization of women, this feminist strategy advocates appropriating the expertise and technology for feminist ends. One advantage of the response of appropriation is that it does not recommend involvement in forms of technology that clearly have disabling and dire outcomes for the deeper feminist project of engaging "in the historical, political, and theoretical process of constituting ourselves as subjects as well as objects of history" (Hartsock 1990, 170).[17] Women who are increasingly immobilized bodily through physical weakness, passivity, withdrawal, and domestic sequestration in situations of hysteria, agoraphobia, and anorexia cannot possibly engage in radical gender performatives of an active public sort or in other acts by which the feminist subject is robustly constituted. In contrast, healthy women who have a feminist understanding of cosmetic surgery are in a situation to deploy cosmetic surgery in the name of its feminist potential for parody and protest.

Working within the creative matrix of ideas provided by Foucault, Kristeva (1982), and Douglas (1966), Judith Butler notes:

> The construction of stable bodily contours relies upon fixed sites of corporeal permeability and impermeability. . . . The deregulation of such (heterosexual) exchanges accordingly disrupts the very boundaries that determine what it is to be a body at all. (1990, 132-33)

As Butler correctly observes, parody "by itself is not subversive" (139) since it always runs the risk of becoming "domesticated and recirculated as instruments of cultural hegemony." She then goes on to ask, in relation to gender identity and sexuality, what words or performances would

> compel a reconsideration of the *place* and stability of the masculine and the feminine? And what kind of gender performance will enact and reveal the performativity of gender itself in a way that destabilizes the naturalized categories of identity and desire? (Butler 1990, 139)

We might, in parallel fashion, ask what sorts of performances would sufficiently destabilize the norms of femininity, what sorts of performances will sufficiently expose the truth of the slogan "Beauty is always made, not born." In response I suggest two performance-oriented forms of revolt.

The first form of revolt involves revalorizing the domain of the "ugly" and all that is associated with it. Although one might argue that the notion of the "ugly" is parasitic on that of "beauty," this is not entirely true since the ugly is also contrasted with the plain and the ordinary, so that we are not even at the outset constrained by binary oppositions. The ugly, even in a beauty-oriented culture, has always held its own fascination, its own particular kind of splendor. Feminists can use that and explore it in ways that might be integrated with a revalorization of being old, thus simultaneously attacking the ageist dimension of the reigning ideology. Rather than being the "culturally enmired subjects" of Butler's analysis, women might constitute themselves as culturally liberated subjects through public participation in Ms. Ugly Canada/America/Universe/ Cosmos pageants *and use the technology of cosmetic surgery to do so.*

Contemplating this form of revolt as a kind of imaginary model of political action is one thing; actually altering our bodies is another matter altogether. And the reader may well share the sentiments of one reviewer of this paper who asked: "Having oneself surgically mutilated in order to prove a point? Isn't this going too far?" I don't know the answer to that question. If we cringe from contemplating this alternative, this may, in fact, testify (so to speak) to the hold that the beauty imperative has on our imagination and our bodies. If we recoil from *this* lived alteration of the contours of our bodies and regard it as "mutilation," then so, too, ought we to shirk from contemplation of the cosmetic surgeons who de-skin and alter the contours of women's bodies so that we become more and more like athletic or emaciated (depending on what's in vogue) mannequins with large breasts in the shop windows of modern patriarchal culture. In what sense are these not equivalent mutilations?

What this feminist performative would require would be not only genuine celebration of but *actual* participation in the fleshly mutations needed to produce what the culture constitutes as "ugly" so as to destabilize the "beautiful" and expose its technologically and culturally constitutive origin and its political consequences. Bleaching one's hair white and applying wrinkle-inducing "wrinkle creams," having one's face and breasts surgically pulled down (rather than lifted), and having wrinkles sewn and carved into one's skin might also be seen as destabilizing actions with respect to aging. And analogous actions might be taken to undermine the "lighter is better" aspect of racist norms of feminine appearance as they affect women of color.

A second performative form of revolt could involve exploring the commodification aspect of cosmetic surgery. One might, for example, envision a set of "Beautiful Body Boutique" franchises, responsive to the particular "needs" of a given community. Here one could advertise and sell a whole range of bodily contours; a variety of metric containers of freeze-dried fat cells for fat implantation and transplant; "body configuration" software for computers; sewing kits of needles, knives, and painkillers; and "skin-Velcro" that could be matched to fit and drape the consumer's body; variously-sized sets of magnetically attachable breasts complete with discrete nipple pumps; and other inflation devices carefully modulated according to bodily aroma and state of arousal. Parallel to the current marketing strategies for cosmetic breast surgeries,[18] commercial protest booths, complete with "before and after" surgical make-over displays for penises, entitled "The Penis You Were Always Meant to Have" could be set up at various medical conventions and health fairs; demonstrations could take place outside the clinics, hotels, and spas of particularly eminent cosmetic surgeons—the possibilities here are endless. Again, if this ghoulish array offends, angers, or shocks the reader, this may well be an

Kathryn Pauly Morgan   47

indication of the extent to which the ideology of compulsory beauty has anesthetized our sensibility in the reverse direction, resulting in the domesticating of the procedures and products of the cosmetic surgery industry.

In appropriating these forms of revolt, women might well accomplish the following: acquire expertise (either in fact or in symbolic form) of cosmetic surgery to challenge the coercive norms of youth and beauty, undermine the power dynamic built into the dependence on surgical experts who define themselves as aestheticians of women's bodies, demonstrate the radical malleability of the cultural commodification of women's bodies, and make publicly explicit the political role that technology can play in the construction of the feminine in women's flesh.

Conclusion

I have characterized both these feminist forms of response as utopian in nature. What I mean by "utopian" is that these responses are unlikely to occur on a large scale even though they may have a kind of ideal desirability. In any culture that defines femininity in terms of submission to men, that makes the achievement of femininity (however culturally specific) in appearance, gesture, movement, voice, bodily contours, aspirations, values, and political behavior obligatory of any woman who will be allowed to be loved or hired or promoted or elected or simply allowed to live, and in any culture that increasingly requires women to purchase femininity through submission to cosmetic surgeons and their magic knives, refusal and revolt exact a high price. I live in such a culture.

NOTES

Many thanks to the members of the Canadian Society for Women in Philosophy for their critical feedback, especially my commentator, Karen Weisbaum, who pointed out how strongly visualist the cosmetic surgery culture is. I am particularly grateful to Sarah Lucia Hoagland, keynote speaker at the 1990 C-SWIP conference, who remarked at my session, "I think this is all wrong." Her comment sent me back to the text to rethink it in a serious way. Thanks also to the two anonymous *Hypatia* reviewers for their frank, helpful, and supportive response to an earlier version of this paper.

1. This paper addresses only the issues generated out of *elective* cosmetic surgery which is sharply distinguished by practitioners, patients, and insurance plans from reconstructive cosmetic surgery which is usually performed in relation to some trauma or is viewed as necessary in relation to some pressing health care concern. This is not to say that the distinction is always clear in practice.

2. I regard the *Hastings Center Report* and *Philosophy and Medicine* as the discipline-establishing journals in mainstream bioethics. The feminist literature to which I am referring includes the double special issue of *Hypatia*, 1989 (vol. 4, nos. 2 and 3), the

anthology *Healing Technology* (Ratcliff 1989), and the entire journal series *Women and Health* and *Women and* Therapy through 1990. With the exception of a paper by Kathy Davis on this topic which has just appeared (1991) the only discussions that *do* exist discuss the case of Quasimodo, the Hunchback of Notre Dame!

3. For a thorough account of how anatomical science has conceptualized and depicted the ideal female skeleton and morphology, see Russett's *Sexual Science: The Victorian Construction of Womanhood* (1989) and Schiebinger's *The Mind Has No Sex? Women in the Origins of Modern Science* (1989), especially the chapter titled "More Than Skin Deep: The Scientific Search for Sexual Difference."

4. Although the particular kind of machine selected as paradigmatic of the human body has shifted from clocks to hydraulics to thermodynamics and now to information-processing models, the Cartesian machine-modeling of the body continues to dominate and is, obviously, the one most congenial to the correlative technologizing of the human body, which literally metamorphoses the body into a machine.

5. I say "virtually all women" because there is now a nascent literature on the subject of fat oppression and body image as it affects lesbians. For a perceptive article on this subject, see Dworkin (1989). I am, of course, not suggesting that compulsory heterosexuality and obligatory maternity affect all women equally. Clearly women who are regarded as "deviant" in some respect or other—because they are lesbian or women with disabilities or "too old" or poor or of the "wrong race"—are under enormous pressure from the dominant culture *not* to bear children, but this, too, is an aspect of patriarchal pronatalism.

6. The desire to subordinate our bodies to some ideal that involves bringing the body under control is deeply felt by many contemporary women (apart from any religious legacy of asceticism). As Bartky (1988) and Bordo (1985, 1989a, 1989b) have noted, this is an aspect of the disembodying desires of anorexic women and women who "pump iron." In the area of cosmetic surgery, this control is mediated by the technology and expertise of the surgeons, but the theme is continually articulated.

7. A similar point regarding femininity is made by Sandra Bartky (1988) in her discussion of "feminine discipline." She remarks that women will resist the dismantling of the disciplines of femininity because, at a very deep level, it would involve a radical alteration of what she calls our "informal social ontology":

> To have a body felt to be "feminine"—a body socially constructed through the appropriate practices—is in most cases crucial to a woman's sense of herself as female and, since persons currently can be only as male or female, to her sense of herself as an existing individual. . . . The radical feminist critique of femininity, then, may pose a threat not only to a woman's sense of her own identity and desirability but to the very structure of her social universe. (Bartky 1988, 78)

8. I view this as a recognizably *political* metamorphosis because forensic cosmetic surgeons and social archaeologists will be needed to determine the actual age and earlier appearance of women in cases where identification is called for on the basic of existing carnal data. See Griffin's (1978) poignant description in "The Anatomy Lesson" for a reconstruction of the life and circumstances of a dead mother from just such carnal evidence. As we more and more profoundly artifactualize our own bodies, we become more sophisticated archaeological repositories and records that both signify and symbolize our culture.

9. For both documentation and analysis of this claim, see Bartky (1988), Bordo (1985, 1989a, 1989b), and Rich (1980).

10. I intend to use "given" here in a relative and political sense. I don't believe that the notion that biology is somehow "given" and culture is just "added on" is a tenable one. I believe that we are intimately and inextricably encultured and embodied, so that a reductionist move in either direction is doomed to failure. For a persuasive analysis of this thesis, see Lowe (1982) and Haraway (1978, 1989). For a variety of political analyses of the "given" as primitive, see Marge Piercy's poem "Right to Life" (1980), Morgan (1989), and Murphy (1984).

11. Although I am cognizant of the fact that many women are entering medical school, the available literature is preponderantly authored by men most of whom, I would infer, are white, given the general demographics of specializations in medical school. I also stress the whiteness here to emphasize the extent to which white norms of beauty dominate the field. I think of these surgeons as akin to "fairy godfathers" to underscore the role they are asked to play to "correct," "improve," or "render beautiful" what girls and women have inherited from their mothers, who can only make recommendations at the level of artifice, not artifact.

12. Space does not permit development of this theme on an international scale but it is important to note the extent to which pharmaceutical "dumping" is taking place in the so-called "developing countries" under the ideological camouflage of "population control and family planning." See Hartman (1987) for a thorough and persuasive analysis of the exploitative nature of this practice.

13. The extent to which ableist bias is at work in this area was brought home to me by two quotations cited by a woman with a disability. She discusses two guests on a television show. One was "a poised, intelligent young woman who'd been rejected as a contestant for the Miss Toronto title. She is a paraplegic. The organizers' lame excuse for disqualifying her: 'We couldn't fit the choreography around you.' Another guest was a former executive of the Miss Universe contest. He declared, 'Her participation in a beauty contest would be like having a blind man compete in a shooting match' " (Matthews 1985).

14. It is important here to guard against facile and ethnocentric assumptions about beauty rituals and mutilation. See Lakoff and Scherr (1984) for an analysis of the relativity of these labels and for important insights about the fact that use of the term "mutilation" almost always signals a distancing from and reinforcement of a sense of cultural superiority in the speaker who uses it to denounce what other cultures do in contrast to "our culture."

15. For the most sustained and theoretically sophisticated analysis of pronatalism operating in the context of industrialized capitalism, see Gimenez (1984). Gimenez restricts her discussion to working-class women but, unfortunately, doesn't develop a more differentiated grid of pronatalist and antinatalist pressures within that economic and social group. For example, in Quebec there are strong pressures on Francophone working class women to reproduce, while there is selective pressure against Anglophone and immigrant working women bearing children. Nevertheless, Gimenez's account demonstrates the systemic importance of pronatalism in many women's lives.

16. One possible feminist response (that, thankfully, appears to go in and out of vogue) is that of feminist fascism, which insists on a certain particular and quite narrow range of embodiment and appearance as the only range that is politically correct for a feminist. Often feminist fascism sanctions the use of informal but very powerful feminist "embodiment police," who feel entitled to identify and denounce various deviations from this normative range. I find this feminist political stance incompatible with any movement I would regard as liberatory for women and here I admit that I side with feminist liberals

who say that "the presumption must be on the side of freedom" (Warren, 1985) and see that as the lesser of two evils.

17. In recommending various forms of appropriation of the practices and dominant ideology surrounding cosmetic surgery, I think it important to distinguish this set of disciplinary practices from those forms of simultaneous Retreat-and-Protest that Susan Bordo (1989a, 20) so insightfully discusses in "The Body and the Reproduction of Femininity": hysteria, agoraphobia, and anorexia. What cosmetic surgery shares with these gestures is what Bordo remarks upon, namely, the fact that they may be "viewed as a surface on which conventional constructions of femininity are exposed starkly to view, through their inscription in extreme or hyperliteral form." What is different, I suggest, is that although submitting to the procedures of cosmetic surgery involves pain, risks, undesirable side effects, and living with a heightened form of patriarchal anxiety, it is also fairly clear that, most of the time, the pain and risks are relatively short-term. Furthermore, the outcome often appears to be one that generally enhances women's confidence, confers a sense of well-being, contributes to a greater comfortableness in the public domain, and affirms the individual woman as a self-determining and risk-taking individual. All these outcomes are significantly different from what Bordo describes as the "languages of horrible suffering" (Bordo 1989a, 20) expressed by women experiencing hysteria, agoraphobia, and anorexia.

18. A booth of this sort was set up in a prominent location at a large "Today's Woman Fair" at the National Exhibition grounds in Toronto in the summer of 1990. It showed "before" and "after" pictures of women's breasts and advertised itself as "The Breasts You Were Always Meant to Have." One special feature of the display was a set of photographs showing a woman whose breasts had been "deformed" by nursing but who had finally attained through cosmetic surgery the breasts "she was meant to have had." I am grateful to my colleague June Larkin for the suggestion of the analogous booth.

REFERENCES

Achilles, Rona. 1988. What's new about the new reproductive technologies? *Discussion paper: Ontario Advisory Council on the Status of Women*. Toronto: Government of Ontario.
Barker-Benfield, G. J. 1976. *The horrors of the half-known life*. New York: Harper and Row.
Bartky, Sandra Lee. 1988. Foucault, femininity, and the modernization of patriarchal power. In *Femininity and Foucault: Reflections of resistance*. Irene Diamond and Lee Quinby, eds. Boston: Northeastern University Press.
Beck-Gernsheim, Elisabeth. 1989. From the pill to test-tube babies: New options, new pressures in reproductive behavior. In *Healing technology: Feminist perspectives*. Kathryn Strother Ratcliff, ed. Ann Arbor: University of Michigan Press.
Berger, John. 1972. *Ways of seeing*. New York: Penguin Books.
Bordo, Susan R. 1985. Anorexia nervosa: Psychopathology as the crystallization of culture. *The Philosophical Forum* 2(Winter): 73-103.
———. 1989a. The body and the reproduction of femininity: A feminist appropriation of Foucault. In *Gender/body/knowledge: Feminist reconstructions of being and knowing*. Alison Jaggar and Susan Bordo, eds. New Brunswick, NJ: Rutgers University Press.

———. 1989b. Reading the slender body. In *Women, science and the body politic: Discourses and representations*. Mary Jacobus, Evelyn Fox Keller and Sally Shuttleworth, eds. New York: Methuen.

Brown, Beverley and Parveen Adams. 1979. The feminine body and feminist politics. *M/F* 3: 35-50.

Brownmiller, Susan. 1984. *Femininity*. New York: Simon and Schuster.

Burk, J., S. L. Zelen, and E. O. Terena. 1985. More than skin deep: A self-consistency approach to the psychology of cosmetic surgery. *Plastic and reconstructive surgery* 6(2): 270-80.

Butler, Judith. 1990. *Gender trouble: Feminism and the subversion of identity*. New York: Routledge.

Changing Faces. 1989. *Toronto Star*. May 25.

Computer used to pick hairstyles. 1989. *Globe and Mail*.

Corea, Gena. 1985. *The mother machine*. New York: Harper and Row.

Cosmetic surgery for the holidays. 1985. *Sheboygan Press*. New York Times News Service.

Davis, Kathy. 1991. Remaking the she-devil: A Critical Look at Feminist Approaches to Beauty. *Hypatia* 6(2): 21-43.

Diamond, Irene and Lee Quinby, eds. 1988. *Feminism and Foucault: Reflections on resistance*. Boston: Northeastern University Press.

Douglas, Mary. 1966. *Purity and danger*. London: Routledge and Kegan Paul; New York: Praeger.

Dworkin, Sari. 1989. Not in man's image: Lesbians and the cultural oppression of body image. *Women and Therapy* 8(1, 2): 27-39.

Easlea, Brian. 1981. *Science and sexual oppression: Patriarchy's confrontation with woman and nature*. London: Weidenfeld and Nicolson.

Facial regeneration. 1990. *Health: A community education service of the Froedtert Memorial Lutheran Hospital*. Supplement to *Milwaukee Journal*, August 26.

Falling in love again. 1990. *Toronto Star*. July 23.

Foucault, Michel. 1979. *Discipline and punish: The birth of the prison*. Alan Sheridan, trans. New York: Pantheon.

———. 1988. Technologies of the self: The political technology of the individual. In *The technologies of the self*. Luther H. Martin, Huck Gutman and Patrick Hutton, eds. Amherst: University of Massachusetts Press.

Fraser, Nancy. 1989. *Unruly practices: Power, discourse, and gender in contemporary social theory*. Minneapolis: University of Minnesota Press.

Gimenez, Martha. 1984. Feminism, pronatalism, and motherhood. In *Mothering: Essays in feminist theory*. Joyce Trebilcot, ed. Totowa, NJ: Rowman and Allenheld.

Goodman, Ellen. 1989. A plastic pageant. *Boston Globe*. September 19.

Griffin, Susan. 1978. The anatomy lesson. In *Woman and nature: The roaring inside her*. New York: Harper and Row.

Haraway, Donna. 1978. Animal sociology and a natural economy of the body politic, Parts I, II. *Signs: Journal of Women in Culture and Society* 4(1): 21-60.

———. 1989. *Primate visions*. New York: Routledge.

Hartman, Betsy. 1987. *Reproductive rights and wrongs: The global politics of population control and contraceptive choice*. New York: Harper and Row.

Hartsock, Nancy. 1990. Foucault on power: A theory for women?. In *Feminism/postmodernism*. Linda Nicholson, ed. New York: Routledge.

Haug, Frigga, ed. 1987. *Female sexualization: A Collective work of memory*. Erica Carter, trans. London: Verso.

Hirshson, Paul. 1987. New wrinkles in plastic surgery: An update on the search for perfection. *Boston Globe Sunday Magazine.* May 24.

Holmes, Helen Bequaert and Laura Purdy, eds. 1989. *Hypatia* Special Issues on Feminist Ethics and Medicine 4(2, 3).

Implants hide tumors in breasts, study says. 1988. *Toronto Star.* July 29. Summarized from article in *Journal of the American Medical Association* July 8, 1988.

Jaggar, Alison, and Susan R. Bordo, eds. 1989. *Gender/body/knowledge: Feminist reconstructions of being and knowing.* New Brunswick, NJ: Rutgers University Press.

Jonas, Hans. 1979. Toward a philosophy of technology. *Hastings Center Report* 9,1(February): 34-43.

Kristeva, Julia. 1982. *The powers of Horror: An essay on abjection.* Leon Roudiez, trans. New York: Columbia University Press.

Lakoff, Robin Tolmach, and Raquel Scherr. 1984. *Face value: The politics of beauty.* Boston: Routledge and Kegan Paul.

Long, strong, perfect nails usually not nature's own. 1988. *Toronto Star.* August 18.

Looking for Mr. Beautiful. 1990. *Boston Globe.* May 7.

Lowe, Marion. 1982. The dialectic of biology and culture. In *Biological woman: The convenient myth.* Ruth Hubbard, Mary Sue Henifin, and Barbara Fried, eds. Cambridge, MA: Schenkman.

Luria, Gina, and Virginia Tiger. 1976. *Everywoman.* New York: Random House.

McCabe, Nora. 1990. Cosmetic solutions. *Homemaker Magazine* (September): 38-46.

Madonna passionate about fitness. 1990. *Toronto Star.* August 16.

Markovic, Mihailo. 1976. Women's liberation and human emancipation. In *Women and philosophy: Toward a theory of liberation.* Carol Gould and Marx Wartofsky, eds. New York: Capricorn Books.

Matthews, Gwyneth Ferguson. 1985. Mirror, mirror: Self-image and disabled women. *Women and disability: Resources for feminist research* 14(1): 47-50.

Mies, Maria. 1988. From the individual to the dividual: In the supermarket of "reproductive alternatives." *Reproductive and Genetic Engineering* 1(3): 225-37.

Morgan, Kathryn Pauly. 1986. Romantic love, altruism, and self-respect: An analysis of Simone De Beauvoir. *Hypatia* 1(1): 117-148.

———. 1987. Women and moral madness. In *Science, morality and feminist theory.* Marsha Hanen and Kai Nielsen, eds. Special issue of the *Canadian Journal of Philosophy* Supplementary Volume 13: 201-226.

———. 1989. Of woman born: How old-fashioned! New reproductive technologies and women's oppression. In *The future of human reproduction.* Christine Overall, ed. Toronto: The Women's Press.

Murphy, Julie [Julien S]. 1984. Egg farming and women's future. In *Test-tube women: What future for motherhood?* Rita Arditti, Renate Duelli-Klein, and Shelley Minden, eds. Boston: Pandora Press.

New bodies for sale. 1985. *Newsweek* May 27.

New profile took 3 years. 1989. *Toronto Star.* May 25.

Osherson, Samuel, and Lorna Amara Singhham. 1981. The machine metaphor in medicine. In *Social contexts of health, illness and patient care.* E. Mishler, ed. New York: Cambridge University Press.

Piercy, Marge. 1980. Right to life. In *The moon is always female.* New York: A. Knopf.

The quest to be a perfect 10. 1990. *Toronto Star.* February 1.

Ratcliff, Hathryn Strother, ed. 1989. *Healing technology: Feminist perspectives.* Ann Arbor: University of Michigan Press.

Raymond, Janice. 1987. Preface to *Man-made woman*. Gena Corea et al., eds. Blooming-ton: Indiana University Press.

Retouching nature's way: Is cosmetic surgery worth it? 1990. *Toronto Star*. February 1.

Rich, Adrienne. 1980. Compulsory heterosexuality and lesbian existence. *Signs: Journal of Women in Culture and Society* 5(4): 631-660.

Rothman, Barbara Katz. 1984. The meanings of choice in reproductive technology. In *Test-tube women: What future for motherhood?*. Rita Arditti, Renate Duelli-Klein, and Shelley Minden, eds. Boston: Pandora Press.

Russett, Cynthia Eagle. 1989. *Sexual science: The Victorian construction of womanhood*. Cambridge: Harvard University Press.

Schiebinger, Londa. 1989. *The mind has no sex? Women in the origins of modern science*. Cambridge: Harvard University Press.

Schoenfielder, Lisa, and Barb Wieser, eds. 1983. *Shadow on a tightrope: Writings by women on fat oppression*. Iowa City: Aunt Lute Press.

Sherwin, Susan. 1984-85. A feminist approach to ethics. *Dalhousie Review*. 64(4): 704-713.

———. 1987. Feminist ethics and in vitro fertilization. In *Science, morality, and feminist theory*. Marcia Hanen and Kai Nielsen, eds. Special issue of *Canadian Journal of Philosophy* Supplementary Volume 13: 265-284.

———. 1989. Feminist and medical ethics: Two different approaches to contextual ethics. *Hypatia* 4(2): 57-72.

Silver, Harold. 1989. Liposuction isn't for everybody. *Toronto Star*. October 20.

Warren, Mary Anne. 1985. *Gendercide: The implications of sex selection*. Totowa, NJ: Rowman and Allenheld.

Warren, Virginia. 1989. Feminist directions in medical ethics. *Hypatia* 4(2): 73-87.

Weldon, Fay. 1983. *The life and loves of a she-devil*. London: Coronet Books; New York: Pantheon Books.

Williams, John, M.D., and Jim Williams. 1990. Say it with liposuction. From a press release; reported in *Harper's* (August).

Woman, 43, dies after cosmetic surgery. 1989. *Toronto Star*. July 7.

[18]

Toward a
Feminist Theory of Disability

SUSAN WENDELL

We need a feminist theory of disability, both because 16 percent of women are disabled, and because the oppression of disabled people is closely linked to the cultural oppression of the body. Disability is not a biological given; like gender, it is socially constructed from biological reality. Our culture idealizes the body and demands that we control it. Thus, although most people will be disabled at some time in their lives, the disabled are made "the other," who symbolize failure of control and the threat of pain, limitation, dependency, and death. If disabled people and their knowledge were fully integrated into society, everyone's relation to her/his real body would be liberated.

In 1985, I fell ill overnight with what turned out to be a disabling chronic disease. In the long struggle to come to terms with it, I had to learn to live with a body that felt entirely different to me—weak, tired, painful, nauseated, dizzy, unpredictable. I learned at first by listening to other people with chronic illnesses or disabilities; suddenly able-bodied people seemed to me profoundly ignorant of everything I most needed to know. Although doctors told me there was a good chance I would eventually recover completely, I realized after a year that waiting to get well, hoping to recover my healthy body, was a dangerous strategy. I began slowly to identify with my new, disabled body and to learn to work with it. As I moved back into the world, I also began to experience the world as structured for people who have no weaknesses.[1] The process of encountering the able-bodied world led me gradually to identify myself as a disabled person, and to reflect on the nature of disability.

Some time ago, I decided to delve into what I assumed would be a substantial philosophical literature in medical ethics on the nature and experience of disability. I consulted *The Philosopher's Index*, looking under "Disability," "Handicap," "Illness," and "Disease." This was a depressing experience. At least 90% of philosophical articles on these topics are concerned with two questions: Under what conditions is it morally permissible/right to kill/let die a disabled person and how potentially disabled does a fetus have to be before it is permissible/right to prevent its being born? Thus, what I have to say here

Hypatia vol. 4, no. 2 (Summer 1989) © by Susan Wendell

Susan Wendell   105

about disability is not a response to philosophical literature on the subject. Instead, it reflects what I have learned from the writings of other disabled people (especially disabled women), from talking with disabled people who have shared their insights and experiences with me, and from my own experience of disability. It also reflects my commitment to feminist theory, which offers perspectives and categories of analysis that help to illuminate the personal and social realities of disability, and which would, in turn, be enriched by a greater understanding of disability.

We need a theory of disability. It should be a social and political theory, because disability is largely socially-constructed, but it has to be more than that; any deep understanding of disability must include thinking about the ethical, psychological and epistemic issues of living with disability. This theory should be feminist, because more than half of disabled people are women and approximately 16% of women are disabled (Fine and Asch 1988), and because feminist thinkers have raised the most radical issues about cultural attitudes to the body. Some of the same attitudes about the body which contribute to women's oppression generally also contribute to the social and psychological disablement of people who have physical disabilities. In addition, feminists are grappling with issues that disabled people also face in a different context: Whether to stress sameness or difference in relation to the dominant group and in relation to each other; whether to place great value on independence from the help of other people, as the dominant culture does, or to question a value-system which distrusts and de-values dependence on other people and vulnerability in general; whether to take full integration into male dominated/able-bodied society as the goal, seeking equal power with men/ able-bodied people in that society, or whether to preserve some degree of separate culture, in which the abilities, knowledge and values of women/the disabled are specifically honoured and developed.[2]

Disabled women struggle with both the oppressions of being women in male-dominated societies and the oppressions of being disabled in societies dominated by the able-bodied. They are bringing the knowledge and concerns of women with disabilities into feminism and feminist perspectives into the disability rights movement. To build a feminist theory of disability that takes adequate account of our differences, we will need to know how experiences of disability and the social oppression of the disabled interact with sexism, racism and class oppression. Michelle Fine and Adrienne Asch and the contributors to their 1988 volume, *Women and Disabilities*, have made a major contribution to our understanding of the complex interactions of gender and disability. Barbara Hillyer Davis has written in depth about the issue of dependency/independence as it relates to disability and feminism (Davis 1984). Other important contributions to theory are scattered throughout the extensive, primarily experiential, writing by disabled women;[3] this work offers vital insights into the nature of embodiment and the experience of oppression.

Unfortunately, feminist perspectives on disability are not yet widely discussed in feminist theory, nor have the insights offered by women writing
about disability been integrated into feminist theorizing about the body. My
purpose in writing this essay is to persuade feminist theorists, especially feminist philosophers, to turn more attention to constructing a theory of disability
and to integrating the experiences and knowledge of disabled people into
feminist theory as a whole. Toward this end I will discuss physical disability[4]
from a theoretical perspective, including: some problems of defining it (here I
will criticize the most widely-used definitions—those of the United Nations);
the social construction of disability from biological reality on analogy with
the social construction of gender; cultural attitudes toward the body which
oppress disabled people while also alienating the able-bodied from their own
experiences of embodiment; the "otherness" of disabled people; the knowledge that disabled people could contribute to culture from our diverse experiences and some of the ways this knowledge is silenced and invalidated. Along
the way, I will describe briefly three issues discussed in disability theory that
have been taken up in different contexts by feminist theory: sameness vs. difference, independence vs. dependency and integration vs. separatism.

I do not presume to speak for disabled women. Like everyone who is disabled, I have a particular standpoint determined in part by both my physical
condition and my social situation. My own disability may be temporary, it
could get better or worse. My disability is usually invisible (except when I use
a walking stick). I am a white university professor who has adequate medical
and long-term disability insurance; that makes me very privileged among the
disabled. I write what I can see from my standpoint. Because I do not want
simply to describe my own experience but to understand it in a much larger
context, I must venture beyond what I know first-hand. I rely on others to
correct my mistakes and fill in those parts of the picture I cannot see.

WHO IS PHYSICALLY DISABLED?

The United Nations offers the following definitions of and distinctions
among impairment, disability and handicap:

> "*Impairment*: Any loss or abnormality of psychological, physio-
> logical, or anatomical structure or function. *Disability*: Any re-
> striction or lack (resulting from an impairment) of ability to
> perform an activity in the manner or within the range consid-
> ered normal for a human being. *Handicap*: A disadvantage for
> a given individual, resulting from an impairment or disability,
> that limits or prevents the fulfillment of a role that is normal,
> depending on age, sex, social and cultural factors, for that in-
> dividual."

> Handicap is therefore a function of the relationship be-
> tween disabled persons and their environment. It occurs when
> they encounter cultural, physical or social barriers which pre-
> vent their access to the various systems of society that are
> available to other citizens. Thus, handicap is the loss or limi-
> tation of opportunities to take part in the life of the commu-
> nity on an equal level with others. (U.N. 1983:I.c. 6-7)

These definitions may be good-enough for the political purposes of the U.N.
They have two advantages: First, they clearly include many conditions that
are not always recognized by the general public as disabling, for example, debilitating chronic illnesses that limit people's activities but do not necessarily
cause any visible disability, such as Crohn's Disease. Second, the definition
of "handicap" explicitly recognizes the possibility that the primary cause of a
disabled person's inability to do certain things may be social—denial of opportunities, lack of accessibility, lack of services, poverty, discrimination—which it often is.

However, by trying to define "impairment" and "disability" in physical
terms and "handicap" in cultural, physical and social terms, the U.N. document appears to be making a shaky distinction between the physical and the
social aspects of disability. Not only the "normal" roles for one's age, sex, society, and culture, but also "normal" structure and function, and "normal"
ability to perform an activity, depend on the society in which the standards of
normality are generated. Paradigms of health and ideas about appropriate
kinds and levels of performance are culturally-dependent. In addition, within
each society there is much variation from the norm of any ability; at what
point does this variation become disability? The answer depends on such factors as what activities a society values and how it distributes labour and resources. The idea that there is some universal, perhaps biologically or medi-
cally-describable paradigm of human physical ability is an illusion. Therefore,
I prefer to use a single term, "disability," and to emphasize that disability is
socially constructed from biological reality.

Another objection I have to the U.N. definitions is that they imply that
women can be disabled, but not handicapped, by being unable to do things
which are not considered part of the normal role for their sex. For example, if
a society does not consider it essential to a woman's normal role that she be
able to read, then a blind woman who is not provided with education in
Braille is not handicapped, according to these definitions.

In addition, these definitions suggest that we can be disabled, but not
handicapped, by the normal process of aging, since although we may lose
some ability, we are not handicapped unless we cannot fulfill roles that are
normal *for our age.* Yet a society which provides few resources to allow disabled people to participate in it will be likely to marginalize *all* the disabled,

including the old, and to define the appropriate roles of old people as very limited, thus handicapping them. Aging is disabling. Recognizing this helps us to see that disabled people are not "other," that they are really "us." Unless we die suddenly, we are all disabled eventually. Most of us will live part of our lives with bodies that hurt, that move with difficulty or not at all, that deprive us of activities we once took for granted or that others take for granted, bodies that make daily life a physical struggle. We need an understanding of disability that does not support a paradigm of humanity as young and healthy. Encouraging everyone to acknowledge, accommodate and identify with a wide range of physical conditions is ultimately the road to self-acceptance as well as the road to liberating those who are disabled now.

Ultimately, we might eliminate the category of "the disabled" altogether, and simply talk about individuals' physical abilities in their social context. For the present, although "the disabled" is a category of "the other" to the able-bodied, for that very reason it is also a politically useful and socially meaningful category to those who are in it. Disabled people share forms of social oppression, and the most important measures to relieve that oppression have been initiated by disabled people themselves. Social oppression may be the only thing the disabled have in common;[5] our struggles with our bodies are extremely diverse.

Finally, in thinking about disability we have to keep in mind that a society's labels do not always fit the people to whom they are applied. Thus, some people are perceived as disabled who do not experience themselves as disabled. Although they have physical conditions that disable other people, because of their opportunities and the context of their lives, they do not feel significantly limited in their activities (see Sacks 1988); these people may be surprised or resentful that they are considered disabled. On the other hand, many people whose bodies cause them great physical, psychological and economic struggles are not considered disabled because the public and/or the medical profession do not recognize their disabling conditions. These people often long to be perceived as disabled, because society stubbornly continues to expect them to perform as healthy people when they cannot and refuses to acknowledge and support their struggles.[6] Of course, no one wants the social stigma associated with disability, but social recognition of disability determines the practical help a person receives from doctors, government agencies, insurance companies, charity organizations, and often from family and friends. Thus, how a society defines disability and whom it recognizes as disabled are of enormous psychological, economic and social importance, both to people who are experiencing themselves as disabled and to those who are not but are nevertheless given the label.

There is no definitive answer to the question: Who is physically disabled? Disability has social, experiential and biological components, present and recognized in different measures for different people. Whether a particular

physical condition is disabling changes with time and place, depending on
such factors as social expectations, the state of technology and its availability
to people in that condition, the educational system, architecture, attitudes
towards physical appearance, and the pace of life. (If, for example, the pace
of life increases without changes in other factors, more people become disabled simply because fewer people can keep up the "normal" pace.)

THE SOCIAL CONSTRUCTION OF DISABILITY.

If we ask the questions: Why are so many disabled people unemployed or
underemployed, impoverished, lonely, isolated; why do so many find it difficult or impossible to get an education (Davis and Marshall 1987; Fine and
Asch 1988, 10-11); why are they victims of violence and coercion; why do
able-bodied people ridicule, avoid, pity, stereotype and patronize them?, we
may be tempted to see the disabled as victims of nature or accident. Feminists
should be, and many are, profoundly suspicious of this answer. We are used to
countering claims that insofar as women are oppressed they are oppressed by
nature, which puts them at a disadvantage in the competition for power and
resources. We know that if being biologically female is a disadvantage, it is
because a social context makes it a disadvantage. From the standpoint of a
disabled person, one can see how society could minimize the disadvantages of
most disabilities, and, in some instances, turn them into advantages.

Consider an extreme case: the situation of physicist Stephen Hawking,
who has had Amyotrophic Lateral Sclerosis (Lou Gehrig's Disease) for more
than 26 years. Professor Hawking can no longer speak and is capable of only
the smallest muscle movements. Yet, in his context of social and technological support, he is able to function as a professor of physics at Cambridge University; indeed he says his disability has given him the *advantage* of having
more time to think, and he is one of the foremost theoretical physicists of our
time. He is a courageous and talented man, but he is able to live the creative
life he has only because of the help of his family, three nurses, a graduate student who travels with him to maintain his computer-communications systems, and the fact that his talent had been developed and recognized before
he fell seriously ill (*Newsweek* 1988).

Many people consider providing resources for disabled people a form of
charity, superogatory in part because the disabled are perceived as unproduc-
tive members of society. Yet most disabled people are placed in a double-
bind: they have access to inadequate resources because they are unemployed
or underemployed, and they are unemployed or underemployed because they
lack the resources that would enable them to make their full contribution to
society (Matthews 1983; Hannaford 1985). Often governments and charity
organizations will spend far more money to keep disabled people in institutions where they have no chance to be productive than they will spend to en-

able the same people to live independently and productively. In addition, many of the "special" resources the disabled need merely compensate for bad social planning that is based on the illusion that everyone is young, strong, healthy (and, often, male).

Disability is also frequently regarded as a personal or family problem rather than a matter for social responsibility. Disabled people are often expected to overcome obstacles to participation by their own extraordinary efforts, or their families are expected to provide what they need (sometimes at great personal sacrifice). Helping in personal or family matters is seen as superogatory for people who are not members of the family.

Many factors contribute to determining whether providing a particular resource is regarded as a social or a personal (or family) responsibility.[7] One such factor is whether the majority can identify with people who need the resource. Most North Americans feel that society should be organized to provide short-term medical care made necessary by illness or accident, I think because they can imagine themselves needing it. Relatively few people can identify with those who cannot be "repaired" by medical intervention. Sue Halpern makes the following observation:

> Physical health is contingent and often short-lived. But this truth eludes us as long as we are able to walk by simply putting one foot in front of the other. As a consequence, empathy for the disabled is unavailable to most able-bodied persons. Sympathy, yes, empathy, no, for every attempt to project oneself into that condition, to feel what it is like not to be ambulatory, for instance, is mediated by an ability to walk (Halpern 1988, 3).

If the able-bodied saw the disabled as potentially themselves or as their future selves, they would be more inclined to feel that society should be organized to provide the resources that would make disabled people fully integrated and contributing members. They would feel that "charity" is as inappropriate a way of thinking about resources for disabled people as it is about emergency medical care or education.

Careful study of the lives of disabled people will reveal how artificial the line is that we draw between the biological and the social. Feminists have already challenged this line in part by showing how processes such as childbirth, menstruation and menopause, which may be represented, treated, and therefore experienced as illnesses or disabilities, are socially-constructed from biological reality (Rich 1976; Ehrenreich and English 1979). Disabled people's relations to our bodies involve elements of struggle which perhaps cannot be eliminated, perhaps not even mitigated, by social arrangements. *But*, much of what is *disabling* about our physical conditions is also a consequence of social arrangements (Finger 1983; Fine and Asch 1988) which could, but do not, either compensate for our physical conditions, or accommodate them so that we can participate fully, or support our struggles and integrate us into the community *and our struggles into the cultural concept of life as it is ordinarily lived.*

Feminists have shown that the world has been designed for men. In North America at least, life and work have been structured as though no one of any importance in the public world, and certainly no one who works outside the home for wages, has to breast-feed a baby or look after a sick child. Common colds can be acknowledged publicly, and allowances made for them, but menstruation cannot. Much of the world is also structured as though everyone is physically strong, as though all bodies are "ideally shaped," as though everyone can walk, hear and see well, as though everyone can work and play at a pace that is not compatible with any kind of illness or pain, as though no one is ever dizzy or incontinent or simply needs to sit or lie down. (For instance, where could you sit down in a supermarket if you needed to?) Not only the architecture, but the entire physical and social organization of life, assumes that we are either strong and healthy and able to do what the average able-bodied person can do, or that we are completely disabled, unable to participate in life.

In the split between the public and the private worlds, women (and children) have been relegated to the private, and so have the disabled, the sick and the old (and mostly women take care of them). The public world is the world of strength, the positive (valued) body, performance and production, the able-bodied and youth. Weakness, illness, rest and recovery, pain, death and the negative (de-valued) body are private, generally hidden, and often neglected. Coming into the public world with illness, pain or a de-valued body, we encounter resistance to mixing the two worlds; the split is vividly revealed. Much of our experience goes underground, because there is no socially acceptable way of expressing it and having our physical and psychological experience acknowledged and shared. A few close friends may share it, but there is a strong impulse to protect them from it too, because it seems so private, so unacceptable. I found that, after a couple of years of illness, even answering the question, "How are you?" became a difficult, conflict-ridden business. I don't want to alienate my friends from my experience, but I don't want to risk their discomfort and rejection by telling them what they don't want to know.[8]

Disabled people learn that many, perhaps most, able-bodied people do not want to know about suffering caused by the body. Visibly disabled women report that curiosity about medical diagnoses, physical appearance and the sexual and other intimate aspects of disability is more common than willingness to listen and try to understand the experience of disability (Matthews 1983). It is not unusual for people with invisible disabilities to keep them entirely secret from everyone but their closest friends.

Contrary to what Sue Halpern says, it is not simply because they are in able bodies that the able-bodied fail to identify with the disabled. Able-bodied people can often make the imaginative leap into the skins of people physically unlike themselves; women can identify with a male protagonist in a story, for example, and adults can identify with children or with people much older than themselves. Something more powerful than being in a different body is at work. Suffering caused by the body, and the inability to control the body, are despised, pitied, and above all, feared. This fear, experienced individually, is also deeply embedded in our culture.

THE OPPRESSION OF DISABLED PEOPLE IS THE OPPRESSION OF EVERYONE'S REAL BODY.

Our real human bodies are exceedingly diverse—in size, shape, colour, texture, structure, function, range and habits of movement, and development—and they are constantly changing. Yet we do not absorb or reflect this simple fact in our culture. Instead, we idealize the human body. Our physical ideals change from time to time, but we always have ideals. These ideals are not just about appearance; they are also ideals of strength and energy and proper control of the body. We are perpetually bombarded with images of these ideals, demands for them, and offers of consumer products and services to help us achieve them.[9] Idealizing the body prevents everyone, able-bodied and disabled, from identifying with and loving her/his real body. Some people can have the illusion of acceptance that comes from believing that their bodies are "close enough" to the ideal, but this illusion only draws them deeper into identifying with the ideal and into the endless task of reconciling the reality with it. Sooner or later they must fail.

Before I became disabled, I was one of those people who felt "close enough" to cultural ideals to be reasonably accepting of my body. Like most feminists I know, I was aware of some alienation from it, and I worked at liking my body better. Nevertheless, I knew in my heart that too much of my liking still depended on being "close enough." When I was disabled by illness, I experienced a much more profound alienation from my body. After a year spent mostly in bed, I could barely identify my body as my own. I felt that "it" was torturing "me," trapping me in exhaustion, pain and inability to do many of the simplest things I did when I was healthy. The shock of this experience and the effort to identify with a new, disabled body, made me realize I had been living a luxury of the able-bodied. The able-bodied can postpone the task of identifying with their *real* bodies. The disabled don't have the luxury of demanding that their bodies fit the physical ideals of their culture As Barbara Hillyer Davis says: "For all of us the difficult work of finding (one's) self includes the body, but people who live with disability in a society that glorifies fitness and physical conformity are forced to understand more fully what bodily integrity means" (Davis 1984,3).

In a society which idealizes the body, the physically disabled are marginalized. People learn to identify with their own strengths (by cultural standards) and to hate, fear and neglect their own weaknesses. The disabled are not only de-valued for their de-valued bodies (Hannaford 1985), they are constant reminders to the able-bodied of the negative body—of what the able-bodied are trying to avoid, forget and ignore (Lessing 1981). For example, if someone tells me she is in pain, she reminds me of the existence of pain, the imperfection and fragility of the body, the possibility of my own pain, the *inevitability* of it. The less willing I am to accept all these, the less I want to know about her pain; if I cannot avoid it in her presence, I will avoid her. I may even blame her for it. I may tell myself that she *could have* avoided it, in order to go on believing that I *can* avoid it. I want to believe I am not like her; I cling to the differences. Gradually, I make her "other" because I don't want to confront my real body, which I fear and cannot accept.[10]

Disabled people can participate in marginalizing ourselves. We can wish for bodies we do not have, with frustration, shame, self-hatred. We can feel trapped in the negative body; it is our internalized oppression to feel this. Every (visibly or invisibly) disabled person I have talked to or read has felt this; some never stop feeling it. In addition, disabled women suffer more than disabled men from the demand that people have "ideal" bodies, because in patriarchal culture people judge women more by their bodies than they do men. Disabled women often do not feel seen (because they are often not seen) by others as whole people, especially not as sexual people (Campling 1981; Matthews 1983; Hannaford 1985; Fine and Asch 1988). Thus, part of their struggle against oppression is a much harder version of the struggle able-bodied women have for a realistic *and positive* self-image (Bogle and Shaul 1981). On the other hand, disabled people who cannot hope to meet the physical ideals of a culture can help reveal that those ideals are not "natural" or "normal" but artificial social creations that oppress everyone.

Feminist theorists have probed the causes of our patriarchal culture's desire for control of the body—fear of death, fear of the strong impulses and feelings the body gives us, fear of nature, fear and resentment of the mother's power over the infant (de Beauvoir 1949; Dinnerstein 1976; Griffin 1981). Idealizing the body and wanting to control it go hand-in-hand; it is impossible to say whether one causes the other. A physical ideal gives us the goal of our efforts to control the body, and the myth that total control is possible deceives us into striving for the ideal. The consequences for women have been widely discussed in the literature of feminism. The consequences for disabled people are less often recognized. In a culture which loves the idea that the body can be controlled, those who cannot control their bodies are seen (and may see themselves) as failures.

When you listen to this culture in a disabled body, you hear how often health and physical vigour are talked about as if they were moral virtues. People constantly praise others for their "energy," their stamina, their ability to work long hours. Of course, acting on behalf of one's health can be a virtue, and undermining one's health can be a vice, but "success" at being healthy, like beauty, is always partly a matter of luck and therefore beyond our control. When health is spoken of as a virtue, people who lack it are made to feel inadequate: I am not suggesting that it is always wrong to praise people's physical strength or accomplishments, any more than it is always wrong to praise their physical beauty. But just as treating cultural standards of beauty as essential virtues for women harms most women, treating health and vigour as moral virtues for everyone harms people with disabilities and illnesses.

The myth that the body can be controlled is not easily dispelled, because it is not very vulnerable to evidence against it. When I became ill, several people wanted to discuss with me what I thought I had done to "make myself" ill or "allow myself" to become sick. At first I fell in with this, generating theories about what I had done wrong; even though I had always taken good care of my health, I was able to find some (rather far-fetched) accounts of my responsibility for my illness. When a few close friends offered hypotheses as to how *they* might be responsible for my being ill, I began to suspect that something was wrong. Gradually, I realized that we were all trying to believe that nothing this important is beyond our control.

Of course, there are sometimes controllable social and psychological forces at work in creating ill health and disability (Kleinman 1988). Nevertheless, our cultural insistence on controlling the body blames the victims of disability for failing and burdens them with self-doubt and self-blame. The search for psychological, moral and spiritual causes of illness, accident and disability is often a harmful expression of this insistence on control (see Sontag 1977).

Modern Western medicine plays into and conforms to our cultural myth that the body can be controlled. Collectively, doctors and medical researchers exhibit very little modesty about their knowledge. They focus their (and our) attention on cures and imminent cures, on successful medical interventions. Research, funding and medical care are more directed toward life-threatening conditions than toward chronic illnesses and disabilities. Even pain was relatively neglected as a medical problem until the second half of this century. Surgery and saving lives bolster the illusion of control much better than does the long, patient process of rehabilitation or the management of long-term illness. These latter, less visible functions of medicine tend to be performed by nurses, physiotherapists and other low-prestige members of the profession. Doctors are trained to do something to control the body, to "make it better" (Kleinman 1988); they are the heroes of medicine. They may like being in the role of hero, but we also like them in that role and try to keep them there, because *we* want to believe that someone can always "make it better."[11] As long as we cling to this belief, the patients who cannot be "repaired"—the chronically ill, the disabled and the dying—will symbolize the

Susan Wendell   115

failure of medicine and more, the failure of the Western scientific project to control nature. They will carry this stigma in medicine and in the culture as a whole.

When philosophers of medical ethics confine themselves to discussing life-and-death issues of medicine, they help perpetuate the idea that the main purpose of medicine is to control the body. Life-and-death interventions are the ultimate exercise of control. If medical ethicists looked more closely at who needs and who receives medical help, they would discover a host of issues concerning how medicine and society understand, mediate, assist with and integrate experiences of illness, injury and disability.

Because of the heroic approach to medicine, and because disabled people's experience is not integrated into the culture, most people know little or nothing about how to live with long-term or life-threatening illness, how to communicate with doctors and nurses and medical bureaucrats about these matters, how to live with limitation, uncertainty, pain, nausea, and other symptoms when doctors cannot make them go away. Recently, patients' support groups have arisen to fill this gap for people with nearly every type of illness and disability. They are vitally important sources of knowledge and encouragement for many of us, but they do not fill the cultural gulf between the able-bodied and the disabled. The problems of living with a disability are not private problems, separable from the rest of life and the rest of society. They are problems which can and should be shared throughout the culture as much as we share the problems of love, work and family life.

Consider the example of pain. It is difficult for most people who have not lived with prolonged or recurring pain to understand the benefits of accepting it. Yet some people who live with chronic pain speak of "making friends" with it as the road to feeling better and enjoying life. How do they picture their pain and think about it; what kind of attention do they give it and when; how do they live around and through it, and what do they learn from it? We all need to know this as part of our education. Some of the fear of experiencing pain is a consequence of ignorance and lack of guidance. The effort to avoid pain contributes to such widespread problems as drug and alcohol addiction, eating disorders, and sedentary lives. People with painful disabilities can teach us about pain, because they *can't* avoid it and have had to learn how to face it and live with it. The pernicious myth that it is possible to avoid almost all pain by controlling the body gives the fear of pain greater power than it should have and blames the victims of unavoidable pain. The fear of pain is also expressed or displaced as a fear of people in pain, which often isolates those with painful disabilities. All this is unnecessary. People *in* pain and knowledge *of* pain could be fully integrated into our culture, to everyone's benefit.

If we knew more about pain, about physical limitation, about loss of abilities, about what it is like to be "too far" from the cultural ideal of the body, perhaps we would have less fear of the negative body, less fear of our own weaknesses and "imperfections," of our inevitable deterioration and death. Perhaps we could give up our idealizations and relax our desire for control of the body; until we do, we maintain them at the expense of disabled people and at the expense of our ability to accept and love our own real bodies.

DISABLED PEOPLE AS "OTHER"

When we make people "other," we group them together as the objects of *our* experience instead of regarding them as fellow *subjects* of experience with whom we might identify. If you are "other" to me, I see you primarily as symbolic of something else—usually, but not always, something I reject and fear and that I project onto you. We can all do this to each other, but very often the process is not symmetrical, because one group of people may have more power to call itself the paradigm of humanity and to make the world suit its own needs and validate its own experiences.[12] Disabled people are "other" to able-bodied people, and (as I have tried to show) the consequences are socially, economically and psychologically oppressive to the disabled and psychologically oppressive to the able-bodied. Able-bodied people may be "other" to disabled people, but the consequences of this for the able-bodied are minor (most able-bodied people can afford not to notice it). There are, however, several political and philosophical issues that being "other" to a more powerful group raises for disabled people.

I have said that for the able-bodied, the disabled often symbolize failure to control the body and the failure of science and medicine to protect us all. However, some disabled people also become symbols of heroic control against all odds; these are the "disabled heroes," who are comforting to the able-bodied because they re-affirm the possibility of overcoming the body. Disabled heroes are people with visible disabilities who receive public attention because they accomplish things that are unusual even for the able-bodied. It is revealing that, with few exceptions (Helen Keller and, very recently, Stephen Hawking are among them), disabled heroes are recognized for performing feats of physical strength and endurance. While disabled heroes can be inspiring and heartening to the disabled, they may give the able-bodied the false impression that anyone can "overcome" a disability. Disabled heroes usually have extraordinary social, economic and physical resources that are not available to most people with those disabilities. In addition, many disabled people are not capable of performing physical heroics, because many (perhaps most) disabilities reduce or consume the energy and stamina of people who have them and do not just limit them in some particular kind of physical activity. Amputee and wheelchair athletes are exceptional, not because of their ambition, discipline and hard work, but because they are in better health than most disabled people can be. Arthritis, Parkinsonism and stroke cause severe disability in far more people than do spinal cord injuries and amputations (Bury 1979). The image of the disabled hero may reduce the "otherness" of a few disabled people, but because it creates an ideal which most disabled people cannot meet, it *increases* the "otherness" of the majority of disabled people.

One recent attempt to reduce the "otherness" of disabled people is the introduction of the term, "differently-abled." I assume the point of using this term is to suggest that there is nothing *wrong* with being the way we are, just different. Yet to call someone "differently-abled" is much like calling her "differently-coloured" or "differently-gendered." It says: "This person is not the norm or paradigm of humanity." If anything, it increases the "otherness" of disabled people, because it reinforces the paradigm of humanity as young, strong and healthy, with all body parts working "perfectly," from which this person is "different." Using the term "differently-abled" also suggests a (polite? patronizing? protective? self-protective?) disregard of the special difficulties, struggles and suffering disabled people face. We are *dis-abled*. We live with particular social and physical struggles that are partly consequences of the conditions of our bodies and partly consequences of the structures and expectations of our societies, but they are struggles which only people with bodies like ours experience.

The positive side of the term "differently-abled" is that it might remind the able-bodied that to be disabled in some respects is not to be disabled in all respects. It also suggests that a disabled person may have abilities that the able-bodied lack in virtue of being able-bodied. Nevertheless, on the whole, the term "differently-abled" should be abandoned, because it reinforces the able-bodied paradigm of humanity and fails to acknowledge the struggles disabled people face.

The problems of being "the other" to a dominant group are always politically complex. One solution is to emphasize similarities to the dominant group in the hope that they will identify with the oppressed, recognize their rights, gradually give them equal opportunities, and eventually assimilate them. Many disabled people are tired of being symbols to the able-bodied, visible only or primarily for their disabilities, and they want nothing more than to be seen as individuals rather than as members of the group, "the disabled." Emphasizing similarities to the able-bodied, making their disabilities unnoticeable in comparison to their other human qualities may bring about assimilation one-by-one. It does not directly challenge the able-bodied paradigm of humanity, just as women moving into traditionally male arenas of power does not directly challenge the male paradigm of humanity, although both may produce a gradual change in the paradigms. In addition, assimilation may be very difficult for the disabled to achieve. Although the able-bodied like disabled tokens who do not seem very different from themselves, they may *need* someone to carry the burden of the negative body as long as they continue to idealize and try to control the body. They may therefore resist the assimilation of most disabled people.

The reasons in favour of the alternative solution to "otherness"—*emphasizing difference* from the able-bodied—are also reasons for emphasizing similarities among the disabled, especially social and political similarities. Disabled people share positions of social oppression that separate us from the able-bodied, and we share physical, psychological and social experiences of disability. Emphasizing differences from the able-bodied demands that those differences be acknowledged and respected and fosters solidarity among the disabled. It challenges the able-bodied paradigm of humanity and creates the possibility of a deeper challenge to the idealization of the body and the demand for its control. Invisibly disabled people tend to be drawn to solutions that emphasize difference, because our need to have our struggles acknowledged is great, and we have far less experience than those who are visibly disabled of being symbolic to the able-bodied.

Whether one wants to emphasize sameness or difference in dealing with the problem of being "the other" depends in part on how radically one wants to challenge the value-structure of the dominant group. A very important issue in this category for both women and disabled people is the value of independence from the help of others, so highly esteemed in our patriarchal culture and now being questioned in feminist ethics (see, for example, Sherwin 1984, 1987; Kittay and Meyers 1987) and discussed in the writings of disabled women (see, for example, Fisher and Galler 1981; Davis 1984; Frank 1988). Many disabled people who can see the possibility of living as independently as any able-bodied person, or who have achieved this goal after long struggle, value their independence above everything. Dependence on the help of others is humiliating in a society which prizes independence. In addition, this issue holds special complications for disabled women; reading the stories of women who became disabled as adults, I was struck by their struggle with shame and loss of self-esteem at being transformed from people who took physical care of others (husbands and children) to people who were physically dependent. All this suggests that disabled people need every bit of independence we can get. Yet there are disabled people who will always need a lot of help from other individuals just to survive (those who have very little control of movement, for example), and to the extent that everyone considers independence necessary to respect and self-esteem, those people will be condemned to be de-valued. In addition, some disabled people spend tremendous energy being independent in ways that might be considered trivial in a culture less insistent on self-reliance; if our culture valued *interdependence* more highly, they could use that energy for more satisfying activities.

In her excellent discussion of the issue of dependency and independence, Barbara Hillyer Davis argues that women with disabilities and those who care for them can work out a model of *reciprocity* for all of us, if we are willing to

learn from them. "Reciprocity involves the difficulty of recognizing each
other's needs, relying on the other, asking and receiving help, delegating responsibility, giving and receiving empathy, respecting boundaries" (Davis
1984, 4). I hope that disabled and able-bodied feminists will join in questioning our cultural obsession with independence and ultimately replacing it with
such a model of reciprocity. If *all* the disabled are to be fully integrated into
society without symbolizing failure, then we have to change social values to
recognize the value of depending on others and being depended upon. This
would also reduce the fear and shame associated with dependency in old
age—a condition most of us will reach.

Whether one wants to emphasize sameness or difference in dealing with
the problems of being "other" is also related to whether one sees anything
valuable to be preserved by maintaining, either temporarily or in the long-
run, some separateness of the oppressed group. Is there a special culture of the
oppressed group or the seeds of a special culture which could be developed in
a supportive context of solidarity? Do members of the oppressed group have
accumulated knowledge or ways of knowing which might be lost if assimilation takes place without the dominant culture being transformed?

It would be hard to claim that disabled people as a whole have an alternative culture or even the seeds of one. One sub-group, the deaf, has a separate
culture from the hearing, and they are fighting for its recognition and preservation, as well as for their right to continue making their own culture (Sacks
1988). Disabled people do have both knowledge and ways of knowing that
are not available to the able-bodied. Although ultimately I hope that disabled people's knowledge will be integrated into the culture as a whole, I suspect that a culture which fears and denigrates the real body would rather silence this knowledge than make the changes necessary to absorb it. It may
have to be nurtured and cultivated separately while the able-bodied culture is
transformed enough to receive and integrate it.

THE KNOWLEDGE OF DISABLED PEOPLE AND HOW IT IS SILENCED

In my second year of illness, I was reading an article about the psychological and philosophical relationship of mind to body. When the author painted
a rosy picture of the experience of being embodied, I was outraged at the presumption of the writer to speak for everyone from a healthy body. I decided I
didn't want to hear *anything* about the body from anyone who was not physically disabled. Before that moment, it had not occurred to me that there was
a world of experience from which I was shut out while I was able-bodied.

Not only do physically disabled people have experiences which are not
available to the able-bodied, they are in a better position to transcend cultural mythologies about the body, because they *cannot* do things that the
able-bodied feel they *must* do in order to be happy, "normal" and sane. For

example, paraplegics and quadriplegics have revolutionary things to teach about the possibilities of sexuality which contradict patriarchal culture's obsession with the genitals (Bullard and Knight 1981). Some people can have orgasms in any part of their bodies where they feel touch. One man said he never knew how good sex could be until he lost the feeling in his genitals. Few able-bodied people know these things, and, to my knowledge, no one has explored their implications for the able-bodied.

If disabled people were truly heard, an explosion of knowledge of the human body and psyche would take place. We have access to realms of experience that our culture has not tapped (even for medical science, which takes relatively little interest in people's *experience* of their bodies). Like women's particular knowledge, which comes from access to experiences most men do not have, disabled people's knowledge is dismissed as trivial, complaining, mundane (or bizarre), *less than* that of the dominant group.

The cognitive authority (Addelson 1983) of medicine plays an important role in distorting and silencing the knowledge of the disabled. Medical professionals have been given the power to describe and validate everyone's experience of the body. If you go to doctors with symptoms they cannot observe directly or verify independently of what you tell them, such as pain or weakness or numbness or dizziness or difficulty concentrating, and if they cannot find an objectively observable cause of those symptoms, you are likely to be told that there is "nothing wrong with you," no matter how you feel. Unless you are very lucky in your doctors, no matter how trustworthy and responsible you were considered to be *before* you started saying you were ill, your experience will be invalidated.[13] *Other* people are the authorities on the reality of your experience of your body.

When you are very ill, you desperately need medical validation of your experience, not only for economic reasons (insurance claims, pensions, welfare and disability benefits all depend upon official diagnosis), but also for social and psychological reasons. People with unrecognized illnesses are often abandoned by their friends and families.[14] Because almost everyone accepts the cognitive authority of medicine, the person whose bodily experience is radically different from medical descriptions of her/his condition is invalidated as a knower. Either you decide to hide your experience, or you are socially isolated with it by being labelled mentally ill[15] or dishonest. In both cases you are silenced.

Even when your experience is recognized by medicine, it is often re-described in ways that are inaccurate from your standpoint. The objectively observable condition of your body may be used to determine the severity of your pain, for instance, regardless of your own reports of it. For example, until recently, relatively few doctors were willing to acknowledge that severe phantom limb pain can persist for months or even years after an amputation. The accumulated experience of doctors who were themselves amputees has begun to legitimize the other patients' reports (Madruga 1979).

When you are forced to realize that other people have more social authority than you do to describe your experience of your own body, your confidence in yourself and your relationship to reality is radically undermined.
What can you know if you cannot know that you are experiencing suffering
or joy; what can you communicate to people who don't believe you know
even this?[16] Most people will censor what they tell or say nothing rather than
expose themselves repeatedly to such deeply felt invalidation. They are silenced by fear and confusion. The process is familiar from our understanding
of how women are silenced in and by patriarchal culture.

One final caution: As with women's "special knowledge," there is a danger
of sentimentalizing disabled people's knowledge and abilities and keeping us
"other" by doing so. We need to bring this knowledge into the culture and to
transform the culture and society so that everyone can receive and make use
of it, so that it can be fully integrated, along with disabled people, into a
shared social life.

CONCLUSION

I have tried to introduce the reader to the rich variety of intellectual and
political issues that are raised by experiences of physical disability. Confronting these issues has increased my appreciation of the insights that feminist
theory already offers into cultural attitudes about the body and the many
forms of social oppression. Feminists have been challenging medicine's authority for many years now, but not, I think, as radically as we would if we
knew what disabled people have to tell. I look forward to the development of
a full feminist theory of disability.[17] We need a theory of disability for the liberation of both disabled and able-bodied people, since the theory of disability
is also the theory of the oppression of the body by a society and its culture.

NOTES

Many thanks to Kathy Gose, Joyce Frazee, Mary Barnes, Barbara Beach, Elliott Gose and
Gordon Renwick for helping me to think about these questions, and to Maureen Ashfield for
helping me to research them. Thanks also to the editors of this issue, Virginia Warren, and two
anonymous reviewers for their work on editing an earlier version of the paper.

1. Itzhak Perlman, when asked in a recent CBC interview about the problems of the disabled, said disabled people have two problems: the fact that the world is not made for people with
any weaknesses but for supermen and the attitudes of able-bodied people.

2. An excellent description of this last issue as it confronts the deaf is found in Sacks 1988.

3. See Matthews 1983; Hannaford 1985; Rooney and Israel (eds.) 1985, esp. the articles by
Jill Weiss, Charlynn Toews, Myra Rosenfield, and Susan Russell; and, for a doctor's theories,
Kleinman 1988.

4. We also need a feminist theory of mental disability, but I will not be discussing mental
disability in this essay.

5. In a recent article in *Signs*, Linda Alcoff argues that we should define "woman" thus: "woman is a position from which a feminist politics can emerge rather than a set of attributes that are 'objectively identifiable.' " (Alcoff 1988, 435). I think a similar approach may be the best one for defining "disability."

6. For example, Pelvic Inflammatory Disease causes severe prolonged disability in some women. These women often have to endure medical diagnoses of psychological illness and the skepticism of family and friends, in addition to having to live with chronic severe pain. See Moore 1985.

7. Feminism has challenged the distribution of responsibility for providing such resources as childcare and protection from family violence. Increasingly many people who once thought of these as family or personal concerns now think of them as social responsibilities.

8. Some people save me that trouble by *telling me* I am fine and walking away. Of course, people also encounter difficulties with answering "How are you?" during and after crises, such as separation from a partner, death of a loved one, or a nervous breakdown. There is a temporary alienation from what is considered ordinary shared experience. In disability, the alienation lasts longer, often for a lifetime, and, in my experience, it is more profound.

9. The idealization of the body is clearly related in complex ways to the economic processes of a consumer society. Since it pre-dated capitalism, we know that capitalism did not cause it, but it is undeniable that idealization now generates tremendous profits and that the quest for profit demands the reinforcement of idealization and the constant development of new ideals.

10. Susan Griffin, in a characteristically honest and insightful passage, describes an encounter with the fear that makes it hard to identify with disabled people. See Griffin 1982, 648-649.

11. Thanks to Joyce Frazee for pointing this out to me.

12. When Simone de Beauvoir uses this term to elucidate men's view of women (and women's view of ourselves), she emphasizes that Man is considered essential, Woman inessential; Man is the Subject, Woman the Other (de Beauvoir 1952, xvi). Susan Griffin expands upon this idea by showing how we project rejected aspects of ourselves onto groups of people who are designated the Other (Griffin 1981).

13. Many women with M.S. have lived through this nightmare in the early stages of their illness. Although this happens to men too, women's experience of the body, like women's experience generally, is more likely to be invalidated (Hannaford 1985).

14. Accounts of the experience of relatively unknown, newly-discovered, or hard-to-diagnose diseases and conditions confirm this. See, for example, Jeffreys 1982, for the story of an experience of Chronic Fatigue Syndrome, which is more common in women than in men.

15. Frequently people with undiagnosed illnesses are sent by their doctors to psychiatrists, who cannot help and may send them back to their doctors saying they must be physically ill. This can leave patients in a dangerous medical and social limbo. Sometimes they commit suicide because of it (Ramsay 1986). Psychiatrists who know enough about living with physical illness or disability to help someone cope with it are rare.

16. For more discussion of this subject, see Zaner 1983 and Rawlinson 1983.

17. At this stage of the disability rights movement, it is impossible to anticipate everything that a full feminist theory will include, just as it would have been impossible to predict in 1970 the present state of feminist theory of mothering. Nevertheless, we can see that besides dealing more fully with the issues I have raised here, an adequate feminist theory of disability will examine all the ways in which disability is socially constructed; it will explain the interaction of disability with gender, race and class position; it will examine every aspect of the cognitive authority of medicine and science over our experiences of our bodies; it will discuss the relationship of technology to disability; it will question the belief that disabled lives are not worth living or preserving when it is implied in our theorizing about abortion and euthanasia; it will give us a detailed vision of the full integration of disabled people in society, and it will propose practical political strategies for the liberation of disabled people and the liberation of the able-bodied from the social oppression of their bodies.

REFERENCES

Addelson, Kathryn P. 1983. The man of professional wisdom. In *Discovering reality*. Sandra Harding and Merrill B. Hintikka, eds. Boston: D. Reidel.

Alcoff, Linda. 1988. Cultural feminism versus poststructuralism: The identity crisis in feminist theory. *Signs: Journal of Women in Culture and Society* 13(3):405-436.

Bullard, David G. and Susan E. Knight, eds. 1981. *Sexuality and physical disability*. St. Louis: C.V. Mosby.

Bury, M.R. 1979. Disablement in society: Towards an integrated perspective. *International Journal of Rehabilitation Research* 2(1):33-40.

Beauvoir, Simone de. 1952. *The second sex*. New York: Alfred A. Knopf.

Campling, Jo, ed. 1981. *Images of ourselves - women with disabilities talking*. London: Routledge and Kegan Paul.

Davis, Barbara Hillyer. 1984. Women, disability and feminism: Notes toward a new theory. *Frontiers: A Journal of Women Studies* VIII(1):1-5.

Davis, Melanie and Catherine Marshall. 1987. Female and disabled: Challenged women in education. *National Women's Studies Association Perspectives* 5:39-41.

Dinnerstein, Dorothy. 1976. *The mermaid and the minotaur: Sexual arrangements and human malaise*. New York: Harper and Row.

Ehrenreich, Barbara and Dierdre English. 1979. *For her own good: 150 years of the experts' advice to women*. New York: Anchor.

Fine, Michelle and Adrienne Asch, eds. 1988. *Women with disabilities: Essays in psychology, culture and politics*. Philadelphia: Temple University Press.

Finger, Anne. 1983. Disability and reproductive rights. *off our backs* 13(9):18-19.

Fisher, Bernice and Roberta Galler. 1981. Conversation between two friends about feminism and disability. *off our backs* 11(5):14-15.

Frank, Gelya. 1988. On embodiment: A case study of congenital limb deficiency in American culture. In *Women with disabilities*. Michelle Fine and Adrienne Asch, eds. Philadelphia: Temple University Press.

Griffin, Susan. 1981. *Pornography and silence: Culture's revenge against nature*. New York: Harper and Row.

Griffin, Susan. 1982. The way of all ideology. *Signs: Journal of Women in Culture and Society* 8(3):641-660.

Halpern, Sue M. 1988. Portrait of the artist. Review of *Under the eye of the clock* by Christopher Nolan. *The New York Review of Books*, June 30:3-4.

Hannaford, Susan. 1985. *Living outside inside. A disabled woman's experience. Towards a social and political perspective*. Berkeley: Canterbury Press.

Jeffreys, Toni. 1982. *The mile-high staircase*. Sydney: Hodder and Stoughton Ltd.

Kittay, Eva Feder and Diana T. Meyers, eds. 1987. *Women and moral theory*. Totowa, NJ: Rowman and Littlefield.

Kleinman, Arthur. 1988. *The illness narratives: Suffering, healing, and the human condition*. New York: Basic Books.

Lessing, Jill. 1981. Denial and disability. *off our backs* 11(5):21.

124   Hypatia

Madruga, Lenor. 1979. *One step at a time*. Toronto: McGraw-Hill.

Matthews, Gwyneth Ferguson. 1983. *Voices from the shadows: Women with disabilities speak out*. Toronto: Women's Educational Press.

Moore, Maureen. 1985. Coping with pelvic inflammatory disease. In *Women and Disability*. Frances Rooney and Pat Israel, eds. *Resources for Feminist Research* 14(1).

Newsweek. 1988. Reading God's mind. June 13. 56-59.

Ramsay, A. Melvin. 1986. *Postviral fatigue syndrome, the saga of Royal Free disease*. London: Gower Medical Publishing.

Rawlinson, Mary C. 1983. The facticity of illness and the appropriation of health. In *Phenomenology in a pluralistic context*. William L. McBride and Calvin O. Schrag, eds. Albany: SUNY Press.

Rich, Adrienne. 1976. *Of woman born: Motherhood as experience and institution*. New York: W.W. Norton.

Rooney, Frances and Pat Israel, eds. 1985. *Women and disability*. *Resources for Feminist Research* 14(1).

Sacks, Oliver. 1988. The revolution of the deaf. *The New York Review of Books*, June 2, 23-28.

Shaul, Susan L. and Jane Elder Bogle. 1981. Body image and the woman with a disability. In *Sexuality and physical disability*. David G. Bullard and Susan E. Knight, eds. St. Louis: C.V. Mosby.

Sherwin, Susan. 1984-85. A feminist approach to ethics. *Dalhousie Review* 64(4):704-713.

Sherwin, Susan. 1987. Feminist ethics and in vitro fertilization. In *Science, morality and feminist theory*. Marsha Hanen and Kai Nielsen, eds. Calgary: The University of Calgary Press.

Sontag, Susan. 1977. *Illness as metaphor*. New York: Random House.

U.N. Decade of Disabled Persons 1983-1992. 1983. *World programme of action concerning disabled persons*. New York: United Nations.

Whitbeck, Caroline. Afterword to the maternal instinct. In *Mothering: Essays in feminist theory*. Joyce Trebilcot, ed. Totowa: Rowman and Allanheld.

Zaner, Richard M. 1983. Flirtations or engagement? Prolegomenon to a philosophy of medicine. In *Phenomenology in a pluralistic context*. William L. McBride and Calvin O. Schrag, eds. Albany: SUNY Press.

[19]

Privacy Beliefs and the Violent Family

Extending the Ethical Argument for Physician Intervention

Nancy S. Jecker, PhD

Privacy beliefs associated with the family impede physicians' response to domestic violence. As a private sphere, the family is regarded as sacred, separate, and hidden from public view. Hence, physicians who look for or uncover violence in the family risk defiling a sacred object and violating norms of noninterference. Privacy beliefs also obfuscate the ethical analysis of physicians' duties to intercede on behalf of battered patients. Ethical principles of beneficence and nonmaleficence have been invoked to justify physicians' duties to abused patients; however, the principle of justice has not been invoked. Ethical analysis of physicians' duties in this area must be broadened to include the principle of justice. Justice is at stake because establishing conditions favorable to self-respect is a requirement of justice, and the response physicians make to battered patients carries important ramifications for supporting patients' self-respect and dignity. If justice forms part of the ethical foundation for physician intervention in domestic violence, mandatory steps that do not transgress the confidentiality of the physician-patient relationship or infringe the patient's autonomy should be taken, such as requiring domestic violence training in medical education and following treatment plans and protocols to identify abuse and provide assistance to battered patients.

(JAMA. 1993;269:776-780)

VIOLENCE is often perpetrated by people a victim knows well. Thus, in the United States, women are more likely to be assaulted, battered, raped, or murdered by a current or former male partner than by all other assailants combined.[1] A 1985 study of intact couples found that approximately one of every eight husbands had performed one or more acts of physical aggression against his female intimate(s) during the survey year, with more than one third of these acts involving severe aggression, such as punching, kicking, choking, beating up, or using a knife or gun.[2] Although spouse abuse takes the form not only of men abusing women but of women abus-

ing men, this article's primary focus will be with spousal abuse of women by men. Women's diminished authority and power within the family have made them more vulnerable to partner violence.[3] Furthermore, when men commit acts of violence against their female partners, their acts are more likely to result in medical injuries than are women's acts of violence toward male partners.[2] That violence occurs with relative frequency and severity within personal relationships poses a special obstacle to preventing it and to interceding on the victim's behalf. The values of family autonomy and privacy are deeply cherished, embedded in our political, social, and cultural heritage and rooted in such fundamental ideals as self-government and freedom from outside interference in diverse spheres of life. The locus of violence also clouds our understanding of the ethical basis for physician intervention.

EXPLAINING MEDICINE'S RELUCTANCE

Although battered persons frequently seek health professionals as help-sources, and more often turn to their physicians for help than to other groups,[4-6] the medical profession has received lower effectiveness ratings from battered women than have lawyers, clergy, police, social service agencies, battered women shelters, and women's groups.[7] Most studies investigating detection and treatment of domestic violence report a large discrepancy between the number of patients who manifest symptoms of living in abusive relationships and the number of patients detected and treated for abuse. Stark et al[8] reported that when physicians said one among 35 of their patients was battered, a more accurate approximation was one in four; when they acknowledged that one injury among 20 resulted from domestic abuse, the actual figure approached one in four; and what they described as a rare occurrence was in reality of "epidemic proportions." Similarly, Kurz[9] found that in 40% of emergency department staff interactions with battered women, staff made no response to abuse. Finally, Warshaw[10] examined the medical records of encounters among medical staff (nurses and physicians) and women whose injuries were highly indicative of abuse and found nondetection, nonintervention, and nonreceptiveness to be the norm.

Scholars attribute physicians' poor record of response to misinformation, to sexism, and to a medical model of disease that focuses on biological or psychiatric causes while overlooking the political and social contexts in which health problems arise. They also maintain that

From the Department of Medical History and Ethics, University of Washington, School of Medicine, Seattle.
Reprint requests to University of Washington, School of Medicine, Department of Medical History and Ethics, SB-20, Seattle, WA 98195 (Dr Jecker).

physicians fail to detect or intervene in domestic violence because they regard the problem as intractable and persistent, experience time constraints that deter asking probing questions, and hold battered women themselves responsible for taking charge of violent relationships.[8,10-14] Although each of these factors sheds light on physicians' response to domestic violence, the reasons underlying this response are multifaceted, and none of these explanations account for it fully. What other factors are relevant? The complex and apparently contradictory nature of medical staffs' attitudes is revealed in a recent study of four hospital emergency services in which 90% of emergency service staff expressed the belief that they should try to identify battered women and 82% considered it "part of their job."[11] However, in 40% of cases the same group failed to respond to domestic violence at all, and in 49% of cases their response was partial and inadequate. What explains the inclination to hold back, despite a desire to help? Commenting on this study, Kurz and Stark[11] hypothesize that medical staff may simultaneously wish to act, yet feel uncomfortable doing so because they regard an inquiry about battering to be "an invasion into 'personal affairs.' "

Attitudes and beliefs related to the private sphere in which domestic violence takes place also emerge as salient in research on primary care physicians' attitudes toward domestic violence. Sugg and Inui[15] examined primary care physicians' response to violence between intimate partners or spouses through a series of open-ended interviews. Privacy concerns were among the most prominent and frequently expressed themes, and often underlay a belief that asking probing questions might offend victims. According to their analysis,[15(pp3158-3159)] fear of offending

often originated in the physician's discomfort with areas that are culturally defined as private.... The uncertainty of whether patients would consider domestic violence a legitimate area to probe was distressing.... Physicians felt that by even broaching the subject of violence, the patient would take offense....

Sugg and Inui conclude, "Not wanting to overstep the boundaries of what is private . . . leaves the physician wary of how to approach the issue."[15(p3160)]

One possible response to a societal norm prohibiting interference in private areas is to recast domestic violence as a public event. For example, Burge identifies "privacy ideology" as an obstacle to family physicians' involvement in domestic abuse. Yet rather than encouraging family physicians to regard

private relationships as susceptible to ethical scrutiny and medical intervention, she recommends that they begin to view violence as "public or criminal behavior," which will enable more open discussion with patients.[16] Similarly, the American Medical Association (AMA) Council on Ethical and Judicial Affairs cites the belief that domestic violence is a private matter as a "common misconception" that should be abandoned.[17] And the former Surgeon General of the US Public Health Service, Antonia Novello,[18] holds that relegating domestic violence to the private realm may contribute to a tendency to minimize its importance. She urges that domestic violence "is not just a 'minor dispute' between spouses or loved ones."

UNDERSTANDING PRIVACY'S MEANING

The foregoing discussion suggests that the beliefs and values we associate with privacy prove an impediment to intervention in domestic violence. Yet explanations referring to privacy are incomplete in the absence of a more precise analysis of privacy's meaning and ethical implications.

Physicians' reported concern about transgressing privacy norms in domestic violence cases stands in stark contrast to the apparent ease with which they routinely intrude in many other areas of patients' private lives. For instance, physicians routinely request that patients disrobe, touch and palpate various parts of patients' bodies, insert fingers and medical instruments into patients' anal and genital orifices, and collect and examine patients' urine and blood. Is it not inconsistent, then, for physicians to regard these incursions into private spaces as justified, yet hesitate to become involved in violent family relationships? To answer this question requires uncovering the meaning and norms associated with privacy generally, and with privacy in family and physician-patient relationships in particular.

Privacy Generally

The *Oxford English Dictionary* identifies the oldest meaning of privacy as referring to activities of a religious nature. Thus, "private" designated the orders of friars that were "withdrawn or separated from the public body."[19] In this sense, what is private bears resemblance to what is sacred. Just as the private sphere demands noninterference, "the sacred is set apart, isolated, untouchable except by special people with special dispensations, and it inspires a respect which demands that a distance be kept from it."[20] "Private" also refers

more generally to any person who acts in a capacity outside public offices and duties. Thus, "private soldier" designated persons without official duties and functions; a private soldier was "without rank or distinction of any kind."[19] A third usage of "private" denotes whatever is hidden away and not open to public scrutiny. Thus, "private" designates things "kept or removed from public view or knowledge; not within the cognizance of people generally; concealed, secret."[19] For example, "private parts" is a term referring to external genitalia that are clothed and covered. What is private is "restricted or intended only for the use or enjoyment of particular and privileged persons."[19] Finally, "private" has come to describe property belonging to a particular person. Thus, the "private house" was "the dwelling-house of a private person, or of a person in his private capacity; which implied or expressed distinction from a public house or inn . . . which are open to the public," and a "private family" designated "the family occupying a private house."[19]

These definitions reveal that privacy's meaning encompasses both descriptive and normative aspects. A descriptive sense of privacy reports specific objects, persons, or places as falling within a private domain. A normative dimension of privacy puts forward an ethical imperative to keep these objects sacred, separate, or hidden. Thus, religious orders and families count as private, and as such their activities are regarded as sacred, set apart, and generally concealed from public view.

Privacy and the Family

In Western civilization, the association of privacy with the family has a distinct history. In ancient Greece, the "family" designated individuals residing together, including both servants and kin who lived under one male head of household.[21] It was contrasted with the public realm of action and agency, in which individuals could be praised, blamed, and held accountable. The family, including the women, children, and slaves who lived exclusively within it, were thought to provide the necessary conditions on which public life rests.[22,23] Thus, the household's value was instrumental, and its main function was to meet the basic needs of citizens (ie, free men). Only through participation in the state did citizens partake of the highest moral good and system of justice.

Although during the 17th and 18th centuries the term "family" designated a large kinship network, by the 19th century it came to refer more narrowly to nuclear family members living together.[21] Activities that had traditionally taken place within the family narrowed as well, as economic production, education, and health care increasingly moved outside the home. By the first half of the 19th century, the family, and the urban middle class family in particular, was increasingly seen as a private or separate sphere, and the related ideas of sacredness and separation became explicitly conjoined with it. Thus, it was in 19th-century America that the so-called doctrine of separate spheres first emerged as a persistent theme.[21] This doctrine held that society was composed of two different and separate spheres. The first sphere was assigned to women and included the family along with specific out-of-home activities, such as charity and ministering to the sick. It was thought to be a realm where morality, love, and self-sacrifice prevailed, and where feelings were allowed free expression. By contrast, the second sphere of business and politics was assigned exclusively to men and was governed by different norms, predominantly the pursuit of power and profit. The public realm was thought to require coldheartedness and self-interest.

The social and political underpinnings of the doctrine of separate spheres are particularly noteworthy. First, separating private associations and an array of "partial publics" from public life enabled these groups to function as bulwarks against totalitarian government.[24] Thus, an imperative to keep private associations free from outside intrusion was interwoven with the ideal of democratic government and limits on excessive government power.[25,26] This imperative extended not only to the family, but to private property as well. Indeed, the privacy rights initially ascribed to heads of household were interpreted as property rights, as a man's wife and children were regarded as belonging to him.

Second, the doctrine of separate spheres reflects the fact that throughout history, the division of public and private spheres has served to reinforce the subordination of women.[27] Women were judged as by nature unsuited to the public realm and denied rights of citizenship within it. Although the family has been viewed as women's proper place, women were treated as naturally subordinate to men within it. Thus, in the 19th century, ascribing privacy rights to the family as a whole, rather than to separate individuals within the family, meant that women (and children) were denied rights against more powerful family members. Domestic violence was a legally sanctioned feature of the patriarchal family, and courts generally upheld the husband's authority to ad-

minister "moderate" punishment, usually defined as anything short of life-threatening or permanent injury.[28,29]

Finally, the sharp distinction drawn between public and domestic realms and the putative protection of the family from outside interferences has meant that ethical principles, such as justice, were generally deemed inapplicable to family relationships. Reflecting this tradition, justice theories typically do not address the family, treating it as a private association, along with churches, universities, and clubs.[30] In modern times this has meant that the family is simultaneously revered as a sentimental and inherently moral haven, while at the same time it is granted immunity from the rules of justice.[31]

Privacy and Medicine

Just as the 19th-century family became identified as a separate sphere, so too medical practice was increasingly constituting itself as a separate and exclusive realm. Thus, it was during the 19th century that American medicine first became a full-time vocation, and physicians attempted to identify themselves as a profession.[32] However, persistent obstacles to establishing professional credibility existed. Dangerous and unsuccessful therapies undermined physicians' prestige, while competition from homeopaths and other medical sects threatened their share of the medical market.[33] In an effort to gain professional repute, physicians increasingly sought to distance themselves from the society at large by emphasizing their exclusive knowledge, training, and skills.[34] Application of the scientific model to medicine not only served to enhance medicine's respectability, but simultaneously reinforced physicians' separation from the public.

The physician-patient relationship itself was increasingly regarded as a private sphere, and norms of privacy and secrecy were applied to it. In its very first Code of Medical Ethics, the newly formed AMA affirmed that the duties of physicians to patients included the requirement that "secrecy and delicacy, when required by peculiar circumstances, should be strictly observed.... The obligation of secrecy extends beyond the period of professional services; —none of the privacies of personal and domestic life ... should ever be divulged by him except when he is imperatively required to do so."[35(p29)]

Treatment of women, especially upper-class women, raised special privacy concerns. The 19th-century ideal of womanhood stressed sexual prudery, and viewing the female patient's body risked embarrassing the patient and overstep-

ping societal norms of modesty and virtue. Practices such as demonstrative midwifery and examination with the vaginal speculum attracted controversy and met with resistance.[36]

Modern medical ethics continues to bring principles of privacy and confidentiality to bear on the physician-patient relationship. The current AMA Principles of Medical Ethics retain the concept of confidentiality. The Principles hold that "A physician shall respect the rights of patients ... and shall safeguard patient confidences within the constraints of the law."[37(p ix)] In its most recent opinion on confidentiality, the AMA Council on Ethical and Judicial Affairs reiterates that "the physician should not reveal confidential communications or information without the express consent of the patient, unless required to do so by law."[38(p25)] More recently, the principle of confidentiality has been conjoined with the principle of autonomy, resulting in heightened recognition of patients' rights to privacy and self-decision.[39]

Implications for Medical Practice

The preceding analysis suggests that distinct privacy claims are at stake when, on the one hand, physicians routinely examine patients' "private parts" but, on the other hand, worry that they may be intruding in a private affair by asking direct and probing questions about family violence. Yet how, more specifically, do family privacy beliefs deter involvement in domestic violence? First, the very identification of the family as "private" implies a norm of noninterference. For "private" not only denotes an activity as falling outside the public realm, it also establishes an ethical imperative not to intrude. Thus, so long as family relationships are represented as private, a special justification for interfering is required.

Second, for a variety of reasons, the special justification to intervene in family matters is more difficult to establish in domestic violence. In other situations, physicians may intervene in family affairs without uncovering violations of traditional ideals of family life. For example, a physician who questions a female patient about sexual functioning or reproductive plans does not risk uncovering wrongful and destructive acts. By contrast, the physician who queries a female patient about abuse admits the possibility that something may be amiss within the family, indeed, searches actively for it. This strains an idealized picture that portrays the family as a sanctuary where love and morality govern. The religious connotations of privacy suggest that ferreting out violent aspects of family life may even be analogous to defiling a once sacred object. In addition, our tradition of assigning privacy rights to the family as a whole, rather than to discrete individuals within the family, makes it natural to think that only the head of the family, traditionally a man, can waive privacy rights and grant permission to intercede.

Finally, the sacred and sentimental qualities associated with the family illuminate reasons behind medicine's tendency to preserve the family when it does intervene.[8] So long as the family is depicted in sentimental terms, as a bastion of love and support, violations of morality and justice occurring within it will remain difficult to acknowledge. Physicians who think in these terms will be less inclined to break the family apart by advising a battered woman to leave her husband or go temporarily to a shelter. Instead, the tendency will be to regard the family as a secure and supportive haven, and thus, an optimal setting for treating a battered woman's depression or chemical dependency, rather than the abuse.

AN ETHICAL ANALYSIS OF PHYSICIANS' DUTIES

Recently, the AMA Council on Ethical and Judicial Affairs identified two ethical principles as forming the foundation of physicians' ethical duty to recognize and respond to family violence.[17] First, the ethical principle of beneficence requires physicians not only to treat the bodily effects of domestic violence, but also to respond to its psychological, social, and spiritual dimensions. These responses are integral to the physician's role when this role is thought to include the broad task of healing the patient. Second, the ethical principle of nonmaleficence, or do not harm, requires physicians to identify domestic violence to avoid prescribing harmful or inappropriate therapies. For example, the prescribing of sedatives or pain medications is commonplace for injured patients, but contraindicated for patients whose injuries are the result of abuse and who are at risk of developing depression and chemical dependency.

The AMA Council's ethical analysis is an important, yet still unfinished, account of physicians' duties in this area. The analysis must be broadened to include the principle of justice, with important implications for the stringency, nature, and basis of physicians' duties. Although the concept of justice is frequently invoked in debates concerning the distribution of scarce resources, its meaning transcends the problem of allocating specific material goods and encompasses broader questions about distributing fundamental liberties, powers, and opportunities. In this context, justice incorporates the conditions that are

necessary for individuals to develop self-respect. Leading philosophers of justice hold that a just society creates institutions that enable the development and exercise of individuals' capacities and foster and protect persons' self-respect. Thus, Rawls[40(p440)] holds that rational persons "would wish to avoid at almost any cost the social conditions that undermine self-respect," regarding self-respect as "perhaps the most important primary good." Nozick[41(p152)] also places the conditions for becoming a self-choosing and self-respecting person at the foundation of justice. He maintains that distributions are unjust whenever they result from fraudulent or exploitive relationships, such as when "people steal from others or defraud them or enslave them ... preventing them from living as they choose...."[41(p152)] These contemporary analyses convey the point that not all harms that people are made to endure carry equal moral weight. Harms that undermine the conditions necessary for self-respect transgress justice standards. Although society cannot guarantee that such harms will not occur, it can create conditions favorable to self-respect. Thus, "what we distribute to one another is esteem, not self-esteem; respect, not self-respect," and a just society can "breed, though it can never guarantee self-respect."[42(p290)]

Within medicine, creating conditions favorable to self-respect calls for protecting patients as much as possible against acts of discrimination, violence, and exploitation. For example, ethical norms prohibiting sexual misconduct in the practice of medicine are required by justice because they protect patients against exploitation.[43] Ethical guidelines barring refusals to treat patients on the basis of their human immunodeficiency virus status express justice duties because they prevent discriminatory practices.[44] In the case of battering, the harms visited on patients are equally weighty, and justice concerns are centrally at stake. Whether or not a physician inquires about abuse and responds effectively to it carries ramifications not only for ensuring beneficial medical treatment and avoiding contraindicated treatments, but also for supporting or squelching an abused individual's authority and ability to effect change. Simply doing nothing can reinforce feelings of humiliation and compound damage already done to the battered patient's sense of self-worth, while keeping intact the abuser's privilege and dominance.

If justice forms part of the basis of physicians' duty to intervene in domestic violence, this carries important ramifications for how we understand the nature of physicians' duties. In comparing duties

of justice with duties of beneficence or nonmaleficence, duties of justice are enforceable and determinate, both with regard to the content of what is required and with regard to the identity of the individual who is the object of the duty. Further, failing to discharge justice-based duties fails to give particular persons their due, whereas failing to fulfill duties of beneficence does not violate what others are owed.[45] Hence, if physicians' duty to assist abused patients is understood to be a matter of justice, rather than solely a matter of beneficence and nonmaleficence, professional or institutional policies may explicitly require physicians to fulfill responsibilities in this area. Moreover, discharging a duty to aid abused patients will entail specific acts toward specific persons.

Translating these points into practical steps demands concerted attention to developing specific strategies. At first glance, it might be thought that the best means of enforcing justice duties is to require by law that physicians report suspected spousal abuse to authorities. There is precedent for such a step, as all states require physicians to report suspected child abuse and neglect.[46] However, as the AMA Council on Ethical and Judicial Affairs notes, spousal abuse differs from child abuse in important respects, and mandatory reporting of spousal abuse violates ethical standards of confidentiality owed to the adult patient.[17(p3192)]

Nonetheless, other mandatory steps are possible that do not transgress duties of confidentiality. In the area of medical education, for example, 53% of US and Canadian medical schools do not offer any instruction about adult domestic violence to medical students.[47] However, studies report that health professionals who receive intensive training about abuse hold stronger beliefs that battered women should be helped and attribute less personal responsibility and blame to abused persons.[48] Intensive domestic violence training should be a mandatory feature of medical education, especially in specialties where physicians more frequently encounter abused patients. There are reasons not only to include domestic violence training in medical education, but to devote special attention to violence against women. Studies document that women are more likely than men to sustain injuries from violent personal relationships and to experience aggressive and severe acts of violence in these relationships.[2,49-51]

Another area where mandatory policies might prove effective is treatment plans and protocols that assist the medical team to identify abuse, validate the abused person's feelings, assess risk, ensure safety, determine the need for legal and social support, and develop follow-up strategies. Protocols addressing such factors have been tried with some success in diverse practice settings.[52,53] As the AMA Council on Scientific Affairs has argued, treatment of symptoms alone is inadequate for victims of violence because it fails to prevent the underlying cause of trauma.[49] Unlike mandatory reporting of spouse abuse, mandatory protocols that require asking direct questions do not infringe on patients' rights. Patients can refuse to answer any questions. And as a recent study[54] indicated, the majority (78%) of patients surveyed in a hospital faculty practice setting favored primary care physicians routinely and directly inquiring about physical abuse, and nearly all (90%) believed phy-

sicians are capable of helping.

Basing physician intervention on the ethical principle of justice is consistent with recognizing the criminal and therefore public nature of battering. It does not obviate prosecution and punishment of persons who batter by bringing them before the criminal justice system. The possibility of abusive conduct being simultaneously a public and a private injustice challenges us to recognize the application of justice to private life. It compels us to acknowledge that private events shape and are shaped by public law.

In closing, it is worth noting that this analysis, which applies justice to relationships in the private sphere, runs contrary to the long history of moral philosophy.[29] This history attests that although nobler virtues have been attributed to

family relationships, justice has rarely been brought to bear. Arguably, contemporary moral theories may force detachment from personal relationships and may be ill suited for developing an ethical analysis of family life.[55] Hence, bioethicists schooled strictly in moral philosophy may not be trained to recognize the harms that occur in violent families as unjust. The best means of addressing domestic violence with the ethical clarity it merits is not to treat the family as a public domain, but instead to reassess the tendency to hold private life immune from ethical scrutiny. Only through questioning the assumptions underpinning ethical analysis can physicians and others contribute to the development of a more just and compassionate response to family violence.

References

1. Council on Scientific Affairs, American Medical Association. Report B of the Council on Scientific Affairs: violence against women. In: Proceedings of the House of Delegates of the American Medical Association. Chicago, Ill: American Medical Association. In press.
2. Straus MA, Gelles RI, eds. *Physical Violence in American Families.* New Brunswick, NJ: Transaction Publishers; 1990.
3. Schechter S, Gary LT. A framework for understanding and empowering battered women. In: Staus MB, ed. *Abuse and Victimization Across the Life Span.* Baltimore, Md: Johns Hopkins University Press; 1990:240-253.
4. Walker LE. *The Battered Woman.* New York, NY: Harper & Row Publishers Inc; 1979.
5. Mehta P, Dandrea LA. The battered woman. *Am Fam Physician.* 1988;37:193-199.
6. Haber JD, Roos C. Effects of spouse abuse and/or sexual abuse in the development and maintenance of chronic pain in women. *Adv Pain Res Ther.* 1985;9:889-896.
7. Bowker LH, Maurer L. The medical treatment of battered wives. *Women Health.* 1987;12:25-45.
8. Stark E, Flitcraft A, Frazier W. Medicine and patriarchal violence. *Int J Health Serv.* 1979;9:461-493.
9. Kurz D. Emergency department responses to battered women. *Soc Probl.* 1987;34:69-81.
10. Warshaw C. Limitations of the medical model in the care of battered women. *Gender Soc.* 1989; 3:506-517.
11. Kurz D, Stark E. Not-so-benign neglect. In: Yllo K, Bograd M, eds. *Feminist Perspectives on Wife Abuse.* Newbury Park, Calif: Sage Publications; 1988:249-265.
12. Gregory M. Battered wives. In: Borland M, ed., *Violence in the Family.* Atlantic Highlands, NJ: Humanities Press; 1976:107-128.
13. *The Federal Response to Domestic Violence.* Washington, DC: US Commission on Civil Rights; 1982.
14. Flitcraft AH. Violence, values, and gender. *JAMA.* 1992;267:3194-3195.
15. Sugg NH, Inui T. Primary care physicians' response to domestic violence. *JAMA.* 1992;267:3157-3160.
16. Burge SK. Violence against women as a health care issue. *Fam Med.* 1989;21:368-373.
17. Council on Ethical and Judicial Affairs, American Medical Association. Physicians and domestic violence. *JAMA.* 1992;267:3190-3193.
18. Novello AC. A medical response to domestic violence. *JAMA.* 1992;267:3132.
19. *The Compact Edition of the Oxford English Dictionary.* New York, NY: Oxford University Press; 1984;2:1388-1389.

20. Simmel A. Privacy. In: *International Encyclopedia of the Social Sciences.* New York, NY: Cromwell, Collier, & Macmillan; 1968;12:480-487.
21. Nicholson L. *Gender and History.* New York, NY: Columbia University Press; 1986.
22. Elshtain JB. Moral women and immoral man: a consideration of the public-private split and its political ramifications. *Polit Soc.* 1974;4:453-473.
23. Elshtain JB. *Public Man, Private Women.* Princeton, NJ: Princeton University Press; 1981.
24. Rosenblum NL. *Another Liberalism.* Cambridge, Mass: Harvard University Press; 1987.
25. Shklar JN. *The Faces of Injustice.* New Haven, Conn: Yale University Press; 1990.
26. Rosaldo MS. The use and abuse of anthropology. *Signs: J Women Culture Soc.* 1980;5:389-417.
27. Okin SM. Gender, the public and the private. In: Held D, ed. *Political Theory Today.* Stanford, Calif: Stanford University Press; 1991:67-90.
28. Rhode D. *Justice and Gender.* Cambridge, Mass: Harvard University Press; 1989.
29. Okin SM. *Justice, Gender, and the Family.* New York, NY: Basic Books Inc Publishers; 1989.
30. Okin SM. Humanist liberalism. In: Rosenblum NL, ed. *Liberalism and the Moral Life.* Cambridge, Mass: Harvard University Press; 1989:39-53.
31. Okin SM. Are our theories of justice gender-neutral? In: Fullinwider RK, Mills C, eds. *The Moral Foundations of Civil Rights.* Totowa, NJ: Rowman & Littlefield; 1986:125-143.
32. Conrad P, Schneider JW. Professionalization, monopoly, and the structure of medical practice. In: Conrad P, Kern R, eds. *The Sociology of Health and Illness.* 3rd ed. New York, NY: St Martin's Press; 1990:141-147.
33. Starr P. *The Social Transformation of American Medicine.* New York, NY: Basic Books Inc Publishers; 1982.
34. Jecker NS, Self DJ. Separating care and cure. *J Med Philos.* 1991;16:285-306.
35. American Medical Association. First code of medical ethics (1847). In: Riser SJ, Dyck AJ, Curran WJ, eds. *Ethics in Medicine: Historical Perspectives and Contemporary Concerns.* Cambridge, Mass: MIT Press; 1977:29-34.
36. Drachman VG. The Loomis trial: social mores and obstetrics in the mid-nineteenth century. In: Reverby S, Rosner D, eds. *Health Care in America: Essays in Social History.* Philadelphia, Pa: Temple University Press; 1979:67-83.
37. Council on Ethical and Judicial Affairs, American Medical Association. Principles of Medical Ethics. In: American Medical Association. *Current Opinions of the Council on Ethical and Judicial Affairs.* Chicago, Ill: American Medical Association; 1992:x.
38. Council on Ethical and Judicial Affairs, Amer-

ican Medical Association. Confidentiality. In: American Medical Association. *Current Opinions of the Council on Ethical and Judicial Affairs.* Chicago, Ill: American Medical Association; 1992:25.
39. *Roe v Wade*, US Supreme Court, 410 US 113, 93 SCt 705. January 22, 1973.
40. Rawls J. *A Theory of Justice.* Cambridge, Mass: Harvard University Press; 1971.
41. Nozick R. *Anarchy, State, and Utopia.* New York, NY: Basic Books Inc Publishers; 1974.
42. Walzer M. *Spheres of Justice: A Defense of Pluralism and Equality.* New York, NY: Basic Books Inc Publishers; 1983.
43. Council on Ethical and Judicial Affairs, American Medical Association. Sexual misconduct in the practice of medicine. In: American Medical Association. *Current Opinions of the Council on Ethical and Judicial Affairs.* Chicago, Ill: American Medical Association; 1992:40.
44. Council on Ethical and Judicial Affairs, American Medical Association. Ethical issues involved in the growing AIDS crisis. *JAMA.* 1988;259:1360-1361.
45. Buchanan A. Justice and charity. *Ethics.* 1987; 97:558-575.
46. Kim DS. How physicians respond to child maltreatment cases. *Health Soc Work.* 1986;11:95-106.
47. Centers for Disease Control. Education about domestic violence in US and Canadian medical schools, 1987-88. *MMWR.* 1989;38:17-19.
48. Rose K, Saunders DG. Nurses' and physicians' attitudes about women abuse. *Health Care Women Int.* 1986;17:427-438.
49. Straus MA, Gelles RI, Steinmetz S. *Behind Closed Doors: Violence in the American Family.* Garden City, NY: Anchor Press; 1980.
50. Council on Scientific Affairs, American Medical Association. Violence against women: relevance for medical practitioners. *JAMA.* 1992;267:3184-3189.
51. Langhinrichsen J, Vivian D. Marital aggression: impact, injury, and health correlates for husbands and wives. *Arch Intern Med.* 1992;152:1178-1184.
52. McFarlane J, Parker B, Soeken K, Bullock L. Assessing for abuse during pregnancy. *JAMA.* 1992; 267:3176-3178.
53. McLeer SV, Anwar RAH. The role of the emergency physician in the prevention of domestic violence. *Ann Emerg Med.* 1987;16:1155-1161.
54. Friedman LC, Samet JH, Roberts MS, et al. Inquiry about victimization. *Arch Intern Med.* 1992; 152:1186-1190.
55. Sommers CH. Filial morality. *J Philos.* 1986; 83:435-456.

[20]

Annu. Rev. Public Health. 1997. 18:401–36
Copyright © 1997 by Annual Reviews Inc. All rights reserved

REFRAMING WOMEN'S RISK:
Social Inequalities and HIV Infection

Sally Zierler

Department of Community Health, Brown University School of Medicine, Box G-A4, Providence, Rhode Island 02912; e-mail: sally_zierler@brown.edu

Nancy Krieger

Department of Health and Social Behavior, Harvard School of Public Health, 677 Huntington Avenue, Boston, Massachusetts 02115; e-mail: nkrieger@hsph.harvard.edu

KEY WORDS: AIDS, gender, racism, poverty, violence

ABSTRACT

Social inequalities lie at the heart of risk of HIV infection among women in the United States. As of December, 1995, 71,818 US women had developed AIDS-defining diagnoses. These women have been disproportionately poor, African-American, and Latina. Their neighborhoods have been burdened by poverty, racism, crack cocaine, heroin, and violence. To explain which women are at risk and why, this article reviews the epidemiology of HIV and AIDS among women in light of four conceptual frameworks linking health and social justice: feminism, social production of disease/political economy of health, ecosocial, and human rights. The article applies these alternative theories to describe sociopolitical contexts for AIDS' emergence and spread in the United States, and reviews evidence linking inequalities of class, race/ethnicity, gender, and sexuality, as well as strategies of resistance to these inequalities, to the distribution of HIV among women.

INTRODUCTION

In 1981, six women in the United States were noted to have an unexplained underlying cellular immune deficiency (70). It was a description of the same phenomenon among five previously healthy young gay white men, however, that prompted the 1981 MMWR report now viewed as the first official recognition of AIDS (23). A retrospective study of underlying causes of death suggested that 48 young women died of AIDS in the years 1980–1981 (30). Although not

401

0163-7525/97/0510-0401$08.00

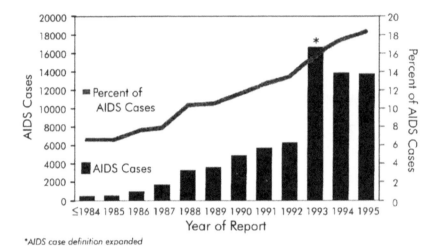

Figure 1 Women with AIDS. Number and percent of adult cases by report year, United States, 1984–1995.

described in that report, we imagine, based on what has been documented since then, that these women were young, between the ages of 15 and 44 years; their neighborhoods were poor and so were they; if they could get work, they were rarely earning wages to meet basic needs for food, child care, clothing, and shelter; mostly they depended on public assistance and men for economic survival. Most were also likely to have been women of color—African-American, Latina, Haitian, American Indian—who were raising young children. Unlike white gay men diagnosed with AIDS, sickness among these women was not unexpected. It was just a part of the ongoing, usual excess morbidity and mortality among the poor and racially oppressed.

Fifteen years later, in 1996, as the proportion of women among AIDS cases continues to rise from 6% in 1984 to 19% in 1995 (Figure 1), the vast majority of women with AIDS in the United States are still poor women of color (Table 1) of whom 75% were recorded as non-Hispanic black or Hispanic women (25). By the end of 1995, a total of 71,818 women with AIDS had been reported to the Centers for Disease Control (CDC). As of 1995, the estimated cumulative incidence in AIDS diagnoses was 12.4/100,000 women. One year earlier, in 1994, HIV infection supplanted heart disease as the third leading cause of death for women age 25 to 44, following cancer and unintentional injuries (26). Among black women in this age group, however, HIV infection ranks as the leading cause of death, accounting for over a fifth of deaths each year since 1993. In 1994, the death rate due to HIV among white women (including white Hispanic women) was 5.7 per 100,000, whereas it was over nine times higher among black women (including black Hispanic women) (51.2 deaths per

Table 1 Cumulative AIDS cases among women and incidence rate of AIDS in 1995 by race/ethnicity

Race/ethnicity	Cumulative number	Among women %	1995 new diagnoses per 100,000 woman-years
Black, not Hispanic	39,270	54.7	119.7
Hispanic	14,703	20.5	61.9
Asian/Pacific Islander	367	0.5	7.8
American Indian/Alaska Native	197	0.3	16.5
White, not Hispanic	17,187	24.0	18.5
Total	71,724	100.0	34.1

Source: CDC, Reference 25.

100,000 black women) (24). These estimates do not adjust for undercounting of HIV-related deaths among women injecting drug users.

What explains the vulnerability of these women to HIV? Why is it that economic deprivation and membership in groups defined, in part, by discrimination are so interwoven with risk of AIDS among women? Or more bluntly, how is it that women's relations with power in personal (as with sexual partners) and public life (as with opportunities for earning a living wage) shape the distribution of HIV in women?

Our central thesis is that the biology of transmission and infection—whether by sex or drugs—is inextricably bound to social and economic relations of race, class, gender, and sexuality. And it is these relations that overwhelmingly account for which women are at risk for HIV infection. Thus, this article, drawing on a variety of theories concerned with health and social justice, reframes HIV occurrence among women as a function of social, economic, and political conditions. We review studies that bring to light underlying causes of risk and discuss how such reframing would affect surveillance and production of knowledge about what drives the epidemic among women. Although we primarily limit this review to research on US women, we believe our framework and its applications are relevant to women in other countries. Our major premise is that the work of public health is not only to reduce human suffering, but to envision and create conditions of human health.

SOCIAL INEQUALITIES AND HIV IN WOMEN: SETTING THE CONTEXT

> The pain in our shoulder comes
> You say, from the damp; and this is also the reason
> For the stain on the wall of our flat.
> So tell us:
> Where does the damp come from?
> Bertolt Brecht (16)

404   ZIERLER & KRIEGER

How we explain and alter occurrence of HIV infection among women depends, in part, on conceptual frameworks that guide the collection and interpretation of data, as well as the design and implementation of policies and programs. To date, much of the literature on women and HIV has relied upon what can be termed biomedical (54, 94, 144), lifestyle (36, 143, 144), and psychological (2, 9, 13, 121, 127) theories of disease causation (Table 2). By contrast, in this article we rely upon four alternative conceptual frameworks to guide our review. These frameworks, summarized in Table 3, are: feminist (43, 75, 146, 147), social production of disease/political economy of health (15, 42, 52, 61, 89), ecosocial theory (82, 86), and human rights (101, 148). Overlapping yet distinct, these frameworks together make connections between disease and inequality on the one hand, and health and social justice on the other.

Economic Inequalities: Relevance of Poverty amidst Wealth

Fundamental to these four alternative frameworks is locating women socially and economically in US society around the time that AIDS emerged in the early 1980s. The deep recession in 1974–75, coupled with a decline in manufacturing jobs in cities, triggered urban fiscal crises that challenged city governments' ability to provide services "for increasingly poor, deteriorating, jobless and crime-ridden neighborhoods" (32). Poverty increased dramatically among residents of the five largest US cities, New York, Chicago, Los Angeles, Philadelphia, Detroit (158). Today, these five cities alone account for nearly a third of all AIDS cases (25).

Social and economic policies under the Reagan Administration (34, 167) dramatically increased spending on military programs and reduced taxation on the wealthy, both of which contributed to a ballooning federal deficit. The deficit, in turn, became justification for congressional and executive action to slash spending on social programs and oppose raising the minimum wage. Added to dramatic reduction in federally sponsored social services and decreased purchasing power of low wages were efforts to overturn affirmative action programs. Taken together, during the years 1980–1988, these actions pushed more than 1.1 million women with children below the poverty line (119). Of note were cutbacks in Aid to Families with Dependent Children (AFDC), the National Health Service Corps, the Community Health Center Program, and the Child Health Assurance Program, all of which had provided health services to poor women and their children. Because women most affected by these cuts were either employed in non-union, part-time, low-paying jobs without fringe benefits, or were unemployed but ineligible for Medicaid, they were unable to afford health insurance for themselves or their children (7). The burden of AIDS among women falls most heavily among the growing ranks of these impoverished women.

SOCIAL INEQUALITIES AND HIV IN WOMEN   405

Economic inequalities occurring in the 1990s, as in prior decades, are further compounded along gender and racial/ethnic lines, in ways that also shape distribution of HIV among women. In 1994, 13.1% of white women, 33.7% of African-American women, and 33.4% of Hispanic women lived below the official poverty line (equal to $7547 for one adult and $15,029 for two adults and two children) (150). Not reflected in these data is the fact that both degree and duration of poverty are more extreme for US black and Hispanic as compared to white populations, and for households headed by women compared to those headed by married couples (149, 150). Highlighting disparities in resources, in 1991, among households in the lowest 20% of the income distribution, the median net worth of black households was $1 and of Hispanic households was $645, compared with $10,257 among white households (50). In 1992, 16% of the black population and 11% of the Hispanic population lived below 50% of the poverty line, as compared to only 4% of the white population. For households with children under age 18, 30% of single female-headed households as compared to 3% of married households lived at 50% of the poverty line. Data from the US Survey of Income and Program Participation (SIPP) further show that between 1991 and 1993, black and Hispanic persons were two to three times more likely than white persons to be poor for one or two months during these two years and were four to five times more likely to be poor for the entire period (135).

The Growing Drug Economy, "War on Drugs," and Racism

Linked to political and economic trends of the 1980s is another social phenomenon directly affecting risk of, and experiences with, HIV infection among women: the increasingly prominent illegal drug economy and federal policies and law enforcement initiatives known as the "war on drugs" (99).

In the midst of decreasing educational and economic opportunity within the legal labor market, the allure of the illegal drug economy as a source of income became more powerful during the early 1980s. New possibilities for profitable mass consumption were also spurred by decreasing costs of production of the coca leaf into crack cocaine. In 1989, the House Select Committee on Narcotics Abuse and Control estimated the value of the drug market to be $100–150 billion annually, twice the US market for oil and half the value of all US currency in circulation (73).

Residents of neighborhoods fraught with economic impoverishment, social disintegration, and boredom were, and continue to be, susceptible to use of psychoactive drugs for relief and stimulation. Not surprisingly, higher prevalence of drug traffic and drug use occurs in such neighborhoods, including drugs linked to risk of HIV infection, such as crack, cocaine, and heroin (93, 99, 109, 151). Among the people living there are economically poor women of color

Table 2 Individual-level frameworks for studies of occurrence and prevention of HIV infection among women

Framework	Key question	Major assumptions	Application of framework to studies
Biomedical	How do humans, as biological organisms, become ill?	Knowledge based on scientific method viewed as objective, value-free, without ideologic or political influence Disease occurrence based on individual susceptibility to biologic, chemical, or physical exposures Population disease patterns are sums of affected individuals Solutions emerge from basic/clinical sciences	Relative efficiency of viral sexual transmission from men to women Vaginal mucosal immunity to HIV infection Female endocrine levels and HIV immunology Female genital tract inflammation and susceptibility to infection Female genital tract inflammation and HIV load HIV vaccine development Vaginal microbicides to prevent HIV infection Reducing HIV viral load
Behavioral/ lifestyle	How do individual behavioral and cultural factors affect health and disease?	Disease occurrence based on individual choices of ways of living Population disease patterns are sums of these individual choices Individuals voluntarily can alter these ways of living	"Mode of transmission" research, primarily sex with men and injection drug use Prostitution as risk factor Cultural factors attributed to membership in racial/ethnic groups
Psychological	What motivates individuals to change behaviors that increase risk for disease?		Measure change/reduction in individual risk-taking with sex and injection drugs

Health belief model	Perceiving behavior as detrimental to health will motivate change Perception of personal susceptibility to disease, severity of disease, and social support influence change
Theory of reasoned action	Intentions influence health behavior Social norms, attitudes, and perceived control affect intentions and influence change
Social cognitive theory	Health behavior is function of social incentives, vicarious learning/expectation Perceived self-efficacy in affecting change influences behavior
Stages of change	Health behavioral change structured by predictable sequence of readiness: precontemplation, contemplation, decision, action, maintenance Stage-specific interventions stimulate change to next stage in sequence

Table 3 Structural-level frameworks for studies of occurrence and prevention of HIV infection among women

Framework	Key question	Major assumptions	Application of framework to studies
Feminist	How do gender inequalities affect health of women (as well as men and children)?	Women's position and experiences in society are determined by social roles and conventions, not by biology. Relations of power between women and men affect health. Interventions to alter distribution of disease include social policies that secure and protect women's economic, legal and physical/sexual autonomy	Gender disparities in power and sexual risk of HIV. Gender-based patterns of injection drug sharing. Gender differences in socially sanctioned sexual expression. Sexual and physical violence against women as determinants of risk of HIV infection. Reproductive autonomy and HIV testing among pregnant women
Social production of disease; political economy of health	How do economic and social relations forged by society's economic, social, and political structure, affect health?	Relative social and economic positioning shapes behaviors. Relations between subordinate-dominant groups affect patterns of disease through material and social inequalities. Population level interventions shift structural conditions that cause material and social deprivation, thus altering societal distribution of disease	Social welfare policy, economic dependence on men, and risk of sexual HIV transmission to women. Social class position and HIV infection in women. Racism and onset of injection drug use among women at risk of HIV infection. Reduction in municipal fire protection, destruction of housing, and HIV incidence among women

Ecosocial	How do developmental and evolutionary biology interact with social, economic, and political conditions to explain population patterns of health, disease, and well-being?	Social relations and ecologic conditions literally incorporate themselves into the body throughout the life course	Thinness of peripubescent vaginal mucosal lining and vaginal susceptibility to HIV infection among girls who depend on older men economically, socially, and sexually Age-specific vaginal tract inflammation and HIV among women in relation to family history of activism in the Civil Rights Movement of the 1960s
Human rights	How do violations of human rights drive population patterns of disease?	Human dignity is a necessary condition for health Preconditions for human dignity imply good health Social, economic, and political conditions that endanger people's health are human rights violations Solutions to violations lie in moral, legal, social, and political challenges to fundamental structures of power	Effect of removing legal barriers to women's education on HIV incidence among women HIV incidence among drug-dependent pregnant women who live in states that criminalize drug use in pregnancy Effect of enforcing domestic violence ordinances and marital rape laws on HIV incidence among women

and the families they support. Young men living in these communities also have been and remain at extremely high risk of violent death, unemployment, and arrest.

Citing data on drug use statistics, during the 1980s the Reagan and Bush Administrations and law enforcement agencies escalated what federal officials and media termed the "war on drugs" (99). Drawing on military and police enforcement, this war on drugs emphasized interdiction, arrest, and imprisonment, an approach that garnered 70% of the $7.8 billion proposed by Bush in his 1989 National Drug Control Strategy. Relatively little money remained to support programs for drug treatment, prevention, and research (99). Political and legal response to the ensuing epidemic of crack use has included mandatory sentencing laws that are biased toward prosecution of poorer people, since crack possession and sale is more feasible than the more expensive powder form of cocaine. For example, distribution of five grams or more of crack, worth about $125 on the street, is a five-year mandatory sentence in prison. In contrast, it would take 500 grams of powder cocaine, worth about $50,000, to receive the same sentence. Reports indicate that 92% of people arrested for crack possession were black, whereas 85% of those arrested for cocaine powder were white (99).

The growing toll of drugs and the war on drugs on lives of women caught up in the drug economy is attested to by data on trends in arrests and incarceration. During the 1980s, most arrests among women had been for economic crimes linked to poverty and the drug economy (20). As a result of these arrest trends, state and federal prison systems reported a 230% increase in the numbers of women in their prisons between 1980 and 1989 (20). According to the Bureau of Justice Statistics, 72% of women in state prisons in 1986 reported a history of drug use, chiefly involving heroin and cocaine (20).

Bureau of Justice statistics further report that black and Hispanic women are disproportionately residents of US prisons and jails (21), most likely a consequence of racially selective enforcement of drug laws. The Washington DC Sentencing Project has released evidence that risk of incarceration is 7 to 44 times greater for black relative to white men, given the same crime (99). Although, to our knowledge, comparable data about women have not been published, a Florida study by the National Association for Prenatal Addiction Research and Education (NAPARE) discovered that physicians were ten times more likely to report black women to state authorities than white women (28), despite the fact that white women test positive for drug use during pregnancy at rates similar to black women (99).

Reflecting combined social forces driving risk of imprisonment and risk of HIV among women, in 1988–89, HIV seroprevalence among incarcerated women across ten US correctional facilities was estimated to be 2.5 to 14.7%

(152). Yet during the same period, the Survey of Childbearing Women estimated overall HIV seroprevalence among US women to be 0.15% (71, 140). Thus, incarcerated women have 16.7 to 98 times the prevalence of HIV relative to the average prevalence of childbearing women measured in the CDC national survey.

FRAMING RISK OF HIV INFECTION AMONG WOMEN: A REVIEW OF THE LITERATURE

Women living with and at high risk of HIV infection by and large have borne the brunt of persistent, and also deepening, forms of economic and social inequality. These inequalities, and women's strategies for living within and against them, make intelligible observed population patterns of HIV among women both in the United States and elsewhere.

To keep in the forefront a vision of women capable of passion and playfulness, of hard work and creativity, of loving parenting and strong kinship, people who desire full participation in society, to be generative and to make a difference in the world, these are the women about whom we are writing. Pushing against such vital possibility are the challenges of economic and political forces and structures that threaten and often take these lives and the lives of their loved ones. Women's struggles with and resistance to social and economic subordination include strategies for survival that bear the burden of drug use, violence, hunger, social disintegration, and sexual risk. It is in this light that we review evidence linking risk of HIV infection among women in the United States to inequalities involving social class, race/ethnicity, gender, and sexuality, guided by the four theories we have described (Table 3): feminist, political economy of health/social production of disease, ecosocial, and human rights. Recognizing how processes of subordination and resistance simultaneously play out at multiple levels over their life course, we accordingly present data, when available, on the embodiment of risk of HIV infection in relation to inequalities manifest at the national or regional, neighborhood, household, and individual level, from childhood to the time at which girls or women become infected by HIV.

Economic Inequalities and HIV in Women

Among the first public health articles to frame women's experience with HIV infection within the larger social and economic conditions in their lives was the Health/PAC Bulletin's powerful commentary by Anastos & Marte in 1989, which drew on both feminist and political economy of health analyses (8). Noting the invisibility of women in the CDC surveillance definition, research agenda, and prevention programs, the authors recounted how public health portrayal of women was as vectors of transmission to babies and to their male sexual partners with little regard for women's right to be seen, to be counted, and to be availed resources that would protect them. By contrast, Anastos & Marte urged that health professionals care about women not because they may be pregnant, mothers, prostitutes, caregivers, or sexual partners, but because women were deserving of good health and fair access to the resources that promote this. The authors wrote not about drug use and sex, but rather, about where women were situated geographically and socially. "... for many women", Anastos & Marte noted, "their address alone places them at risk ... poor black and Latina women are at unduly high risk for infection, whatever their life-style, because poverty and lack of resources and opportunity keep them in areas of high HIV seroprevalence" (8, p. 10).

Few studies have linked regional economic conditions in the United States with prevalence of HIV. Among them is a set of studies by Drucker (45) and Wallace (154, 155). Building upon a political economy of health framework, they dissect relationships between urban crises in housing, depleted city budgets, poor schools, and unemployment, and how these economic conditions led to dislocation of residents, dissolution of family and other social networks, and spread of AIDS. One study, for example, employed analytic techniques of population and community ecology, quantitative geography, and epidemiology to link reduction in public services to poor neighborhoods in the Bronx to subsequent high concentrations of HIV prevalence (154). Between 1972 and 1976, during the severe economic recession of the 1970s, the New York City Fire Department reduced staff by 30% within geographic areas with high fire rates and high population density. These neighborhoods were also among the poorest in the city, lacking in political influence to maintain services. "By 1980, 50 to 80% of housing had been destroyed, a figure unprecedented in an industrialized nation not involved in total war. Where communities once lived, hulks of burned and abandoned buildings and vacant lots remained ... Both the devastated zones and nearby communities experienced rising rates of homicide, suicide, drug and alcohol abuse, HIV infection and AIDS ... the fate of the South Bronx reflects the vulnerability to HIV infection created by processes of urban decay already widespread in many US cities" (154).

Three additional US studies provide population-based evidence of strong relationships between incidence of AIDS in large urban areas and neighborhood level income (55, 74, 136). Linking AIDS incidence data to 1990 census-based socioeconomic data from the zip code or census tract level, these studies analyzed socioeconomic inequalities in AIDS occurrence within three cities: Philadelphia, PA (54), Newark, NJ (74), and Los Angeles, CA (136). They found that incidence of AIDS was between 2 and 13 times higher in low-income areas compared to high-income areas. Although one study reported an inverse relationship between AIDS incidence and income among four racial/ethnic groups (white, black, Hispanic, and Asian/Pacific Islander Americans) (136), none of these studies reported results for incidence of AIDS among women, nor did they analyze AIDS or neighborhood income data in relation to issues of urban economies or policies.

Although incidence of HIV and AIDS among women in the United States in relation to social class remains undocumented, several studies have noted conditions of poverty and accompanying economic challenges in the lives of women with or at risk of HIV infection. For example, an ongoing five-year NIDA study to reduce HIV occurrence among women who have injected drugs and smoked crack described the extent of social and material deprivation among 887 women from low-income, inner-city neighborhoods in Los Angeles (18). Most of the women received their primary economic support from male sex partners, or from public assistance programs. Nearly all of the women reported a monthly income of less than $1000. Similar levels of economic poverty have been reported by two ongoing national cohorts of women living with HIV infection, based on populations of women from ten major US cities: the HIV Epidemiology Study (HERS) and the Women's Interagency HIV Study (WIHS). Together enrolling nearly 3000 women with HIV infection and a comparison group of approximately 1000 seronegative women, these two studies confirm that most women with HIV in the United States are living and caring for children amidst severe poverty (10, 108).

Feminist analyses, moreover, would suggest that women with or at risk of HIV infection might be economically more destitute than their male counterparts. Supporting this contention, data from the NIDA National AIDS Demonstration Research (NADR) programs, enrolling 6609 women injection drug users, has shown that women are much less likely to be earning a legal income than men and therefore more reliant upon other means of support. Nearly 30% of the women were dependent upon male partners for economic support, and 42% said they relied on illegal means of income, mostly involving sex work. These women were also two times more likely than men to have children living with them (19), implying that their already low incomes needed to be stretched that much further.

Similarly, an interview-based study (41) of 428 women and 2470 men diagnosed with AIDS in 11 US states measured education, recent household income, and current employment. Women fared worse than men for all three aspects of socioeconomic position. Overall, half the women had not completed high school, most were unemployed, and 77% had an annual household income of less than $10,000. Suggesting that black women experienced more severe deprivation than white women, nearly all black women versus three quarters of the white women had an annual family income under $10,000. Additionally, among women living with AIDS and reporting injection drug use histories, black women were nearly two times more likely not to have completed high school than US black women, overall, based on US census data (63% vs 32%); for white women, the corresponding proportions were more similar (29% versus 20%). The authors noted that although employment and income data may have reflected consequences of AIDS rather than conditions at time of diagnosis, their report included data on persons infected with HIV but free of AIDS-defining symptoms. Among this subgroup, 84% of women and 58% of men were unemployed. Further supporting the hypothesis that associations of social class and HIV progression were not simply a consequence of job loss due to illness, a Canadian study based on white gay men (131) measured social class in relation to job category and income before men were aware of their HIV status and before they had symptomatic disease. That study found a direct inverse relation between social class and rate of disease progression.

Because of paucity of US research explicitly examining women's risk of HIV infection in relation to economic inequality and economic policies, we mention briefly several non-US studies that explore these issues. One relevant analysis of social class and HIV in Brazil described conditions comparable to women in US cities (96). This cross-sectional study of 600 women in three cities who depended on sex with men for money, drugs, or gifts at least once in the previous month found that lower social class position was associated with higher prevalence of HIV infection. In fact, women in the lowest social class stratum were more than four times more likely to have HIV infection relative to women in higher social class stratum (17% versus 4%), independent of HIV prevalence in the cities where women lived and worked.

Also documenting the centrality of women's economic resources and strategies for survival in relation to HIV infection are several anthropologic case studies and ethnographies conducted outside of the United States (52, 53, 118, 132). For example, Farmer has tracked rising water from construction of a hydroelectric plant that dammed Haiti's largest river to spread of AIDS among families forced to relocate from their original farmlands to higher, less fertile ground. In a context of deepening poverty, Farmer tells the story of women becoming sexually involved with men who might offer women alternatives to destitution in their lives. As said by Acephie Joseph, who later died of AIDS, "... I looked around and saw how poor we all were, how the old people were finished.... It was a way out, that's how I saw it" (53, p. 389). Political economy of health analyses of AIDS as a disease of development have linked spread of HIV to global economic interests structured by the World Bank and International Monetary Fund (11, 52, 78, 97, 132). Schoepf, for example, has described how women in Zaire have survived amidst macroeconomic conditions that underscore already pervasive gender inequality in the labor market and in childbearing decision-making. Strapped with responsibilities for childcare and wage-earning amidst extreme conditions of poverty, women "engage in ... activities in the informal sector," usually involving sex for material sustenance, sometimes at the request of their families for purchasing land or building materials or to repay debts. Men, less constrained by caring for children, have sought wages from jobs that involved traveling or living away from home for long periods of time. These labor migrations became a source of HIV infection among men as they sought sexual contact with women or men along their routes. Upon returning home, these men then introduced HIV into their families (132). Analyses of women and AIDS in Zimbabwe (11) and South Africa (78) have reported comparable findings.

Finally, use of race/ethnicity as a marker for social class has been inferred by a number of US studies (26, 37). The underlying assumption has been that higher rates of HIV infection among populations of color reflect the greater poverty among them than among white populations. However, not having explicit data on social class to support such an interpretation conflates issues of class position with another important dimension of racial/ethnic categories: racism.

Race/Racism and HIV in Women

To our knowledge, no published studies have expressly measured racism in the lives of women at risk for, or living with, HIV infection. Among epidemiologic studies and commentaries proposing to measure "racial" differences in HIV risk or disease progression, investigators have interpreted their findings in at least one of four ways: first, that racial/ethnic differences reflect underlying biologic differences (for example, see Reference 95, 129); second, that race/ethnicity is a marker for social class position; third, that racial/ethnic categories reflect culture; and fourth, that racial/ethnic disparities result from social processes of racial domination, subordination, and resistance, reflected in US histories of expropriation, conquest, slavery, and discrimination.

Interpreting racial/ethnic differences as markers for biological differences is problematic because race is not a biologic construct but a social one. The notion that race/ethnicity denotes biological groups with genetic distinctions has long been discounted scientifically, and we refer our readers to some of the many books and articles on this subject (35, 80, 84). As this scholarship has demonstrated, racial categories instead have been created by oppressive systems of race relations that emphasize distinctions based on selective physical characteristics. The weak link between these characteristics and so-called race-specific diseases accounts for only a minute percentage of each racial group's overall morbidity and even less of their mortality (120). Sickle cell anemia, for example, the one known potentially fatal black-linked disease, accounted for only 0.3% of the 37% higher age-adjusted death rate in 1977 for the US black as compared to white population (35).

Second, although disparities in socioeconomic conditions may partially explain racial/ethnic inequalities in health, these racial/ethnic differences in AIDS incidence persist within class strata (136). Persistence of these differences may reflect residual confounding due to inadequate measurement of socioeconomic position, noneconomic aspects of racial discrimination, or differences in cultural practices unrelated to inequality. We recognize that important dimensions of race/ethnicity derive from shared culture, ancestry, and also, histories of racial/ethnic domination and struggle (1, 35, 104). To speak, however, of "African-American", "Hispanic", or less commonly "white" or "Anglo", culture obscures large differences among people from different countries and from different regions within those countries (including the United States) and also reduces rich, complex, and heterogeneous histories, customs, and norms to a single experience. What people in a subordinated racialized group do share, however, that has bearing on HIV risk is their membership in a racially oppressed group, although the history and structure of their oppression may differ. The conflation of "culture" with sociopolitical conditions that force community and individual adaptation to discrimination and dehumanization is not useful. First, it continues to hold accountable, solely, the "communities" of African-American and Hispanic/Latino people for the dangerous conditions in their lives, without mention of how these conditions have been shaped by white Euro-Americans; and second, it reinforces a legacy of scientific racism, promulgated by basic and social scientists, that there are inherent cultural norms that drive the racial/ethnic distribution of HIV as well as other damaging conditions. [See, for example, Rushton & Bogaert's sociobiological account of racial differences in AIDS susceptibility (129) and Leslie's rebuttal (91), addressing both biological and cultural determinism.]

How might racism affect HIV risk in women? Although no empirical studies on racism against women and HIV have been published to date, we hypothesize that both economic and noneconomic forms of racism create conditions affecting women's risk. First, several commentaries on racial/ethnic disparities in AIDS have called attention to economic inequalities rooted in racial discrimination as a cause of HIV infection (38, 63, 64, 72, 83, 104, 145, 160). Following a political economy of health framework, these commentaries emphasize that excess relative risk of AIDS among communities of color, notably African-American and Latina people, reflect underlying forces of discrimination in employment, housing, earning power, and educational opportunity (72, 122, 145). Living amidst such constraints, social and economic strategies for work, play, and love may involve more risk for drug use, partnerships with drug users, and income-earning strategies that include sex and drugs than among people living free of constraints imposed by racial subordination.

SOCIAL INEQUALITIES AND HIV IN WOMEN   417

Second, noneconomic expressions of racism could increase risk of HIV infection among women. In response to daily assaults of racial prejudice (51)
and denial of dignity (59), women may turn to readily available mind-altering
substances for relief as well as for self-medication from depression (12, 33).
Seeking sanctuary from racial hatred through sexual connection as a way to
enhance self-esteem, gain social status, and feel emotional comfort may offer
rewards so compelling that condom use becomes less of a priority (76). Women
would be at particular risk if such drug and sexual activities occurred within
communities affected by residential hypersegregation into deteriorating neighborhoods. Such segregation, enforced by racial discrimination in housing and
limited economic options, creates concentrated pockets of HIV prevalence and
other sexually transmitted diseases. These other sexually transmitted diseases,
untreated in a context of inaccessible health care services or inhospitable treatment by providers, have been implicated as cofactors for vaginal susceptibility
to HIV infection (103). Additionally, racism construed as a psychosocial stress-
or might increase biological susceptibility to infection, since studies have found
that social stressors may impair immune function (see Reference 76 for a review of this research). Although studies have not yet measured how racism and
resistance to racism may affect women's risk of infection, effects of racism on
health in other contexts have begun to be measured and demonstrated in relation
to elevated blood pressure (85, 157) and impaired mental health (33, 44, 110).

Although not specific to women, some research has documented how recent
awareness of atrocities of scientific misconduct in the 40-year Tuskegee Syphilis
Study has carried over into suspicion of the origins of AIDS and motives for
public health and medical interventions (38, 72, 145). Concerns about genocide
may be an understandable barrier to trusting knowledge and recommendations
emerging from scientific research, which may in turn have delayed prevention
action among people of color. A 1990 survey of 1054 African-American church
members conducted by the Southern Christian Leadership Conference reported
that 35% of people believed that AIDS was a mechanism of racial genocide;
30% were unsure if this was true (122). In addition, public health messages
that women with HIV should use condoms and not become pregnant ignore
a legacy of sterilization abuse and other forms of population control against
women of color. As Levine & Dubler wrote: "One need not accept the concept
of an active governmental policy of genocide to appreciate the power of the loss
of a generation of men through societal neglect and the community's desire to
replace them through the birth of a new generation" (92a, p. 335).

On the other hand, racial injustice may be a basis for collective resistance
and generating responses that protect communities from HIV infection. Some
investigators have recognized the power of social networks in affecting social

change among subordinated groups (45, 63, 104). As Friedman has noted, this approach moves

> beyond the common view of minorities as deprived and subordinated, and thus, as less able than whites to protect themselves against the epidemic, while recognizing that blacks and Hispanics are indeed subjected to relations of dominance and inequality that leave them with lower levels of material resources and of formal education than whites. . . . In addition to deprivation, subordination, and pathology, however, minorities are constantly developing resources and dynamics of their own that aid their individual and collective struggles for survival, dignity, and happiness (63, p. 456; see also Reference 114).

For example, in the AIDS Community Demonstration Project in New York, women sex workers organized with HIV investigators to bring effective race-conscious messages for rebuilding community at the same time as they teach women how to protect themselves from HIV transmission.

Gender Inequalities in Relation to Sex, Violence, and Drugs

Women's risk of HIV infection may also be linked to both economic and noneconomic forms of gender-based inequality, especially as these pertain to sex, violence, and illicit drugs. Economic forms of gender inequality that increase HIV risk are apparent in relation to women's socially structured dependence on men for material and economic resources. Such dependence comes from economic and family structures that preclude women from comparable wages and access to jobs, as well as from compensation for responsibilites of child and other family care. As we review, a number of studies have documented how such dependence translates into women being in the difficult position of having to risk loss of income, food, housing, and social nurturing requiring money (such as theater, traveling, music, and recreation) to prevent HIV infection with men who may not be willing to use condoms. Even if not dependent on men for material support, women may depend on the social and personal esteem that comes from being in a heterosexual couple. Before adulthood, young girls' vulnerability to experiences of gender-based violence, such as incestuous sexual and physical abuse, lay the groundwork for drug and alcohol addiction and dissociated sexuality in which women may not be aware of their right and capability to claim when, how, and with whom they are sexual. And finally, gendered social roles play out in the social experience of drug use, just as they do in other aspects of women's everyday lives.

The proportion of AIDS cases in women attributed to sex with men has steadily increased from 15% in 1983 to 38% in 1995. In 1995, among women reported to have acquired AIDS from sex with men, 37% of cases were attributed to sex with men who injected drugs. The remainder of AIDS cases among women having sex with men were attributed to sex with a partner with HIV infection whose risk was unreported or unknown (54%), sex with a bisexual man (7%), sex with a transfusion recipient (1%), and sex with a man with hemophilia (1%) (25). Although injection drug use remains the predominant mode of transmission among women with AIDS in the Northeast, the number of women reported to have acquired HIV from sex with men exceeds the number infected through injection drug use in the South, the Midwest, and the West. Noninjection drugs, in particular smokeable freebase cocaine ("crack"), have been linked to male sexual transmission of HIV to women (27, 48, 65). Among crack users, the practice of exchanging drugs for sex with multiple partners has led to intersecting epidemics of syphilis and HIV, each enhancing transmission of the other (27, 48).

GENDER INEQUALITY AND SEX   Women's experiences of sex with men may include unsafe sex with the possibility of HIV transmission within a context that is about mutual and loving expression of shared desire. However, when expressions of sexuality preclude condom use because of fear of loss of material support for women or their children, or because of beliefs that women should not make sexual demands of men, or because of fear that male sexual partners will react violently to discussions of low risk sex, it is gender inequality that is driving women's risk of HIV infection.

Evidence of these connections comes from studies documenting that economic dependence on men who are primary partners affects women's perception of or practice in influencing partners' use of condoms (4, 29, 117). A study of African-American women in Los Angeles found that women who depended on their male partners for financial assistance for housing were more likely to have sex without condoms than women who did not depend on men for economic reasons (161). By contrast among women who expressly have sex with male clients for economic purposes, condom use was more frequent in that setting than with their primary partners (96).

Noneconomic disparities between women and men also affect risk. Amaro summarized interviews with 2527 Latina women in the Northeast United States on reasons for engaging in sex with men who do not use condoms. Women "expressed feelings of powerlessness, low self-esteem, isolation, lack of voice, and inability to affect risk reduction decisions or behaviors with their partners" (4). Studies have also found that condom use was less likely when women reported needing men for social status (117) or physical protection because they lived on the streets (56), or when teenage and young women were sexual with older men (3, 100).

GENDER-BASED VIOLENCE   As feminist and human rights analyses emphasize, girls and women can be victimized by men regardless of economic circumstances. Political economy of health and ecosocial approaches further

420   ZIERLER & KRIEGER

contextualize these experiences by theorizing how state-sponsored, public, and private expressions of violence interact with material and social deprivation over women's life course.

In the case of women and HIV infection, past and present experiences with violence can affect risk in several ways. First, childhood sexual abuse, noted repeatedly to have occurred in alarming prevalence among women currently infected as well as women living amidst conditions of increasing risk for infection, has profound, long-term impacts on psychological and physical health. Most relevant to HIV risk are sequelae that include high-risk sex, prostitution, crack use, injection drug use, recurrent sexual assault, homelessness and incarceration (77, 87, 115, 134, 159, 164, 166). Studies of incarcerated women (6, 39), homeless women (56), women in drug treatment programs (159) as well as active drug-dependent women (17, 115, 164, 166) enrolled in street outreach studies report prevalences of early sexual abuse ranging from 30 to 80%. Among women living with HIV infection, nearly half report forced sexual experiences in childhood or teenage years (40, 153, 163, 166). The preponderance of evidence that childhood and adolescent sexual abuse predisposes young women to drug using and sexual experiences links this trauma to HIV risk.

Teenage girls and women most at risk for HIV infection are likely to have witnessed or been affected by violence in their neighborhoods. Among 246 Detroit inner-city, mostly African-American youth ages 18–23, a group at high risk for HIV infection, 42% had seen someone shot or knifed, 22% had seen someone killed, and 9% had seen more than one person killed (133). Studies from other cities (47, 57, 142) find similar estimates of exposure, even among very young children. One in ten children (average age 2.7 years) attending Boston City Hospital had witnessed a shooting or stabbing before the age of six, half in the home and half in the street (142). In a recent study of young adult women prisoners' experiences with violence, over 85% reported at least one victim experience, nearly 70% reported abuse by male sexual partners, and 75% reported being robbed, or physically or sexually assaulted by strangers (88).

A second link between violence and HIV infection in women is how violence or fear of violence affects women's ability to protect themselves sexually (66, 163). Studies of over 2000 women in drug treatment programs and women who were sexual partners of male injection drug users in San Juan, Juarez, Boston, Los Angeles, and San Diego found that 42% of women were sexual with men who physically hurt them; 45% were sexual with men who threatened women with violence; and 21% said they had sex with men because of fear of physical harm if they refused (17). A recent Baltimore study of risk of partner violence among women during their most recent childbearing year revealed that women living in the poorest neighborhoods with high unemployment and high HIV

SOCIAL INEQUALITIES AND HIV IN WOMEN   421

prevalence were found to be most at risk for partner violence (112). A study of Brazilian sex workers further found that 23% of women reported fear of violence if they insisted that clients wear condoms, and the prevalence of this concern tripled when requesting condom use with men whom they regarded as "non clients" (96).

A third connection between HIV experiences and violence emerges in a context of homelessness among women. Twenty-two to 86% of homeless women cite domestic abuse as their reason for being homeless (56, 106, 168), and without a safe place to live, women faced dangers of street life that included exposure to HIV from rape, sex for economic survival, and drugs. A study of women who had been homeless for at least three months (56) reported that 15% had been raped while homeless in the last year. Interestingly, the authors noted that homeless women with the least risk for HIV infection were those who asserted that they did not have male "protectors" in the streets.

A fourth implication of these data, although not directly related to women's risk of HIV infection, is that if women at risk for HIV infection are living within relationships that include violence, then women already infected may be living in similar conditions. In fact, studies bear this out. In the WIHS multisite cohort study of HIV-infected women, 67% reported sexual or physical violence by a current or past partner, and in nearly a third of women this occurred in the past year. Prevalence of partner violence in this cohort heightened to 83% among women who were current injection drug users and 81% among women who depended on sex for money, drugs, or shelter (40). Limited empirical data, moreover, indicate that women's disclosure of HIV infection itself may be a trigger for partner violence (68, 128). Because of these findings, Rothenberg and others (68, 111) have proposed that state-level policies of partner notification may be dangerous to women. This danger stems from a premise that disclosure obligations may risk harm to women if they are required to inform violent sexual partners of possible exposure to HIV infection (111, 128). Further arguing against the ethics of mandatory partner notification is evidence that the risk of violence women face by disclosing their HIV status is greater than the risk their male partners face of female-to-male sexual transmission of HIV (113).

In considering issues of gender-based violence in the lives of women at risk of or living with HIV infection, a political economy of health framework further underscores that men inflicting this violence are also likely to be living amidst conditions of economic and social hardship. We emphasize men inflicting violence against women because research documents that this is the dominant form of interpersonal violence against women. To our knowledge, lesbian interpersonal violence has not been described in relation to HIV (163) in the published literature. Sharing with women positions of similar class and racial/ethnic inequalities, men additionally carry distinct gendered authority and social roles that, in a context of poverty, have limited room for healthy expression. As people who may use violence against women, these men also may have experienced assaults against their own humanity through racial discrimination, economic impoverishment, and the social alienation that accompanies it. Thus, the brutally logical concurrence of violence and HIV happens within a larger structural control of social and economic resources and their distribution.

GENDER INEQUALITIES AND ILLICIT DRUGS   Gender inequalities may affect social patterning of illicit drug use that has bearing on women's risk of HIV infection. This social patterning spans from onset to dependency and extends to drug treatment. A number of studies have observed that heterosexual teenage girls and women were more likely to begin and to continue drug use with boyfriends and male partners. Men, on the other hand, were more likely to begin and then continue to share drugs with male friends and associates (5, 19, 46, 126, 138).

Effect of these patterns of women's risk may depend on characteristics of social networks and HIV prevalence in the region where these networks form (60). Friedman and colleagues (62) reported that among injection drug users living in a high HIV-seroprevalence area who had been injecting drugs for less than ten years, women were more likely than men to become HIV infected. This observation was most apparent among women using drugs in "high-risk networks" (defined as social networks that included older, and therefore more likely to have HIV, injectors, or injectors only recently known to women, suggesting more rapid turnover in network members and thus exposure to a greater number of high-risk injectors over time). One study reported that women injectors with at least three different male sex partners in the past six months were 5.1 times more likely to seroconvert than women injectors with less than three partners over that period (137).

Preliminary findings from ethnographic research note that once a pattern of regular drug use has begun, women's networks are more likely to depend on men for locating, purchasing, and bringing home drugs (P Case, personal communication). Women's autonomy in exercising options for harm reduction, for example, through needle exchange programs, or for drug treatment, may be met with resistance by male partners. Studies have documented that, compared to men, women were less likely to receive support from primary partners and from family members for seeking treatment from drug addiction (5, 14).

In fact, recent reports from needle exchange projects suggest that women's positions in social networks of drug use reflect larger social roles and expectations (114). Women tend to present at needle exchange sites at lower proportions than men, with various sites reporting 25 to 32% are women (98). In part, this may reflect a lower proportion of women injection drug users, but

SOCIAL INEQUALITIES AND HIV IN WOMEN   423

also, women may not use needle exchange sites for several reasons related to gender. First, in a heterosexual construct, social norms dictate that men handle tasks of obtaining drugs and syringes for their women sexual partners (P Case, personal communication). In a Boston needle exchange study, 70% of women who shared syringes reported sharing only with their male sexual partner, in contrast to 16% of men reporting sharing syringes with their female sexual partners (P Case, preliminary data). A second reason for women's lower attendance is that their male partners may not allow them to participate in needle exchange programs, as suggested by a communication about a San Francisco needle exchange program. One woman stated, "He told me either he goes [to the needle exchange site] or nobody goes" (S Murphy, personal communication, Women, Inc., San Francisco). Women at this site also reported being intimidated by male drug and sexual partners who threatened to withhold drugs and sterile equipment if women tried to get them for themselves (156; S Murphy, personal communication). A third reason women have reported not scoring drugs or visiting needle exchange sites was because the neighborhoods where they would have had to travel were too dangerous. Related to this were reports from the San Francisco program that women felt harrassed as they waited in line to exchange their needles because of men wanting women to give them drugs or to have sex with them. Fourth, public identity as a drug user carries more stigma for women than for men (66, 126), thereby reducing women's willingness to be seen in programs exclusively designated as needle exchange sites. S Murphy of Prevention Point, a San Francisco needle exchange program, tells this story (personal communication): To improve women's access to clean needles, a San Francisco program created an indoor needle exchange site for women at an existing multiservice women's center. Thus, women attending the site for needles were not identifiable as drug users merely because they came to the center. Still, as one of the organizers of this site noted, women at first were reluctant to use the program. To encourage their attendance, the program offered grocery vouchers. The resulting increased attendance included men who were also hungry for food, for when they learned that this site was giving out grocery vouchers, some dressed as women so that they would be able to feed themselves as well as obtain clean needles.

An additional way gender can affect women's safer use of drugs and opportunities for treatment is that women who are mothers risk criminalization for their drug dependence and subsequent loss of their children. At the same time, treatment programs for pregnant and parenting women are relatively few and often full. A New York City survey of 78 drug treatment centers (29) found that 54% of them excluded pregnant women, and 87% denied services to pregnant crack users, even if they had Medicaid insurance to pay for them. Thus, criminalization of both drug use and pregnancy in a context of drug dependence force women to hide their drug use (124), which in turn limits their access to whatever programs might be available to them and their children, prolonging use and increasing risk of HIV infection (79, 92).

Sexual Identity as a Source of Inequality in Lesbian Risk for HIV Infection

Five instances of female-to-female sexual transmission of HIV have been documented in the literature (102, 107, 116, 123, 130). In a review of AIDS cases in women who reported sexual contact only with other women (n = 164), 152 women (93%) injected drugs and 12 (7%) had a history of a blood transfusion before March 1985; no cases were attributed to female-to-female sexual transmission of HIV (31). In a serosurvey of 498 women who have sex with women recruited through public venues, 1.2% were HIV infected; all infected women reported either a history of injection drug use or sexual contact with men (90). Data from the National AIDS Demonstration Project reported 2.1% HIV seropositivity among women injecting drug users who had sex with women (60). The authors attributed this level of infection to social networks of women drug users who were likely to have shared drug injection equipment and to have had sexual activities with women and men who were sexual with men.

Inequalities involving sexual identity may also affect women's risk. Legal rights of lesbians and gay men are not protected by federal law, although some states and municipalities have laws that prohibit discrimination in the areas of housing, employment, and public accommodation. Nearly half of states in the United States have sodomy laws that are selectively enforced against gay people, and although lesbians are rarely prosecuted under these laws, their continued legitimacy underscores a social message that sexual intimacy and love between women is unacceptable, and even perhaps dangerous to society. In such a climate, women who identify as lesbian who also are living in conditions of poverty, drug dependence, and reliance on sex work for economic support, face considerable challenges in avoiding HIV infection.

To our knowledge, no studies have examined how sexual identity as lesbian may influence risk of HIV infection. The sparse data published or presented to date on lesbians and HIV infection suggest that apart from sexual identity and frequency of sex with men, lesbians share similar conditions of poverty and gender and racial/ethnic subordination as women who identify as heterosexual and bisexual (165). Because data on sexual identity were not included for most published studies on HIV infection in women, distinctions between identity (as lesbian, bisexual, or heterosexual) and practice (sex with women, with men, or both) have been blurred. These distinctions may matter, since women who identify as lesbian may have experiences of social isolation and discrimination in addition to those resulting from class, gender, and racial/ethnic position (141, 165).

The two largest ongoing cohorts of women living with HIV infection have reported that 18% (165) and 25% (10) have had sex with other women, but across both studies, less than a fifth of women reporting sex with women actually identified as lesbian. Moreover, between 10 and 20% of these lesbian-identified women reported recent sexual activity with men (among women in the WIHS, 11% of HIV positive and 9% of uninfected lesbians, and among women in the HERS, 19% of seropositive and 14% of seronegative women reported sex with men in the previous six months).

Community-based agencies may be unaware that their messages to women for HIV prevention typically assume heterosexual identity; by excluding those who identify as lesbian, these agencies may erroneously signal that lesbians are not at risk. Furthermore, safer sex messages directed to lesbians have emphasized prevention of woman-to-woman transmission despite the fact that the overwhelming experience of lesbians with AIDS is in a context of injection drug use and sex with men (10, 49, 90, 162, 165).

Thus, labels of sexual identity, seen in this larger context, hardly distinguish sexual and drug using behavior as markers for HIV risk, apart from self-evident differences in distribution of gender of sexual partners. What stands out instead are the shared difficult experiences of lesbian, bisexual, and heterosexual women living amidst severe material and social deprivation.

RESEARCH RECOMMENDATIONS

Returning to our initial question—what accounts for the distribution of HIV among women in the United States—the data we have reviewed offer an explanation for causes of HIV incidence among women. Fundamental determinants of HIV risk among women are social inequalities involving class, race/ethnicity, gender, and sexuality. These inequalities and women's responses to them explain why women most afflicted by AIDS in the United States are predominantly African American and Latina women living in conditions of economic hardship. In this context, women's rightful efforts toward creating lives replete with love, meaningful work, and economic security within safe households, workplaces, and neighborhoods may be thwarted into desperate strategies for survival that increase risk of exposure to HIV in infected semen or infected blood. Continued efforts to explain biologic mechanisms to reduce susceptibility and to develop effective vaccines and therapeutics to reduce viral replication are critical. This review emphasizes HIV infection as a biologic expression of inextricably connected social experience.

Research explicitly investigating how social inequalities structure women's risk of HIV is in its infancy and needs to be expanded. Inherent in women's risk are how social inequalities affect lives of men and women who are their family,

friends, acquaintances, drug partners, and lovers. Women with and at risk
of HIV are mothers, daughters, lovers, caregivers, companions, workers, vital
members of their communities, part of the fabric of our society. Their deaths
leave behind bereaved friends, relatives, and lovers, as well as an ever-growing
number of orphans, estimated to be as high as 125,000–150,000 children by
the year 2000 (22, 92, 105). To staunch these losses means developing social and biological (69, 139) strategies to prevent HIV from entering women's
bodies.

Surveying the first decade of public health efforts to understand and prevent
the AIDS epidemic, Freudenberg concluded, "The future direction of this epidemic depends as much on what happens in the political arena as it does on
new discoveries in the laboratories or on hospital wards. . . . AIDS prevention
effort has to be connected with a vision of a better world" (58, p. 70). Research
and interventions primarily concerned with measuring and promoting use of
condoms and clean needles, or sustaining energy of AIDS workers, and even
"mobilizing communities to protect themselves," Freudenberg notes, will not
be enough. Rather than promoting mostly defensive approaches that focus on
"the negative image of protecting oneself from a deadly disease," he calls on us
to imagine what it would mean to live in a world without AIDS, and to connect
our daily lives to making it happen. The vision he invokes is one

> where every one is entitled to comprehensive education about sexuality, drugs, and health;
> a world where those who need treatment for drug addiction can get it on demand; a world
> where basic health care is a right, not a privilege; a world where gay men and lesbians,
> women and people of color, are not discriminated against; a world where alternatives to
> drug use exist for the young people this country; a world where no one has to die on the
> streets because there is no home for them (58, p. 70).

What would it mean for epidemiologists and other public health researchers
to integrate this vision into the daily work of HIV surveillance, research, and
prevention efforts? Here, we draw upon social justice frameworks described
earlier and in Table 3 to develop measurable surveillance tools and research
questions.

To begin, surveillance data on HIV and AIDS among women can be linked
to existing databases that routinely document social, economic, and political
conditions at local, state, and federal levels. A conceptually valid and cost-
effective approach to adding socioeconomic data to HIV/AIDS surveillance
records would be linking street addresses of cases to existing census data, using
the technique of geocoding (81). Census-based socioeconomic data at the level
of census block-groups, which on average contain 1000 people, provide more
valid descriptions than census tracts, which on average contain 4000 people.
Block-groups, thus, tend to be more homogeneous with respect to social and
economic composition.

SOCIAL INEQUALITIES AND HIV IN WOMEN   427

Geocoding HIV/AIDS surveillance data to incorporate census-based socio-economic information would permit characterizing socioeconomic conditions of neighborhoods (at the block-group level), and also of state economic areas and regional economies, in relation to trends in HIV incidence and AIDS diagnoses. The same could be done with other routinely monitored health outcomes related to the AIDS epidemic, such as tuberculosis and selected sexually transmitted diseases. Census data are rich in description of conditions of poverty, including population density, class composition, household income, percent of female heads of household, of adults with less than high school education, of persons with income at a certain percentage of the poverty line, home ownership, and more.

Other linkages to surveillance data on incidence of HIV and AIDS among women at the level of census block-groups include police data on frequency of domestic violence calls within block-group boundaries, court records documenting frequency of restraining orders for streets within those block-groups, arrests and charges for drug-related activities, for prostitution, and for more explicit economic crimes, such as check forgery. Availability of civil services such as fire, police, public libraries, community centers, grass-covered parks, well-designed recreational equipment in playgrounds, and functional street lighting are examples of resources in neighborhoods that provide protection from, as well as alternatives to, drug-related crime. At the county, state, and regional level, it would also be possible to analyze data on occurrence of HIV among women in relation to public assistance programs, tax policies, and levels of industrialization and deindustrialization. One application would be to develop what Friedman has named "AIDS impact statements," similar to the environmental impact statements that are now required to anticipate effects of diverse economic policies upon the environment (61).

Second, research studies, in part driven by descriptions emerging from expanded surveillance data, would require development of methodologies for valid measures of women's various experiences with discrimination and subordination, as well as experiences with creative responses and resistance to inequality. Furthermore, such data would provide public health professionals with empirical documentation to advance legislative and regulatory action to reduce HIV transmission as well as other diseases that are endemic or may emerge amidst conditions of material and social deprivation, such as prematurity and infant mortality, other effects of drug and alcohol use, violence, hypertension, and asthma, among many others. Examples of social determinants that are measurable for studies of occurrence of HIV infection among women are listed in Table 4. We recommend measurement of these categories at the individual, household, neighborhood, and regional level and over women's life course. Highlighting resistance and adaptation strategies as well as subordination, these

Table 4   Measuring* social inequalities in relation to HIV in women

Economics	Political/legal factors	Race/ethnicity and racism	Gender

Income and work
  Sources (legal and illegal)
  Nature of work (doing what, with, and for whom)
  Number of people supported on income
  Amount/month
Health insurance
Proportion of income for food, housing, drugs (illicit/prescribed)
Level of income in relation to poverty line and fluctuations
Experiences with hunger, homelessness, insufficient heat
Housing status: rent, own, none
Household crowding
Use of public/private transport; own or access to car
Education credentials
Literacy level in primary language and English
Access to recreation and culture
State-level: tax base; budget for education, housing, welfare and other social services, art/culture
	Voter participation
	Awareness of legal rights
	Awareness of public officials
	Neighborhood/community work: awareness/involvement/activism
	Workplace organizing/activism
	Lobbying/social advocacy work
	Awareness of eligibility for benefits/resources and how to access them
	Legal access to and use of clean needles/syringes
	Interactions with police
	Arrest/incarceration experience
	
	Violence
	Exposure to street, workplace or public violence (witness, victim, participant)
	Gang membership
	Own/carry gun or other weapon
	Nature of violence
	Response to violence
		Self-identity vs how perceived by others
		Awareness of ancestry and family origins/roots
		Participation in civil rights movement (past and current racial justice work)
		Racial/ethnic pride
		Cultural/ethnic social resources (community groups/churches)
		Racial/ethnic composition of neighborhood/block-group
		Race/ethnicity of elected officials
		Experience with racially motivated violence
		
		Networks
		Family, friends, sexual partners
		Spiritual
		Work-related
		Drug-related: distribution, use, recovery
		Turnover of network membership
			Uses of sex: social, economic
			Sexual identity
			Sexual fulfillment
			Reproductive autonomy
			Awareness and use of services to support women's sexual and reproductive health
			Involvement in women's groups (political, social, health-related)
			Parenting and other care-giving responsibilities
			Gender-based violence: sexual, physical, verbal threats
			Gender-based control: economic and social
			Gender-based discrimination
			Lesbian-based discrimination
			Marital/partner status

*Pattern over life course (childhood to present); at level of individual, household, network, neighborhood, region.

Table 5 FDR's Economic Bill of Rights

The right to a useful and remunerative job in the industries, or shops or farms or mines of the Nation
The right to earn enough to provide adequate food and clothing and recreation
The right of every farmer to raise and sell his [*sic*] products at a return which will give him and
 his family a decent living
The right of every businessman [*sic*], large and small, to trade in an atmosphere of freedom
 from unfair competition and domination by monopolies at home or abroad
The right to adequate medical care and the opportunity to achieve and enjoy good health
The right to adequate protection from the economic fears of old age, sickness, accident,
 and unemployment
The right to a good education
All of these rights spell security. And after this war is won we must be prepared to move
 forward, in the implementation of these rights, to new goals of human happiness and well-being

Excerpt from Franklin Delano Roosevelt, 11th annual *State of the Union Address*, Jan. 11, 1944 (see Reference 34, p. 98).

determinants pertain to women's experiences regarding: knowledge of and exercise of political and legal rights; racial/ethnic identity and racism; gender, sexual identity, and gender and sexual inequalities involving sex, violence, and drug use; public and private violence; and social networks.

During the 1930s, in the midst of the Great Depression, President Franklin Delano Roosevelt established the New Deal to improve conditions among the one third of the nation that was then ill-fed, ill-clothed, ill-housed. In 1944, Roosevelt's State of the Union address envisioned a postwar economy embodying an economic bill of rights (see Table 5). Tens of millions of people in this country have yet to realize these rights. Today, we continue to need full employment at decent wages, progressive taxation, quality public education, health insurance for all, a safety net for the unemployed and retired, full political participation, and elimination of discrimination (67, 158). In a nation as wealthy as the United States, we have the economic and social resources to reduce sharply inequalities that perpetuate the AIDS epidemic. Shifts in wealth and poverty in the United States in the 1980s and 1990s, the decade of this epidemic, reflect political and economic decisions; they—and the trends in AIDS they have fostered—are not immutable or inevitable.

It is likely that the moment of HIV transmission into women's bodies is a very private moment—whether in the embrace of a lover or shared injection of a drug. Yet the chosen or imposed isolation of this moment hardly measures the enormous public force that culminates in this irrevocable transference of viral particles. This review, in offering theoretical frameworks that contextualize HIV infection among women within social, economic, and political structures, calls for greater emphasis on naming and measuring the impact of these public forces on such private moments.

430   ZIERLER & KRIEGER

ACKNOWLEDGMENTS

We thank Pascale Wortley of the CDC/AIDS Division for her contributions to the epidemiologic overview section and for her comments on an earlier draft. Among our internal reviewers, we are particularly grateful to Sam Friedman for his thoughtful comments, and to Jonathan Mann for his support. Conceptualization of this article occurred while Sally Zierler was a Fellow at the Institute for Health and Social Justice in Cambridge, Massachusetts; she thanks the staff: Ophelia Dahl, Paul Farmer, Roger Grande, Jim Kim, Kristin Nelson, Bill Rodriguez, and Loune Viaud. Over the years, many women and men on HIV advisory boards, in activist groups, and in AIDS research studies offered lively, passionate, and insightful perspectives that are woven throughout this article.

> Visit the *Annual Reviews home page* at
> http://www.annurev.org.

Literature Cited

1. Airhihenbuwa CO, DiClemente RJ, Wingood GM, Lowe A. 1992. HIV/AIDS education and prevention among African-Americans: a focus on culture. *AIDS Educ. Prev.* 4:267–76
2. Ajzen I, Fishbein M. 1980. *Understanding Attitudes and Predicting Social Behavior.* Englewood Cliffs, NJ: Prentice Hall
3. Alan Guttmacher Institute. 1994. *Sex and America's Teenagers.* New York: Alan Guttmacher Inst.
4. Amaro H. 1995. Love, sex and power. *Am. Psychol.* 50:437–47
5. Amaro H, Hardy-Fanta C. 1995. Gender relations in addiction and recovery. *J. Psychoact. Drugs* 27:325–37
6. American Correction Association. 1990. *The Female Offender: What Does the Future Hold?* Laurel, MD: Am. Correct. Assoc.
7. Amott T. 1993. *Caught in the Crisis: Women and the US Economy Today.* New York: Monthly Rev. Press
8. Anastos K, Marte C. 1989. Women–the missing persons in the AIDS epidemic. *Health/PAC Bull.* Winter:6–15
9. Bandura A. 1977. Self-efficacy: toward a unifying theory of behavioral change. *Psychol. Rev.* 84:191–215
10. Barkan S, Deaumant C, Young M, Stonis LF, Lucy M, et al. 1996. *Sexual identity and behavior among women with female sexual partners in the Women's Interagency HIV Study (WIHS).* Int. AIDS Conf., 11th, Vancouver, Canada (Abstr.)
11. Basset M, Mihloyi M. 1994. Women and AIDS in Zimbabwe: The making of an epidemic. See Ref. 83a, pp. 125–39
12. Battle S. 1990. Moving targets: alcohol, crack and black women. In *The Black Women's Health Book: Speaking for Ourselves,* ed. EC White, pp. 251–56. Seattle, WA: Seal Press
13. Becker MH. 1974. The health belief model and sick role behavior. *Health Educ. Monogr.* 2:409–19
14. Beckman L, Amaro H. 1986. Personal and social difficulties faced by women and men entering alcoholism treatment. *J. Stud. Alcohol* 47:220–28
15. Black D, Morris JN, Smith C, Townsend P. 1985. *Inequalities in Health: The Black Report.* Harmondsworth: Penguin
16. Brecht B. 1976. A worker's speech to a doctor (c. 1938). In *Poems 1913–1965,* ed. J Willett, R Manheim, pp. 292–93. New York: Methuen
17. Brown VB. 1995. *HIV infection in women: models of intervention for violence against women.* Women HIV Infect. Conf., Washington, DC (Abstr. TD2–122)
18. Brown VB, Melchior CR, Huba GJ. 1994. Mandatory partner notification of HIV test results: psychological and social

SOCIAL INEQUALITIES AND HIV IN WOMEN   431

issues for women. *AIDS Public Policy J.* 9:86–92

19. Brown VB, Weissman G. 1993. Women and men injection drug users: an updated look at gender differences and risk factors. In *Handbook on Risk of AIDS Injection Drug Users and Sexual Partners*, ed. BS Brown, GM Beschnes, Natl. AIDS Res. Consort. Westport, CT: Greenwood Press

20. Bureau of Justice Statistics. 1991. *Women in Prison*. Washington, DC: US Dep. Justice

21. Bureau of Justice Statistics. 1995. *Prisoners in 1994*. Washington, DC: US Dep. Justice

22. Caldwell MB, Fleming PL, Oxtoby MJ. 1992. Estimated number of AIDS orphans in the United States [letter]. *Pediatrics* 90:482

23. Cent. Dis. Control. 1981. Pneumocystis pneumonia—Los Angeles. *MMWR* 30: 250–52

24. Cent. Dis. Control Prevent. 1995. Update: AIDS among women-United States, 1994. *MMWR* 44:81–84

25. Cent. Dis. Control Prevent. 1996. 1995 *HIV/AIDS Surveillance Report*. Atlanta, GA: US DHHS, PHS, 7 (no. 2)

26. Cent. Dis. Control Prevent. 1996. Update: mortality attributable to HIV infection among persons aged 25–44 years–United States, 1994. *MMWR* 45:121–25

27. Chiasson MA, Stoneburner RL, Hildebrandt DS, Ewing WE, Telzak EE, Jaffee HW. 1991. Heterosexual transmission of HIV-1 associated with use of smokeable freebase cocaine (crack). *AIDS* 5:1121–26

28. Chasnoff IJ, Landress HJ, Barrett ME. 1990. The prevalence of illicit drug or alcohol use during pregnancy and discrepancies in mandatory reporting in Pinellas County, Fla. *N. Engl. J. Med.* 322:1202–6

29. Chavkin W, Driver C, Forman P. 1989. The crisis in New YOrk City's perinatal services. *NY State J. Med.* 12:658–63

30. Chu SY, Buehler JW, Berkelman RL. 1990. Impact of the human immunodeficiency virus epidemic on mortality in women of reproductive age, United States. *JAMA* 264:225–29

31. Chu SY, Hammett TA, Buehler JW. 1992. Update: epidemiology of reported cases of AIDS in women who report sex only with other women, United States, 1980–1991. *AIDS* 6:518–19

32. Cluster D, Rutter N. 1980. *Shrinking Dollars, Vanishing Jobs*, p. 66. Boston, MA: Beacon Press

33. Cochran SD, Mays VM. 1994. Depressive distress among homosexually active African-American men and women. *Am. J. Psychol.* 51:524–29

34. Collins S. 1996. *Let Them Eat Ketchup! The Politics of Poverty and Inequality.* New York: Monthly Rev. Press

35. Cooper R, David R. 1986. The biological concept of race and its application to public health and epidemiology. *J. Health Polit. Policy Law* 11:97–116

36. Coreil J, Levin JS, Jaco EG. 1985. Life style–an emergent concept in the sociomedical science. *Cult. Psychiatry Med.* 9:423–37

37. Curtis JR, Patrick DL. 1993. Race and survival time with AIDS: a synthesis of the literature. *Am. J. Public Health* 83:1425–28

38. Dalton HL. 1989. AIDS in blackface. *Daedalus* 115:205–27

39. De Groot A, Zierler S, Stevens J. 1995. *Sexual abuse histories among incarcerated women in Massachusetts.* Presented at Women HIV Infect. Conf., Washington, DC

40. Deamant C, Cohen M, Markan S, Richardson J, FitzGerald G, et al. 1996. Prevalence of domestic violence and childhood abuse among women wtih HIV and high risk uninfected women. *Int. AIDS Conf., 11th, Vancouver, Canada* (Abstr.)

41. Diaz T, Chu SY, Buchler JW, Boyd D, Checko PJ. 1994. Socioeconomic differences among people with AIDS: results from a multistate surveillance project. *Am. J. Prev. Med.* 10:217–22

42. Doyal L. 1979. *The Political Economy of Health* London: Pluto Press

43. Doyal L. 1994. HIV and AIDS: putting women on the global agenda. In *AIDS: Setting a Feminist Agenda*, ed. L Doyal, J Naidoo, T Wilton, pp. 11–29. London: Taylor & Francis

44. Dressler WW. 1993. Health in the African American community: accounting for health inequalities. *Med. Anthropol. Q.* 7:325–45

45. Drucker E. 1990. Epidemic in the war zone: AIDS and community survival in New York City. *Int. J. Health Serv.* 20:601–5

46. Dwyer R, Richardson D, Ross MW, Wodak A, Miller ME, Gold J. 1994. A comparison of HIV risk between women and men who inject drugs. *AIDS Educ. Prev.* 6:379–89

47. Dyson J. 1990. The effect of family violence on children's academic performance and behavior. *J. Natl. Med. Assoc.* 82:17–22

48. Edlin BR, Irwin KL, Faruque S, McCoy CB, Word C. 1994. Intersecting

432   ZIERLER & KRIEGER

epidemics: crack cocaine use and HIV infection among inner-city young adults. *New Engl. J. Med.* 331:1422–27

49. Einhorn L, Polgar M. 1994. HIV risk behavior among lesbian and bisexual women. *AIDS Prev. Educ.* 6:514–23

50. Eller TJ. 1994. Household wealth and asset ownership: 1991. *US Bur. Census Curr. Popul. Rep.*, pp. P70–34. Washington, DC: US GPO

51. Essed P. 1991. *Understanding Everyday Racism: An Interdisciplinary Theory.* Newbury Park, CA: Sage

52. Farmer P, Conners M, Simmons J, eds. 1996. *Women, Poverty and AIDS.* Monroe, Me: Common Courage Press

53. Farmer P, Lindenbaum S, Good MJD. 1993. Women, poverty and AIDS: an introduction. *Cult. Med. Psychiatry* 17:387–97

54. Fee E, Krieger N. 1993. Understanding AIDS: historical interpretations and the limits of biomedical individualism. *Am. J. Public Health* 83:1477–86

55. Fife D, Mode C. 1992. AIDS incidence and income. *J. Acquir. Immun. Defic. Syndr.* 5:1105–10

56. Fisher B, Hovell M, Hofstetter CR, Hough R. 1995. Risks associated with long-term homelessness among women: battery, rape, and HIV infection. *Int. J. Health Serv.* 25:351–69

57. Fitzpatrick K, Boldizar J. 1993. The prevalence and consequences of exposure to violence among African-American youth. *J. Am. Acad. Child Adol. Psychol.* 32:424–30

58. Freudenberg N. 1994. AIDS prevention in the United States: lessons from the first decade. See Ref. 83a, pp. 61–72

59. Friedman SR. 1991. Alienated labor and dignity denial in capitalist society. In *Critical Perspectives in Sociology,* ed. B Berberoglu, pp. 83–91. Dubuque, IA: Kendall/Hunt Publ.

60. Friedman SR, Jose B, Deren S, Des Jarlais DC, Neaigus A. 1995. Risk factors for human immunodeficiency virus seroconversion among out-of-treatment drug injectors in high and low seroprevalence cities. The National AIDS Research Consortium. *Am. J. Epidemiol.* 142:864–74

61. Friedman SR, Neigus A, Jose B, Curtis R, Goldstein M. et al. 1997. Network and sociohistorical approaches to the HIV epidemic among drug injectors. In *Impact of AIDS. Psychological and Social Aspects of HIV Infection.,* ed. J Catalan, B Hedge, L Sherr. Chur, Switz.: Harwood Acad. Publ.

62. Friedman SR, Neaigus A, Jose B, Goldstein M, Curtis R, et al. 1993. Female injecting drug users get infected sooner than males. *Int. Conf. AIDS, Berlin, Germany, 9th.* (Abstr. PO-DO3–3512)

63. Friedman SR, Sotheran JL, Abdul-Quader A, Primm BJ, Des Jarlais DC, et al. 1987. The AIDS epidemic among Blacks and Hispanics. *Milbank Q.* 65: 455–99

64. Friedman SR, Stepherson B, Woods J, Des Jarlais DC, Ward TP. 1992. Society, drug injectors, and AIDS. *J. Health Care Poor Underserved* 3:73–89

65. Fullilove RE, Fullilove MT, Bowser BP, Gross SA. 1990. Risk of sexually transmitted disease among black adolescent crack users in Oakland and San Francisco, Calif. *JAMA* 263:851–55

66. Fullilove MT, Golden E, Fullilove RE, Lennon R, Porterfield D, et al. 1992. Crack cocaine and high risk behaviors among sexually active adolescents. *J. Adolesc. Health* 14:295–300

67. Galbraith JK. 1996. *The Good Society: The Humane Agenda.* Boston: Houghton Mifflin

68. Gielen AC, O'Campo P, Faden R, Eke A. 1995. *Women with HIV: disclosure concerns and experiences.* Presented at Women and HIV Infect. Conf., Washington, DC (Abstr. TA1–88)

69. Gollub EL, Stein ZA. 1993. Commentary: the new female condom–item 1 on a women's AIDS prevention agenda. *Am. J. Public Health* 83:490–500

70. Guinan ME, Hardy A. 1987. Epidemiology of AIDS in women in the United States: 1981 through 1986. *JAMA* 257: 2039–42

71. Gwinn M, Pappaioanou M, George R, et al. 1991. Prevalence of HIV infection in childbearing women in the United States. *JAMA* 265:1704–8

72. Holmes MD. 1991. Editorial: AIDS in communities of color. *Am. J. Prev. Med.* 7:461–63

73. House Select Comm. Narc. Abuse Control. 1989. *Narcotics Abuse and Control Report,* 101st Congr., Washington, DC: GPO

74. Hu DJ, Frey R, Costa SJ, et al. 1994. Geographical AIDS rates and sociodemographic variables in Newark, New Jersey, metropolitan area. *AIDS Public Policy J.* 9:20–25

75. Hubbard R. 1990. *The Politics of Women's Biology.* New Brunswick, NJ: Rutgers Univ. Press

76. Ickovics JR, Rodin J. 1992. Women and AIDS in the United States: epidemiol-

ogy, natural history, and mediating mechanisms. *Health Psychol.* 11:1–16

77. James J, Meyerding J. 1977. Early sexual experience and prostitution. *Am. J. Psychiatry* 134:1381–85

78. Jochelson K, Mothibeli M, Leger J-P. 1994. Human immunodeficiency virus and migrant labor in South Africa. See Ref. 83a, pp. 141–58

79. Karan L. 1989. AIDS perception and chemical dependence treatment needs of women and their children. *J. Psychoact. Drugs* 21:396–99

80. King JC. 1981. *The Biology of Race.* Berkeley, CA: Univ. Calif. Press

81. Krieger N. 1992. Overcoming the absence of socioeconomic data in medical records: validation and application of a census-based methodology. *Am. J. Public Health* 82:703–10

82. Krieger N. 1994. Epidemiology and the web of causation: has anyone seen the spider? *Soc. Sci. Med.* 39:887–903

83. Krieger N, Appleman R. 1986. *The Politics of AIDS.* Oakland, CA: Frontline Publ.

83a. Krieger N, Margo G, eds. 1994. *AIDS: The Politics of Survival.* Amityville, NY: Baywood

84. Krieger N, Rowley D, Hermann AA, Avery B, Phillips MT. 1993. Racism, sexism and social class: implications for studies of health, disease and well-being. *Am. J. Prev. Med.* 9 (Suppl. 2):82–122

85. Krieger N, Sidney S. 1996. Racial discrimination and blood pressure: the CARDIA study of young black and white adults. *Am. J. Public Health* 86:1370–78

86. Krieger N, Zierler S. 1996. Accounting for health of women. *Curr. Issues Public Health* 1:251–56

87. Ladwig GB, Andersen MD. 1989. Substance abuse in women: relationship between chemical dependency of women and past reports of physical and/or sexual abuse. *Int. J. Addict.* 24:739–54

88. Lake ES. 1993. An exploration of the violent victim experiences of female offenders. *Violence Vict.* 8:41–51

89. Laurell AC. 1989. Social analysis of collective health in Latin America. *Soc. Sci. Med.* 28:1183–91

90. Lemp GF, Jones M, Kellogg TA, Nieri GN, Anderson L, et al. 1995. HIV seroprevalence and risk behaviors among lesbians and bisexual women in San Francisco and Berkeley, California. *Am. J. Public Health* 85:1549–552.

91. Leslie C. 1990. Scientific racism: reflections on peer review, science and ideology. *Soc. Sci. Med.* 32:891–905

92. Levine C. 1995. Orphans of the HIV epidemic: unmet needs in six US cities. *AIDS Care* 1(Suppl. 7):S57–62

92a. Levine G, Dubler N. 1990. Uncertain risk and bitter realities. *Milbank Q.* 68:321–51

93. Lillie-Blanton M, Anthony JC, Schuster CR. 1993. Probing the meaning of racial/ethnic group comparisons in crack cocaine smoking. *JAMA* 269:993–97

94. Lock M, Gordon D, eds. 1988. *Biomedicine Examined.* Dordrecht: Kluwer

95. Lucey DR, Hendrix C, Andrzejewski C, Melcher GP, Butzin CA, et al. 1992. Comparison by race of total serum IgG, IgA, and IgM with CD4+ T-cell counts in North American persons infected with the human immunodeficiency virus type 1. *J. Acquir. Immun. Defic. Syndr.* 5:325–32

96. Lurie P, Fernandes MEL, Hughes V, Arevalo EL, Hudes ES, et al. 1995. Socioeconomic status and risk of HIV-1, syphilis and hepatitis B infection among sex workers in Sao Paulo State, Brazil. *AIDS* 9(Suppl.):S31–S37

97. Lurie P, Hintzen P, Lowe RA. 1995. Socioeconomic obstacles to HIV prevention and treatment in developing countries: the roles of the International Monetary Fund and the World Bank. *AIDS* 9:539–46

98. Lurie P, Reingold AL, Bowser B, Chen D, Foley J, et al. 1993. *The Public Health Impact of Needle Exchange Programs in the United States and Abroad.* San Francisco, CA: Univ. Calif. Press. Vol. 1

99. Lusane C. 1991. *Pipe Dream Blues: Racism & the War on Drugs.* Boston, MA: South End Press

100. Males MA. 1995. Adult involvement in teenage childbearing and STD. *Lancet* 340:64–65

101. Mann JM, Gostin L, Gruskin S, Brennan T, Lazzarini Z, Fineberg HV. 1994. Health and human rights. *Health Hum. Rights* 1:6–23

102. Marmor M, Weiss LR, Lyden M. 1986. Possible female-to-female transmission of human immunodeficiency virus (letter). *Ann. Intern. Med.* 105:969

103. Mayer KH, Anderson DJ. 1995. Heterosexual HIV transmission. *Infect. Agents Dis.* 4:273–84

104. Mays VM, Cochran SD. 1987. Acquired immunodeficiency syndrome and Black Americans: Special psychosocial issues. *Public Health Rep.* 102:224–31

105. Michaels D, Levine C. 1992. Estimates of the number of motherless youth orphaned by AIDS in the United States [see comments]. *JAMA* 268:3456–61

106. Mills C, Ota H. 1989. Homeless women with minor children in the Detroit

metropolitan area. *Soc. Work* 34:185–89

107. Monzon OT, Capellan JMB. 1987. Female-to-female transmission of HIV (letter). *Lancet* 2:40–41

108. Moore J, Solomon L, Schoenbaum E, Schuman P, Boland R, et al. 1995. *Factors associated with stress and distress among HIV-infected and uninfected women.* Presented at HIV and Women Conf., Washington, DC (Abstr.)

109. National Institute on Drug Abuse. 1991. *National Household Survey on Drug Abuse: Population Estimates.* Washington, DC: US GPO. DHHS Publ. No. 91–1732

110. Neighbors HW, Jackson JS, Broman C, Thompson E. 1996. Racism and the mental health of African Americans: the role of self and system blame. *Ethn. Dis.* 6:167–75

111. North RL, Rothenberg KH. 1993. Partner notification and the threat of domestic violence against women with HIV infection. *N. Engl. J. Med.* 329:1194–96

112. O'Campo P, Gilen A, Faden R, Xue X, Kass N, Wang M. 1995. Violence by male partners against women during the childbearing year. *Am. J. Public Health* 85:1092–97

113. Padian N, Shiboski SC, Jewell NP. 1991. Female-male transmission of human immunodeficiency virus. *JAMA* 266:1664–67

114. Paone D, Caloir S, Shi Q, Des Jarlais DC. 1995. Sex, drugs, and syringe exchange in New York City: women's experiences. *JAMA* 50:109–14

115. Paone D, Chavkin W, Willets I, Friedmann P, Des Jarlais DC. 1992. The impact of sexual abuse: implications for drug treatment. *J. Women's Health* 1:149–53

116. Perry S, Jacobsberg L, Fogel K. 1989. Orogenital transmission of HIV. *Ann. Intern. Med.* 111:951–52

117. Pivnick A. 1993. HIV infection and the meaning of condoms. *Cult. Med. Psychiatry* 17:431–53

118. Pivnick A, Jacobson A, Eric K, Doll L, Drucker E. 1994. AIDS, HIV infection, illicit drug use within inner-city families and social networks. *Am. J. Public Health* 84:271–74

119. Plotnick RD. 1993. Changes in poverty, income inequality, and the standard of living in the United States during the Reagan years. *Int. J. Health Serv.* 23:347–58

120. Polednak AP. 1989. *Racial and Ethnic Differences in Disease.* New York: Oxford Univ. Press

121. Prochaska J, DiClemente C, Norcross J. 1992. In seach of how people change. *Am.*

Psychol. 47:1102–14

122. Quinn SC. 1993. AIDS and the African American woman: the triple burden of race, class, and gender. *Health Educ. Q.* 20:305–20

123. Rich JD, Buck A, Tuomala RE, Kazanjian PH. 1993. Transmission of human immunodeficiency virus infection presumed to have occurred via female homosexual contact. *Clin. Infect. Dis.* 17:1003–5

124. Robbins C. 1989. Sex differences in psychosocial consequences of alcohol and drug abuse. *J. Health Soc. Behav.* 30:117–30

125. Roberts S. 1994. Gap between rich and poor in New York grows wider. *New York Times,* Dec. 26, p. 20

126. Rosenbaum M. 1979. Difficulties in taking care of business: women addicts as mothers. *Am. J. Drug Alcohol Abuse* 6:431–46

127. Rosenstock IM, Strecher V, Becker M. 1988. Social learning theory and the health belief model. *Health Educ. Q.* 15:175–83

128. Rothenberg KH, SJ Paskey. 1995. The risk of domestic violence and women with HIV infection: implications for partner notification policy, and the law. *Am. J. Public Health* 85:1569–76

129. Rushton JP, Bogaert AF. 1989. Population differences in susceptibility to AIDS: an evolutionary analysis. *Soc. Sci. Med.* 28:1211–20

130. Sabatini MT, Patel K, Hirshman R. 1984. Kaposi's sarcoma and T-cell lymphoma in an immunodeficient woman: a case report. *AIDS Res.* 1:135–37

131. Schechter MT, Hogg RS, Aylward B, Craib KSP, Le TN, Montaner JSG. 1994. Higher socioeconomic status is associated with slower progression of HIV infection independent of access to health care. *J. Clin. Epidemiol.* 47:59–67

132. Schoepf BG. 1993. Gender, development, and AIDS: a political economy and culture framework. *Women Int. Dev. Annu.* 3:53–85

133. Schubiner H, Scott R, Tzelepis A. 1993. Exposure to violence among inner-city youth. *J. Adolesc. Health* 14:214–19

134. Schwarcz SK, Bolan GA, Fullilove MT, McCright J, Fullilove R, et al. 1992. Crack cocaine and the exchange of sex for money or drugs. *Sex. Transmit. Dis.* 19:7–13

135. Shea M. 1995. Dynamics of economic well-being: poverty, 1991–1993. In *US Bureau of the Census, Current Population Reports,* Washinton, DC: US GPO

136. Simon PA, Hu DJ, Diaz T, Kerndt PR. 1995. Income and AIDS rates in Los Angeles County. *AIDS* 9:281–84

137. Solomon L, Astemborski J, Warren D, Munoz A, Cohn S, et al. 1993. Differences in risk factors for human immunodeficiency virus type 1 seroconversion among male and female intravenous drug users. *Am. J. Epidemiol.* 137:892–98

138. Sotheran JL, Wenston JA, Rockwell R, Des Jarlais D, Friedman SR. 1992. *Injecting drug users: why do women share syringes more often than men?* Presented at Am. Public Health Assoc., Washington, DC

139. Stein ZA. 1995. More on women and the prevention of HIV infection. *Am. J. Public Health* 85:1485–1488

140. Steinberg S, Davis S, Gwinn M. 1995. *Prevalence of HIV among childbearing women in the United States, 1989–1993.* Abstr. [WE2–55]. Presented at HIV Infect. Women, Washington, DC

141. Stevens PE. 1993. Lesbians and HIV: clinical, research, and policy issues. *Am. Orthopsychol. Assoc.* 63:289–94

142. Taylor L, Zuckerman B, Harik V, Groves BM. 1994. Witnessing violence by young children and their mothers. *J. Dev. Behav. Pediatr.* 15:120–23

143. Terris M. 1980. The lifestyle approach to prevention: editorial. *J. Public Health Policy* 1:5–9

144. Tesh S. 1988. *Hidden Arguments: Political Ideology and Disease Prevention Policy.* New Brunswick, NJ: Rutgers Univ. Press

145. Thomas SB, Quinn SC. 1991. The Tuskegee Syphilis Study, 1932–1972: implications for HIV education and AIDS risk education programs in the Black community. *Am. J. Public Health* 81:1498–504

146. Thomas VG. 1994. Using feminist and social structural analysis to focus on health of poor women. *Women Health* 22:1–15

147. Treichler PA. 1988. AIDS, gender, and biomedical discourse: current contests for meaning. In *AIDS: The Burdens of History*, eds. E Fee, DM Fox, pp. 190–266. Berkeley, CA: Univ. Calif. Press

148. *Universal Declaration of Human Rights.* 1948. Adopted and proclaimed by UN Gen. Assem. Resol. 217A (III). Dec. 10

149. US Bureau of the Census. 1992. *Current Population Reports, Series P70–26. Extended Measures of Well-Being: Selected Data from the 1984 Survey of Income and Program Participation.* Washington, DC: US GPO

150. US Bureau of the Census. 1996. *Current Population Reports, Series P60–189, Income, Poverty, and Valuation of Noncash Benefits: 1994.* Washington, DC: US GPO

151. US Dep. Health and Human Serv. 1985. *Report of the Secretary's Task Force on Black and Minority Health.* Washington, DC: US GPO

152. Vlahov D, Brewer TF, Castro KG, Narkunas JP, Salive ME, et al. 1991. Prevalence of antibody to HIV-1 among entrants to US correctional facilities. *JAMA* 265:1129–32

153. Vlahov D, Wientge D, Moore J, Flynn C, Schuman P, et al. 1996. *Violence among women with or at risk for HIV infection.* Abstr. Presented at Int. AIDS Meet., 11th, Vancouver, Canada HERE

154. Wallace R. 1988. A synergism of plagues: "Planned shrinkage", contagious housing destruction, and AIDS in the Bronx. *Environ. Res.* 47:1–33

155. Wallace R, Wallace D. 1995. US apartheid and the spread of AIDS to the suburbs: a multi-city analysis of the political economy of spatial epidemic threshold. *Soc. Sci. Med.* 41:333–45

156. Wenger L, Murphy S. 1995. *Barriers to needle exchange: a case for expanded services and legislative reform.* Presented at Am. Public Health Assoc., San Diego, CA

157. Williams DR. 1992. Black-white differences in blood pressure: the role of social factors. *Ethn. Dis.* 2:126–41

158. Wilson WJ. 1987. *The Truly Disadvantaged: The Inner-City, The Underclass, and Public Policy*, p. 46. Chicago, IL: Univ. Chicago Press

159. Worth D, Paone D, Chavkin W. 1993. From the private family domain to the public health forum: sexual abuse, women and risk for HIV infection. *SIECUS Rep.* 21:13–17

160. Worth D, Rodriguez R. 1987. Latina women and AIDS. *SEICUS Rep.* 15:5–7

161. Wyatt GE, Dunn KM. 1991. Examining predictors of sex guilt in multiethnic samples of women. *Arch. Sex. Behav.* 20:471–85

162. Young RM, Weissman G, Cohen JB. 1992. Assessing risk in the absence of information: HIV risk among women injection-drug users who have sex with woman. *AIDS Public Policy J.* 7:175–83

163. Zierler S. 1997. Hitting Hard: HIV and violence against women. In *Gender Politics of HIV*, ed. J Manlowe, N Goldstein.

436   ZIERLER & KRIEGER

New York: New York Univ. Press. In press

164. Zierler S, Feingold L, Laufer D, Velentgas P, Kantrowitz-Gordon I, Mayer K. 1991. Adult survivors of childhood sexual abuse and subsequent risk of HIV infection. *Am. J. Public Health* 81:572–75

165. Zierler S, Moore J, Solomon L, Schuman P, Schoenbaum E, et al. 1995. *Sexuality among a cohort of HIV seropositive and seronegative women.* Presented at HIV and Women Conf., Washington, DC (Abstr.)

166. Zierler S, Witbeck B, Mayer K. 1996. Sexual violence and HIV in women. *Am. J. Prev. Med.* 12:304–10

167. Zinn H. 1995. *A Peoples History of the United States 1492–Present.* New York: Harper Perennial

168. Zorza J. 1991. Women battering: A major cause of homeless. *Clearinghouse Rev.* 25:420–29

Name Index

For Product Safety Concerns and Information please contact our EU representative GPSR@taylorandfrancis.com
Taylor & Francis Verlag GmbH, Kaufingerstraße 24, 80331 München, Germany

T - #0133 - 160425 - C0 - 244/166/25 - PB - 9781138730403 - Gloss Lamination